Chile
& Easter Island

Carolyn Hubbard
Brigitte Barta
Jeff Davis

LONELY PLANET PUBLICATIONS
Melbourne • Oakland • London • Paris

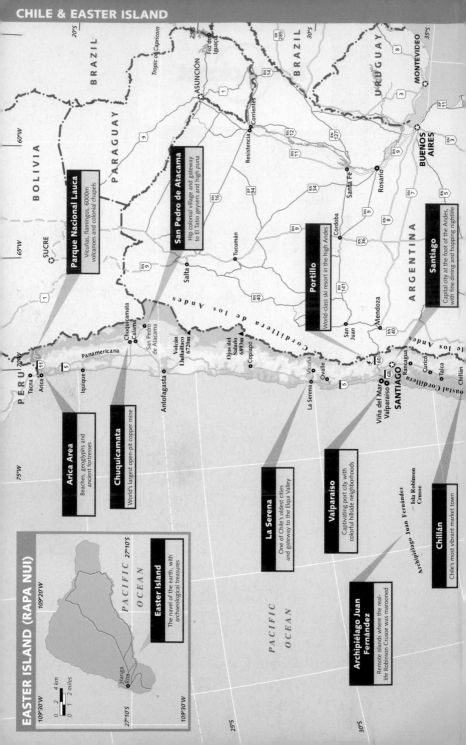

CHILE & EASTER ISLAND

Parque Nacional Lauca
Vicuñas, flamingos, 6000m volcanoes and colonial chapels

San Pedro de Atacama
Hip colonial village and gateway to El Tatio geysers and high puna

Portillo
World-class ski resort in the high Andes

Santiago
Capital city at the foot of the Andes, with fine dining and hopping nightlife

Arica Area
Beaches, geoglyphs and ancient fortresses

Chuquicamata
World's largest open-pit copper mine

La Serena
One of Chile's oldest cities and gateway to the Elqui Valley

Valparaíso
Captivating port city with colorful hillside neighborhoods

Chillán
Chile's most vibrant market town

Archipiélago Juan Fernández
Remote islands where the real-life Robinson Crusoe was marooned

Easter Island
The navel of the earth, with archaeological treasures

EASTER ISLAND (RAPA NUI)

0   2   4 km
0 1 2 miles

Hanga Roa

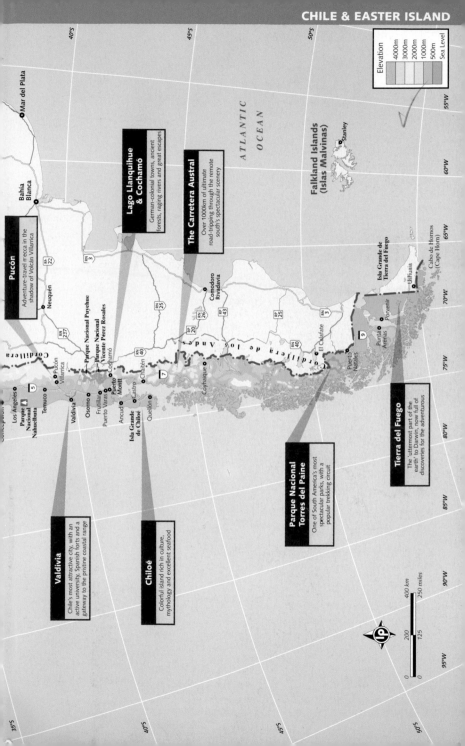

Elevation

| 4000m |
| 3000m |
| 2000m |
| 1000m |
| 500m |
| Sea Level |

ATLANTIC OCEAN

Falkland Islands (Islas Malvinas)

Stanley

Mar del Plata

Bahía Blanca

Neuquén

Pucón

Adventure-travel mecca in the shadow of Volcán Villarrica

Lago Llanquihue & Cochamó

German-colonial towns, ancient forests, raging rivers and great escapes

The Carretera Austral

Over 1000km of ultimate road-tripping through the remote south's spectacular scenery

Comodoro Rivadavia

Isla Grande de Tierra del Fuego

Ushuaia

Cabo de Hornos (Cape Horn)

Porvenir

Punta Arenas

El Calafate

Puerto Natales

Coyhaique

Chaitén

Cochamó

Puerto Varas
Frutillar
Puerto Montt
Castro
Ancud

Quellón

Isla Grande de Chiloé

Valdivia
Osorno
Temuco
Pucón
Villarrica

Parque Nacional Puyehue
Parque Nacional Vicente Pérez Rosales

Los Angeles

Parque Nacional Nahuelbuta

Concepción

Cordillera de los Andes

Cordillera

Tierra del Fuego

The uttermost part of the earth to Darwin, now full of discoveries for the adventurous

Parque Nacional Torres del Paine

One of South America's most spectacular parks, with a popular trekking circuit

Valdivia

Chile's most attractive city, with an active university, Spanish forts and a gateway to the pristine coastal range

Chiloé

Colorful island rich in culture, mythology and excellent seafood

RN 22
RN 3
RN 227
RN 25
RN 26
RP 43
RP 25
RN 3
RN 20
RN 40
RN 40
7
9
5

0   200   400 km
0   125   250 miles

35°S
40°S
45°S
50°S
55°S
60°S

40°S
45°S
55°W
60°W
65°W
70°W
75°W
80°W
85°W
90°W
95°W

Chile & Easter Island
6th edition – May 2003
First published – July 1987

Published by
Lonely Planet Publications Pty Ltd ABN 36 005 607 983
90 Maribyrnong St, Footscray, Victoria 3011, Australia

Lonely Planet Offices
Australia Locked Bag 1, Footscray, Victoria 3011
USA 150 Linden St, Oakland, CA 94607
UK 10a Spring Place, London NW5 3BH
France 1 rue du Dahomey, 75011 Paris

Photographs
Many of the images in this guide are available for licensing from
Lonely Planet Images.
W www.lonelyplanetimages.com

Front cover photograph
Torres del Paine National Park, Chile (Galen Rowell/Corbis)

ISBN 1 74059 116 X

text & maps © Lonely Planet Publications Pty Ltd 2003
photos © photographers as indicated 2003

Printed by The Bookmaker International Ltd
Printed in China

Although the authors and Lonely Planet try to make the information as accurate as possible, we accept no responsibility for any loss, injury or inconvenience sustained by anyone using this book.

Contents

MIDDLE CHILE   126

NORTE GRANDE   176

NORTE CHICO   229

LA ARAUCANÍA & THE LAKES DISTRICT   259

CHILOÉ 326

AISÉN & THE CARRETERA AUSTRAL 344

MAGALLANES & TIERRA DEL FUEGO 374

ARCHIPIÉLAGO JUAN FERNÁNDEZ 411

EASTER ISLAND (RAPA NUI) 421

LANGUAGE 443

GLOSSARY 448

THANKS 453

INDEX 457

MAP LEGEND 464

CHILE & EASTER ISLAND MAP INDEX

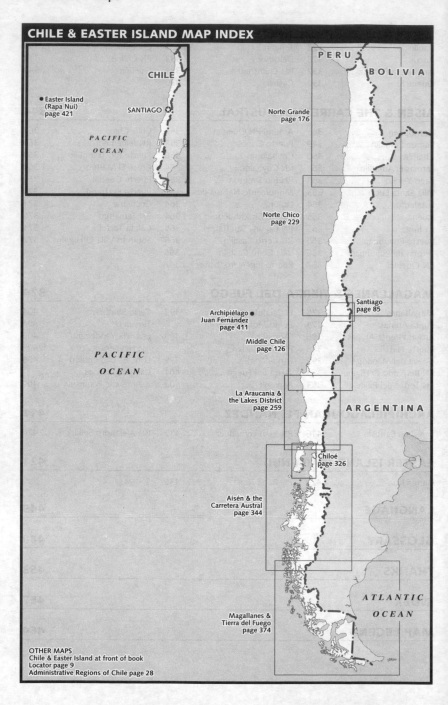

PERU

BOLIVIA

CHILE

● Easter Island
(Rapa Nui)
page 421

SANTIAGO

PACIFIC

OCEAN

Norte Grande
page 176

Norte Chico
page 229

Santiago
page 85

Archipiélago ●
Juan Fernández
page 411

Middle Chile
page 126

PACIFIC

OCEAN

La Araucanía &
the Lakes District
page 259

ARGENTINA

Chiloé
page 326

Aisén & the
Carretera Austral
page 344

ATLANTIC

OCEAN

Magallanes &
Tierra del Fuego
page 374

OTHER MAPS
Chile & Easter Island at front of book
Locator page 9
Administrative Regions of Chile page 28

The Authors

Carolyn Hubbard

Raised in Canada, Australia and Washington State, Carolyn kept the adventure going, studying in Spain and Mexico before and during university and then living and working in New York City and Barcelona afterwards, meanwhile traveling around Europe, Morocco and Southeast Asia. After landing back in the USA, she worked as a senior editor at Lonely Planet's US office. When memories of living beyond office walls grew too vague, she branched out to explore new challenges, including massage therapy, substitute teaching, volunteering and dashing to Chile and Argentina to research sections of Lonely Planet's *South America on a shoestring, Argentina, Uruguay & Paraguay* and this current edition. For the moment, she lives in the Bay Area of California.

Brigitte Barta

Brigitte was born in Wellington, New Zealand, and has lived in seven countries on three continents. After spending five years in San Francisco, she now has one foot planted on Lesvos, Greece, and another in Melbourne, Australia, and is about to embark on her biggest journey: motherhood. In addition to *Chile*, Brigitte is the coauthor of Lonely Planet's *Greece* and *Greek Islands*.

Jeff Davis

Born in Alabama, Jeff grew up mostly in Columbus, Georgia. He attended college in Illinois and studied music, chemical engineering and finally – in a desperate bid to avoid the real world – writing. As an environmental engineer, Jeff has worked in Central America reducing air pollution from factories. He now lives in Cincinnati, Ohio, with his wife and occasional travel companion, Rina. His Lonely Planet credits include work on the books *Georgia & the Carolinas, Central America on a shoestring, USA* and *Canada*.

FROM THE AUTHORS

Carolyn Hubbard Research trips wouldn't be possible or half as enjoyable if it weren't for those people met on the way who bring insight, ease and laughter to each day. To all of you (more than I can list) who make Chile magical, thank you: Marcella Castillo, of CTS for assistance beyond expectation; Marco Vergara, of Navimag; Steve Anderson, of CHIP Travel; Marcelo Díaz, of America's Travel in San Francisco; Britt Lewis & Sandra Echegaray, of Austral Adventures, Chiloé; Willy Stone and Gabriela, of Sernatur in Coyhaique; Gerson Reyes and family, in Punta Arenas; Hernán Jofre and Rodrigo Bahamondez, of Big Foot, Puerto Natales; and Ina Bredfeldt, on Isla Robinson Crusoe. Thanks to Max Bello of Valdivia for making forests all the more alive and to Peter Keller, whose knowledge on Chile's protected areas provided valuable insight, recommendations and caulking to the text. To my coauthors, Jeff Davis and Brigitte Barta, thanks for bringing the pieces together. Much gratitude is extended to Wayne Bernhardson for his previous research and writing on Chile and to Lonely Planeteers Robert Reid and Wendy Smith for the opportunity and support. A warm thank you to Mum for the lake cabin getaway.

Brigitte Barta Many people were extremely generous with their time and knowledge during my research. I wouldn't have survived the task at hand without help from the amazing Marcela Castillo and her sidekicks, Rodrigo Mendes and Rodrigo Gomez, at the Chilean Travel Service (CTS). Other little helpers who kept my head above water include Franz Schubert, Peter Krinner and Margot Martinez Epulef, from Casa Chueca; Simon, from La Casa Roja; Patty Esquerré Dal Borgo, of Verde Que te Quiero Verde; and Yerko Ivelic, of Cascadas Expediciones. Karen Gilchrist, of Ruta del Vino (Valle del Maule), and Thomas Wilkins and staff, at Viñas de Colchagua, gave me a taste for Chilean wine. Many thanks to Free Molina Silva and family, whose hospitality and friendship knew no bounds. Buddies Grant Phelps, Nathan Petersen and Unai Etxeberria also kept my spirits up. Also, one thousand thank-yous to Patricia, at Sarita Colonia, who found my wallet and returned it intact. Coordinating author Carolyn Hubbard was a joy to work with, as were LPers Wendy Smith, Annette Olson, Wendy Taylor and Robert Reid. Thanks lots to Dermot Burgess for taking my photo.

Jeff Davis Thanks to the many *Chilenos* and fellow travelers who helped me during my trip, especially those who did not laugh too loudly at my Spanish. Special thanks go to Clark Stede and Manuela Paradeiser for the respite at Hacienda Los Andes, and to Barbara Knapton for addressing queries after my trip. Many Sernatur staff were helpful in answering my never-ending questions, especially Arlette Levy Arensburg, in Copiapó; Mirna Cortés Arrouch, in Calama; and Alicia Díaz, in La Serena. A special salute goes to my past and present colleagues at Lonely Planet: Kate Hoffman, who introduced me to travel guidebook writing; Robert Reid, who patiently and professionally got this project going; coordinating author Carolyn Hubbard, who offered indispensable advice on the field research; and editors Jeff Campbell and Wendy Taylor, who massaged my words and made me look better without complaining at all. Most of all, thanks to my wonderful and patient wife, Rina, who in many ways deserves coauthor, or at least coeditor, credit on my sections. Because of her, coming home is the best part of any journey.

This Book

A team of writers came together to produce this 6th edition of *Chile & Easter Island*. Coordinating author Carolyn Hubbard wrote and updated the introductory chapters, as well as La Araucanía & the Lakes District, Archipiélago de Chiloé, Aisén & the Carretera Austral, Magallanes & Tierra del Fuego and Archipiélago Juan Fernandez. Brigitte Barta took charge of the Santiago and Middle Chile chapters, while Jeff Davis was responsible for Norte Grande, Norte Chico and Easter Island.

The first two editions of the book were written by Alan Samalgalski. Wayne Bernhardson researched, wrote and updated the 3rd, 4th and 5th editions.

From the Publisher

This edition of *Chile* was produced in Lonely Planet's US office. Robert Reid got the ball rolling and passed on commissioning editor duties to Wendy Smith and series publishing manager duties to Maria Donohoe. Graham Neale was the regional cartographer, and maps were drawn by Annette Olson and Kat Smith at Fineline Mapping. Wendy Taylor served as coordinating editor and applied her copyediting expertise to the first half of the book; Jeff Campbell edited the rest of the regional chapters. Kanani Kauka and Paul Sheridan proofread the book. Emily Douglas laid out the pages, with help from layout editor Valerie Sinzdak. Candice Jacobus designed the color wraps, and Ruth Askevold created the cover. Ken della Penta made the index.

Foreword

ABOUT LONELY PLANET GUIDEBOOKS

The story begins with a classic travel adventure: Tony and Maureen Wheeler's 1972 journey across Europe and Asia to Australia. There was no useful information about the overland trail then, so Tony and Maureen published the first Lonely Planet guidebook to meet a growing need.

From a kitchen table, Lonely Planet has grown to become the largest independent travel publisher in the world, with offices in Melbourne (Australia), Oakland (USA), London (UK) and Paris (France).

Today Lonely Planet guidebooks cover the globe. There is an ever-growing list of books and information in a variety of media. Some things haven't changed. The main aim is still to make it possible for adventurous travelers to get out there – to explore and better understand the world.

At Lonely Planet we believe travelers can make a positive contribution to the countries they visit – if they respect their host communities and spend their money wisely. Since 1986 a percentage of the income from each book has been donated to aid projects and human rights campaigns, and, more recently, to wildlife conservation.

> Although inclusion in a guidebook usually implies a recommendation, we cannot list every good place. Exclusion does not necessarily imply criticism. In fact, there are a number of reasons why we might exclude a place – sometimes it is simply inappropriate to encourage an influx of travelers.

UPDATES & READER FEEDBACK

Things change – prices go up, schedules change, good places go bad and bad places go bankrupt. Nothing stays the same. So, if you find things better or worse, recently opened or long-since closed, please tell us and help make the next edition even more accurate and useful.

Lonely Planet thoroughly updates each guidebook as often as possible – usually every two years, although for some destinations the gap can be longer. Between editions, up-to-date information is available in our free, quarterly *Planet Talk* newsletter and monthly email bulletin *Comet*. The *Upgrades* section of our website (W www.lonelyplanet.com) is also regularly updated by Lonely Planet authors, and the site's *Scoop* section covers news and current affairs relevant to travelers. Lastly, the *Thorn Tree* bulletin board and *Postcards* section carry unverified, but fascinating, reports from travelers.

Tell us about it! We genuinely value your feedback. A well-traveled team at Lonely Planet reads and acknowledges every email and letter we receive and ensures that every morsel of information finds its way to the relevant authors, editors and cartographers.

Everyone who writes to us will find their name listed in the next edition of the appropriate guidebook and will receive the latest issue of *Comet* or *Planet Talk*. The very best contributions will be rewarded with a free guidebook.

We may edit, reproduce and incorporate your comments in Lonely Planet products such as guidebooks, websites and digital products, so let us know if you don't want your comments reproduced or your name acknowledged.

How to contact Lonely Planet:
Online: e talk2us@lonelyplanet.com.au, W www.lonelyplanet.com
Australia: Locked Bag 1, Footscray, Victoria 3011
UK: 10a Spring Place, London NW5 3BH
USA: 150 Linden St, Oakland, CA 94607

Introduction

Let's cut straight to what most people know about Chile: it's skinny, it's long, it's a string-bean country. It is a 4300km strip of all coast on one side and almost all mountain on the other, reaching from Peru to Cape Horn. Its shape alone makes it an alluring destination – travelers can attempt the challenge of going from point to point without ever needing to double back. It's the utmost in linear exploration, with chances for adventure that surpass many destinations.

But what Chile has to offer isn't so cut and dry. This country has a crazy mix of activities

to keep you going for far longer than you have planned. Can't decide whether to visit a desert, surf the waves at hidden beaches, study pre-Columbian art, soak in natural hot springs, spoil yourself at a seaside spa, tour wineries, ride a horse around a volcano, kayak a river or fjord, take to fly-fishing, trek through the Andes or retrace the steps of Magellan and Darwin? Chile is the destination for you – you can do it all here. But don't limit a trip to the spring and summer: the Andes offer top-notch skiing in the Southern Hemisphere's winter months.

Chile's official heart is Santiago, one of South America's most important business centers and a bustling city with superb restaurants and nonstop nightlife. Nearby beach resorts Valparaíso, Viña del Mar and La Serena, as well as the Andes, all offer accessible escapes and loads of fun. Northern Chile holds the world's driest desert, the Atacama, which boasts pastel salt flats, fuming geysers and Inka geoglyphs. Crystal-clear skies in the north have made this area of Chile home to some of the world's most important astronomical observatories. Wine-lovers flock to the country's central valleys, which are speckled in vineyards but are also home to little-visited mountain parks and beaches. To the south, Chile sparkles lush green – a spectacle of forest, lake and volcano, woven together by rivers and undulating farmland. The island of Chiloé is a charm that is becoming more and more a travelers' draw for its intriguing ocean lore, seafood, and unique island culture. The Carretera Austral takes the true adventurer on a gravel road-romp through some of the most inaccesible parts of the country, to impenetrable rainforest, to the raging Río Futaleufú and down into the barren Patagonia steppe. At the foot of the country, the jumble of fjords and the miles of milky-blue glaciers are upstaged only by the crowning jewel of Torres del Paine, a national park with spectacular granite pillars. For those able to go the extra mile, Easter Island (Rapa Nui) mystifies, Isla Robinson Crusoe lets the most urban of us play castaway, and Antarctica awakens our spirit of discovery.

For centuries, world explorers – from Magellan to D'Agostini, Darwin and Shackleton – extoled the beauty of the country's wildness: this is Chile's symbolic heart and what modern-day adventurers come seeking. Juxtaposed to this is an impressive orderliness, in part due to the strong European influence, that makes traveling in Chile easy (but more costly): Transportation is top-notch; the towns and cities, though often architecturally boring, are clean and straightforward; and most travelers agree that Chile is remarkably safe. And, hands down, the highlight of any trip here is getting to know the Chilenos, who are proud of their country's beauty and eager to make travelers feel welcome and at home.

Don't come expecting tantalizing cuisine or obvious indigenous culture, but do come with hiking boots, a raincoat and a desire to get your heart thumping while you ride the waves, raft the rivers, trek the trails, sail over desert, swim the lakes, ski the slopes or simply ogle out the window at all that crazy geography and vast wild going by.

Now, the next decision to make: Which way will you go first – north or south?

Facts about Chile

HISTORY
Indigenous Cultures
Archaeological digs at Monte Verde, near Puerto Montt, uncovered perishables, basalt points and grass twine that were recorded to be 14,800 years old. Amazingly preserved, thanks to a peat bog that covered the dwelling, the findings at Monte Verde have challenged the theory that the Americas were first populated by the Clovis people, who came from Asia by crossing the Bering land bridge some 14,000 years ago and moving south. The Monte Verde site provides an alternative theory that the first peoples either used a coastal route to travel south (the land would have been covered in ice, forbidding an overland route) or that humans arrived on the continent much earlier. It also shows a Paleo-Indian culture that was based more on permanent dwellings and plant cultivation than on nomadic game hunting.

By the 16th century, when Europeans first arrived, a number of groups with differing customs and economies inhabited the region. In the canyons of the desert north, sedentary Aymara farmers cultivated maize in transverse valleys irrigated by the rivers descending from the Andes. At higher elevations, the Aymara grew potatoes and tended flocks of llama and alpaca. To the south, beyond the Río Loa, Atacameño peoples practiced a similar livelihood, while Chango occupied coastal areas from Arica almost to the Río Choapa, south of present-day La Serena. Diaguita Indians inhabited the interior of this latter region, which comprises the drainages of the Copiapó, Huasco and Elqui Rivers.

Inka rule barely touched the central valley and the forests of the south, where Picunche and Mapuche fiercely resisted incursions from the north. The Picunche lived in permanent agricultural settlements, while the Mapuche, who practiced shifting cultivation, were more mobile and much more difficult for the Inkas, and later the Spaniards, to subdue. Several groups closely related to the Mapuche – the Pehuenche, Huilliche and Puelche – lived in the southern lakes region, while the Cunco fished and farmed on the island of Chiloé and along the shores of the gulfs of Reloncaví and Ancud.

South of the Chilean mainland, numerous small populations subsisted through hunting and fishing – the Chonos, Qawashqar (Alacalufes), Yamaná (Yahgan), Tehuelche and Ona (Selk'nam). These isolated archipelagic peoples long avoided contact with Europeans, but once colonization occurred, they were horrifically wiped out; very few remain today.

Spanish Invasion
In 1494, the papal Treaty of Tordesillas ratified the Spanish-Portuguese division of the Americas, granting all territory west of Brazil to Spain, which rapidly consolidated its formal authority and, by the mid-16th century, dominated most of an area extending from Florida and Mexico to central Chile. In the same period, most of South America's important cities were founded, including Lima, Peru; Santiago, Chile; Asunción, Paraguay; and La Paz, Bolivia.

Spain's successful invasion of the Americas was accomplished by groups of adventurers, lowlifes and soldiers-of-fortune. Few in number, the conquerors were determined and ruthless, exploiting factionalism among indigenous groups and frightening native peoples with their horses, vicious dogs and firearms; but their greatest ally was infectious disease, to which the natives lacked immunity.

Before Francisco Pizarro, the conqueror of the Inka Empire in Peru, was assassinated in 1541, he assigned the task of conquering Chile to Pedro de Valdivia. Valdivia's expedition left Peru in 1540, crossed the desert and reached Chile's fertile Mapocho Valley in 1541. There, he subdued local Indians and found the city of Santiago, on February 12. Only six months later, the Indians counterattacked, destroying the town and nearly wiping out the settlers' supplies. But the Spaniards held out, and six years later their numbers had grown to nearly 500. Meanwhile, they founded settlements at La Serena and Valparaíso. Valdivia also worked southward, founding Concepción, Valdivia and Villarrica. By the time of his death at the battle of Tucapel in 1553, at the hands of Mapuche forces led by the famous *caciques* (chiefs) Caupolicán and Lautaro, Valdivia had laid the groundwork for a new society.

Colonial Society

The Spaniards' primary goal was the acquisition of gold and silver, and they ruthlessly appropriated precious metals through outright robbery when possible, and by other, no less brutal, means when necessary. El Dorado, the legendary city of gold, proved elusive, but the Spaniards soon realized that the true wealth of the New World consisted of the large Indian populations of Mexico, Peru and other lands.

Disdaining physical labor themselves, the Spaniards exploited the indigenous populations of the New World through the *encomienda* system, best translated as 'entrustment,' by which the Crown granted an individual Spaniard *(encomendero)* rights to Indian labor and tribute in a particular village or area. In theory, Spanish legislation required the encomendero to reciprocate by giving the Indians lessons on the Spanish language and the Catholic religion, but in practice, imperial administration was inadequate to ensure compliance or to stop the worst abuses.

The encomienda system failed when Indian populations declined rapidly from epidemic disease. Isolated for at least 10,000 years from Old World diseases, the Indians could not withstand the onslaught of smallpox, influenza, typhus and other such killers: in some parts of the New World, these diseases reduced the native population by more than 95%.

In northern Chile (then part of Peru), the Spaniards successfully developed an encomienda system. The large indigenous population in this area was easily subdued and controlled, ironically because they were more highly organized and more accustomed to similar forms of exploitation. In hierarchical states such as the Inka empire, the Spaniards easily replaced the established local authority.

The Spaniards also established dominance in central Chile, but the semisedentary and nomadic peoples of the south mounted vigorous resistance, and even into the late 19th century the area remained unsafe for white settlers. Crossing the Andes, the Mapuche had tamed the feral horses

that had multiplied rapidly on the fine pastures of the Argentine pampas; they soon became expert riders, which increased their mobility and enhanced their ability to strike.

Even in places where Spanish supremacy went unchallenged, Indians outnumbered Spaniards. Since few women accompanied the early settlers, Spanish men, especially of the lower classes, had both formal and informal relationships with Indian women; the resulting *mestizo* children, of mixed Spanish and Indian parentage, soon outnumbered the Indian population as many of the natives died through epidemics, forced-labor abuses and warfare.

Rise of the Latifundio

Chile was too remote for adequate imperial oversight, and despite the Crown's disapproval, Valdivia rewarded his followers with enormous land grants, some stretching from the Andes to the Pacific. More than anywhere else in the Americas, the system of control resembled the great feudal estates of Valdivia's Spanish homeland of Extremadura. Such estates *(latifundios)*, many intact as late as the 1960s, became an enduring feature of Chilean agriculture and the dominant force in Chilean society.

As the encomienda system declined, Chile's neo-aristocracy had to look elsewhere for labor. The country's growing mestizo population, who were systematically excluded from land ownership, provided the solution. Landless and vagrant, these ostensible Spaniards soon attached themselves as *inquilinos* (tenant farmers) to the large rural estates, which evolved from livestock ranches *estancias* into agricultural haciendas or, as they became more commonly known in Chile, *fundos*.

In becoming inquilinos, laborers and their families also became personally dependent on the *hacendado* (master) for certain rights. Paying little or no rent, they could occupy a shack on the estate, graze livestock on its more remote sections, and cultivate a patch of land for household use. In return, they provided labor during annual rodeos and watched out for their master's interests.

Later immigrants, especially Basques, became a major influence from the late 17th century to the end of the colonial era. Surnames such as Eyzaguirre, Urrutia and Larraín became prominent in Chilean commerce, and these families purchased many landed estates, including those publicly auctioned after being confiscated when the Spaniards expelled the Jesuits. Basque families adopted the pseudo-aristocratic values of the early landed gentry and have remained important in Chilean politics, society and business.

In colonial times, mining and business brought greater wealth than did land. Only after political independence from imperial Spain did Chile's agricultural economy begin to flourish.

Independence Movements

Within a few decades of Columbus' Caribbean landing, Spain possessed an empire twice the size of Europe, stretching from California to Cape Horn. Yet the empire disintegrated in less than two decades; by the late 1820s, only Puerto Rico and Cuba remained in Spanish hands.

Many factors contributed to the rise of Latin American independence movements that began between 1808 and 1810. One was the emergence of the *criollo* (creole) class – American-born Spaniards who soon distinguished themselves from the Iberians. In every Latin American country, the development of a definable American identity increased people's desire for self-government. Of equal importance, influential criollo merchants resented Spain's rigid mercantile trade system. To facilitate tax collection, Madrid decreed that all trade to the mother country must pass overland through Panama to the Caribbean and Havana, rather than directly by ship from the port of Valparaíso. This cumbersome system hampered the commerce of Chile and other Spanish colonies and eventually cost Spain its empire.

Revolutionary Wars

During colonial times, the formal jurisdiction of the Audiencia de Chile stretched roughly from present-day Chañaral in the north to Puerto Aisén in the south; it also encompassed the trans-Andean Cuyo region of modern Argentina, comprising the provinces of Mendoza, San Juan and San Luis. The Audiencia was an administrative subdivision of the much larger Viceroyalty of Peru, whose capital, Lima, was South America's most important city. But Chile was distant from Lima and developed in near isolation

from Peru, with an identity distinct from its northern neighbor.

Independence movements throughout South America united to expel Spain from the continent by the 1820s. From Venezuela, a criollo army under Simón Bolívar fought its way across the Andes to the Pacific and then south toward Peru. José de San Martín's Ejército de los Andes (Army of the Andes) – nearly a third of them liberated slaves – marched over the *cordillera* (mountain range) from Argentina into Chile, occupied Santiago and sailed north to Lima.

San Martín's army also included numerous Chileans who had fled the reimposition of Spanish colonial rule after the Napoleonic Wars. The Argentine liberator appointed Bernardo O'Higgins second-in-command of his forces. O'Higgins, the illegitimate son of an Irishman who had served the Spaniards as Viceroy of Peru, became supreme director of the new Chilean republic. San Martín helped drive Spain from Peru, transporting his army in ships either seized from the Spaniards or purchased from Britons or North Americans. British and North American merchants also financed the purchase of arms and ammunition, knowing that expulsion of the Spaniards would create new commercial opportunities. Scotsman Thomas Cochrane, a colorful former Royal Navy officer, founded and commanded Chile's navy.

Early Republic

Spanish administrative divisions provided the framework for the political geography of the new South American republics. At independence, Chile was but a fraction of its present size, consisting of the *intendencias* (administrative units of the Spanish Empire) of Santiago and Concepción and sharing ambiguous boundaries with Bolivia in the north, Argentina to the east, and the hostile Mapuche nation south of the Río Biobío. Chile lost the trans-Andean region of Cuyo to the Provincias Unidas del Río de la Plata (United Provinces of the River Plate), forerunner of modern Argentina.

Although other Latin American countries emerged from the wars with severe economic difficulties, Chile quickly achieved a degree of political stability, permitting rapid development of agriculture, mining, industry and commerce. Regional quarrels were less serious and violent than they were, for example, in Argentina. Despite social and economic cleavages, the population was relatively homogeneous and less afflicted by racial problems than most other Latin American states. The country was well situated to take advantage of international economic trends; the port of Valparaíso, for instance, became an important outlet for Chilean wheat, which satisfied the unprecedented demand of the California gold rush.

O'Higgins dominated Chilean politics for five years after formal independence in 1818, enacting political, social, religious and educational reforms, but the landowning elite that first supported him soon objected to increased taxes, abolition of titles and limitations on the inheritance of landed estates. Pressured by military forces allied with the aristocracy, he resigned in 1823 and went into exile in Peru. He died there in 1842, never having returned to his homeland.

Apart from deposing the Spaniards, political independence did not alter the structure of Chilean society, which was dominated by major landowners. The embodiment of landowning interests was Diego Portales, a businessman who, as interior minister, was a de facto dictator until his execution after an uprising in 1837. His custom-drawn constitution centralized power in Santiago and established Roman Catholicism as the state religion. It also limited suffrage to literate and propertied adult males and established indirect elections for the presidency and the Senate; only the lower Chamber of Deputies was chosen directly by voters. Portales' constitution lasted, with some changes, until 1925.

War of the Pacific

Also known as the Chile-Peruvian War, the War of the Pacific (1879–84) began after Bolivia prohibited a Chilean company from exploiting the nitrate deposits in the then-Bolivian-owned Atacama. Chile retaliated by taking over the port of Antofogasta, which was also then part of Bolivia, and declared war on Peru, Bolivia's ally. By the end of 1874, Chile had seized control of Bolivia's only coastal access, plus the Tacna and Arica provinces of Peru.

Territorial Expansion & Political Reform

From the mid-19th century, railroad construction began to revolutionize internal transport. Military triumphs over Peru and Bolivia in the War of the Pacific and treaties with the Mapuche (1881) incorporated the nitrate-rich Atacama and temperate southern territories under Chilean authority. At the same time, however, Chile had to abandon its claims to most of enormous, sparsely populated Patagonia to Argentina.

Santiago's intervention in the Atacama, ostensibly to protect the interests of Chilean nationals laboring in the nitrate fields, proved a bonanza. Just as guano financed Peruvian independence, so nitrates brought prosperity to Chile, or at least to certain sectors of Chilean society. British, North American and German investors supplied most of the capital.

Ever since the California gold rush (1849), Valparaíso had been a critical port. Soon the nitrate ports of Antofagasta and Iquique also became important in international commerce, until the opening of the Panama Canal in 1914 nearly eliminated traffic around the Horn, and the later development of petroleum-based fertilizers made mineral nitrates obsolete.

Chile also sought a broader Pacific presence, and annexed the tiny, remote Easter Island (Isla de Pascua, or Rapa Nui) in 1888.

Chile emerged from the War of the Pacific enriched not only by Atacama's nitrates but also, later, by copper. Mining expansion created a new working class, as well as a class of nouveaux riches, both of which challenged the political power of the landowning oligarchy.

The first political figure to tackle the dilemma of Chile's badly distributed wealth and power was President José Manuel Balmaceda, elected in 1886. Balmaceda's administration undertook major public works projects: expanding the rail network and building new roads, bridges and docks; extending telegraph lines and postal services; and improving hospitals and schools.

Balmaceda's policies met resistance from a conservative Congress, which in 1890 rejected his budget, voted to depose him and appointed Naval Commander Jorge Montt to head a provisional government. More than 10,000 Chileans died in the ensuing civil war, in which Montt's navy controlled the country's ports and eventually defeated the government, despite army support for Balmaceda. After several months' asylum in the Argentine embassy, Balmaceda shot himself.

Although they weakened the presidential system, Balmaceda's immediate successors continued many of his public works projects and also opened Congress to popular rather than indirect elections. Major reform, though, wouldn't come until after WWII.

20th Century

Despite economic hardship due to a declining nitrate industry, the election of President Arturo Alessandri Palma was a hopeful sign for Chile's working class. To reduce landowners' power, he proposed greater political autonomy for the provinces, and land and income taxes to finance social benefits to improve working conditions, public health, education and welfare. Congressional conservatives obstructed these reforms, though, and army opposition forced Alessandri's resignation in 1924.

For several years, the dictatorial General Carlos Ibáñez del Campo occupied the presidency and other positions of power, but his misguided or miscarried economic policies (exacerbated by global depression) led to widespread opposition, forcing him into Argentine exile in 1931.

After Ibáñez's ouster, Chilean political parties realigned. Several leftist groups briefly imposed a socialist republic and merged to form the Socialist Party. Splits between Stalinists and Trotskyites divided the Communist Party, while splinter groups from existing radical and reformist parties created a bewildering mix of new political organizations. For most of the 1930s and '40s the democratic left dominated Chilean politics, and government intervention in the economy through Corfo, the state development corporation, became increasingly important.

Meanwhile, the US role in the Chilean economy also grew steadily, since German investment had declined after WWI and development of synthetic nitrates undercut British economic influence. In the first two decades of the 20th century, North American companies had gained control of the copper mines, the cornerstone – then and now – of the Chilean economy. WWII augmented the demand for Chilean copper, promoting economic growth even as Chile remained neutral in the conflict.

Politics of Land Reform

In the 1920s as much as 75% of Chile's rural population still depended on haciendas that controlled 80% of the prime agricultural land. Inquilinos remained at the mercy of landowners for access to housing, soil and subsistence. Their votes belonged to landowners, who used them to influence Congress and maintain the existing land tenure system.

As protected industry expanded and the government promoted public works, employment increased and the lot of urban workers improved. The lot of rural workers, however, deteriorated rapidly – real wages fell, forcing day laborers to the cities in search of work. Inquilinos suffered reduced land allotments, seed and fertilizer supplies, as well as reduced rights to graze animals, and yet they had to supply more labor. Given abundant labor, haciendas had little incentive to modernize, and production stagnated – a situation that changed little until the 1960s.

In 1952, the former dictator Ibáñez del Campo won the presidency and, surprisingly, tried to curtail landowners' political power by reducing their control over the votes of their tenants and laborers; he also revoked an earlier law banning the Communist Party, but his government faltered in the face of high inflation and partisan politicking.

In 1958, socialist Salvador Allende headed a new leftist coalition known as FRAP (Frente de Acción Popular, or Popular Action Front), while Jorge Alessandri, son of Arturo Alessandri, represented a coalition between the conservative and liberal parties. Eduardo Frei Montalva represented the recently formed Democracia Cristiana (Christian Democrats), a reformist party whose goals resembled those of FRAP but whose philosophical basis was Catholic humanism.

Alessandri won the election with less than 32% of the vote, while Allende managed 29% and Frei 21%, the best showing ever by a Christian Democrat. An opposition Congress forced Alessandri to accept modest land-reform legislation, beginning a decade-long battle with the haciendas. Alessandri's term saw little concrete progress in this matter, but the new laws provided a legal basis for the expropriation of large estates.

The Day the Earth Shook

In southern Chile, those old enough to remember May 22, 1960, can recall exactly what they were doing at 7:11pm when the earthquake hit. Measuring 8.6 on the Richter scale and with an epicenter off the coast of Valdivia, the quake shook Chile from Concepción to southern Chiloé, destroying most of the coastal towns' colonial buildings, changing the coastline and causing US$550 million in damage. One thousand people were killed. In Chiloé, 200 locals fearing the shaking earth took to the seemingly safer ocean in their fishing boats only to be engulfed in the tsunami-ravaged waters just moments later.

Fourteen hours after the earthquake hit, the tsunami crashed into the Waiakea area of Hilo, Hawaii, about 10,000km away, causing 61 deaths and US$24 million in damage. It continued westward to the Honshu coast of Japan, destroying villages, killing 200 people and causing US$50 million in damage.

In Chile, aftershocks continued the next day. In the Andes, land and rock slides blocked Río San Pedro, creating an artificial lake and turning pasture into swamp; coastal streets and railway lines turned to beachfront. Two days after the first shock, Volcán Puyehue erupted in a dramatic blast, changing vast stands of forests and pasturelands into a desert landscape of sand dunes and lava rivers. As you travel, you can witness the earthquake's impact: many coastal cities are cluttered with quickly built slapdash '60s block architecture; near Ancud, Chiloé, railway foundations jut out at low tide; and when you ask anyone about the earthquake, you'll see them take in a longer breath, remembering the day, and then tell their own story of where they were when it hit.

Christian Democratic Period

The 1964 presidential election was a choice between Allende and Frei, who also drew support from conservative groups who detested the leftist physician. During the campaign, both FRAP and the Christian Democrats promised agrarian reform, supported rural unionization and promised an end to the hacienda system. Frei won with 56%, as Allende, undermined by leftist factionalism, polled only 39%.

Genuinely committed to social transformation, the Christian Democrats attempted to control inflation, improve the balance of payments between imports and exports, implement agrarian reform and improve public health, education and social services. Their policies, however, threatened both the traditional elite's privileges and the radical left's working-class support. Fearful of losing their influence, the FRAP coalition urged faster and more radical action.

The Christian Democrats had other difficulties. In the last years of Jorge Alessandri's presidency, the country's economy had declined, and limited opportunities in the countryside drove the dispossessed to the cities, where spontaneous squatter settlements or *callampas* (mushrooms), sprang up almost overnight. As the Christian Democrats inherited these problems, one common response was to attack the visible export sector, dominated by US interests; President Frei advocated 'Chileanization' of the copper industry (getting rid of foreign investors in favor of Chileans), while Allende and his backers supported the industry's 'nationalization' (placing the industry under state control).

The Christian Democrats also faced challenges from violent groups such as the MIR (Movimiento de Izquierda Revolucionario, or Leftist Revolutionary Movement), which had begun among upper-middle-class students in Concepción, a southern university town and important industrial center. MIR's activism appealed to coal miners, textile workers and other urban laborers who formed the allied Frente de Trabajadores Revolucionarios (Revolutionary Workers Front). Activism also caught on with peasants who longed for land reform. Other leftist groups supported strikes and land seizures by Mapuche Indians and rural laborers.

Frei's reforms were too slow to appease the leftists and too rapid for the conservative National Party, and even for some Christian Democrats. Despite improved living conditions for many rural workers and impressive gains in education and public health, the country was plagued by increasing inflation, dependence on foreign markets and capital, and inequitable income distribution. The Christian Democrats could not satisfy rising expectations in Chile's increasingly militant and polarized society.

Allende's Rise to Power

As the presidential election approached in 1970, the new leftist coalition UP (Unidad Popular, or Popular Unity) chose Allende as its candidate. The UP's radical program included the nationalization of mines, banks and insurance companies, plus the expropriation and redistribution of large landholdings.

The other major candidates were Christian Democrat Radomiro Tomic (too left-wing for conservatives) and aged Jorge Alessandri, standing for the National Party. In one of Chile's closest elections ever, Allende won a plurality of 36%, while Alessandri drew 35% and Tomic 28%. Under the constitution, if no candidate obtained an absolute majority, Congress had to confirm the result and could in theory choose the runner-up, although by custom it had never done so. Since no party had a congressional majority, Christian Democrats pressured Allende for constitutional guarantees to preserve the democratic process in return for their support. Agreeing to these guarantees, Allende assumed the presidency in October 1970.

Allende's own multiparty coalition of socialists, communists and radicals disagreed on the new government's objectives. Lacking any real electoral mandate, he faced an opposition Congress and a suspicious US government, and right-wing extremists even advocated his overthrow by violent means.

Allende's economic program, accomplished by evading rather than confronting Congress, included the state takeover of many private enterprises and massive income redistribution. By increasing government spending, the new president expected to stimulate demand and encourage private enterprise to increase production and reduce unemployment, thereby bringing the country out of recession. This worked briefly, but apprehensive businessmen and landowners, worried over expropriation and nationalization, sold off stock and disposed of farm machinery and livestock. Industrial production nose-dived,

leading to shortages, hyperinflation and black marketeering.

Peasants, frustrated with an agrarian reform that favored collectives of inquilinos (resident laborers who had rights to a small patch of land for household use) over sharecroppers (contract farmers who owed half their crop to the hacienda) and afuerinos (outside laborers), seized land, and agricultural production fell. The government had to use scarce foreign currency to import food.

Chilean politics grew increasingly polarized and confrontational, as many of Allende's supporters resented his indirect approach to transformation of the state and its economy. MIR intensified its guerrilla activities, and stories circulated in Santiago's factories about the creation of armed communist organizations.

Expropriation of US-controlled copper mines and other enterprises, plus conspicuously friendly relations with Cuba, provoked US hostility. Later, hearings in the US Congress indicated that President Richard Nixon and Secretary of State Henry Kissinger had actively undercut Allende by discouraging credit from international finance organizations and providing both financial and moral support to his opponents. Until the late 1980s, except during the Carter administration, the US maintained friendly relations with the Chilean military.

Faced with such difficulties, the government tried to forestall conflict by proposing clearly defined limits on nationalization. Unfortunately, neither extreme leftists, who believed that only force could achieve socialism, nor their rightist counterparts, who believed only force could prevent it, were open to compromise.

Rightist Backlash

In late 1972, independent truckers led a widespread strike by an alliance of shopkeepers, professionals, bank clerks, right-wing students and even some urban and rural laborers. The strikers, supported by both the Christian Democrats and the National Party, threatened the government's viability and demanded that plans for a state-owned trucking enterprise be abandoned. As the government's authority crumbled, a desperate Allende invited constitutionalist army commander General Carlos Prats to occupy the critical post of interior minister, and he included an admiral and an air force general in his cabinet. Despite the economic crisis, results of the March 1973 congressional elections demonstrated that Allende's support had actually increased since 1970 – but the unified opposition nevertheless strengthened its control of Congress, underscoring the polarization of Chilean politics. In June 1973 there was an unsuccessful military coup.

The next month, truckers and other rightists once again went on strike, supported by the entire opposition. Having lost military support, General Prats resigned, to be replaced by the relatively obscure General Augusto Pinochet Ugarte, whom both Prats and Allende thought loyal to constitutional government. On September 11, 1973, Pinochet unleashed a brutal *golpe de estado* (coup d'état) that overthrew the UP government and resulted in Allende's death (an apparent suicide) and the death of thousands of Allende supporters.

Police and the military apprehended thousands of leftists, suspected leftists and sympathizers. Many were herded into Santiago's National Stadium, where they suffered beatings, torture and even execution. Hundreds of thousands went into exile.

The military argued that force was necessary to remove Allende because his government had fomented political and economic chaos and because he himself was planning to overthrow the constitutional order by force. Certainly, inept policies brought about this 'economic chaos,' but reactionary sectors, encouraged and abetted from abroad, exacerbated scarcities, producing a black market that further undercut order. Allende's record of persistently standing for election and his pledge to the opposition implied commitment to the democratic process, but his inability or unwillingness to control factions to his left terrified the middle class as well as the oligarchy. His last words, part of a radio address just before the attacks on the government palace, La Moneda, expressed his ideals but underlined his failure:

My words are not spoken in bitterness, but in disappointment. There will be a moral judgment on those who have betrayed the oath they took as soldiers of Chile....They have the might and they can enslave us, but they cannot halt the world's social processes, not with crimes, nor with guns....May you go forward in the knowledge that, sooner rather than later, the great avenues will open once again, along which free citizens will march in order to build a better society. Long live Chile! Long live the people! Long live the workers! These are my last words, and I am sure that this sacrifice will constitute a moral lesson that will punish cowardice, perfidy and treason.

Military Dictatorship

Many opposition leaders, some of whom had encouraged the coup, expected a quick return to civilian government, but General Pinochet had other ideas. From 1973 to 1989, he headed a durable junta that dissolved Congress, banned leftist parties and suspended all others, prohibited nearly all political activity and ruled by decree. Assuming the presidency in 1974, Pinochet sought to reorder the country's political and economic culture through repression, torture and murder. The Caravan of Death, a group of military that traveled by helicopter from town to town, mainly in northern Chile, killed many political opponents, many of whom had voluntarily turned themselves in. Detainees came from all sectors of society, from peasant to professional (including doctors, lawyers and university professors). About a thousand people 'disappeared' during the 17-year regime.

The CNI (Centro Nacional de Informaciones, or National Information Center) and its predecessor DINA (Directoria de Inteligencia Nacional, or National Intelligence Directorate) were the most notorious practitioners of state terrorism. International assassinations were not unusual – a car bomb killed General Prats in Buenos Aires a year after the coup, and Christian Democrat leader Bernardo Leighton barely survived a shooting in Rome in 1975. Perhaps the most notorious case was the 1976 murder of Allende's foreign minister, Orlando Letelier, by a car bomb in Washington, DC.

By 1977 even air force general Gustavo Leigh, a member of the junta, thought the campaign against 'subversion' so successful that he proposed a return to civilian rule, but Pinochet forced Leigh's resignation, ensuring the army's dominance and perpetuating himself in power. By 1980, Pinochet felt confident enough to submit a new, customized constitution to the electorate and wagered his own political future on it. In a plebiscite with narrow options, about two-thirds of the voters approved the constitution and ratified Pinochet's presidency until 1989, though many voters abstained in protest.

Return to Democracy

Political parties began to function openly again in 1987. In late 1988, trying to extend his presidency until 1997, Pinochet held another plebiscite, but this time voters rejected him. In multiparty elections in 1989, Christian Democrat Patricio Aylwin, compromise candidate of a coalition of opposition parties known as the Concertación para la Democracia, defeated Pinochet protégé Hernán Büchi, a conservative economist.

Consolidating the return to democracy, Aylwin's relatively uneventful four-year term expired in 1994; in late 1993, Chileans elected Eduardo Frei Ruiz-Tagle, son of the late president Eduardo Frei Montalva, to a six-year term. Despite uninterrupted civilian government, the military retains considerable power and the constitution institutionalizes this, at least in the short term. Pinochet's senate appointees, with help from elected conservatives, can still block reform, and he himself assumed a senate seat upon retirement from the army in 1997 – at least in part because it conferred immunity from prosecution in Chile.

The September 1998 arrest of General Pinochet in London at the request of Spanish judge Báltazar Garzón, who was investigating deaths and disappearances of Spanish citizens in the aftermath of the 1973 coup, caused an international uproar.

In response to the arrest, US President Clinton requested the release of files showing 30 years of US government covert aid to undermine Allende and create the stage for the coup d'état. Pinochet was put under house arrest, and for four years, lawyers argued whether or not he was able to stand trial for crimes committed by the Caravan of Death based on his health and mental condition. Both the Court of Appeals (in 2000) and the Supreme Court (2002) ruled him unfit to stand trial, thereby ending any judicial effort to hold him accountable. As a consequence of the court's decision – that he suffers from dementia – Pinochet stepped down from his post as lifetime senator, finally ending his political career.

GEOGRAPHY & CLIMATE

Many Chileans delight in recounting the joke that after God made most of South America he took what was left over – bits of desert, mountain, valley, glacier, rainforest, coast and mountain – and created Chile, a slinky thin country that extends some 4300km from Peru in the north to the Strait of Magellan in the south, but averages less than 200km wide.

The most obvious feature in Chile is the long Andean chain, which began forming in the Paleocene epoch, about 60 million years ago. By the Pleistocene Epoch, two million years ago, the Andes had fully formed (reaching a height above 6000m in some areas). Most of southern Chile was covered in glaciers, and northern Chile was still under the ocean. Today, the effect of this time is evident in the barren north's salt flats and in the south's deep glacially carved lakes, gently curved moraine hills, and impressive glacial valleys.

Chile's geography is most often described in terms of horizontal chunks. **Norte Grande** (Big North) extends from the Peruvian border to the province of Chañaral and is dominated by the Atacama Desert. Despite its aridity and tropical latitude, the Atacama is a remarkably temperate desert: The region gets an average of only 0.10cm of rainfall a year, with and annual high temperatures range from 17°C to 24°C (63°F to 76°F) and lows from 11°C to 17°C (52°F to 63°F). The climate is moderated by the cool, north-flowing Humboldt Current, which parallels the coast. High humidity produces an extensive cloud cover and thick fogs known as *camanchaca*, which condense on coastal–range escarpments. Cities such as Arica, Iquique and Antofagasta, which occupy narrow coastal plains, are sustained by transverse river valleys, subterranean water sources and springs, and diversions of distant streams. Toward the Bolivian border, the canyons of the *precordillera* (foothills) lead to the *altiplano*, or high steppe, and to high mountain passes.

South of Chañaral, the **Norte Chico** (Little North), whose approximate southern boundary is the Río Aconcagua, is a transition zone from desert to scrub and occasional forest. Major river valleys, such as Valle Elqui, allow for agriculture. In those rare years of substantial rainfall, the landscape erupts with wildflowers.

South of the Río Aconcagua begins the fertile heartland of **Middle Chile**, through which the Valle Central (Central Valley) extends. This area, supporting Chile's main agricultural and wine-growing region, is home to the country's capital, Santiago (with at least a third of the country's population), the ports of Valparaíso and San Antonio, and the bulk of the country's industry and employment, plus important copper mines. Temperatures here average around 28°C (82°F) in January and 10°C (50°F) in July; the rainy season lasts from May to August.

The **Lakes District**, from Río Biobío to the Seno de Reloncaví, undulates with green pastureland, temperate rainforest, and many foothill lakes. It also has a score of snow-capped volcanoes. Average temperatures are 14°C (57°F) in summer and 4°C (40°F) in winter, but the region receives about a whopping 3m of rainfall annually, most of which dumps between May and September, but no month is excluded. The strong easterly winds here, usually quite warm, are known as *puelches*. Winters are snowy, making skiing great but border passage through the mountains difficult.

The country's largest island, **Chiloé** hangs off the continent near Puerto Montt, and is vulnerable to the Pacific winds and storms that thrash at its 180km-long western coast. The smaller islands between Chiloé and the mainland make up the archipelago and stay relatively protected in the Golfo de Ancud, but there's no escaping the rain: The archipelago gets up to 150 days of rain a year.

Across from Chiloé, the **Aisén** region has fjords, roaring rivers, thick forests and high peaks: Anyone who has been to Alaska or New Zealand will note similarities. At about 45° S, just before Coyhaique, the Andes jog west to meet up with the Pacific and the Campo de Hielo Norte:, 300,000 hectares of northern ice field, where 19 major glaciers coalesce, nourished by the more than 5000mm of rain and snow that fall here each year. To the east, the land transitions from mountainous rainforest to dry windy Patagonia steppe – this is where you'll find Coyhaique and other Patagonia towns. Lago General Carrera, considered to be the deepest lake in South America, takes up 224,000 hectares, a third of which lies in Argentina, where it is known as Lago Buenos Aires.

The Campo de Hielo Sur, the southern continental ice field, separates the mainland from **Magallanes and Tierra del Fuego**, which comprises about 30% of the country's territory. Temperatures in summer average just 11°C (52°F), and in winter about 4°C (40°F), but wind chill can make it feel even lower. The weather is highly changeable (they say expect four seasons in a day), and the incessant winds can be brutal, although they do allow for fewer cloudy days in winter. Tapering into the wet foot of the continent, glaciers, fjords, ice fields and mountains all join together in a marvelous puzzle before reaching the Magellan Strait and Tierra del Fuego. The eastern flat pampas extend through northern Tierra del Fuego, until abruptly halted in the south by the Cordillera Darwin.

See also the Climate Charts at the end of this chapter.

ECOLOGY & ENVIRONMENT

Chile is considered to be one of the least sustainable countries in the world, indiscriminately using its natural resources to improve economic growth, often allowing foreign companies to do the exploiting. However, Chileans are becoming more aware of the environmental issues and the government's lack of foresight. International awareness and concern has also grown, and a variety of international foundations now support environmental projects in Chile. It remains to be seen if the government can adopt more environmentally friendly practices.

For most Chileans, the single most palpable environmental issue is the cloud of smog that so often hangs over the city of Santiago, which sits in a basin between two mountain ranges. In 2002, the city was ranked as the second most polluted city in the Americas. Outlying communities are the worst off; Padahuel, the home of the international airport, is considered to have the highest level of pollution. The smog, which on some days is so severe that schoolchildren are kept from participating in physical education and older citizens are advised to stay indoors, stems from the growing number of private automobiles, the presence of diesel buses and the concentration of polluting industries. Efforts have been made to reduce air pollution, for example, by improving the quality of public transport vehicles and by creating no-drive days for private vehicles.

From Region VIII south, native forest continues to lose ground to plantations of fast-growing exotics, such as eucalyptus and

Monterey pine. Native forests of araucaria (monkey-puzzle trees) and alerce (a long-living conifer resembling the redwood) have declined precipitously over the past decades.

Throughout the south, the burgeoning salmon-farming industry has drawn criticism for polluting both freshwater and saltwater areas. Another issue is the intensive use of agricultural chemicals and pesticides to promote Chile's flourishing fruit exports, which during the southern summer furnish the Northern Hemisphere with fresh produce. Water contamination and air pollution caused by the mining industry are also major concerns throughout the country.

The growing hole in the ozone layer over Antarctica has become such an issue that medical authorities recommend wearing protective clothing and heavy sunblock to avoid cancer-causing ultraviolet radiation, especially in Patagonia.

Environmental Organizations

As an increasingly environmentally conscious country, Chile has a number of organizations dedicated to conservation and education. For those looking to get involved, try contacting such places to inquire about volunteer opportunities. One of the best stories of an organization that has brought

foreigners and Chilean together to work on conservation is **École**, in the Lakes District. Started by a few Californians who saw how the logging of Chile's native forests was strikingly similar to the devastation of their own native forests of Humboldt County, the member-oriented group has been supremely successful in raising awareness. They run one of the most popular places to stay in Pucón – it is both a meeting point and place to learn more about what's happening to Chile's forests. To learn more about École, see the Pucón section of the La Araucanía & the Lakes District chapter, or contact the organizations that support it (AFI) and organizations that were spawned by it (Fundación Lahuen), both listed below.

Most environmental conservation groups have offices in Santiago.

Ancient Forests International (AFI; ☎/fax 707-923-3015; Box 1850, Redway, CA 95560 USA) Has close links to Chilean forest-conservation organizations and helps raise awareness and funding.

Coalición para la Conservación de la Cordillera de la Costa (☎ 063-257-673; W www.ccc.terra.cl; Carlos Anwandter 624, Casa 4, Valdivia) Focuses on protecting the Valdivian rainforest along the coastal range through education campaigns.

Codeff (Comité Pro Defensa de la Fauna y Flora; ☎ 02-274-7461, fax 02-251-8433;

Chile's Endangered Rivers

In its drive toward modernization, Chile has had to deal with limited energy resources. Successive Chilean governments have made a conscious decision to encourage hydroelectricity. On the face of it, this is a wise decision: in many areas, heavy spring snowmelt in the high Andes feeds raging transverse rivers that pass through narrow canyons; many sites are ideal for dams. Unfortunately, these dam projects also have major social, cultural, environmental and economic drawbacks.

The most internationally notorious project has been the construction, by the powerful electrical utility Endesa, of a series of dams on the Río Biobío, which is revered by rafters and kayakers as one of the world's finest white-water rivers. The Panque, the first of seven dams to be built on the upper Biobío, is expected to provide a substantial percentage of Chile's hydroelectricity. Objections from Pehuenche communities, stemming from Endesa's inadequate environmental-impact report, stalled construction but have been unable to stop it permanently.

The Biobío is not the only river under threat. Residents in the area of Chile's other world-class white-water site, the Futaleufú, near the Argentine border southeast of Chaitén, were shocked to learn that Endesa and two other hydroelectric utilities had filed claims on water rights to the river's flow – without any fanfare. In response, the locals have formed their own Corporación de Defensa y Desarollo del Río Futaleufú (Codderfu), seeking to create a nationally recognized and protected river corridor. Their supporters include Codeff, Grupo de Acción por el Biobío and the US-based FutaFriends (see Environmental Organizations, under Ecology & Environment, in this chapter).

W *www.codeff.cl; Luis Uribe 2620, Ñuñoa, Santiago)* Campaigns to protect the country's flora and fauna, especially endangered species. Trips, seminars and work projects are organized for volunteers.

Defensores del Bosque Chileno *(☎ 02-204-1914;* **W** *www.elbosquechileno; Diagonal Oriente 1413, Ñuñoa)* Focuses on defending and conserving the native forests through information campaigns, environmental education programs, lobbying, promoting planting of native species over exotics, and taking legal action against logging interests.

Fundación Ayacara *(☎ 02-232-3407;* **e** *info@ ayacara.org; PO Box 100-9, Providencia, Santiago)* Implements forest conservation, scientific research, education and alternative production within the remote Ayacara community on the Huequi Peninsula, in Aisén.

Fundación Lahuen *(☎ 02-278-0237; Orrego Luco 054, Providencia)* Protects native forests at their private park, El Cañi, and organizes environmental education programs.

FutaFriends *(☎ 406-586-3460;* **W** *futafriends.org; PO Box 1942, Bozeman, MT 59771 USA)* Works with Chilean partners to support viable economic alternatives to a potential dam in the Futaleufú River Valley.

Greenpeace Pacífico Sur *(☎ 02-343-7788, fax 02-204-0162;* **W** *www.greenpeace.cl; Eleodoro Flores 2424, Ñuñoa, Santiago)* Focuses on forest conservation, ocean ecology and dealing with toxic waste.

Grupo de Acción por el Biobío *(☎ 02-737-1420;* **e** *gabb@huelen.reuna.cl; Ernesto Pinto Lagarrigue 112, Recoleta, Santiago)* Continues an impressive fight against damming projects on the Biobío and protecting the threatened Pehuenche people.

FLORA & FAUNA

Bounded by ocean, desert and mountain, Chile is home to a unique environment that developed much on its own, creating a number of endemic species.

The northern coastal deserts are virtually devoid of vegetation except in river valleys. The cacti at slightly higher elevations include the candelabra cactus, which grow well spaced apart and reach heights of up to 5m. These give way to the patchy grasslands of the very high altiplano, where there are also scrub forests of queñoa *(Polylepis tarapacana)*. Within the desert, the tamarugo once covered thousands of square kilometers. Within the altiplano you can spot members of the Camelid family – guanaco, vicuña, llama and alpaca (see the boxed text 'The New World Camelids,' in the Norte Grande chapter) – as well as the ostrich-like rhea (called ñandú in Spanish) and the viscacha (a wild relative of the chinchilla). Parque Nacional Lauca, in the northern altiplano, contains a variety of bird life, from Andean gulls and giant coots to three species of flamingo.

From the Norte Chico through most of Middle Chile, the native flora consists mostly of shrubs whose sclerophyllous (glossy) leaves help conserve water during the long dry season. At some higher elevations in the coastal range, there are forests of southern beech *(Nothofagus* species). Few stands of the endemic Chilean palm still exist, but you can find some in Parque Nacional La Campana.

South of the Biobío, the distinctive araucaria is related to Northern Hemisphere pines, while at the southern end of the lakes region, the alerce *(Fitzroya cupressoides)*, belonging to the cypress family, has become the focus of international conservation efforts. Throughout, the Valdivian temperate rainforest provides a substantial variety of plants and trees. In the Andes, the wide-ranging puma has been seen, although rarely, as have *jaivas*, or wild boars. The rare and diminutive deer, *pudú*, hides out in thick forests throughout the south. The awkward looking ibis, which makes a loud knocking call, is seen in pastures, while the *chucao*, a small red bird, is heard more than seen. The *queltehue*, with black, white and grey markings, has a loud call used to protect its ground nests. If there's a bird that will wake you up at any hour, it's this one.

On Chiloé and in Aisén, the *nalca* is the world's largest herbaceous plant, with enormous leaves that grow from a single stalk. The inner stalk of younger plants can be eaten. Off the northwestern coast of Chiloé is a colony of Humboldt and Magellanic penguins.

In the far south of Aisén and Magallanes, verdant upland forests consist of several species of the widespread genus *Nothofagus*, while on the eastern plains of Magallanes and Tierra del Fuego, decreased rainfall supports extensive grasslands. Reserva Nacional Tamango, near Cochrane, has the largest concentration of the elusive *huemul* (Andean deer). Guanaco, now protected, have made a successful comeback within Torres del Paine, where rheas, *caiquenes* (upland geese) and several species of foxes can also be spotted. Colonies of Magellanic penguins and cormorants are found near Punta Arenas. The legendary Andean condor is widespread though not numerous.

Chile's long coastline features many marine mammals, including sea lions, otters and fur seals.

Easter Island (Rapa Nui) has a rich marine life, while the Juan Fernández Archipelago is a major storehouse of biological diversity that has been named a Unesco Biosphere Reserve.

Protected Areas

Since the establishment of Parque Nacional Vicente Pérez Rosales in the mid-1920s, Chile's national parks have become a major international attraction. But this attraction has not played out in numbers. With the exception of Torres del Paine, Chile's protected areas are underutilized. Hikers have their pick of trails, and solitude is easily found – if you avoid the summer high season of January and February. As part of its 'Sistema Nacional de Areas Silvestres Protegidas del Estado' (Snaspe; or National System of State-Protected Wild Areas), the government has created a variety of parks and reserves that are administered by Conaf, mostly but not exclusively in the Andean range.

Before leaving Santiago, travelers should visit Conaf's central information office (☎ 390-0282; **w** www.conaf.cl; Av Bulnes 291) for inexpensive maps and brochures, which may be in short supply in the parks themselves. Regional Conaf offices, listed in the appropriate city entries, will sometimes assist in transportation to more isolated areas.

Protected areas under Snaspe jurisdiction are divided into categories: *Parques nacionales* (national parks; 32 sites) are generally extensive areas with a variety of natural ecosystems; *reservas nacionales* (national reserves; 43 sites) are areas open to economic exploitation on a sustainable basis and may include some relatively pristine areas; and *monumentos naturales* (natural monuments; 12 sites) are smaller but more strictly protected, usually with a single outstanding natural feature.

Chilean law also permits the creation of private nature reserves, which are categorized as *Áreas de protección turística* (tourist protection areas), which are usually private lands where management practices limit economic exploitation in the interest of scenic resources; and *santuarios de la naturaleza* (nature sanctuaries), which are primarily intended for research.

Combined, these protected areas cover almost 14 million hectares, or about 18% of

The Elusive Huemul

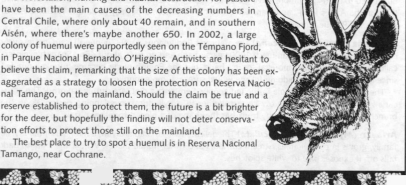

The docile huemul is a national symbol. It's also the world's fifth most endangered species of deer and could disappear from mainland Chile in the next 10 years if its natural habitat in the southern Andes is not protected.

Deforestation, hunting and habitat destruction for pasture have been the main causes of the decreasing numbers in Central Chile, where only about 40 remain, and in southern Aisén, where there's maybe another 650. In 2002, a large colony of huemul were purportedly seen on the Témpano Fjord, in Parque Nacional Bernardo O'Higgins. Activists are hesitant to believe this claim, remarking that the size of the colony has been exaggerated as a strategy to loosen the protection on Reserva Nacional Tamango, on the mainland. Should the claim be true and a reserve established to protect them, the future is a bit brighter for the deer, but hopefully the finding will not deter conservation efforts to protect those still on the mainland.

The best place to try to spot a huemul is in Reserva Nacional Tamango, near Cochrane.

the country. Of this, 8.4 million hectares are national parks, or about 10.7% of the country. (In comparison, the USA has 33.3 million hectares of parks, which represent 3.6% of the land area.) In 2000, about one million people (18% of which were foreign) visited Chile's parks and reserves, a 32% leap from the previous year. However,

Seeing the Forest for the Trees

> 'Anyone who hasn't been in the Chilean forest doesn't know this planet.'
> — Pablo Neruda

Subjected to large-scale burning by colonists in the 19th century and desiccation by timber companies in the 20th century, Chile's native forests have a history of being under attack and are now in peril of being wiped out entirely in unprotected areas. Long stuck in a tug-of-war between logging and ecological interests, Chile's southern forests are a topic of controversy, politics, conservation and consumerism.

Of the earth's temperate rainforests, southern Chile boasts the second largest (the most extensive is in the USA's Pacific Northwest). Other substantial ones are in New Zealand's South Island and in Australia's Tasmania. These southern areas, once all connected in the landmass Gondwanaland, are home to broadleaf evergreens and southern beech, known as Nothofagus.

Chile's temperate rainforest can be divided, north to south, into the Valdivian (40° to 45° latitude), from about Valdivia to Chaitén; and the Magellanic (45° to 55° latitude), from the beginning of the icefields to the southernmost point of Tierra del Fuego. With an average of 2.5m of rainfall, overcast summers, few fires and moderate changes to the climate, the Valdivian Rainforest is prime ground for this ecosystem. At lower elevations along the coast is a labyrinth of evergreens, such as coihue, ulmo, canelo, tineo and tepa, rising above impenetrable thickets of the bamboo-like quila and tepú, and hugged by epiphytes and climbing vines, including bromeliads and the giant hydrangea. At higher elevations the three varieties of evergreen coihue and deciduous lenga dominate. Farther south, the Magellanic Rainforest exists in more extreme conditions, which allow only a few tree species to exist. The Magellanic coihue dominates, but other southern beech are abundant, such as ñirre and lenga, and the Guaitecas cypress.

The other type of forest, equally breathtaking and home to the most unique tree of all, is the Araucaria Forest (37° to 40° latitude), in the Andes from Región XIII (Volcán Antuco) to Región X (Volcán Villarrica) and on the coast in the Nahuelbuta Range.

Alerce (Fitzroya cupressoides) The alerce (indigenous names are 'lahuen' and 'lahal') is the king of the forests: it's one of the longest-living trees in the world. Trees up to 4000 years old have been found, and they can grow up to 50m. Travelers from California may note its resemblance to the giant sequoia. The needles are triangular and grow in superimposed scales. Until the late 19th century, alerces grew throughout the Lakes District and northern Patagonia. The wood's excellent quality led to overexploitation, leaving only a few pure *alerzales* (clusters of alerces) left. Go admire them in the Andes from Lago Llanquihue south to Chaitén, especially in Parque Nacional Alerce Andino and Parque Pumalín.

Araucaria (Araucaria araucana) The araucaria (indigenous name: 'pehuén') is an impressively old species of conifer that can reach 1000 years of age and grow to about 45m. Spanish explorers called the tree *paragua* (umbrella) for its shape, but the English name became 'monkey puzzle,' since its structure and forbidding foliage would surely stump a monkey.

The *piñones* seeds, a staple in the indigenous Pehuenche diet, are nuttily flavorful. The araucaria's wide, spiky needles grow close together in a cylindrical, overlapping design along the branches. The bark on the stubby trunk has the shape of a pieced-together puzzle.

Arrayán (Myrceugenella apiculata) The delicate rust-colored arrayán, a member of the myrtle family, grows in coastal areas, stream corridors and other humid places. Where the smooth bark falls off, it exposes pale to white splotches.

Conaf receives an annual budget of only US$5 million from the government to spend on protected lands. In comparison, the USA's Yellowstone and Yosemite National Parks have budgets of around US$20 million each.

For information on books about Chile's parks, see the Books section of the Facts for

Seeing the Forest for the Trees

Canelo (Drimys winteri) Sacred to the Mapuche and one of the oldest of the angiosperms (flowering plants) ever found, the canelo grows to 25m in mainly humid sectors from the Río Limarí, in the north, to Tierra del Fuego. The leaves are long, wide and smooth, while the flowers are small and white, and grow in bunches. Tea made from the leaves eases stomachaches.

Ciprés de la Cordillera (Austrocedrus chilensis) The coniferous cordilleran cypress grows from Aconcagua to the south of Chiloé in mountainous areas up to 2000m and in dry, exposed volcanic zones. Pure stands are common, but it can also be found in forests of roble. It can range from 20m to 25m in height, with trunk widths up to 2m, often bifurcated near the base. The needles are flat.

Ciprés de las Guaitecas (Pilgerodendron uviferum) From the Valdivian Coastal Range to Tierra del Fuego, the Guaitecas cypress thrives in very humid, marshy zones. Resembling the alerce, it dominates forests of coihue and canelo and is often found with an understory of *tepuales* (see Tepú, later). Trees as old as 3000 years may have existed in the south before being burned. Today, one can find trees up to 40m in height and 1m in diameter. The needles have a more square point than the alerce.

Coihue (Nothofagus dombeyi) This perennial evergreen southern beech, along with two other varieties – the Chilote coihue *(N. nitida)* and Magellanic coihue *(N. betuloides)* – grace a lot of the forests, including almost half of all trees in the Magellanic Rainforest. It grows to 40m, with widths up to 4m and equally thick branches. You'll find it in damp sites, from sea level to timberline, but mostly at high elevations. The bark is dark gray and rough, and the leaves are small, with sharply pointed, sawtooth edges.

Lenga (N. pumilio) The lenga grows at high elevations, around 1500m above sea level, in Regiones VII to X, but grows closer to sea level farther south, where it grows with ñirre. Pure stands protected from the wind can reach 25m in height. In higher, more exposed altitudes, where it grows alongside coihue and araucaria, the trees are more stunted.

Ñirre (N. antarctica) Ñirre is one of the few species tolerant of the wet, cold climate of the extreme south of Tierra del Fuego. But this deciduous southern beech also grows in high-elevation forests of south-central Chile and at lower elevations in Patagonia. Look for it in rocky areas that are uninviting to most growth. It is short and bushlike with spindly branches and wide, rounded ridged leaves.

Tepa (Laureliopsis philippiana) Similar to a laurel, the tepa can grow to 30m and is usually found above 500m in the Valdivian Rainforest, down to Región XI. The leaves have a slight citrus smell, and the trunk, to which climbing vines cling, has a white mossy appearance.

Tepú (Tepualia stipularis) The shrubby tepú grows in swampy areas and is an important part of the Guaitecas cypress forest understory in southern Chile. The trees often grow in thick clusters, called *tepuales*.

Ulmo (Eucryphia cordifolia) The ulmo, which grows as tall as 45m, grows mainly in damp regions in the Coastal Range from sea level to 700m and as far south as southern Chiloé. It can be found in forests of coihue, tepa and roble. Look for a tall, straight trunk, dark-green rounded leaves, and in the summer, tiny white flowers with four petals. Be sure to try some of the very flavorful honey *miel de ulmo*.

— information for this text provided by Maximiliano Bello of WWF in Valdivia and Ken Wilcox's *Chile's Native Forests: A Conservation Legacy*, published by Ancient Forest International

the Visitor chapter. The following list highlights most of the protected areas as presented in this guide. See the regional maps and chapters for details.

Norte Grande

PN Lauca In the northern region of Tarapacá, east of Arica, 138,000-hectare Lauca has active and dormant volcanoes, clear blue lakes with abundant bird life and extensive steppes that support flourishing populations of the endangered vicuña, a wild relative of the llama and alpaca.

MN Salar de Surire Huge nesting colonies of flamingos make this salt flat of 11,300 hectares home.

PN Volcán Isluga Rarely visited and relatively inaccessible, this 175,000-hectare park in the altiplano of Iquique, bears many similarities to Lauca, but its cultural resources may be even more impressive.

RN Los Flamencos Seven scattered sectors in and around San Pedro de Atacama, covering almost 74,000 hectares, protect a variety of salt lakes and high-altitude lagoons that host several species of flamingos, as well as eerie desert landforms and hot springs.

Norte Chico

PN Pan de Azúcar Set in the coastal desert of the regions of Antofagasta and Atacama, this 44,000-hectare park features a stark but beautiful shoreline that is home to pelicans, penguins, otters and sea lions, plus unique vegetation that draws moisture from the coastal fog.

PN Nevado de Tres Cruces Encompassing 62,000 hectares east of Copiapó, in the high Andes along the Argentine border, the park includes a 6330m-high namesake peak. Also in this park is the even more prominent 6900m-high Ojos del Salado, a prime climber's destination that was once thought to be higher than Argentina's Aconcagua, which is the highest peak in the Western Hemisphere.

PN Llanos de Challe On the coastal plain of the Norte Chico, the 45,000-hectare Llanos de Challe is the best site to view the spectacular 'flowering of the desert' after one of the region's rare heavy rains.

RN Pingüino de Humboldt Breeding populations of Humboldt penguin and many other seabirds are protected in this 859-hectare reserve, which consists of several offshore islands.

PN Fray Jorge This ecological 'island' of cloud forest spans 10,000 hectares and protects this type of humid forest, which is usually found several hundred kilometers to the south.

Middle Chile

PN La Campana Easily accessible both from Santiago and Valparaíso/Viña del Mar, this 8000-hectare park protects tranquil forests of native oaks and Chilean palms.

RN Río Clarillo Only 45km from Santiago and suitable for a day trip, these 10,000 hectares encompass a variety of Andean ecosystems.

RN Río de los Cipreses In the Andes east of Rancagua, best known for the massive El Teniente copper mine, these 37,000 hectares are the area's outstanding escape.

RN Radal Siete Tazas A virtual staircase of falls and pools along the Río Claro is the major attraction of the 7700-hectare reserve in the precordillera of Talca.

RN Altos del Lircay Spectacular views of the Andean divide and its many hiking trails, including a loop trek to Radal Siete Tazas, make this 17,000-hectare reserve a clear central-Chilean highlight.

PN Laguna del Laja In the Andean foothills of Region VIII, 12,000-hectare Laja has a great deal to offer: waterfalls, lakes, volcanoes, bird life and numerous hiking trails.

PN Nahuelbuta In the high coastal range of Region IX, these 7000 hectares preserve the area's largest remaining araucaria forests.

La Araucanía & the Lakes District

PN Tolhuaca At the end of a narrow mountain road east of the town of Victoria and north of Curacautín, 6400-hectare Tolhuaca is a remote forested getaway in the headwaters of the Río Malleco. The park suffered forest fire damage in early 2002.

PN Conguillío In the Andean portion of the Araucanía, these 61,000 hectares feature mixed forests of araucaria, cypress and southern beech surrounding the active, snowcapped Volcán Llaima. The park suffered forest fire damage in early 2002.

PN Huerquehue Small but scenic, this 12,500-hectare park has excellent hiking trails through araucaria forests, with outstanding views of Volcán Villarrica.

PN Villarrica One of the region's gems, the smoking symmetrical cone of Volcán Villarrica overlooks the lake nearby resort towns. Its 61,000 hectares are popular with trekkers and climbers in summer, and with snowboarders and skiers in winter.

PN Puyehue One of the country's most visited parks, 107,000-hectare Puyehue is only 80km from the city of Osorno and is home to two hotsprings resorts, a ski resort and a variety of rugged hikes through forest and striking volcanic desert, which was created when Volcán Puyehue erupted in 1960.

PN Vicente Pérez Rosales Founded in 1926, this is Chile's oldest national park. Its 254,000 hectares include the spectacular lake, Lago Todos los Santos.

PN Alerce Andino Just 50km from Puerto Montt, the 40,000-hectare Alerce Andino preserves stands of alerce trees.

Chiloé

PN Chiloé On the remote western shore of Chiloé, this 43,000-hectare park features sweeping dunes, broad sandy beaches, blue lagoons and the forbidding forests that fostered the island's colorful folklore.

Aisén

PN Hornopirén Largely undeveloped, this 48,000-hectare park rewards determined hikers with verdant rainforest and secluded lakes.

PN Queulat These 154,000 hectares of truly wild evergreen forest, mountains and glaciers stretch across 70km of the Carretera Austral.

RN Coyhaique Despite its proximity to its city namesake (it's less than an hour's walk away), this 2150-hectare reserve is wild and attractive, with exceptional views of the surrounding area.

RN Río Simpson Straddling the highway between Coyhaique and Puerto Aisén, this 41,000-hectare reserve is a pleasant and accessible destination with verdant forests, waterfalls and a spectacular canyon.

RN Cerro Castillo Wild, high and remote, the 180,000-hectare Cerro Castillo, south of Coyhaique, is increasingly popular with hikers.

RN Tamango Officially known as RN Lago Cochrane, this 7000-hectare reserve protects a transitional area to Patagonia steppe, home to the elusive huemul.

Magallanes & Tierra del Fuego

PN Laguna San Rafael Glaciers reach the sea at this park, which is one of Chile's most impressive and part of the Campo de Hielo Norte (northern Patagonian ice field).

PN Bernardo O'Higgins Largely inaccessible, this massive 3.5-million-hectare park straddles the Patagonian ice fields.

PN Torres del Paine Chile's showpiece and an Unesco Biosphere Reserve, Torres' 181,000 hectares is home to a wealth of wildlife, including the Patagonian guanaco, a wild relative of the Andean llama. It is 150km from Puerto Natales.

RN Magallanes Above Punta Arenas, this is a 13,500-hectare hilly forest of southern beech.

PN Pali Aike Near the Argentine border, this 5000-hectare park is one of southern South America's major sites for the study of early human habitation.

PN Archipiélago de Juan Fernández This three-island archipelago (9500 hectares) is an ecological treasure with a great variety of endemic plants.

PN Rapa Nui An archaeological wonder known for its huge, enigmatic stone statues (the *moai*), close to half of this Polynesian island (also known as Easter Island) is protected as a national park.

Private Protected Areas

A 1994 Chilean law permits the creation of private nature reserves, more officially known as 'wild protected areas of private property.' However, no 'private parks' have yet to be declared, due to legal and bureaucratic complications. The most notable private protected area is Parque Pumalín in the Aisén region. Pumalín officials have proposed that the property be declared a nature sanctuary (a category established in 1970 as part of the National Monuments Law), which would need approval from the Ministry of Education. Other important private reserves are Alto Huemul, in Region VII; El Cañi, near Pucón; Monte Verde, on Isla Riesco north of Punta Arenas; and Bahía Yendegaia, on Tierra del Fuego. In all, there are about 104 privately protected areas throughout Chile. Codeff (see Environmental Organizations, earlier) maintains a database of the properties, all of which have joined together to create *Red de Areas Protegidas Privadas* (Network of Private Protected Areas).

Marine Parks

While considered the latest breakthrough in conservation, the creation of marine parks first began when the Navy declared three areas off the shores of Easter Island as an underwater park. Another one has been established near Viña del Mar. Conama, the Comisión Nacional del Medio Ambiente (National Environmental Commission), which promotes environmental sustainability, has also proposed developing one near Reserva Nacional Pingüino de Humboldt. There's also talk of creating one at the Juan Fernández archipelago.

GOVERNMENT & POLITICS

Chile's constitution, ratified by the electorate in a controversial plebiscite in 1980 – and further amended in 1989, '93 and '97 – is a custom document that was largely the work of Pinochet-supporter Jaime Guzmán. It provides for a popularly elected president, who is both Chief of State and Head of Government and serves a term of six years, and a bicameral Congress, with a 46-member Senado (Senate) and a 120-member Cámara de Diputados (Chamber of Deputies); eight senators are 'institutional,' appointed by the president and not subject to popular vote.

The current president, Ricardo Lagos, who was the Public Works Minister in Frei's administration, is considered to be a moderate leftist and is the first elected president from the Socialist party since 1988. Pressures to strengthen the economy and his own plans of improving transportation routes obscure his original, more ecological and socialist, platform. The next election is scheduled for December 2005. Top choices for that election include Joaquin Lavín, who was narrowly defeated in the last election and is now Santiago's mayor, and Soledad Alvear, the current foreign minister. Although the president continues to reside in Santiago and work at the Palacio de la Moneda there, Congress meets in Valparaíso.

Administratively, the country consists of 12 numbered regions, plus the Metropolitan Region, which includes the capital of Santiago and its surroundings. Each region has a formal name, but they are most commonly referred to by their Roman numerals, starting with I (Tarapacá) and counting to XII (Magallanes y la Antártica Chilena). See the Administrative Regions of Chile map. The regions are administered by appointed 'intendentes' and are subdivided into provinces, which are further subdivided into *comunas*, the units of local government. Traditionally, Chilean politics is highly centralized; most important decisions are made in Santiago, with little input from other regions.

Political Parties

The range and variation of political parties and their incessant transformations make it difficult for any but the most experienced observer to follow Chilean electoral politics. In the 1989 elections, 17 parties with little in common except their opposition to Pinochet formed an unlikely coalition known as the Concertación para la Democracia (CPD), choosing Christian Democrat Patricio Aylwin as a compromise candidate for the pres-

ADMINISTRATIVE REGIONS OF CHILE

I	Región de Tarapacá
II	Región de Antofagasta
III	Región de Atacama
IV	Región de Coquimbo
V	Región de Valparaíso (includes Easter Island & Archipiélago Juan Fernández)
✪	Región Metropolitana de Santiago
VI	Región del Libertador General Bernardo O'Higgins
VII	Región del Maule
VIII	Región del Biobío
IX	Región de La Araucanía
X	Región de Los Lagos
XI	Región de Aisén del General Carlos Ibáñez del Campo
XII	Región de Magallanes y Antártica Chilena

Easter Island (Rapa Nui)
Archipiélago Juan Fernández
SANTIAGO

PERU
BOLIVIA
IQUIQUE
ANTOFAGASTA
COPIAPÓ
LA SERENA
VALPARAÍSO
SANTIAGO
RANCAGUA
PACIFIC OCEAN
TALCA
CONCEPCIÓN
TEMUCO
ARGENTINA
PUERTO MONTT
COYHAIQUE
ATLANTIC OCEAN
PUNTA ARENAS

0   150   300 km
0   90   180 miles

idency. Aylwin easily defeated Pinochet's reluctant protégé Hernán Büchi, who stood for the Renovación Nacional (RN; a direct descendant of the conservative National Party), and independent businessman Francisco Errázuriz, a right-wing populist.

Today, the Concertación remains the ruling coalition. Member parties of the coalition are the Partido Demócrata Cristiano (PDC, Christian Democratic Party), the Partido Socialista (PS, Socialist Party) and the similar Partido por la Democracia (PPD, Party of Democracy). The opposing right-wing coalition is known as the Alianza por Chile (APC, Alliance for Chile). The two parties allied with this coalition, but rivals to each other, are the Unión Demócrata Independiente (UDI, Independent Democratic Union) and the Renovación Nacional (RN). The latter has moved toward the center and condemned the Pinochet-era human rights violations. The right wing of Chilean society now supports mainly the UDI, which is run by Joaquín Lavín, Santiago's mayor and a possible 2005 presidential candidate.

The Military

Military service is obligatory for males (though university students can get out of it), but there is growing sentiment for eliminating conscription.

All the services enjoy wide autonomy – the civilian president lacks authority over their chiefs or even junior officers – and are highly disciplined, cohesive and far more loyal to their commanders than to the civilian head of state.

A legal provision guarantees that 10% of the profits from state copper sales are used for arms purchases.

Human Rights

Despite the military's self-serving amnesty laws, human rights issues have not gone away. The last few years have seen a recurring theme: military personnel are indicted on human rights violations that occurred following the 1973 coup and then are amnestied a few years later. While this frustrates human rights advocates, each trial brings more awareness, both nationally and internationally, to the horrors of the coup and the politics that protect its perpetrators. The biggest news of the past few years was the London arrest of former dictator Pinochet on charges

of torture, followed by court proceedings in Chile, where it was eventually determined that Pinochet suffered from dementia and could not stand trial.

Another blow for human rights was Supreme Court Judge Ariztia's opposition to allowing the extradition of five ex-DINA (Directora de Inteligencia Nacional, or National Intelligence Directorate) agents as suspects in the 1974 assassination of General Prats, citing that the case did not have sufficient evidence to accuse them. This ruling came just weeks after the courts also decided to amnesty members of the Pinochet-era death squad 'Comando Conjunto.'

Judge Juan Guzmán, who has brought many human rights cases to light, continues the fight to indict those responsible for the Caravan of Death and the murders immediately following the coup. An ongoing investigation into the murder of Charles Horman, a US journalist who learned too much about the coup and was killed (most likely with the help of the CIA), led Guzmán to request that Henry Kissinger, Secretary of State under the Nixon administration at the time of the coup, respond to a series of questions about his involvement in the murder and stand trial. Declassified documents in the USA show further evidence of Nixon's role in the 1973 coup.

Another human rights issue is the plight of the country's disenfranchised indigenous communities. Pehuenche communities along Río Biobío have lost ancestral lands to the hydroelectricity projects; and along the coast north of Valdivia south to Osorno, Huilliche communities are losing their homes to the coastal-highway and logging interests. Chilean law both protects the rights to ancestral land and promotes the increase in energy resources to meet the country's needs – two laws that are now being pitched against each other.

ECONOMY

Until very recently, the Chilean economy had improved greatly on a macro scale, enjoying a decade of uninterrupted growth at rates of 6% or higher, but close economic ties across the Pacific made the country especially vulnerable to the Asian meltdown of 1998. The elite have benefited more from economic growth than the poor, and unemployment stands at around 9%. Countless city dwellers earn a precarious subsistence as street vendors. In 2001 it was estimated that 20% lived below the poverty line, with just fewer than 6% living in extreme poverty, a marked improvement since 1990's rate of 13%.

Chile's most important trading partners are the European Union, USA, Japan, Argentina and Brazil. The export economy is now more diverse and less vulnerable to fluctuations in international markets; the mining sector, for instance, no longer relies exclusively on copper but also produces less-traditional commodities, such as lithium. Still, Chilean copper represents nearly 40% of the country's exports, and a slump in the US economy directly affects Chile. Over the last few years, Chile became the world's second leading producer of fresh and processed salmon, fishmeal and fish oil. The increased production flooded the international market, caused drastic price cuts and irritated the Alaskan and Norwegian salmon sector. Salmon is now the country's fourth largest export and exceeded the export of grapes and pinewood to the USA in 2001. Fish flour accounts for about 2% of all exports.

Forest products are a rapidly growing but increasingly controversial sector, given the country's declining native forests, the apparent unsustainability of the present level of exports, and dubious reforestation programs of fast-growing exotic species such as Monterey pine and eucalyptus. Still, wood products and chips account for 11% of the country's exports. In the last seven years, Chile has become the fifth largest exporter of wine worldwide and stands to increase production in years to come.

Chile is an associate member of Mercosur and has a free-trade agreement with Canada. The current administration continues to seek inclusion in Nafta and signed a free-trade agreement with the EU in 2002. These developments have been met with much concern, especially about the effects that increased exploitation would have on Chile's environment.

POPULATION & PEOPLE

About 75% of Chile's population lives in just 20% of the country's total area – in the main agricultural region of Middle Chile. This region includes Gran Santiago (the capital and its suburbs), where over a third of the country's estimated 15.1 million people reside.

More than 85% of Chileans live in cities, a marked increase of 17% in the last 10 years.

According to Chile's 2002 census, the northernmost region of Tarapacá saw a 25% population growth in the past 10 years. On the southern extreme, Magallanes grew by only 6%. In Aisén, the person-per-square-kilometer ratio is 1:1. In the Region Metropolitana, that ratio is 392:1. Population figures given in this book are based on the preliminary findings of the 2002 census. Some figures may represent the city or town plus its surrounding communities. The regional population breakdown is as follows:

Region	Population
I	430,000
II	493,000
III	252,000
IV	600,000
V	1,540,000
RM	6,000,000
VI	774,000
VII	904,000
VIII	1,854,000
IX	865,000
X	1,061,000
XI	87,000
XII	152,000

Chile's people are mainly of Spanish ancestry, but the Irish and English also made a mark. Germans began immigrating in 1848 and left quite a stamp on the Lakes District. Other immigrants came from France, Italy, Croatia (especially to Magallanes and Tierra del Fuego) and Palestine. The northern Andean foothills are home to around 20,000 Aymara and Atacameño peoples. Over 900,000 are or consider themselves Mapuche (population statistics vary widely as a consequence), many of whom consider the south (La Araucanía) their home. Their name stems from the words *mapu* for 'land,' and *che* for 'people.' About 2000 Rapa Nui, of Polynesian ancestry, live on Easter Island.

EDUCATION

Chile's 95% literacy rate is one of Latin America's highest. Most children attend elementary school, which is free and compulsory, but school attendance drops for middle levels, mainly due to children in rural areas needing to work to help support the family, and also due to teenage pregnancy. Public spending on education increased 84% from 1989 to 1996, spurred on under the Aylwin presidency and the then–education minister Ricardo Lagos, but spending still falls short of Chile's needs. Increasing levels of private and subsidized schools are widening the social gap in the country.

Traditionally, universities are free and open, but after the 1973 coup, the military government privatized the universities. Its sweeping reform of the 1980s reduced state funding, raised student fees and downgraded or eliminated ostensibly 'subversive' careers, such as sociology and psychology. The Universidad de Chile was a particular target because of its reputation for aggressive dissent. It underwent further downsizing during the Frei administration. While students are again free to study 'subversive' careers, tuition costs are a main concern, especially since a system of student loans has yet to be developed. The military reform of higher education made it easy to open private 'universities,' but most of these are glorified trade schools with part-time faculty, limited curriculum and dubious standards. Some, however, are rapidly improving.

ARTS
Poetry
Pablo Neruda and Gabriela Mistral, both Nobel Prize–winning poets, are major figures in Chilean, Latin American and world literature. Much of Neruda's work is available in English translation, such as *Heights of Macchu Picchu*, *Canto General*, and *Passions and Impressions*.

Vicente Huidobro (1893–1948), a contemporary of Neruda's, never achieved the same level of acclaim but is studied in Chile's classrooms as one of the founders of modern Spanish-language poetry, represented in works *Altazor*, *Poemas Árticos* and *Ecuatorial*.

Gabriela Mistral's work is not as easily translated as Neruda's. US poet Langston Hughes translated some in *Selected Poems of Gabriela Mistral*. For an interpretation of her work, try Margot Arce de Vásquez's *Gabriela Mistral, the Poet and Her Work*.

Nicanor Parra, who still lives in Chile, has drawn Nobel Prize attention. *De Hojas de Parra* and *Poemas y antipoemas* are his most well known. Jorge Teillier, a bohemian character quick to the bottle, wrote of teenage angst and solitude. His work has been translated and analyzed by Carolyne Wright in *In Order to Talk with the Dead*.

Fiction
Chile's most famous literary export is Isabel Allende (1942–), niece of the late president Salvador Allende, who weaves 'magical realism' into stories with Chilean historic reference, such as *House of the Spirits*, *Of Love and Shadows*, *Eva Luna*, *Daughter of Fortune* and *Portrait in Sepia*.

José Donoso (1924–96) wrote of the fragile social facades. His *Curfew* offers a portrait of life under the dictatorship through the eyes of a returned exile, while *Coronación*, made into a film, deals with one dynasty's loss of wealth and status.

Antonio Skármeta's (1940–) *I Dreamt the Snow Was Burning* is a novel of the early postcoup years, but he has become famous for his novel *Burning Patience*, adapted into the award-winning Italian film *Il Postino* (The Postman).

Luis Sepúlveda (1949–) is one of Chile's most prolific writers, with such books as *The Name of the Bullfighter*, a tough stylish noir set in Germany and Chile with loads of political intrigue involving Nazi gold and ex-communist agents and interesting perspectives on exile; and the novella *The Old Man Who Read Love Stories*, a fictional account of life and society on Ecuador's Amazonian frontier.

Roberto Ampuero (1953–) writes mystery novels, such as *El Alemán de Atacama*, whose main character, Cayetano Brulé, is a Valparaíso-based Cuban expatriate detective who gets around the country.

Marcela Serrano (1951–) is considered to be one of the best Latina authors in the last decade, with works such as *Antigua Vida Mia*, *Nosotras Que Nos Queremos Tanto* and *Lo Que Está en Mi Corazón*, all of which focus on women's issues in political, social and psychological circles.

Pedro Lemebel (1950–) writes of homosexuality, transgender issues and other controversial subjects with top-notch shock value that has some Chileans applauding: His novel *Tengo Miedo Torero* was selected as Chile's 'novel of the year' for 2001.

Younger writers developing a style far from the 'magical realism' that brought Latin literature to the international scene include Alberto Fuguet (1964–), whose novella *Sobredosis* has been considered the spark that set off the 'new Chilean narrative'. *Mala Onda*, a story of excessive drug use and addiction, has also earned acclaim and scowls. Andrea Maturana (1969–) takes a more erotic approach to the new narrative in *(des)encuentros, (des)esperados*.

Music

Chile's contemporary music spans from the revolutionary tunes of the 1960s and '70s to Andean folklore to today's one-hit-wonder sexy crooners and hip-hoppers.

La Nueva Canción Chilena (New Chilean Song Movement) grew as the country's folk singers lyricized about the social hopes and political issues of the time. Its most legendary figure is Violeta Parra, best known for her enduring theme *Gracias a la Vida* (Thanks to Life). Her children Isabel and Angel, also performers, established the first of many *peñas* (musical and cultural centers) in Santiago in the mid-1960s. The movement also gave strength to performers

The Paths of Mistral & Neruda

Gabriela Mistral and Pablo Neruda have opened a window to Chile and Latin America through their poetry.

They were contemporaries, but of different generations; Mistral was born in 1889, Neruda in 1904. Both belonged to the provinces: Mistral to the remote Elqui Valley of the Norte Chico, Neruda to the southern city of Temuco, though his birthplace was Parral, in the heartland province of Maule, and he lived in Santiago, Valparaíso and a small beach community at Isla Negra. Both poets used pseudonyms: Gabriela Mistral's given name was Lucila Godoy Alcayaga; Pablo Neruda's was Neftalí Ricardo Reyes Basoalto. Both adopted their aliases out of timidity: the young rural schoolmistress Lucila Godoy sat in the audience at Santiago's Teatro Municipal while a surrogate received a prize for her series *Sonnets on Death,* in memory of a young suitor who had committed suicide; Neftalí Reyes feared the ridicule of his working-class family.

Both enjoyed literary success at a young age. The government rewarded both with diplomatic posts that subsidized their creative writing; as a consequence, both traveled extensively and became celebrities outside the South American continent, which hadn't produced a Nobel Prize winner in literature until Mistral's award in 1945. In 1971, Neruda became the third Latin American writer to receive the Swedish Academy's prize (Guatemalan novelist Miguel Angel Asturias was the second, in 1967).

Despite these similarities, the two poets were very different in other respects. After the death of her beloved, Mistral never married, and instead devoted her life to children and their education at schools from La Serena to Punta Arenas. When she taught in Temuco, the young Neruda and his friends worshipped her. She even traveled abroad to reform the Mexican system of public instruction. She lived austerely, but her stern features masked the sensitivity of a woman whose poetry was compassionate and mystical. Though friendly with political figures, most notably President Pedro Aguirre Cerda, her politics were not a matter of public controversy.

Neruda, by contrast, became a flamboyant figure whose private life was public knowledge, who built eccentric houses and filled them with outlandish objects, and whose politics more than once landed him in trouble. Unlike the somber Mistral, his face was usually smiling, often pensive, but never grim. While consul in Java in the 1930s, he married a Dutch woman, left her for Delia del Carril (a decade older than himself) a few years later, and after nearly 20 years left Delia for the much younger Matilde Urrutia. For her, he built and named La Chascona (her nickname, for her unruly mane of hair), his Santiago house at the foot of Cerro San Cristóbal.

such as Victor Jara, and groups Quilapayún and Inti-Illimani.

Immediately following the coup, many musicians were imprisoned. Victor Jara was brutally murdered in the National Stadium. Quilapuyún and Inti-Illimani happened to be touring in Europe, where they stayed in exile, acquiring international reputations for both their music and their political commitment, and furthered international awareness of the military regime. Other music groups (mainly rock groups) also went into exile and found similar success, such as Paris-based Los Jaivas, Los Prisioneros, and La Ley (based in Mexico).

Los Prisioneros broke up for a long time, but have since reunited and started a whole new fan base. La Ley has won a Grammy for best alternative rock group. Based in Sweden, DJ Mendez enjoys more fame in Europe than in his home country, but is gaining more attention. Nicole, a spunky young, multiplatinum singer, is signed up on Madonna's Latin music label. Alberto Plaza's life-affirming *Que Cante La Vida* has become another national treasure.

The Paths of Mistral & Neruda

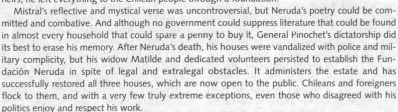

After Franco's rebels defeated the Spanish republic, the Chilean diplomat devoted his energies to helping refugees escape the dictator's revenge. In Spain he had made a personal commitment to the Communist Party, although he did not enroll officially until his return to Chile, where he was elected senator for Tarapacá and Antofagasta, the mining provinces of the Norte Grande. After managing Gabriel González Videla's successful presidential campaign of 1946, he fell afoul of the president's caprice and went into hiding and then exile in Argentina, escaping by foot and horseback across the southern Andes.

After González Videla left office, Neruda returned to Chile and continued his political activities without reducing his prolific output of poetry. In 1969 he was the Communist candidate for the presidency, but he withdrew in support of Salvador Allende's candidacy and later became Allende's ambassador to France. He received the Nobel Prize during his tenure in France. Neruda died less than a fortnight after the military coup of 1973.

For all his wealth, Neruda never forgot his modest origins nor abandoned his political convictions, and he did not consider his privileged lifestyle incompatible with his leftist beliefs. Lacking heirs, he left everything to the Chilean people through a foundation.

Mistral's reflective and mystical verse was uncontroversial, but Neruda's poetry could be committed and combative. And although no government could suppress literature that could be found in almost every household that could spare a penny to buy it, General Pinochet's dictatorship did its best to erase his memory. After Neruda's death, his houses were vandalized with police and military complicity, but his widow Matilde and dedicated volunteers persisted to establish the Fundación Neruda in spite of legal and extralegal obstacles. It administers the estate and has successfully restored all three houses, which are now open to the public. Chileans and foreigners flock to them, and with a very few truly extreme exceptions, even those who disagreed with his politics enjoy and respect his work.

Gabriela Mistral, meanwhile, remains a modest but reassuring presence in Chilean life and literature. Every day, thousands of Santiago's citizens pass the mural of Gabriela and her 'children' on the Alameda, at the base of Cerro Santa Lucía, while many more pay her homage at the museum bearing her name in the village of Vicuña, in her native Elqui Valley. Even more are reminded every day of her, each time they take out a 5000-peso note, colloquially referred to as 'una Gabriela.' Although she died in New York, she is buried in her natal hamlet of Montegrande.

— **Wayne Bernhardson**

A Bit of Chile on the MP3

Load up the MP3 with some of Chile's well-known artists. Here's a list to get you going:

Rock and Pop
La Ley – *Doble Opuesto; Unplugged*
Los Prisioneros – *El Caset Pirata*
Nicole – *Viaje Infinito*
DJ Mendez – *DJ Mendez – Latino for Life*

Ballads
Pablo Herrera – *Hasta La Luna*
Miriam Hernández – *Solo Lo Mejor – 20 Éxitos*
Alberto Plaza – *15 Años – En Vivo*

Folk
Illapu – *Sereno: Andean Panpipe Instrumentals*
Inti Illimani – *Inti-Illimani: Antología en Vivo, Lejania, Amar de Nuevo*
Violeta Parra – *Songs of Violeta Parra; Las Últimas Composiciones*
Victor Jara – *Te Recuerdo, Victor, Tributo a Victor Jara* (variety of artists singing Jara's songs)

Despite this goldmine of talent, most airwaves play sugary international pop standards rather than promoting their own country's talent.

Film

Before the 1973 coup, Chilean cinema was among the most experimental in Latin America and is now returning to reclaim some of this status. Director Alejandro Jodorowsky's surrealistic *El Topo (The Mole)*, an underground success overseas, included a performance by Country Joe and the Fish. Then-exiled director Miguel Littín's *Alsino and the Condor* (1983), nominated for an Academy Award as Best Foreign Film, is readily available on video. Following the end of the military dictatorship, Ricardo Larrain's debut film *La Frontera* (1991), presented the issues of internal exile during the regime, using symbolic references to cast a powerful message. It attracted some of the largest movie crowds in Chile's recent history. Movie themes continued to deal with the after effects of the regime with Gonzalo Justiniano's *Amnesia* (1994). Through the story of a Chilean soldier forced to shoot prisoners, Justiniano

challenges a society more inclined to simply forget the past atrocities.

Director Gustavo Graef-Marino's *Johnny 100 Pesos*, based on a true story about a group of robbers who become trapped in a Santiago high-rise, made a favorable impression at 1994's Sundance Film Festival. Paris-based Raúl Ruiz, another exile, has been prolific in his adopted country but only recently released his first English-language film, the psychological thriller *Shattered Image* (1998), which drew mostly tepid and critical reviews for its portrayal of a woman unable to distinguish between dream and reality. More recent films deal with the corruption and decay within a growing consumer society. *Taxi Para Tres* (2001), by Orlando Lubbert, is a sharp comedy about the mess a couple of bandits and their heisted taxi and driver get into after the taxi breaks down in a slum. *La Fiebre del Loco* (2001) by Andrés Wood, pokes fun at the frenzy that occurs each year during the short locos (abalone) fishing season in Patagonia.

José Donoso's novel *La Coronación*, about the fall of a family dynasty caused by the patron's desires for a 17-year-old and his psychological unraveling, was made into a well-acclaimed movie by veteran director Silvio Caiozzi in 2000.

The movie that has had the most success bringing Chileans back to their own directors is *El Chacotero Sentimental (The Sentimental Teaser;* 1999), which won 18 national and international awards. The movie tracks the true story of a frank radio host whose listeners start to reveal on the airwaves all sorts of complicated and passionate love stories.

Antonio Skármeta's novel *Burning Patience* was the template for British director Michael Radford's award-winning Italian-language film *Il Postino (The Postman,* 1994), a fictional exploration of Pablo Neruda's counsel to a shy but love-struck mail carrier.

Several films about Chile deal with politics to a greater or lesser degree. Costa-Gavras' *Missing* (1982), with Jack Lemmon and Sissy Spacek, was based on Thomas Hauser's book *The Execution of Charles Horman: An American Sacrifice*, which chronicled the disappearance of a US journalist following the coup. Ben Kingsley and Sigourney Weaver starred in Roman Polanski's English-language adaptation of Chilean playwright Ariel Dorfman's work *Death and the Maiden*

(1994), which takes place in an unspecified South American country after the fall of a dictator.

Painting & Sculpture

Chile's best-known living painter is Paris-based Roberto Matta (born 1911), the Latin American artist most closely identified with surrealism. Jesuit-educated in Chile, he went to France in 1934 to study architecture with Le Corbusier, but he has also lived in New York and Mexico City. Influenced by Mexican landscapes, his painting is nevertheless more abstract than that influence would suggest; he has also worked in media such as sculpture and engraving.

Among Chile's notable contemporary artists are Máximo Pincheira, whose grim works deal with the anxieties of life under the dictatorship, María José Romero (daughter of painter Carmen Aldunate), whose 'frivolous' oils, as she has called them, deal more with personal than political issues, and Mario Irarrázaval (born 1940).

SOCIETY & CONDUCT

Chile has a strong European influence. On the surface, it's a conservative society, mainly because of the influence the Catholic Church holds over the government and the media. But underneath this increasingly thin veneer, Chile is going through some radical social changes. The lack of a law making divorce legal doesn't keep families together as much as it has increased the acceptance of couples living together and having children out of wedlock. Dress is usually conservative, but coffee-bar waitresses are scantily clad, and following fashion is more important than covering up.

The lack of freedom of expression (Chile is considered one of the worst in Latin America) has made some Chileans find new outlets to defy the church's conservative oppression. One of the more 'expressive' gestures happened on a bitterly cold morning in 2002, when US artist Spencer Tunick advertised his need for 400 souls to pose naked for a photo shoot and over 3000 showed up. A concern that the country's social fabric is wearing thin has troubled government officials. While most Chileans are quite proud of their heritage, there's a palpable lack of patriotism and an increasing level of individualism.

What this means to the average traveler is that finding something that is uniquely Chilean can be difficult. Festivals have mostly a regional or community influence. Travelers will also find many Chileans genuinely interested to learn about other parts of the world, and willing visitors can spend hours in compare-and-contrast conversations. While most travelers want to talk about Pinochet and the issues of human rights, most Chileans would rather discuss the latest Santiago scandal or Argentina's woes.

Especially in the south, but not exclusively, Chileans can be sincerely hospitable. Being invited into someone's home for tea or to participate in daily activities is not uncommon. They trust most foreigners a great deal, at times more than they trust other Chileans. Prejudice against foreigners does exist,

Saludos y Besitos

Upon greeting and leaving, cheek kisses are often exchanged between men and women and between women. This lovely way of breaking the ice is also a subtle art, so those who hail from countries of handshakes and high-fives need a lesson or two.

The kiss is more of a cheek sweep: Rather than puckering up and smacking the other's cheek, both parties gently touch cheek to cheek and send the kiss to the air. If, however, one party wants to show an added level of endearment, the kiss is placed on the cheek. If one party wishes to show attraction to the other, the kiss is sometimes planted just a bit closer to the mouth. The action is always performed with the right cheek, and handshakes may add to the greeting. If, for whatever reason, you don't feel right or comfortable sweeping cheeks with him or her, use a simple handshake instead. Between men, the kissing is replaced with a hearty handshake and sometimes a pat to the shoulder.

And if that kiss does turn into something more, remember Chile still doesn't have a divorce law....

however, especially towards young backpackers from Israel. Sometimes assumed racist, this prejudice has derived from the traveling styles of some young Israelis clashing with Chile's social codes.

When calling or answering the telephone, the proper salutation is '*aló*' or '*hola*' (hello). Start any conversation with the usual pleasantries before getting to the point.

Travelers should be circumspect in their behavior around indigenous peoples, especially in areas like the altiplano of Arica, around San Pedro de Atacama, and in the Mapuche south. Aggressive picture-taking and rowdiness may be particularly offensive.

RELIGION

About 90% of Chileans are Roman Catholic, but evangelical Protestantism is rapidly gaining converts. There are also Lutherans,

Jews, Presbyterians, Mormons and Pentecostals. Catholicism has provided Chile with some of its most compelling cultural monuments, such as the colonial adobe churches of the Norte Grande, Santiago's Catedral Metropolitana and colonial Iglesia San Francisco, and the modest but dignified shingled chapels of Chiloé. Countless roadside shrines, some of them extraordinary examples of folk art, also testify to the pervasiveness of religion.

The church's influence on the government and society has kept Chile the only democratic country in the world without a divorce law, though annulments are not unusual for those who can pay for the legal maneuvering. A new divorce law under consideration by Congress would make the system of requesting a divorce one of the world's most conservative. The government has found it difficult to institute critically important sex-education programs due to ecclesiastical opposition.

CLIMATE CHARTS

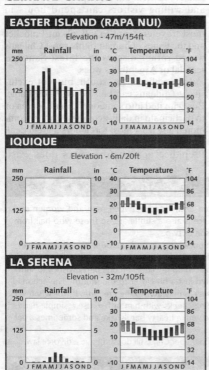

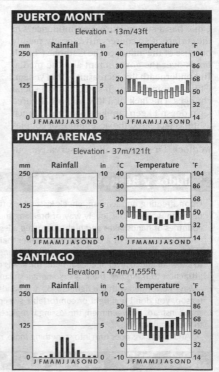

Facts for the Visitor

SUGGESTED ITINERARIES

The most important thing to remember when planning your trip in Chile is that traveling from point to point can eat up a day. LanChile offers an air pass that is both economical and convenient. Also consider that if your interest lies in the extreme north or south, arriving in Chile from either Peru (north) or Argentina (south) may be more advantageous.

Another important point is to realize that Chile has a very well-trodden gringo trail. The fact that nearly everything is on or near one or two major highways, with frequent and comfortable bus service, has made for a very marked trail. To seek out less-traveled areas will require more time. Chile is much more of an activity-oriented destination than a sightseeing one, and so it's important to consider in advance what you might want to do: Hiking? Rafting? Skiing? Paragliding? Horseback Riding? The Activities section in this chapter provides information on the many outdoor pastimes you can enjoy.

One Week

Concentrate on one area. If you want to stick around Santiago, plan on two days in the city, then take off for the nearby Andes (especially during the ski season). If you aren't too interested in the capital, consider hopping on a plane the same day you arrive. In the north, San Pedro de Atacama or Arica, which are good jumping-off points for trips to Parque Nacional Lauca, are the main destinations. In the south, head to Temuco or Puerto Montt to access the Lakes District, or go the distance to Punta Arenas to get to Parque Nacional Torres del Paine.

Two to Three Weeks

Now you can diversify. In two weeks you can take a whirlwind of the north and south (remember you'll lose days in getting to/from points), or add in a trip to Easter Island. Still, concentrating on one area will afford a more fulfilling stay. Two weeks in the north can allow you to take in San Pedro de Atacama and Parque Nacional Lauca, plus some side trips. In the south you could stay in the Lakes District to enjoy activities aplenty and visit

the island of Chiloé; or take a four-day ferry ride through the fjords, followed by hiking in Parque Nacional Torres del Paine; or travel the Carretera Austral. Adding an extra week allows for a less frantic trip.

One Month

With four weeks, you can easily split the country into four: around Santiago, the north, south and Easter Island, or any combination of those four. In the north, add the beach resort of La Serena, Valle Elqui and Reserva Nacional Los Flamencos. In the south, add in Valdivia, a boat trip to Bariloche (Argentina), a trip through Chiloé and rafting on the Futaleufú.

Or if you prefer to focus on the heart of Patagonia, add in a trip to Tierra del Fuego, a side trip to El Calafate (Argentina), or a drive around Lago General Carrera.

Two Months

Consider a long-term car rental, or a purchase, and hit the road. With two months you can drive the length of the country and see all the top spots, plus dig into some of the less-visited areas. Spend time on the altiplano, enjoy relaxing at beaches around Santiago and taking in the city's ambiance, check out wineries and markets in Middle Chile, see how many thermal baths you can find in the Lakes District, cross over the Andes a couple of times to check out Argentine destinations, trek the circuit at Torres del Paine, then ferry back up to Puerto Montt, barrel back to Santiago and hop a plane to Easter Island to relax for a week.

PLANNING
When to Go

The country's geographical variety can make a visit rewarding in any season. Santiago and Middle Chile are best in the verdant spring (September through November) or during the fall harvest (late February into April), while popular natural attractions such as Parque Nacional Torres del Paine, in Magallanes, and the Lakes District are best in summer (December through March). Chilean ski resorts draw many visitors from July through September.

The Atacama Desert is temperate and attractive at any time of year, although nights are always cold at higher altitudes. In the northern altiplano, summer is the rainy season, but this usually means only a brief afternoon thunderstorm. Still, the dry spring months are probably best for explorations off the main highways.

Easter Island is cooler, slightly cheaper and far less crowded outside the summer months. The same is true of the Juan Fernández Archipelago, which can be inaccessible if storms crop up; March is an ideal time for a visit.

In the south, the summer's long days (December to February) permit outdoor activities, despite the unpredictable weather, but the spring months of November and December and autumn months of March and April can be nearly as good.

Maps

International Travel Maps & Books (ITMB) publishes *Southern South America*. At a scale of 1:4,000,000, it includes most of Chile, as does its *Argentina*, at an identical scale. ITMB also publishes maps of Easter Island at 1:30,000 and Tierra del Fuego at 1:750,000.

Several useful maps of Chile are available from kiosks and street vendors in the main towns and cities. Atlas de Chile's *Plano de Santiago y Mini Atlas Caminero de Chile, 1995* combines an indexed plan of the capital (1:25,000) with a respectable highway map (1:2,000,000). Inupal's *Gran Mapa Caminero de Chile* provides comparable highway coverage but lacks city maps.

The Instituto Geográfico Militar's *Guía Caminera* (1992) is a reasonably good highway map in a convenient ring-binder format, with scales ranging from 1:500,000 to 1:1,500,000; it also includes several city maps at varying scales. If you can find it, the IGM's *Plano Guía del Gran Santiago* (1997) is the local equivalent of *London A-Z*, at a scale of 1:20,000.

The IGM's 1:50,000 topographic series is valuable for trekkers, although maps are out of date and those of some sensitive border areas (where most national parks are) may not be available. Individual maps cost about US$15 each in Santiago, available from **IGM** (☎ 02-460-6800; Dieciocho 369, Centro; open 9am-5:30pm Mon-Fri), just south of the Alameda.

The popular Turistel guidebook series (see Guidebooks, later in this chapter) contains detailed highway maps and excellent plans of Chilean cities and towns, but lacks scales.

JLM Mapas *(Mapas Matassi; ☎ 02-236-4808;* w *www.jlmmapas.cl; General del Canto 105, Oficina 1506, Providencia, Santiago)* publishes maps for all major regions and trekking areas at scales ranging from 1:50,000 to 1:500,000. Catering mainly to tourists, the maps are widely distributed, easy to use and provide decent information, but they don't claim to be perfectly accurate.

In most major Chilean cities, the Automóvil Club de Chile (Acchi) has an office that sells maps, although not all of them are equally well stocked. If you belong to an auto club at home, ask for a discount.

What to Bring

Chile is a mostly temperate, midlatitude country, and seasonally appropriate clothing for North America or Europe will be equally suitable here. In the desert north, lightweight cottons are a good idea, but at the higher elevations of the Andes and in Patagonia, you should carry warm clothing even in summer. From Temuco south, rain is possible at any time of the year, and a small, light umbrella is useful in the city (but not in the gales of Magallanes, where heavier rain gear is desirable). In winter, budget hotels in the south may not provide sufficient blankets, so a warm sleeping bag is a good idea even if you're not camping.

There is little prejudice against backpackers who travel respectfully, and during the summer, many young Chileans themselves visit remote parts of the country on a shoestring budget. The selection and quality of outdoor equipment are improving, but prices are still relatively high compared to North America or Europe, so it's better to bring camping gear from home.

Personal preference largely determines the best way to carry your baggage. A large zip-up bag or duffel with a wide shoulder strap is convenient for buses, trains and planes but is awkward to carry for long distances. A backpack is most convenient if you expect to do a lot of walking. Internal frame packs, with a cover that protects the straps from getting snagged in storage on buses or planes, can be a good compromise.

Don't overlook small essentials like a Swiss Army knife, needle and thread, a small pair of scissors, contraceptives, sunglasses and swimming gear. Basic supplies such as toothbrushes and toothpaste, shaving cream, shampoo and tampons are readily available, except in very small, remote places. Visitors staying in budget hotels and traveling on buses or trains will find a good pair of earplugs useful. It's also a good idea to carry toilet paper at all times, since many Chilean bathrooms lack it.

Travelers interested in wildlife, particularly birds, should remember to bring a pair of binoculars.

See Health, later in this chapter, for a list of medical items to bring.

TOURIST OFFICES

Every regional capital and some other Chilean cities have a local representative of Sernatur, the national tourist service, while many municipalities have their own tourist office, usually on the main plaza or at the bus terminal. In some areas, these offices may be open during the summer only.

Abroad, Chile is remarkably lacking in tourism information. Consulates in major cities may have a tourist representative, but the more accessible and comprehensive information will be found through specialized travel agencies and on the Internet. Chile has a few general travel agencies that work with affiliates around the world. **Chilean Travel Service** (CTS; ☎ 02-251-0400, fax 251-0423; ⓦ www.ctsturismo.cl; Antonio Bellet 77, Providencia, Santiago) has exceptionally helpful, well-informed, and multilingual staff and can organize accommodations and tours all over Chile through your local travel agency. Staff are also happy to provide general information on Santiago and the rest of Chile.

VISAS & DOCUMENTS
Passports & Visas
Except for nationals of Argentina, Brazil, Uruguay and Paraguay, who need only their national identity cards, passports are obligatory. Citizens of Canada, the UK, the USA, Australia, New Zealand and most Western European countries need passports only. Do not arrive at the border without one, or you may be sent back to the nearest Chilean consulate.

The Chilean government collects a US$100 'reciprocity' fee from arriving US citizens in response to the US government's imposition of a similar fee on Chilean citizens applying for US visas; this payment applies only to tourists arriving by air and is valid for the life of the passport. Canadians pay US$55, Australians US$34. Payment must be made in US cash and for the exact amount; officials rarely have change.

It is advisable to carry your passport: Chile's *carabineros* (police) can demand identification at any moment, and many hotels require you to show your passport upon check-in.

If your passport is lost or stolen, notify the carabineros, ask them for a police statement, and notify your consulate as soon as possible.

Tourist Cards On arrival, visitors receive a tourist card and entry stamp that allow a stay of up to 90 days but are renewable for an additional 90. To renew an expiring tourist card, make a visit to the **Departamento de Extranjería** (☎ 02-550-2400; ⓔ visas@interior .gov.cl; Agustinas 1235, Centro, Santiago; open 8:30am-2pm Mon-Fri). Take with you photocopies of your passport and tourist card. You may also visit the Departamento de Extranjería in any of Chile's regional capitals. However, since this now costs about US$100 and requires standing in lines for several hours, many visitors prefer a quick dash across the Argentine border and back.

If you plan on staying longer than six months, it's simplest to make a brief visit to Argentina, Peru or Bolivia, then return and start your six months all over again. There is no formal obstacle to doing so, although border officials sometimes question returnees from Mendoza, Argentina, to determine whether they are working illegally in Chile. Do not lose your tourist card, which border authorities take very seriously; for a replacement, visit the **Policía Internacional** (☎ 02-737-1292; General Borgoño 1052, Independencia, Santiago; open 8:30am-5pm Mon-Fri), near the old Mapocho station.

Onward Tickets
Theoretically, Chile requires a return or onward ticket for arriving travelers, and some airlines may ask for evidence of an onward ticket if the date of your return ticket is beyond the initial 90-day tourist-card limit.

However, some travelers report having crossed numerous Chilean border posts, including international airports, dozens of times over many years without ever being asked for an onward ticket.

Travel Insurance

Insurance bought at relatively small cost can pay great benefits if you get sick. Look for a policy that will pay return travel costs and reimburse you for lost air tickets and other fixed expenses if you become ill. Such policies often cover losses from theft as well (a policy that protects baggage and valuables like cameras and camcorders is a good idea). The international travel policies handled by STA or other budget-travel organizations are usually a good value. Keep insurance records separate from your other possessions in case you have to make a claim.

Driver's Licenses & Permits

Bring along an International Driving Permit. Some rental car agencies don't require one, but others do, so it's best to have one on hand. Carabineros at highway checkpoints or on the road are generally firm but courteous and fair, with a much higher reputation for personal integrity than most Latin American police. *Never* attempt to bribe them.

Permits for temporarily imported tourist vehicles may be extended beyond the initial 90-day period, but not all customs officials are aware of this; it may be easier to cross the border into Argentina and return with new paperwork.

Foreigners residing in Chile may obtain a Chilean driver's license through the municipality in which they live.

Hostel Card

Many towns in Chile have a Hostelling International affiliate. **Asociación Chilena de Albergues Turísticos Juveniles** *(☎/fax 02-233-3220;* e *hostelling@hostelling.cl; Hernando de Aguirre 201, Oficina 602, Providencia, Santiago)* distributes hostel cards, which cost US$25 for a new issue or US$15 for a renewal and the staff should have lists of lodgings. Cards can also be purchased at the **Santiago hostel** *(Cienfuegos 151).*

Photocopies

All important documents (passport data page and visa page, credit cards, travel insurance policy, air/bus/train tickets, driving license etc) should be photocopied before you leave home. Leave one copy with someone at home and keep another with you, separate from the originals.

It's also a good idea to store details of your vital travel documents in Lonely Planet's free online Travel Vault in case you lose the photocopies or can't be bothered with them. Your password-protected Travel Vault is accessible online anywhere in the world – create it at w www.ekno.lonely planet.com.

EMBASSIES & CONSULATES
Chilean Embassies & Consulates

Chile has diplomatic representation in most parts of the world; those listed here are the ones most likely to be useful to intending visitors.

Australia
(☎ 06-6286 2430) 10 Culgoa Circuit, O'Malley, ACT 2606
(☎ 02-9299 2533) National Market Centre, 44 Market St, 18th floor, Sydney 2000
(☎ 03-9654 4982) Level 43, Nauru House, 80 Collins St, Melbourne 3000

Canada
(☎ 613-235-4402) 50 O'Connor St, Suite 1413, Ottawa, Ontario
(☎ 416-924-0106) 2 Bloor St W, Suite 1801, Toronto, Ontario
(☎ 514-861-8006) 1010 St Catherine W, Suite 731, Montréal, Québec
(☎ 604-681-9162) 1185 W Georgia, Suite 1250, Vancouver, BC

France
(☎ 01-4705 4661) 64 Blvd de la Tour Maubourg, Paris, 75007

Germany
(☎ 069-550194) Humboldstrasse 94, Frankfurt
(☎ 030-2044990) Leipzigerstrasse 63, Berlin

New Zealand
(☎ 4-471 6270) 19 Bolton St, Wellington

UK
(☎ 207-580 1023) 12 Devonshire Rd, London

USA
(☎ 202-331-5057) 1140 Connecticut Ave NW, Suite 703, Washington, DC 20036
(☎ 212-980-3366) 866 United Nations Plaza, Room 302, New York, NY 10017
(☎ 310-785-0047) 1900 Avenue of the Stars, Suite 1250, Los Angeles, CA 90067
(☎ 415-982-7662) 870 Market St, Suite 1058, San Francisco, CA 94102
(☎ 305-373-8623) 1110 Brickell Ave, Suite 616, Miami, FL 33131

(☎ 708-654-8780) 875 N Michigan Ave, Suite 3352, Chicago, IL 60611

Embassies & Consulates in Chile

The following countries maintain embassies in Santiago (we've also listed a couple UK missions outside Santiago):

Argentina
(☎ 02-635-9863) Vicuña Mackenna 41, Centro

Australia
(☎ 02-228-5065) Gertrudis Echeñique 420, Las Condes

Bolivia
(☎ 02-232-8180) Av Santa María 2796, Las Condes (see the Santiago map)

Canada
(☎ 02-362-9660) Nuevo Tajamar 481, 12th floor, Las Condes

France
(☎ 02-225-1030) Av Condell 65, Providencia

Germany
(☎ 02-463-2500) Agustinas 785, 7th floor, Centro

Israel
(☎ 02-246-1570) San Sebastián 2812, 5th floor, Las Condes

New Zealand
(☎ 02-290-9802) Isidora Goyenechea 3516, Las Condes

Peru
(☎ 02-235-2356) Calle Padre Mariano 10, Oficina 309, Providencia

UK
(☎ 02-370-4100) Av El Bosque Norte 0125, 3rd floor, Las Condes
(☎ 032-255-113) Blanco 1199, 5th floor, Valparaíso
(☎ 061-211-535) Cataratas de Niaguara 01325, Punta Arenas

USA
(☎ 02-232-2600) Andrés Bello 2800, Las Condes

Argentine consulates in other cities include the following:

Puerto Montt
(☎ 065-253-996) Cauquenes 94, 2nd floor

Punta Arenas
(☎ 061-261-912) 21 de Mayo 1878

Bolivian consulates in other cities include the following:

Arica
(☎ 058-231-030) Patricio Lynch 298

Calama
(☎ 055-344-413) Vicuña Mackenna 1984

Iquique
(☎ 057-421-777) Gorostiaga 215, Dept E

Peruvian consulates in other cities include the following:

Arica
(☎ 058-231-020) San Marcos 785

Iquique
(☎ 057-411-584) Zegers 570, 2nd floor

Concepción
(☎ 041-224-644) Barros Arana 176, 2nd floor

CUSTOMS

There are no restrictions on import and export of local and foreign currency. Duty-free allowances include 400 cigarettes or 50 cigars or 500g of tobacco, and 2.5L of alcoholic beverages and perfume for personal use. Though Chilean officials generally defer to foreign visitors, travelers crossing the border frequently and carrying electronic equipment like camcorders or laptop computers should keep a typed list of these items, with serial numbers, stamped by authorities.

Your Own Embassy

It's important to realize what your own embassy – the embassy of the country of which you are a citizen – can and can't do to help you if you get into trouble. Generally speaking, it won't be much help in emergencies if the trouble you're in is remotely your own fault. Remember that you are bound by the laws of the country you are in. Your embassy will not be sympathetic if you end up in jail after committing a crime locally, even if such actions are legal in your own country.

In genuine emergencies, you might get some assistance, but only if other channels have been exhausted. For example, if you need to get home urgently, a free ticket home is exceedingly unlikely – the embassy would expect you to have insurance. If you have all your money and documents stolen, it might assist with getting a new passport, but a loan for onward travel is out of the question.

Some embassies used to keep letters for travelers or have a small reading room with home newspapers, but these days, the mail-holding service has usually been stopped, and even newspapers tend to be out-of-date.

Inspections are usually routine, although some travelers have had to put up with more thorough examinations because of drug smuggling from Peru and Bolivia. Travelers from Regiones I and XII, both of which enjoy *zona franca* (duty-free) status, are subject to internal customs inspections when leaving those regions.

At international borders, officials of the SAG (Servicio Agrícola-Ganadero; Agriculture and Livestock Service) rigorously check luggage for fruit and organic products, the importation of which is strictly controlled to prevent the spread of diseases and pests that might threaten Chile's booming fruit exports.

Photographers should note that at major international border crossings such as Los Libertadores (the crossing from Mendoza, Argentina) and Pajaritos (the crossing from Bariloche, Argentina), Chilean customs officials put baggage through X-ray machines; do not leave your film in your luggage.

MONEY
Currency
The unit of currency is the peso (Ch$). Bank notes come in denominations of 500, 1000, 2000, 5000, 10,000 and 20,000 pesos. Coin values are 1, 5, 10, 50, 100 and 500 pesos, although one-peso coins are rare. In small villages, it can be difficult to change bills larger than Ch$1000.

Exchange Rates
Exchange rates are usually best in Santiago. Generally, only Santiago will have a ready market for European currencies. Throughout the book we have used the exchange rate of 600 pesos to US$1, but recessions across Latin America have created some fluctuation. Paying a bill with US cash will occasionally be acceptable, for example at hospedajes or at luxury hotels; however the exchange rate they offer may not be to your advantage. Other than that, expect to pay all transactions in the local currency.

Many top-end hotels publish rates in US dollars with a lower exchange rate than the daily one. Compare the rates carefully to determine whether paying in pesos or US cash is the more favorable option. Paying attention will pay off.

The following exchange rates, current as of November 2002, provide an idea of relative values:

country	unit	pesos
Argentina	Arg$1	Ch$200
Australia	A$1	Ch$395
Bolivia	Bol1	Ch$95
Canada	C$1	Ch$450
euro	€1	Ch$710
Japan	¥100	Ch$590
New Zealand	NZ$1	Ch$350
Peru	Sol1	Ch$195
UK	UK£1	Ch$1120
USA	US$1	Ch$710

For the most current information, see *Estrategia* (Chile's equivalent of the *Wall Street Journal* or *Financial Times*), the financial pages of *El Mercurio*, or the online *Santiago Times*. Conversion rates are also available at W www.xe.net/ucc/full.shtml.

Exchanging & Carrying Money
Accessing funds through an ATM, known as *un Redbanc* is by far the easiest and most convenient way of carrying money while in Chile. Machines are found in many towns (with the exception of Chile's Pacific Islands). They don't charge commission and give decent exchange rates.

Few banks will exchange cash dollars (and usually US$ only), but *casas de cambio* (exchange houses) in Santiago and more tourist-oriented destinations will exchange, but they also charge some commission or have less agreeable rates. More costly purchases can sometimes be paid in US cash. Chile has no black market, but some businesses may give an especially favorable exchange rate for purchases in US cash. There is nothing illegal about this.

Traveler's checks are the least convenient way to go. Except at the American Express representative in Santiago, hardly anyone wants to exchange traveler's checks, and those that do offer poor rates. Carrying a combination of all three forms is wise (traveler's checks are a more secure back-up), but depositing funds into a debit account before going will be most useful.

Credit cards – American Express, Visa and MasterCard – are accepted in most established businesses, but travelers shouldn't depend on them. Business owners may also charge more to cover the charge they have to pay for the transaction. They can be useful to show 'sufficient funds' before entering another South American country, or in an emergency.

To receive money from abroad, have your home bank send a draft. Money transferred by cable should arrive in a few days; Chilean banks will give you your money in US dollars on request. Western Union offices can be found throughout Chile, usually adjacent to the post office.

Security

Chile is not a high-crime country, but pickpocketing is not unknown, and travelers should avoid carrying large amounts of money in vulnerable spots such as the back pocket. Money belts and leg pouches are two secure means of carrying cash and other important documents.

Costs

Chile is not a cheap country by South American standards, but modest lodging, food and transport are still more economical than in Europe or North America. Chile's very structured tourist season means that from late December to mid-March, prices for traveler's services are higher than any other time of the year. Taking a trip just weeks before or after the official season means great bargains on many accommodations and with tour operators.

Shoestring travelers should budget a minimum of US$25 per day for food and lodging, but if you purchase food at markets or eat at modest restaurants, you may be able to get by more cheaply. It's possible to lunch economically at some very fine restaurants that offer fixed menus.

Mid-range travelers can do very well on about US$50 per day, though some of the best family-style accommodations are better values than mid-range hotels. Visitors willing to splurge can enjoy some incredible values.

Tipping & Bargaining

In restaurants, it's customary to tip about 10% of the bill except in exclusively family-run places, which rarely expect a tip. In general, waiters and waitresses are poorly paid, so if you can afford to eat out, you can afford to tip, and even a small *propina* will

be appreciated. Taxi drivers do not require tips, although you may round off the fare for convenience.

In general, bargaining is not part of Chilean culture. At handicrafts markets some can occur, but it is usually based on discounting extra purchases rather than lowering the price of one item. Hotel prices are generally fixed and prominently displayed, but during the off-season or a slow summer, discounts are often given; for long-term stays, it is definitely possible to ask for a discount. It's worth asking if the first price quoted is their best.

Taxes & Refunds

At many mid-range and top-end hotels, payment in US dollars (either cash or credit) legally sidesteps the crippling 18% IVA (*impuesto de valor agregado*, or value-added tax). If there is any question as to whether IVA is included in the rates, clarify before paying. A few places that get only a handful of foreign visitors can't be bothered with the extra paperwork, but most find it advantageous to be able to offer the discount.

POST & COMMUNICATIONS

Correos de Chile's postal services are reasonably dependable but sometimes rather slow. Over the past decade or so, telephone infrastructure has gone from Paleolithic to postmodern and is probably the best on the continent. Every major city and most tourist-oriented areas have Internet and email access.

Postal Rates

Within Chile, an ordinary letter costs about US$0.45. An airmail letter or postcard costs about US$0.45 to North America and US$0.50 to Europe and Australia.

Addresses

In Chilean cities and towns, names of streets, plazas and other features are often very long and elaborate, such as Calle Cardenal José Maria Caro or Avenida Libertador General Bernardo O'Higgins, but are usually shortened in writing and speech, and on maps. So the former might appear on a map as JM Caro, or just Caro, while the latter might appear as Avenida Gral O'Higgins, Avenida B O'Higgins, just O'Higgins or even by a colloquial alternative (Alameda).

Some addresses include the expression *local* (locale) followed by a number, for example Cochrane 56, Local 5. 'Local' means it's one of several offices at the same street address. Some street numbers begin with a zero, eg, Bosque Norte 084. This confusing practice usually happens when an older street is extended in the opposite direction, beyond the original number 1. If, for example, street numbers are increasing from north to south, El Bosque Norte 084 will be north of El Bosque 84, which will be north of El Bosque 184.

The abbreviation 's/n' following a street address stands for *sin número* (without number) and indicates that the address has no specific street number.

Sending Mail
Chilean post offices are open 9am to 6pm weekdays and 9am to noon Saturdays. Send important overseas mail *certificado* (registered) to ensure its arrival. Mail that appears to contain cash is unlikely to arrive at its final destination.

Sending parcels is straightforward, although a customs official may have to inspect your package before a postal clerk will accept it. Vendors in or near the post office will wrap parcels upon request. International courier services are readily available in Santiago, less so outside the capital. To send packages within Chile, the bus system is a much more reliable service, called *encomienda*. Simply take the package to a bus company that goes to the destination. Label the package clearly with the destination and the name of the person who will pick it up.

Receiving Mail
You can receive mail via *lista de correos* or poste restante (equivalent to general delivery) at any Chilean post office. Santiago's American Express office offers client mail services, while some consulates will also hold correspondence for their citizens. To collect your mail from a post office (or from American Express or an embassy), you need your passport as proof of identity. Instruct your correspondents to address letters clearly and to indicate a date until which the post office should hold them; otherwise, they may be returned or destroyed. There is usually a small charge, about US$0.25 per item.

Chilean post offices maintain separate lists of correspondence for men and women, so check both if your correspondent has not addressed the letter 'Señor,' 'Señora' or 'Señorita.' If expected correspondence does not arrive, ask the clerk to check under every possible combination of your initials. There may be particular confusion if correspondents use your middle name, since Chileans use both paternal and maternal surnames for identification, with the former listed first.

Telephone
Chile's country code is ☎ 56. All telephone numbers in Santiago and the Metropolitan Region have seven digits; all other telephone numbers have six digits except for certain toll-free and emergency numbers. The toll-free number for the carabineros is ☎ 133, ambulance is ☎ 131. You'll reach directory assistance at ☎ 103.

Chilean telephone services are among the best and cheapest in the world. Entel, Telefónica (CTC) and several other carriers offer domestic and international long-distance services throughout most of the country. In Regiones X and XI, the unrelated Telefónica del Sur provides most long-distance service. Because of the so-called multicarrier system, whereby a number of companies compete for long-distance services, charges for both foreign and domestic calls can be remarkably cheap. In this book Entel and Telefónica (CTC) offices are listed, not necessarily because they have the best rates (often the independents centers have better rates), but because they are more established and convenient – you won't have to ask the operator to place the call first.

Each telephone company installs its own public phones with their own system of payment. Many take coins, but increasingly, phone booths use only magnetic phone cards. A local call costs Ch$100 (about US$0.20) for five minutes, but outside peak hours (8am to 8pm weekdays, 8am to 2pm Saturdays) costs only Ch$50. Calls to cell phones are expensive and may require more coins to initiate the call. A liquid-crystal readout indicates the remaining credit on your call. When it reaches zero and you hear a beeping sound, insert another coin unless you plan to finish soon. Public phones do not make change, but if there is at least Ch$50 credit remaining, you may make another call by pressing a button rather than inserting another coin.

Telefónica (CTC) uses magnetic pre-paid phone cards, while Entel's 'Entel Ticket' uses a toll-free number and password system. *Cobro revertido* (reverse-charge or collect) calls overseas are simple: dial the number of the carrier, then ☎ 182 for an operator. Most Entel and CTC offices close by 10pm.

Cell Phones Cell phone numbers have seven digits, prefixed by ☎ 09. When making a cell-to-cell phone call, drop the 09 prefix, but if making a cell to landline call, add the landline's prefix (or area code). Numbers are often duplicated, so not adding the area code often means calling up a stranger. For those who just must have a cell phone handy, they can be purchased for as little as US$50 and can be charged up by credit card, or more conveniently by prepaid phone cards sold at kiosks and call centers. Cell phones have a 'caller-pays' format. Calls between cell and landlines are expensive and quickly eat up prepaid card amounts.

Fax & Telegraph
Entel, Telefónica, Telex-Chile and VTR offer telegraph and fax services; there are also many small private offices with fax service. Prices are very reasonable.

Email & Internet Access
Internet cafés are found throughout Chile, even in some towns so tiny they seem out of place. The easiest and most secure way to read and send email is to set up a free Web-based email account such as Hotmail or Yahoo. Your regular Internet service provider will most likely also provide Web-based email services. Rates at Internet cafés range from US$2 to US$4 per hour. The farther off the beaten path and the farther south you go, the slower the connection will become.

DIGITAL RESOURCES
The World Wide Web is a rich resource for travelers. You can research your trip, hunt down bargain airfares, book hotels, check on weather conditions or chat with locals and other travelers about the best places to visit (or avoid!).

Lonely Planet's website (**w** www.lonely planet.com) has succinct summaries on traveling in Chile; postcards from other travelers; and the Thorn Tree bulletin board, where you can ask questions before you go or dispense advice when you get back. You can also find travel news and updates to many of our most popular guidebooks, and the subWWWay section links you to the most useful travel resources elsewhere on the Web.

The best overall search engine for information on Chile is created by the Latin American Network Information Center (**w** www.lanic.utexas.edu/la/chile), which has lists of sites dealing with government, politics, culture, environment and loads more. Throughout the book, we have listed relevant websites or email addresses for those with reliable service. The following lists provide good tips and background information as well.

w www.gochile.cl – general tourist information for the whole country

w www.prochile.com – tourism and business promoters

w www.sernatur.cl – information from the national tourism organization

w www.gaychile.com – for all things gay, from issues to hot spots

w www.chiloeweb.cl – best source of information about the island of Chiloé

w www.netaxs.com/~trance/rapanui.html – Easter Island's website

w www.mapulink.org – loads of information on Mapuche history, issues and events

BOOKS

See the Arts section of the Facts about Chile chapter for information on Chilean literature and reading recommendations. For books relating to Easter Island, see that chapter, toward the end of this book.

Different publishers in different countries publish most books in different editions. As a result, a book might be a hardcover rarity in one country while it's readily available in paperback in another. Fortunately, bookstores and libraries can do a search by title or author, so your local bookstore or library is best place to advise you on the availability of the following recommendations.

Lonely Planet

Additional guidebooks can supplement or complement this one, especially if you are visiting countries other than Chile. Lonely Planet's guidebook series includes the following titles: *Argentina, Uruguay & Paraguay; Buenos Aires; Ecuador & the Galápagos Islands; Bolivia; Peru;* and *Brazil.* Budget travelers covering a large part of the continent should look for *South America on a shoestring.*

Trekkers may want to check out Lonely Planet's *Trekking in the Patagonian Andes,* with detailed descriptions and maps of extensive walks in Chile, plus others across the border in Argentina. Lonely Planet's *Latin American Spanish phrasebook* is helpful for beginners. If you're planning your first big trip, you may want to check out Lonely Planet's *Read This First: Central & South America.* The Read This First series, aimed at first-time travelers, is packed with useful predeparture information on planning, buying tickets, visa applications and health issues. A section (with full-color maps) is devoted to Chile.

Guidebooks

While we've done our best to showcase all that Chile has to offer, the country just has so much that a supplementary guide focusing on activities is a worthwhile purchase. *Chile Experience* (2001), by Josh Howell, is a comprehensive look at Chile from all sides, with background information from Turistel (in English) and loads of details on just about every outdoor activity possible. *Adventure Handbook Central Chile* (2001), by Franz Schubert & Malte Sieber, is another comprehensive activity guide written by folks who have lived and loved the country for years. *Chile and Argentina: Backpacking and Hiking* (1998), by Tim Burford & John Dixon, has information about hiking and camping in the Southern Cone countries.

One of the most useful sources of information is the annually updated Turistel guide series, published (in Spanish only) by Telefónica (CTC) with separate volumes on the north, center and south of the country, plus an additional volume on camping and campgrounds that has more detailed maps of some important areas. Oriented toward motorists, Turistel guides provide excellent highway and city maps (the latter beautifully drawn, despite frequent minor errors and the absence of scales) and thorough background information, but they rarely cover budget accommodations.

For English-speakers, William C Leitch's eloquent survey *South America's National Parks* contains a valuable chapter on the history and natural history of half a dozen of Chile's most popular parks. Conaf's *Guía de Parques Nacionales* provides general descriptions, transportation options and facilities of all the protected areas, but lacks decent maps and trail details. Jürgen Rottmann's bilingual *Bosques de Chile/Chile's Woodlands,* published in cooperation with the World Wide Fund for Nature, is a well-illustrated, generalist's introduction to the country's forests and fauna. Also worth reading is *La Tragedia del Bosque Chileno,* edited by Adriana Hoffman. Ancient Forest International's *Chile's Native Forests: A Conservation Legacy,* by Ken Wilcox, provides an accessible overview to the history and description of Chile's forests and the environmental issues affecting them.

Decent bird-watching guides include Mark Pearman's *Essential Guide to Birding in Chile,* Nigel Wheatley's *Where to Watch Birds in South America,* Martín R de la Peña and Maurice Rumbold's *Birds of Southern South America and Antarctica,* or Braulio Araya and Sharon Chester's *Birds of Chile: A Field Guide.* Those competent in Spanish should look for the *Guía de Campo de las Aves de Chile,* by Araya and Guillermo Millie.

For details on nature in the far south, *Fauna-Flora y Montaña Torres del Paine,* by Gladys Garay N & Oscar Guineo N provides colorful detail of the regions flora and fauna; although only in Spanish, it is still a useful reference.

Travel Literature

The classic Charles Darwin's *Voyage of the Beagle* is a perfect companion for any trip to Chile, with memorable descriptions of the areas of his travels that are as fresh as if he'd just disembarked the Navimag ferry.

Sara Wheeler's *Travels in a Thin Country* is humorous and sometimes insightful. Novelist/journalist Luis Sepúlveda's *Full Circle: A South American Journey* is a hybrid work combining an exile's political insights on his own country with travel observations.

Ariel Dorfman's *Heading South, Looking North* is the personal and political memoir of a bicultural activist who is also one of contemporary Chile's major literary figures.

Patagonia has been a favored topic by many, and books of its history and characters make great reads while down in the Southern Cone. Although Bruce Chatwin's classic *In Patagonia* deals more with Argentina than with Chile, it's one of the most informed syntheses of life and landscape about any part of South America.

The Last Cowboys at the End of the World: The Story of the Gauchos of Patagonia, by Nick Reding, is a sharp, insightful and engagingly written study of the overlooked culture of Chile's southern gauchos, based on the author's time living with them.

There is a voluminous amount of literature on Rapa Nui; see that chapter for more details.

History & Politics

For an account of early European exploration of Chile and other parts of South America, see JH Parry's *Discovery of South America* (1979). Another good source is Edward J Goodman's *Explorers of South America* (1992).

Uruguayan journalist-historian Eduardo Galeano presents a bitter indictment of European invasion and its consequences in *The Open Veins of Latin America, Five Centuries of the Pillage of a Continent* (1973).

Publishing works on the Allende years is a minor industry in its own right, and as in the 1970s, it's still hard to find a middle ground. Try *Allende's Chile* (1977), by Edward Boorstein, a US economist who worked for the UP government. A more recent and wide-ranging attempt to explain the UP's failure is Edy Kaufman's *Crisis in Allende's Chile: New Perspectives* (1988).

For a Marxist analysis of US involvement in the campaign against Allende, try *The United States and Chile: Imperialism and the Overthrow of the Allende Government* (1975), by James Petras & Morris Morley. For a more thorough historical perspective, see Robert J Alexander's *Tragedy of Chile* (1978).

Joan Jara, the English wife of murdered folk singer Victor Jara, has written a personal account of life during the 1960s and '70s in *Victor: An Unfinished Song* (1983). The death of a politically involved US citizen in the 1973 coup was the subject of Thomas Hauser's book *The Execution of Charles Horman: An American Sacrifice* (1978), which implicated US officials and was the basis of the film *Missing*.

The assassination of Orlando Letelier, a career diplomat and foreign minister under Allende, has been the subject of several books, including John Dinges & Saul Landau's *Assassination on Embassy Row* (1980) and Taylor Branch & Eugene Popper's *Labyrinth* (1983).

Chile: The Pinochet Decade, by Phil O'Brien & Jackie Roddick (1983), covers the junta's early years, concentrating on the economic measures of the Chicago Boys.

A riveting account of an exile's secret return is Colombian writer Gabriel García Márquez's *Clandestine in Chile* (1987), which tells the story of filmmaker Miguel Littín's secret working visit to Chile in 1985. Argentine writer Jacobo Timerman, famous for criticism of his country's military dictatorship of the late 1970s, has written *Chile: Death in the South* (1987).

March Cooper, a contributing editor to *The Nation* and Allende's translator before the coup, covers Chile's politics and its debilitating effects on society from the coup to today's cynical consumer society in the insightful and poignant *Pinochet and Me: A Chilean Anti-Memoir* (2002).

Mateo Martinic is the leading historian of the Magallanes area; his summary *History of Magallanes* is worth a read. For those traveling to Tierra del Fuego, pick up *History of Indigenous Peoples,* by Ramón Lista.

NEWSPAPERS & MAGAZINES

The single best resource of Chilean news in English is the *Santiago Times*, available by fax or email subscription through the **Chile Information Project** (☎ *02-777-5376, fax 735-2267;* W *www.chipnews.cl; Casilla 53331, Correo Central, Santiago).* Santiago's English-language *News Review* (☎ 02-236-1424; Almirante Pastene 202) is hard to find outside the capital, but try upscale hotels in the regions.

El Mercurio (W www.elmercurio.cl), the capital's oldest and most prestigious daily, follows a conservative editorial policy but has a diverse letters section, excellent cultural coverage and an outstanding Sunday travel magazine; its *Wikén* supplement, which comes out Fridays, is a guide to entertainment in the capital. *Mercurio*'s parent corporation also owns *La Segunda, La Tercera, Ultimas Noticias* and sleazy *La Cuarta* with more derriere than discourse.

La Nación is the official government daily. *Estrategia* (W www.estrategia.cl) is the daily voice of Chile's financial community and the best source on trends in the exchange rate. Despite passing the 'Press Law,' which safeguards public freedom of expression and opinion, and eliminates restrictions on the press, freedom of the press is still elusive. Two private enterprises own Chile's most distributed news sources. Filling a void, the alternative *The Clinic* provides the most open and cutting-edge editorials and satire about politics and Chilean society.

Rocinante is a monthly magazine highlighting trends in arts, culture and society (mainly in Santiago). *Siete +7* is a weekly that takes a liberal-to-left-leaning view on the nation's news. *Opus Gay*, playing off the conservative Opus Dei branch of the Catholic church, is Chile's first magazine oriented toward gays and other socially disenfranchised groups.

RADIO & TV

Radio broadcasting is less regulated than before, and there are many stations on both AM and FM bands, most of which are in Santiago, and many of which are still strongly influenced by the Catholic church. Television stations include the government-owned Televisión Nacional (TVN) and the Universidad Católica's Channel 13, considered to be the most conservative, plus several private stations. Cable or satellite hookups are increasingly common, and most hotels and *hospedajes* have a hookup if they have a TV.

Chile's most famous television personality is Mario Kreuzberger, popularly known as 'Don Francisco,' host of the weekly variety program *Sábado Gigante*, which is also seen on Spanish-language TV stations in the USA. The portly, multilingual Don Francisco, whose smiling visage endorses products on billboards throughout the country, also hosts the annual *Teletón* to raise money for disabled children. The most popular national *telenovelas* (soap operas) are *Amores de Mercado* and *El Circo de Las Montini*.

PHOTOGRAPHY & VIDEO

Duty-free zones at Iquique (Región I, Norte Grande) and Punta Arenas (Región XII, Magallanes) are good places to replace a lost or stolen camera. Kodak and Fuji have stores throughout Chile. Agfa film is a more economical and decent alternative. Color slide film is harder to come by and expensive but can be found in Iquique's zona franca. To be on the safe side, wait to develop photos until your return home.

At high altitudes, especially in northern Chile, the bright tropical sun can wash out photographs; a polarizing filter is virtually essential. Photographers should be particularly circumspect about indigenous peoples, who often resent the intrusion. When in doubt, don't do it.

At major international border crossings such as Los Libertadores (from Mendoza, Argentina) and Pajaritos (from Bariloche, Argentina), Chilean customs officials put baggage through X-ray machines; do not leave your film in your luggage.

TIME

For most of the year, Chile is four hours behind GMT, but from mid-December to late March, because of daylight saving time (summer time), the difference is three hours. The exact date of the changeover varies from year to year. Because of Chile's great latitudinal range, this means that the summer sunrise in the desert tropics of Arica, where the durations of day and night are roughly equal throughout the year, occurs after 8am. Easter Island is two hours behind the mainland.

ELECTRICITY
Electric current operates on 220 volts, 50 cycles. In Santiago, numerous electrical supply stores on Calle San Pablo, west of the Puente pedestrian mall, sell transformers for appliances.

WEIGHTS & MEASURES
The metric system is official. For motorists, it's common to find tire pressure measured in pounds per square inch, and the Chilean military often uses feet as a standard measure, for instance, for airport elevations.

LAUNDRY
In most towns, there is drop-off laundry service. Most charge by the basket rather than by weight. Expect to pay about US$5 per basket for wash, dry and fold. Many *hospedajes* offer laundry service at a similar rate, and most request that washing not be done in the bathrooms. Self-service *lavanderías* (laundries) are difficult to find – probably because the price to have someone else do it is quite minimal.

TOILETS
Pipes and sewer systems in older buildings are quite fragile: used toilet paper should be discarded in wastebaskets. Cheaper accommodations and public toilets rarely provide toilet paper, so carry your own wherever you go. Better restaurants and cafés are good alternatives to public toilets, which are often dirty.

HEALTH
In general, Chile presents few serious health hazards. US residents can call the **Centers for Disease Control's International Traveler's Hotline** (☎ *404-332-4559*), where, by punching in the country's phone code (56 for Chile), you can get recorded information on vaccinations, food and water, and current health problems. They also have a fax-back service and a website.

Medical Kit Checklist

All standard medications are available in well-stocked pharmacies. Many common prescription drugs can be purchased legally over the counter in Chile. However, it's wise to carry a small medical kit with you. This should include the following:

Aspirin or paracetamol (acetaminophen in the USA) – for pain or fever

Antihistamine – for allergies (eg, hay fever); to ease the itch from insect bites or stings and to prevent motion sickness

Cold and flu tablets, throat lozenges and nasal decongestant

Multivitamins – for long trips during which dietary vitamin intake may be inadequate

Antibiotics – for traveling well off the beaten track. See your doctor, as they must be prescribed, and carry the prescription with you.

Loperamide or diphenoxylate – 'blockers' for diarrhea

Prochlorperazine or metaclopramide – for nausea and vomiting

Rehydration mixture – to prevent dehydration, which may occur, for example, during bouts of diarrhea. This is particularly important when traveling with children.

Insect repellent, sunscreen, lip balm and eye drops

Calamine lotion, sting-relief spray or aloe vera – to ease irritation from sunburn and insect bites or stings

Antifungal cream or powder – for fungal skin infections and thrush

Antiseptic – for cuts and grazes

Bandages, Band-Aids (plasters) and other wound dressings

Water-purification tablets or iodine

Scissors, tweezers and a thermometer – Note that mercury thermometers are prohibited by airlines.

Travelers who wear glasses should bring an extra pair and a copy of their prescription. Losing your glasses can be a real nuisance, although in many places you can get new spectacles made up quickly, cheaply and competently.

If you require a particular medication, take an adequate supply and a copy of the prescription, with the generic rather than the brand name. Many US and European prescription items are available over the counter in Chile.

Predeparture Preparations

Vaccinations Chile doesn't require vaccinations for entry from any country, but visitors to nearby tropical countries should definitely consider prophylaxis against typhoid, malaria and other diseases. Typhoid, polio, tetanus and hepatitis immunization are also recommended. All vaccinations should be recorded on an International Health Certificate, available from your physician or health department.

Typhoid protection lasts three years and is useful if traveling in rural areas. You may suffer side effects such as pain at the point of injection site, fever, headache and general discomfort.

A complete series of oral polio vaccines is essential if you haven't ever had them before. Tetanus and diphtheria boosters are necessary every 10 years and are highly recommended.

Injections of gamma globulin, not a vaccine but a ready-made antibody, provide some protection against infectious hepatitis (hepatitis A).

Malaria does not exist in Chile, but if you are coming from a malarial zone, you should continue to take antimalarial drugs for six weeks.

Travel Health Guides Lonely Planet's handy, pocket-size *Healthy Travel: Central and South America* is packed with useful information including pretrip planning, emergency first aid, immunization and disease information and advice on what to do if you get sick on the road.

For basic health information when traveling, a good source is Richard Dawood's *Travellers' Health: How to Stay Healthy Abroad* (1994). Another possibility is David Werner's *Where There Is No Doctor* (1992).

Food & Water

Salad greens and other fresh, unpeeled vegetables are safe to eat, but eating raw shellfish is not advisable. Santiago's drinking water is adequately treated, and you can drink tap water in most parts of the country without problems, but Santiago's drinking water, although adequately treated, has a high mineral content and can cause stomach upset. If you have any doubts, stay with bottled mineral waters.

Take precautions in rural areas, where latrines may be close to wells and untreated water may be taken from rivers or irrigation ditches. Water in the Atacama Desert and its cities has a strong mineral taste.

Geographical & Climatic Considerations

Jet Lag Jet lag is experienced when a person travels by air across more than three time zones (each time zone usually represents a one-hour time difference). It occurs because many of the functions of the human body (such as temperature, pulse rate and the emptying of the bladder and bowels) are regulated by internal 24-hour cycles. When we travel long distances rapidly, our bodies take time to adjust to the 'new time' of our destination, and we may experience fatigue, disorientation, insomnia, anxiety, impaired concentration and a loss of appetite. These effects will usually be gone within three days after arrival, but to minimize the impact of jet lag, do the following:

- Rest for a couple of days prior to departure.
- Try to select flight schedules that minimize sleep deprivation; arriving late in the day means you can go to sleep soon after you arrive. For very long flights, try to organize a stopover.
- Avoid excessive eating (which bloats the stomach) and alcohol (which causes dehydration) during the flight. Instead, drink plenty of noncarbonated, nonalcoholic drinks, such as fruit juice or water.
- Avoid smoking.
- Make yourself comfortable by wearing loose-fitting clothes and by bringing an eye mask and ear plugs to help you sleep.
- Try to sleep at the appropriate time for the time zone you are traveling to.

Motion Sickness Eating lightly before and during a trip will reduce the chances of motion sickness. If you are prone to motion sickness, try to find a place that minimizes movement – near the wing on aircraft, close to midships on boats, near the center on buses. Fresh air usually helps; reading and cigarette smoke hurt. Commercial motion-sickness preparations, which can cause drowsiness, have to be taken before the trip commences. Ginger (available in capsule form) and peppermint (including mint-flavored sweets) are natural preventatives.

Altitude Sickness Lack of oxygen at high altitudes (over 2500m) affects most people to some extent. The effect may be mild or severe and occurs because less oxygen reaches the muscles and the brain at high altitudes, requiring the heart and lungs to compensate by working harder. Symptoms of Acute Mountain Sickness (AMS) usually develop during the first 24 hours at a high altitude but may be delayed up to three weeks. Mild symptoms include headache, lethargy, dizziness, difficulty sleeping and loss of appetite. AMS may become more severe without warning and can be fatal. Severe symptoms include breathlessness; a dry, irritative cough (which may progress to the production of pink, frothy sputum); severe headache; lack of coordination and balance; confusion; irrational behavior; vomiting; drowsiness and unconsciousness. There is no hard-and-fast rule as to what is too high: AMS has been fatal at 3000m, although 3500m to 4500m is the usual range.

Treat mild symptoms by resting at the same altitude until recovery, usually a day or two. Paracetamol or aspirin can be taken for headaches. If symptoms persist or become worse, however, *immediate descent is necessary;* even 500m can help. Drug treatments should never be used to avoid descent or to enable further ascent.

The drugs acetazolamide and dexamethasone are recommended by some doctors for the prevention of AMS; however, their use is controversial. They can reduce the symptoms, but they may also mask warning signs; severe and fatal AMS has occurred in people taking these drugs. In general, we do not recommend them.

To prevent acute mountain sickness:

• Ascend slowly – have frequent rest days, spending two to three nights at each rise of 1000m. If you reach a high altitude by trekking, acclimatization takes place gradually, and you are less likely to be affected than if you fly directly to a high altitude.

• Sleep at a lower altitude than the greatest height reached during the day. Also, once above 3000m, care should be taken to not increase the sleeping altitude by more than 300m per day.

• Drink extra fluids. The mountain air is dry and cold, and moisture is lost as you breathe. Evaporation of sweat may occur unnoticed and result in dehydration.

• Eat light, high-carbohydrate meals for more energy.

• Avoid alcohol, as it may increase the risk of dehydration.

• Avoid sedatives.

Heat Exhaustion & Sunburn Although Chile is mostly a temperate country, its northern regions lie within the tropic of Capricorn, and the sun's nearly direct rays can be devastating, especially at high altitude. In the desert, summer temperatures are usually not oppressive, but dehydration can still be a serious problem. Drink plenty of liquids and keep your body well covered with light cotton clothing. Wear a hat that shades your head and neck. Damage to the ozone layer has increased the level of ultraviolet radiation in southern South America, so protection from the sun is especially important – use an effective sunscreen on exposed parts of your body and good-quality sunglasses. Sweating can also lead to a loss of salt, so adding some salt to your food can be a good idea. Salt tablets should be taken only to treat heat exhaustion caused by salt deficiency.

Hypothermia Hypothermia occurs when the body loses heat faster than it can produce it, causing the core temperature of the body to fall. It is surprisingly easy to progress from very cold to dangerously cold due to a combination of wind, wet clothing, fatigue and hunger, even if the air temperature is above freezing. At high altitudes and in Patagonia, changeable weather can leave you vulnerable to exposure: after dark, temperatures can drop from balmy to below freezing, while a sudden soaking and high winds can lower your body temperature rapidly; in such places, always be prepared for cold, wet or windy conditions. Make sure to bring layers of clothing; some of it should be water-resistant.

It is best to dress in layers; silk, wool and some of the new artificial fibers are all good insulating materials. A hat is important, as a lot of heat is lost through the head. A strong, waterproof outer layer (and a 'space' blanket for emergencies) is essential. Carry basic supplies, including food containing simple sugars to generate heat quickly and fluid to drink.

Symptoms of hypothermia are exhaustion, numb skin (particularly toes and fingers), shivering, slurred speech, irrational or violent behavior, lethargy, stumbling, dizzy spells, muscle cramps and violent bursts of energy. Irrationality may take the form of sufferers' claiming they are warm and trying to take off their clothes.

To treat mild hypothermia, first get the victims out of the wind and/or rain, remove their clothing if it's wet and replace it with dry, warm clothing. Give them hot liquids – not alcohol – and some high-kilojoule, easily digestible food. Do not rub victims: instead, allow them to slowly warm themselves. This should be enough to treat the early stages of hypothermia. The early recognition and treatment of mild hypothermia is the only way to prevent severe hypothermia, which is a critical condition.

Diarrhea & Dysentery

Simple things – such as a change of water, food or climate – can cause a mild bout of diarrhea, but a few rushed toilet trips with no other symptoms is not indicative of a major problem.

Dehydration is the main danger with any diarrhea – particularly for children, who can dehydrate quite quickly. Under all circumstances, *fluid replacement* (at least equal to the volume being lost) is the most important thing to remember. Soda water, weak black tea with a little sugar, or soft drinks allowed to go flat and diluted 50% with clean water are all good. Many cafés in Chile serve chamomile tea *(aguita de manzanilla)* or other herbal teas thought to help stomach upsets. With severe diarrhea, a rehydrating solution is preferable to replace lost minerals and salts. Commercially available oral rehydration salts (ORS) are very useful; add them to boiled or bottled water. In an emergency, you can make up a solution of six teaspoons of sugar and a half teaspoon of salt per liter of boiled or bottled water. You need to drink at least the same volume of fluid that you are losing through bowel movements and vomiting. Urine is the best guide to the adequacy of replacement – if you have small amounts of concentrated urine, you need to drink more. Keep drinking small amounts often. Stick to a bland diet as you recover.

Lomotil or Imodium can be used to bring relief from the symptoms, although they do not actually cure the problem. Only use these drugs if you do not have access to toilets, eg, if you *must* travel. Note that these drugs are not recommended for children under the age of 12 years.

Antibiotics may be required in treating diarrhea that is watery, with blood or mucus and/or accompanied by a fever.

The recommended drugs for bacterial diarrhea (the most likely cause of severe diarrhea in travelers) are norfloxacin (400mg twice daily for three days) or ciprofloxacin (500mg twice daily for five days). These are not recommended for children or pregnant women. The drug of choice for children would be co-trimoxazole (dosage is dependent on weight; a five-day course is given). Ampicillin or amoxycillin may be given during pregnancy, but medical care is necessary.

Giardiasis Commonly known as Giardia, and sometimes 'beaver fever,' this intestinal parasite, *Giardia lamblia*, is present in contaminated water. Symptoms include stomach cramps, nausea, a bloated stomach, watery and foul-smelling diarrhea, and frequent gas. Giardiasis can appear several weeks after you have been exposed to the parasite. The symptoms may disappear for a few days and then return; this can go on for several weeks. Avoid drinking dirty water.

Sexually Transmitted Diseases

Sexual contact with an infected partner spreads these diseases. While abstinence is the only certain preventative, condoms are also effective. Gonorrhea and syphilis are the most common of these diseases; sores, blisters or rashes around the genitals and discharge or pain when urinating are common symptoms. Symptoms may be less obvious – or even absent – in women. The symptoms of syphilis eventually disappear completely, but the disease can cause severe problems in later years. Both gonorrhea and syphilis can be treated effectively with antibiotics.

There are numerous other sexually transmitted diseases, and effective treatment is available for most. However, there is no cure for either herpes or the far more serious AIDS.

HIV/AIDS

AIDS (Acquired Immune Deficiency Syndrome) is most commonly transmitted by unsafe sexual activity – in Chile, this is the source of about 85% of all cases.

AIDS can also be spread by dirty needles (vaccinations, acupuncture and tattooing are potentially as dangerous as intravenous drug use if the equipment is not clean) or through infected blood transfusions. If you need an injection or a blood test (obligatory if you are a driver involved in an auto accident), purchase a new syringe from a pharmacy and ask the doctor or nurse to use it.

Fear of HIV infection should never preclude treatment for serious medical conditions. Although there may be a risk of infection, it is very small indeed. A good resource for help and information is the US **Centers for Disease Control AIDS hotline** (☎ 800-343-2347). In Santiago contact the **Corporación Chilena de Prevención del Sida** (☎ 02-222-5255; General Jofré 179, Santiago) or **Información sobre Sida y Enfermedades de Transmisión Sexual** (☎ 02-736-5542; Melipilla 3432, Conchalí, Santiago), which also provides medical and legal advice.

Women's Health

Gynecological Problems Poor diet, lowered resistance due to the use of antibiotics for stomach upsets and even contraceptive pills can lead to vaginal infections when traveling in hot climates. Yeast infections, characterized by rash, itch and discharge, can be treated with a diluted vinegar or even lemon-juice douche or with yogurt. Nystatin suppositories are the usual medical prescription. Trichomonas is a more serious infection with a discharge and a burning sensation when urinating. Male sexual partners must also be treated; if a vinegar-water douche is not effective, seek medical attention.

Pregnancy The first three months of pregnancy are riskiest time to travel, since most miscarriages occur during this trimester. The last three months should also be spent within reasonable distance of good medical care. Pregnant women should avoid all unnecessary medication, but vaccinations and malarial prophylactics should still be taken where possible. Take additional care to prevent illness and pay particular attention to diet and nutrition.

WOMEN TRAVELERS

The strong cultural thread running throughout Latin America, that of *machismo* (chauvinism), is much more subtle in Chile than in other countries. Women hold prominent positions in government, political parties and corporations, yet still have trouble receiving equal degrees of respect as given to their male counterparts. Female journalists have written some highly respected books analyzing the political and social upheaval caused by the dictatorship. Demoted to home and fashion sections of the newspapers during the regime, these women kept a low profile but copious notes while watching their male peers lose jobs or seek exile.

In general, there's a great deal of respect for women, but sometimes that machismo thread gets the better of even the best of men. Foreign women traveling alone may be the object of flirtation. This is usually in the form of a simple *piropo* (compliment) that can be acknowledged with little to worry about. Flirting back, however, will often be interpreted as a green light for them to show a bit more interest.

Chilean women sometimes first consider a foreign woman as competition or a threat to their relationship. This puts a damper on developing friendships with Chilean women, but after a few conversations this discomfort usually fades.

While most men are respectful, there are those who behave inappropriately. If the catcalls become too aggressive, responding aggressively, '¿Me estás hablando a mí?' ('Are you talking to me?'), will probably shame the fellow to silence. Unwelcome physical contact, particularly on crowded buses or trains, is not unusual, but if you're physically confident, a slap or a well-aimed elbow should discourage any further incident. If a man sitting next to you on an overnight bus makes you feel unsafe or uncomfortable, ask to be reseated.

Single women checking in at low-budget hotels, both in Santiago and elsewhere, may feel uncomfortable and unwelcome, since prostitutes may frequent such places. If you like the place, however, ignore the discomfort and it should disappear. But do make sure the doors lock.

For women traveling alone, Chile is safer than most other Latin American countries, and safer than the US and many areas of Europe. This doesn't mean you can be complacent, however. Outside the larger cities, women traveling alone are objects of curiosity, since Chilean women generally do not travel alone. Interpret questions about family or reasons you are alone as expressions of concern.

Should you hitchhike, exercise caution and especially avoid getting into a vehicle with more than one man. Though hitchhiking is never totally safe, it is much safer in pairs. Lonely Planet does not recommend hitchhiking.

GAY & LESBIAN TRAVELERS

While Chile is a strongly Catholic country and many frown upon homosexuality, there are enclaves of tolerance, most notably in Santiago. Since Chilean males are often more physically demonstrative than their counterparts in Europe or North America, behaviors like a vigorous embrace will seem innocuous. Likewise, lesbians walking hand-in-hand will attract little attention, since Chilean women frequently do so, but this would be very indiscreet behavior for males. The website gaychile.com is a fine resource with lodging recommendations, listings of basic services – legal, medical and otherwise, plus information on the nightlife in Santiago. **Tempo Travel** (☎ 02-281-8547; e novellus@tempotravel.cl; Almirante Pastene 7, Oficina 54, Providencia, Santiago) can provide all sorts of help to plan a gay-friendly trip through the country. While in Santiago, keep an eye out for Opus Gay, a magazine covering gay issues around Chile.

Chile's main gay-rights organization is **Movimiento Unificado de Minorías Sexuales** (MUMS; ☎ 02-737-0892; w www .orgullogay.cl; Alberto Reyes 063, Providencia, Santiago).

DISABLED TRAVELERS

Travelers with disabilities may find Chile somewhat difficult; in particular those in wheelchairs will find the narrow sidewalks, which are frequently in a state of disrepair, difficult to negotiate. Crossing streets can also be a problem, though most Chilean drivers are courteous toward individuals with obvious handicaps. Law now requires new public buildings to provide disabled access, but public transport remains poor in this regard – though the Metro's new Línea 5 has been retrofitted.

Santiago's **Tixi Service** (☎ 800-223-097 toll-free) caters specifically to disabled individuals, with hydraulic elevators to accommodate wheelchairs. Trips within the capital generally cost around US$12.

SENIOR TRAVELERS

Senior travelers should encounter no particular difficulties traveling in Chile, where older citizens typically enjoy a great deal of respect. On crowded buses, for instance, most Chileans will readily offer their seat to an older person. Elderhostel (see Organized Tours in the Getting There & Away chapter) organizes quality tours of the country geared to senior travelers.

TRAVEL WITH CHILDREN

Chile is child-friendly in terms of safety, health, people's attitudes and family-oriented activities. For small children, a folding stroller is a good idea, especially where there is a chance of getting lost in crowds. People are also very helpful on public transport; often someone will give up a seat for parent and child, but if that does not happen, an older person may offer to put the child on his or her lap.

In terms of food and health, there are no special concerns in most of the country, but bottled water may be a good idea for delicate stomachs. Most restaurants offer a wide variety of dishes suitable for children (vegetables, pasta, meat, chicken, fish), and Chilean cuisine is generally bland despite the occasional hot sauce. Portions are abundant enough that smaller children probably will not need separate meals, and there is usually no problem in securing additional cutlery.

In general, public toilets are poorly maintained; always carry toilet paper, which is almost nonexistent. While a woman may take a young boy into the ladies' room, it would be socially unacceptable for a man to take a girl into the men's room.

Unless you are traveling by plane, remember that distances are long and trips seem endless, so bring a comfortable blanket and enough toys and games to amuse your child. Santiago and most other cities have large public parks with playgrounds, so it's easy for children to make international friendships. There are also many activities specifically for children; consult newspapers like *El Mercurio* for listings.

For general information on the subject, look for Lonely Planet's *Travel with Children* (1995), by Cathy Lanigan & Lonely Planet cofounder Maureen Wheeler.

DANGERS & ANNOYANCES

Chile is much safer than most other South American countries and many other parts of the world, but certain precautions will nevertheless reduce risks and make your trip more enjoyable.

Personal Security & Theft

Although many Chileans find street crime alarming, personal security problems are minor compared with many other South American countries. Truly violent crime is still unusual in Santiago; men or women can travel in most parts of the city at any time of day or night without excessive apprehension. The crowded Metro and buses can be havens for pickpockets, however.

Valparaíso has a reputation for robberies in some of its southern neighborhoods. Summer is the crime season in beach resorts like Viña del Mar, Reñaca and La Serena. Though these are by no means violent places, be alert for pickpockets and avoid leaving valuables on the beach while you go for a swim.

Take precautions against petty theft, such as purse snatching. Be especially wary of calculated distractions, such as someone tapping you on the shoulder or spilling something on you, since these 'accidents' are often part of a team effort to relieve you of your backpack or other valuables. Grip your bag or purse firmly, carry your wallet in a front pocket and avoid conspicuous displays of expensive jewelry. Valuables such as passports and air tickets can be conveniently carried in a light jacket or vest with one or two zip-up or button-up pockets. Money belts and neck pouches are common alternatives, though some travelers find them uncomfortable; an elastic leg pouch is less cumbersome but can get very sweaty in hot weather.

Baggage insurance is a good idea. Since the doors to rooms in many budget hotels have only token locks or none at all, do not leave valuables such as cash or cameras in your room. You may want to bring your own lock. Lower to mid-range accommodations usually have secure left-luggage areas, while upscale hotels often have secure strongboxes in each room.

Natural Hazards

Volcanic activity is unlikely to pose any immediate threat to travelers, since volcanoes usually give some notice before a big eruption. A few popular resorts are especially vulnerable, particularly the town of Pucón, at the base of Volcán Villarrica.

Earthquakes are another matter, since they occur without warning. Local construction often does not meet seismic safety standards; adobe buildings tend to be especially vulnerable.

Many of Chile's finest beach areas have dangerous offshore rip currents, so ask before entering the water and be sure someone on shore knows your whereabouts. Most accessible beaches post signs about the possibility of swimming. Look for signs that say *apto para bañar* (swimming okay) and *no apto para bañar* (swimming not okay) or *peligroso* (dangerous). When in doubt, ask people before jumping in.

Dogs & Bugs

Stray dogs are a growing problem in Chile. These are often not your emaciated, mongrel variety, but well-fed purebreds, and – especially in the south – an impressive number of German shepherds. Chile doesn't have much of a spaying or neutering program (most Chileans think it immoral to chop the *cojones* off any beast) and, in more rural areas, locals may purchase the dogs and coddle them as puppies, but let them fend for themselves later on. In tourist towns, dogs sniff out the foreign tourists and follow them everywhere: They know who'll pet them and feed them half an empanada. Packs of dogs prowl the streets and can be intimidating but are rarely dangerous. Dog attacks do happen, unfortunately, usually to kids. If driving, be prepared for dogs barking and running after the bumper. Slow down a bit, but don't make abrupt moves – the dog will back off soon enough.

In the summer months, southern Chile gets plagued with pesky biting horseflies called *tábanos*. Bring along insect repellent and wear light-colored clothing.

LEGAL MATTERS

Chile's *carabineros* (police) are professional and polite in ordinary circumstances.

Carabineros can demand identification at any time, so carry your passport. Throughout the country, the toll-free emergency telephone number for carabineros is ☎ 133.

Chileans often refer to carabineros as *pacos*, a disrespectful (though not obscene) term that should *never* be used to a policeman's face.

Members of the military take themselves seriously, so avoid photographing military installations. If you are involved in any automobile accident, your license (usually your international permit) will be confiscated until the case is resolved, although local officials will usually issue a temporary driving permit within a few days. A blood-alcohol test is obligatory; purchase a sterile syringe at the hospital or clinic pharmacy when the carabineros take you there. After this, you will be taken to the police station to make a statement and then, under most circumstances, released. Ordinarily you cannot leave Chile until the matter is resolved; consult your consulate, insurance carrier and a lawyer at home.

Carabineros do not harass drivers for minor equipment violations but can be uptight about parking violations. You should *never* attempt to bribe the carabineros, whose reputation for institutional integrity is high.

BUSINESS HOURS

Shops in Chile open by 9am, but they often close at about 1pm for two to three hours for lunch then reopen until 8pm or 9pm. Government offices and businesses have a more conventional 9am to 6pm schedule. Banks are open 9am to 2pm weekdays.

PUBLIC HOLIDAYS & SPECIAL EVENTS

Throughout the year but especially in summer, Chileans from Arica to Punta Arenas celebrate a variety of local and national cultural festivals. Other than religious holidays such as Easter and Christmas, the most significant are mid-September's Fiestas Patrias, but many localities have their own favorites.

National holidays, when government offices and businesses are closed, are listed below. There is pressure to reduce these or to eliminate so-called sandwich holidays, which many Chileans take between an actual holiday and the weekend, by moving some of them to the nearest Monday.

Año Nuevo (New Year) January 1

Semana Santa (Easter Week) March or April

Día del Trabajo (Labor Day) May 1

Glorias Navales (commemorating the naval Battle of Iquique) May 21

Día de San Pedro y San Pablo (St Peter & St Paul's Day) June 29

Asunción de la Virgen (Assumption) August 15

Día de la Independencia Nacional (National Independence Day) September 18

Día del Ejército (Armed Forces Day) September 19

Día de la Raza (Columbus Day) October 12

Todo los Santos (All Saints' Day) November 1

Inmaculada Concepción (Immaculate Conception) December 8

Navidad (Christmas Day) December 25

ACTIVITIES

Chile has an increasing number of Santiago-based agencies specializing in adventure travel; See Organized Tours, in the Getting Around chapter, for more information.

Cycling & Mountain Biking

An increasing number of travelers are taking to Chile's length on mountain bike. It's an alluring idea, to be able to go straight for so long and through such a variety of landscape. Most large towns have bike repair shops and sell basic parts, but packing a comprehensive repair kit is essential. The Panamericana has undergone a major revamping and the shoulder, while still narrow in areas, is at least paved. And while biking the Ruta 5 is a popular goal, mountain bikers can enjoy fabulous trips in the Lakes District, circling lakes and accessing pristine areas with limited public transport. The Carretera Austral attracts more cycling groups every year. It's a great route through fantastic scenery. See the Getting Around chapter for more details.

Skiing & Snowboarding

Chile has some world-class ski resorts, many with the price to match. Most of them are within an hour's drive of Santiago, including La Parva, El Colorado and Valle Nevado. Portillo, the site of several downhill speed records, is northeast of Santiago near the Argentine border crossing to Mendoza. Termas de Chillán, just east of Chillán, is a fun spot with a more laid-back feel to it, while Parque Nacional Villarrica, near the resort town of Pucón, has the added thrill of skiing on a smoking volcano. Antillanca, in Parque Nacional Puyehue, east of Osorno, has incredible views. Those last three have the added bonus of being close to hot springs to soak in after a hard day of descents. Once-closed La Burbuja, in Parque Nacional Vicente Pérez Rosales, east of Puerto Varas, makes skiing Volcán Osorno possible again. Coyhaique has its own small resort, while Punta Arenas can lay claim to having one of the few places where one can ski with an ocean view. 'First descents' of Chilean Patagonia's numerous mountains is a growing, but obviously limited, trend.

Hiking & Trekking

The number-one reason to come to Chile is most definitely to get off the roads and into nature – on foot. Most of the national parks and reserves have decent trail networks, although many travelers will be alarmed at how few there are in comparison to the amount of protected land. (Conaf's insufficient funding means that for years they've had to focus more on maintaining what they already have rather than developing the trail systems.) But opportunities are not limited to the national parks: A growing number of private reserves, plus undeveloped rural properties, have trails that are just as good. Some regional Conaf offices have published decent trail maps, and the Matassi maps also have trail indicators on their more specific tourist-oriented maps. What follows barely touches the extent of the possibilities but should tantalize enough to pack those boots.

In the north, Parque Nacional Lauca has a number of intriguing hikes, as does desert oasis San Pedro Atacama. Escaping Santiago's fog is easy with jaunts to nearby El Morado or Parque Nacional La Campana. Altos de Lircay, in Chile's middle, has a great backcountry circuit. The offerings amp up farther south, with far too many places to mention, but hikes through Conguillío, along the Valdivian coast, and around Volcán Puyehue – with out-of-place and out-of-this-world Sahara-like landscapes, natural hot springs and geyser fields – are highlights of the Lakes District.

Within the northern corner of Patagonia, Cochamós valley, though not protected as a park, has enticing treks through the 'Yosemite of the south,' while Pumalín has a number of great day hikes and is steadfastly developing multiday hikes as well.

In the heart of Patagonia, Torres del Paine is by far Chile's most popular destination, with a network of transportation, *refugios* and campsites that allow for day hikes and multiday circuit treks. Recent overcrowding in summer months, however, has challenged the experience of 'bonding with nature.' Tierra del Fuego's Dientes de Navarino is another circuit that's inconvenient to get to, but well worth it, as are less exhausting hikes anywhere around magical Isla Navarino.

Hiking in Isla Juan Fernández is a highlight for anyone who makes it there, with a system of independent and guided hikes through steep terrain filled with endemic plants and birds. And Easter Island's magic lures some travelers to trek its circumference.

Hikers and trekkers visiting the Southern Hemisphere for the first time should look for a compensated needle compass such as the Recta DP 10; Northern Hemisphere compasses can be deceptive as an indicator of direction in far southern latitudes.

Mountaineering

Chile has great mountaineering country, ranging from the Pallachatas volcanoes of the northern altiplano to Ojos del Salado, east of Copiapó, the numerous volcanic cones of Araucanía and Los Lagos and Torres del Paine.

Climbers intending to scale border peaks like the Pallachatas or Ojos del Salado must have permission from Chile's **Dirección de Fronteras y Límites** (Difrol; ☎ 02-671-4110, fax 697-1909, 672-2536; e difrol3@minrel .cl; Bandera 52, 5th floor, Santiago). It's possible to request permission prior to arriving in Chile; a request form can be accessed on the agency's website (w www.difrol.cl).

For other information on climbing and help with the bureaucracy, contact the

Federación de Andinismo (☎ 02-222-9140; Almirante Simpson 77, Providencia, Santiago).

Horseback Riding

Saddling up and following in the path of Chile's *huasos* is a fun and easy way to experience the wilderness. Except in the far north, opportunities can be found just about everywhere. While many rural workers use horses like machines, a great many others, along with landowners and adventure-travel outfitters, revere the animals and treat them exceptionally well. Most places offer first-time riders preliminary lessons before taking to the trails. Favorites for single- or multiday treks are: Valle de Elqui, around Pucón, Parque Nacional Puyehue, Cochamó and Torres del Paine.

Surfing

Chile's almost endless coastline offers plenty of surfing possibilities, but only at Arica is the water comfortably warm, so wet suits are imperative. Rough surf and rip currents make some areas inadvisable, and it's best not to surf alone anywhere.

Many of the best surfing areas are in or near Arica, Iquique and Antofagasta in the Norte Grande; the paving of coastal Ruta 1 has opened this area to surfers, but has also brought mountains of trash from careless campers. Pichilemu, in Región V, is another popular area.

Rafting & Kayaking

Water lovers can plan a trip through Chile's south using its rivers, lakes, fjords and inlets as their routes quite easily. And whitewater enthusiasts agree that Chile's rivers are world-class for both rafting and kayaking. While hydroelectric projects are mercilessly taming the Biobío, the Futaleufú has plenty of Class V challenges. Other popular runs are down Río Petrohue and Río Trancura in the Lakes District and Río Simpson and Río Baker in the Aisén region. Even near Santiago, the Cajón del Maipo, offers a decent run.

Sea-kayaking spots include the fjords in Parque Pumalín and around the sheltered bays of Chiloé. For details on North American operators that arrange trips, see the Organized Tours section in the Getting Around chapter.

Diving

Chile is not known for diving or snorkeling, since even the tropical segments of its long coastline experience cold currents. The best places for diving are its Pacific island possessions – the Juan Fernández Archipelago and Easter Island – and offshore islands like Isla Damas in Reserva Nacional Pingüino de Humboldt.

Paragliding

Conditions in and near Iquique – steep coastal escarpment, rising air currents and the soft, extensive dunes, make it an ideal area for paragliding *(parapente)*, a sport that is taking off quite quickly.

Cultural Touring

In an effort to create alternative economic resources for indigenous peoples and farmers, the governmental departments overseeing small business (Sercotec) and farming development (Indap) have helped promote tourism in rural areas. Known as 'etnoturismo', 'agroturismo' or 'turismo rural', possibilities include camping or homestays; workshops in music, medicinal herbs or cooking; or helping out on farms. This is a great way to get off the gringo trail and enjoy the country's oft-overlooked cultures. Organized networks are in the south, most notably in Chiloé, Lago Ranco, and around Pucón and Temuco, but the trend is growing in other parts of the country. A list of participants working with Indap can be found on their website (ⓦ www.indap.cl/turismo; click Vacaciones) or ask municipal tourist offices for details.

COURSES

Spanish-language courses can be found in Santiago, Iquique, Pucón and Coyhaique. Most have both short- and long-term courses, plus one-on-one instruction.

With Chilean headquarters at Coyhaique, the **National Outdoor Leadership School** (NOLS; ☎ 307-332-5300, fax 307-332-1220; ⓔ admissions@nols.edu; ⓦ www.nols.edu; 284 Lincoln St, Lander, WY 82520, USA) offers a 75-day 'Semester in Patagonia' program, emphasizing mountain wilderness skills, sea kayaking and natural-history courses, with university credit available. They also organize a five-week mountaineering course in the Campo de Hielo Norte (northern icefield).

Santiago's **Vinoteca** (☎ 02-335-2349, *Isidora Goyenechea 2966, Las Condes)* organizes wine courses for groups of up to 10 people on a regular basis as well as on request. The cost per person is about US$70.

WORK

It's increasingly difficult to obtain residence and work permits for Chile. Consequently, many foreigners do not bother to do so, but the most reputable employers will insist on the proper visa. If you need one, go to the **Departamento de Extranjería** (☎ 02-550-2400; *Agustinas 1235, Santiago; open 8:30am-2pm Mon-Fri).*

A good orientation to working and living in Chile, including suggestions on obtaining residence and starting a business, is *The International Settler*, an informational booklet published by the *News Review*, Santiago's weekly English-language newspaper. If you're unable to find it around town, try to contact the **News Review** (☎ 02-236-1424; ⓒ newrevi@mcl.cl; *Almirante Pastene 202, Providencia, Santiago).*

It is not unusual for visiting travelers to work as English-language instructors in Santiago. Industries with an international trading focus, such as salmon farming and fishmeal processing, have a growing need for English-language instruction. Puerto Montt has a number of language schools. Wages aren't very good, and full-time employment is hard to come by without a commitment to stay for some time.

Options for volunteer work are worth exploring, especially with social and environmental organizations. Two good sources to consult are the comprehensive, biannual *Directorio de Instituciones de Chile* (popularly known as the 'Guía Silber' after its publisher, Silber Editores), a directory of political, labor, church, cultural and other institutions both official and nongovernmental; and the annual *Directorio de Organizaciones Miembros* published by Renace (Red Nacional de Acción Ecológica), a loosely affiliated network of environmental organizations throughout the country.

ACCOMMODATIONS

Chile's broad spectrum of accommodations ranges from hostels and campgrounds to five-star luxury hotels. Where you stay will depend on your budget and your standards, where you are, and how hard you look, but you should be able to find something reasonable. You may also find yourself invited into Chilean homes and generally should not hesitate to accept this hospitality.

Reservations

Nearly all hotels, even the cheapest, have telephones, and many have fax machines, so it's easy to make reservations. While reservations are usually unnecessary, if you'll be arriving at an awkward hour or during the peak summer season or a holiday weekend, they can be a good idea.

Camping

Most organized campgrounds are designed with the family or small group in mind. Sites are large and clustered close together and have excellent facilities: hot showers, toilets, laundry, restaurants or snack bars, and ample room around a firepit for the essential *asado*. The pricing structure also reflects this design, charging a steep sum by site rather than by person. Often, singles and couples can arrange a discounted per person rate, but if not, staying in a basic *hospedaje* will be cheaper. This is true both at private campgrounds and in national parks, where concessionaires control the franchise. In some remote parts of Chile, there is free camping, but drinkable water and sanitary facilities are often lacking.

Sernatur's Santiago headquarters has a free pamphlet called *Camping* that lists and describes family-oriented campgrounds throughout Chile. Turistel's annually updated camping guide has detailed information on campgrounds within protected areas, accompanied by excellent maps.

For comfort, invest in a good, dome-style tent with a rain fly before coming to South America, where camping equipment is more expensive. With a good tent, a three-season sleeping bag should be adequate for almost any weather conditions. If heading to Patagonia, make sure to have a synthetic, not down, sleeping bag, which will dry more quickly in the unpredictable weather. A camp stove that can burn a variety of fuels is a good idea, since white gas *(bencina blanca)* is available only at chemical supply shops or hardware stores. Firewood is a limited and often expensive resource. Bring or buy mosquito repellent, since many campsites are near rivers or lakes.

Servicentros along Ruta 5, the Panamericana, have spacious lots suitable for parking and sleeping – if the maneuvers of 18-wheelers don't disturb your sleep. In addition to clean toilet facilities (for which there is a token charge), most of these places offer hot showers for less than US$1.

Refugios

Within some national parks, Conaf maintains rustic shelters, or *refugios* for hikers and trekkers, that unfortunately lack upkeep due to Conaf's limited budget. In some of the more popular parks, most notably Torres del Paine, concessions manage more comfortable refugios with bunks, mattresses, showers and even restaurants, but charge dearly for their use. Private reserves may also have refugios set up along their trails.

Cabins

In resort towns, near national parks, and in many campgrounds, *cabañas* are great value for small groups of travelers. Most come with a private bathroom and fully-equipped kitchens, allowing for a great deal more privacy and a chance to cook your own food.

Casas de Familia & Rural Homestays

In summer, especially from Temuco south, families often rent rooms to visitors. A *casa de familia* can be an excellent bargain with access to cooking and laundry facilities, hot showers and Chilean hospitality. Tourist offices often maintain lists of such accommodations. Increasingly, families in rural areas, including indigenous communities, are taking in tourists. See Cultural Touring, under Activities, earlier in this chapter, for more information.

Hostels

Most towns along the gringo trail have a hostel *albergue* with Hostelling International (HI) affiliation. Some are the typical youth hostel setup, with dorm beds, common kitchens and living spaces, as well as shared baths, while others are hotels or more established *hospedajes* with rooms set aside for hostelers to share. Most places don't insist on a HI card, but charge a bit more for non-members. The local affiliate of Hostelling International, **Asociación Chilena de Albergues Turísticos Juveniles** (☎/fax 02-233-3220;

e) *hostelling@hostelling.cl; Hernando de Aguirre 201, Oficina 602, Providencia, Santiago)* distributes hostel cards, which cost US$25 for a new issue or US$15 for a renewal. The Santiago HI hostel also sells the cards and has lists of affiliates in the country.

The second system is coordinated by the **Dirección General de Deportes y Recreación** (*Digeder;* ☎ 02-655-0090, fax 343-0669; *Fidel Oteíza 1956, 5th floor, Providencia),* whose *albergues juveniles* cater mainly to schoolchildren and students on holiday and occupy temporary sites at sports stadiums, campgrounds, schools or churches. Usually open in January and February only, they charge a mere few dollars per night for a dormitory bed, making them just about the cheapest accommodations in Chile. Remember, however, that you'll be sharing space with some very energetic, amped-up youth whose priority is not to get enough sleep before the next day's hike. Local tourist offices should be able to refer you to them. Note that the translation *hostal* can refer to a hotel.

Hospedajes & Residenciales

The difference between a *hospedaje* and *residencial* is vague and shouldn't affect a decision on where to stay. Both offer very reasonable accommodations. Rooms are usually modest but clean with foam-mattress beds, rock-hard foam-filled pillows, clean sheets and blankets. During high season, some request that rooms be shared. However, only specifically in dorm-style lodging, will they mix men and women in shared rooms. Never hesitate to ask to see a room before making a decision.

Bathrooms and shower facilities are usually shared, but a few will have rooms with private bath, usually with a double bed for couples. Mostly in the north, but not exclusively, you may have to ask them to turn on the *calefón* (hot-water heater) before taking a shower.

Breakfast usually comes included in the price. If you grow weary of Nescafé and white bread, you may be able to negotiate a slightly lower rate and skip the breakfast. In very touristy spots, such as San Pedro de Atacama and Pucón, breakfast is rarely included in the price.

Some places (and most often those considered 'residenciales') cater to clients who intend only *very* short stays – say two hours or so, such as couples with no other indoor alternative for their passion or prostitutes. Except for occasional noise, the proximity of such activities should not deter you, even if you have children.

Hotels & Motels

Hotels vary from one-star austerity to five-star luxury, but correlation between these categories and their standards is less than perfect; many one-star places seem to be a better value than their three- and four-star brethren. In general, hotels provide a room with private bath, often a telephone and a TV, increasingly with cable or satellite service. Normally they will have a restaurant; breakfast is often, but not always, included in the price.

In some areas, motels are what North Americans and Europeans expect: rural or suburban roadside accommodations with convenient parking. However, the term 'motel' can also be a euphemism for a place catering almost exclusively to unmarried couples (or individuals married to others) with no other alternative for privacy. The external decor usually makes it obvious what sort of place a given establishment is. With safe parking and rather economical rates, these love shacks can make decent, if not entertaining, options for those with their own wheels. Within cities, its counterpart is known as a *hotel parejero*.

Long-Term Rentals

For long-term rentals in Santiago, check listings in Sunday's *El Mercurio* or in the weekly classified paper *El Rastro*. In resorts such as Viña del Mar, La Serena or Villarrica, several travelers together could consider renting an apartment to keep costs down. In towns such as Valdivia and La Serena, people line the highway approaches in summer to offer houses and apartments. You can also check the tourist office or local papers.

FOOD

Markets piled high with fresh fruits and vegetables, and stalls of every shape and size of fish and shellfish, are found throughout Chile. However, the average restaurant in Chile rarely takes advantage of this bounty. In fact, Chilean food can get downright boring, and the best way to beat the palate blues is to find a place to cook your own

meals once in a while. Restaurants in Santiago's Barrio Bellavista and in Pucón, plus a handful of upscale restaurants around the country, are about the only places that show culinary creativity.

Where cooking is as much social as nutritional, Chiloé has the most unique cuisine, including *curanto*, a hearty stew of shellfish, chicken, pork, lamb, beef and potato, served with chapalele or milcao (potato breads).

Fast-food chains – both imports and Chile's own – can be found around the country. Dino's is a good bet for sandwiches, while Bavaria is more like a glorified Denny's.

Meals

Do not hesitate to ask waiters for an explanation of any dish. It is customary – and expected – to leave a 10% tip. The menu is *la carta*; the bill is *la cuenta*.

Breakfast In budget lodgings, breakfast *(desayuno)* usually comprises toast *(pan tostado)* or white rolls with butter *(mantequilla)* and jam *(mermelada)*, tea or coffee. Some places may offer eggs *(huevos)*, which can be served fried *(frito)*, scrambled *(revuelto)*, soft-boiled *(pasado)*, poached *(a la copa)* (well done is *bien cocidos)* or hard-boiled *(duros)*. In the southern Lakes District, where breakfasts tend to be much heartier, you are served a slice of küchen (German-style cake) as well as bread.

Lunch & Dinner Many places offer a cheap set meal *(comida corrida* or *almuerzo del día)* for lunch *(almuerzo* or *colación)* and, less often, for dinner *(cena)*. The most basic is usually two hearty plates, heavy on meat and carbos, and a simple dessert. *Cocinerías* or *comedores*, small, cheap restaurants often found around the markets, can often have tastier daily specials than the more staid, linen-service *clubs de unión*. Another worthwhile lunch spot is the *casino de bomberos* (fire station restaurant), which offers inexpensive meals. Note that the best meal is often at lunch, the most important meal of the day, when more people eat out and the kitchen is more active. Many basic restaurants prepare their fish by frying it in heavy oil, which besides its dietary shortcomings also destroys the flavor; on request, however, most will prepare fish *al vapor* (steamed) or *a la plancha* (grilled). Certain shellfish, mainly locos and centolla, may be in *veda* (closed season) because of overexploitation. Restaurants claiming to serve them fresh during that time are being unethical either by purchasing them in the first place or by serving you morsels from the freezer. Check first.

Popular lunch and dinner alternatives are *parrillas*, restaurants that grill everything from steak to sausages over charcoal, and *pizzerías* that, with the exception of a few, pale in comparison to most other pizza-eating countries.

Vegetarian Concerns

Menus can be quite limiting to the truly vegetarian. Consider bringing along some multivitamins. Most restaurants have side dishes of vegetables – such as mashed potatoes, spinach or boiled carrots and peas – that you can order as a main dish. When explaining that you don't eat meat, it's helpful to say it is due to an allergy *(alergia)* or some health reason. Many of the white-bread rolls served at restaurants and *hospedajes* are made with lard. Top tourist destinations, such as San Pedro de Atacama, Pucón and Puerto Varas, do have vegetarian or veggie-friendly restaurants.

Ordering

The lists below should give a basic introduction to what's on the menu. Regional variety does exist. In towns that see lots of foreign tourists, restaurants often have an English-language menu, the translations of which can be brilliant.

Sandwiches

palta – avocado

queso – cheese

ave – chicken

churrasco – steak

jamón – ham

aliado – cold cheese and ham

Barros Jarpa – ham and melted cheese, named after a Chilean painter known for consuming them in large quantities

Barros Luco – steak with melted cheese, the favorite of Ramón Barros Luco, who was president from 1910 to 1915

chacarero – beefsteak with tomato and other vegetables

completo – a hot dog with absolutely everything

Basics

empanada – a tasty turnover; the most common empanada fillings are *pino* (ground beef with just a bit of hard-boiled egg and olive) and *queso* (cheese), but some specialized places offer quite a variety of stuffings, from seafood to veggies. Empanadas are made either *al horno* (baked) or *fritas* (fried).

humitas – corn tamales, frequently wrapped in corn husks and steamed

sopaipilla – a deep fried batter bread made from squash and flour

pebre – similar to Mexican salsa, a tasty condiment of chopped tomatoes, onion, garlic, chili peppers, cilantro, oil and lemon juice

cazuela – stew of potato or maize with a piece of beef or chicken

caldo or *sopa* – soup

pastel de choclo – maize casserole filled with vegetables, chicken and beef, available during the summer maize harvest

lomo a lo pobre – enormous slab of beef topped with two fried eggs and buried in French fries

ajiaco – spiced beef stew

ensalada – salad

ensalada surtido – mixed salad, with fresh greens plus cold cooked sweet beets, corn or peas and carrots

ensalada chilena – sliced tomatoes and white onions served with oil and salt

Seafood

almejas – clams

calamares – squid

camarones grandes – prawns

camarones – shrimp

cangrejo or *jaiva* – crab

centolla – king crab

cholgas – mussels

erizos – sea urchins

machas – razor clams

mariscos – shellfish

ostiones – scallops

ostras – oysters

pescado – fish

picoroco – giant barnacle

pulpo – octopus

caldillo de … – hearty soup of a variety of fish (often *congrio* or conger eel), spiced up with lemon, cilantro and garlic

ceviche – raw fish or shellfish, usually 'cooked' in lemon juice, but now usually steam cooked (for health reasons) and served cold with lemon juice and chopped onion

chupe de ... – a 'stew' of some sort of seafood, cooked in a thick sauce of butter, bread crumbs, cheese and spices

paila marina – a fish and shellfish chowder

DRINKS
Soft Drinks & Water
Chileans guzzle prodigious amounts of soft drinks, from the ubiquitous Coca Cola to 7-Up, Sprite and sugary local brands such as Bilz. Mineral water, both carbonated *(con gas)* and plain *(sin gas)*, is widely available, but tap water is potable almost everywhere.

Fruit Juices
Fresh *jugos* (juices) are excellent and vary depending on the season. For fresh-squeezed orange juice, order *jugo de naranja exprimido*. Other common choices are *toronja* (grapefruit), *damasco* (apricot), *piña* (pineapple), *mora* (blackberry), *maracuyá* (passion fruit) and *sandía* (watermelon). The distinctively Chilean *mote con huesillo* is a delicious and refreshing drink of rehydrated peaches in nectar and is served with barley kernels. Countless street vendors throughout the country sell it in the summer.

Licuados are milk-blended fruit drinks; on request they can be made with water. Common flavors are banana, *durazno* (peach) and *pera* (pear). Unless you like yours *very* sweet, ask them to hold the sugar ('sin azúcar, por favor').

Coffee & Tea
While the situation is improving, Chilean coffee will dismay serious caffeine addicts. The gut-wrenching instant Nescafé is the norm in most households and at budget restaurants and accommodations. *Café con leche* is literally milk with coffee – a teaspoonful (or packet) of Nescafé dissolved in

---

Chilean Wine: New World Wine-Making with Old Roots

Chilean wine is on everyone's lips. From London to Los Angeles to Lisbon, it's being consumed and talked about, partly because it's great wine that's often very affordable and partly because of a concerted effort on the part of the local industry to embrace modern methods, experimental plantings and shrewd marketing strategies.

The tradition of wine-making came with the *conquistadores* and clergy, who brought the black *país* grape from Europe in the mid-16th century. However, *país* is good only for simple table wine, and it was not until it became fashionable in the mid-19th century for local mining barons to source noble root stock from Bordeaux that serious wine-making got its start. Chile's cabernet sauvignon, merlot, and carmenére – a variety no longer found in Europe – all date from that era, as do big names like Underraga, Cousiño and Concha y Toro.

It wasn't until the 1980s that the Chilean wine industry embraced the idea of small boutique wineries, with vineyards that had previously been selling all their grapes to the giant companies around Santiago deciding to bottle their own. These days many of the old vineyards still exist but there's also an awful lot of planting going on, particularly in the Colchagua Valley, where some growers are experimenting with dry hillside plots.

It's pretty much accepted that Chile's best wines are its reds – especially its ungrafted cabernet sauvignon – but there's currently a lot of buzz around the long-lost carmenére grape, which was wiped out in Europe with the phylloxera (an aphid-like insect) plague in the 1860s and only recently rediscovered in Chile after centuries of masquerading as merlot. In general, look for vintages belonging to odd years, which in the 1990s were all hot and dry. A locally published wine guide is Fred Purdy's *Gringo's Guide to Chilean Wine*.

Chile's wine-growing takes place in seven river valleys: Valle de Elquí, near La Serena; Valle de Maipo, near Santiago; Valle de Casablanca, near Valparaíso; Valle de Rapel, which is further broken into the Valle de Colchagua (around Santa Cruz) and the Valle de Cachapoal (near Rancagua); Valle de Curicó; Valle de Maule, near Talca; and Valle de Itata, near Chillán. Of these, Valle de Maipo, Valle de Colchagua and Valle de Maule offer the best opportunities for visitors to learn about winemaking – see those sections for details.

— Brigitte Barta

hot milk. *Café solo* or *café negro* is coffee with hot water alone. ost cafés and upscale restaurants and hotels have espresso drinks. An *espresso* is the usual one shot. A *cortado* is a shot with a splash of hot milk; you can order these *chico* (small – or one shot) or *grande* (large – two shots and with more milk).

Tea is normally served black, with at least three packets of sugar. If you prefer just a touch of milk, a habit most Chileans find bizarre, ask for *un poquito de leche* Asking for *té con leche* (tea with milk) means getting a tea bag submerged in warm milk. *Yerba mate*, or 'Paraguayan tea,' is consumed to some degree in Patagonia, but not as much as in the River Plate countries (Argentina, Uruguay and Paraguay). Herbal teas *(aguitas)* such as *manzanilla* (chamomile), *rosa mosqueta* and *boldo* are on offer anywhere and often use the leaves or flowers rather than the bagged tea. Because of their digestive properties, these are usually ordered after a meal.

Pisco

If you leave Chile without being offered or trying a *pisco sour* you might actually have been in Argentina. Pisco is a potent grape brandy made from distilled grapes with a high sugar content, grown in the dry soils of the Copiapó and Elquí Valleys. It's also Chile's most popular drink. Dinners often start with a *pisco sour* – a mix of pisco, lemon juice, powdered sugar and egg white to make it foamy. Premixed sours are available, and some bars and restaurants try to get away with serving that instead of the real thing. The best ones are made by bartenders who shake it by hand until the ice melts and the sugar completely dissolves. Bar and club hoppers often order *piscola*, a mix of pisco and cola to keep them going all night. Pisco may also be served with ginger ale *(chilcano)* or vermouth *(capitán)*. Popular brands are Capel, Tres Erres and Los Artesanos del Cochiguaz. Higher-end brands are Mistral and Monte Fraile.

Beer & Specialty Drinks

Escudo and Cristal are the most popular beers, and it's hard to tell the difference between them. Becker is another decent choice, but *Kuntsmann*, started by German colonists in Valdivia, is by far the best, making both ale *and* lager. Draft beer goes by its German name *schop*, which is cheaper and often better than the bottled options.

Chileans have concocted their share of specialized alcoholic drinks. *Gol* is a translucent mixture of butter, sugar and milk, left to ferment for a fortnight. It's drunk in the south, mostly in private homes, and not readily available in restaurants. *Licor de oro*, found in Chiloé, uses a similar base of fermented milk, but adds in other secret ingredients. *Guinda* is a cherrylike fruit that is the basis of *guindado*, with brandy, cinnamon, and cloves. *Murtillado* is a similar concept, with the blueberrylike fruit *murtilla*. *Chicha* is fermented apple cider, found throughout the south. A popular holiday drink is the powerful but sweet *cola de mono* ('tail of the monkey'), which consists of *aguardiente* (cane alcohol), coffee, cloves and vanilla.

ENTERTAINMENT
Cinemas

Except in the deep of Patagonia, most major cities have a multiplex movie theater showing blockbuster films. These are usually shown in the original language, with subtitles. Repertory houses, cultural centers and universities show classics or less commercial films.

Performing Arts

The fine performing arts are not very prevalent in Chile, but throughout the country you'll find some theater and dance, performed mostly by community organizations or Santiago-based touring groups. Santiago has several good choices, as do cities with a strong university scene, such as Valdivia. Folkloric dance shows are often held during the town festivals in January and February.

Bars & Clubs

The nightlife scene in Chile has little to distinguish it from similar scenes in North America, Australia or Europe. Unlike the US, however, things here don't get going until about 11pm and last until sunrise. You won't find a lot of 'authentic' culture playing out, and so far, nobody, thank goodness, has tried to merge the national dance *cueca* with hip-hop. Chileans themselves say they aren't much into dancing, at least not like their northern and eastern neighbors, but still there's plenty of nightlife to go round.

Some bars are staging grounds for local bands, but most are meeting points for friends to gather and down a few Escudos or piscolas before heading to the dance clubs *(discote-*

cas). More and more, elements of architecture and design are sneaking into the bar scene and creating some elaborate affairs, a great showing of Chile busting out some expression. Dance clubs are barren echo chambers before 2am and only really get thumping around 3am or 4am. Most are found outside of town limits, or, in the case of port towns, in the more industrial sectors closer to the water. A number of cities also have salsa dancing clubs, or *salsatecas*. Keeping track of what places are hip is impossible; ask the locals where everyone's going these days.

Clubs de noche (nightclubs) are most often tacky, glitzy affairs.

Live Music

Santiago's most prestigious music venues, like the Teatro Municipal and the Teatro de la Universidad de Chile, are the main sites for classical concerts. See the Santiago chapter for details.

Chile's best-known rock groups play at stadium venues in Chile's largest cities, but most international rock concerts take place only in Santiago.

Peñas are nightclubs whose performers offer unapologetically political material based on folk themes. The famous *Nueva Canción Chilena* (New Chilean Song Movement) had its origins in the peñas of the 1960s.

Summer cultural festivals, which take place throughout Chile from mid-January to mid-February, are heaps of fun and should definitely be sought out if you're in the area. From cookouts to folk music, jazz festivals to songfests, rodeos to races, they are pure, down-home fun.

SPECTATOR SPORTS

By far the most popular spectator sport is soccer. The professional season begins in March and ends in November, though the playoffs run almost until Christmas.

The most popular teams are Colo Colo (named for the legendary Mapuche *cacique*), Universidad de Chile and the more elitist Universidad Católica. Followers of Colo Colo are popularly known as *garras blancas* (the white claws), while those of the Universidad de Chile are called *los de abajo* (the underdogs).

Other popular spectator sports include tennis, boxing, horse racing and basketball. Internationally, the best-known Chilean athletes are soccer forwards Iván Zamorano (a star with Spain's Real Madrid and Italy's Inter Milan) and Marcelo Salas, and tennis player Marcelo (Chino) Ríos, who was ranked No 1 in the world for a brief period of time.

Rodeos take place in the spring and summer, mainly in the northern and central areas.

SHOPPING

Artisans' *ferias* can be found throughout the country. In the north, woolen goods are similar to those in Bolivia and Peru, using alpaca and llama wool. In Chiloé and Patagonia, sheep-wool goods, such as thick fishermen's sweaters and blankets, are plentiful and great deals. In the Araucanía, look for jewelry based on Mapuche designs, possibly the most unique item in Chile, but also possibly the least produced. They also produce quality weavings and basketry. Items with lapis lazuli can be found in many places, but check the quality of the setting and silver used – things are often only silver plated and very soft. In the Lakes District, artisans carve wooden plates and bowls out of the hardwood *raulí*.

After trying many of Chile's wines, taking home a few bottles is tempting. Stick to the boutique wineries that you can't find in your own country, or pick up bottles of pisco, which is much more difficult to find outside of Chile. Other artisanal edibles include *miel de ulmo*, a very aromatic and tasty honey special to Patagonia, *mermelada de murtilla*, a jam made of a red blueberrylike fruit, and canned papayas from Norte Chico. As long as such goods are still sealed, there shouldn't be a problem going through international customs.

Many cities have good antiques markets, most notably Santiago's Mercado Franklin and Valparaíso's Plaza O'Higgins. Flea markets are commonly known as *Ferias Persas* (Persian Fairs).

Getting There & Away

Chile has direct overseas air connections from North America, the UK, Europe and Australia/New Zealand. Another alternative is to fly to a neighboring country like Argentina, Bolivia or Peru and continue to Chile by air or land. International flights within South America, however, tend to be costly unless purchased as part of intercontinental travel, but there are real bargain roundtrip fares between Buenos Aires and Santiago.

AIR

Always reconfirm onward flights or return bookings by the specified time – at least 72 hours before departure on intercontinental flights. Otherwise you risk missing your flight because of rescheduling or being classified as a 'no-show.'

Most long-distance flights to Chile arrive at Santiago, landing at **Aeropuerto Internacional Arturo Merino Benítez** (☎ 02-601-9709) in the suburb of Pudahuel. There are also flights from neighboring countries to regional airports such as Arica, Iquique, Temuco, Puerto Montt and Punta Arenas.

LanChile is the national carrier, with the most extensive system of connecting internal routes. Many major international airlines have offices or representatives in Santiago, including:

Aerolíneas Argentinas (☎ 02-639-5001, 800-200-508) Moneda 756, Centro

Air France (☎ 02-290-9300, 690-1540) Alcántara 44, 6th floor, Las Condes

Alitalia (☎ 02-378-8230) Av El Bosque Norte 0107, Oficina 21, Las Condes

American Airlines (☎ 02-679-0000) Huérfanos 1199, Centro • Av El Bosque Norte 0107, Local 11, Las Condes • Santa Magdalena 90, Providencia

Avianca (☎ 02-270-6600) Santa Magdalena 116, Local 106, Providencia

British Airways (☎ 02-330-8600) Isidora Goyenechea 2934, Oficina 302, Las Condes

Canadian Airlines International (☎ 02-688-3656) Huérfanos 1199, Centro

Copa (☎ 02-200-2100) Fidel Oteíza 1921, Oficina 703, Providencia

Cubana de Aviación (☎ 02-274-1819) Fidel Oteíza 1971, Oficina 201, Providencia

Iberia (☎ 02-870-1070) Bandera 206, 8th floor, Centro

KLM (☎ 02-233-0991) San Sebastián 2839, Oficina 202, Las Condes

LanChile (☎ 02-526-2000) Huérfanos 926 • (☎ same) Providencia 2006

Líneas Aéreas de Costa Rica (Lacsa; ☎ 02-235-5500) Manuel Barros Borgoño 105, 2nd floor, Providencia

Lloyd Aéreo Boliviano (LAB; toll-free ☎ 02-600-200-2015, 688-8678) Moneda 1170, Centro

Lufthansa (☎ 02-630-1655) Moneda 970, 16th floor, Centro

Plunatel (☎ 02-707-8000, fax 332-0541) Av El Bosque Norte 0177, 9th floor, Las Condes

Qantas (☎ 02-232-9562) Isidora Goyenechea 2934, Oficina 301, Las Condes

SAS (☎ 02-233-3585) Fernández 128, Oficina 502, Providencia

Swissair (☎ 02-244-2888) Alfredo Barros Errázuriz 1954, Oficina 810, Providencia

Varig (☎ 02-707-8000) Av El Bosque Norte 0177, Oficina 903, Las Condes

Tickets

From almost everywhere, South America is a relatively expensive destination to fly to, but discount fares can reduce the bite considerably. If possible, take advantage of sea-

---

Warning

The information in this chapter is particularly vulnerable to change: Prices for international travel are volatile, routes are introduced and canceled, schedules change, special deals come and go, and rules and visa requirements are amended. You should check directly with the airline or a travel agent to make sure you understand how a fare (and ticket you may buy) works, and be aware of the security requirements for international travel.

The upshot of this is that you should get opinions, quotes and advice from as many airlines and travel agents as possible before you part with your hard-earned cash. The details given in this chapter should be regarded as pointers and are not a substitute for your own careful, up-to-date research.

sonal discounts and try to avoid peak times such as Christmas, New Year's or Easter. Advance purchase for a given period of time, usually two to six months, will normally provide the best, but not necessarily most flexible, deal.

The plane ticket will probably be the single most expensive item in your budget, and buying it can be intimidating. It is always worth putting aside a few hours to research the current state of the market. Start shopping for a ticket early – some of the cheapest tickets must be purchased months in advance, and some popular flights sell out early. Talk to recent travelers – they just might be able to stop you from making some of the same old mistakes. Look at the ads in newspapers and magazines, consult reference books, and watch for special offers.

Airlines can supply information on routes and timetables, but they do not supply the cheapest tickets except during fare wars and the competitive low season. Travel agents are usually a better source of bargains. Whether you go directly through an airline or use an agent, always ask the representative to clarify the fare, the route, the duration of the journey and any restrictions on the ticket.

Most major airlines have ticket 'consolidators' who offer substantial discounts on fares to Latin America, but things change so rapidly that even newspaper listings can be quickly out of date. Among the best sources of information are the Sunday travel pages of major dailies like the *New York Times*, the *Los Angeles Times* or the *San Francisco Chronicle*. Most cities' weekly free newspapers also have good travel pages. If you're in a university town, look for bargains in the campus newspapers. There will usually be a listing for a local affiliate of the student travel agency STA; you needn't be a student to take advantage of their services. See regional sections in this chapter for discount travel agencies and bucket shops.

Similar listings are available in the travel sections of the magazines like *Time Out* and *TNT* in the UK, or the Saturday editions of newspapers like the *Sydney Morning Herald* and the *Age* in Australia. Ads in these publications offer cheap fares, but don't be surprised if they happen to be sold out when you contact the agents. They're usually low-season fares on obscure airlines with conditions attached.

Cheap fares fall into two distinct categories: official and consolidator. Official ones have a variety of names, including advance-purchase fares, budget fares, Apex, and super-Apex. Consolidator tickets are simply discounted tickets that the airlines release through selected travel agents (not through airline offices). The cheapest fares are often nonrefundable and require an extra fee for changing your flight. Many insurance policies will cover this loss if you have to change your flight for emergency reasons. Roundtrip (return) tickets usually work out cheaper than two one-way fares – often *much* cheaper.

Discounts on such fares are often available from travel agents, but usually not in Latin America, where discount ticketing is unusual. Standby can be a cheap way of getting from Europe to the USA, but there are no such flights to Chile or other parts of South America. Foreigners in Chile may pay for international air tickets in local currency, but the disappearance of differential exchange rates has eliminated any incentive to do so.

One of the cheapest options for getting to Chile is on a courier flight: You surrender some of your baggage allowance and accompany business equipment or documents in return for a significantly discounted fare. If the courier company is really desperate and needs someone to fly on very short notice, you may even score a free flight. The major drawbacks (in addition to being limited to carry-on baggage) are restricted travel dates, the often short travel periods allowed and the limited number of gateway airports in Europe (London) and North America (New York, Miami, Los Angeles, San Francisco, Chicago, Orlando and Washington, DC). Also, it's difficult to get more than one courier ticket for the same flight, so if you want to travel with someone, you'll both have to juggle your schedules (possibly with different courier companies) or fly on different days.

Courier flights are occasionally advertised in the newspapers, or you can contact airfreight companies listed in the phonebook. You may even have to go to the air-freight company to get an answer – the companies aren't always keen to give out information over the phone. For more information, contact the **International Association of Air**

Travel Couriers (IAATC; ☎ 561-582-8320) in the USA or visit its website at Ⓦ www .courier.org. Joining this organization does not guarantee that you'll get a courier flight. See also the USA and the UK & Europe sections, below.

You may decide to pay more than the rock-bottom fare by opting for the safety of a better-known travel agent. Established firms such as worldwide STA Travel and Canada's Travel Cuts are viable alternatives, offering good prices to most destinations.

Once you have your ticket, write down its number, together with the flight numbers and other details, and keep the information in a separate location. If the ticket is lost or stolen, this will help you get a replacement. Remember to buy travel insurance as early as possible.

Round-the-World & 'Circle Pacific' Tickets Some of the best deals for travelers visiting many countries on different continents are Round-the-World (RTW) tickets. Itineraries from the USA, Europe or Australia that include five or six stopovers (including Santiago) start from US$2000 or US$2500 and go up to US$4000 or more. Fares can vary widely; to get an idea, check out Ⓦ www.airtreks.com and use their calculator to find approximate fares for whatever destinations you pick. Similar 'Circle Pacific' fares allow excursions between Australasia and Chile, often with a stop at Easter Island. These types of tickets are certain to have restrictions, so check the fine print carefully.

Baggage & Other Restrictions

On most domestic and international flights, you are limited to two checked bags. There could be a charge if you bring more or if the size of the bags exceeds the airline's limits. It's best to check with the individual airline if you are worried about this. On some international flights, the luggage allowance is based on weight, not numbers; again, check with the airline.

If your luggage is delayed upon arrival (which is rare), some airlines will give a cash advance to purchase necessities. If sporting equipment is misplaced, the airline may pay for rentals. Should the luggage be lost, it's important to submit a claim. The airline

doesn't have to pay the full amount of the claim; rather, they can estimate the value of your lost items. It may take them anywhere from six weeks to three months to process the claim and pay.

Travelers with Special Needs

If you have special needs of any sort – vegetarianism or other dietary restrictions, a broken leg, dependence on a wheelchair, responsibility for a baby, fear of flying – let the airline know as soon as possible so that they can make arrangements accordingly. You should remind them when you reconfirm your booking (at least 72 hours before departure) and again when you check in at the airport. It may also be worth telephoning the airlines before making your booking to find out how they can handle your particular needs.

Airports and airlines can be helpful, but need advance warning. Most international airports provide escorts from check-in desk to plane where needed, and there should be ramps, lifts, accessible toilets and accessible phones. Aircraft toilets, on the other hand, are likely to present a problem; discuss this with the airline at an early stage and, if necessary, with a doctor.

Guide dogs for the blind will often have to travel in a specially pressurized baggage compartment with other animals, away from their owner; smaller guide dogs may be admitted to the cabin. All guide dogs are subject to the same quarantine laws (six months in isolation, etc) as any other animal when entering or returning to rabies-free countries such as the UK or Australia (although UK regulations have recently eased up: see Ⓦ www.londonandessex.demon .co.uk/pets.htm for details).

Deaf travelers can ask for airport and inflight announcements to be written down for them.

Children under two years old travel for 10% of the standard fare (free on some airlines) as long as they don't occupy a seat, although they get no baggage allowance. 'Skycots' should be provided by the airline if requested in advance; these will take a child weighing up to about 10kg (22lb). Children between two and 12 years old can usually occupy a seat for half fare and do get a baggage allowance. Strollers can often be taken as hand luggage.

Departure Tax

Chilean departure tax for international flights is US$26 or its equivalent in local currency. For domestic flights, there is a departure tax of about US$6.50.

Note that *arriving* US air passengers pay a one-time fee of US$65, valid for the life of the passport. Chilean authorities imposed this fee after US officials increased a visa application fee for Chilean nationals and have since applied it to Australians, who pay US$34, and Canadians, who pay US$55. This must be paid in cash and in US dollars. Also note that the officials collecting the fee most often won't make change; bring exact cash.

The USA

From the USA, the principal gateways to South America are Miami, New York and Los Angeles, Atlanta and Dallas. Airlines that serve Santiago from the USA include Lan-Chile, Aerolíneas Argentinas (via Buenos Aires), American, Copa (via Panama), Avianca (via Bogotá and Buenos Aires), Delta, Líneas Aéreas de Costa Rica (Lacsa) and Varig (via Brazil). Note that United Airlines suspended flights to and from Chile in late 2002, but service may be resumed in the future.

One alternative to landing in Santiago is to fly to Lima (Peru) and on to the Peruvian border city of Tacna, or to Arica (in northern Chile). For visitors to the Atacama Desert, this would save a long trip north from Santiago. Depending on the season, the fare ranges from US$600 to US$900.

Travelers can check their local branch of **STA Travel** (☎ 800-777-0112; W *www.sta travel.com)*, also known as Council Travel, which offers cheap flights, insurance and other travel services.

For cheap courier flights, contact the **Air Courier Association** (☎ 877-707-9658; W *www.cheaptrips.com; 350 Indiana St, Suite 300, Golden, CO 80401)*. Other reliable courier companies include **Now Voyager** (☎ 212-431-1616, fax 334-5253; 74 Varick St, Suite 307, New York, NY 10013)*. For up-to-date information on courier companies and fares, contact the **International Association of Air Travel Couriers** (☎ 561-582-8320, fax 582-1581; W *www.iaatc.com; PO Box 1349, Lake Worth, FL 33460)*; its US$45 annual membership fee includes a bimonthly newsletter.

Canada & Mexico

Canadian Airlines offers good connections to Santiago from Toronto via Miami (US$600 to US$800) and from Vancouver via Los Angeles (US$700 to US$900). **Travel Cuts** (☎ 800-667-2887; W *www.travelcuts.com)* is Canada's national student-travel agency and has offices in all major cities.

Aeroméxico and LanChile combine for eight flights weekly from Mexico City (US$700 to US$900). LanChile also flies twice weekly to Cancún.

The UK & Europe

It is no longer necessarily cheaper to fly through New York or Miami than it is to go directly from Europe. The only European nonstop is from Madrid to Santiago. Otherwise, many airlines have flights from major European cities to Santiago via Buenos Aires, Rio de Janeiro or São Paulo.

Discount air travel is big business in London. Advertisements for many travel agencies appear in the travel pages of the weekend broadsheet newspapers, in *Time Out*, in the *Evening Standard* and in the free magazine *TNT*. Advertised fares from London to Santiago have fallen recently and now start as low as £380 roundtrip.

For students or travelers under the age of 26, a popular travel agency in the UK is **STA Travel** (☎ 020-7361-6262; W *www.sta travel.co.uk; 86 Old Brompton Rd, London SW7)*, with branches throughout the UK.

Since bucket shops come and go, it's worth inquiring about their affiliation with the Association of British Travel Agents (ABTA), which will guarantee a refund or alternative if the agent goes out of business. The following are reputable London bucket shops:

Campus Travel (☎ 0870-240-1010; W *www.campus travel.co.uk) 52 Grosvenor Gardens, London SW1W 0AG*

Journey Latin America (☎ 020-8747-3108; W *www.journeylatinamerica.co.uk) 12 & 13 Heathfield Terrace, Chiswick, London W4 4JE*

South American Experience (☎ 020-7976-5511; W *www.sax.mcmail.com) 47 Causton St, London SW1P 4AT*

STA Travel (☎ 020-7361-6262; W *www.statravel.com) 86 Old Brompton Rd, London SW7 3LQ*

Trailfinders (☎ 020-7938-3939; W *www.trail finder.com) 194 Kensington High St, London W8 7RG*

Travelers interested in courier flights between London and Buenos Aires should contact **British Airways Travel Shop** (☎ *0870-606-1133;* w *www.baworldcargo.com/info; look under 'services')*. You can also try the International Association of Air Travel couriers (see the USA, earlier, for contact information).

Continental Europe

The following travel agencies are good possibilities for bargain fares from Continental Europe:

France – *Nouvelles Frontières* (☎ *08-03-33-33-33, Minitel 3615 NF;* w *www.nouvelles-frontieres.com) 87 Boulevard de Grenelle 75738, Paris Cedex 15*

Germany – *STA Travel* (☎ *030-311-0950;* w *www.statravel.com) Goethestrasse 73, Berlin* (☎ *069-430191) Bergerstrasse 118, 60316, Frankfurt*

Italy – *CTS* (☎ *06-462-0431) Via Genova 16, Rome*

Netherlands – *NBBS* (☎ *020-624-0989) Rokin 38, Amsterdam; Malibu Travel* (☎ *020-623-6814) Damrak 30, Amsterdam*

Spain – *Tive* (☎ *91-543-02-08) Fernando de Católico 86, Madrid*

Switzerland – *SSR Travel* (☎ *01-261-29-55) Leonhardstrasse 10, 8001 Zurich*

Australia & New Zealand

LanChile and Qantas share a flight from Sydney, stopping in Auckland, to Santiago. The flight continues on to Buenos Aires. Air New Zealand does the same from Auckland. A roundtrip ticket from Australia to Santiago averages around A$1700 in low season, A$1900 in high season.

Travelers can also take a Qantas flight to Tahiti, from where they can take the Lan-Chile flight to Santiago that stops at Easter Island. LanChile has a few offices in Australia, including Sydney (☎ 02-9244-2333), at 64 York St, and Melbourne (☎ 03-9920-3881), 310 King St. Qantas' direct flights to Buenos Aires permits a side trip to another South American city, say Santiago, with Aerolíneas Argentinas.

STA Travel (☎ *1-300-360-960 in Australia;* w *www.statravel.com)* is a good place to find bargain airfares, and you don't have to be a student to use their services or to get the good deals. Check their website for the location closest to you.

Asia & Africa

Carriers serving Santiago from Asia, usually via North America, include All Nippon Airways (with LanChile) via Los Angeles and Varig (via Brazil). Varig also flies to Johannesburg via São Paulo.

Malaysia Airlines (with LanChile) connects Santiago with Kuala Lumpur via Buenos Aires, Johannesburg and Capetown, while South African Airways (with British Airways) flies from Santiago to Johannesburg via Buenos Aires, São Paulo and Rio de Janeiro.

South America

Peru LanChile and Lacsa have daily flights from Lima to Santiago for about US$380 one way, but there are many discount roundtrip fares. Peruvian domestic airline Aerocontinente flies from Lima to the southern city of Tacna, only 50km from the Chilean border city of Arica, for US$90 one way. Crossing overland from Tacna and flying from Arica to Santiago is substantially cheaper than flying nonstop from Lima to Santiago.

Bolivia LanChile flies daily from Santiago to La Paz (US$210) via Iquique and Arica. LAB flies weekdays from Santiago to Iquique and La Paz, once or twice weekly to Arica and Santa Cruz or La Paz, and to Iquique and Santa Cruz.

Argentina Many airlines fly between Santiago and Buenos Aires from about US$120 one way. European airlines that pick up and discharge most of their passengers in Buenos Aires try to fill empty seats by selling roundtrips between the Argentine and Chilean capitals for around US$160 – not much more than the bus fare. Even if you throw away the return portion, one-way passengers still come out ahead.

There are also LanChile (twice daily) flights from Santiago to Mendoza (around US$110 one way, with discount roundtrips for as little as US$90), and to Córdoba (twice daily, US$110 one way, but with discount roundtrips for as little as US$139). TAN, the regional carrier of Argentina's Neuquén province, connects Puerto Montt with Neuquén, Bariloche and Mendoza. In Patagonia from November through mid-March, Aerovías DAP flies from Punta Arenas to

Río Grande and Ushuaia in Tierra del Fuego, and from Puerto Natales to El Calafate.

Other Countries LanChile flies from Santiago to Guayaquil, Ecuador; Bogotá, Colombia (US$730); Caracas, Venezuela (US$470); Asunción, Paraguay, in conjunction with TAM, and to São Paulo and Rio de Janeiro, Brazil (US$400), and from Iquique to Asunción three times weekly in conjunction with TAM.

Avianca links Santiago with Bogotá daily, either nonstop or via Buenos Aires. Pluna and LanChile fly to Montevideo, the Uruguayan capital. TransBrasil and Varig fly to Brazilian destinations.

LAND

Chile has a handful of border crossings with Peru and Bolivia and many with Argentina, only a few of which are served by public transportation. Chile's Ministerio de Obras Públicas (MOP; Public Works Ministry) continues to improve border crossings to these countries, but especially those to Argentina, to facilitate contact with the Mercosur free-trade zone. Photographers should note that at major land borders, such as Los Libertadores complex between Santiago and Mendoza, and the Pajaritos crossing between Osorno and Bariloche, Chilean customs officials X-ray the baggage of arriving bus passengers. Most international buses depart from (and arrive at) Terminal de Buses Santiago. There are direct buses to every country on the continent except the Guianas and Bolivia, but only masochists are likely to attempt the 4½- to 10-day marathons to destinations like Quito, Ecuador (US$110); Bogotá, Colombia (US$160); and Caracas, Venezuela (US$200). The most common destinations are served by the following bus companies, all located in the Terminal de Buses Santiago:

Brazil
Cata ☎ 02-779-3660
Chilebus International ☎ 02-776-5557

Argentina
Buses Ahumada ☎ 02-778-2703
Turismo Nevada ☎ 02-776-4116
Andesmar ☎ 02-776-2416
Pluma ☎ 02-779-6054
El Rápido ☎ 02-779-0316
Tas Choapa ☎ 02-779-4925

Sample trip times and costs are:

destination	duration in hours	cost
Bariloche, Argentina	28	US$36
Buenos Aires, Argentina	22	US$65
Córdoba, Argentina	17	US$57
Mendoza, Argentina	7	US$25
São Paulo, Brazil	72	US$112
Río de Janeiro, Brazil	55	US$110
Asunción, Paraguay	30	US$70
Lima, Peru	48	US$70
Montevideo, Uruguay	25	US$70

From Terminal Santiago, travelers can hop on taxi *colectivos* to Mendoza, which are only slightly more expensive (about US$28) and far quicker than buses – and drivers may stop on request for photo opportunities on the spectacular Andean crossing. Prices may be open to haggling outside the peak summer season.

Peru

Tacna to Arica is the only overland crossing between Peru and Chile. There is a choice of bus, taxi or train. For details, see Arica, in the Norte Grande chapter.

Bolivia

Road connections between Bolivia and Chile have improved dramatically, with the highway from Arica to La Paz completely paved and the route from Iquique to Colchane, and beyond to Oruro and La Paz, well under way. There is bus service on both routes, but more on the former.

The only train is a weekly service from Calama to the border village of Ollagüe, with connections to Oruro and La Paz; there is a parallel, but mostly unpaved, highway here.

It's possible to travel from Uyuni, Bolivia to San Pedro de Atacama via the Portezuelo del Cajón, near the juncture of the Chilean, Bolivian and Argentine borders, but no regularly scheduled public transport exists in this area. See San Pedro de Atacama, in the Norte Grande chapter, for details on organized trips to Uyuni.

Argentina

Except in Patagonia, every land crossing to Argentina involves crossing the Andes. There is public transportation on only a few of these crossings, and some passes are closed in winter.

Calama to Jujuy & Salta Ruta 27 over the Paso de Jama is now the main route over the Andes via San Pedro de Atacama and has regular bus service (advance booking is advisable, as seats are limited). Slightly farther south, on Ruta 23, motorists will find the 4079m Paso de Lago Sico a reasonable summer alternative that goes to Salta without passing through Jujuy, but the route just north, across the Paso de Huaytiquina, is more difficult. Chilean customs are at San Pedro de Atacama or Toconao.

There is an occasional Argentine passenger train from Salta to the border at Socompa, but only freight service beyond, although the uncomfortable Chilean freight will sometimes carry passengers to the abandoned station of Augusta Victoria (where it's possible to hitch to Antofagasta), or to Baquedano on Ruta 5 (the Panamericana), where it's easy to catch a bus.

Copiapó to Catamarca & La Rioja There is no public transportation over the 4726m Paso de San Francisco, but an increasing amount of vehicle traffic is using this improving route.

La Serena to San Juan Dynamited by the Argentine military during the Beagle Channel dispute of 1978–79, the 4779m Paso del Agua Negra is open for automobile traffic once again, but the road is rough. Bus services continue to use Los Libertadores crossing west of Mendoza. It is a good bicycle route, however, and tours from La Serena may carry passengers to hot springs on the Argentine side.

Santiago or Valparaíso to Mendoza & Buenos Aires Many bus companies service this most popular of crossing points between the two countries, along Ruta 60 through the Los Libertadores tunnel. Taxi colectivos are faster, more comfortable and only slightly more expensive. Winter snow sometimes closes the route, but rarely for long.

Talca to Malargüe & San Rafael Occasional minibuses now use Ruta 115 to cross the 2553m Paso Pehuenche, southeast of Talca. A new crossing is under considera-

tion from Curicó over the 2938m Paso del Planchón, also to San Rafael.

Southern Mainland Routes There are a number of scenic crossings from Temuco south to Puerto Montt, some involving bus-boat shuttles. These are popular in summer, so make advance bookings whenever possible.

Temuco to Zapala & Neuquén
This route crosses the Andes over the 1884m Paso de Pino Hachado, directly east of Temuco via Curacautín and Lonquimay, along the upper Río Biobío. A slightly more southerly route is the 1298m Paso de Icalma. Both have occasional bus traffic in summer.

Temuco to San Martín de los Andes
The most popular route from Temuco passes Lago Villarrica, Pucón and Curarrehue en route to the Paso de Mamuil Malal (known to Argentines as Paso Tromen). On the Argentine side, the road skirts the northern slopes of Volcán Lanín. There is regular summer bus service, but the pass is closed in winter.

Valdivia to San Martín de los Andes
This route starts with a bus from Valdivia to Panguipulli, Choshuenco and Puerto Fuy, followed by a ferry across Lago Pirehueico to the village of Pirehueico. From Pirehueico a local bus goes to Argentine customs at 659m Paso Huahum, where travelers can catch a bus to San Martín.

Osorno to Bariloche via Paso Cardenal Samoré
This crossing, commonly known as Pajaritos, is the quickest land route in the southern Lakes District, passing through Parque Nacional Puyehue on the Chilean side and Parque Nacional Nahuel Huapi on the Argentine side. It has frequent bus service all year.

Puerto Montt/Puerto Varas to Bariloche
Very popular in summer but open all year, this bus-ferry combination via Parque Nacional Vicente Pérez Rosales starts in Puerto Montt or Puerto Varas. A ferry goes from Petrohué, at the west end of Lago Todos Los Santos, to Peulla, and a bus crosses 1022m Paso de Pérez Rosales to Argentine immigration at Puerto Frías. After crossing Lago Frías by launch, there's a short bus hop to Puerto Blest on Lago Nahuel Huapi and another ferry to Puerto Pañuelo (Llao Llao). From Llao Llao, there is frequent bus service to Bariloche.

Southern Patagonian Routes Since the opening of the Carretera Austral (Southern Highway) south of Puerto Montt, it's become more common to cross between Chile and Argentina in this area. There are also several crossing points in extreme southern Patagonia and Tierra del Fuego.

Puerto Ramírez to Esquel

There are two options here. From the village of Villa Santa Lucía, on the Camino Austral, there is a good lateral road that forks at Puerto Ramírez, at the southeastern end of Lago Yelcho. The north fork goes to Futaleufú, where a bridge crosses the river to the Argentine side where you can catch colectivos to Esquel. The south fork goes to Palena and Argentine customs at Carrenleufú, which has bus service to Corcovado, Trevelin and Esquel. Customs and immigration are much more efficient at Futaleufú.

Puerto Cisnes to José de San Martín

At Villa Amengual, a lateral off the Camino Austral climbs the valley of the Río Cisnes to Paso de Río Frías and the Argentine province of Chubut. This crossing may close because there is so little traffic.

Coyhaique to Comodoro Rivadavia

There are several buses per week, often heavily booked, from Coyhaique to Comodoro Rivadavia via Río Mayo. For private vehicles, there is an alternative route via Balmaceda to Perito Moreno via the 502m Paso Huemules.

Puerto Ingeniero Ibáñez to Perito Moreno

This route follows the north shore of Lago General Carrera (Lago Buenos Aires on the Argentine side). There is no public transport, but since all vehicles must pass through the *carabineros* (national police) post on the lakefront in Puerto Ibáñez, patient waiting may yield a lift.

Chile Chico to Los Antiguos

From Puerto Ibáñez, take the ferry to Chile Chico on the southern shore of Lago Carrera and a bus to Los Antiguos, which has connections to the Patagonian coastal town of Caleta Olivia or south to El Chaltén or El Calafate. There is also a narrow mountain road with regular bus services to Chile Chico from Cruce El Maitén at the southwestern end of Lago General Carrera.

Cochrane to Bajo Caracoles

Perhaps the most desolate crossing in the Aisén region, 647m Paso Roballos links the hamlet of Cochrane with a flyspeck outpost in Argentina's Santa Cruz province.

Puerto Natales to Río Turbio & El Calafate

Frequent buses connect Puerto Natales to the Argentine coal town of Río Turbio, where many Chileans work; from Río Turbio there are further connections to Río Gallegos and El Calafate. All year, but far more frequently in summer, there are buses from Puerto Natales to El Calafate, the gateway to Argentina's Parque Nacional Los Glaciares, via Paso Río don Guillermo.

Punta Arenas to Río Gallegos

Daily, many buses travel on the improved highway between Punta Arenas and Río Gallegos. It's a six-hour trip because of slow customs checks and a rough segment of Argentine Ruta Nacional (RN) 3.

Punta Arenas to Tierra del Fuego

From Punta Arenas, a 2½-hour ferry trip or a 10-minute flight takes you to Porvenir, on Chilean Tierra del Fuego, where there are two buses weekly to the Argentine city of Río Grande, which has connections to Ushuaia. Direct buses travel from Punta Arenas to Ushuaia via the more northerly, more frequent and shorter ferry crossing at Primera Angostura.

Puerto Williams to Ushuaia

Because of local commercial-political intrigues, mostly on the Argentine side, passenger boat service from Puerto Williams, on Isla Navarino (reached by plane or boat from Punta Arenas) to the Argentine city of Ushuaia is sporadic, undependable and frequently interrupted.

ORGANIZED TOURS

As the adventure-travel boom continues and more people want to get out of the bus and onto trails, a lot of agencies have sprung up to meet the demand. Chile is a popular destination, but most agencies focus on Patagonia and usually take in Argentine Patagonia as well. The prices quoted do not include international travel. When choosing, ask what transport costs they do include. Also ask how much time you'll actually be where you want to be. Chile's geography means that a couple of days at least can be eaten up in travel time, and most spend a couple of days hanging out in Santiago before heading up, down or across the Pacific.

From the USA & Canada

Adventure & Culture Trips The following lists recommended agencies focusing on 'adventure' travel – usually trekking and culture.

Wilderness Travel (☎ 510-558-2488, 800-368-2794; ⓦ www.wildernesstravel.com; 1102 9th St, Berkeley, CA 94710) Trips with a focus on hiking and exploration. They offer a 9-day Futaleufú Trail (US$2995) and 16-day Peaks of Patagonia (US$3600) trip. Also ask about sea kayaking trips in Pumalín and the Straits of Magellan.

Wildland Adventures (☎ 206-365-0686, 800-345-4453, fax 206-363-6615; ⓦ www.wildland .com; 3516 NE 155th St, Seattle, WA 98155) Has 9- to 14-day trips in southern Patagonia and Tierra del Fuego (US$2195-4410); the longer trip includes a 4-day cruise on *Mare Australis*. Prices include all internal land and air transport. They also have customized trips taking in northern highlights, Lakes District and Easter Island.

Chilean Andean Snow Adventures *(CASA; ☎ 510-919-9241, 888-449-2272; W www.casatours.com; 187 Purdue Ave, Kensington, CA 94708)* Specializes in ski trips from July to October with 8- to 15-day tours (US$1350-1795) that include entrance to a bunch of ski resorts, *asados* (barbecues) with local skiers, chances to backcountry ski and avalanche-awareness classes. Prices include lift tickets, guides and in-country transport and lodging (meals not included). They also organize first descents on Patagonia's hard-to-get-to mountains.

Myths and Mountains *(☎ 775-832-5454, 800-670-6984; W www.mythsandmountains.com; 976 Tee Court, Incline Village, NV 89451)* Has trips with an emphasis on culture and wildlife. Includes wine tours, Torres del Paine trekking, homestays on farms, learning about *huaso* (cowboy) culture and rodeos, and ski trips to El Portillo. Trips range from 7 to 17 days (US$1550-4000, includes full travel insurance) or can be customized for more in-depth experiences.

Far Horizons Archaeological & Cultural Trips *(☎ 505-343-9400, 800-552-4575, fax 505-343-8076; W www.farhorizon.com; PO Box 91900, Albuquerque, NM 87199-1900)* Specializes in trips to Rapa Nui, including one during the Tapati festival, led by well-known scholars of the island's archaeology and culture. The company's excursions also take in important archaeological sites in the Norte Grande. Combined, the 16-day trip costs US$5495, including airfare to/from the island. They spend more days on the island than many other agencies.

'Soft Adventure' For those who want to experience the wild but want to be wined and dined as well, the following offer quality programs.

Off the Beaten Path *(☎ 406-586-1311, 800-445-2995, fax 406-587-4147; W www.offthebeaten path.com; 7 East Beall, Bozeman, MT 59715)* Has multiactivity trips to Patagonia, emphasizing cultural and natural history and guided by company owners and locals. Fifteen-day tours cost US$5700. Customized trips, including ones with a fly-fishing emphasis, are also organized.

Nature Expeditions International *(☎ 800-869-0639; W www.naturexp.com; 7860 Peters Rd, Suite F103, Plantation, FL 33324)* Has upscale soft adventure and cultural tours, with a 16-day tour of Chile, including an optional glacier cruise (US$5180) and a tour to Easter Island (about five nights on the island; US$2150).

Mountain Travel Sobek *(☎ 510-527-8100, 800-227-2384; W www.mtsobek.com; 6420 Fairmount Ave, El Cerrito, CA 94530)* Emphasizes trekking in Patagonia. Offers three different tours ranging from 11 to 17 days (US$2590-5150).

Kayaking & Rafting Trips Tour outfitters focusing on the Futaleufú provide a lot more than just river descents. While the white water is the main stage, most outfitters own their own properties with different style camps and a variety of activities, such as mountain biking, fishing, horseback riding and waterfall rappeling. When deciding, ask about transport to Futaleufú and how many actual days of water time are included.

Earth River Expeditions *(☎ 845-626-2665, 800-643-2784, fax 845-626-4423; W www.earth river.com; 180 Towpath Rd, Accord, NY 12404)* Run by Eric Hertz and Chilean Robert Currie, pioneer Futa rafters who made the first commercial descent. Ten-day excursions (US$2700) include transport from Puerto Montt and about four days of rafting (plus chances to kayak), as well as loads of outdoor adventures, including ropes courses, at their different camps, including a 'cave' camp and a tree-house camp.

Expediciones Chile *(☎ 970-328-1476, 888-488-9082; W www.raftingchile.com; PO Box 4869, Eagle, CO 81631)* Started by Chris Spelius, an Olympic kayaker. The company runs Class IV and V white-water descents from December through March, ranging from 6 to 8 days (US$1900-2500).

Bio Bio Expeditions *(☎ 800-246-7238; W www .bbxrafting.com; PO Box 2028, Truckee, CA 96160)* Runs trips out of their Adventure Spa Base Camp, with sauna, hot tub, hot showers and massage. Rafting and kayaking trips are catered depending on expertise, and they run a well-regarded kayaking school. Their La Cascada camp, accessed by horseback, is next to a waterfall on the banks of the Río Azul, from where clients can kayak or ride horses along the river back to the main camp.

Senior Travelers Folks over 50 may want to check out organizations that cater to them. Here are two of the most established.

Eldertreks *(☎ 416-588-5000, 800-741-7956, fax 416-588-9839; W www. eldertreks.com; 597 Markham St, Toronto, Ontario M6G2L7)* For the fit 50-and-over crowd, there's a 15-day trip hiking trip around Chilean Patagonia (US$3395). With an extension to Easter Island, not including flight from Santiago, the price is US$4565.

Elderhostel *(☎ 877-426-8056; W www.elder hostel.com; 11 Ave de Lafayette, Boston, MA 02111)* Operates several two-week tours including Patagonia and the Lakes District, starting in Buenos Aires and ending in Santiago; the Chilean heartland; the Atacama Desert; and the Mapuche territory.

From the UK & Europe

Most UK or European organized tours take in much more of South America than just Chile. Here are a couple that have well-recommended trips to Chile, especially Patagonia.

Journey Latin America (☎ 020-8747-3108, fax 8742-1312; w www.journeylatinamerica.com; 12 & 13 Heathfield Terrace, Chiswick, London W4 4JE) Offers both basic tours with simple hotels and public transport and more upscale packages. They also lead activity-based tours.

Explore Worldwide (☎ 0125-276-0000, fax 276-0001; w www.exploreworldwide.com; 1 Frederick St, Aldershot, Hants GU11 1LQ) Arranges trips taking in Chilean and Argentine Patagonia.

From Australia

World Expeditions (☎ 02-9264-3366, fax 9261-1974; w www.worldexpediciones .com.au; 441 Kent St, Sydney, NSW 2000) has tours to South America that mostly include Andean treks. Also consider hooking up with a US- or European-based group once in South America.

Getting Around

From Arica down to Puerto Montt, traveling in Chile is (quite literally) straightforward, with flights and buses making connections up and down to the north-south cities continuously. What is a bit less convenient, but improving, is service widthwise, from the coast to the Andes, and south of Puerto Montt, where the country turns into a route-challenged knit of fjord, glacier and mountain. But, with a former Public Works minister as president, improving roads, making new ones (some contentious) and revamping the railways are all priorities. You can expect easy travel around Chile.

AIR

You may want to avoid tiresome and time-consuming backtracking by taking an occasional flight. For instance, you can travel overland through Chilean and Argentine Patagonia to Tierra del Fuego and then fly from Punta Arenas to Puerto Montt or Santiago. The return flight should be no more expensive than a combination of bus fares and accommodations.

Domestic Air Services

Most cities have domestic airports with commercial air service, except for some larger cities near Santiago and towns near other major cities. Santiago's Aeropuerto Internacional Arturo Merino Benítez has a separate domestic terminal; Santiago also has smaller airfields for air taxi services to the Juan Fernández Archipelago. Major domestic airports are in Arica, Iquique, Calama, Copiapó, La Serena, Temuco, Valdivia, Puerto Montt, Balmaceda (Coyhaique) and Punta Arenas.

Currently LanChile is the only major airline with domestic flights. They offer as several daily northbound to Antofagasta, Calama, Iquique and Arica, as well as southbound to Puerto Montt and Punta Arenas. They also fly two or three times weekly to Easter Island. Some of their flights are managed by their franchise LanExpress.

LanChile is a frequent-flyer partner of American Airlines. Do not be surprised, however, if credits for Chilean international and domestic flights fail to show up on your quarterly mileage statements – be sure to save your tickets and boarding passes so you'll be able to corroborate your flights when you return home.

Minor regional airlines include Aerolíneas DAP, which connects Punta Arenas with Tierra del Fuego, Puerto Williams and Antarctica; Lassa, which flies to the Juan Fernández Archipelago; and several air taxi companies that connect isolated settlements in the Aisén region, south of Puerto Montt.

Purchasing & Air Passes

The best rates with LanChile are found on their website (W www.lanchile.com), on which weekly specials give cut-rate deals, especially on well-traveled routes such as Puerto Montt to Punta Arenas. Purchasing a roundtrip on the Internet (even if planning to use only one way) is often cheaper than buying a one-way ticket from a LanChile agent. The prices quoted to Easter Island are also substantially less expensive than the regular rate. The Internet has had its glitches though, and the agents in LanChile offices are instructed to not help with any Internet purchases or customer-service issues. You can ask for the telephone number for the Internet service and call to confirm your purchase.

The other way to cut costs, and the most popular with foreign travelers, is the Lan-Pass. For US$250, LanChile offers a 'Visit Chile Pass,' valid for 30 days, that includes three separate flight coupons, each additional coupon costing US$60, up to a maximum of six total. The only restriction on the pass is that you can't go to the same destination twice. For example, if after that first flight to Punta Arenas, you return to Santiago and just have to go again, your coupons will not be accepted. The above price applies to those who also purchase a LanChile flight to get to Chile. If you fly with another airline, the pass costs US$350, and US$80 for each additional coupon. Passes must be purchased outside Chile, are available only to foreigners and nonresidents of Chile, and do not include travel to Easter Island. Fares to Easter Island, however are discounted (US$645 roundtrip) if you purchase your international flight with

LanChile. To give you an idea of the savings of the pass, here are some average prices of one-way flights from Santiago:

destination	one-way fare
Antofagasta	US$230
Arica	US$256
Calama	US$229
Concepción	US$117
Copiapó	US$170
Coyhaique	US$230
Iquique	US$245
La Serena	US$122
Puerto Montt	US$197
Punta Arenas	US$332
Temuco	US$157

BUS

Most Chilean cities have a central bus terminal, but in some, the companies have separate offices, which tend to be within a few blocks of each other. The bus stations are well organized, with destinations, schedules and fares prominently displayed. Major highways and some others are paved (except for large parts of the Carretera Austral south of Puerto Montt), but many secondary roads are gravel or dirt. Buses on main roads are comfortable, and nearly all are well maintained, fast and punctual. They generally have toilet facilities and often serve coffee, tea and even meals on board; if not, they make regular stops. By European or North American standards, fares are a bargain. On back roads, which include about 70,000km of gravel or dirt roads, transport is slower, and buses, or *micros,* are less frequent, older and more basic.

Long-distance buses have a variety of seating arrangements, with differing levels of comfort: *Pullman* has 44 ordinary reclining seats, two on each side of the aisle; *executivo* and *semi-cama* usually mean 32 seats, providing extra legroom and calf rests; while *salón cama* sleepers seat only 24 passengers, with only three seats per row and additional legroom. If you have any doubt about the type of service offered, ask for a seat diagram.

Normally departing at night, these premium bus services cost upwards of 50% more than ordinary buses, but on long hauls like Arica to Santiago, they merit consideration. Regular buses are also comfortable

enough for most purposes, however. Smoking is prohibited on buses throughout the country.

Except during the holiday season (Christmas, January, February, Easter and mid-September's patriotic holidays), it is rarely necessary to book more than a few hours in advance. On very long trips, like Arica to Santiago, or rural routes with limited services (along the Carretera Austral, for instance), advance booking is a good idea.

The largest bus company in Chile is Tur Bus. Known for being extremely punctual and equally anal, they have the most service around the country. Frequent travelers can pay US$5 to become card-carrying members of the Tur Bus club, which provides a 10% discount on one-way fares (if paying in cash), a phone or Internet reservation system, and a tad more attention at the counter. You can join at any Tur Bus office.

The nerve center of the country, Santiago has four main bus terminals, from which buses leave to northern, central, and southern destinations.

Fares can vary dramatically among companies, so explore several possibilities. Promotions *(ofertas)* can reduce normal fares by half; student reductions by 25%. Discounts are common outside the peak summer season, and bargaining may even be possible. Try it if the bus is leaving soon and appears to have empty seats. Fares between important destinations are listed throughout this book.

destination	hours	Pullman	salón cama
Antofagasta	18	US$31	US$42
Arica	28	US$38	US$56
Castro	19	US$27	US$45
Chillán	6	US$9	n/a
Concepción	8	US$14	n/a
Copiapó	11	US$20	US$30
Iquique	26	US$37	US$46
La Serena	7	US$15	US$22
Osorno	14	US$19	US$32
Puerto Montt	16	US$20	US$35
Punta Arenas	60	US$100	n/a
Temuco	11	US$14	US$29
Valdivia	13	US$17	US$32
Valparaíso	2	US$4	n/a
Villarrica	13	US$15	US$29
Viña del Mar	2	US$4	n/a

Terminal San Borja

This terminal (☎ 02-776-0645; Alameda 3250, Barrio Brasil; Ⓜ Estación Central) is at the end of the shopping mall alongside the main railway station. The ticket booths are divided by region, with destinations prominently displayed. Destinations are from Arica down to the Cordillera around Santiago.

Región I & II

Carmelitas	☎ 02-778-7579
Flota Barrios	☎ 02-778-7076
Los Corsarios	☎ 02-778-7070
Pullman Fichtur	☎ 02-778-7070
Tas Choapa	☎ 02-778-6830

Región III & IV

Buses Lit	☎ 02-778-6857
Diamantes de Elqui	☎ 02-778-7073
Libac	☎ 02-778-7071
Tas Choapa	☎ 02-778-6827

Región V, including the Cordillera

Ahumada	☎ 02-779-4224
Cóndor	☎ 02-778-7089
Flota Imperial	☎ 02-778-4224
Tas Choapa	☎ 02-778-6827
Tur Bus	☎ 02-778-7336

Terminal de Buses Alameda

This terminal (☎ 02-776-2424, cnr Alameda & Jotabeche; Ⓜ Universidad de Santiago) is home to Tur Bus and Pullman Bus (see the Santiago map for location). For northern destinations and central coastal, contact Pullman Bus; for middle Chile, Pullman del Sur; and for every destination along the Panamericana, Tur Bus.

Pullman Bus	☎ 02-778-1185
Pullman del Sur	☎ 776-2426
Tur Bus	☎ 02-778-0808

Terminal de Buses Santiago

This terminal, also referred to as Terminal de Buses Sur, (☎ 02-779-1385; Alameda 3850), is between Ruiz Tagle and Nicasio Retamales (see the Santiago map). It has the most service to the central coast, southern destinations – the Lakes District and Chiloé – and international destinations (discussed in the Getting There & Away chapter).

South

Ahumada	☎ 02-778-2703
Bus Norte	☎ 02-779-5433
Buses Jac	☎ 02-776-1582
Cóndor	☎ 02-680-6900

Cruz del Sur	☎ 02-779-0607
Igi Llaima	☎ 02-779-1751
Inter Sur	☎ 02-270-7500
Lit	☎ 02-779-5710
Panguisur	☎ 02-778-1278
Queilen	☎ 02-764-5769
Tas Choapa	☎ 02-779-4694
Tur Bus	☎ 02-776-3690
Turibús	☎ 02-779-0607

Middle Chile & Central Coast

Andimar	☎ 02-779-3810
Buses Al Sur	☎ 02-779-2305
Cruzmar	☎ 02-776-7794
Inter Sur	☎ 02-270-7500

North

Flota Barrios	☎ 02-776-0665

Terminal Los Héroes

This terminal, on Tucapel Jiménez near the Alameda, in the Centro, is a much more convenient and less chaotic terminal. There's also Internet service upstairs. Some long-distance buses from Terminal de Buses Santiago make an additional stop for passengers.

North

Flota Barrios	☎ 02-696-9322
Libac	☎ 02-698-5974
Los Diamantes de Elquí	☎ 02-696-9321
Tas Choapa	☎ 02-696-9326

South

Cruz del Sur/Pullman Sur	☎ 02-696-9324
Tas Choapa	☎ 02-696-9326

Argentina

Buses Ahumada/Fénix Int'l	☎ 02-696-9337
Tas Choapa	☎ 02-696-9326

Torres de Tajamar

A business center, Torres de Tajamar (Av Providencia 1100) has ticket offices for many buses, including Buses Jac, Fénix, Libac, Los Corsarios, Pullman Bus, Tas Choapa, Tramaca and Tur Bus.

TRAIN

After felling thousands of hectares of native forest in the early 20th century to make room for railway lines running from Santiago to Puerto Montt, Chile's railroad has remained relatively abandoned. Southbound trains from Santiago pass through Talca and Chillán to Temuco; a spur that leaves the main longitudinal line at Chillán provides direct service from Santiago to Concepción, but that's the extent of it. The current administration, however, has designs to bring the lines to the south back to life by 2005.

With the exception of the Calama-Oruro line between Chile and Bolivia, there are no long-distance passenger services north of Santiago. It's difficult but not impossible to travel by freight from Baquedano (on the Panamericana northeast of Antofagasta) to the border town of Socompa, and on to Salta, in Argentina.

The **Empresa de Ferrocarriles del Estado** (EFE; ☎ 02-376-8500; ⓦ www.efe.cl) runs southbound passenger service from Santiago to Chillán, Concepción, Temuco and intermediates. EFE also runs frequent commuter service between Santiago and Rancagua. Trains to Chillán and Temuco leave at night.

Trains have three classes: *economía, salón* and *cama. Cama* refers to 'sleeper' class, which has upper and lower bunks; the latter are more expensive. The charming between-the-wars sleepers that were a trip highlight for some travelers have been replaced with modern models. The current rates average about US$1 per hour for *economía,* US$2 per hour for *salón,* and US$3 per hour for a lower bunk (to Concepción or Temuco), but are subject to change as improvement are made to the system.

All trains from Santiago depart from the Estancia Central. Tickets can be purchased at that **ticket office** (☎ 02-376-8500; Alameda 3170, Centro; open 7am-9:45pm daily) and at **Metro Universidad de Chile** (☎ 02-688-3284; open 9am-8pm Mon-Fri, 9am-2pm Sat).

CAR & MOTORCYCLE

If aiming to really explore off the beaten path, or if your time is limited, having a vehicle is a good idea.

In some areas – such as the Atacama Desert, the Carretera Austral or on Easter Island – a car is definitely the best way to get around. Security problems are minor, but always lock your vehicle, and leave valuables out of sight. Note that because of smog problems, there are frequent restrictions on private vehicle use in Santiago and the surrounding region; usually these are organized according to the terminal digit of the license plate of the car.

Motorists with their own vehicles should be aware that a customs regulation which once stipulated that the 90-day import permit for foreign vehicles could not be extended (unlike tourist cards) is no longer in effect. Also, some border officials routinely issue 180-day permits. Not all customs officials are aware of this change, however, and it may be easier to leave the country and return.

The Panamericana has undergone substantial improvements, but it comes at a cost: toll booths *(peajes)* now chop the highway into paying sections. There are two types: tolls to pay to use a distance of the highway (around US$2 to US$3), and the tolls you pay to get off the highway to access a lateral to a town or city (US$0.70). Paying the former sometimes voids the need to pay the latter. You'll notice distance markers every 5km along Chile's two major roads, the Panamericana and the Carretera Austral, and you may be given directions that refer to these kilometer markers.

Road Rules

While Chileans sometimes drive carelessly or a bit too fast (especially in the cities), if you have come from Argentina, you will think them saints. Most Chilean drivers are courteous to pedestrians and rarely willfully do anything dangerous. Driving after dark is not advisable, especially in rural areas in southern Chile, where pedestrians, domestic animals and wooden carts are difficult to see on or near the highways. If you are involved in an automobile accident, consult the entry under Legal Matters, in the Facts for the Visitor chapter. In contrast to neighboring Argentina, Chile's carabineros enforce speed limits with US$75 fines; bribing them is not an option.

Road Atlases

The annual Turistel guides, detailed in the guidebooks entry in the Facts for the Visitor chapter, are a good source on recent changes, particularly with regard to newly paved roads.

Road Assistance

The **Automóvil Club de Chile** (Acchi; ☎ 02-431-1000; Andres Bello 1863, Santiago) has offices in most major Chilean cities, provides useful information, sells maps and rents cars. It also offers member services and grants discounts to members of its foreign counterparts, such as the American Automobile Association (AAA) in the USA or the

Automobile Association (AA) in the UK. Acchi also has a **member services office** (☎ 02-225-3790; Fidel Oteíza 1960, Providencia, Santiago). Membership includes free towing and other roadside services within 25km of an Automóvil Club office.

Costs

Driving costs will be cheaper than in Europe but more expensive than in the USA.

The price of *bencina* (gasoline) ranges from about US$0.50 to US$0.70 per liter, depending on the grade, while *gas-oil* (diesel fuel) is somewhat cheaper. The 93-octane *común* is available both unleaded *(sin plomo)* and leaded *(con plomo)*, while 95- and 97-octane grades are invariably unleaded.

Rental

Major international rental agencies like Hertz, Avis and Budget have offices in Santiago (see that chapter for details), as well as in major cities and other tourist areas. The Automóvil Club also rents cars at some of its offices. To rent a car, you must have a valid driver's international license, be at least 25 years of age (some younger readers have managed to rent cars, however) and present either a major credit card (such as Master-Card or Visa) or a large cash deposit. Travelers from the USA, Canada, Germany and Australia are not required to have an international driver's license to rent a car in Chile, but to avoid confusion and ensure a rental, it is best to carry one.

Even at smaller agencies, basic rental charges are now very high, with the cheapest and smallest vehicles going for about US$50 to US$65 per day with 150km to 200km included, or sometimes with unlimited mileage. Adding the cost of insurance, petrol and IVA *(impuesto de valor agregado,* the value-added tax, or VAT), it becomes very pricey indeed to operate a rental vehicle without several others to share expenses. Weekend or weekly rates, with unlimited mileage, are a better bargain. Small vehicles with unlimited mileage cost about US$340 to US$450 per week, while 4WD vehicles cans cost US$100 per day. Some companies will give discounts for extended rentals, say a month or more.

One-way rentals can be awkward or impossible to arrange. Some companies, most notably Hertz, will arrange such rentals but

with a substantial drop-off charge. With smaller, local agencies, this is next to impossible. Some of these smaller agencies will, however, usually arrange paperwork for taking cars into Argentina, so long as the car is returned to the original office. There may be a substantial charge, up to US$150, for taking a car into Argentina; Chilean insurance is not valid in Argentina.

When traveling in remote areas, where fuel may not be readily available, carry extra fuel. Rental agencies often provide a spare *bidón* (fuel container) for this purpose.

Purchase

If you are planning on spending several months in Chile, purchasing a car merits consideration. However, it has both advantages and disadvantages. On the one hand, driving is more flexible than taking public transport and is likely to be cheaper than multiple rentals; reselling it at the end of your stay can make it even more economical. On the other hand, any used car can be a risk, especially on the many rugged back roads. Fortunately, even the smallest hamlet seems to have a competent and resourceful mechanic.

Chile's domestic automobile industry is insignificant – nearly 90% of vehicles are imported – but good imported vehicles are available at prices higher than in Europe or the USA, though more reasonable than in Argentina. Japanese and Korean vehicles such as Toyota and Hyundai are especially popular, but Argentine Peugeots are also common. Parts are readily available, except for some older models. Do not expect to find a reliable used car for less than about US$3000, and expect to pay much more for recent models.

If you purchase a car, you must change the title within 30 days; failure to do so can result in a fine of several hundred dollars. In order to buy a vehicle, you must have a RUT (Rol Unico Tributario) tax identification number, available through Impuestos Internos, the Chilean tax office; issuance of the RUT takes about 10 days. The actual title transfer is done at any notary through a *compraventa* for about US$10.

All vehicles must carry so-called *seguro obligatorio* (minimum insurance), which covers personal injuries up to a maximum of about US$3000 at a cost of about US$20 per year. All companies issue these policies, which run from April 1 to March 31 of the following year. Additional liability insurance is highly desirable.

Since Chilean policies are not valid in Argentina, but Argentine policies are valid in Chile and other neighboring countries, it is worth buying a reasonably priced Argentine policy across the border if you plan to visit several countries.

Note that, while many inexpensive vehicles are for sale in the duty-free zones of Regiones I and XII (Tarapacá and Magallanes); only legal permanent residents of those regions may take a vehicle outside of those regions, for a maximum of 90 days per calendar year.

Shipping a Vehicle

Given its openness toward foreign trade and tourism, Chile is probably the best country on the continent to ship an overseas vehicle to. To find a reliable shipper, check the yellow pages of your local phone directory under Automobile Transporters. Most transporters are more accustomed to arranging shipments between North America and Europe than from North America or Europe to South America, so it may take some of them time to work out details. When shipping a vehicle into Chile, do not leave anything whatsoever of value in the vehicle if at all possible. Theft, of tools in particular, is very common.

For shipping a car from Chile back to your home country, try the consolidator **Ultramar** (☎ 02-630-1000, fax 698-6552; e mail box@ultramar.cl; Moneda 970, 18th floor, Santiago).

BICYCLE

Cycling is an increasingly popular way to tour Chile. A mountain bike *todo terreno* or a touring bike with beefy tires is essential. There are many good routes, but the weather can be a drawback. From Temuco south, it is changeable and you must be prepared for rain; from Santiago north, especially in the Atacama, water sources are infrequent. In some areas, the wind can slow your progress to a crawl; north to south is generally easier than south to north, but some readers report strong headwinds southbound in summer. Roads leading into the mountains can be challenging even for a vehicle; pushing yourself and stocked panniers up a long, winding

uphill road can be quite the character-builder. Chilean motorists are usually courteous, but on narrow, two-lane highways without shoulders, passing cars can be a real hazard. The newly paved sections of the Panamericana have a wider shoulder, but the constant trucks and fumes, especially in central Chile, can be a deterrent, if not a danger.

Car ferries in Patagonia often charge a fee to carry a bike on, but not if it's in the back of someone's pickup. Ask kindly if you see an empty back; most people are receptive to the idea. Throughout Chile, towns have bike repair shops. Bike rental shops aren't as prolific, but *hospedajes* throughout the country run by expat Swiss-Germans seem to have them.

Long-distance bus companies are usually amenable to stashing a bike in the luggage hold. On domestic airlines, bikes are allowed and account for the one allotted piece of checked luggage if disassembled and boxed. If assembled, they are considered 1½ pieces of luggage. If you have something else to check, the bike will be considered extra luggage and will be charged by weight. Readers interested in detailed information on cycling in South America can find more material in Walter Sienko's *Cycling in Latin America*.

HITCHHIKING

Chile is probably the safest country for hitchhiking in South America. It's certainly safer than in the USA and some parts of Europe. A major drawback, however, is that Chilean vehicles are often packed with families, and waits for a lift can be long. Truck drivers will often help backpackers. At *servicentros* on the outskirts of Chilean cities on the Panamericana, where truckers gas up their vehicles, it is often worth soliciting a ride. That said, hitching is never entirely safe, and Lonely Planet does not recommend it. Travelers who decide to hitchhike should understand that they are taking a small but potentially serious risk. People who do choose to hitchhike will be safer if they travel in pairs and let someone know where they are planning to go.

Women can and do hitchhike alone but should exercise caution and should especially avoid getting into a car with more than one man. In Patagonia, where distances are great and vehicles few, hitchhikers should expect long waits and carry warm, windproof clothing. In the Atacama you may wait for some time, but almost every ride will be a long one. It's also a good idea to carry some snack food and a water bottle, especially in the desert north.

FERRY

From Puerto Montt south, Chilean Patagonia and Tierra del Fuego is accessed by a system of ferries. (Most bus services between Puerto Montt and Coyhaique pass through Argentina). Taking a ferry is an almost essential part of experiencing this part of Chile. Unfortunately, the end of the high season also marks limited ferry service. Navimag's enormously popular ferry service from Puerto Montt to Puerto Natales is one of the continent's great travel experiences. The information that follows lists just the basic ferry service. Also on offer are a handful of exclusive tour operators that run their own cruises; since they require preliminary planning (and a lot more money), they are listed below under Organized Tours. More details on the routes below are given under the respective destination.

Companies running passenger ferries are:

Navimag (☎ 02-442-3120, fax 203-5025; w www .navimag.com; Av El Bosque Norte 0440, 11th floor)

Transmarchilay (toll-free ☎ 02-600-600-8687, fax 02-234-4899; w www.transmarchilay.cl; Providencia 2653, Local 24)

Catamaranes del Sur (☎ 02-333-7127, fax 232-9736; w www.catamaranesdelsur.cl; Isidora Goyenechea 3250, Oficina 802)

Naviera Sotramin (☎ 067-233-515, 234-240; Simón Bolívar 254, Coyhaique)

Mar del Sur (☎ 067-231-255; Baquedano 146-A, Coyhaique)

Transbordador Austral Broom (☎ 61-218-100, fax 212-126; Av Bulnes 05075)

Puerto Montt to Chaitén – Navimag and Transmarchilay run car-passenger ferries from Puerto Montt to Chaitén. Catamaranes del Sur runs a high-speed passenger catamaran three times a week.

Puerto Montt to Puerto Chacabuco – Navimag and Transmarchilay operate services from Puerto Montt to Puerto Chacabuco, with bus service continuing on to Coyhaique, and on to Parque Nacional Laguna San Rafael.

Puerto Montt to Puerto Natales – Navimag ferries *Puerto Edén* and *Magallanes* depart Puerto Montt weekly, taking about four days to reach Puerto Natales. Erratic Patagonian weather can play havoc with schedules.

La Arena to Puelche – Transmarchilay's shuttle ferry, about 45km southeast of Puerto Montt, runs back and forth constantly, connecting two northerly segments of the Carretera Austral all year.

Hornopirén to Caleta Gonzalo – Transmarchilay ferries sail from the last mainland stop southbound on the Carretera Austral, to Caleta Gonzalo, about 60km north of Chaitén. Service is limited in the off-season.

Mainland to Chiloé – Ferries run between Pargua to Chacao, at the northern tip of Chiloé.

Chiloé to Chaitén – Transmarchilay and Navimag run ferries between the port of Quellón, on Chiloé, and Chaitén. Catamaranes del Sur runs a passenger catamaran from Castro to Chaitén.

Chiloé to Puerto Chacabuco – Navimag's ferry *Alejandrina* puddle-jumps down to Puerto Chacabuco.

Puerto Chacabuco to Puerto Natales – Navimag's ferry *Magallanes* stops in Puerto Chacabuco before continuing on to Puerto Natales.

Puerto Ibáñez to Chile Chico – Naviera Sotramin and Mar del Sur operate automobile/passenger ferries across Lago General Carrera, south of Coyhaique. There are shuttles from Chile Chico to the Argentine town of Los Antiguos.

Punta Arenas to Tierra del Fuego – Austral Broom runs ferries from Punta Arenas' ferry terminal Tres Puentes to Porvenir; from Punta Delgada, east of Punta Arenas, to Bahía Azul; and from Tres Puentes to Puerto Williams, on Isla Navarino.

Puerto Williams to Ushuaia – Things might be looking up for this most necessary and stymied connection. Contact Austral Broom for latest developments.

LOCAL TRANSPORT
To/From the Airport

In Santiago and main cities, inexpensive (US$1.60 to US$2) airport buses are frequent, but travelers who carry heavy luggage might take advantage of door-to-door airport services for around US$6 to US$7.50. See the Santiago chapter for more details.

Top-end hotels usually provide a shuttle for their clients.

Bus

Even small towns have extensive bus systems that can seem chaotic to the novice rider. Buses, *(micros)*, are clearly numbered and usually carry a placard indicating their final destination. Since many identically numbered buses serve slightly different routes, pay attention to these placards. On boarding, mention your final destination, and the driver will tell you the fare and give you a ticket. Do not lose this ticket, which may be checked en route.

Bus fares in Santiago, the most expensive in the country, are around Ch$210 (approximately US$0.40). Automatic machines are currently being installed, but the process has been slower than authorities would prefer.

Train

Both Santiago and Valparaíso have commuter rail networks. The former runs from Rancagua, capital of Región VI, to Estación Central, on the Alameda in Santiago; while the latter runs from Quillota to Viña del Mar and Valparaíso. For details, see the respective city entries.

Metro

Santiago is the only Chilean city with a subway, the Metro. It is efficient, clean and cheap. For details, see the Santiago chapter.

Taxi

Most Chilean cabs are metered, but fares vary. In Santiago, it costs Ch$300 (about US$0.60) to *bajar la bandera* ('lower the flag'), plus Ch$100 (US$0.20) per 200m. Each cab carries a placard indicating its authorized fare.

In some towns, such as Viña del Mar, cabs may cost twice as much. In others, such as Coquimbo, meters are less common, so it is wise to agree upon a fare in advance if possible. Drivers are generally polite and honest, but there are exceptions. Tipping is not necessary, but you may tell the driver to keep small change.

Nearly all Chilean cities also have *taxi colectivos*, which cover fixed routes and are faster than buses and less expensive than regular taxis.

ORGANIZED TOURS

Chile has an increasing number of agencies specializing in adventure travel around the country; most have offices in Santiago and summer offices in the location of their trips. Others have year-round offices in the specific location.

Altué Active Travel (☎ 02-233-2964, fax 233-6799; w www.altue.com; Encomenderos 83, 2nd floor, Las Condes, Santiago), Chile's pioneer in adventure tourism, arranges trips involving just about every activity throughout the country. One of their specialties is sea kayaking and cultural trips in Chiloé. When the desert blooms, they arrange quality treks to the north.

Austral Adventures (☎/fax 065-625-977; w www.austral-adventures.com; Lord Cochrane 432, Ancud, Chiloé) specializes in yacht cruises aboard the personable and comfortable *Cahuella*, taking in the Pumalín fjords and the smaller islands of Chiloé. Most of the guides are knowledgeable and friendly US and European expats. Customized trips including a variety of activities are arranged throughout southern Chile, as are in-depth cultural trips around Chiloé, with an emphasis on rural tourism and cuisine.

Azimut 360 (☎ 02-236-3880, fax 235-3085; w www.azimut.cl; General Salvo 159, Providencia) specializes in overland trips in the Atacama, mountain biking in the altiplano and multiactivity trips in Patagonia.

Big Foot Adventure Patagonia (☎ 061-414-611; Bories 206, Puerto Natales) is a well-reputed agency that focuses on trekking, mountaineering, kayaking and glacier hiking in Torres del Paine and the Cordillera Sarmiento.

Cascada Expediciones (☎ 02-861-1777, fax 861-2222; w www.cascada-expediciones .com; Camino Al Volcán 17710, Guayacán, San José de Maipo), one the largest tour companies, runs a variety of adventure trips throughout the country, including custom day and weekend excursions in the mountains near Santiago, horseback expeditions across the Andes, tours of the Juan Fernández Archipelago, treks near Pucón and in Torres del Paine, explorations of the Atacama Desert and the northern altiplano, sea-kayaking stints in the fjords of Chiloé, dives at Easter Island and white-water rafting and kayaking trips on the Futaleufú.

Cruceros Australis (☎ 02-442-3110, fax 203-5173; w www.australis.com; Av El Bosque Norte 0440, 11th floor, Las Condes, Santiago) arranges week-long luxury cruises on the 130-passenger *Mare Australis* between Punta Arenas and Ushuaia. The route to Ushuaia takes four nights and stops at Marinelli Glacier, Islote Tucker, Serrano and D'Agostini Glaciers, Bahía Yendegaia and Puerto Williams. The route back to Punta Arenas takes three nights and goes to Cabo de Hornos, Wulala, Garibaldi Glacier and Isla Magdalena. The cruises are expensive – rates based on double occupancy start at US$1150 in low season (September to October and April) and reach US$2530 in high-season (mid-December through February) – but all meals are included, and they do offer a chance to visit parts of the region that are otherwise very difficult and even more expensive to reach independently. Also on board are knowledgeable guides to explain the cultural and physical history of the area. It's possible to do the leg between Punta Arenas and Ushuaia or vice-versa separately and, obviously, less expensively.

Explora (☎ 02-206-6060, fax 228-4655; ⓦ www.explora.com; Américo Vespucio Sur 80, 5th floor, Las Condes, Santiago) offers all-inclusive packages, including luxury accommodations and excursions, in Parque Nacional Torres del Paine and in and around San Pedro de Atacama. They also have contact numbers in the USA (☎ 212-501-8779, 800-858-0855).

Mountain Service (☎ 02-201-2680; ⓦ www.mountainservice.cl; PO Box 233, Correo 35, Providencia, Santiago) focuses on mountaineering at Ojos del Salado and bird-watching tours.

Pared Sur (☎ 02-207-3525, fax 207-3159; ⓦ www.paredsur.cl; Juan Estéban Montero 5497, Las Condes, Santiago) focuses on mountain biking with trips from Parque Nacional Lauca to Tierra del Fuego and lots of places in between.

Patagonia Connection (☎ 02-225-6489, fax 274-8111; ⓦ www.patagonia-connection .com; Fidel Oteíza 1921, Oficina 1006, Providencia, Santiago) offers luxury package trips to Termas de Puyuhuapi Hotel & Spa, in the Aisén region, including either a ground tour of the Carretera Austral or a trip aboard the luxury catamaran Patagonia Express to Laguna San Rafael. The tours run from four to six days. Double rates for the 'Austral Road' range from US$1400 to US$2400; the 'South of Silence' package, including the full-day catamaran excursion to Laguna San Rafael and a night in Puerto Chacabuco, rates range from US$2520 to US$3860. Other packages with more focus on spa treatments are available. Package rates include ground transfer (from Chaitén or Coyhaique) and boat transfers, lodging, meals, use of spa facilities, kayaks and rainforest excursions.

Skorpios (☎ 02-231-1030, fax 232-2269; ⓦ www.skorpios.cl; Augusto Laguia Norte 118, Las Condes, Santiago) runs tours aboard their fleet of luxury cruisers from Puerto Montt and Puerto Chacabuco to Laguna San Rafael, stopping in their own private reserve with hot springs. See the departure destinations for more details.

Yak Expediciones (☎ 227-0427; ⓦ www .yakexpediciones.cl) specializes in sea kayaking and white-water rafting with small groups.

Santiago

☎ 02 • pop 4,650,000

Compared to other cities in Latin America, Santiago feels distinctly European. Its stately, dignified boulevards and neoclassical architecture, swanky high-rise suburbs, efficient metro system and, above all, general state of orderliness reflect a culture that is hardworking, prosperous and business-minded. Santiaguinos tend to be polite, well-dressed (a little too conservatively perhaps) and somewhat restrained, despite their predilection for staying out late.

It's true, especially in winter, that smog frequently lurks overhead – a recent survey found that 79% of inhabitants dream of moving elsewhere to escape the pollution (and, more positively, that 69% would happily pay to improve air quality) – but the city has plenty of distractions. Anyone interested in eating out will find Chile's most inventive cuisine here, and once night falls, the city's veil of drabness lifts, and things quickly come to life in select little corners.

One of the best things about Santiago is its proximity to the mighty Andes. There's something kind of great about being smack in the middle of a metropolis and then looking up and seeing, to your surprise, the second-highest mountain range in the world just a few miles away.

HISTORY

Although conquistador Pedro de Valdivia laid out a regular grid of streets from the present-day Plaza de Armas, early 'Santiago del Nuevo Extremo' was little more than a besieged hillside camp. Just six months after Valdivia founded it in 1541, Mapuche warriors almost obliterated it, and colonists nearly starved under Indian pressure.

By the late 16th century, Santiago was a settlement of just 200 houses, inhabited by not more than 700 Spaniards and mestizos, plus several thousand Indian laborers and servants. Despite their precarious position, wealthy *encomenderos* emulated European nobility, acquiring platoons of servants and importing products from Europe and China.

By the late 18th century, Santiago began to acquire the infrastructure of a proper city, as new *tajamares* (dikes) restrained the Río

Mapocho and as improving roads were able to handle increasing commerce between the capital and the port of Valparaíso. At the same time, authorities sponsored various

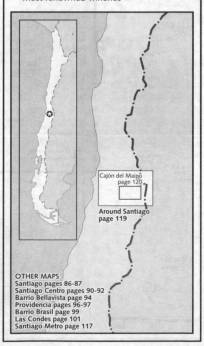

Cajón del Maipo page 120

Around Santiago page 119

SANTIAGO

SANTIAGO

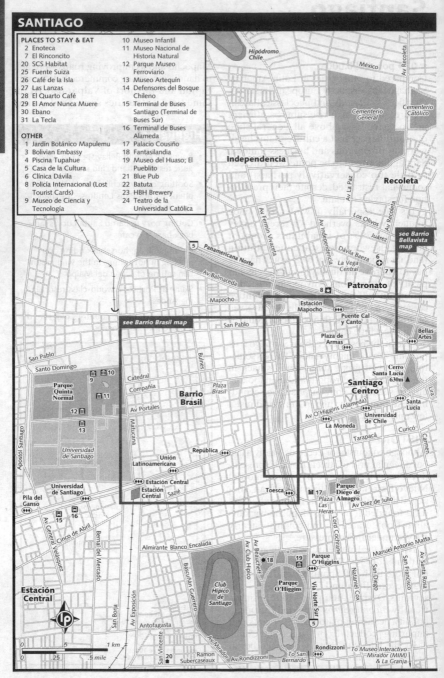

PLACES TO STAY & EAT
2 Enoteca
7 El Rinconcito
20 SCS Habitat
25 Fuente Suiza
26 Café de la Isla
27 Las Lanzas
28 El Quarto Café
29 El Amor Nunca Muere
30 Ebano
31 La Tecla

OTHER
1 Jardín Botánico Mapulemu
3 Bolivian Embassy
4 Piscina Tupahue
5 Casa de la Cultura
6 Clínica Dávila
8 Policía Internacional (Lost
   Tourist Cards)
9 Museo de Ciencia y
   Tecnología

10 Museo Infantil
11 Museo Nacional de
   Historia Natural
12 Parque Museo
   Ferroviario
13 Museo Artequín
14 Defensores del Bosque
   Chileno
15 Terminal de Buses
   Santiago (Terminal de
   Buses Sur)
16 Terminal de Buses
   Alameda
17 Palacio Cousiño
18 Fantasilandia
19 Museo del Huaso; El
   Pueblito
21 Blue Pub
22 Batuta
23 HBH Brewery
24 Teatro de la
   Universidad Católica

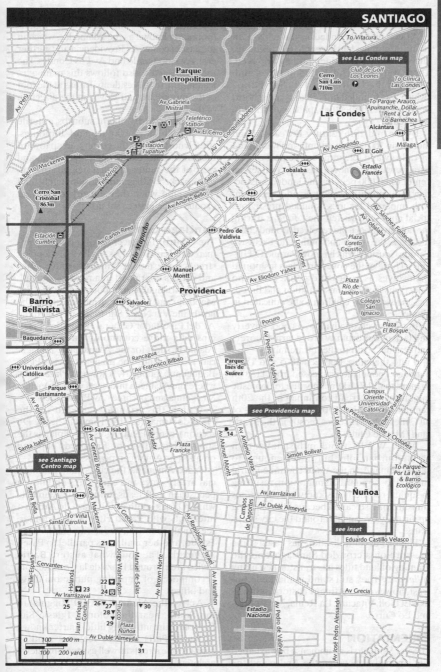

beautification projects to please the land-owning aristocracy.

As colonial rule ended in the early 19th century, Santiago had barely 30,000 residents, and city streets remained largely unpaved. There were few schools and libraries and, although the Universidad de San Felipe (which was founded in 1758 as a law school) provided an intellectual spark, cultural life was bleak.

By the mid-19th century, the capital had more than 100,000 inhabitants and was linked by railway and telegraph to the port of Valparaíso, which was now a bustling commercial center of 60,000 people. The landed aristocracy built sumptuous houses, adorned them with imported luxuries, founded prestigious social clubs and visited their *fundos* during the holidays. Social life revolved around clubs, the track, the opera and outings to exclusive Parque Cousiño (which is now Parque O'Higgins). Those of the governing class fashioned themselves as ladies and gentlemen who valued civilized customs, tradition and breeding, and sent their children to be educated in Europe.

But not everyone had it so good. Poverty and lack of opportunity drove farm laborers and tenants north to the nitrate mines – and also into the cities: Between 1865 and 1875, Santiago's population increased from 115,000 to more than 150,000, mainly due to domestic migration. This trend continued in the 20th century and, by the 1970s, more than 70% of all Chileans lived in cities, mostly in the heartland (Middle Chile).

After WWII, rapid industrialization created urban jobs, but never enough to satisfy demand. In the 1960s continued rural turmoil fostered urban migration, resulting in squatter settlements known as *callampas* (mushrooms, so called because they sprang up virtually overnight) around the city's outskirts.

Planned decentralization has eased some pressure on a crowded Santiago, and the granting of land titles has transformed many *callampas*. They still stand in marked contrast, however, to affluent eastern suburbs like El Golf, Vitacura, La Reina, Las Condes and Lo Curro.

ORIENTATION

Greater Santiago is an immense bowl-shaped city jammed in between the Andes and the coastal cordillera. The most important axis is the east-west thoroughfare Av O'Higgins (popularly known as the Alameda), which in the east becomes Av Providencia and, farther east, Av Apoquindo and Av Las Condes. The metro's Línea 1 also follows this main axis, leading 'up' to the residential areas at the foot of the mountains and 'down' in the direction of the coast.

The city's most affluent suburbs, a sterile forest of high-rise apartment buildings, stretch northeast of the center and up toward the Andes. The less fortunate live south and west of the center in quiet neighborhoods, some packed with grand mansions left behind by the elite when they embarked on their exodus to the eastern suburbs.

Santiago Centro

The Centro, the epicenter of the city's commerce and civic business, is a hive of shopping streets, government buildings, universities and offices contained in a relatively small, roughly triangular area bounded by the Río Mapocho and woodsy Parque Forestal to the north, the Vía Norte Sur to the west, and the Av del Libertador General Bernardo O'Higgins (it's more commonly known as the Alameda, short for the 'Alameda de las Delicias') to the south. The triangle's apex is Plaza Baquedano, popularly known as **Plaza Italia**, where the Alameda intersects with Av Vicuña Mackenna and becomes Av Providencia.

Within this triangle, centered on the **Plaza de Armas** (see the Things to See & Do section), central Santiago's street plan is the standard grid that the Spaniards imposed on all their American possessions.

Paseo Ahumada, the city's main commercial artery since the early days and now a pedestrian mall, leads south to the Alameda, while a block south of the Plaza de Armas it intersects with **Paseo Huérfanos**, another, seemingly identical, pedestrian mall. **Paseo Estado**, another mall, runs parallel to Paseo Ahumada. The somewhat austere **Barrio Cívico** area, around Plaza de la Constitución, is composed of imposing public buildings and offices.

Across the Alameda (Av O'Higgins) to the South, near the colonial Iglesia San Francisco, the intriguing little quarter known as **Barrio París Londres** features winding cobblestone streets as well as mock-medieval architecture.

Barrio Santa Lucía

Cerro Santa Lucía, one of Santiago's most pleasant parks, overlooks the Alameda between the Plaza de Armas and Plaza Italia and gives its name to the trendy **Barrio Santa Lucía** (also known as Barrio Lastarria), where you'll find dim, intimate little bars, fine restaurants, bookshops and a remarkably quiet pseudo-Parisian streetscape.

Barrio Bellavista

Across the canal-like Mapocho and huddling under the enormous Cerro San Cristóbal, Barrio Bellavista is one of Santiago's liveliest neighborhoods – at least at night. Its narrow residential-seeming streets teem with up-scale, interesting places to eat and drink. Pío Nono, the main drag, is lined with a busy street market hawking the usual handicrafts and hippie accoutrements – it is not the nicest slice of the neighborhood. Many of the best places are tucked away on side streets. Just northwest of Barrio Bellavista, the **Recoleta** neighborhood has a few Middle Eastern restaurants and a market of sorts where you can buy cheap clothes.

Providencia

Across the river from Bellavista, the Alameda becomes Av Providencia and leads into the somewhat upscale neighborhood of Providencia.

Providencia is considerably calmer than the Centro, but there's plenty of street life and even a few decent restaurants. Av Providencia is lined with shops, fast-food joints and, increasingly as it continues north, mirror-glass high-rise edifices and malls. Most of the side streets are bordered with trees, and there are some nice old apartment buildings, lending the whole area a European flavor.

The neighborhood is also home to the bizarre nightlife zone known as Suecia, a fake village full of noisy bars, clubs and drunkards.

Barrio Brasil

West of the Vía Norte Sur, Barrio Brasil is an enclave of mock-Baroque early-20th-century architecture that is presently experiencing an urban renaissance. It's a buzzing area filled with students and is a good place for budget accommodations. The barrio's centerpiece is **Plaza Brasil**, which gets especially lively on weekends. Other landmarks include the quake-damaged, neo-Gothic **Basílica del Salvador** (1892), at the corner of Barroso and Huérfanos, and the gargoyle-festooned headquarters of Club Colo Colo (a soccer club), at Cienfuegos 41.

Beside Barrio Brasil, closer to the Alameda, the minuscule Barrio **Concha y Toro** is a quaint area with cobblestone streets and buildings that look like they've been lifted from a fairytale. Farther west and south are the green spaces of Parque Quinta Normal and Parque O'Higgins, both popular weekend refuges for Santiaguino families.

Las Condes

Las Condes marks the beginning of the exclusive 'Sanhattan' *comunas* that lead east from Providencia. The area's soulless modernity is the pride and joy of the city, which might explain why so many top-end hotels are marooned out here. It's worth a visit just to see where every Santiaguino with aspirations wants to live, and there is something intriguing, even spooky, about its well-groomed sparseness. Amongst the '80s and '90s high-rises, there are a couple of restaurant strips with pretenses to a kind of street life, namely Av El Bosque Norte, Av Apoquindo and Av Isidora Goyenechea, collectively known as El Golf.

Beyond Las Condes, in Vitacura and Lo Barnechea, things get even more spread out; without a car, you will not get far.

Ñuñoa

Increasingly fashionable Ñuñoa is southeast of Providencia. It has an active cultural life centered around Plaza Ñuñoa, and its simple single-family houses and tree-lined streets recall what other parts of the capital have lost in the rush to build high-rises. The restaurants and nightspots around the plaza get very busy on weekends, and foreign students from the Universidad de Chile's nearby Macul campus add a cosmopolitan element. Buses for Ñuñoa depart from the west side of Plaza Italia. See the Santiago map for points of interest in Ñuñoa.

INFORMATION

For the addresses of diplomatic representatives of overseas and neighboring countries, see the Facts for the Visitor chapter.

SANTIAGO

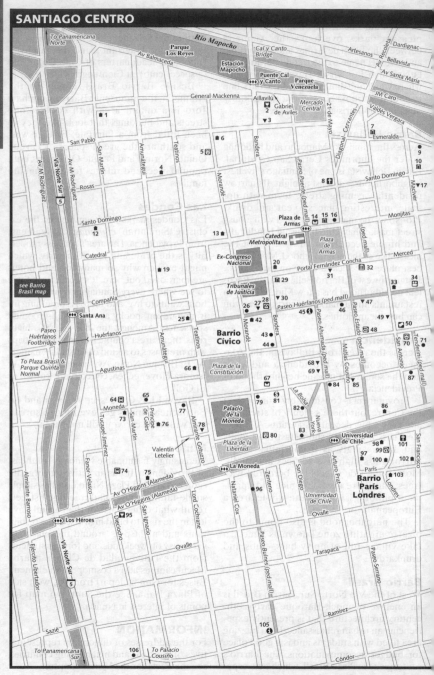

SANTIAGO CENTRO

Río Mapocho

To Panamericana Norte

Parque Los Reyes

Av Balmaceda

Cal y Canto Bridge

Artesanos

Dardignac

Bellavista

Av Recoleta

Av Santa María

Estación Mapocho

Puente Cal y Canto

Parque Venezuela

JM Caro

General Mackenna

Ailavilú

Gabriel de Aviles

Mercado Central

Valdés Vergara

21 de Mayo

Esmeralda

Paseo Puente (ped mall)

Diagonal Cervantes

Santo Domingo

Maciver

San Pablo

Teatinos

San Martín

Amunátegui

Av M Rodríguez

Av M Rodríguez

Rosas

Morandé

Bandera

Santo Domingo

Plaza de Armas

Monjitas

Santo Domingo

Catedral

Catedral Metropolitana

Plaza de Armas

Merced

Ex-Congreso Nacional

Portal Fernández Concha

Compañía

Tribunales de Justicia

Paseo Huérfanos (ped mall)

Paseo Ahumada (ped mall)

Paseo Estado (ped mall)

San Antonio

Tenderini (ped mall)

Santa Ana

Paseo Huérfanos Footbridge

Huérfanos

Barrio Cívico

Matías Cousiño

To Plaza Brasil & Parque Quinta Normal

Agustinas

Plaza de la Constitución

Moneda

Príncipe de Gales

Tucapel Jiménez

San Martín

Almirante Cochrano

La Bolsa

Nueva York

Valentín Letelier

Palacio de la Moneda

Plaza de la Libertad

Universidad de Chile

San Francisco

Barrio París Londres

Londres

La Moneda

Natanieel Cox

Zenteno

San Diego

Arturo Prat

Paris

Av O'Higgins (Alameda)

Lord Cochrane

Av O'Higgins (Alameda)

Los Héroes

Diez Ocho

San Ignacio

Universidad de Chile

Ovalle

Via Norte Sur

Ejército Libertador

Almirante Barroso

Fanor-Velasco

Ovalle

Tarapacá

Paseo Bulnes (ped mall)

Ramírez

Paseo Serrano

Saziè

To Panamericana Sur

To Palacio Cousiño

Cóndor

see Barrio Brasil map

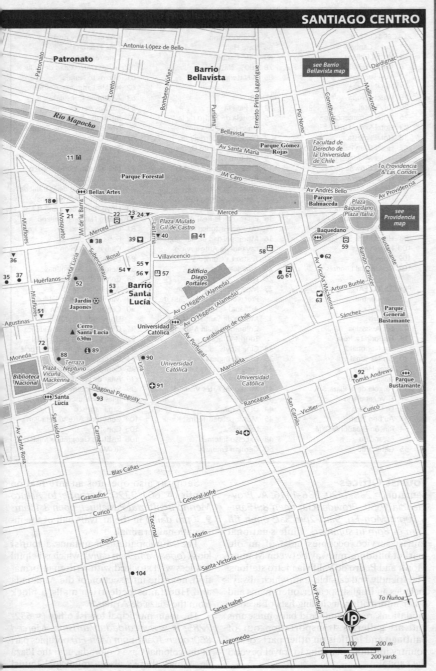

SANTIAGO CENTRO

SANTIAGO CENTRO

PLACES TO STAY
1 Hotel Caribe
4 Hostal Indiana
6 Nuevo Hotel
12 Majestic Hotel
13 Hotel España
19 Hotel Europa
20 City Hotel
25 Hotel Panamericano
33 Hotel Santa Lucía
38 Hotel Foresta
42 Hotel Gran Palace & Libro's
53 Hotel Montecarlo
60 Hotel Crowne Plaza
66 Hotel Carrera
73 Hotel di Maurier
75 Hotel Diego de Almagro
76 Residencia Tabita
86 Hotel Libertador
97 Hotel Fundador
98 Hotel Plaza San Francisco
100 Hotel Vegas
102 Hotel París
103 Residencial Londres

PLACES TO EAT
3 Bar Central
17 Da Carla
21 Kintaro
23 Les Assassins
24 Emporio La Rosa
27 Bar Nacional 2
30 Bar Nacional 1
31 Chez Henry
36 Izakaya Yoko
40 Pérgola de la Plaza & R
47 El Vegetariano
49 Le Due Torri
51 Au Bon Pain
54 Rincón Español & Café
   Escondido
55 Gatopardo

56 Don Victorino
68 Café Haití
69 Café Caribe
78 100% Natural
85 El Naturista

OTHER
2 La Piojera
5 Escuela de Teatro de la
   Universidad de Chile
7 Posada del Corregidor
8 Templo de Santo Domingo
9 Instituto Goethe
10 Casa Manso de Velasco
11 Palacio de Bellas Artes &
   Museo de Arte
   Contemporáneo (MAC)
14 Main Post Office
15 Palacio de la Real Audiencia
   (Museo Histórico Nacional)
16 Municipalidad de Santiago
18 Lavandería Autoservicio
22 Teatro La Comedia
26 American Airlines
28 Entel
29 Museo Chileno de Arte
   Precolombino (Real Casa de
   Aduana)
32 Museo de Santiago (Casa
   Colorada); Main Municipal
   Tourist Office
34 Cine Hoyts
35 Librería Inglesa
37 Feria Chilena del Libro
39 Bar Berri
41 Museo de Artes Visuales
43 Iberia
44 DHL Express
45 Municipalidad Tourist Kiosk
46 LanChile
48 Axcesso Internet
50 German Embassy

52 Ascensor (Elevator)
57 Cine El Biógrafo
58 Cine Alameda
59 Teatro Universidad de Chile
61 Micros to Ñuñoa
62 Natalis Language Center
63 Argentine Consulate
64 Tur Bus Aeropuerto
65 Instituto Chileno-
   Norteamericano de Cultura
67 Post Office
70 Teatro Municipal
71 United Airlines
72 Instituto Chileno-Británico
74 Terminal Los Héroes
77 Departamento de Extranjería
   (Tourist Card Extensions)
79 Lloyd Aéreo Boliviano (LAB)
80 Teatro Nacional Chileno
81 Cambios Afex
82 Bolsa de Comercio
83 Club de La Unión
84 Lufthansa
87 Aerolíneas Argentinas
88 Centro de Exposición de
   Arte Indígena
89 Municipal Tourist Office
90 Centro de Extensión de la
   Universidad Católica
91 Clínica Universidad Católica
92 Andes Escuela de Español
93 Centro Artesanal Santa Lucía
94 Posta Central
95 Confitería Las Torres
96 Altar de la Patria
99 Sonnets Internet
101 Iglesia y Museo Colonial de
   San Francisco
104 Centro de Arte Violeta Parra
105 Conaf
106 Instituto Geográfico Militar
   (IGM)

Tourist Offices

Sernatur (☎ 236-1420, 236-1416; Av Providencia 1550, Providencia; open 8:45am-6:30pm Mon-Fri, 9am-2pm Sat; open till 7pm or 8pm in summer), Chile's national tourist service, occupies most of an old market building, midway between Manuel Montt and Pedro de Valdivia metro stations. The friendly and capable staff, which always includes an English speaker, offers maps and other information, including lists of accommodations, restaurants and bars, museums and art galleries, transportation out of Santiago and leaflets on other parts of the country for those planning to travel beyond the capital.

Sernatur also operates an **information booth** (☎ 601-9320; Aeropuerto Arturo Merino Benítez at Pudahuel; open 8:15am-9:30pm daily) in the arrivals hall of the international terminal.

The Municipalidad maintains a **tourist kiosk** (open 9am-9pm daily), which is helpful but less well stocked with written information, near the intersection of the Ahumada and Huérfanos pedestrian malls, a block from the Plaza de Armas.

The **main municipal tourist office** (☎ 632-7785; ⓦ www.cuidad.cl/turismo; Merced 860; open 10am-6pm Mon-Fri) occupies part of the colonial Casa Colorada, near the Plaza de Armas; there's also a **municipal tourist**

office (☎ 664-4216, 664-4220; W www
.ciudad.cl/turismo; Terraza Neptuno; open
Mon-Thur 9am-1:30pm & 3pm-6pm, Fri
9am-1:30pm & 3pm-5pm) on Cerro Santa
Lucía, close to the Alameda. It offers free, informative 1½-hour guided tours, in Spanish
and English, Thursdays at 11am. These
include a visit to Vicuña Mackenna's tomb
and the traditional midday cannon shot.

All these offices distribute free maps detailing the Centro, Providencia and other
inner comunas of the capital, with the main
metro stations included. More detailed maps
are available from the Municipalidad for
about US$2, but the best city map is San-
tiago, by Mapas de Matassi (☎ 236-4808;
General del Canto 105, Oficina 1506, Providencia), also available at various bookstores
and travel agencies around town.

For trekking and mountaineering information, as well as inexpensive maps and other
national-parks publications (in Spanish), visit
Conaf (Corporación Nacional Forestal; ☎ 390-
0282, 390-0125; W www.conaf.cl; Paseo
Bulnes 291, Centro; open 9:30am-5:30pm
Mon-Thur, 9:30am-4:30pm Fri).

Money

Ubiquitous ATMs have made exchange
houses less important than they used to be,
but numerous cambios on Agustinas, between
Bandera and Ahumada, still change traveler's
checks and foreign cash. There are also exchange facilities and ATMs in Providencia
and at the airport, where rates are notably
lower – change minimal amounts at the
airport unless you're arriving on a weekend.

Cambios pay slightly less for traveler's
checks than for US cash, but they do not
usually charge any additional commission.
It's still possible to locate street changers
by strolling down Paseo Ahumada, but for
the most part this is no longer necessary.

The local Thomas Cook representative is
Turismo Tajamar (☎ 232-9595; Orrego Luco
023, Providencia), which deals only with re-
placing lost or stolen checks.

To exchange American Express traveler's
checks, head to Blanco Viajes (☎ 636-9100;
General Holley 148, Providencia). Cambios
Afex (Moneda 1140, Centro) changes checks
for cash. If you lose your credit cards or traveler's checks, call Diner's Club (☎ 600-231-9999)
or the representative for Visa, MasterCard
and American Express (☎ 671-7003).

Post & Communications

The main post office (Plaza de Armas; open
8am-10pm Mon-Fri, 8am-6pm Sat), on the
north side of the plaza, handles poste
restante. Street vendors at the entrance sell
envelopes and postcards and will also wrap
parcels for a small fee. There is also a post
office in the Centro at Moneda 1155 and in
Providencia at Av Providencia 1466.

For international courier services, try
Federal Express (☎ 231-5250; Av Providencia 1951, Providencia; Ⓜ Pedro de Valdivia)
or DHL Express (Bandera 204, Centro).

For overseas calls, go to one of the many
Entel (Paseo Huérfanos 1133, Centro • Av
11 de Septiembre 1919, Providencia; open
9am-6:30pm daily) offices. Telefónica (CTC)
also has long-distance offices in the Centro
and at metro stations.

For Internet access, visit Axcesso Internet
(Agustinas 869, Galería Imperio, 2nd floor,
Centro; Ⓜ Universidad de Chile; open 7am-
11pm daily; US$1.70/hr), which has 60 com-
puters and fast connections, or Dity Office
(☎ 269-2610; Fidel Oteíza 1930, Providencia;
Ⓜ Pedro de Valdivia; open 9am-7pm daily;
US$2/hr). Sonnets Internet (Londres 43,
Centro; Ⓜ Universidad de Chile; open 9am-
9pm daily; US$1.50/hr), with fast connec-
tions and cheap rates, has become a meeting
place, thanks to the friendly Dutch owner.

Travel Agencies

Santiago seems to have travel agencies on
nearly every corner in the Centro, especially on streets such as Agustinas, Teatinos
and Huérfanos, and in affluent Providencia. For good prices on air tickets, contact
the Student Flight Center (☎ 335-0395, fax
335-0394; e stflictr@ctc-mundo.net; Av
Hernando de Aguirre 201, Oficina 401,
Providencia; Ⓜ Tobalaba).

The Chilean Travel Service (CTS; ☎ 251-
0400, fax 251-0423; W www.ctsturismo.cl;
Antonio Bellet 77, Providencia; Ⓜ Pedro
de Valdivia) has exceptionally helpful, well-
informed, multilingual staff and can organize
accommodations and tours all over Chile.
Staff are also happy to provide general information on Santiago and the rest of Chile.

Several agencies specialize in adventure
and ecotourism excursions. For more information, see the Cajón del Maipo entry at the
end of this chapter and Organized Tours in
the Getting Around chapter.

Bookstores & Newsstands

Santiago's largest and best-stocked bookstore is the **Feria Chilena del Libro** (*Paseo Huérfanos 623, Centro;* Ⓜ *Universidad de Chile*), a fine place to browse an excellent selection of books in both Spanish and English; there are several other branches scattered around town.

For new books in English, try **Librería Inglesa** (☎ *632-5153; Paseo Huérfanos 669, Local 11* • ☎ *231-6270; Av Pedro de Valdivia 47, Providencia*).

For a nearly complete selection of Lonely Planet titles, and many other books in English, pay a visit to **Librería Eduardo Albers** (☎ *218-5371; Av Vitacura 5648, Vitacura*). Take any bus out to Av Vitacura from Av

Santa María, which runs along the north bank of the Río Mapocho.

Behind the grape arbor at the Phone Box Pub, **Librería Chile Ilustrado** (☎ *235-8145; Av Providencia 1652, Providencia; open 9:30am-1:30pm & 4pm-7:30pm Mon-Fri, 10am-1:30pm Sat*) has a superb selection of books on Chilean history, archaeology, anthropology and folklore. It specializes in rare materials, but has much general-interest stock. Two other booksellers occupy the same complex: **Books** (☎ *235-1205*), with used but fairly expensive English-language paperbacks, and the feminist bookshop **Lila**.

Gaia Centro de Difusión Ecológica (*Orrego Luco 54, Centro*) stocks books on flora, fauna and environmental issues, as well as

BARRIO BELLAVISTA

PLACES TO STAY & EAT
4 Rodizio
5 La Bohème
9 Ali Baba
10 El Tallarín Gordo
11 El Caramaño
16 El Otro Sitio
20 Di Simoncelli
21 Tasca Mediterránea
22 Rinconcito Peruano
25 Venezia
26 Apart Hotel Monteverde
27 Etniko
28 Galindo
29 Azul Profundo
33 Muñeca Brava
36 Donde La Elke
37 Sarita Colonia
38 Como Agua para Chocolate
39 Zen
40 Cava de Dardignac
41 El Antojo de Gauguin

OTHER
1 Santuario Inmaculada Concepción
2 Terraza Bellavista
3 Havana Salsa
6 Cooperativa Almacén Campesina
7 Escuela Violeta Parra
8 Bokhara
12 Tadeo
13 La Chascona (Museo Neruda)
14 Teatro La Feria
15 Bunker
17 La Feria
18 Da Lua
19 Centro de Idiomas Bellavista
23 Tantra Lounge
24 Arte del Mundo
30 La Casa en el Aire
31 Teatro Bellavista
32 Altazor
34 Chile Information Project
35 Teatro El Conventillo
42 Lapiz Lazuli
43 Chilean Rent a Car

To Cementerio Católico
Cerro San Cristóbal 869m
Estación Cumbre Teleférico
To Casa de la Cultura & Enoteca
Parque Metropolitano
Funicular
Jardín Zoológico
Plaza Caupolicán
Parque Forestal
Río Mapocho
Parque Gómez Rojas
Facultad de Derecho de la Universidad de Chile
To Providencia & Las Condes
see Santiago Centro map
see Providencia map
Plaza Baquedano (Plaza Italia)
To Santiago Centro
Baquedano
Providencia

coffee-table books and postcards. **N'aitún** (☎ 671-8410; Av Ricardo Cumming 453), in Santiago's Barrio Brasil, is a leftist bookstore/ community center that doubles as a venue for live music and theater; drinks and snacks are available as well.

For magazines and newspapers, try **Libro's** (☎ 699-0319; Paseo Huérfanos 1178, Centro • ☎ 232-8839; Av Pedro de Valdivia 039, Providencia). Foreign newspapers and magazines, including some in English, are also available at two kiosks at the junction of the Ahumada and Huérfanos pedestrian malls. If a newspaper appears to have been around more than a few days or if pages are missing, haggle over the price.

Cultural Centers
Where passenger trains to Viña del Mar and Valparaíso once arrived and departed, the **Estación Mapocho** (☎ 361-1761; cnr Bandera & Balmaceda; Ⓜ Puente Cal y Canto) is now Santiago's main cultural center, offering live theater, concerts, exhibits and a café. The center also hosts special events such as the annual book fair. It's on the south bank of the Río Mapocho at the north end of Bandera.

The **Centro de Extensión de la Universidad Católica** (☎ 222-0275; Alameda 390, Centro; Ⓜ Universidad Católica), **Centro de Arte Violeta Parra** (☎ 635-2387; Carmen 340, Centro), **Instituto Cultural de Providencia** (☎ 209-4341; Av 11 de Septiembre 1995, Providencia) and **Centro Cultural de España** (☎ 235-0657; Av Providencia 927, Providencia; Ⓜ Salvador) all host lectures, art and photo exhibits, and films.

The **Instituto Chileno-Norteamericano de Cultura** (☎ 696-3215; Moneda 1467, Centro) and the **Instituto Chileno-Británico** (☎ 638-2156; Santa Lucía 124, Centro) both have libraries with English-language newspapers and periodicals.

Laundry
Dry cleaners are abundant, but self-service laundries can be hard to find. At most of these, 'self-service' means dropping off your clothes and picking them up later. Most hotels will do laundry for a reasonable price.

Lavandería Autoservicio (☎ 632-1772; Monjitas 507, Centro; US$5/load) can have your clothes washed and dried two hours after drop-off. **Lavandería San Miguel** (☎ 699-5376; Moneda 2296, Barrio Brasil;

Ⓜ República) and **Laverap** (Av Providencia 1645, Providencia; Ⓜ Pedro de Valdivia) also provide speedy laundry services.

Medical Services
In an emergency, go to the **Posta Central** (☎ 634-1650; Av Portugal 125, Centro; Ⓜ Universidad Católica), which has English-speaking personnel. Private clinics include the **Clínica Universidad Católica** (☎ 633-4122; Lira 40, Centro), the **Clínica Dávila** (☎ 735-4030; Av Recoleta 464, Recoleta) and the **Clínica Las Condes** (☎ 211-1002; Lo Fontecilla 411, Las Condes).

Dangers & Annoyances
Santiago has a growing reputation for pickpockets, especially in the Centro (the first two blocks of San Antonio going north from Alameda are notorious), around Mercado Central (near the river) and on Cerro Santa Lucía. Be alert but not obsessed with personal security, and take special care with your belongings when seated at sidewalk cafés in heavily traveled areas. Women should avoid walking alone at night, and it's probably safest to avoid walking through parks at night, even in groups.

Every year, around the September 11 anniversary of the 1973 coup, Providencia's Av 11 de Septiembre becomes the site of very contentious demonstrations, and many visitors prefer to avoid the area at that time.

THINGS TO SEE & DO
Plaza de Armas & Barrio Cívico
Plaza de Armas, the city's historic center, is a bustling square flanked by a clutch of colonial and neoclassical buildings, including the main post office (1882; the site of the city's first house, which belonged to Pedro de Valdivia), the Museo Histórico Nacional (see Museums, next) in the **Palacio de la Real Audiencia** (1804), the **Municipalidad de Santiago** (town hall; 1785) and the **Catedral Metropolitana** (1745), which has an ornate interior. The eastern and southern sides of the plaza are edged with busy arcades containing little shops, restaurants and wildly popular hot-dog stands. Half a block east of the plaza, the ochre-colored, colonial **Casa Colorada** (1769) houses the Museo de Santiago (see Museums) and a tourist office.

The run of fancy civic buildings continues west of the plaza, where you'll find the garden-ensconced **Ex-Congreso Nacional** *(Morandé 441)* (1876), now the Foreign Ministry, and, fronting on Compañía, the **Tribunales de Justicia** (law courts). Across the street, the late-colonial **Real Casa de Aduana** *(royal customhouse; cnr Bandera & Compañía)* houses the outstanding Museo Chileno de Arte Precolombino (see Museums).

Two blocks northeast of Plaza de Armas, the 1765 **Posada del Corregidor** *(Esmeralda 749)* is a whitewashed, two-story adobe with an interesting wooden balcony; it was once an inn. Nearby, the similar **Casa Manso de Velasco** *(Santo Domingo 699)*, dating from 1730, is another colonial gem.

Two blocks west, on the corner of Santo Domingo and 21 de Mayo, the **Templo de Santo Domingo** is an impressive-looking church. Originally dating from 1557, it was destroyed and rebuilt numerous times after earthquakes and fires; the present building was last renovated in 1963.

Santiago's main shopping zone is just south of Plaza de Armas, in a grid of pedestrian malls that are all disorientatingly similar. The main drag, **Paseo Ahumada**, leads south from the plaza along with the parallel **Paseo Estado**, and both are crossed by **Paseo Huérfanos** one block to the south. These pedestrian malls are not particularly interesting, but it's worth exploring the lovely old *galerías* (shopping arcades) that lead off them.

Southwest of the plaza, between Teatinos and Morandé, grassy **Plaza de la Constitución** offers unobstructed views of the mighty late-colonial **Palacio de La Moneda**, which occupies an entire block. Designed by Italian architect Joaquín Toesca and formerly the presidential residence (originally the colonial mint), La Moneda was badly damaged by air force attacks during the 1973 military coup. It was restored before the return to democracy and now houses presidential offices, though the president does not reside here. On alternate days at 10am, *carabineros* hold a changing-of-the-guard ceremony outside. On the opposite side of La Moneda, on the Alameda, **Plaza de la Libertad** faces the **Altar de la Patria**, which crowns the crypt of Chilean liberator General Bernardo O'Higgins.

East of Palacio de la Moneda, the triangular 1917 **Bolsa de Comercio** *(stock exchange; La Bolsa 64)* and the 1925 **Club de La Unión** *(Alameda 1091)*, where Santiago's stockbrokers hold their power

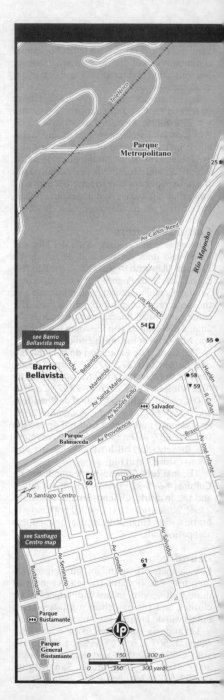

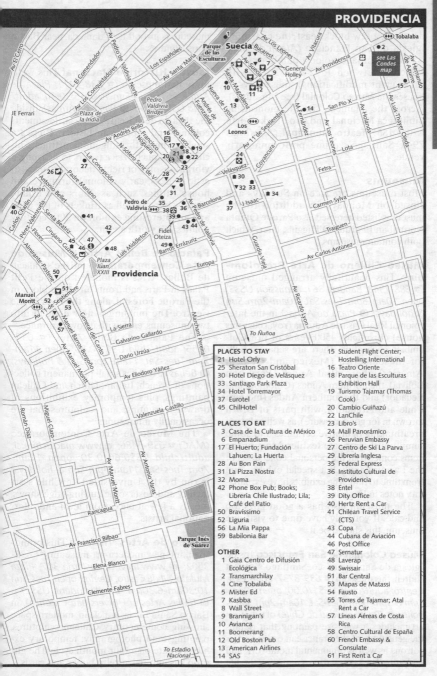

PLACES TO STAY
21 Hotel Orly
25 Sheraton San Cristóbal
30 Hotel Diego de Velásquez
33 Santiago Park Plaza
34 Hotel Torremayor
37 Eurotel
45 ChilHotel

PLACES TO EAT
3 Casa de la Cultura de México
6 Empanadium
17 El Huerto; Fundación
   Lahuen; La Huerta
28 Au Bon Pain
31 La Pizza Nostra
32 Moma
42 Phone Box Pub; Books;
   Librería Chile Ilustrado; Lila;
   Café del Patio
50 Bravíssimo
52 Liguria
56 La Mia Pappa
59 Babilonia Bar

OTHER
1 Gaia Centro de Difusión
   Ecológica
2 Transmarchilay
4 Cine Tobalaba
5 Mister Ed
7 Kasbba
8 Wall Street
9 Brannigan's
10 Avianca
11 Boomerang
12 Old Boston Pub
13 American Airlines
14 SAS

15 Student Flight Center;
   Hostelling International
16 Teatro Oriente
18 Parque de las Esculturas
   Exhibition Hall
19 Turismo Tajamar (Thomas
   Cook)
20 Cambio Guiñazú
22 LanChile
23 Libro's
24 Mall Panorámico
26 Peruvian Embassy
27 Centro de Ski La Parva
29 Librería Inglesa
35 Federal Express
36 Instituto Cultural de
   Providencia
38 Entel
39 Dity Office
40 Hertz Rent a Car
41 Chilean Travel Service
   (CTS)
43 Copa
44 Cubana de Aviación
46 Post Office
47 Sernatur
48 Laverap
49 Swissair
51 Bar Central
53 Mapas de Matassi
54 Fausto
55 Torres de Tajamar; Atal
   Rent a Car
57 Líneas Aéreas de Costa
   Rica
58 Centro Cultural de España
60 French Embassy &
   Consulate
61 First Rent a Car

lunches, are also elegant buildings of note. Across the Alameda (take the metro underpass), a few blocks east, the charming **Iglesia de San Francisco** *(Alameda 834)* is one of Santiago's oldest buildings (constructed between 1572 and 1628, with subsequent modifications); these days, it houses the **Museo Colonial** (see Museums). Across the Alameda sits the monolithic **Biblioteca Nacional**, and two blocks north is the 1857 **Teatro Municipal** *(Agustinas 794)*, Santiago's prime performing-arts venue.

Museums

Most museums are free on Sundays and closed on Mondays. In addition to the museums listed here, see also Parque Quinta Normal and Parque O'Higgins, later, which both contain museums.

Museo Chileno de Arte Precolombino This beautifully arranged museum *(☎ 688-7348; Bandera 361; admission US$3; open 10am-6pm Tues-Sat, 10am-2pm Sun & holidays; ⓜ Plaza de Armas)* in the late-colonial Real Casa de Aduana (royal customs house) chronicles 4500 years of pre-Columbian civilization. There are separate halls for Mesoamerica (Mexico and Central America), the central Andes (Peru and Bolivia), the northern Andes (Colombia and Ecuador) and the southern Andes (modern Chile and Argentina, with parts of Brazil thrown in for good measure), as well as lots of breathtaking figurative ceramics and some sumptuously intricate textiles. Most of the items come from the personal collections of the Larraín family, but special exhibits run from time to time. The exhibits have explanatory notes in English.

The museum also has a good giftshop and café. If you only have time to visit one museum, this should be it.

Museo Colonial de San Francisco Inside Iglesia de San Francisco, Santiago's oldest church, this museum *(☎ 639-8737; Londres 4, Centro; adult/child US$1/0.50; open 10am-1pm & 3pm-6pm Tues-Sat, 10am-2pm Sun & holidays; ⓜ Universidad de Chile)* of religious art includes a wall-size painting that details the genealogy of the Franciscan order and its patrons, as well as ornamental metalwork and sculpture. The several rooms depicting the life

of St Francis of Assisi will test the endurance of all but the most earnestly devout. The museum is just off the Alameda, near Barrio París Londres.

Museo Histórico Nacional This well-presented museum *(☎ 638-1411; Plaza de Armas 951; Tues-Sun 10am-5:30pm; adult/child US$1/0.50; ⓜ Plaza de Armas)*, inside the Palacio de la Real Audencia, documents colonial and republican history. There's a small room with indigenous artifacts, including Mapuche *rewe* (stairs to heaven); a vibrant display of richly decorated ecclesiastic objects; early colonial furniture and house fittings, such as doors and ornate window bars, as well as trinkets of the elite; and an interesting exhibit on 20th-century politics. It's worth a visit.

Palacio de Bellas Artes & Museo de Arte Contemporáneo Santiago's Palacio de Bellas Artes is modeled on the Petit Palais in Paris and fronts an entire block in the Parque Forestal, along the river in the Centro. The building is now divided into two museums, each with its own entrance.

The Palacio de Bellas Artes *(☎ 633-0655; adult/child US$1/0.50; open 11am-7pm Tues-Sat, 11am-2pm Sun & holidays; ⓜ Bellas Artes)* has small permanent collections of French, Italian, Dutch and Chilean paintings, plus temporary exhibitions of drawings, paintings and sculptures that are occasionally interesting.

The Museo de Arte Contemporáneo *(MAC; ☎ 639-5486; ⓦ www.mac.uchile.cl; adult/child US$0.60/0.30; open 11am-7pm Tues-Sat, 11am-4pm Sun & holidays)* is run by the Universidad de Chile's art faculty and hosts some cutting-edge shows, mostly a few at once, from local and international artists.

Museo de Artes Visuales This brand-spanking-new modern-art museum *(☎ 638-3502; ⓦ www.mavi.cl; Lastarria 307, Plaza Mulato Gil de Castro, Centro; open Tues-Sun 10:30am-6:30pm; adult/student US$2/1; ⓜ Bellas Artes or Universidad Católica)*, in Barrio Santa Lucía, is a clean, modern space showing contemporary Chilean sculptures, paintings and photography; temporary exhibits rotate on a four-month cycle. The gift shop has unusual jewelry, books and cards.

Museo de la Solidaridad Salvador Allende Housed in an old mansion with a pretty central courtyard, this museum (☎ 681-4954; W *www.mssa.cl; Herrera 360, Barrio Brasil;* ⓜ *Unión Latinoamericana; admission by donation; open 10am-7pm Tues-Sun)* is a '70s art time-capsule. Having begun in 1971 with donations from artists around the world in sympathy with Chile's socialist experiment, the museum went underground after the coup of 1973 – the entire collection spent 17 years in the warehouses of the Museo de Arte Contemporáneo, awaiting the return of civilian rule.

The main attractions are works by Matta, Miró, Tapies, Calder and Yoko Ono, though there's also some fabulous geometric art.

While the paintings and sculptures themselves are less overtly political than one might expect, the museum also includes a multimedia station for viewing the history of Allende and the Unidad Popular.

Museo Interactivo Mirador This bold and dramatic interactive park and museum *(MIM;* ☎ *294-3955;* W *www.mim.cl; Sebastapol 90, La Granja; adult/child US$5/3; open Tues-Sun 9:30am-6:30pm; tickets sold until 5:30pm;* ⓜ *Mirador)* features striking architecture of curved concrete and polished copper, and the sculptural, landscaped 11-hectare grounds are reason enough for a visit. Inside there are climb-aboard mechanical toys, funny mirrors,

BARRIO BRASIL

PLACES TO STAY
1 Residencial del Norte
6 La Casa Roja
12 Hostelling International Hostel
13 Hotel Tokyo
23 Residencial Mery
25 Residencial Alemana

PLACES TO EAT
4 Manos Morenos
5 Ocean Pacific's
7 Peperone
8 Las Vacas Gordas
11 Plaza Garibaldi
14 Tongoy
15 Ostras Squella
17 Puente de los Suspiros

OTHER
2 N'aitún
3 Museo de la Solidaridad Salvador Allende
9 Basílica del Salvador
10 Instituto Chileno de la Lengua
16 Lavandería San Miguel
18 Club Colo Colo
19 Blondie
20 La Cueva
21 Teatro Carrera
22 Centropuerto (Airport Buses)
24 Terminal San Borja

wind tunnels, old sombrero-making machines, music rooms, art workshops, play areas for kids under six years old, a diet-assessor and a bed of nails that you can nap on – and that's not half of it.

If you're feeling peckish, there's a café and a large restaurant on site. The museum is in the southern comuna of La Granja, with a spectacular Andes backdrop. To get there, take the metro to Mirador; at the exit, cross Av Mackenna Oriente and follow Mirador Azul until its end; then turn left and follow the signs.

Museo de Santiago Part of the colonial Casa Colorada, this quaintly amateurish little museum (☎ 633-0723; Merced 860, Centro; adult/child US$0.80/0.30; open 10am-6pm Tues-Fri, 10am-5pm Sat, 11am-2pm Sun & holidays) documents the capital's growth from its modest beginnings. Permanent exhibits include maps, paintings, colonial garb, models and dioramas. Adults will find it all a bit of a yawn, but kids might get a kick out of it.

Museo Nacional de Historia Natural This natural-history museum (☎ 681-4095; adult/child US$1/0.50; open 10am-5:30pm Tues-Sun) is in Quinta Normal, a huge park west of the center of town (see the Santiago map). It contains some fun old-style dioramas, an enormous butterfly collection and a sampling of dinosaur bones, including bone fragments of the giant Pleistocene ground sloth known as the 'milodon' from the famous cave near Puerto Natales in southern Chile (see the Magallanes chapter).

Palacio Cousiño

Originally of Portuguese descent, the prominent Cousiño-Goyenechea family enjoyed successes in wine and coal and silver mining that enabled them to build Santiago's most glorious mansion, dating from 1871. The house is embellished with French-style artwork and features one of the country's first elevators. The palacio (☎ 698-5063; Dieciocho 438; ⓜ Toesca; adult/child US$2/1; open 9:30am-1:30pm & 2:30pm-5pm Tues-Fri, 9:30pm-1:30pm Sat & Sun) is south of the Alameda, near Parque Diego de Almagro, in Santiago Centro. The admission price includes excellent guided tours in Spanish or English. See the Santiago map for location.

La Chascona (Museo Neruda)

Named after the unruly hair of the poet's widow, Matilde Urrutia, Pablo Neruda's eclectic shiplike house sits on a shady cul-de-sac at the foot of Cerro San Cristóbal, a short distance off Pío Nono in Barrio Bellavista. Neruda was an obsessive collector, and the contents of his house include a beautiful bar from Marseille, Bauhaus furniture and other intriguing knickknacks collected on his travels.

The **Fundación Neruda**, which looks after La Chascona (☎ 737-8712; Márquez de La Plata 0192; adult/child US$5/2.50; open 10am-6pm Tues-Sun), conducts tours of La Chascona on a first-come, first-served basis. The tours last an hour and are very thorough.

Cementerio General

Chile's distant and recent history is on display here, where the tombs of figures such as José Manuel Balmaceda, Salvador Allende and diplomat Orlando Letelier are reminders of political turmoil from the 19th century to the present. **Memorial del Detenido Desaparecido y del Ejecutado Político**, a memorial to the 'disappeared' victims of the Pinochet dictatorship, was erected in 1994.

The Cementerio General (open until sundown daily) is at the north end of Av La Paz, north of the Río Mapocho via the Cal y Canto bridge.

Parks & Gardens

Cerro Santa Lucía Honeycombed with gardens, footpaths and fountains, Cerro Santa Lucía (known to the Mapuche as Huelén) has been a handy hilltop sanctuary from the bustle of Santiago since 1875. At its base, on the Alameda, sits a large stone engraved with the text of a letter in which Pedro de Valdivia extolled the beauty of the newly conquered territories to Spain's King Carlos V. Also, fronting the Alameda, at the southwest corner of Cerro Santa Lucía, is the highly ornamented **Terraza Neptuno**, with fountains and curving staircases that ascend to the summit.

From the center of town, it's an easy walk to the east end of Huérfanos, where a glass *ascensor* (elevator) carries passengers up the steep hillside, or you can take a short ride on the metro to the Santa Lucía stop. The park has acquired a reputation for nighttime muggings but is generally safe during the day. Still, visitors should not be complacent.

For information about guided tours of Cerro Santa Lucía, see Tourist Offices, earlier.

Parque Metropolitano (Cerro San Cristóbal) Crowned by a 36m statue of the Virgin Mary, 869m-tall Cerro San Cristóbal towers above Santiago from the north side of the Mapocho, in Barrio Bellavista. Reached by funicular railway, *teleférico* (aerial tramway), bus, car or foot, it dominates Parque Metropolitano, central Santiago's largest open space and a major recreational resource for residents of the capital.

The most direct route to San Cristóbal's summit is via the **funicular** *(adult/child US$2/1.20 roundtrip; 1pm-8pm Mon, 10am-*

8pm Tues-Sun), which climbs 485m from Plaza Caupolicán, at the north end of Pío Nono in Bellavista.

The funicular makes an intermediate stop at the **Jardín Zoológico** *(zoo; US$2.60/0.85 adult/child; 10am-6pm Tues-Sun),* which has a modest collection of neglected exotic animals; improvements are supposedly under way. The climb continues to the **Terraza Bellavista**, where, on a rare clear day, there are extraordinary views of the city. At the summit proper, Pope John Paul II said Mass at the **Santuario Inmaculada Concepción** during his Santiago visit in 1984.

A short walk from the Terraza is the Estación Cumbre, the start of the 2000m-long **teleférico** *(adult/child US$2.30/1.20 roundtrip; open 2:30pm-6:30pm Mon-Fri,*

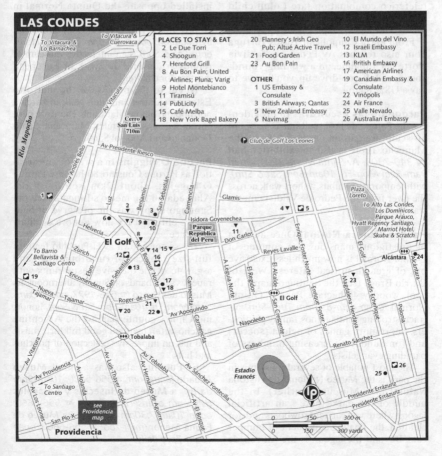

LAS CONDES

To Vitacura &
Lo Barnechea

To Vitacura &
Cuerovaca

Río Mapocho

Cerro ▲
San Luis
710m

PLACES TO STAY & EAT
2 Le Due Torri
4 Shoogun
7 Hereford Grill
8 Au Bon Pain; United Airlines; Pluna; Varig
9 Hotel Montebianco
11 Tiramisú
14 PubLicity
15 Café Melba
18 New York Bagel Bakery

20 Flannery's Irish Geo Pub; Altué Active Travel
21 Food Garden
23 Au Bon Pain

OTHER
1 US Embassy & Consulate
3 British Airways; Qantas
5 New Zealand Embassy
6 Navimag

10 El Mundo del Vino
12 Israeli Embassy
13 KLM
16 British Embassy
17 American Airlines
19 Canadian Embassy & Consulate
22 Vinópolis
24 Air France
25 Valle Nevado
26 Australian Embassy

Club de Golf Los Leones

Av Vitacura

Av Andrés Bello

Av Presidente Riesco

Plaza
Loreto

To Alto Las Condes,
Los Dominicos,
Parque Arauco,
Hyatt Regency Santiago,
Marriot Hotel,
Skuba & Scratch

Luz

Benjamin

San Sebastián

Carmencita

Glamis

Isidora Goyenechea

Parque
República
del Peru

Don Carlos

Reyes Lavalle

Enrique Foster Norte

El Golf

Alcántara   24

Helvecia

Zurich

Ebro

Encomenderos

El Golf

Nueva Tajamar

Tajamar

San Sebastián

El Bosque Norte

Carmencita

A Leguía Norte

El Regidor

El Alcalde

San Crescente

Enrique Foster Sur

Magdalena Hendaya

Gertrudis Echenique

Polonia

To Barrio
Bellavista &
Santiago Centro

19

Roger de Flor

Carmencita

Napoleón

Tobalaba

Callao

Renato Sánchez

Av Vitacura

Av Providencia

Av Luis Thayer Ojeda

Av Tobalaba

Av Hernando de Aguirre

Av Sánchez Fontecilla

El Bosque

Presidente Errázuriz

Estadio
Francés

25

26

To Santiago
Centro

Av Holanda

Av Los Leones

San Pío X

Presidente Errázuriz

see
Providencia
map

Providencia

0   150   300 m

0   150   300 yards

10:30am-7:30pm Sat, Sun & holidays, in winter open Fri-Sun only), which goes from Cerro San Cristóbal, via Tupahue, to a station near the north end of Av Pedro de Valdivia Norte (about 1200m from the Pedro de Valdivia metro station; many of the sites are on the Santiago map).

At the Tupahue teleférico station is the **Piscina Tupahue**, a large and lovely swimming pool. A short walk east from Tupahue are an art museum called the **Casa de la Cultura** *(open 9am-5pm daily)*, Santiago's **Enoteca** (a restaurant with wine tastings) and the **Jardín Botánico Mapulemu** (botanical garden). Further east, there's another large pool at **Piscina Antilén**, reachable only by bus or on foot.

From either direction, the funicular-teleférico combination fare (adult/child US$3.30/1.60) is a good way to orient yourself to Santiago's complex geography.

From Plaza Caupolicán, Buses Tortuga Tour also reaches Av Pedro de Valdivia Norte via Tupahue, on a winding, roundabout road. If you drive up, you'll have to pay a US$2.80 toll.

Parque de las Esculturas In Providencia, the **Parque de las Esculturas** is an open-air sculpture garden on the banks of the Mapocho. There is also an **exhibition hall** *(☎ 340-7303; Av Santa María 2201; open 9am-6pm Mon-Fri, 10am-6pm Sat & Sun)*, with temporary exhibits, a short walk across the river from the Pedro de Valdivia metro station.

Parque Quinta Normal Once an area of prestigious mansions, the comuna of Quinta Normal is now much less exclusive but of great historical interest. West of Barrio Brasil (see the Santiago map), the cool, woodsy 40-hectare Parque Quinta Normal *(open 8am-8:30pm Tues-Sun)* attracts strolling Santiaguinos, family picnickers, impromptu games of pelota (soccer) and (on Sundays) increasing numbers of parading evangelists.

The most notable of several museums in the park is the **Museo Nacional de Historia Natural** (see Museums, earlier). In the middle of the park, there's an artificial lagoon where you can rent rowboats and, for children, the floating equivalent of bumper cars. Beyond the lagoon is the **Museo de Ciencia y Tecnología** *(☎ 681-6022; adult/ child US$1.25/0.90; open 10am-5:30pm Tues-Fri, 11am-6pm Sat & Sun)*, which has interactive exhibits on astronomy, geology and other aspects of science and technology. Other museums in the park include the **Museo Infantil** *(☎ 681-6022; admission free; open 9:30am-5pm Mon-Fri)*, which allows access only for children two to five years old, and, near the southern entrance, the open-air **Parque Museo Ferroviario** *(☎ 681-4627; adult/child US$1.25/0.85; open 10am-5:30pm Tues-Fri, 11am-6pm Sat & Sun)*, which is filled with lovingly maintained steam locomotives.

Across from the southern entrance, housed in an offbeat glass structure designed for the Paris Exhibition of 1889 and dismantled and installed opposite the Quinta Normal in the early 20th century, the **Museo Artequín** *(☎ 681-8687; Av Portales 3530; admission by donation; open 9am-5pm Tues-Fri, 11am-6pm Sat & Sun)* is an interactive museum of replica art, mostly the work of European masters, for children.

To get to the park, take the metro to Estación Central and then walk or catch a northbound bus up Matucana. There are park entrances on Av Portales, Matucana, Santo Domingo and Apóstol Santiago.

Parque O'Higgins In a previous incarnation as Parque Cousiño, 80-hectare Parque O'Higgins, about 2km south of the Alameda on the metro's Línea 2 (see the Santiago map), was the preserve of Santiago's elite, but it's now a more egalitarian place.

The sector known as **El Pueblito** features full-size replicas of rural buildings and a gaggle of inexpensive restaurants with raucous salsa bands on Sunday afternoons. Its **Museo del Huaso** *(☎ 556-1927; open 10am-5pm Mon-Fri, 10am-2pm Sat & Sun)*, honoring Chile's counterpart to the Argentine gaucho, often features good folkloric music and has an impressive collection of ponchos and hats.

El Pueblito also has a small **Museo Acuario** *(aquarium; ☎ 556-5680; 10am-9pm daily)*, a **Museo de Insectas y Caracoles** *(Museum of Insects & Snails; ☎ 556-6660; open 10am-7:30pm daily)* and a **Museo de Fauna Menor** *(mini-zoo; ☎ 556-6660; open 10am-7pm daily)*.

The fantastically named **Fantasilandia** *(☎ 689-3035, Beaucheff 938; open 2pm-8pm Tues-Fri, 11am-8pm Sat & Sun in summer, 11am-8pm Sat, Sun and holidays only rest of year)* is a children's amusement park. Admission, which includes unlimited rides, is free for children who are shorter than 90cm; those between 91cm and 140cm pay US$7.50; all others pay US$8.50.

To get to Parque O'Higgins, take Línea 2 of the metro to Parque O'Higgins station and walk west.

Parque por La Paz In the mostly working-class comuna of Peñalolén, in Santiago's eastern foothills, the onetime estate of Villa Grimaldi was the main detention and torture center for now-imprisoned General Manuel Contreras' notorious DINA (National Intelligence Directorate). The compound was razed by the military to cover up evidence in the last days of the Pinochet dictatorship, and it has been converted into a memorial park *(open 11am-8:30pm Tues-Sun)*. It's a powerful testament; you need only read the descriptions and see the names of the dead and disappeared to imagine what happened here.

Parque por La Paz is in the 8300 block of José Arrieta near La Capilla. Take bus No 242 from Av Providencia, No 433 from Plaza Italia, or No 337 from Estación Central, on the Alameda.

LANGUAGE COURSES

For intensive (and not inexpensive) language courses, try the **Centro de Idiomas Bellavista** *(☎ 735-7651; Crucero Exéter 0325, Bellavista)*.

Escuela Violeta Parra *(☎ 735-8240; e vioparra@chilesat.cl; Ernesto Pinto Lagarrigue 362-A)*, also in Bellavista, has drawn praise for emphasizing the social context of language instruction by arranging field trips to community and environmental organizations, vineyards and the like, as well as tours to nearby national parks. Two-week intensive courses with four 45-minute sessions per day cost US$216. Classes have a maximum of seven students. The school can also arrange for homestays (from US$10/night), and individual classes are also available.

Instituto Goethe *(☎ 638-3185; w www .goethe.de/hs/sao/spspanen.htm; Esmeralda 650)*, in central Santiago, offers intensive

Spanish-language courses consisting of three weeks of 25 classes (45 minutes) per week for US$275; classes are available for beginning, intermediate and advanced students, with a maximum of twelve students per class. Classes are no larger than 10 to 12 students.

Natalis Language Center *(☎ 222-8721; w www.natalislang.com; Vicuña Mackenna 6, 7th floor)* is another centrally located alternative. Here, a 100-hour intensive course (four to five weeks) costs US$400, with a maximum of five students per class. One-on-one conversation classes are also possible.

Instituto Chileno de la Lengua *(ICHIL; ☎ 697-2728; w www.cmet.net/ichil; Riquelme 226, Barrio Brasil)* offers classes (maximum 10 students) at four different levels. A one-month intensive course, including 100 lessons, accommodations with a family and excursions, is US$610. Private lessons are US$15/hour.

Andes Escuela de Español *(☎ 635-4776; e info@latinimmersion.com; Tomás Andrews 074; m Baquedano)*, in Providencia, is the local Latin Immersion school. Classes have a maximum of five students, and homestay accommodations can be organized by the school. A two-week course is US$340, with 20 hours of classes per week.

ORGANIZED TOURS

If your time is limited, consider an organized tour of Santiago and its surroundings.

Casa Colorada tourist office *(☎ 632-7783; w www.cuidad.cl/turismo; Merced 860)* offers free walking tours of the central area Tuesday mornings at 10:30am and Wednesday afternoons at 3pm; a separate museum tour (US$1) takes place at the same times. A church circuit departs Mondays at 10:30am. All tours accommodate English speakers. You can also take a tour of Cerro Santa Lucía from the tourist office on Cerro Santa Lucía on Thursdays at 11am.

TurisTour *(☎ 551-9370; e operaciones@ turistour.cl)* runs tours of the capital (US$22), excursions to Viña del Mar and Valparaíso (US$30), visits to wineries (US$24/30 half/ full day), visits to Isla Negra and Pomaire (US$50) and ski trips to Farellones, Valle del Nevado and Portillo (see Ski Resorts in the Around Santiago section, later).

Sportstour *(☎ 549-5200, 09-325-0606; e mailbox@sportstour.cl; Moneda 970, 14th floor)* has similar offerings.

The friendly folks at **Chilean Travel Service** (CTS; ☎ 251-0400; w www.ctsturismo.cl; Antonio Bellet 77, Providencia) offer a range of bus tours with multilingual guides, including half-day panoramic city tours (from US$28, two-person minimum) and a half-day visit to Concha y Toro winery and the Cajón del Maipo (starts at US$35, two-person minimum). Full-day trips (US$46, two-person minimum) to Valparaíso, Viña del Mar and Isla Negra, or to ski resorts, are also available.

The **Chile Information Project** (CHIP; ☎ 777-5376; w www.chip.cl; Av Santa María 227, Oficina 12), on the north side of the Río Mapocho, offers an unusual, human rights–oriented 'Historical Memory' tour that includes visits to Parque por La Paz (see that section under Parks & Gardens, earlier) and, for a different point of view, the Fundación Pinochet. Prices for a half-day tour start from US$25, while a full-day tour, including lunch, costs US$55 to US$95, depending on the number of passengers. Chip also offers tours in the vicinity of Santiago, including Neruda's Isla Negra and regional vineyards.

For other tours and activities outside the city, see the Around Santiago section.

SPECIAL EVENTS

Santiago hosts a variety of special events throughout the year. January's **Festival del Barrio Brasil** highlights an area currently undergoing a major renewal, with exhibitions, theater, dance and music in Plaza Brasil. Late in the month, in the suburban comuna of San Bernardo, the five-day **Festival Nacional del Folclore** celebrates traditional Chilean music and dance.

In late March, Aeropuerto Los Cerrillos, southwest of town (see the Santiago Metro map), is the site of the **Feria Internacional del Aire y del Espacio**, a major international air show attended by an odd combination of arms merchants and the general public.

On May 4, the **Gran Premio Hipódromo Chile** (at the Hipódromo Chile, see the Santiago map) determines Chile's best three-year-old race horses. Over the course of the winter, several other racing events take place here and at the Club Hípico de Santiago, south of Barrio Brasil.

Rodeo season starts in the first week of September, though most events take place in Rancagua, 90 miles south of Santiago. Call Federación del Rodeo Chileno at ☎ 02-699-0115 for details or check w www.rodeo chileno.cl.

The **Feria Internacional de Artesanía**, held in the Centro's Parque General Bustamente in the first week of November and organized by the Universidad Católica, is the city's best crafts festival.

Santiago's annual **Feria Internacional del Libro** takes place the last week of November in the Estación Mapocho, near the river. Though not so large as Buenos Aires' festival, it attracts authors from throughout the country and the continent, including big names such as Peru's Mario Vargas Llosa and Argentina's Federico Andahazi. In addition, new and antiquarian books are sold.

PLACES TO STAY

Santiago has a good range of accommodations, from hostels in grand old mansions to soaring deluxe hotels, but make sure you seriously consider location as well as amenities – it's no fun if you're stuck miles from transportation, restaurants and nightlife. The Centro, while close to the action in daylight hours, is actually very dead at night, and some of the fancy upscale hotels are a long taxi ride from just about everywhere.

Budget

Santiago has abundant budget lodging, especially north and west of the Centro, but the nicest areas with budget beds are Barrio Brasil and Barrio Paris Londres. Also, language schools (see that section, earlier) can usually arrange cheap homestays with families.

Hostels La Casa Roja (☎ 696-4241; e info@ lacasaroja.tie.cl; Av Agustinas 2113, Barrio Brasil; dorm beds US$5.80, singles & doubles US$15, breakfast US$2.50), a splendid 19th-century mansion, is the new kid on the block. This Australian-owned hostel is a good hub for travelers looking to hook up and share experiences. There are elegant lounge areas, including pleasant patios, as well as a large back garden and a communal kitchen. Internet access is free for the first 20 minutes, and the hostel is happy to store luggage without charge. Anyone interested in historic architecture and a communal atmosphere should look no further. Reservations are recommended.

SCS Habitat (☎ 683-3732; e scshabitat@ yahoo.com; San Vicente 1798; dorm beds US$6, breakfast US$1.50) is in an inconvenient neighborhood about 10 minutes south of Barrio Brasil's Estación Central by *micro* or taxi. The US-run lodging is a bit scruffy and cramped but still popular, mainly because the manager is a good information resource. To get there from Estación Central, take micro 335, 358 or 360 down Exposición to San Vicente and walk east one block. See the Santiago map for location.

The **Hostelling International Hostel** (☎ 671-8532, 688-6434, fax 672-8880; e histgoch@entelchile.net; Cienfuegos 151, Barrio Brasil; ⓜ Los Héroes; dorm beds members/nonmembers US$9/11; singles/ doubles US$18/20) is a custom-built facility in a convenient location. There are 120 beds in four- and six-bed rooms with locking closets. Common areas are ample, including a pleasant cafeteria, TV lounge and patio, and there's a quick, inexpensive laundry service. If the hostel is not crowded, it's possible to have a dorm room all to yourself for about double the bed rate. If you're not a member, note that guests automatically become members after six nights.

Hotels, Hospedajes & Residenciales Santiago's cheapest hotels are in a seedy neighborhood near the Estación Mapocho – around General Mackenna, Amunátegui, San Pablo and San Martín – where accommodations range from squalid to basic and acceptable. Single women may feel uncomfortable here late at night, especially on General Mackenna, where many prostitutes hang out. If you can afford it, it's worth shelling out a few extra bucks to stay in Barrio Brasil or Barrio Paris Londres.

Hotel Indiana (☎ 671-4251; Rosas 1343, Centro; per person without/with private bath US$5/6.50), a dilapidated house with dependable hot water, is Santiago's Israeli hangout. It's really pretty grimy, and there are signs everywhere asserting petty house rules, but some travelers don't seem to mind.

Nuevo Hotel (☎ 671-5698; San Pablo 1182/Morandé 791, Centro; beds US$5 with shared bath) is cheap but nothing flashy, and the rooms are insecure – store your valuables safely.

Hotel Caribe (☎ 696-6681; San Martín 851, Centro; per person US$7.50) has dark, spartan rooms and dingy shared bathrooms. This labyrinthine hotel is popular with travelers even though it's incredibly run down. Ask for a room at the back or upstairs, since foot traffic makes the lobby and passageway a bit noisy.

Residencia Tabita (☎ 671-5700, fax 696-9492; Príncipe de Gales 81, Centro; per person with shared bath US$10, including breakfast) is closer to the Alameda. It's run by an aged Marilyn Monroe lookalike and is a definite step up from the cheapest places. It's centrally located, the rooms are large and clean, and there's plenty of lounging space with TV and stereo. The tiki-style dining room is a highlight.

Residencial del Norte (☎ 695-1876, fax 696-9251; Catedral 2207, Barrio Brasil; ⓜ Santa Ana or República; per person US$10 with shared bath & breakfast) has a nice family atmosphere. The rooms are enormous, with ample furniture and balconies, but the numerous micros passing nearby can be noisy.

Residencial Alemana (☎ 671-2388; Av República 220; ⓜ República; per person shared bath US$11.50, including breakfast) is a well kept, charming Old World place in a neighborhood full of university buzz; it's one of the nicest budget options.

Residencial Mery (☎ 696-8883; Pasaje República 36; US$13/18 per person with shared/private bath) is closer to the metro than Residencial Alemana but is rather bland.

Residencial Londres (☎/fax 638-2215; Londres 54; ⓜ Universidad de Chile; singles/doubles/triples with shared bath US$11/22/32.50, doubles/triples with private bath US$25/37, breakfast US$1) is a popular place in atmospheric Barrio París Londres, south of the Alameda near Iglesia San Francisco. It's an outstanding value, with beautiful, clean, secure rooms with parquet floors and antique furniture, as well as pleasant and helpful staff. Make reservations or arrive early, since it fills up quickly – singles are almost impossible to get. There's no heating, so unless you're part polar bear, this isn't the best option in winter.

Hotel París (☎ 639-4037; París 813; ⓜ Universidad de Chile; singles/doubles start at US$23/27 with private bath, breakfast US$1.60) doesn't have the charm of Residencial Londres, but it's not a bad option at all. The rooms are small but clean and comfy, though some are a little dark. Internet access is available for US$1.30 an hour.

Mid-Range

Santiago's mid-range accommodations are mostly in the Centro, though a couple have managed to carve out a niche in Providencia, and there are some great places in Barrio Santa Lucía. Many of these hotels have nice, simple little rooms with private bath, telephone, TV and heating, and breakfast is usually included in the room rate.

The professionally run **City Hotel** (☎/fax 695-4526; Compañía 1063, Centro; singles/doubles US$24/30 with private bath and TV; ⓜ Plaza de Armas), smack in the middle of the Centro, has a certain Gotham City-esque appeal, with original, polished Art Deco fittings, huge bathrooms and friendly staff. The rooms are a little bit worn but are a great value.

Hotel di Maurier (☎ 695-7750, fax 696-6193; Moneda 1510, Centro; singles/doubles with shared bath US$21/25, with private bath US$27/33) is well kept and convenient to the airport bus, but most of the rooms are small and dark.

Hotel Europa (☎ 695-2448, fax 697-1378; Amunátegui 449, Centro; singles/doubles US$27/34 with breakfast) offers small, simple but tidy rooms.

Apart Hotel Monteverde (☎ 777-3607, fax 737-0341; Pío Nono 193, Barrio Bellavista; singles/doubles US$26/39 with kitchenette & breakfast), pretty much the only hotel in Bellavista, is an ugly boxy place but not a bad value; note that the street is noisy into the wee hours on weekends.

Hotel Foresta (☎/fax 639-6262, fax 632-2996; Subercaseaux 353, Centro; singles/doubles US$30/36 with private bath, phone, cable & minibar) is in the interesting Barrio Santa Lucía, close to happening bars and restaurants. The hotel is cute and cozy and a first-rate choice.

Hotel Tokyo (☎ 698-4500; Almirante Barroso 160, Barrio Brasil; singles/doubles US$35/45) has spacious gardens and an English-speaking owner who will exchange books. Prices include breakfast; it's an excellent value, though it can get a little cool in winter.

Hotel Santa Lucía (☎ 639-8201, fax 633-1844; Huérfanos 779, 4th floor, Centro;

singles/doubles US$36/42 with TV, telephone, strongbox, refrigerator & private bath) is a good value and is central. Rooms are pleasant and have glistening bathrooms.

Hotel Montecarlo (☎ 639-2945, fax 633-5577; Subercaseaux 209, Centro; singles/doubles US$41/48) is in Barrio Santa Lucía and has jolly staff. The rooms are fitted out with bizarre faux-Deco furniture – the beds are really something to behold.

ChilHotel (☎ 235-0713, fax 264-1323; ⓔ info@chilhotel.cl; Cirujano Guzmán 103, Providencia; ⓜ Manuel Montt; singles/doubles US$42/45) is the cheapest option in Providencia. The rooms are very small but clean and comfortable, as long as you don't mind a sterile aesthetic, and the staff speak some English. The rates are discounted by as much as 25% when the hotel isn't busy.

Hotel Libertador (☎ 639-4212, fax 633-7128; Alameda 853, Centro; singles/doubles US$42/51) has been refurbished with colonial-looking furniture and is comfortable, if a little bland; street noise can be a problem.

Hotel Gran Palace (☎ 671-2551, fax 695-1095; Huérfanos 1178, Centro; singles/doubles from US$45/55, including breakfast & cable) is quite a bargain, with friendly staff and fancy-pants rooms.

Hotel Panamericano (☎ 672-3060; Teatinos 320, Centro; singles/doubles US$45/55) is a trifle noisy and suffers from surly management, but the rooms aren't bad.

Hotel Vegas (☎ 632-2498, fax 632-5084; Londres 49, Centro; ⓜ Universidad de Chile; singles/doubles US$48/55, breakfast US$6), in beautiful Barrio París Londres, is one of Santiago's better mid-range bargains, despite a slightly cheesy remodeling job. Rooms are comfy and heated.

Hotel España (☎ 698-5245; Morandé 510, Centro; ⓜ Morandé or Plaza de Armas; singles/doubles with private bath & cable TV US$55/65, including breakfast & Internet) is central and newly renovated though somewhat corporate and kitschy.

Top End

Santiago has an abundance of expensive, first-rate hotels, including well-known international chains, mostly in Providencia and Las Condes. They usually offer gourmet restaurants, cafés, bars and money-exchange services for their clients. Some of the best-value places are at the low end of the range.

Hotel Montebianco (☎ *233-0427, fax 233-0420; Isidora Goyenechea 2911, Las Condes; singles/doubles from US$64/82, including breakfast; discounts for longer stays*) is a sparkling place that has rooms with attractive attached patios. Rooms are air-conditioned and come with cable TV and telephone. The friendly staff speak English, and the hotel offers excursions to the coast, the mountains and other interesting spots.

Hotel Diego de Velásquez (☎/fax *234-4400;* e *htldiego@tnet.cl; Guardia Vieja 150, Providencia;* Ⓜ *Pedro de Valdivia or Los Leones; singles/doubles US$65/75 with breakfast, cable, phone & minibar*) has very spacious rooms with views of the city lights. The hotel is well run, and the staff speak English.

Hotel Diego de Almagro (☎ *672-6002; Alameda 1485, Centro; standard/executive rooms US$66/86, including breakfast*) is a modern hotel that sprouts out of the ornate Palacio Rivas in the Barrio Cívico. The rooms are nicely decorated, and the hotel sports a pool, restaurant, café and bar.

Majestic Hotel (☎ *695-8366, fax 697-4051; Santo Domingo 1526, Centro; singles/doubles US$70/80, including breakfast;* Ⓜ *Santa Ana*) has staff who will bend over backward to please and superb Indian food (see Places to Eat, Santiago Centro). Rooms have coffee-making facilities, and there's a pool. Noise from the nearby freeway might be a problem for insomniacs.

Hotel Orly (☎ *231-8947, fax 252-0051; Av Pedro de Valdivia 27, Providencia;* Ⓜ *Pedro de Valdivia; singles/doubles US$75/95, including breakfast*), in a handsome older building, reflects the Providencia of more dignified, less commercial times. Rooms are a little small, mainly because they're well padded with floral curtains and boofy cushions, but the hospitable staff are a big plus.

Hotel Torremayor (☎ *234-2000, fax 234-3779; Av Ricardo Lyon 322, Providencia; room/suite US$80/130, including breakfast*) is comfortable and run by nice people. Rooms with a desktop computer cost only a few dollars more than regular rooms. There's also a fine Italian restaurant.

Eurotel (☎/fax *232-7178;* w *www.eurotel .cl; Guardia Vieja 285, Providencia;* Ⓜ *Los Leones; singles & doubles US$99, including breakfast*) is a swish French-owned hotel. It oozes 21st-century chic and offers all sorts of

useful extras, including 24-hour Internet access and spring-water dispensers in the passageways. The rooms are spacious, quiet and comfortable, with extra-large bathrooms. Discounts of 10% and more are often given on the rack rates, especially for stays of a week a more.

Hotel Carrera (☎ *698-2011, fax 672-1083;* e *hotelcarrera@carrera.cl; Teatinos 180, Centro; regular/executive rooms US$110/140, including breakfast*) is a venerable hotel overlooking Plaza de la Constitución. Built in 1940 and with exquisite Art Deco details, this is a beautiful, grand place. The rooms are classically decorated and sumptuous; the suite-like executive rooms are even plusher, with bathrooms double the size of most hotel rooms. The hotel has three restaurants, a rooftop pool and a gym.

Sheraton San Cristóbal (☎ *233-5000, fax 234-1729; Av Santa María 1742; standard/ executive rooms start at US$120/140, children stay free*) is set in peaceful surroundings north of the Mapocho, close to Providencia. It is one of the city's best hotels, with business center, boutiques and shops, a beauty parlor, doctor, florist, fitness center, indoor and outdoor pools, tennis court, golf course, bars, restaurant and babysitting.

Hotel Plaza San Francisco (☎ *639-3832, fax 639-7826;* e *fcohotel@entelchile.net; Alameda 816, Centro; rooms start at US$145 in winter, more expensive in summer*) has a reputation for fine food and wine and excellent service. The rooms are woody, with tapestries, fine furniture and modern conveniences. Its award-winning restaurant is well known for its new Chilean cuisine. The wine shop stocks a daunting selection of Chilean wines at wholesale prices.

Hotel Fundador (☎ *632-2566; Serrano 34, Centro; singles/doubles/suites for US$150/170/230, including breakfast*), on the edge of the quaint Barrio París Londres, is a top-class place with a gym, swimming pool and business center. Rooms are plushly furnished and come with all modern conveniences.

Hyatt Regency Santiago (☎ *218-1234, fax 218-2513; Av Kennedy 4601; singles/ doubles US$155/175, including breakfast*) is a gleaming golden tower in Las Condes. All rooms offer spectacular views of Santiago and the Andes.

Marriott Hotel (☎ 426-2000, fax 426-2001; Av Presidente Kennedy 5741, Las Condes; rooms start at US$198) is the city's newest hotel. It features cafés, restaurants, bars and lounges, 24-hour room service, childcare services, a hair salon, a full business center, an outdoor pool and a health club.

Santiago Park Plaza (☎ 233-6363, fax 233-6668; Ricardo Lyon 207, Providencia; Ⓜ Los Leones; singles/doubles start at US$210/220, including breakfast; children under seven stay free) is lushly furnished with dark woods, Persian rugs and soft lighting. Rooms feature fireplace and fresh flowers, bathrobe and bath slippers, in addition to the usual comforts. Executive rooms and all suites come with full multimedia computer, video-conference camera and color printer.

Hotel Crowne Plaza (☎ 638-1042, fax 633-6015; Alameda 136, Centro; rooms from US$239) has been remodeled and comes with business centers, an outdoor pool and rooftop tennis courts, as well as pleasant bars and restaurants. The rooms are nicely appointed, and staff are efficient and polite.

PLACES TO EAT

The best selection of restaurants is in Barrio Santa Lucía, Barrio Bellavista and the comunas of Providencia and Las Condes.

While most restaurants offer up traditional Chilean food – which is heavy on the meat and seafood and light on the vegetables – you can also find very good Italian, Indian, Middle Eastern, Japanese, Mexican and Peruvian places.

Bear in mind that Chileans eat their main meal in the middle of the day, between 1pm and 3pm, and then don't head out to eat at night until after 10pm. With the exception of fast-food joints and cafés that serve *onces* (sandwiches, cakes, tea and coffee), most restaurants close their doors between 3:30pm and 9pm. Also, your options will be severely limited on Sundays, when even fast food can be hard to find.

Santiago Centro

For cheap snacks, pastries and drinks, there's a string of stand-up places in the **Portal Fernández Concha**, on the south side of the Plaza de Armas, serving empanadas, *completos* (hot dogs), sandwiches and fried chicken.

One of Santiago's best lunch options is the wrought-iron **Mercado Central** (open 6am-4pm Sun-Thur, 6am-8pm Fri, 6am-6pm Sat; Ⓜ Cal y Canto), which is these days mostly taken over by seafood restaurants (the main vegetable market is across the Puente Cal y Canto at the huge La Vega Central).

Donde Augusto (☎ 672-2829; Local 66 & 166), in the Mercado Central, is the most obviously appealing option for fish and shellfish, though the food is not dramatically different from what's served at the smaller, cheaper places on the periphery.

Chez Henry (☎ 696-6612; Portal Fernández Concha 962; meals start at US$6) is highly regarded and popular. The traditional Chilean menú includes *cazuela de ave* (US$5.80) and *arroz valenciana* (US$7.50), which is cooked to perfection and packed with seafood, chicken and pork. Ready-made items from the take-away deli are cheaper and just as good.

Bar Central (San Pablo 1063) serves cheap, generous portions of excellent seafood and is also popular with locals.

Bar Nacional 1 (☎ 695-3368; Bandera 317), serving inexpensive Chilean specialties such as *pastel de choclo*, is a lively sparkling place that's a favorite with office workers. It's also a bar and has a good range of wines, and the fresh juices are delicious. Cheerful bow-tied waiters add extra jolliness. **Bar Nacional 2** (☎ 696-5986; Huérfanos 1151) is a nearby branch.

Au Bon Pain (Miraflores 235) serves reliable sandwiches and croissants.

100% Natural (☎ 697-1860; Valentín Letelier 1319), directly west of La Moneda, is a good central place for *onces*, juices and sandwiches.

El Naturista (☎ 698-4122; Moneda 846 • Vitacura 2571; lunch US$5) is another vegetarian place. The range of dishes is daunting (pizzas, pancakes, lasagne etc; all around US$3.50), but the food is on the bland side and the setting lacks any cozy ambience. One plus: the mint tea is made with fresh leaves.

El Vegetariano (☎ 639-7063; Huérfanos 827, Local 18), in an arcade off Huérfanos, serves fresh juices, salads, pasta (US$3) and rice dishes that are all vegetarian, but don't expect anything terribly delicious – it's all a bit tasteless.

Restaurant Majestic (☎ 695-8366; Santo Domingo 1526), in the Majestic Hotel, is the place to go for exquisite Indian food in sumptuous surroundings. The extensive menu stretches from tandoori to curries, and you'll want to order everything – go with a group of friends so you can share dishes. Service is formal but not overly fussy. Expect to pay around US$20 per person.

Le Due Torri (☎ 633-3799; *San Antonio 258*) has a super-stylish front room with a terrazzo floor and wood-paneled walls, but the menu offers standard, slightly soggy Italian food with no surprises. It's fairly pricey, with risotto al mare going for US$11; skip the salads, which are nothing special.

Da Carla (☎ 633-5201; *MacIver 577; meals US$20 per person*) is a classy, formal Italian place with starched table cloths; naturally, it is rather expensive.

Barrio Santa Lucía

Just south of the Mapocho there's a cluster of restaurants (and bars) in a happening neighborhood in and around Plaza Mulato Gil de Castro, on Lastarria near Merced. Aside from the places listed here, there are a few tiny **Middle Eastern cafés** on Merced that serve excellent sweets, spinach empanadas and Turkish coffee.

Emporio La Rosa (☎ 638-9257; *Merced 291*) is a sunny grocery and café. It stocks superb bread and pastries and also sells pasta and hard-to-find essentials like caviar, paté and Nutella.

Pérgola de la Plaza (☎ 639-3604; *Lastarria 321; lunch specials US$6*) has tasty lunches that are great bargains, and there's a nice patio area where you can soak up sun.

Don Victorino (☎ 639-5263; *Lastarria 138*) is one of several venues that offer excellent lunches at moderate prices; service is first-rate, and there's a nice relaxed atmosphere inside.

In the same category as Don Victorino is nearby **Gatopardo** (☎ 633-6420; *Lastarria 192; meal US$16*), which serves French-nuanced continental cuisine in some cozy surrounds.

Rincón Español (☎ 633-9466; *Rosal Interior 346*), in a cul-de-sac off Rosal, is an earthy cavernous place serving Spanish tapas and meals.

R (☎ 664-9844; *Lastarria 307; lunch US$7.50*) is a quirky yet elegant spot serving inventive, relatively inexpensive food. Highlights include chicken stuffed with prunes (US$8) and flounder with a walnut and butter sauce (US$11).

Les Assassins (☎ 638-4280; *Merced 297-B; lunch US$7*), where French cuisine is the rule, offers outstanding fixed-price lunches. The downstairs is tobacco-free.

Izakaya Yoko (☎ 632-1954; *Merced 456; meals US$5-6*) has cheap, just passable sushi; you'll find much classier stuff in Bellavista and Las Condes.

Kintaro (☎ 638-2448; *Monjitas 460*) is a popular little Japanese place; sushi for two costs only about US$9.

Barrio Bellavista

North of the Mapocho, a short walk from the Baquedano metro station, Pablo Neruda's old haunts offer great dining. Many, though not the best, restaurants line both sides of Pío Nono between the bridge and Plaza Caupolicán.

El Rinconcito (*Manzano & Dávila Baeza*) is in Recoleta's Patronato district, a bit to the west (see the Santiago map). It's a very cheap Middle Eastern *picada* (informal family restaurant) run by a Lebanese immigrant who arrived by way of Chicago; it's an excellent place for hummus, falafel and the like.

Di Simoncelli (*Dardignac 197*) is basic and unglamorous, with cheap pasta dishes and set lunches.

Donde La Elke (☎ 735-0526; *Dardignac 68*) is a bright little café-like place serving very good inexpensive set lunches (US$2.80).

Venezia (☎ 737-0900; *Pío Nono 200*) is a moderately priced Chilean *picada* (informal family restaurant) where Neruda used to eat. It has a great old-time atmosphere.

Galindo (☎ 771-0116; *Dardignac 098*) is a traditional, bohemian place that was one of Neruda's favorites. It's refreshingly unpretentious, and though the food is standard Chilean fare, it's reliable and hearty.

El Antojo de Gauguin (☎ 737-0398; *Pío Nono 69*) is a cozy Mediterranean restaurant and one of few places in the area that offers fixed-price lunches on Saturdays.

La Bohème (☎ 737-4110; *Bombero Núñez 336*) is a casual French bar-eatery frequented by the thirty-something crowd. Try the onion soup (US$3.60) or the quiche (US$4.60).

Zen (☎ 737-9520; Dardignac 0175; lunch US$10) is a fairly traditional Japanese place with unflashy, minimalist décor.

Cava de Dardignac (☎ 777-6268; Dardignac 0191; dishes US$8) is a Portuguese wine bar/restaurant with a simple, re-strained interior; soothing bossa nova music hovers in the background.

Sarita Colonia (☎ 737-0242; Dardignac 50) is a magical, velvet-curtains kind of place. Daring and woman-run, it serves up great drinks and superb food, including sushi and ceviche. The upstairs lounge area is a feast for the eyes and has plenty of sofas to sink into.

Azul Profundo (☎ 738-0288; Constitución 0111) serves fine seafood amid elaborate maritime décor that gives you the impression you're under water. Though it's one of the more expensive places in Bellavista, it's quite reasonable nonetheless. Try the ceviche (US$6.60), the *ostiones* or *machas parmesana* (US$8), or the *risotto de mariscos* for two (US$18).

Etniko (☎ 732-0119; Constitución 172) is the favorite cool, stylie place of the moment. It functions as a bar as well as a restaurant, and there's a striking low-lit central courtyard. Overall, the mood is mellow, even though there's usually a DJ spinning. The food has an Asian bent; large wok stirfries (US$6.60) and sushi (US$5-7) are the standouts.

Ali Baba (☎ 732-7036; Santo Filomena 102; closed Sun; appetizers & salads US$5; main courses US$6-12, meze tablas for two US$13) is a beautifully decked-out, woman-owned Lebanese-Palestinian restaurant offering lots of delicious vegetarian options, as well as exotic meat and fish dishes. With 24 hours' notice, special 'masa' dishes such as couscous (US$7) can be prepared. There's an extensive wine list, and you're welcome to smoke a waterpipe. On Fridays, the restaurant is enlivened with music and dancing, and a fortune-teller sometimes drops in to read coffee grounds.

Muñeca Brava (☎ 732-1338; Mallinkrodt 170) features live jazz and specializes in fine meats, including *parrillada* (US$20 for two people). The interior is a bit brassy, but it sets the right mood.

Como Agua para Chocolate (☎ 777-8740; Constitución 88), designed by the same architect as Azul Profundo, is a magical Mexican place with imaginative, colorful décor and great use of natural light. The menu was created in consultation with the founder of Barrio Brasil's Plaza Garibaldi.

Rinconcito Peruano (☎ 735-0634; Antonia López de Bello 60; opens 8pm) is a vast place serving outstanding Peruvian food.

El Otro Sitio (☎ 777-3059; Antonia López de Bello 53) is another good Peruvian place, though the décor is not as fetching as Rinconcito Peruano.

El Caramaño (☎ 737-7043; Purísima 257) has very good Chilean food and friendly service.

Tasca Mediterránea (☎ 737-1542; Purísima 161) offers a range of Meditteranean dishes and has a laid-back atmosphere.

Rodizio (☎ 777-9240; Bombero Núñez 388; all-you-can-eat US$23) is a snazzy Brazilian *parrilla*.

El Tallarín Gordo (☎ 737-8567; Purísima 254) serves Italian food but lags behind Bellavista's more innovative locales.

Providencia

Empanadium (☎ 333-1748; Av Suecia 0735), tucked in among the pubs on busy Suecia, is open 24 hours and serves over 20 different varieties of empanada (around US$1). It's great for a quick stand-up bite.

Au Bon Pain (☎ 233-6912; Av Providencia 1936; Ⓜ Pedro de Valdivia), the chain, serves predictable sandwiches and croissants and is a good option for a fast bite.

For ice cream, go to **Bravíssimo** (☎ 235-2511; Av Providencia 1406), near Manuel Montt station. Besides insanely huge sundaes, there are surprisingly excellent sandwiches and baguettes, though the '80s color-clash ice-cream parlor décor is kind of hard to take; sunglasses might help.

La Mia Pappa (☎ 235 1302; Av 11 de Septiembre 1351; pasta US$2, menú del dia US$2) is a incredibly popular all-you-can-eat pasta joint – you'll have to fight for a table at lunchtime. The food is freshly prepared and not bad, though it has a definite cafeteria flavor to it.

In an interesting part of Providencia with winding streets and old, opulent apartment buildings, **Babilonia Bar** (☎ 236-0360; Av José Infante 28; lunch US$4.50) is a chic little restaurant with simple wooden furniture and a relaxed comfortable vibe. Simple, delicious food is the order of the day.

MoMa (☎ 232-6278; Guardia Vieja 208) is a tiny place with a straight-edged moderne interior. It serves drinks and Japanese food; the US$6 lunch menú is great value.

Café del Patio (☎ 236-1251; Av Providencia 1670, Local 8-A; ⓜ Manuel Montt) has an exciting vegetarian and seafood menu; servings are huge, so consider splitting one dish between two. The mushrooms with rice and salad (US$7.50) is filling, subtle and delicious.

The **Phone Box Pub** (☎ 235-9972; Av Providencia 1670; ⓜ Manuel Montt; lunch US$7-8) has a grapevine arbor patio that's a pleasant sanctuary from the busy avenue outside. Homesick Brits will find Santiago's best pub lunches here.

El Huerto (☎ 233-2690; Orrego Luco 054; ⓜ Pedro de Valdivia) serves up imaginative meatless meals so good that even carnivores flock here. The smaller menu at its adjacent café, **La Huerta**, offers similar food at much lower prices.

Casa de la Cultura de México (☎ 334-3848; Bucarest 162; ⓜ Los Leones), affiliated with Mexico's diplomatic mission, features outstanding regional dishes rather than Tex-Mex borderlands food; it also sells superb crafts and runs a bookstore.

Liguria (☎ 235-7914; Av Providencia 1373; ⓜ Manuel Montt) is a sweetly decorated place with gingham tablecloths, little floral lampshades and walls covered in old photos and pictures. But don't be fooled by all the flowery flourishes – this is one of the rowdiest places around, attracting a chattery afternoon crowd that knows how to mingle. The food has an Italian tilt and is a definite cut above regular Santiago fare, though it's not particularly pricey. The waiters are sharp, and there's a lengthy wine list.

La Pizza Nostra (☎ 231-9853; Av Providencia 1975; dishes US$8) is chainlike but is open when most other places are closed (eg, on Sunday). It offers a good range of pastas (most of which are overly creamy), pizzas and salads, as well as excellent fresh juices.

Barrio Brasil

West of the Vía Norte Sur, Barrio Brasil's dining scene is a combination of older, traditional restaurants and newer, more innovative eateries that rival Bellavista's restaurants but are substantially cheaper. The nearest metro stations are Los Héroes and República.

Las Vacas Gordas (☎ 697-1066; Cienfuegos 280) is buzzing place always packed with happy meat-eaters tucking into large steaks. As well as fabulous *parrillada*, it serves seafood (including a good ceviche) and pasta, and the service is excellent. There's none of the musty atmosphere that you find at many restaurants serving traditional food – everything is fresh, bright and efficient. Make sure you call ahead.

Ocean Pacific's (☎ 697-2413; Av Ricardo Cumming 221) is a reasonably priced, family-style seafood restaurant with excellent, friendly service and particularly delicious homemade bread.

Ostras Squella (☎ 699-4883; Ricardo Cumming 94), close to Ocean Pacific's, is slightly pricey but known for the high quality of its seafood.

The popular **Tongoy** (☎ 697-1144; Bulnes 91) serves up fish dishes in atmospheric old-style surroundings.

Plaza Garibaldi (☎ 699-4278; Moneda 2319, Centro) is moderately priced and has great Mexican dishes and margaritas.

Puente de los Suspiros (☎ 696-7962; Av Brasil 75; lunch US$6) is one of Santiago's best Peruvian bargains.

Manos Morenos (☎ 681-9355; Maipú 363; formerly Puro Chile) combines imaginative décor with upscale Chilean, Peruvian and Spanish food. The focus is on seafood, but all sorts of things are available.

Peperone (☎ 687-9180; Huérfanos 1954) is a supercute candlelit neighborhood café serving tea, coffee, beer, fresh juices and 20 different kinds of empanadas (around US$1).

Ñuñoa

Plaza Ñuñoa offers a mix of solid traditional eateries and funky new dining establishments. To get to Plaza Ñuñoa from elsewhere in the city, take bus Nos 212, 338 or 382 from Plaza Italia (the area around Plaza Baquedano), 433 from Alameda and Vicuña Mackenna, 606 from the Terminal de Buses Santiago, 600 from Estación Central or 243 from Compañía. Metrobús directly connects Estación Salvador with Plaza Ñuñoa.

Fuente Suiza (☎ 204-7199; Irarrázaval 3361) has been around forever and is famous for its fried empanadas and large, succulent *lomo* (pork) sandwiches.

Las Lanzas (Trucco 25) is a popular no-frills picada with an excellent lunchtime menú.

El Quarto Café (☎ 225-1495; Trucco 35; meals US$4.50) has a healthy lunch menú featuring rarities such as Caesar salad and lentil soup.

El Amor Nunca Muere (☎ 274-9432; Trucco 43; open dinner only) is an informal place offering French and international dishes, including crêpes and fondue.

Café de la Isla (☎ 341-5389; Irarrázaval 3465) is an interesting Cuban eatery with good sandwiches and excellent juices.

Ebano (☎ 209-5220; Manuel de Salas 123) specializes in soul food, though it dishes out sushi and fusion food as well. It's also a bar.

La Tecla (☎ 274-3603; Doctor Johow 320) is a groovy bar and snackeria with pancakes, pizzas and so on.

Las Condes

Most Las Condes eateries are near the Tobalaba metro station, on El Bosque Norte, Apoquindo and Isadora Goyenechea. It's a strangely desolate area without a lot of community spirit, but some of the city's best restaurants, mostly purpose-built affairs, are out here.

At the low end of the scale, the complex of fast-food outlets at the **Food Garden** (Av El Bosque Norte & Roger de Flor) contains a number of decent, inexpensive snack places, including the juice bar **Jugomanía**.

More fast food is available at **Au Bon Pain** (☎ 366-9145; Av El Bosque Norte 0177 • ☎ 331-5048; Av Apoquindo 3575), which has two branches in Las Condes, both serving their standard sandwiches and croissants.

New York Bagel Bakery (☎ 246-3060; Roger de Flor 2894) actually seems like it's been transplanted from New York. It has great bagels with substantial fillings and is one of the best options if you're looking for fast food in this neighborhood.

Café Melba (☎ 232-4546; Don Carlos 2988) serves North American breakfasts all day and is a popular lunch spot.

Putting the heart back into Las Condes, **Tiramisú** (☎ 233-1995; Isadora Goyenechea 3141) is a warm little place with exceptionally delicious and adventurous thin-crust pizzas. If you're suffering from vegetable deprivation, it's worth trekking out here to try the superb arugula pizza (US$7).

Flannery's Irish Geo Pub (☎ 233-6675; Encomenderos 83; lunch US$5-7) has a cozy pub atmosphere with big tables and log fires. The lunches are a good value, and it's a popular weekend hangout. It's one of the few places in Chile with Guinness on tap, making it something of a gringo favorite.

PubLicity (☎ 246-6414; Av El Bosque Norte 0155) is a slightly cheesy pub-style joint that's very popular. It serves decent meals ranging from simple sandwiches to more elaborate fare.

Le Due Torri (☎ 231-3427; Isidora Goyenechea 2908) is a venerable Italian restaurant serving traditional fare.

Shoogun (☎ 231-1604; Enrique Foster Norte 172) is a top-notch Japanese restaurant with an elegant woody interior and a long menu. Sushi for two is US$26, while a sashimi lunch box is US$15. During the week there's an US$8 lunch menú.

Stylish **Cuerovaca** (☎ 206-3911; El Mañío 1659, cnr Av Vitacura), farther north in Vitacura, is the place for a classy meat feast. It's not cheap, but you get plenty of top-quality moo for your money.

In the thick of El Bosque, **Hereford Grill** (☎ 231-9117; Av El Bosque Norte 0355) is another expensive place that attracts beef-eaters.

ENTERTAINMENT

Santiago's main nightlife districts are Barrio Bellavista (Ⓜ Baquedano), Providencia's Av Suecia (Ⓜ Los Leones), Plaza Ñuñoa (most easily reached by bus or taxi) and Barrio Brasil (Ⓜ República & Unión Latinoamericana), though other venues are scattered throughout the city, and there are a few discos out in the Las Condes hills. Remember that, in any event, the metro closes at 10:30pm – around the time most of these places open.

Although venues are listed here in categories, the lines are blurry; it's often difficult to distinguish a pub from a club from a bar. To make matters even more complicated, many bars are also great spots for a bite to eat; see Places to Eat for details.

Bars

La Piojera (☎ 698-1682; Aillavilú 1030, Centro) is a rowdy, cavernous drinking hall near the Mercado Central. It's packed with atmosphere and chicha drinkers, even during the day.

Low-ceilinged **Bar Berri** (☎ 638-4734; Rosal 321, Centro), in Barrio Santa Lucía, is one of Santiago's liveliest, most informal bars;

if you're with a gang of friends, it'll be hard to get past their offer of a bottle of pisco, four mixers and four empanadas for US$20. It also has good, inexpensive lunches.

Café Escondido (☎ 632-7356; *Rosal Interior 346, Centro*) is hidden away in a cul-de-sac in the cute Barrio Santa Lucía neighborhood. It's a cozy place that's good for a relaxed chat and a glass of wine; good salads and other small dishes round out the experience.

La Casa en el Aire (☎ 735-6680; *Antonia López de Bello 0125, Bellavista*) lets you absorb theater, poetry and live music, as well as a few drinks.

Other Bellavista venues featuring music include **Altazor** (☎ 777-9651; *Antonia López de Bello 0189*) and **Da Lua** (*Antonia López de Bello 0126*).

Brannigans (☎ 232-5172; *Av Suecia 035*) and the **Old Boston Pub** (☎ 231-5169; *General Holley 2291*) are two pub-themed bars in the Suecia late-night ghetto.

La Cueva (☎ 681-8489; *Alameda 2733;* Ⓜ *Unión Latinoamericana*) is a meeting spot for Barrio Brasil's student and goth crowd.

HBH Brewery (☎ 204-3075; *Irarrázaval 3176, Ñuñoa*) is a laid-back microbrewery with two styles of beer. It's a popular hangout for students.

Blue Pub (☎ 223-7132; *19 de Abril 3526, Ñuñoa*) has live music, tarot-card readings and a happy hour beginning at 10pm.

Dance Clubs

Most Santiago dance clubs close their doors in February and move up to Valparaíso and

Viña del Mar – worth bearing in mind before you shell out for a taxi to Alto Las Condes. Also, don't bother showing up to any of these places earlier than 1am; a serious night out for Santiaguinos involves staying out till the sun comes up.

The bunch of clubs clustered on and around Av Suecia (Ⓜ Los Leones) in Providencia form Santiago's most concentrated club precinct. There's something eerily artificial and Disney-like about Suecia, as most bars have distinct 'themes,' though it's not always easy to figure out exactly what they are and, once inside, you'll probably find them all pretty much the same. Many of the clubs hold happy hours (two drinks for the price of one), until midnight in some cases, and serve decent if unexceptional food. Nearly all have live music (usually cover versions of international hits), and most dance floors jump to commercial Latin music.

Among the clubs around Suecia are **Boomerang** (☎ 334-5081; *General Holley 2285*), **Mister Ed** (☎ 231-2624; *Av Suecia 0152*), **Kasbba** (☎ 231-7419; *Av Suecia 081*) and **Wall Street** (☎ 232-5548; *General Holley 99*), but there are many, many more.

Tantra Lounge (☎ 732-3268; *Ernesto Pinto Lagarrigue 154, Bellavista*) is where the cool folk go after drinks at Etniko. The music here is strictly techno and house.

La Feria (☎ 777-1685; *Constitución 275, Bellavista*) is the place to go for electronic music.

Bunker (☎ 777-3760; *Bombero Núñez 159, Bellavista*) is one of the venues that

---

Coffee with Legs

Some of Santiago's best espresso and cocoa is served in stand-up cafés in the Centro such as **Café Haití** (*Ahumada 140*) and **Café Caribe** (*Ahumada 120*), almost next door, both of which have many other branches around town.

Some women feel uncomfortable in this kind of coffee bar, which is colloquially referred to as a *café con piernas* (café with legs), since most of them attract a male clientele by requiring their young female staff to dress in tight, revealing minidresses. These cafés are a genuine Chilean invention and apparently have men flocking from all over South America to visit them. While usually very tame, there does seem to be an ascending scale of risqueness; the serious stuff takes place in the cafés with mirror-glass windows (often in arcades), which are pretty much male-only venues. In these tinted-window establishments, the waitresses are likely to be wearing the skimpiest and sheerest of bras and knickers in environs enhanced by disco lights and pumping music. Despite the strip-club ambience, no alcohol is served (at least, that's the official story), and the only things customers can buy are nonalcoholic beer and hot, strong espresso (at least, that's the official story).

makes Bellavista the focus of Santiago's gay life.

Bokhara (☎ 732-1050; Pío Nono 430, Bellavista) is primarily a gay venue. It's relatively small – although mirrors make it seem larger and livelier.

Tadeo (Ernesto Pinto Lagarrigue 282, Bellavista) has a spacious dance floor and attracts a mid-20s crowd.

Havana Salsa (☎ 737-1737; Dominica 142, Bellavista) cleverly recreates the ambience of Old Havana, encouraging even neophytes to salsa, and also serves good food.

Fausto (☎ 777-1041; Av Santa María 0832, Providencia; Ⓜ Salvador) is a stylish, multilevel club with techno-pop music and a gay crowd.

Blondie (☎ 300-9333, 300-3153; Alameda 2879, Barrio Brasil; Ⓜ Unión Latinoamericana) occupies a spectacular old theater. A massive video screen looms over the dance floor, which is awash with goths dancing like bats and Brit-pop fans looking cute in skinny ties. The music alternates between '80s (alternative and mainstream) and more recent British sounds. This is the place to discover Santiago's dark side.

Teatro Carrera (Alameda 2145, cnr Concha y Toro, Barrio Brasil), another ornate old theater, is even more gothicky than Blondie, with nary a Brit-pop kid in sight.

Confitería Las Torres (☎ 698-6220; Alameda 1570, Centro; Ⓜ Los Héroes), an Old World place dating from 1879, has live tango music on weekends. The stage set features enormous blowups of Argentine tango legend Carlos Gardel, and the walls are lined with photographs of Chilean presidents – perhaps the only place in the world where portraits of Allende and Pinochet hang side by side.

Batuta (☎ 274-7096; Jorge Washington 52, Ñuñoa) is a pub-disco with live music as well.

Skuba (☎ 243-1108; Paseo San Damian; Av Las Condes 11271), out in the hills, is popular with young snoots in their mid-20s and early 30s; dress is semiformal and up-to-the-minute.

Scratch (Centro de Eventos, Av Las Condes 10690), also in outer Las Condes, attracts a late-teens to early-20s crowd.

Music & Theater

Teatro Municipal (☎ 369-0282; Agustinas 794, Centro; box office open 10am-7pm Mon-Fri,

10am-2pm Sat & Sun) is the most prestigious performing-arts venue, with offerings from opera and symphony orchestras to musicals. Members have priority, so seats can be hard to come by.

Teatro Universidad de Chile (☎ 634-5295; Baquedano 043, Centro; Ⓜ Baquedano) presents a fall season of ballet and orchestral and chamber music, but it also hosts occasional popular music concerts; acoustics are excellent.

Other venues in the center include the **Escuela de Teatro de la Universidad de Chile** (☎ 634-5295; Morandé 750); the **Teatro Casa Amarilla** (☎ 672-0347; Balmaceda 1301), in the Estación Mapocho cultural center; and the **Teatro Nacional Chileno** (☎ 671-7850; Morandé 25).

Teatro La Comedia (☎ 6391-523; Merced 349; open Thur-Sun), near Cerro Santa Lucía, is well established.

Known for experimental theater, Barrio Bellavista is home to companies such as **Teatro El Conventillo** (☎ 777-4164; Bellavista 173), **Teatro Bellavista** (☎ 735-6264; Dardignac 0110) and **Teatro La Feria** (☎ 737-7371; Crucero Exéter 0250).

Teatro Oriente (☎ 231-7151; Av Pedro de Valdivia 099), in Providencia, doubles as a cinema. Tickets are also available at Av 11 de Septiembre 2214, Oficina 66.

Teatro de la Universidad Católica (☎ 205-5652; Jorge Washington 26) gets much of the credit for Plaza Ñuñoa's renaissance.

Cinemas

There are usually half-price discounts at theaters on Wednesdays.

Santiago's most central multiplex is **Cine Hoyts** (☎ 664-1861; Paseo Huérfanos 735, Centro). **Teatro Oriente** (☎ 231-7151; Pedro de Valdivia 099, Providencia) is another commercial cinema.

Art-house cinemas include **Centro de Extensión de la Universidad Católica** (☎ 686-6516; Alameda 390, Centro); **Cine Alameda** (☎ 639-2479; Alameda 139); **Cine El Biógrafo** (☎ 633-4435; Lastarria 181, Centro), in Barrio Santa Lucía; and **Cine Tobalaba** (☎ 231-6630; Av Providencia 2563, Providencia).

SPECTATOR SPORTS

Club de Huasos Gil Letelier (☎ 563-5848; Carlos Valdovinos 2951, San Joaquin; US$2) holds rodeos in March and September. As this club is in the suburbs, the easiest way to get there is by car.

Soccer

Santiago has several first-division soccer teams: Universidad de Chile, Colo Colo and Universidad Católica. Major matches usually take place at the **Estadio Nacional** (☎ 238-8102; Av Grecia 2001), southeast of the center (see the Santiago map). Any match involving Colo Colo is likely to be fairly exciting, as they have the biggest fan base. Tickets can be bought at the stadium.

Horse Racing

Santiago has two racecourses. The **Hipódromo Chile** (☎ 270-9237; Av Independencia 1715) is at Fermín Vivaceta, north of the Mapocho in the comuna of Independencia (see the Santiago map). Races take place here every Saturday from 2:30pm and on alternate Thursdays.

There's also the grand-looking **Club Hípico de Santiago** (☎ 693-9600; Almirante Blanco Encalada 2540; Ⓜ Unión Latinoamericana), south of the Alameda near Parque O'Higgins (see the Santiago map). Races take place here every Monday from 2:30pm and on alternate Wednesdays.

SHOPPING

Santiago's shops are usually open 9am to 8pm Monday to Friday and 9am to 2pm Saturday, often closing 1pm to 2pm for lunch. Malls and department stores are generally open 10am to 9pm daily.

The Centro's main shopping streets are the busy, pedestrianized Ahumada and Huérfanos, both lined with shoe shops (sorry girls, don't get your hopes up) boutiques and department stores. There's a lot of repetition along these streets, and you may feel as if you're walking in circles even if you're not. Investigate the old galerías for interesting little specialist shops.

Malls & Markets

In keeping with their taste for all things modern and shiny, Chileans love to flock to disorienting, modern shopping centers, including the **Mall Panorámico** (☎ 233-2244; cnr Av 11 de Septiembre & Av Ricardo Lyon, Providencia; Ⓜ Pedro de Valdivia); **Parque Arauco** (☎ 299-0500; Av Kennedy 5413, Las Condes; Ⓜ Escuela Militar); **Apumanque**

(☎ 246-2614; Av Manquehue Sur 31); and the more exclusive **Alto Las Condes** (☎ 299-6999; Av Kennedy 9001). Most of these shopping centers have free shuttles from upscale hotels in the Centro and eastern suburbs. Buses also run from Escuela Militar metro station.

For cheap (though not necessarily great-quality) new clothes, head to the marketlike area known as Patronato, west of Bellavista between Patronato and Manzano streets. Santiago has recently been seized by a passion for second-hand European and North American clothing, and you'll see signs blaring 'Ropa Europea' everywhere you look, particularly along the Alameda near Barrio Brasil. The garments are a complete grab-bag – often nothing special – usually arranged in no particular order.

Wine

Wine shops specializing in Chilean wine are mostly out in Las Condes, including **Vinopolis** (☎ 232-3814; ⓦ www.vinopolis.cl; El Bosque Norte 038), which has very helpful staff, and **El Mundo del Vino** (☎ 244-8888; Isidora Goyenechea 2931), which also stocks wines from elsewhere in the world and offers tastings.

Crafts

Santiago is a hub for handicrafts from all over the country, including handwoven alpaca shawls, Mapuche silver jewelry, lapis lazuli, black pottery and copperware.

For a good selection of indigenous crafts from the Mapuche and Aymara people, as well as from Rapa Nui, visit the **Centro de Exposición de Arte Indígena** (☎ 664-1352; Alameda 499, Centro), at the southwestern corner of Cerro Santa Lucía. Across the Alameda, the **Centro Artesanal Santa Lucía** (Carmen & Diagonal Paraguay) has similar stuff.

Bellavista is also a good area to scout for crafts, both at Pío Nono's nightly and weekend street fair and at shops such as the **Cooperativa Almacén Campesina** (☎ 737-2117; Purísima 303), which stocks beautiful shawls and scarves, as well as pottery and jewelry. Several shops specialize in lapis lazuli jewelry, including **Lapiz Lazuli** (Pío Nono 3). For antiques, try rummaging at **Arte del Mundo** (☎ 735-2507; Dardignac 67), though it's a pretty mixed bag.

The artisans' village at **Centro Artesanal de Los Dominicos** (☎ 245-4152; Av Apoquindo 9085; open 11am-7:30pm daily year-round), at the Dominican monastery in Las Condes, boasts Santiago's largest crafts selection, with goods imported from throughout the country and also made on site. There are also tempting little cafés, and, on weekends, folk music and dancing. Handmade parchment lampshades, jewelry, ceramics, alpaca woolens, copperware, *huaso* horsegear and antique furniture are amongst the goodies you'll find for sale. The quickest way to get there is to take the metro to Escuela Militar and then catch a taxi (US$4) or bus (look for one marked 'Los Dominicos') out along Av Apoquindo. It's also possible to catch bus No 327 from Av Providencia, No 344 from the Alameda or Av Providencia, No 229 from Catedral or Compañía or No 326 from Alameda and Miraflores.

Another market, open in summer only, is the **daily crafts market** on the north side of Av Providencia, at the exit from the Pedro de Valdivia metro station.

In the eastern comuna of Lo Barnechea, beyond Vitacura, the **Feria San Enrique** (☎ 243-4758) features antiques and bric-a-brac, artwork and crafts with a minimum of kitsch. The crafts fair proper starts around 11:30am Sundays, from October through December only. From San Pablo or Compañía in Santiago Centro, or from Av Providencia, take bus No 203, 205 or 206.

GETTING THERE & AWAY

Many major international airlines have offices or representatives in Santiago. See the Air section in the Getting There & Away chapter for a complete list. For a list of LanChile's Santiago offices, as well as sample one-way domestic coach airfares from Santiago, see the Air section in the Getting Around chapter.

For information regarding international buses departing and arriving in Santiago, see the Land section in the Getting There & Away chapter. For a discussion of Santiago's bus terminals, ticket offices, sample fares and bus companies serving various destinations in Chile, see the Bus section in the Getting Around chapter.

For information on trains leaving Santiago, see Train in the Getting Around chapter.

GETTING AROUND
To/From the Airport

Aeropuerto Internacional Arturo Merino Benítez (☎ 601-9001, 601-9709; also known as Pudahuel), which also serves as the airport for most domestic flights, is 26km west of Santiago Centro. Note that although Línea 1 of the metro ends in Pudahuel, the metro does *not* reach the airport.

The cheapest transportation to the airport, **Buses Centropuerto** (☎ 601-9883), charges only US$1/1.80 one-way/return from Plazoleta Los Héroes, outside the Los Héroes metro station in Barrio Brasil. Buses run about every 20 minutes between 5:30am and 10pm.

Slightly more expensive, **TurBus Aeropuerto** (☎ 671-7380; Moneda 1529, Centro) charges US$2/3.50 one-way/roundtrip, and has buses every 15 minutes on weekdays, and every 30 minutes after 8:30pm and on weekends. The trip takes at least a half-hour, depending on traffic. In addition, buses depart from the Tur Bus terminal (Terminal Alameda) every 30 minutes from 6:30am to 9pm daily.

Buses from the airport leave from the front of the international terminal and will drop you at the city terminus at Plazoleta Los Heróes, or at marked stops along the Alameda if you wish to disembark farther west.

Minibuses belonging to **TransVip** (☎ 677-3000), **Delfos** (☎ 766-2290) and **Transfer** (☎ 777-7707) carry passengers door-to-door between the airport and any part of Santiago for US$5-7, depending on the distance from the airport. At the airport, tickets can be purchased in the arrivals hall. Departing passengers should call the day before their flight if possible, but the minibuses will sometimes pick up on short notice.

Taxi fares are negotiable; a cab to or from the Centro can cost anywhere from about US$12 (if your Spanish is good) to US$20, and may be shared.

Bus

Santiago's yellow exhaust–spewing buses (known as *micros*) go everywhere cheaply, but it takes a while to learn the system; check the destination signs in their windows or ask other passengers waiting at the stop. Many buses now have signed, fixed stops, especially in the Centro, but that doesn't necessarily mean they won't stop at other points. Fares vary slightly depending on the bus, but most are US$0.50 per trip; hang on to your ticket, since inspectors may ask for it.

Metro

Carrying nearly a million passengers daily, Santiago's metro system has three separate lines that interlink, and extensions are under construction. For destinations along these lines, it's far quicker to take the metro than a city bus, which must contend with the capital's narrow, congested streets. The metro operates 6:30am to 10:30pm Monday to Saturday, and 8am to 10:30pm Sundays and holidays, but the ticket booths close about 15

minutes before the trains stop running (one good reason to buy a multitrip ticket). Trains are clean, quiet and frequent, but at most hours it's difficult to get a seat.

Fares vary depending on the time of day. The discounted rate (US$0.45) is available 6:30am to 7:15am, 9am to 6pm and 7:30pm 10pm; the normal rate (US$0.60) applies 7:15am to 9am and 6pm to 7:30pm. Tickets can be purchased from agents at each station; a *boleto inteligente* (multitrip ticket) covers 10 trips and costs about US$5.

Tickets have a magnetic strip on the back. After slipping your ticket into a slot, pass through the turnstile and continue to the platform; your ticket is not returned. No ticket is necessary to exit the system.

SANTIAGO METRO

Car

Keep in mind that a car is less useful in Santiago than on excursions beyond the city, since traffic is congested, and parking is difficult and expensive. However, Santiago has dozens of car rental agencies, from internationally known franchises to lesser-known local companies that tend to be cheaper. For rate details, see the Getting Around chapter. Be sure to call around for good deals.

Many companies have airport offices at Pudahuel in addition to the city offices listed below:

Alamo (☎ 225-3061) Av Francisco Bilbao 2486, Providencia

Atal (☎ 235-9222, fax 236-0636) Av Costanera Andrés Bello 1051, Providencia

Automóvil Club de Chile (Acchi; ☎ 212-5702, 274-6261, fax 229-5295) Av Vitacura 8620, Vitacura

Budget (☎ 362-3232, 362-3200) Bilbao 1439, Providencia

Chilean (☎/fax 737-9650; w www.chileanrentacar.cl) Bellavista 0183, Bellavista

Dollar (☎ 202-5510) Av Kennedy 8292, Vitacura

First (☎ 225-6328) Rancagua 0514, Providencia

Hertz (☎ 235-9666, fax 236-0252) Av Andrés Bello 1469, Providencia

Colectivo

Taxi colectivos are, in effect, five-passenger buses on fixed routes. They are quicker and more comfortable than most buses and not much more expensive – about US$0.75 within Santiago city limits, although some colectivos to outlying suburbs such as Puente Alto are a bit dearer. Taxi colectivos resemble ordinary taxis but have an illuminated roof sign indicating their destination and a placard in the window stating the fixed fare.

Taxi

Santiago has abundant metered taxis – black with yellow roofs. Fares vary, but it costs about US$0.25 to *bajar la bandera* ('drop the flag,' ie, start the meter) and about US$0.12 per 200m. Most Santiago taxi drivers are honest, courteous and helpful, but a few will take roundabout routes, and a handful have 'funny' meters.

There is also a system of radio taxis, which can be slightly cheaper. Hotels and restaurants are usually happy to make calls for clients.

Bicycle

Except in poorer barrios and upscale neighborhoods, not many people ride bicycles within the city because of the dense auto traffic, narrow streets and the propensity for cars to take the right-of-way. Recreational cyclists often use sidewalks.

Around Santiago

There are many worthwhile sights outside the capital proper but still within the Región Metropolitana, as well as others outside the region but near enough for reasonable day trips.

POMAIRE

In this small, dusty village near Melipilla, southwest of Santiago, skilled potters spend the days at their wheels producing unique and remarkably inexpensive ceramics. A punchbowl with half a dozen cups, for instance, costs only about US$10. Unfortunately, most items are too large and fragile for travelers to take home, but it's still worth a day trip from the capital for a tour and a small souvenir.

The town is also known for its tasty, typically Chilean food. For lunch, try **Las Tinagas** or **La Greda** (☎ 831-1166; *Manuel Rodríguez 251*), which both serve traditional food, including parrillada.

From Santiago, take **Buses Melipilla** (☎ 776-2060; US$1.50) from Terminal San Borja, Alameda 3250, in Barrio Brasil near metro station Estación Central. The trip takes about an hour.

CAJÓN DEL MAIPO

Southeast of the capital, easily accessible by public transportation, the Cajón del Maipo (Río Maipo canyon) is one of the main weekend recreation spots for Santiaguinos. The canyon is an excellent place for camping, hiking, climbing, cycling, white-water rafting and skiing.

Two main access routes climb the canyon: on the north side of the river, a good paved road passes from the suburban comuna of La Florida to San José de Maipo and beyond, while another narrower, less-traveled paved route follows the south side of the river from Puente Alto. The southern route crosses the river and joins with the

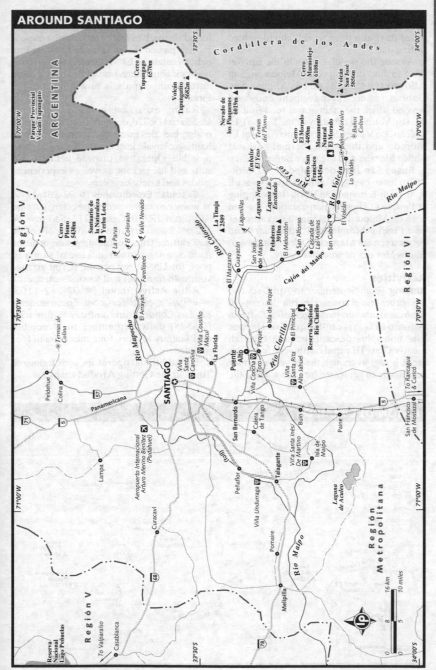

AROUND SANTIAGO

other just beyond San José de Maipo. In winter, these roads are sometimes snowed in for days at a time, so call ahead before setting out.

Among the popular stops in the canyon are San José de Maipo, El Melocotón, San Alfonso and Cascada de Las Animas, San Gabriel (where the pavement ends and beyond which the main gravel road follows the Río Volcán, a tributary of the Maipo), El Volcán, Lo Valdés, Monumento Natural El Morado and the rustic thermal baths at Baños Morales and the nicer Baños Colina.

Buses San José de Maipo (☎ 02-697-2520) leave every 30 minutes, from 6am till 9pm, from Terminal San Borja (but stopping at Parque O'Higgins metro station) for San José de Maipo. The 7:15am bus continues on to Baños Morales daily in January and February; from March to October it runs to Baños Morales on weekends only.

Activities

Rafting From September to April, several adventure-travel companies run descents of the Maipo in seven-passenger rafts, from San Alfonso to Guayacán-Parque Los Héroes. The hour-plus descent, passing through mostly Class III rapids with very few calm areas, is rugged enough that it's common for passengers to get tossed into the water. Still,

it's perhaps less hazardous than it was when the first kayakers descending in the 1970s found themselves facing automatic weapons as they passed the grounds of General Pinochet's estate at El Melocotón (the narrow bedrock chute here, one of the river's more entertaining rapids, is now known as 'El Pinocho').

Rafting excursions cost anywhere from US$25 to US$120, depending on whether the outing includes lunch and transport to/from Santiago; kayak descents and lessons are also possible. Operators provide helmets, wet suits and life jackets, as well as experienced guides and safety kayakers.

Cascadas Expediciones (☎ 02-861-1777; w www.cascada-expediciones.com; Camino Al Volcán 17710, Casilla 211, San José de Maipo), based in Cajón del Maipo, offer full-day rafting trips, including transportation from Santiago, lunch and use of sauna or pool, for US$70 per person. If you arrange your own transport and food, it's cheaper.

Altué Active Travel (☎ 02-232-1103; w www.chileoutdoors.com; Encomenderos 83, Las Condes) runs half-day rafting trips (US$25) daily September to December and January to April for a minimum of four people.

For additional operators, see Organized Tours in the Getting Around chapter.

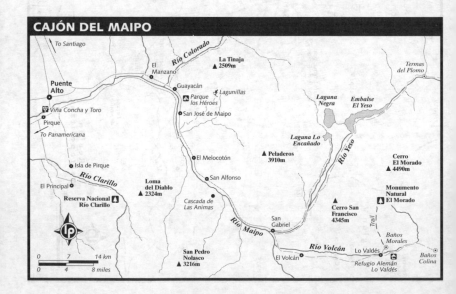

CAJÓN DEL MAIPO

Hiking Besides rafting, **Cascadas Expediciones** *(see Rafting, above)* runs full-day hiking tours in the areas, including transport to and from Santiago and lunch, for US$53-73 per person, depending on the hike. In winter they take people snowshoeing up to Baños Colina.

Altué Active Travel *(see Rafting, above)* arranges day hikes to El Morado; call for details.

Horseback Riding In addition to hiking and rafting, **Cascadas Expediciones** *(see Rafting, above)*, in association with **Cascada de la Animas** (see San Alfonso, below), runs horseback rides ranging from two hours to 12 days, including one that crosses the Andes into Argentina and another that travels along the spine of the Andes to Parque Nacional Los Cipreses in the south. Call for prices. A day of riding in the Cajón del Maipo costs around US$94.

Skiing Ranging from 2250m to 2580m above sea level, the small ski resort (four lifts, 13 runs) at Lagunillas, 84km southeast of Santiago via San José de Maipo, is a very modest counterpart to the region's other high-powered resorts. Accommodations are available through the **Club Andino de Chile** *(☎ 02-269-0898; US$10 per person)* or in nearby San Alfonso, but it's also an easy day trip from the capital.

In winter only **Buses Manzur** *(☎ 777-4284)* runs at 7:15am Wednesday, Saturday and Sunday to the Lagunillas ski area from Baquedano metro station on Plaza Italia.

See Ski Resorts, at the end of this chapter, for information on other snowsport opportunities around Santiago.

Pirque

One of the gateways to the Cajón, Pirque is an easygoing village just beyond Puente Alto. On weekends a crafts fair features leather workers, goldsmiths and silversmiths. Cyclists will find the paved but narrow route up the south bank of the Maipo much less crowded and more pleasant than the north-bank route.

Chile's largest winery, **Viña Concha y Toro** (see the 'Viñas Santiaguinas' boxed text) occupies spacious grounds here. About 3km east of Concha y Toro, on the road up the south side of the Cajón, there is a string of restaurants (see Places to Stay & Eat, later).

The quickest way to Pirque is to take Línea 5 of the metro to the end of the line at Bellavista de La Florida, then catch metrobus No 74 or 80, or a taxi colectivo at Paradero 14, just outside the station.

RN Río Clarillo

One of the closest nature reserves to Santiago, 13,000-hectare Río Clarillo *(admission Mon-Fri US$4, Sat & Sun US$5.80; open 8:30am-7pm Dec-Mar, till 6pm Apr-Nov)* is a scenic tributary canyon of the Cajón del Maipo, 23km southeast of Pirque. Its primary attractions are the river and the forest, with sclerophyllous (hard-leafed) tree species unique to the area. In addition to abundant bird life, the endangered Chilean iguana also inhabits the reserve.

Metrobus No 8 from Bellavista de La Florida metro station in Santiago drops passengers at the entrance to the Reserve Nacional Río Clarillo (US$0.80, 90 minutes). The buses depart every 10 minutes.

San Alfonso

San Alfonso is home to **Cascada de las Animas** *(☎ 02-861-1303, 861-4019, fax 02-861-1833; ⓦ www.cascadadelasanimas.cl)*, a 3500-hectare private nature reserve and working horse ranch. This is a popular place on weekends and in summer, but it is much quieter during the week and off-season. Hiking, white-water rafting and horseback riding are the main activities on offer, but there is also a large unchlorinated pool filled with natural spring water, and a sauna and massage facility. Natural healing programs and excursions to local parks and hotsprings are available too. The ranch has been operating horseback-riding trips for 25 years (see Horseback Riding, above, for details).

About 20m up the well-marked turnoff to Cascada de las Animas, one of the Cajón's oddest sights is the collection of **antique railcars** and operating miniature railway belonging to José Sagall, known as 'Pepe Tren' to his neighbors. About 100m farther down the road stands the **old station** for the military railroad that, until the 1960s, carried Santiaguino weekenders up the Cajón.

Cascada de Las Animas has a lovely, shady **campground** *(US$8/5 adult/child)*

Viñas Santiaguinas

While Santiago's growth has displaced many of the wineries that once surrounded the capital, it has spared some, even within the city limits. Although the following wineries can accommodate visits with advance warning, they are much more focused on production than courting the tourist dollar, though this is changing as wineries construct purpose-built tasting rooms, restaurants and other facilities. For approximate locations for the following, see the Around Santiago map.

Within Santiago city limits, in the comuna of Macul, is **Viña Cousiño Macul** (☎ 284-1011 anexo 45; Av Quilín 7100, Peñalolén; free tours Mon-Sat by reservation). You'll need to pay for tastings. There's also a **sales office** (open 9am-1pm & 2pm-6pm Mon-Fri, 9am-1pm Sat). To get there, take bus No 210 from the Alameda, or bus No 39, 391 or 703 from Santo Domingo along Américo Vespucio Sur.

Also within Santiago is **Viña Santa Carolina** (☎ 450-3000; Rodrigo de Araya 1341), in the comuna of Macul, near the Estadio Nacional; it dates from 1875. Although the sprawling capital has displaced the vineyards themselves, the historical casco (main house) of the Julio Pereira estate and the bodegas (cellars) are still here, open to the public only with 24 hours' advance notice. When calling, ask for 'relaciones públicas,' and try to avoid getting passed on to the voicemail system. Taxi colectivos along Av Vicuña Mackenna pass within easy walking distance.

Chile's largest winery, **Viña Concha y Toro** (☎ 821-7069; w www.conchaytoro.com; Virginia Subercaseaux 210, Pirque) occupies spacious grounds at Pirque, the gateway to Cajón del Maipo. Tours (US$4) of the vineyards and cellars in English take place at 11:30am and 3pm weekdays, and 10am and noon Saturday. A tour of the homestead (depicted on Santa Emiliana labels) is included. Call four days in advance to be sure of a spot. To get there, take the metro to Bellavista de La Florida and then catch blue metrobus 74.

Viña Santa Inés/De Martino (☎ 819-2062; w www.demartino.cl; Manuel Rodríguez 229; 10:30am-1:30pm & 3pm-6:30pm Mon-Fri, 10:30am-1:30pm Sat), in Isla de Maipo, about an hour southwest of Santiago, has excellent tours run by enologists and is one of the nicest places to visit. The winery, which has started making organic wines, has a lovely Tuscan-style vinoteca. There are two types of tours: one for the 'knowledgeable' (US$10, including tasting of two reserve wines) and one for 'fanatics' (US$20, with a tasting of four premium wines). A tour and lunch with unlimited reserve wine costs US$35. Tours in English take place at noon Monday to Saturday and must be reserved at least a day in advance. Buses for Isla de Maipo leave from Terminal San Borja.

In the village of Alto Jahuel, south of the capital and east of Buin, is **Viña Santa Rita** (☎ 821-2707 for reservations; Camino Padre Hurtado 0695). Tours (US$6) take place five times daily Tuesday through Friday and at 12:30pm and 3:30pm weekends; they include a tasting, and there is also an excellent restaurant. By public transport, the simplest way to get here is to take Línea 2 to the end of the line at Lo Ovalle and catch metrobus No 56, which passes the winery entrance.

About 34km southwest of the capital, on the old Melipilla highway between Peñaflor and Talagante, are the grounds and buildings of **Viña Undurraga** (☎ 372-2900; open 10am-4pm Mon-Fri). The vineyard was started in 1885 by Francisco Undurraga, who introduced most varietal rootstock to Chile. Reservations are obligatory. **Buses Peñaflor** (☎ 776-1025; US$1) covers this route from the Terminal San Borja; be sure to take the smaller Talagante micro rather than the larger Melipilla bus, which doesn't go to the winery. Buses leave every five minutes, and the trip takes 45 minutes.

that can be as much as 20% to 50% cheaper April to August. Also, there are cute **cabañas** (US$67 for 4 people), with logfires and a fully equipped kitchen. Larger cabins are also available, and discounts are offered on weekends and from March to August.

A lively **restaurant/bar** serves adventurous food and has a spectacular terrace with views over the valley.

Buses Cajon del Maipo (☎ 697 2520) runs from Parque O'Higgins metro station to San Alfonso (US$1, five hours) every 30 minutes. By car, it takes only two hours to make the trip from Pqrque O'Higgins to San Alfonso.

Monumento Natural El Morado

Only 93km from Santiago, this relatively small (3000 hectares) but very scenic park *(admission US$2; closed May-Sept)* rewards visitors with views of the Glaciar San Francisco and 4490m-tall Cerro El Morado from sparkling **Laguna El Morado**, a two-hour hike from the humble luke warm hot springs of **Baños Morales**. Although it's a stiff climb at the beginning, the trail soon levels off; motivated hikers can continue to the base of Glaciar El Morado, on the lower slopes of the cerro. There are free **campsites** around the lake.

Conaf maintains a small information office at the park entrance, where rangers collect admission. Rental horses are available for about US$5 per hour at Baños Morales, where there's also **camping** and simple accommodations.

In summer, Buses Manzur (see Baños Colina, next) goes to Baños Morales.

Turismo Arpue *(☎ 02-211-7165)* runs buses on Saturday and Sunday beginning at 7:30am from Santiago's Plaza Italia (the Baquedano metro station) directly to Baños Morales; the fare is US$5. Call the bus company in advance to confirm departure times, as the schedule is subject to change.

Baños Colina

The road ends at **Baños Colina** *(☎ 02-209-9114; US$15 per person, including campsite)*, where there are lovely cascading springs overlooking the valley. There are also horse rentals; the border is about a six-hour ride away, but only group trips planned far in advance may cross to Argentina here.

From October to mid-May, **Buses Manzur** *(☎ 02-777-4284)* runs to the baths from Plaza Italia on Wednesday, Saturday and Sunday at 7:15am. Try also **Buses Cordillera** *(☎ 02-777-3881)* from Terminal San Borja.

Places to Stay & Eat

See the Lagunillas (under Skiing), Cascada del Las Animas (under San Alfonso) and Monumento Natural El Morado sections for information about accommodations in those places.

Overlooking the Cajón from a southside perch above the Río Volcán, across from Baños Morales and surrounded by poplars, the **Refugio Alemán Lo Valdes** *(☎ 02-232-0476; e info@refugioaleman.com; US$39/48 per person with breakfast/half-board)* is a popular weekend destination throughout the year. Travelers with their own sleeping bags can crash in the attic for US$11, and the refugio's **restaurant** serves good meals and *onces*.

Casa Bosque *(☎ 02-871-1570; Camino El Volcán 16829)*, in Guayacán, is a popular, crazy-looking Gaudí-esque affair serving tender beef imported from Uruguay, Paraguay and Argentina.

La Petite France *(☎ 02-861-1967; Camino al Volcán 16096; closed Mon; meals US$17 per person)*, in Guayacán, is a charming place with excellent French food, such as slow-roasted pork with onion marmelade. It suffered a bad fire in 2002 but plans to reopen.

There is a bunch of restaurants in Pirque, all very popular on weekends, most notably **La Vaquita Echá** *(☎ 02-854-6025; Ramón Subercaseaux)*, famed for its *pastel de choclo* and *cazuela de ave.*

SKI RESORTS

Chile has acquired an international reputation among skiers, and Chile's best downhill skiing is to be found in Middle Chile's high cordillera, primarily clustered up in the valley of the Río Mapocho beyond Farellones, and along Ruta 60 to Mendoza, Argentina (for information on Portillo, the resort on this route, see the Middle Chile chapter). Most ski areas are above 3300m and treeless; the runs are long, the season is long, and the snow is deep and dry. Snowboarders are welcome at all the resorts.

World-class skiing is not far from the capital.

The season generally runs from June to early October. Most resorts adjust their rates according to season. Low season is generally mid-June to early July and mid-September to early October, while high season is early July to mid-September, as well as weekends and public holidays, but this varies wildly depending on the hotel and ski field. For current conditions, check the English-language *Santiago Times* online at **W** www.chip.cl.

SkiTotal (☎ *02-246-6881;* **W** *www.ski total.cl; Av Apoquindo 4900, Local 42-46, Las Condes*) arranges transportation (US$10/30 from city/airport) to all of the resorts, leaving at 8:45am and returning at 5:30pm. They also rent equipment (US$20-26 for full package) for prices slightly cheaper than on the slopes and offer ski lessons and accommodations (from US$42).

KL Adventure Ski (☎ *02-217-9101;* **W** *www.klchile.com; Av Las Condes 12207, Las Condes*) heads to the slopes daily at 8:30am, returning at 5:30pm; it also rents ski and snowboarding equipment (US$15-20 per day) and carries out repairs.

Ski Ahorro (☎ *02-229-4532; Av Las Condes 9143, Las Condes)* runs transport to the resorts (US$8/17/25 from office/hotel/airport) and also offers equipment rental (US$13-20 for full package).

Transport to and from the international airport in Santiago costs US$60 roundtrip with **Andina del Sud** (☎ *02-697-1010).*

See the Cajón del Maipo section, earlier for information about skiing at Lagunillas, and the Middle Chile chapter for information about the Termas de Chillán resort.

Farellones/El Colorado

Farellones and El Colorado are close enough together to be considered a single destination. Farellones was Chile's first ski resort and has some quaint old cabins and interesting restaurants, though these days the actual skiing takes place higher up at neighboring El Colorado; a couple of lifts link the two resorts. Farellones/El Colorado combined offers 19 lifts climbing to 3333m above sea level, with 22 different runs and a vertical drop of 903m. Daily lift tickets cost US$33, with discounts for children and seniors; season passes are also available.

There is lodging at **Hotel Posada El Farellones** (*singles/doubles US$70/100, including three meals & transport to the slopes*), which

also has cheaper rooms with shared bathroom, and at **Apartments Gerona/Andorra** (☎ *02-217-9101;* **e** *adventure@klchile.com; 1-/2-bed apartments start at US$840/1200 per week, more in high season*).

For information in Santiago, contact **Centro de Ski El Colorado** (☎ *02-246-3344, fax 206-4078;* **e** *ski-colorado@ ctcinternet.cl; Av Apoquindo 4900, Local 47/48, Las Condes*), which is also the point of departure for direct transport.

La Parva

Only 4km from Farellones, La Parva is a family-oriented place, with many private cottages and condos. Elevations on La Parva's 30 separate runs range from 2662m to 3650m (968m vertical drop).

Daily lift tickets range from US$22.50 in low season to US$28 in high season; multiday, weekly and seasonal passes are also available. It's also possible to buy an interconnected lift ticket (US$33/38 low/high season) with the Valle Nevado resort (see below).

The **Hotel Condominio Nueva La Parva** (☎ *655-1881; apartments for 6/8 people US$2000/2600 per week; more in high season*) is good for families and groups of friends, as is **KL Adventure La Parva** (☎ *217-9101;* **e** *adventure@klchile.com; per person from US$350/380 per week low/high season*). For the most current information, contact **Centro de Ski La Parva** (☎ *02-264-1466, fax 264-1569; La Concepción 266, Oficina 301, Providencia*).

Valle Nevado

Another 14km beyond Farellones, Valle Nevado is a well-planned, high-altitude ski area, ranging from 2805m to 3670m, with 27 runs up to 3km in length. It's Chile's newest ski area and tends to pull an international crowd. Full-day lift tickets are US$24/30 low/high season. Multiday tickets are also available. Rental equipment is available on site, and there's also a ski school.

The resort has three hotels, all of a high standard. Rates at resort hotels include half-board, lift tickets and parking.

Hotel Valle Nevado (*singles/doubles US$217/175 low season, US$434/310 high season*) is the most exclusive place to stay.

Hotel Puerta del Sol (*singles/doubles US$171/161 low season, US$356/319 high* *season)* is less expensive and offers a family environment.

Hotel Tres Puntas *(singles/doubles US$128/100 low season, US$263/192 high season)* is even cheaper and appeals to young people.

The resort has eight **restaurants**, all of a high standard.

For hotel bookings at the resort, contact **Valle Nevado** (☎ 02-206-0027, fax 208-0695; e info@vallenevado.com; *Gertrudis Echeñique 441, Las Condes)*. Valle Nevado also has toll-free numbers in the USA (☎ 800-669-0554) and Canada (☎ 888-301-3248).

KL Adventure Condos Mirador del Inca (☎ 217-9101; e adventure@klchile.com; *low/high season US$185/470 per person per week)* is close to the resort's other amenities; rates do not include lift tickets or meals.

Middle Chile

Chile's heartland is dominated by the fertile central valley, which at its widest extends just 70km between the Andean foothills and the coastal range. Only at the southern edge does the valley floor extend to the Pacific. Endowed with rich alluvial soils, a pleasant Mediterranean climate and Andean meltwater for irrigation, this is Chile's chief farming region, ideal for orchards and vineyards, and for growing cereal.

Middle Chile contains almost 75% of the country's population and most of its industry. Nearly a third of the region's inhabitants live in the sprawling capital, but Middle Chile also includes the major port of Valparaíso and Chile's most famous resort, the 'garden city' of Viña del Mar. Copper mines dot the sierras, while just north of Río Biobío, Concepción (a manufacturing center) and its port, Talcahuano (also home to a naval base), play a key role in the national economy.

Throughout the region, the imposing Andean crest is never far out of sight, and although Argentina is just over the mountain range, the Los Libertadores tunnel northeast of Santiago is the only all-season crossing to Argentina.

Valparaíso & the Central Coast

Northwest of Santiago, Valparaíso and its scenic coastline play a dual role in Chile. Valparaíso is a vital port and one of South America's most distinctive cities, while Viña del Mar and other coastal towns to its north are favorite summer playgrounds.

VALPARAÍSO
☎ 32 • pop 270,000
Growing spontaneously along the sea and up the surrounding coast range, Valparaíso – 'Valpo' for short – more closely resembles a medieval European harbor than a 21st-century commercial port. Often called 'La Perla del Pacífico' (Pearl of the Pacific), Chile's second-largest city occupies a narrow, wave-cut terrace and rises up

the overhanging precipitous cliffs and hills. The colorful barrios and shantytowns that

Highlights

- Riding *ascensores* and exploring *cerros* in the quirky port city of Valparaíso
- Visiting stunning wine country near Santa Cruz in the Colchagua Valley and near Talca in the Maule Valley
- Surfing and hanging out in the far-flung coastal town of Pichilemu
- Hiking through the PN La Campana to see stands of the exotic Chilean palm
- Driving up the spectacular coast road north of Viña del Mar to quaint seaside towns
- Hiking and horseback-riding through beech forest to high Andean peaks in PN Altos del Lircay and PN Radal de Siete Tazas
- Shop, stroll and enjoy the vibrant energy at Chillán's finest and most colorful market

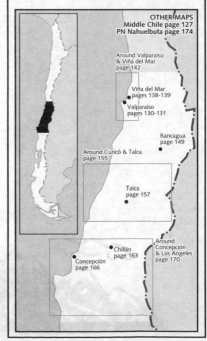

OTHER MAPS
Middle Chile page 127
PN Nahuelbuta page 174

Around Valparaíso & Viña del Mar page 142

Viña del Mar pages 138-139

Valparaíso pages 130-131

Rancagua page 149

Around Curicó & Talca page 155

Talca page 157

Around Concepción & Los Angeles page 170

Chillán page 163

Concepción page 166

MIDDLE CHILE

MIDDLE CHILE

cover the hills are linked to the city center by meandering roads, footpaths, staircases and *ascensores* (funicular elevators).

Compared to the hillside areas, the commercial center, built on landfill behind the waterfront, feels somewhat dark and claustrophobic, with sinuous narrow streets and run-down, imposing 19th-century architecture.

In parts of the city where residents pay no garbage tax because their home values are so low, trash tends to pile up; but other areas are improving rapidly. Some neglected older houses are being restored, particularly on Cerro Concepción.

History

Valparaíso's population at independence (in 1818) was barely 5000, but demand for Chilean wheat (brought on by the California gold rush) prompted such a boom that shortly after the mid-18th century the city's population was about 55,000. Completion of the railroad from Santiago helped to boost the city's population further, and by 1880 it exceeded 100,000. As the first major port of call for ships coming around Cape Horn, the city had become a commercial center for the entire Pacific coast and the hub of Chile's nascent banking industry.

A major earthquake in 1906 destroyed many downtown buildings, though some impressive 19th-century architecture remains. The opening of the Panama Canal, soon after, was an economic blow, as European shipping avoided the longer, more arduous Cape Horn route. Furthermore, Chilean exports of mineral nitrates declined as Europeans found synthetic substitutes, indirectly affecting Valparaíso by further reducing the region's maritime commerce. The Great Depression of the 1930s was a calamity, as demand for Chile's other mineral exports declined. Not until after WWII was there significant recovery, as the country began to industrialize.

Valparaíso remains less dependent on tourism than neighboring Viña del Mar, but many Chilean vacationers make brief excursions to the city from nearby beach resorts. Despite port expansion, the city's congested location has diverted cargo south to San Antonio, which handles nearly twice the volume of Valparaíso. The navy's conspicuous presence remains an important factor in the economy.

Orientation

Valparaíso has an extraordinarily complicated layout that probably only a lifetime resident could completely fathom, but there is an obvious divide between the residential hill neighborhoods and the flat area below, known as El Plan, which contains the business district, shopping streets, market areas and spacious plazas. In the city's congested commercial center, pinched between the port and the hills, nearly all major streets parallel the shoreline, which curves north as it approaches Viña del Mar. Av Errázuriz runs the length of the waterfront, alongside the railway, before merging with Av España, the main route to Viña. The main shopping district runs from Plaza Anibal Pinto east to Plaza Victoria.

Downtown's focal point is Plaza Sotomayor, facing the port, though it's not particularly abuzz. Several other plazas have a much more vibrant street life. Families frequent Plaza Victoria, for instance, for its lively playground, while Plaza O'Higgins is the site of one of Chile's finest antique markets.

Behind and above the downtown area, Valparaíso's many hills are a rabbit's warren of steep footpaths, zigzag roads and blind alleys, where even the best map will fail the visitor. Most of the hills *(cerros)* have their own unique identity; for instance, Cerro Concepción was once the prime place to live and has particularly lovely buildings, while neighboring Cerro Alegre has a bohemian feel. Cerro Playa Ancha is lively and working class, despite its mansions. The municipal tourist office's map offers some interesting walking routes that traverse various neighborhoods.

Information

The colorful hill neighborhoods and the area around the Mercado Central have a reputation for petty street crime – local people warn against any ostentatious display of wealth – but with the usual precautions, these areas are safe enough, at least during daylight. Exercise all reasonable caution, avoid poorly lit areas at night and, if possible, walk with a companion.

Valparaíso has an enthusiastic municipal **Departamento de Turismo** (☎ 221-001; *Condell 1490; open 8:30am-2pm & 3:30pm-*

Taking a break from the waves on Chile's coast

PAUL KENNEDY

Backpacking in PN Torres del Paine

WOODS WHEATCROFT

Climbing Volcán Villarrica, near Pucón

SHANNON NACE

Hitting the trails in the high Andes

CHRIS BARTON

Chilean flamingos flying over Laguna del Negro Francisco in PN Nevado Tres Cruces

Magellanic penguins on Isla Magdalena

The endangered vicuña

A smooth-billed ani catching a ride on a capybara, the world's largest rodent

5:30pm Mon-Fri). Its **visitor center** (☎ 236-322; open 10am-7pm daily) at the Centro de Difusión on Muelle Prat (the pier), near Plaza Sotomayor, employs friendly and well-informed personnel, including English speakers, and distributes free city maps.

There is also an office (open 10am-2pm & 3-6pm Tues-Sun) in the Terminal Rodoviario (bus station), and on Plaza Victoria (open summer only).

Valparaíso's exchange houses include **Inter Cambio** (Plaza Sotomayor) and **Cambio Exprinter** (Prat 895).

The post office is on Prat at its junction with Plaza Sotomayor. There are long-distance telephone services at **Telefónica (CTC)** (Esmeralda 1054 • Av Pedro Montt 2023), and at the bus station. There's also **Entel** (Condell 1495 • cnr Av Pedro Montt & Cruz). **Chilexpress** (Av Brasil 1456) has fax, telephone and courier services. **DHL** (☎ 881-299; Plaza Sotomayor 55) is another useful courier service.

World Next Door Ciber Cafe (☎ 227-148; Blanco 692; open 8:30am-8pm; US$1.30/hr), near Plaza Sotomayor, is a great Internet café with a superfast connection and student discounts. Up on Cerro Concepción, **Valparaíso Mi Amor** (☎ 749-992; Papudo 612; US$1.50/hr) is open late.

Lavanda Cafe (Almirante Montt 454), on Cerro Alegre, is the place to do laundry; you can also get coffee and food here.

Hospital Carlos van Buren (☎ 254-074; Av Colón 2454) is at the corner of San Ignacio.

LanChile (☎ 251-441, fax 233-374; Esmeralda 1048) has an office is downtown.

Things to See & Do

El Plan The commercial zone between the hills and the sea, called El Plan, contains most of the city's monuments, as well as lively plazas and shopping streets. It may not be the most distinctive part of the city, but it's where the action is.

Plaza Sotomayor is the official heart of the city, though it's a bit dingey and lacks the relaxed outdoorsy atmosphere of Valpo's other plazas. Landmarks in and around Plaza Sotomayor include the **Primera Zona Naval**, an impressive structure with a mansard roof; **Monumento a los Héroes de Iquique**, a subterranean mausoleum paying tribute to Chile's naval martyrs; the **Aduana Nacional** (customhouse); and **Estación Puerto**, the

rather ugly terminal for Merval commuter trains, which has some murals. **Muelle Prat**, the touristy pier at the foot of Plaza Sotomayor, is a lively place on weekends. It has a helpful tourist kiosk and a handicrafts market, the **Feria de Artesanías** (open 10am-8pm Thur-Sun). Small boats offer tours of the harbor for about US$1.50. Do not photograph any of the numerous Chilean naval vessels at anchor, or you may find yourself in military custody.

Plaza Matriz is Valparaíso's historic core, directly uphill from the Mercado Central, where El Plan narrows and the distinctive hills architecture starts to take shape. The plaza's major landmark is the **Iglesia Matriz**, a national monument dating from 1842. This is the fourth church to occupy this site since the construction of the original chapel in 1559.

Southeast of Plaza Sotomayor, where Prat and Cochrane converge to become Esmeralda, the Edificio Turri narrows to the width of its namesake clock tower, the **Reloj Turri**. Topped by a mansard roof at Esmeralda and Ross, the neoclassical **El Mercurio de Valparaíso** (1903) is the home of Chile's oldest continuously published newspaper (since 1827, predating the building itself).

At Independencia and Huito, the neoclassical **Palacio Lyon** (1881), once a private mansion, now houses the city's natural history museum and the municipal art gallery. One block east is vibrant **Plaza Victoria**, with tempting cake shops on its perimeter and a fun-filled atmosphere, especially in the early evening. Overlooking Plaza Victoria, on Edwards between Av Pedro Montt and Chacabuco, is the **Iglesia Catedral de Valparaíso**, the largest church.

At the east end of downtown, opposite Plaza O'Higgins and the bus terminal, the most imposing landmark is the controversial **Congreso Nacional** (open 3pm-5pm Fri when in session), built in 1990 and overlooking **Plaza O'Higgins**. Mandated by Pinochet's 1980 constitution, which moved the legislature away from the Santiago-based executive branch, this was the last major public-works project of the dictatorship, at a cost of US$100 million. The edifice was built on the site of one of Pinochet's boyhood homes. Since the return to constitutional government, the location of the legislature has been a notable inconvenience – rapid physical communication between the two cities is

MIDDLE CHILE

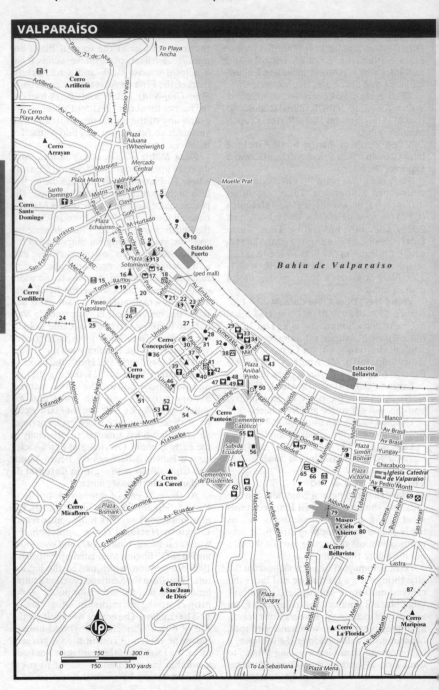

VALPARAÍSO

To Playa
Ancha

Paseo 21 de Mayo

Artillería

1

Cerro
Artillería

To Cerro
Playa Ancha

Av Carampangue

Antonio Varas

2

Cerro
Arrayan

Plaza
Aduana
(Wheelwright)

Márquez

Mercado
Central

Valdivia

Muelle Prat

Plaza Matriz

Santo
Domingo

San Martín

Matriz

Cerro
Santo
Domingo

San Francisco Carrasco

Pascal

Clave

Goñi

5

M Hurtado

Plaza
Echaurren

Serrano

Cochrane

Blanco

7

Bahía de Valparaíso

6

9

Estación
Puerto

V Hugo

12

Merlet

Plaza
Sotomayor

13

10

Cerro
Cordillera

15

16

14

17

Av Tomás Ramos

19

18

(ped mall)

Castillo

24

Paseo
Yugoslavo

25

20

Higuera

26

21

22

23

Av Errázuriz

Prat

Señorit

Carreño

Ross

Esmeralda

27

29

33

28

31

32

34

Pudeto

35

Mar

Urriola

Cerro
Concepción

30

37

38

Lautaro Rosas

39

Conceptión

41

42

Plaza
Aníbal
Pinto

43

Estación
Bellavista

Cerro
Alegre

Urriola

36

40

46

47

48

49

Medrano

Estanque

Morrison

Monte Alegre

Templeman

51

52

53

Cumming

50

Higgins

Bellavista

Blanco

54

Av Almirante Montt

Elias

Cerro
Panteón

Cementerio
Católico

55

Av Brasil

Av Brasil

Yungay

Atahualpa

Subida
Ecuador

56

Salvador Donoso

Condell

58

57

Plaza
Simón
Bolívar

E Ramírez

59

Hurto

Chacabuco

61

Av Akemania

Cerro
La Carcel

Cementerio
de Disidentes

65

66

67

64

Plaza
Victoria

Iglesia Catedral
de Valparaíso

Av Pedro Montt

68

Carrera

Edwards

Las Heras

69

Cerro
Miraflores

Atahalpa

Plaza
Bismark

62

63

Mackenna

79

Museo
a Cielo
Abierto

80

Cumming

Av Ecuador

Av Yerbas Buenas

Buenos Aires

Aldunate

C Newman

Cerro
Bellavista

Lastra

86

87

Cerro
San Juan
de Dios

Plaza
Yungay

Ricardo Ferrari

Bernardo Ramos

Mena

Cerro
Mariposa

To La Sebastiana

Plaza Mena

Cerro
La Florida

Av Baquedano

0   150   300 m

0   150   300 yards

VALPARAÍSO

PLACES TO STAY
25 Anita's Bed and Breakfast
30 Casa Latina
36 Casa Aventura
40 Casa Familiar Carrasco
48 Hotel Brighton
56 Hotel Puerta del Alcalá
59 Hotel Puerto Principal
75 Residencial Veracruz
76 Casa Familiar Mónica
   Venegas
82 Hostal Kolping
83 Hotel Casa Baska

PLACES TO EAT
4 Los Porteños No 2
5 Bote Salvavidas
21 La Rotonda
23 Bar Inglés
31 Café Turri
37 Color Café
46 Le Filou de Montpellier
50 Café Riquet
51 El Rincón Sueco
53 Lavanda Cafe
64 Jota Cruz
68 Vitamin Service
72 Marco Polo
77 Pizzería Napoletana
85 Nuevo Restaurant
   O'Higgins

OTHER
1 Museo Naval y Marílimo
3 Iglesia Matriz
7 Feria de Artesanías

8 La Playa
9 Aduana Nacional
10 Visitor Center
11 Iglesia San Francisco
12 Monumento a los Héroes
   de Iquique
13 Inter Cambio
14 DHL
15 Museo del Mar Lord
   Cochrane
16 Primera Zona Naval
17 Post Office (Correos de
   Chile)
18 Valparaíso Eterno; World
   Next Door Ciber Cafe
19 Tribunales (Law Courts)
22 Cambio Exprinter; Reloj
   Turri
26 Palacio Baburizza (Museo
   de Bellas Artes)
28 El Mercurio de Valparaíso
29 La Piedra Feliz
32 LanChile
33 Tortus
34 Puerto Bahía
35 Centro Cultural
   Valparaíso/Quintil; Centro
   Cine
38 Telefónica (CTC)
39 Iglesia San Pablo
41 Valparaíso Mi Amor
42 Iglesia Luterana
43 Roland Bar
45 Mirador Diego Portales
47 Bar Kabala
49 Cinzano

52 Café Vinilo
55 Leo Bar
57 La Cueva Pancho Pirata
58 Chilexpress
61 Mr Egg
62 Emile Dubois
63 West
65 Entel
66 Municipalidad;
   Departamento de Turismo
67 Palacio Lyon (Natural
   History Museum; Municipal
   Art Gallery)
69 Mercado Artesanal
   Permanente
70 Telefónica (CTC)
71 Cine Hoyts
73 Entel
74 Terminal Rodoviario
80 Sala Herbert Jonckers
81 Antiguidades El Abuelo

84 Teatro Municipal
88 Hospital Carlos van Buren

ASCENSORES
2 Ascensor Artillería
6 Ascensor Cordillera
20 Ascensor El Peral
24 Ascensor San Augustín
27 Ascensor Concepción
   (Turri)
44 Ascensor Barón
54 Ascensor Reina Victoria
60 Ascensor Lecheros
78 Ascensor Larraín
79 Ascensor Espíritu Santo
   (Bellavista)
86 Ascensor Florida
87 Ascensor Mariposa
89 Ascensor Polanco
90 Ascensor Monjas
91 Ascensor Cerro La Cruz

MIDDLE CHILE

To Viña
del Mar

Av España

Cerro
Barón

Av Diego Portales

Muelle Barón

Estación
Barón

Feria
Persa
Barón
45
44

Magallanes

Cerro
Lecheros

60

Av Errázuriz
Av Errázuriz

Blanco

Av Brasil
Av Brasil

El Plan

Yungay

Chacabuco

Av Argentina

Eusebio Lillo

78

Cerro
Larraín

70

71
72
73

Rawson

12 de Febrero

Av Pedro Montt

74

75

76

77

Victoria

83

84

Plaza
O'Higgins

Congreso
Nacional

Cerro
Rodríguez

81

Parque
Italia

82

Independencia

Simón Bolívar

Morris

Av Uruguay

Ross

Rancagua

Plaza
Radomiro

Av Francia

Freire

Vergara

Cruz

Av Colón

San Ignacio

88

Retamo

Barroso

Juana

Simpson

89

Cerro
Molino

Cerro
Monjas

90

Van Buren

Blas Cuevas

Pocuro

Hontaneda

Casablanca

Av Santos Ossa

Plaza
Esmeralda

91

Cerro La Cruz

Parque
El Litre

Cerro de la Merced

11

85

only possible by helicopter, and a number of legislators have been busted for speeding on Ruta 68 between the two cities. Talk of returning the Congreso to Santiago, hitherto opposed by conservative elements, has been gaining steam, but such action would leave Valparaíso with an unanticipated contemporary historical monument – or a white elephant.

Plaza O'Higgins is also the site of the **Teatro Municipal** (municipal theater) and of the city's best **antiques market** on weekends.

Hills of Valparaíso Valparaíso is undoubtedly the single most distinctive city in Chile and one of the most intriguing in all of South America. It's possible to spend hours riding the 15 *ascensores* (funicular elevators), built between 1883 and 1916, and strolling back alleys. Some of the ascensores are remarkable feats of engineering – **Ascensor Polanco**, on the east side of Av Argentina, rises vertically through a tunnel. Each ascensor has its own unique opening hours, and the price of a ride varies from 60 to 120 pesos (it's usually a few pesos cheaper to descend than go up). Mostly they're run by characterful old folk who have been collecting change and pulling levers all their lives.

One of the best areas for urban explorers is Cerro Concepción, a pleasant neighborhood that has wall-to-wall two-story houses with brightly painted corrugated iron facades and pitched roofs. Along with Cerro Alegre, next door, this area is undergoing something of a renaissance and has interesting places to stay and eat. The easiest way to get to Cerro Concepción is by taking **Ascensor Concepción** *(open 7am-8:30pm)*, the oldest elevator in the city (it originally ran on steam power). Also known as Ascensor Turri, it climbs the slopes from the corner of Prat and Almirante Carreño, across from the landmark clock tower known as the Reloj Turri.

Reached by **Ascensor El Peral** *(open 7am-8pm)*, near the Tribunales (law courts) just off Plaza Sotomayor, Cerro Alegre is home to the **Palacio Baburizza** (1916), housing the city's fine arts museum but presently undergoing an overdue renovation. From here, it's possible to loop over to Cerro Concepción, or vice versa. One block north of Plaza Sotomayor, **Ascensor Cordillera** *(open 6am-11:30pm)* climbs Cerro Cordillera to the Museo del Mar Lord Cochrane (see Museums, later).

Above the Feria Persa Barón (flea market), reached by **Ascensor Barón**, the **Mirador Diego Portales** offers a panorama of the city toward the west; nearby, the bell tower of the historic **Iglesia San Francisco** (1845) served as a landmark for approaching mariners, who gave the city its common nickname 'Pancho' (a diminutive of Francisco).

Other ascensores worth a ride include the **Acensor Espiritu Santo** (sometimes called Ascensor Bellavista), near Plaza Victoria, which climbs up to the Museo a Cielo Abierto (see Museums) and La Sebastiana (see next section); and **Ascensor Artillería**, which hauls you up to Museo Naval y Marítimo.

For a quick, inexpensive tour of Valparaíso's hills, catch the Verde Mar 'O' *micro* (city bus) on Serrano near Plaza Sotomayor, and take it all the way to Viña del Mar (US$0.50). This bus also passes Pablo Neruda's Valparaíso home, now a museum (see La Sebastiana, next).

La Sebastiana Pablo Neruda probably spent less time at La Sebastiana (☎ 256-606; *Ricardo Ferrari 692; adult/student US$3.75/2; open 10:30am-2:30pm & 3:30pm-6pm Tues-Sun, till 7pm Jan & Feb)*, his least-known and least-visited house, than at La Chascona or Isla Negra, but he made it a point to watch Valparaíso's annual New Year's fireworks from his lookout on Cerro Bellavista.

Restored and open to the public, La Sebastiana (Fundación Neruda) may be the best destination for Neruda pilgrims – it's the only one of his three houses that visitors can wander around at will without having to subject themselves to regimented tours that seem out of character with the informal poet. In addition to the usual assemblage of oddball artifacts within the house, the Fundación Neruda has built a Centro Cultural La Sebastiana alongside it, with rotating exhibitions, a café and a souvenir shop.

To reach La Sebastiana, take Verde Mar bus 'O' or 'D' on Serrano near Plaza Sotomayor and disembark in the 6900 block of Av Alemania, a short walk from the house. Alternatively, take Acensor Espiritu Santo (sometimes called Ascensor Bellavista) near Plaza Victoria and ask directions.

Neruda's most famous house, with an extensive collection of maritime memorabilia, is at Isla Negra (see Around Valparaíso & Viña del Mar).

Museums Frankly, Valparaíso's museums are nothing to write home about. If you're pushed for time, you're better off exploring the *cerros* and having fun on the ascensores.

Once a private mansion, the neoclassical Palacio Lyon (1881) merits a visit in its own right, but also houses two of the city's museums. Most of the natural-history specimens in the **Museo de Historia Natural** *(☎ 257-441; Condell 1546; adult US$1; open 10am-1pm & 2pm-6pm Tues-Fri, 10am-6pm Sat, 10am-2pm Sun & holidays)* are mediocre, but the upper exhibition halls compensate with interesting dioramas on the story of Chile's pre-Hispanic cultures and their environments. There is also fine material on the oceans and their future, a subject of great importance to a maritime country such as Chile. In the basement of the building, but with a separate entrance, the **Galería Municipal de Arte** *(municipal art gallery; ☎ 220-062; Condell 1550; admission free; open 10am-7pm Mon-Sat)* hosts temporary art exhibits throughout the year.

Designed for an Italian nitrate baron but named after the Yugoslav who purchased it from him, the Art Nouveau Palacio Baburizza (1916) houses the city's **Museo de Bellas Artes** *(fine-arts museum; ☎ 252-332; donations welcome; open 9:30am-6pm Tues-Sun)*, which is currently undergoing renovation. The palace is noteworthy for imaginative woodwork, forged-iron details and a steeply pitched central tower. Set among attractive gardens, the building and its grounds alone justify a visit. On Cerro Alegre's Paseo Yugoslavo, the museum is reached by Ascensor El Peral from Plaza Sotomayor.

The **Museo del Mar Lord Cochrane** *(☎ 213-124; Merlet 195; admission free; open 10am-6pm Tues-Sun mid-Mar to mid-Sept, 10am-1pm & 3pm-8pm mid-Sept to mid-Mar)*, with a stunning patio overlooking the harbor, was built in 1842 for Lord Thomas Cochrane but was never occupied by him. The building, a tile-roofed, colonial-style house above Plaza Sotomayor, held Chile's first astronomical observatory – however unlikely a place to observe the heavens Valparaíso might seem, given its constant fog. The house itself is more interesting than the exhibits, which are mostly temporary displays of photos and paintings. Ring the bell if the gate is locked. To reach the museum, take Ascensor Cordillera from

the west side of Plaza Sotomayor and walk east to Merlet.

One of the few Chilean museums with sufficient resources for acquisitions and truly professional presentation, Chile's shipshape **Museo Naval y Marítimo** *(☎ 283-749; adult US$0.80; open 10am-6pm Tues-Sun)* is a military museum that focuses on the War of the Pacific (specifically honoring naval hero and national icon Arturo Prat), but there are also major displays on Lord Cochrane (the navy's founder), Admiral Manuel Blanco Encalada (an independence-era naval fighter) and other lesser figures. The most interesting displays deal with voyages around the Horn, giving credit to sailors of every European country. To get to the museum, take **Ascensor Artillería** *(open 7am-11:30pm)* from the triangular Plaza Aduana (also known as the Plaza Wheelwright). At the top of the ascensor, Paseo 21 de Mayo offers souvenir stands, a small café with an attractive terrace and outstanding views of the port to the east.

Between 1969 and 1973, students from the Universidad Católica's Instituto de Arte created the **Museo a Cielo Abierto**, comprised of 20 brightly colored abstract murals that cover numerous hillside sites on Cerro Bellavista. It is reached by Ascensor Espíritu Santo. Concentrated on Calle Aldunate and Paseos Guimera, Pasteur, Rudolph and Ferrari, Valparaíso's 'open sky museum' adds a welcome spot of color to an otherwise run-down area.

Special Events

Año Nuevo (New Year's) is one of Valparaíso's biggest events, thanks to the massive fireworks display that brings hundreds of thousands of spectators to the city.

April 17, which marks the arrival of the authorization of the *cabildo* (town council) of Valparaíso in 1791, is the city's official day (imperial Spain's snail-paced bureaucracy and slow communications across the Atlantic delayed receipt of the authorization for more than three years).

Places to Stay

Nearby Viña del Mar has a broader choice of accommodations in all categories, but Valparaíso has a few alternatives, the most interesting of which are *hospedajes* (guesthouses) in the scenic hills. Phone ahead before visiting any of these places, which fill up quickly and can be difficult to find.

Residencial Veracruz (☎ 253-583; Av Pedro Montt 2881; singles/doubles US$8/12; tiny single US$3), located opposite the Congreso Nacional, is very friendly and has nice rooms.

Casa Familiar Mónica Venegas (☎ 215-673; Av Argentina 322; US$8/10 per person without/with breakfast), near the bus terminal, is comfortable and amiable. There is some space for negotiation, especially when it's not crowded.

Casa Aventura (☎/fax 755-963, e casatur @ctcinternet.cl; Pasaje Gálvez 11; US$10 per person, including breakfast), on Cerro Alegre, is a comfortable, airy backpackers' hostal run by a friendly couple who also organizes hiking trips and Spanish courses. The breakfast features fresh fruit, homemade cheese and real coffee, and there's a fully equipped kitchen where guests can cook their own food. To get there, walk up Urriola until it's intersected by Alvaro Besa to the right and tiny Pasaje Galvez to the left; the hostal is the first door along Pasaje Galvez.

Casa Familiar Carrasco (☎ 210-737; Abtao 668; US$12 per person), up on Cerro Concepción, has a cheerful pink and green exterior. The rooms are simple but very clean. There are spectacular vistas from the rooftop deck (an ideal spot to see New Year's fireworks).

Casa Latina (☎ 494-622; Papudo 462; US$13 per person, with breakfast & shared bath), also on Cerro Concepción, is family-oriented, with simple but clean rooms; take Ascensor Concepción (Turri) to get there.

Anita's Bed & Breakfast (☎ 239-327; Higueras 107; US$13 per person, including breakfast), on Cerro Alegre, is a stunning old house with large, bright, beautifully decorated rooms. Anita is a quite a character to boot.

Hostal Kolping (☎ 216-306; Vergara 622; singles/doubles with private bath US$13/20, including breakfast), on the south side of Plaza Italia, is clean, secure and not too far from the bus station.

Hostal Casa Baska (☎ 234-036; Victoria 2449; singles/doubles US$20/23) is in a noisy area and has very spartan rooms, but it's close to the bus station.

Hotel Puerto Principal (☎ 745-629; Huito 361; singles/doubles US$30/33, with private bath, telephone, TV & breakfast), near Plaza Victoria, is clean and central.

Hotel Puerta del Alcalá (☎ 227-478, fax 745-642; Pirámide 524; singles & doubles US$48) is a business-oriented hotel lacking the charm of the hillside places, but if you can't survive without cable and minibar, this is your best bet.

Hotel Brighton (☎/fax 223-513; Pasaje Atkinson 151; rooms with sea view US$60, including breakfast), atop Cerro Concepción, is a bright-yellow, peak-roofed confection with great views of the city and harbor. Despite its classic Valparaíso architecture, it's a new building, fitted with recycled materials. Though the hotel looks great, it suffers from poor management and Fawlty Towers–type maintenance – saggy beds, heaters that don't work, doors that don't lock, and intermittent hot water. And you better have all morning to waste while you wait for your breakfast to be served.

Places to Eat

Valparaíso is full of traditional old bars and restaurants offering classic food and loads of atmosphere.

Vitamin Service (☎ 212-689; Pedro Montt 1746) is a classic family-oriented salón de té serving scrumptious sandwiches and fresh juices.

Los Porteños No 2 (☎ 252-511; Valdivia 169), near Mercado Central, has large portions and specializes in seafood. The prices are very reasonable.

At the **Mercado Central**, the 2nd-floor marisquerías (seafood restaurants) charge less than US$3 for three-course meals featuring fried fish.

Color Café (Papudo 526), on Cerro Concepción, serves delicious vegetarian food, tea and coffee.

Jota Cruz (☎ 211-225; Condell 1466; open 2:30pm to 4am) is the place to go late at night for bow-tied service and chorrillana (a piled plate of spicy pork, onions and egg, buried under a blanket of chips) – one serving easily feeds two. The décor is good and quirky.

Marco Polo (☎ 256-512; Av Pedro Monte 2199) is another old-time cafeteria. It has a definite Italian bent, serving a range of homemade pasta dishes, including vegetarian cannelloni (US$5.60) and fettuccine with fresh pesto. It also has excellent coffee, onces, sandwiches, juices and ice cream.

If you're still in an Italian mood, head to **Pizzería Napoletana** (☎ 233-683), opposite the Congreso. Here you will find the genuine article, unlikely as that may seem.

Le Filou de Montpellier (☎ 224-663; *Av Almirante Montt 382; menú US$4.60*) is a cute-as-sixpence restaurant run by a mad Frenchman. The food is an excellent value and definitely exotic for Chile. The lunch menu changes daily but typically might include quiche Lorraine, roast turkey stuffed with prunes in a cognac and port sauce, and dessert. It's up on Cerro Alegre.

Café Riquet (*Plaza Anibal Pinto 1191; lunch menú US$8.30*) is a nice traditional place that's just right for lunch or *onces*.

Bar Inglés (☎ 214-625; *Cochrane 851; fresh fish dishes US$6*) is a classic old favorite with dark wood, white tablecloths and lots of atmosphere. There are entrances on both Cochrane and Blanco.

La Rotonda (☎ 217-746; *Prat 701; daily lunch special US$10*) has excellent seafood and service. Consider splitting à la carte dishes from the extensive menu – portions are huge.

If you're looking for a change, try **El Rincón Sueco** (☎ 594-851; *Lautaro Rosas 510*), up on Cerro Alegre, which serves Swedish fare, including meatballs and baked potatoes (okay, so it's not that much of a change...).

Nuevo Restaurant O'Higgins (☎ 256-115; *Barroso 506; lunch US$7, fish US$6.50, paella for 2 US$15*) is a spacious, gracious place with a popular Sunday lunch, though it's also open in the evenings.

Bote Salvavidas (☎ 251-477; *Muelle Prat s/n*) is a pricey seafood restaurant on the waterfront.

Café Turri (☎ 252-091; *Templeman 147*), fronting on Paseo Gervasoni at the upper exit of Ascensor Concepción (Turri), is a touristy, piped-music kind of place, but its seafood has a good reputation. The views from its terraces are grand.

For a quick espresso, tea or sandwich on Cerro Alegre, head to **Lavanda Cafe** (*Almirante Montt 454*), which is run by the tallest man in Chile and doubles as a laundry.

Entertainment

In the happening Cerro Alegre neighborhood, **Café Vinilo** (☎ 09-864-9906; *Almirante Montt 448; opens at 9pm*) is an old butcher shop refurbished by its architect and textile-designer owners; it's a stylish place to meet the locals.

Cinzano (☎ 213-043; *Anibal Pinto 1182*) is a rowdy little place that dates back to 1896; the walls are covered in photos of sinking ships, and old crooners with golden voices perform tango tunes in the evenings. If you're very hungry, try the *chorrillana*, which is big enough for two.

Bar Kabala (☎ 229-940; *Almirante Montt 16*) is a relaxed spot for a drink; there's live music on Saturday nights at 11:30pm.

Valparaíso Eterno (☎ 255-605; *Señoret 150, 2nd floor*) drips with bohemian atmosphere and usually has live music.

Roland Bar (☎ 235-123; *Av Errázuriz 1152*) is an old restaurant now serving as an interesting nightspot.

The cute café/bar in **Centro Cultural Valparaíso** (*Esmeralda 1083*) is a cozy place worth a look.

Pirate fans should check out **La Cueva Pancho Pirata** (☎ 236-140; *Pudeto 489*).

Subida Ecuador is a pub strip stretching along Av Ecuador. Most of the pubs along here are noisy and seem fairly characterless, but if you feel like bar-hopping without having to hop too far, this is the place to do it. Long-standing venues include **Mr Egg** (☎ 257-534; *Subida Ecuador 50*), **West** (☎ 291-498; *Subida Ecuador 121*) and the subdued **Emile Dubois** (☎ 213-486; *Subida Ecuador 144*).

Leo Bar (*Subida Ecuador 24*) is a dark, denlike bar with chess players and a laid-back vibe.

Closer to the waterfront there's another nightlife zone, this one more about dancing than drinking (though, of course, there's usually a fair amount of overlap).

Puerto Bahía (*Errázuriz 1090*) is a huge, hard-core salsoteca.

La Piedra Feliz (☎ 256-788; *Errázuriz 1054*) is a tango place with live music.

Tortus (*Blanco 1049*) is much quieter, with acoustic one-act shows.

La Playa (*Cochrane 568*) is popular with students and serves cheap pitchers of beer.

Cine Hoyts (☎ 594-709; *Av Pedro Montt 2111*), with five screens, shows current films.

Centro Cine (☎ 216-953; *Esmeralda 1083*), part of the Centro Cultural Valparaíso, an art house theater.

Teatro Municipal (☎ 214-654; *Av Uruguay 410*) hosts live theater and concerts.

Sala Herbert Jonckers (☎ 221-680; *Av Colón 1712*) also offers live theater.

MIDDLE CHILE

Shopping

On weekends and holidays, the tremendous **Feria de Antiguedades y Libros La Merced** *(Plaza O'Higgins)* takes place. Prices aren't cheap, but the selection of books and antiques is outstanding. A more general-interest **flea market** *(Plaza Radomiro Tomic)* is on the median strip between the lanes of Av Argentina, and offers some Mapuche crafts among the usual post-industrial dreck. There's also a modest **Feria de Artesanías** near Plaza Prat.

Antiguidades El Abuelo *(☎ 217-032; Independencia 2071)* is packed with oddball bits and pieces from the Chile of times past.

For handicrafts, visit the **Mercado Artesanal Permanente** *(cnr Av Pedro Montt & Las Heras)*. Valparaíso may be the best city in Chile for flea markets, such as the **Feria Persa Barón** *(open 9am-11pm daily)*, on Av Argentina where it becomes Av España.

Getting There & Away

Nearly all bus companies have offices at Valparaíso's Terminal Rodoviario **bus station** *(☎ 939-646, 237-209, 213-246; Av Pedro Montt 2800)*, across from the Congreso Nacional. Because services from Valparaíso and Viña del Mar are almost identical, most information appears here.

For Santiago, **Tur Bus** *(☎ 939-646 in Valpo, ☎ 882-621 in Viña)* has the most departures. Some Viña buses go direct to Santiago, while others go via Valparaíso, but the fare is identical. Other companies traveling to Santiago include **Cóndor** *(☎ 212-927 in Valpo, ☎ 882-345 in Viña)*, **Sol del Pacífico** *(☎ 213-776 in Valpo, ☎ 883-156 in Viña)*, **Sol del Sur** *(☎ 252-211 in Valpo, ☎ 687-277 in Viña)*, **Tas Choapa** *(☎ 252-921 in Valpo, ☎ 882-258 in Viña)* and **Pullman Lit** *(☎ 237-290 in Valpo, ☎ 690-783 in Viña)*.

Bus companies traveling to coastal and interior destinations in the northern sector of the region, such as Quintero, Papudo and La Ligua, include **Buses La Porteña** *(☎ 216-568; Molina 366)*, **Cóndor** *(☎ 212-927)* and **Sol del Pacífico** *(☎ 288-577)*.

Buses running to Los Andes include **Buses JM** *(☎ 256-581)*, **Pullman Bus** *(☎ 253-125)* and **Buses Dhino's** *(☎ 221-298)*.

Pullman Bus Lago Peñuelas *(☎ 224-025)* goes to Algarrobo and nearby Isla Negra (for Neruda's house).

Note that some northbound long-distance buses, especially ones that travel at night, involve connections with buses from Santiago, which can mean waiting on the Panamericana – ask before buying your ticket.

Tur Bus *(☎ 939-646 in Valpo, ☎ 882-621 in Viña)* covers north- and southbound routes on the Panamericana. **Buses Zambrano** *(☎ 258-986 in Valpo, ☎ 883-942 in Viña)*, **Pullman Bus** *(☎ 256-898 in Valpo, ☎ 680-424 in Viña)*, **Flota Barrios** *(☎ 253-674 in Valpo, ☎ 882-725 in Viña)*, **Chile Bus** *(☎ 256-325 in Valpo, ☎ 881-187 in Viña)* and **Fénix Pullman Norte** *(☎ 257-993 in Valpo)* follow the Panamericana north to Iquique, Arica and intermediate points. **Transportes Lasval** *(☎ 214-915 in Valpo, ☎ 684-121 in Viña)* serves the cities of the Norte Chico, primarily Ovalle and La Serena/Coquimbo.

Buses Norte *(☎ 258-322)* goes south to Temuco, Valdivia, Osorno and Puerto Montt, and makes connections in Santiago with Turibús for Punta Arenas. **Tas Choapa** *(☎ 252-921 in Valpo, ☎ 882-258 in Viña del Mar)*, **Buses Lit** *(☎ 237-200 in Valpo, ☎ 690-783 in Viña)*, **Cóndor** *(☎ 212-927 in Valpo, ☎ 882-345 in Viña)* and **Intersur** *(☎ 212-297)* go to points on the Panamericana as far south as Puerto Montt. **Sol del Sur** *(☎ 252-211 in Valpo, ☎ 687-277 in Viña)*, **Buses JM** *(☎ 256-581 in Valpo, ☎ 883-184 in Viña)* and **Sol del Pacífico** *(☎ 213-776 in Valpo, ☎ 883-156 in Viña)* go to Talca, Chillán, Concepción and Los Angeles.

Valparaíso and Viña both have direct services to Argentina, bypassing Santiago. Carriers with daily departures to Buenos Aires via Mendoza include **El Rápido** *(☎ 257-587 in Valpo, ☎ 685-474 in Viña)*, **Buses TAC** *(☎ 258-922 in Valpo, ☎ 685-767 in Viña)* and **Buses Ahumada** *(☎ 216-663)*. **Tur Bus** *(☎ 939-646 in Valpo, ☎ 882-621 in Viña)* and **Fénix Pullman Norte** *(☎ 257-993 in Valpo)* run to Mendoza, as does **Tas Choapa** *(☎ 252-921 in Valparaíso, ☎ 882-258 in Viña del Mar)*, which continues to San Juan and Córdoba. **Buses Pluma** *(☎ 258-322)* runs to Mendoza, Rosario and the Brazilian cities of Florianópolis, São Paulo and Rio de Janeiro (US$112). **Buses Géminis** *(☎ 258-322)* goes to La Paz, Bolivia (US$80).

The following table gives prices and journey times from Valparaíso to major destinations in South America:

destination	duration in hours	cost
Antofagasta	15	US$29
Algarrobo	1	US$2
Arica	24	US$40
Buenos Aires (Ar)	19	US$50
Chillán	10	US$12
Concepción	10	US$13
Córdoba (Ar)	16	US$43
Iquique	20	US$35
Isla Negra	1½	US$3
La Ligua	1	US$2
Los Andes	2	US$4
Los Angeles	10	US$14
Mendoza (Ar)	8	US$17
Osorno	14	US$24
Ovalle	6	US$12
Puerto Montt	16	US$27
São Paolo (Br)	72	US$106
Santiago	2	US$4
Talca	6	US$8
Temuco	11	US$18

Getting Around

Valparaíso and Viña del Mar are pretty much contiguous, connected by countless local buses (about US$0.50), slightly more expensive taxi colectivos, and the Merval train (US$0.40).

Metro Regional de Valparaíso (Merval) operates regular commuter trains within the Valparaíso-Viña area and to the towns of Quilpué, Villa Alemana and Limache. The area's endemic traffic congestion makes the frequent, inexpensive service between Valparaíso and Viña a superior alternative to either bus or taxi, but bear in mind that services cease at around 10pm. Valparaíso's **Estación Puerto** (☎ 217-108; Plaza Sotomayor 711) is at the corner of Errázuriz, with additional stations at Bellavista (on Errázuriz between Pudeto and Molina) and at Muelle Barón.

Driving in Valparaíso makes little sense, but cars can be useful for visiting beach resorts to the north or south. Most car rental agencies are in Viña del Mar, but in Valparaíso try **Rosselot Rent a Car** (☎ 254-842; Victoria 2675).

VIÑA DEL MAR
☎ 32 • pop 299,000

Viña del Mar (Viña for short) has long been Chile's premier beach resort, but it's also a bustling commercial center. Only a short bus ride north of Valparaíso, it is popularly known as the Ciudad Jardín (Garden City) for reasons obvious to any visitor; beginning with Av España's Reloj de Flores (Clock of Flowers), whose blooms greet visitors at the entrance to town, Viña's manicured subtropical landscape of palms and bananas contrasts dramatically with the colorful disorder of its blue-collar neighbor. Many moneyed Chileans and other wealthy Latin Americans own houses here.

Colonial Viña was the hacienda of the prominent Carrera family, who sold it to a Portuguese businessman named Alvarez in the mid-19th century. Alvarez's daughter and sole heir later married into the Vergara family, who have bestowed their name upon many city landmarks. Soon thereafter, Viña's role as the country's Pacific playground began as the railroad linked Valparaíso with Santiago; the *porteños* of Valparaíso, many of them foreigners, now had easy access to the beaches and broad green spaces to the north, and soon built grand houses and mansions away from the cramped harbor city.

With construction of hotels and the subdivision of the sector north of the Estero Marga Marga, Viña became an increasingly attractive and popular weekend destination for Santiaguinos. Viña, though, has recently lost popularity to competing resorts such as La Serena (see the Norte Chico chapter). Visitors hoping for balmy summer weather are often disappointed; Viña and the entire central coast are subject to cool fogs that don't burn off until early afternoon, and ocean temperatures are downright chilly.

Orientation

Viña consists of two distinct sectors: an established, prestigious area of traditional mansions south of the Estero (estuary) Marga Marga, and a newer, more regular residential grid to its north. Several bridges, most notably Puente Libertad, connect the two sectors. North of the heavily polluted Marga Marga, most streets are identified by number and direction, either Norte (north), Oriente (east) or Poniente (west). Av Libertad separates Ponientes from Orientes. These

MIDDLE CHILE

streets are usually written as a numeral, but are sometimes spelled out, so that 1 Norte may also appear as Uno Norte.

The commercial center of Viña is south of the Marga Marga, on Plaza Vergara and Avs Arlegui and Valparaíso, which parallel the river. South of Alvarez is a zone of turn-of-the-20th-century mansions that belonged to the Santiago and Viña elite, whose centerpiece is the famous Quinta Vergara (see below). Viña's main attractions, of course, are the white-sand beaches that stretch northward from the northern bank of the Estero Marga Marga to the suburbs of Reñaca and Concón. The permanent crafts stalls along Pasaje Cousiño are a good place to search for jewelry, copperware and leather goods.

Information

The municipal **Central de Turismo e Informaciones** (☎ 269-330; Av Marina, open 9am-7pm Mon-Sat in summer, 9am-2pm & 3pm-7pm Mon-Fri, 10am-2pm & 4pm-7pm Sat rest of year) is at the junction of Avs Libertad and Marina, just north of Plaza Vergara. The tourist office distributes an adequate city map and a monthly calendar of events for both cities. There's another **municipal tourist office** (☎ 713-800; cnr Villanelo & Valparaíso; open 10am-2pm, 3pm-6pm Mon-Sat), though its main focus is promoting travel to Mendoza, in Argentina.

Sernatur (☎ 882-285, fax 684-117; Av Valparaíso 507, 3rd floor; open 8:30am-5:30pm

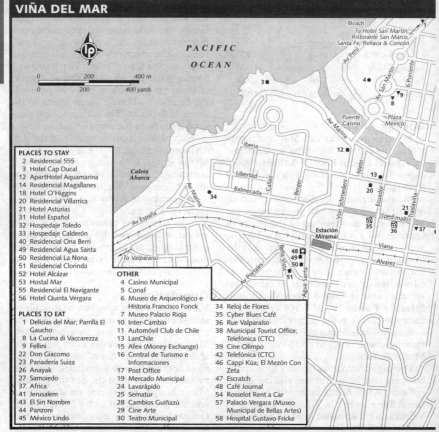

VIÑA DEL MAR

PACIFIC OCEAN

Beach
To Hotel San Martín,
Ristorante San Marco,
Santa Fe, Reñaca & Concón

Caleta Abarca

Estación Miramar

PLACES TO STAY
2 Residencial 555
3 Hotel Cap Ducal
12 ApartHotel Aquamarina
14 Residencial Magallanes
18 Hotel O'Higgins
20 Residencial Villarrica
21 Hotel Asturias
31 Hotel Español
32 Hospedaje Toledo
33 Hospedaje Calderón
40 Residencial Ona Berri
49 Residencial Agua Santa
50 Residencial La Nona
51 Residencial Clorinda
52 Hotel Alcázar
53 Hostal Mar
55 Residencial El Navigante
56 Hotel Quinta Vergara

PLACES TO EAT
1 Delicias del Mar; Parrilla El Gaucho
8 La Cucina di Vaccarezza
9 Fellini
22 Don Giacomo
23 Panadería Suiza
26 Anayak
27 Samoiedo
37 Africa
41 Jerusalem
43 El Sin Nombre
44 Panzoni
45 México Lindo

OTHER
4 Casino Municipal
5 Conaf
6 Museo de Arqueológico e Historia Francisco Fonck
7 Museo Palacio Rioja
10 Inter-Cambio
11 Automóvil Club de Chile
13 LanChile
15 Afex (Money Exchange)
16 Central de Turismo e Informaciones
17 Post Office
19 Mercado Municipal
24 Lavarápido
25 Sernatur
28 Cambios Guiñazú
29 Cine Arte
30 Teatro Municipal
34 Reloj de Flores
35 Cyber Blues Café
36 Rue Valparaíso
38 Municipal Tourist Office; Telefónica (CTC)
39 Cine Olimpo
42 Telefónica (CTC)
46 Cappi Kúa; El Mezón Con Zeta
47 Escratch
48 Café Journal
54 Rosselot Rent a Car
57 Palacio Vergara (Museo Municipal de Bellas Artes)
58 Hospital Gustavo Fricke

MIDDLE CHILE

Mon-Fri) has an entrance that's a little difficult to find, and the staff cater more to businesses than individuals.

The **Automóvil Club de Chile** *(Acchi; ☎ 689-505; 1 Norte 901)* is just north of the Marga Marga.

For US cash or traveler's checks, try **Cambios Guiñazú** *(Arlegui 686)* or **Inter-Cambio** *(1 Norte 655-B)*.

The **post office** is at the northwest side of Plaza Vergara, near Puente Libertad. **DHL** *(Av Libertad)*, between 8 and 9 Norte, offers international courier services.

Telefónica (CTC) *(Valparaíso 628 • cnr Valparaíso & Villanelo • cnr Av Libertad & 1 Norte)* has a few long-distance offices scattered around town.

The **Cyber Blues Café** *(☎ 690-529; Av Valparaíso 196)* offers Internet access.

Conaf *(☎ 970-108; 3 Norte 541)* has information on protected areas such as Parque Nacional La Campana.

For laundry services, go to **Lavarápido** *(Arlegui 440)*.

Hospital Gustavo Fricke *(☎ 680-041; Alvarez 1532)* is east of downtown, at the corner of Cancha.

Summer is the pickpocket season, so keep a close eye on your belongings, especially on the beach.

Museums
Specializing in Easter Island archaeology and Chilean natural history, the small

VIÑA DEL MAR

MIDDLE CHILE

Museo de Arqueológico e Historia Francisco Fonck (☎ 686-753; 4 Norte 784; adult/child US$1.70/0.30; open 9:30am-6pm Tues-Fri, 9:30am-2pm Sat, Sun & holidays) features an original *moai* (Easter Island statue) from Chile's remote Pacific possession at the approach to its entrance. It also has Mapuche silverwork, Peruvian ceramics, a good insect room and lots of stuffed birds.

The **Museo Palacio Rioja** (☎ 689-665; Quillota 214; adult/child US$0.30/0.15; open 10am-1:30pm & 3pm-5:30pm Tues-Sun), an elegant century-old mansion, is now a municipal museum. It also hosts films and musical performances; pleasant sounds from the downstairs conservatory of music sometimes waft out to the mansion's beautiful formal gardens.

Quinta Vergara

Once the residence of the prosperous Alvarez-Vergara family, now a public park, the grounds of the magnificently landscaped Quinta Vergara (open 7am-7pm daily) contain the Venetian-style **Palacio Vergara**, which dates from 1908. The building houses the **Museo Municipal de Bellas Artes** (☎ 684-137; open 10am-2pm & 3pm-6pm Tues-Sun).

Frequent summer concerts at the Quinta's amphitheater complement the celebrated Festival Internacional de la Canción (see Special Events). The only entrance to the grounds is on Errázuriz at the south end of Quinta.

Jardín Botánico Nacional

Chile's national botanical garden (☎ 672-566; adult/child US$1.20/0.30; open 9am-7pm Tues-Sun in summer, 10am-6:30pm daily rest of year) comprises 61 hectares with over 3000 native and exotic plant species.

It's in the southeast part of town. From Viana in downtown Viña, take Bus No 20 east to the end of the line, then cross the bridge and walk about 10 minutes; the Jardín Botánico is on your left.

Special Events

Viña del Mar's most popular attraction is the annual Festival Internacional de la Canción (International Song Festival), resembling a Spanish-speaking version of the insipid Eurovision Song Contest and held every February in the amphitheater of the Quinta Vergara. Every evening for a week,

everything stops as Chileans without tickets gaze transfixed at TV sets in their homes, and in cafés, restaurants and bars.

Places to Stay

Prices rise in summer, but outside the peak months of January and February, supply exceeds demand (except on major holidays such as Easter and mid-September's Fiestas Patrias). March is an especially good month to visit; the weather is ideal but most Chileans have finished their holidays.

Budget Budget travelers will find several alternatives on or near Agua Santa, as well as downtown near the bus terminal.

Well-located and professional **Hotel Asturias** (☎ 032-691565, Av Valparaíso 299) takes HI cardholders for US$10 per person.

Residencial Agua Santa (☎ 901-531; Agua Santa 36; peak season US$10 per person) is in an attractive blue Victorian building.

Residencial Clorinda (☎ 623-835; Av Portales 47; singles/doubles with shared bath US$10/20) has a host of wonderful outdoor patios with great views; there are also laundry facilities, and guests can use the kitchen.

Residencial La Nona (☎ 663-825; Agua Santa 48; US$13 per person, including breakfast) is brightly painted and run by a nice family.

Residencial Ona Berri (☎ 688-187; Av Valparaíso 618; rooms with shared/private bath US$10/17, including breakfast) has sunny, pleasant rooms and is very central.

Near the bus terminal, across the street from each other, are two friendly, comfortable family lodgings.

Hospedaje Calderón (☎ 970-456; Batuco 147; US$10 per person) and **Hospedaje Toledo** (☎ 881-496; Baluco 160, US$10 per person).

Residencial Magallanes (☎ 685-101; Arlegui 555; US$12 per person with shared bath), set back from the street, is a friendly, family-run place.

Residencial El Navigante (☎ 482-648; Prieto Nieto 0332; US$12/8 per person with/ without breakfast), near the grounds of the Quinta Vergara, is a family-run bargain in an old, rambling mansion.

Hostal Mar (☎ 884-775; Alvarez 868; singles/doubles US$13/27 with breakfast) is a pleasant place shaded by trees.

Residencial Villarrica (☎ 881-484; Arlegui 172; singles/doubles US$14/21 with shared bath) is also a good choice, with bright, spacious rooms.

Mid-Range Although close to the beach, **ApartHotel Aquamarina** (☎ 978-845; Von Shroeders 14; singles/doubles US$18/42) is on a somewhat noisy street. But it does have large, comfortable apartments with fully equipped kitchen and separate dining/lounge room.

Hotel Quinta Vergara (☎ 685-073, fax 691-978; Errázuriz 690; singles/doubles US$25/35, including breakfast) has a great location and a spiffy exterior; the rooms themselves are adequate but nothing flash.

Residencial 555 (☎/fax 972-240; 5 Norte 555; singles/doubles US$26/43 with private bath, breakfast, cable & phone) has lovely, spotless rooms in an old house on a quiet tree-lined street.

Top End Opposite Plaza Vergara and close to Estación Viña del Mar, **Hotel Español** (☎ 685-860; Plaza Parroquia 391; doubles US$42) is nice and central.

Hotel Alcázar (☎ 685-112; Alvarez 646; singles & doubles US$50) has comfortable rooms but is on a noisy street.

Hotel O'Higgins (☎ 882-016; Plaza Vergara s/n; singles/doubles from US$66/82, with breakfast) is a venerable place, where you can run up a huge room-service bill without working up a sweat. It's worth mentioning, though, that this 1934 landmark is past its prime, and the service could stand improvement as well.

Hotel Cap Ducal (☎ 626-655, fax 665-478; Av Marina 51; singles/doubles US$80/85) is an Art Deco, shipshaped building set out on a concrete foundation in the surf ('It's not next to the sea, it's on the sea'), dating from 1936. The rooms are gorgeous and cozy, with a balcony and huge windows looking out to sea.

Hotel San Martín (☎ 689-191; San Martín 667; singles/doubles from around US$90/117) offers top-end accommodations. Rooms are small but offer lovely views of Playa Acapulco.

Places to Eat
Panadería Suiza (Arlegui & Villanelo) has good, cheap pastries and küchen.

For good sandwiches, coffee and desserts, try **Anayak** (☎ 680-093; Quinta 134) or **Samoiedo** (☎ 684-610; Valparaíso 637).

Panzoni (☎ 682-134; Paseo Cousiño 12-B) features friendly service and fine Italian specialties; it's especially popular for lunch.

México Lindo (☎ 692-144; Paseo Cousiño 136, 2nd floor) serves Tex-Mex specialties such as enchiladas and burritos but it's no great shakes.

Jerusalem (☎ 687-608; Quinta 259) is a stand-up place with tasty felafel sandwiches and other Middle Eastern fare.

El Sin Nombre (Cousiño s/n) has cheap lunches but zero atmosphere.

Africa (☎ 882-856; Av Valparaíso 324) has a novel grass-hut décor and serves meat dishes and sandwiches.

Ristorante San Marco (☎ 975-304; San Martín 597), **Don Giacomo** (☎ 688-889; Villanelo 135, 2nd floor; lasagna and pasta dishes US$1.70) and **La Cucina di Vaccarezza** (☎ 975-790; Av San Martín 180) all serve Italian specialties.

Fellini (☎ 975-742; 3 Norte 880) is Franco-Italian, with excellent fish.

Delicias del Mar (☎ 901-837; San Martín 459) is a good, but expensive, Basque seafood restaurant.

It's hard to get past the scenery at hotel **Cap Ducal** (☎ 626-655, fax 665-478; Av Marina 51; meal per person US$30), a stunning, shiplike place with sweeping views of the horizon, an open fireplace and a backlit bar built of bottles, but it's also well respected for its seafood.

Parrilla El Gaucho (Av San Martín & 5 Norte) serves full parrilladas.

Santa Fe (☎ 691-719; 8 Norte 303) is a popular but expensive Tex-Mex restaurant.

Entertainment
Café Journal (☎ 666-654) , at the corner of Santa Agua and Alvarez, near Estación Miramar, is popular with the alternative crowd.

There is a cluster of pubs in Pasaje Cousiño, including **Cappi Kúa** (☎ 977-331; Pasaje Cousiño 11, Local 4) and **El Mezón con Zeta** (☎ 690-494; Pasaje Cousiño 9), which has live music.

Viña has a plethora of nightclubs. **Scratch** (☎ 978-219; Bohn 970) is the most well known.

The **Casino Municipal** (☎ 689-200; Av San Martín 199; cover US$6; open 6pm-early morning daily), overlooking the beach on the north side of the Marga Marga, offers opportunities to squander your savings on slot machines, bingo and card games – in between dinner and cabaret entertainment. Formal attire is required.

First-run movies often hit Viña even before Santiago. Try the two-screen **Cine Olimpo** (☎ 711-607; Quinta 294). **Cine Arte** (☎ 882-798; Plaza Vergara 142) shows less commercial films.

Teatro Municipal (☎ 681-739; Plaza Vergara s/n) stages plays, concerts and movies – mostly retrospectives and art films.

Horse-racing takes place at the **Valparaíso Sporting Club** (☎ 689-393; Av Los Castaños 404).

Getting There & Away

LanChile (☎ 690-365; Ecuador 80) has an office, but all flights leave from Santiago.

Viña's **bus terminal** at Valparaíso and Quilpué, four long blocks east of Plaza Vergara, has undergone a major renovation. Services are virtually identical to those from Valparaíso, and all northbound and international services from the port capital stop in Viña (see Valparaíso's Getting There & Away section for details).

Getting Around

Running along Arlegui, frequent local buses marked 'Puerto' or 'Aduana' link Viña with Valparaíso.

For easier connections to Valparaíso, the Metro Regional Valparaíso (Merval) has two stations: **Estación Miramar** (Alvarez & Agua Santa) and **Estación Viña del Mar**, at the southeast corner of Plaza Sucre.

In summer the Viña area is congested and impossible to park in. However, for car rentals, try **Rosselot** (☎ 382-888; Alvarez 762).

AROUND VALPARAÍSO & VIÑA DEL MAR
Lo Vásquez

Every December 8, Chilean authorities close Ruta 68, as nearly half a million pilgrims converge on this small town's **Santuario de la Inmaculada Concepción**, 32km southeast of Valparaíso and 68km northwest of Santiago. Masses take place hourly from 6pm the night before until 8pm on the 8th.

Isla Negra

Even more outlandish than La Chascona in Santiago, Pablo Neruda's favorite house (☎ 035-461-284; admission US$4 with English-speaking guide; open 10am-8pm Tues-Sun in summer, 10am-2pm & 3pm-6pm Tues-Fri, 10am-8pm Sat & Sun rest of year) sits on a rocky ocean headland between Valparaíso and Cartagena. Once vandalized by agents of the Pinochet dictatorship, it now houses the Museo Neruda, holding the poet's collections of bowsprits, ships in bottles, nautical instruments, wood carvings and other memorabilia. His tomb is also here. Isla Negra is not, by the way, an island.

Reservations are imperative, since there are up to 40 tours daily led by guides,

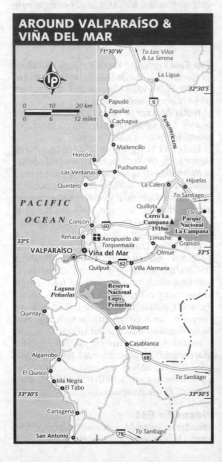

AROUND VALPARAÍSO & VIÑA DEL MAR

whose interest and competence vary greatly. Outside the summer months, Isla Negra tours are more relaxed. Tours last only half an hour, but visitors are permitted to hang around and photograph the grounds as long as they like.

Pullman Bus Lago Peñuelas (☎ *032-224-025; US$2; 1½ hrs*) leaves from the main bus terminal in Valparaíso. You can also catch a bus from Santiago's Terminal Sur. Unfortunately, Neruda's house is poorly signposted from the bus stop; ask for directions.

Reñaca & Concón

Among the beach towns north of Viña are overbuilt suburbs such as **Reñaca**, which has the area's most pleasant and extensive beach – though the foreshore is unfortunately crowded with multitiered apartment buildings.

Concón, just north of Reñaca, has a couple of beaches that are popular with surfers. Bodyboarders frequent Playa Negra, while surfers go to Playa de Ritoque, farther north, toward Quintero. Concón is also known for its informal seafood restaurants. **La Picá Horizonte** (☎ *032-903-665; San Pedro 120, Concón*), at Caleta Higuerillas, is one of the best. It's a little hard to find but worth the effort. From the Muelle de Pescadores (Fishermen's Pier), climb the steps (behind Restaurant El Tiburón) and, at the top, walk one short block left along the dirt road to San Pedro. On Sunday afternoons it can be hard to get a table.

Quintero

Another 23km beyond Concón, Quintero is a peninsular beach community that was once part of Lord Cochrane's hacienda. It has a nice relaxed seaside feel and is popular with families. There are interesting covelike beaches nestled between rocks.

Hotel Monaco (☎ *032-930-939; 21 de Mayo 1530; US$6 per person with shared bath, doubles with private bath US$30*) has some bargain rooms. From its fabulous architecture, you can tell that it must once have been a very fine place.

Residencial Victoria (☎ *032-930-208; Vicuña Mackenna 1460; US$10 per person*) is not too bad and has a good picada.

Residencial María Alejandra (☎ *032-930-266; Lord Cochrane 157; singles with shared bath US$10*) has reasonable accommoda-tions. Rooms with private bath are only slightly more expensive.

Residencial Brazilian (☎ *032-930590; 21 de Mayo 1336; singles/doubles US$20/36*), though a bit drab, has decent rooms and attractive gardens; rates include breakfast.

You'll find dozens of seafood **picadas** along 21 de Mayo.

North of Quintero, the town of **Las Ventanas** has a petroleum port and a scary-looking power plant – but there's no reason to pause there, as things get much nicer just a few kilometers beyond.

Horcón

Across the bay to the north, the quaint working port of Horcón is also something of a hippie colony. Its short, narrow beach is nothing special, but nearby **Playa Cau Cau** is the place for beach volleyball, bodysurfing and the like. Horcón's clutter of cheap seafood restaurants rank among the area's best. Try **El Ancla**, which also offers accommodations. **Roty Schop**, on the beach, has good fried seafood empanadas.

Sol del Pacífico buses from Viña go directly here.

Maitencillo

Maitencillo's long, sandy beaches – Playa Larga and Playa Aguas Blancas – attract many visitors. It's a big town packed with holiday homes, but it has retained a pleasant low-key vibe. Playa Caleta is a cute little beach with fishing boats.

Many places offer accommodations; try **Cabañas Maitencillo** (☎ *032-772-307; Carmen 63; doubles US$30*), which has very clean, comfy cabins at the northern end of town.

Cachagua

Cachagua, a tiny settlement 10km north of Maitencillo, lacks hotels but has plenty of summer houses and a couple of restaurants, most notably **Entre Olas**. Just opposite the attractive crescent beach is **Isla Cachagua**, one of the central coast's major seabird breeding sites and home to over 2000 Humboldt penguins, as well as a colony of sea lions.

Zapallar

At Zapallar, the most exclusive of Chilean beach resorts, about 80km north of Viña, multimillion-dollar houses (many of them historic mansions) cover the densely wooded hillsides from the beach nearly to the ridgetops. The beach is a secluded, gently curving arc of yellow sand in a sheltered cove. **La Caleta de Pescadores**, where the fishermen sell their catch, is near the large rock at the southwestern end of the beach; a short walk around the promontory leads to **Plaza del Mar Bravo**, where huge waves crash with a splash onto interesting rocks.

Residencial La Terraza (☎ *033-741-026, 711-409; Alcalde 142; singles/doubles high season US$40/50, low season US$24/30)* is two short blocks west of the highway that connects with the Panamericana and is a stiff climb from the beach. It also has a good restaurant.

Hotel Isla Seca (☎ *033-741-221; Camino Costero s/n; singles/doubles US$95/135, more with ocean view)* is a classy place set amid Zapallar's mansions. Its restaurant is stylishly decorated with black and white tiles on the floor, drapey tablecloths and heavy velvet curtains; the house specialty is fresh fish and shellfish and local desserts. Expect to pay about US$23 per person for a meal.

Il Parador (☎ *033-790-514; Carretera F30 E Norte 5680; rooms US$50/150 low/high season, including breakfast)* is an extraordinary, architecturally distinctive hotel overlooking the ocean about 10km north of Zapallar. The rooms have elegantly restrained furnishings and exquisite views. Designed by Matias Klotz, one of Chile's most interesting architects, the hotel has a supercool one-lane swimming pool excavated into the hillside, and there's a rooftop helipad. The hotel also has a bar and restaurant, the latter serving elaborate seafood and fusion cuisine (lunch menú US$10).

Restaurant César (☎ *033-741-507; Rambla s/n)* is on the beach, where the view commands premium prices and is popular with upper-income Chileans.

El Chiringuito (☎ *033-741-024; Caleta de Pescadores; fish mains US$8)* is the relaxed alternative to Zapallar's fancy restaurants. Though the seafood is superb, it's worth a visit just to check out the restaurant's spectacular location by the water and its interior, which has a wall of windows and a floor carpeted with loose, crushed scallop shells; there's also a cozy logfire.

Papudo

Papudo, 10km north of Zapallar, is a lot less exclusive than Zapallar and has a wider range of accommodations, but high-rise apartment buildings are starting to crowd the waterfront. Sheltered Playa Chica and the long Playa Grande are the main attractions, linked together by Av Irarrázaval. The town center is up the hill from the waterfront, clustered around a plaza – this part of Papudo feels much more like a traditional Chilean town than a beach resort.

Residencial La Plaza (☎ *033-791-391; Chorrillos 119; US$10 per person)* is a small, friendly, family-run lodging that maintains the same prices all year. Room rates include private bath and breakfast, and are even less with shared bath.

Hotel La Abeja (☎ *033-791-116; Chorrillos 36; rooms from US$25)* is an old-style guesthouse with simple cabaña-style rooms; it's also famous for its empanadas.

Hotel Carande (☎ *033-791-105, fax 791-118; Chorrillos 89; singles/doubles US$20/37 with breakfast)* is a nice place, with better rooms than La Abeja.

Several beachfront restaurants and pubs line Irarrázaval, most notably **Banana** and **Caleta Papudo**. At Caleta Zapallar, just beyond the yacht club, there's a **shellfish market**, which may have hot food on offer as well.

Buses up and down the coast connect Papudo with Valparaíso, Viña del Mar and intermediates, and with La Ligua.

La Ligua

Inland from Papudo, where the landscape opens out onto rolling golden hills, motorists and bus passengers passing on the Panamericana will notice vendors hawking the famous *dulces* (sweets) of La Ligua, a modest but tidy agricultural town. The cakes and pastries – filled with *manjar*, a soft caramel made from condensed milk – really are La Ligua's only claim to fame, though it does have a museum, and there's a good artisans' market on the Plaza de Armas.

The **Museo de La Ligua** (☎ *033-714-143; Pedro Polanco 698; admission US$0.40; open 9am-1pm & 3:30pm-7pm Mon-Fri, 10am-2pm Sat)* is an interesting archaeological museum. Once the city slaughterhouse, this well-organized and remodeled building recreates a burial site in the Diaguita-Inka style, with materials uncovered in downtown La Ligua. It also displays a selection of materials from the 19th-century mining era and historical photographs of the city's early days.

Budget accommodations are available at **Residencial Regine I** (☎ 033-711-192; *Esmeralda 27; rooms with shared bath US$7*) and **Residencial Regine II** (☎ 033-711-192; *Condell 360; rooms with private bath US$11*).

Hotel Anchimallén (☎ 033-711-683; *Ortiz de Rosas 694; singles/doubles US$33/44; with private bath and breakfast*) is modern and well managed.

Restaurant Lihuén (☎ 033-711-143; *Ortiz de Rosas 303*) has good sandwiches and outstanding ice cream.

The **bus terminal** is on Papudo between Pedro Polanco and Uribe; frequent buses connect La Ligua with Santiago, and with the coastal towns of Papudo and Zapallar.

PN La Campana

Parque Nacional La Campana, halfway between Santiago and Valparaíso, contains the highest mountains in the coastal cordillera, including Cerro La Campana (1880m), climbed by Charles Darwin in 1834. It occupies 8000 hectares in a nearly roadless segment of the coastal range that once belonged to the Jesuit hacienda of San Isidro. In geological structure and vegetation, its jagged scrubland resembles the mountains of Southern California and protects remaining stands of the deciduous roble de Santiago (*Nothofagus obliqua*), the northernmost species of the common South American genus, and the Chilean palm (*Jubaea chilensis*).

The Chilean palm, also known as the palma de coquitos for its tasty fruits (they are just like miniature coconuts), grows up to 25m in height and measures up to 1.5m in diameter. At age 60 it flowers for the first time, and it can live to be 1000 years old. It used to cover the coastal range, but it declined greatly in the 19th century because it was exploited for its sugary sap, obtained by toppling the tree and stripping it of its foliage. Each palm yielded up to 90 gallons of sap, which cutters concentrated into treacle by boiling. In some parts of the park you can see the ruins of ovens that were used for this purpose; there are also old-fashioned charcoal kilns.

Profuse wildflowers and a reliable water supply make spring the best time for a visit, but the park is open all year.

La Campana (*admission US$2.50*) has Conaf stations at each entrance, where rangers collect the entrance fee and sometimes have maps. The largest of these stations is at **Granizo** (☎ 033-44-1342; *open 9am-5:30pm daily*), on the south side of the park near Olmué; the other is at **Ocoa** (*open 9am-5:30pm Sat-Thur, 9am-4:45pm Fri*).

Cerro La Campana Thousands of Chileans and increasing numbers of foreign visitors reach the summit of La Campana every year. On a clear day, the view from La Campana, stretching from the ships at anchor in the Pacific harbor to the Andean summit of Aconcagua, is spectacular.

It's possible to hitchhike or drive to the abandoned mine site at the end of the road leading into the park from the Granizo entrance, considerably shortening the hike to the summit, but it's much more interesting and rewarding to hike the trail all the way from the park entrance. Figure at least four hours to the top and three hours back down.

From Granizo, 373m above sea level, the abruptly steep trail to the summit climbs 1455m in only 7km – an average grade of nearly 21%. Fortunately, most of the hike is in shade, and there are three water sources en route: Primera Aguada, at an elevation of 580m; Segunda Aguada; and the abandoned mine site, where the trail continues to the summit.

At the point where the trail skirts a granite wall, prior to the final vertiginous ascent, is a plaque commemorating the 101st anniversary of Darwin's climb. At another point slightly beyond this, the Club Montañés de Valparaíso has placed another plaque, honoring climbers who died in 1968 when an earthquake unleashed a landslide.

Sturdy, sensible footwear is essential, as parts of the trail are slippery even when dry; sneakers can be awkward.

Ocoa Reached by a rough gravel road from the village of **Hijuelas** on the Panamericana, Ocoa is the northern entrance to La Campana. This part of the park seems almost tropical, with mighty Chilean palms adding a very exotic element.

At **Casino**, 2km beyond the park entrance, a good walking trail connects Palmas de Ocoa with Granizo, 14km to the north. To reach the high saddle of the **Portezuelo de**

Granizo takes about two hours of steady hiking through the palm-studded canyon of the Estero Rabuco. On clear days, the Portezuelo offers fine views. The trail forks at the Portezuelo: the lower branch plunges into **Cajón Grande**, a canyon with deciduous *roble* forest, while the other follows the contour westward before dropping into Granizo.

Also at Ocoa, another foot trail leads 6km to **Salto de la Cortadera**, an attractive waterfall that is best during the spring runoff. Ask the rangers for directions to the trailhead.

Places to Stay & Eat There are formal camping areas *(US$10 for up to 6 people)* at Granizo, Cajón Grande and Ocoa. Backcountry camping is not permitted.

The most convenient lodgings are in Olmué, which is popular on weekends.

Hostería Copihue *(☎ 033-441-544; Diego Portales 2203, Olmué; singles/doubles US$43/67 with breakfast; half-board and full-board options also available)* offers spic-and-span rooms, well-groomed grounds, two pools, a gym, tennis courts and a restaurant.

Hostería Aire Puro *(☎ 033-441-381; Av Granizo 7672, Olmué; doubles US$27 with breakfast; lunch menu US$4)* has simple cabins.

Getting There & Away La Campana is easily accessible from both Santiago and Viña del Mar, and it's a pretty drive to either entrance. Local transport (Agdabus) to Granizo leaves every 20 minutes from Limache and Olmué, which are connected by regular bus with Santiago and Valparaíso/Viña. From the Valparaíso and Viña area, **Ciferal Express** *(☎ 953-317; US$1; 1¾ hours)* goes to within about a kilometer of the Granizo entrance every 30 minutes in season; the easiest place to catch the bus is on 1 Norte in Viña.

Direct access to Sector Ocoa is more problematic. Almost any northbound bus from Santiago will drop you at Hijuelas (there is a sharp and poorly marked turnoff to the park just before the bridge across the Río Aconcagua), but from there, you will have to hitch or walk 12km to the park entrance, or else hire a taxi (about US$10).

Several operators run hiking trips in the park. **Andes Trek** *(☎ 032-956-052, 09-327-6593; e andestrek@andestrek.cl)* offers day hikes starting from the oak forest in

Granizo and ending up at the Palmas de Ocoa, with full transportation and a barbecue lunch provided. They also run day hikes to the summit of La Campana and overnight horseback-riding trips up Mt Roble, the highest mountain in the coastal cordillera. From October to April, **Altué Active Travel** *(☎ 02-232-1103, fax 233-6799; Encomenderos 83, Las Condes, Santiago)* runs full-day tours to climb Cerro La Campana.

Aconcagua Valley

The fertile Aconcagua Valley is fed by the Río Aconcagua, which flows west from the highest mountain in the Americas – Cerro Aconcagua (6959m) – to Concón (just north of Viña del Mar). Scenic Hwy 60 runs along the length of the valley and across the Andes to Mendoza, Argentina.

LOS ANDES
☎ 34 • pop 60,200

Founded in 1791 by Ambrosio O'Higgins, Los Andes is a friendly foothill town along the international highway to the legendary ski resort at Portillo, near the Argentine border, and the Argentine city of Mendoza. Its mountain backdrop adds a bit of drama.

The town has a helpful municipal **Quiosco Turístico** *(☎ 421-121; Av Santa Teresa 333; open 10am-2pm & 4pm-8pm Mon-Fri, 10am-6pm Sat & Sun)* near the archaeological museum. The **post office** *(cnr Santa Rosa & Esmeralda)* and **Entel** *(Esmeralda 463)* are both on the main plaza. If you need medical attention go to **Hospital San Juan de Dios** *(☎ 421-121, 421-666; Avs Argentina & Hermanos Clark)*.

Things to See & Do

For a small provincial museum, Los Andes' **Museo Arqueológico** *(☎ 420-115; Av Santa Teresa 398; admission US$1; open 10am-8pm Tues-Sun)* features surprisingly good presentations on pre-Hispanic local cultures and also exhibits material on forensic anthropology, colonial times and the cultures of the Inka, Mapuche and Easter Islanders. The curator, who once lived in the USA, has translated the exhibit captions into English.

Across the street, dating from the early 19th century but reconstructed during the 1920s, the **Museo Antiguo Monasterio del Es-**

píritu Santo *(Av Santa Teresa 389; open 10am-6pm daily)* formerly served as the Convento Carmelitas Descalzas del Espíritu Santo de los Andes, a retreat for Carmelite nuns. It was home to Santa Teresa de los Andes, beatified in 1993; it also includes materials on Laura Vicuña, who legend says willed herself to die at the age of 12, in 1906, in atonement for her widowed mother's taking a married lover.

From 1912 to 1918, Gabriela Mistral taught classes at the former **Colegio de Niñas** *(Girls' School; Esmeralda 246)*, now the Círculo Italiano.

On the first Saturday of each month, a little steam train *(☎ 09-882-0675, 09-319-3454; US$13)* travels east to Río Blanco through the mountains, departing at 10am and returning at 5pm. The trip takes two hours. Call ahead to reserve a spot, as the train can only take 25 passengers.

Places to Stay & Eat
Hotel Central *(☎ 421-275; Esmeralda 278; rooms with private bath US$13)* is friendly but rundown, and some rooms lack windows.

Hotel Don Ambrosio *(☎ 420-441; Freire 472; singles/doubles US$23/33, with private bath, TV & breakfast)* is on the bland side but has tidy, comfy rooms that are a good value.

Hotel Plaza *(☎ 421-169, fax 426-029; Rodríguez 370; singles/doubles US$31/33)* is the best option; rooms are comfortable, heated and come with balcony and cable TV. The hotel's entrance faces the north side of the Plaza de Armas at Esmeralda 353 despite its formal street address. The café is a good choice for breakfast.

Hosteria Rucahue *(☎ 406-366; General del Canto 98; rooms with bathroom US$32, including breakfast)*, a few blocks from the center of town, is spotless and well run, if a bit sterile. The hotel has a restaurant and can organize excursions to the mountains.

Roka Pizza *(☎ 407-653; Maipu 599)* is a tropical-style joint with pizza napolitana for US$1.30.

Donde Bahía Pacífico *(Santa Rosa 596; menú US$2)* specializes in seafood.

Centro Español *(O'Higgins 674)*, half a block from the museum and somewhat upscale, has a good daily fixed-price lunch and a beautiful tiled patio.

Círculo Italiano *(Esmeralda 246)* serves Italian food in an interesting old building (see Things to See & Do).

El Guatón *(☎ 423-596; Av Santa Teresa 240)* is the place for *parrillada*.

La Golosita *(Esmeralda 247)* is the best spot for coffee and ice cream.

Getting There & Away
Los Andes' bus station is in the old train station at the end of Av Carlos Díaz, the northern extension of Av Santa Teresa. **Buses Ahumada** *(☎ 421-227; Yerbas Buenas 650)* has a separate terminal.

Companies with buses to Santiago (US$4) and Valparaíso/Viña (two hours, US$3) include **JM Directo** *(☎ 406-484)*, **Pullman Bus** *(☎ 032-253-125)*, Buses Ahumada, **Buses Dhino's** *(☎ 032-221-298)* and **Sol del Pacífico** *(☎ 032-213-776)*, which continues on to Talca, Chillán and Concepción once a day. There are buses every two hours or so to Mendoza, Argentina with Buses Ahumada. **Buses Tac** *(☎ 034-407-355)* runs to the Portillo ski resort four times a day.

PORTILLO
Known for its dry powder, Chile's most famous ski resort is the site of several downhill speed records. It's the most exclusive of the resorts, with top-notch service and an international crowd. Altitudes range from 2590m to 3310m on its 12 runs, the longest of which is 1.5km, and the slopes are well groomed. Lifts run from both sides of the Laguna del Inca, the bright blue alpine lake that forms the centerpiece of the resort.

Hotel Portillo *(bunks with shared bath US$490/790 low/high season per week; bunks with private bath US$610/1185 low/high season per week; rooms per person low season from US$890 per week)* is not cheap, but prices include four meals per day and eight days of lift tickets, and bunks come with five ski lessons.

Additional services include a ski school, ice-skating rink, heated outdoor swimming pool, sauna and massage, gymnasium, yoga classes, shops, cinema, disco, bars and childcare. Meals are available in the hotel restaurant, which has superb views of Laguna del Inca.

Moderately priced accommodations are available in the city of Los Andes, below the snow line, 69km to the west. For those not staying at the resort, daily lift tickets are US$34.

For more information, contact the **Centro de Ski Portillo** *(☎ 263-0606, fax 263-0595;*

MIDDLE CHILE

e *ptours@skiportillo.com; Renato Sánchez 4270, Las Condes, Santiago;* Ⓜ *Escuela Militar).* From the USA, call toll-free ☎ 800-829-5325.

Buses Tac *(☎ 034-407-355)* runs from the Los Andes bus station to Portillo year-round at 10am, 10:30am, 11:30am and 1pm. Transportation from Santiago can be arranged with **KL Adventure Ski** *(☎ 02-217-9101, Av Las Condes 12207).*

Southern Heartland

South of Santiago, squeezed between the Andes and the coastal cordillera, the central valley is Chile's fruit bowl, with a Mediterranean climate and endless orchards and vineyards – this region produces almost all of Chile's wine. The Andes in this sector are spectacular, with deciduous beech forests climbing their slopes, and broad gravel-bedded rivers descending into the valley. Most of the large settlements in this area are agricultural service towns that make good bases for excursions to the hinterland.

RANCAGUA
☎ 72 • pop 212,200

Rancagua is not the most interesting town in Central Chile. The regional economy mostly relies on the huge El Teniente copper mine, in the Andes to the east, and the city is something of a cultural wasteland – it's the only regional capital without a university. Despite its shortcomings, Rancagua can boast that it's the capital of Chilean rodeo. It's also close to the hot springs resort of Termas de Cauquenes and to Reserva Nacional Río de los Cipreses, a popular Andean retreat.

Orientation & Information
Like most cities of colonial origin, Rancagua has a standard grid pattern, centered on Plaza de los Héroes. Between Av San Martín and the plaza, the commercial street of Independencia is a pedestrian mall; street names change on each side of San Martín, but street numbering does not.

Sernatur *(☎ 230-413, fax 232-297; Germán Riesco 277, 1st floor; open 8:30am-5:15pm Mon-Fri)* has an office one block east of Plaza de los Héroes. **Automóvil Club de Chile** *(Acchi,* ☎ *239-930; Ibieta 09)* is on the eastern outskirts.

The **post office** *(Campos)* is between Cuevas and Independencia. **Telefónica** *(San Martín 440)* has a long-distance office, as does **Entel** *(Independencia 468).*

If you need cash, there are numerous ATMs, including the Banco Estado on Independencia at the corner of Bueras.

For information regarding national parks, visit **Conaf** *(☎ 297-505; Cuevas 480, 1st floor).*

The local laundry, **Lava Express** *(☎ 241-738; Av San Martín 270)* charges US$1.30 for 1kg, including ironing.

Rancagua's **Hospital Regional** is on Av O'Higgins, between Astorga and Campos.

Things to See & Do
The **Iglesia de la Merced** *(cnr Estado & Cuevas)* is a national monument dating from 1854, when it served as the Convento y Templo de la Merced de Rancagua. During the battle of Rancagua, the building was headquarters for O'Higgins' patriots. Another religious landmark, the **Iglesia Catedral** *(cnr Estado & Plaza de los Héroes)* dates from 1861 but is fairly run-of-the-mill.

In a colonial house, the **Museo Regional** *(☎ 221-254; adult US$1, free Tues; open 10am-6pm Tues-Fri, 9am-1pm Sat, Sun & holidays)* covers O'Higgins' role in Chilean independence. It also displays a selection of colonial religious artwork.

Special Events
In early autumn (late March), the **Campeonato Nacional de Rodeo** *(national rodeo championship; Medialuna de Rancagua, Av España)* takes place. If planning to stay in Rancagua at this time, make hotel reservations early; otherwise, make it a day trip from Santiago.

Places to Stay & Eat
Hotel España *(☎ 230-141; Av San Martín 367; singles/doubles US$25/33 with private bath & breakfast)* is both the cheapest and the nicest place to stay in Rancagua. Quite a haven from the busy street on which it fronts, it somehow has a fresh tropical feel, with rooms arranged around two patios. Breakfast is served in a splendid dining room decorated with Victorian flourishes. The staff are warm and friendly to boot.

Hotel Turismo Santiago (☎ 230-860, fax 230-822; Av Brasil 1036; singles/doubles US$39/59 with breakfast & cable) is a business-style place with surprisingly nice rooms, but it's not in the nicest part of town.

Hotel Camino del Rey (☎ 239-765, fax 232-314; Estado 275; singles/doubles US$57/80) has a promising antique facade, but its interior wins no points for style; rooms are a little tatty and overpriced.

Bavaria (☎ 241-241; Av San Martín 255), the local branch of the countrywide chain serving reasonably priced sandwiches and standard Chilean food, is reliable but uninspiring.

Reina Victoria (Independencia 667; lunch US$3) is a cheery café with waitresses in orange uniforms; aside from coffee, it has good lunches and excellent ice cream.

Guy (☎ 226-053; Astorga 319; lunch menu US$10) is an informal, country-style French restaurant, the likes of which is difficult to find in Chile.

Torito (Zañartu 323) is a parrilla with a good atmosphere.

Entertainment

Retro Bar (☎ 243-556; Av San Martín 226) gets busy on weekends but is otherwise fairly quiet.

Getting There & Away

Bus Rancagua's bus station (Dr Salinas 1165) is just north of the Mercado Central, but Tur Bus and Buses Al Sur use their own terminals.

The focus at the main station is mostly on regional services. Carriers operating out of the station include **Via Tur** (☎ 234-502) to Los Angeles, Puerto Montt and intermediates, and **Buses Nilahue** (☎ 229-358) and **Andimar** (☎ 237-818), which both go to coastal destinations, including Pichilemu (US$4) via Santa Cruz (US$2).

There are buses every 10 or 15 minutes to Santiago (US$2, one hour) with **Buses al Sur** (☎ 230-340; O'Carrol 1039) and **Tur Bus** (☎ 241-117; Calvo & O'Carrol), which both have their own terminals.

Train Rancagua's train station (☎ 225-239; Av Viña del Mar) is between O'Carrol and Carrera Pinto. Metrotrén runs commuter

MIDDLE CHILE

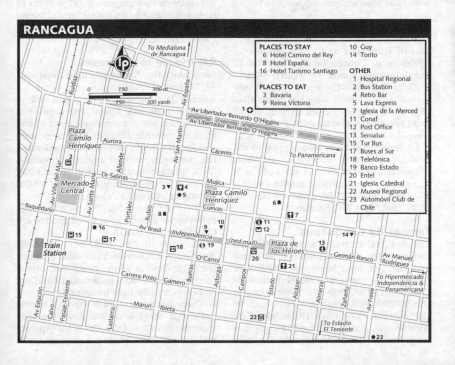

RANCAGUA

0   150   300 m
0   150   300 yards

PLACES TO STAY
6   Hotel Camino del Rey
8   Hotel España
16 Hotel Turismo Santiago

PLACES TO EAT
3   Bavaria
9   Reina Victoria

10 Guy
14 Torito

OTHER
1   Hospital Regional
2   Bus Station
4   Retro Bar
5   Lava Express
7   Iglesia de la Merced
11 Conaf
12 Post Office
13 Sernatur
15 Tur Bus
17 Buses al Sur
18 Teléfonica
19 Banco Estado
20 Entel
21 Iglesia Catedral
22 Museo Regional
23 Automóvil Club de Chile

To Medialuna de Rancagua
Plaza Camilo Henríquez
Mercado Central
Plaza Camilo Henríquez
Plaza de los Héroes
Train Station
To Panamericana
To Hipermercado Independencia & Panamericana
To Estadio El Teniente

Ruidiaz, Aurora, Allende, Dr Salinas, Portales, Rubio, Independencia, O'Carrol, Carrera Pinto, Gamero, Bueras, Astorga, Campos, Estado, Alcázar, Almarza, Zañartu, Av Freire, Av Viña del Mar, Av Santa María, Av San Martín, Av España, Av Libertador Bernardo O'Higgins, Cáceres, Mujica, Cuevas, Av Brasil, Germán-Riesco, Av Manuel Rodriguez, Baquedano, Av Estación, Calvo, Pasaje-Teniente, Lastarria, Maruri, Ibieta, (ped mall) trains to Santiago (US$2) every hour or so. EFE's long-distance passenger services, connecting Santiago with Chillán (US$7, three per day), Concepción (US$10, at least once daily) and Temuco (US$13, at least once daily), also stop at Rancagua.

AROUND RANCAGUA
Chapa Verde
Some 50km northeast of Rancagua via a mostly paved highway, Chapa Verde (☎ 294-255; daily lift ticket US$23/18 high/low season) is less famous than more prestigious ski centers such as Portillo and Valle Nevado, but it has four lifts and eight runs and is 2870m above sea level. Created for Codelco (the national copper company) workers but open to the public, its facilities include a ski school, rental equipment, a café and a restaurant.

This is a day trip only, and since the road to Chapa Verde is not open to the public, visitors must take Codelco buses from the Hipermercado Independencia (☎ 217-651; Av Manuel Ramírez 665, Local 5, Rancagua) at 9am on weekdays, or 8am to 9:30am on weekends. Buses return at 5pm.

Sewell
The company town of Sewell, 55km northeast of Rancagua and at an altitude of 2600m, housed mining families from the El Teniente copper mine between 1904 and 1975. El Teniente is the world's largest subsurface copper mine and has more than 1500km of tunnels. Sewell itself is now a ghost town and a monument to 20th-century company-town architecture.

El Teniente and Sewell are open to the public for organized tours only, and visitors to the mine must be over 14 years of age. If you want to visit, contact Codelco (☎ 072-292-000; Millan 220, Rancagua • ☎ 02-690-3000; Huérfanos 120, Santiago).

Termas de Cauquenes
The medicinal waters at Cauquenes' thermal springs, in the Andean foothills 28km east of Rancagua, have been venerated since pre-Hispanic times. The Hotel Termas de Cauquenes (☎ 072-899-010; singles/doubles US$70/100 with breakfast) dates back to 1885 and is a grand affair. The lodgings are comfortable, and the surrounding gardens are pretty. The hotel's dining room overlooks

the Cachapoal River and offers a popular Sunday lunch (US$15).

If you can't afford to stay at Cauquenes, you can just visit the thermal baths (open 8am-7:30pm; US$6, more with Jacuzzi) for the day. To get there take Buses Machali (☎ 072-244-662; Andén 12) from Rancagua's bus station, daily at 11:15am, returning at 7:45am and 5pm.

Hacienda Los Lingues
This hacienda (☎ 02-235-5446; w www .loslingues.com; singles/doubles/suites US$217/236/458 with breakfast), dating from the 17th century, is one of Chile's oldest horse-breeding farms and is still owned by the original family. These days it continues to be a working farm but also offer pricey luxury accommodations.

Riding, mountain biking, hiking, tennis, swimming and fly-fishing are all possible on its extensive grounds at an extra cost. Day visits (US$26 per person with lunch, including welcome drink, a tour of the main house and a look at the horses) are also possible, but call first.

Hacienda Los Lingues is 32km south of Rancagua, reached by a short gravel lateral just south of the town of Pelequén on the Panamericana.

RN Río de los Cipreses
Set among the Andean foothills, this lush 37,000-hectare park contains a variety of volcanic landforms, hanging glacial valleys with waterfalls, and fluvial landscapes. The reserve is home to extensive forests of fragrant cypress, olivillo and other native tree species; its wildlife includes puma, guanaco, fox, vizcacha, condor and the tricahue, Chile's largest native parrot. In altitude, the park ranges from 900m to the 4900m summit of Volcán El Palomo.

There are also indigenous rock drawings in the upper canyon – but you'll need to ask Conaf's help to find them.

The park entrance (US$2.50/1.20 adult/child; open 8:30am-8pm Dec-Mar, 8:30am-6pm Apr-Nov) is at the north end of the reserve, along a badly maintained dirt road, and is open in daylight hours only.

There are several trails throughout the park, but the finest is a day hike that ascends the valley of the Río de los Cipreses to Uriarte, where there's a nice campsite

(US$7 per tent), and then continues to Lake Piuquenes.

No direct public transport exists, but visitors can take a bus as far as Termas de Cauquenes (see the Termas de Cauquenes section earlier in this section) and walk or hitch another 15km to the park entrance.

SANTA CRUZ
☎ 72 • pop 33,000

This unspoiled town in the heart of the stunning Colchagua Valley is the locus of area's winemaking activities. It's the kind of place where you'll see real live *huasos* (cowboys) going about their business, but it also has one of Chile's best museums and a classy new hotel built in traditional style. A lively **Fiesta de la Vendimia** (grape-harvest festival) takes place in the plaza at the beginning of March.

The main street, Rafael Casanova, leads from the bus terminal to the pretty central plaza, where there's a helpful Sernatur **information kiosk** *(open 10am-1pm & 3pm-6pm Mon-Fri, 10am-2pm Sat)*. There's an **Entel** *(Casanova 344)* office next to the taxi colectivo stand.

The **Museo de Colchagua** *(☎ 821-010; w www.museocolchagua.cl; Errázuriz 145; admission US$4/0.85 adult/child; open 10am-6pm Tues-Sat)* is the largest private museum in Chile. The sheer number of exhibits is astounding, and just when you think you've reached the last room you realize there's *more*. The well-displayed collection includes unusual fossils; amber-trapped insects; Mapuche textiles; masses of pre-Columbian anthropomorphic ceramics from all over Latin America; exquisite gold work; and conquistador equipment, documents and maps. There are also beautiful religious artifacts, and a whole room is dedicated to *huaso* gear (including guitars). The last stretch, preceded by a massive showroom of old carriages and vintage cars, is an outdoor display of steam-driven machinery and wine-making equipment.

The **Museo San Jose del Carmen de El Huique** *(☎ 933-083; admission US$1.60; open 11am-5pm Wed-Sun, till 6pm in summer)*, 28km north of Santa Cruz in El Huique, is a beautifully preserved hacienda dating from 1829. Buses for El Huique leave the Santa Cruz bus station (see the end of this section) at 8:30am, 1pm and 3pm.

Hotel Santa Cruz Plaza *(☎ 821-010, fax 823-445; e reservas@hscp.cl; Plaza de Armas 286; singles/doubles US$90/105)*, opposite the town's plaza, is a new hotel designed in colonial style. It's a stunning place with a richly decorated interior and lovely grounds (including a full-to-the-brim pool surrounded by lush vegetation). It's also home to the town's best **restaurant**. Rates include a regal breakfast spread with highlights such as clove-scented quince compote, fresh cheese, roasted meats and fancy cakes. Visitors interested in wine should ask about the hotel's wine-route program (US$130), which includes one night's accommodations, breakfast, lunch and dinner, and visits to vineyards as well as to the Museo de Colchagua and El Huique.

Sombreria Santa Cruz *(☎ 822-257; Rafael Casanova 344)* is the place to saddle up and buy *huaso* gear; there's everything from spikey spurs and wooden stirrups to ponchos, hats, boots and whips.

If you want to buy wine, visit the *vinoteca* at the Hotel Santa Cruz Plaza – all of its wines are from Colchagua.

Santa Cruz's **bus terminal** *(Rafael Casanova 478)* is about four blocks west of the town plaza. **Buses Nilahue** *(☎ 825-582)* and **Buses Andimar** *(☎ 841-081)* travel from Santa Cruz to Pichilemu (US$2, two hours), San Fernando and Santiago every half-hour or so.

PICHILEMU
☎ 72 • pop 12,000

Pichilemu has been a popular beach resort since the beginning of the 20th century, when Agustín Ross Edwards bought land here and established a rail link with Santiago in an attempt to lure holidaymakers.

These days Pichilemu is known for its surfing, and when it hosts the **Campeonato Nacional de Surf** (national surfing championship) each summer at Punta de Lobos, 6km south of town, spectators come in droves.

There are still vestiges of the resort's early heyday, most obviously the fantastical hotel/casino known as the **Palacio Ross**, which Ross built to fuel his dream, and the adjacent well-clipped Parque Ross. The town has a wild-west, edge-of-the-world feel about it, with dusty streets and old tumble-down buildings.

Ruta del Vino Valle de Colchagua

The Colchagua Valley – blessed with deep loamy soils, abundant water, dry air, bright sunshine and cool nights – has a reputation for producing some of the country's best wines (especially reds), and its **Ruta del Vino** (☎ 823-199; e rv@uva.cl; Plaza de Armas 140) was Chile's first organized wine route.

There are currently nine wineries involved in the wine route, and all are making large investments in tasting rooms and other facilities for visitors. The wineries are: Viña Bisquertt, Viña Casa Lapostalle, Viña Casa Silva, Viña Luis Felipe Edwards, Viña Montes, Viña MontGras, Viña Santa Laura, Viña Siegel-El Crucero and Viña Viu Manent. All visits to wineries must be organized through Ruta de Vino 24 hours in advance. Three types of tour are offered. An express tour (from US$25 per person, depending on numbers) includes a visit to two wineries, with tastings of two wines at each winery, a bilingual guide and transport within the valley. A half-day tour (from US$30) visits three wineries, or two wineries and a museum, while a full-day tour (from US$40) adds lunch at Hotel Santa Cruz Plaza. Special tailormade tours are also available.

Three of the best wineries to visit are **Viu Manent** (☎ 072-858-751; w www.viumanent.cl), a third-generation winery known for its top-class wines, especially its malbec; **Viña Bisquertt**, which has beautiful old colonial buildings, a palm-lined drive and antique carriages in the tasting room; **Viña Santa Laura**, a tiny boutique winery with a gorgeous tasting room in the fragrant cellar; and **Viña Montes**, owned by Chile's most famous enologist, Aurelio Montes.

Not all wineries belong to the Ruta del Vino. It is possible to visit **Viña La Posada** (☎ 822-589; e laposada@entelchile.net; Rafael Casanova 570; 2-person apartment US$25 with breakfast), right in Santa Cruz, independently. It's one of the valley's oldest wineries and has a cozy tasting room furnished with antiques. Originally an old inn, it still provides accommodations and meals for visitors. Call ahead if you want to have lunch (US$8-13). There's also a lovely little shop selling locally produced ceramics and alpaca shawls.

Information

The **Oficina de Información Turística** (☎ 841-017; Municipalidad, Angel Gaete 365) also has a kiosk at the corner of Angel Gaete and Anibal Pinto, open in summer only. The **post office** (Av Ortúzar 568) is on the main drag, as is **Telefónica (CTC)** (Av Ortúzar 349).

Places to Stay & Eat

Gran Hotel Ross (☎ 841-038; Av Ross 130; rooms & cabañas US$10 per person) is an extraordinary old rambling place opposite Parque Ross. It has an elegant dining room and a cute bar, but the rooms are musty and verging on derelict; the cabins are a better option.

Hotel Asthur (☎ 841-495; e asthur@starmedia.com; Av Ortúzar 540; singles/doubles US$12/25 with breakfast & private bath), next door to the post office, is a huge place with a big common space that has a great view; there's also a pool, laundry, bar and restaurant. The rooms are a little on the dark side but quite pleasant nonetheless.

Hotel Chile España (☎ 841-270; Av Ortúzar 255; singles/doubles US$12/20 with shared bath, US$16/25 with private bath, all rates include breakfast) caters to surfers and is highly praised. Prices with shared bath are about 20% less, and there are also substantial off-season discounts. The owner can organize interesting farm tours that involve cheese-making and aphrodisiac drinks.

El Balaustro (☎ 842-458; Av Ortúzar 289; menú US$4), next door to Hotel Chile España, is a welcoming place with pretty good seafood, steak and chicken, as well as empanadas and other snacks.

Costa Luna (☎ 842-905; sushi starts at US$2) is a 20-minute walk (or a short taxi ride) south of town, on the beachfront. The walk is worth it if you're tired of run-of-the-mill food, for here, you will find sushi and Mediterranean seafood dishes.

Getting There & Away

The **Terminal de Buses** (☎ 841-709; cnr Av Millaco & Los Alerces) is inconveniently located on the outskirts; ask to be let off at the corner of Santa Maria and Ortúzar, which is the nearest bus stop to the center of town. **Buses Andimar** (☎ 841-081; Av Ortúzar 483) and **Buses Nilahue** (☎ 02-779-7379) run frequent buses between Pichilemu and Santa Cruz (US$2, two hours) and San Fernando (US$3, three hours), where there are connections north to Rancagua (US$4, four hours) and Santiago (US$6, five hours), and south to Curicó, Talca and Chillán.

Around Pichilemu

About 20km south of Pichilemu is the surf spot and fishing village of **Bucalemu**, where several residenciales have singles for about US$10. Try **Hotel Casablanca** (☎ 072-342-235; Av Celedonio Pastene s/n). From Bucalemu, it's possible to make a two- to four-day beach trek – camping along the way – to the seaside village of **Llico**, a popular windsurfing spot with frequent bus connections to Curicó.

CURICÓ

☎ 75 • pop 120,300

Curicó, most famous for its Festival de la Vendimia (wine harvest festival), which lasts three days in mid-March, is a service center for surrounding orchards and vineyards and not a major attraction in its own right. But it's a good base for excursions to nearby wineries, coastal areas like Vichuquén and parts of the Andes that are visited by relatively few foreigners, such as the Reserva Nacional Radal Siete Tazas.

The town's palm-studded Plaza de Armas is one of Chile's prettiest, with an eccentric, early-20th-century wrought-iron bandstand on stilts, and there's a nice park at Cerro Carlos Condell with a public swimming pool. The area around the Mercado Central is lively pretty much all week and is worth checking out.

Information

Curicó has no formal tourist office, but in summer there's a **Sernatur kiosk** (Edificio Servicios Públicos, Carmen 556; open daily 9am-6:30pm) on the east side of the plaza. It's understaffed and lacks space but does its best.

The local branch of **Automóvil Club de Chile** (Acchi; ☎ 311-156; Chacabuco 759) is especially helpful.

You can change US cash and traveler's checks at **Forex** (Carmen 497). There are many ATMs, including **Banco de Crédito** (Merced 315).

The **post office** (Carmen 556) is opposite the Plaza de Armas. If you need to make phone calls, try **Entel** (Av Camilo Henríquez 414 • Peña 650).

Places to Stay & Eat

Hotel Prat (☎ 311-069; Peña 427; singles/ doubles US$9/18 with shared bath, US$12/23 with private bath, including breakfast) is the friendly budget pick. Rooms vary – some are large, bright and comfortable, with high ceilings, while others are dark and drab. The showers are hot, there's a shady grape arbor over the patio, and it's become a good meeting place.

Residencial Rahue (☎ 312-194; Peña 410; US$9 per person) is a comfy, brightly painted alternative to Hotel Prat.

Hotel Turismo (☎ 310-823; Carmen 727; singles/doubles US$41/55) is surprisingly stylish for a little town like Curicó. There's a wonderful lounge area with a massive log-burning fireplace, and the charming rooms have large windows and a private balcony overlooking a beautiful garden, as well as bathtub big enough to swim in.

If you're game, there are plenty of cheap, hole-in-the-wall **picadas** near the Mercado Central.

Bavaria (☎ 319-972; Yungay 615), close to Plaza de Armas, has espresso coffee and reliable standard fare.

El Aleman (Peña 879), near the market, is open late and not bad for the usual mayo-laden sandwiches and snacks if you're hungry and desperate.

El Fogon Chileno (☎ 325-592; Montt 399) is a favorite place for parrilladas, but beware of the live entertainment.

Centro Italiano (☎ 310-482; Estado 531; lunch US$3) serves good food but can be a bit intimidating.

Getting There & Away

Bus Nearly all companies use the Terminal de Buses at the west end of Calle Prat, across from the railway station. Buses to Santiago (US$4, 2½ hours) leave about every half-hour. **Buses Bravo** (☎ 312-193) goes to Lago Vichuquén and the coastal resort of Iloca (US$1.60), while **Buses Hernández** (☎ 491-607, 491-179) goes to interior destinations such as Molina and Radal Siete Tazas. **Buses**

MIDDLE CHILE

Díaz (☎ 311-905) goes to Santiago (US$4, 2½ hours), as does **Andimar** (☎ 312-000), which also goes to Pichilemu, San Fernando and Temuco. **P del Sur** (☎ 02-776-2426) also has buses to Santiago but travels to coastal destinations, Talca (US$1.60) and Rancagua (US$2.50) as well.

The companies that have their own terminals are **Buses Lit** (☎ 315-648; cnr Av Manso de Velasco & Buen Pastor) and **Tur Bus** (☎ 312-115; Av Manso de Velasco 0106), both southeast of town near the Panamericana.

Micros to Molina (for wineries and RN Radal Siete Tazas) leave almost continuously from in front of the train station.

Train Passenger trains between Santiago and Temuco stop at Curicó's **train station** (☎ 310-028; Maipú 657), at the west end of Calle Prat, four blocks west of the Plaza de Armas. There are five trains a day north to Rancagua (US$2-3) and Santiago (US$3-4) and five trains a day south to Talca (US$2), Chillán (US$3-5) and Temuco (US$7-10). Once a day a train runs to Concepción (US$6-7).

AROUND CURICÓ
Lago Vichuquén & RN Laguna Torca
In the coast range only a short distance from the Pacific, Lago Vichuquén is a natural lake that is a popular center for water sports. Nearby is Reserva Nacional Laguna Torca, a 604-hectare reserve that is home to breeding populations of black-necked swans, coscoroba swans and more than a hundred other bird species. In especially wet years, the two lakes join to form a single extensive coastal wetland.

Conaf maintains a **Centro de Información Ambiental** at Laguna Torca, where it collects admission (US$1.50). There is a US$10 charge for **camping** in rustic sites with cold showers; fires and music are not permitted.

The village of **Vichuquén**, on the road from Curicó just before Lake Vichuquén, is a very pretty colonial town that features well-preserved architecture.

RN Radal Siete Tazas
In the upper basin of the Río Claro southeast of Molina, Reserva Nacional Radal Siete Tazas marks an ecological transition between the drought-tolerant Mediter-

ranean vegetation to the north and the moist evergreen forests to the south.

Its major scenic attraction is a stunning series of cascading waterfalls and pools that the Río Claro has carved out of black basalt rock. The falls and pools at Siete Tazas (literally, Seven Cups) are accessible via a short footpath through pretty beech forest. Another trail leads to a viewpoint for the Salto de la Leona, a waterfall that drops more than 50m from a narrow gorge to the main channel of the Río Claro. The same trail continues down to the river itself. There are longer hiking trails up Cerro El Fraile and at Valle del Indio, and it's also possible to trek across the drainage of the Río Claro to exit at Reserva Nacional Altos del Lircay (see the Reserva Nacional Altos del Lircay section, later in this section), taking about two days, but not without a guide.

At Parque Inglés, the entrance to the reserve, Conaf maintains a **Centro de Información Ambiental** (open 9am-8:30pm Dec-Feb, 9am-7pm Mar-Nov; US$1.50) where it collects the entrance fee.

Places to Stay & Eat Free, rustic campgrounds with cold running water are available at Radal and Parque Inglés, though these tend to get dirty in high season. There are also private camping grounds on the way to the park, including **Radal Eco Adventure** (sites US$21, 5 people per site), 1km from the road to Radal Siete Tazas and 45km from Molina (look for signs on your right). The sites are spacious and have stunning views. Rates include firewood, spring water and hot wine at night.

Hostería Flor de la Canela (☎ 075-491-613; triples with private bath US$33), near the Conaf headquarters at Parque Inglés, offers accommodations from December to March.

A **kiosk** sells basic supplies, but it's best to bring food with you. White flags hanging at houses along the way indicate places to buy pan amasado (homemade bread).

Getting There & Away Reserva Nacional Radal Siete Tazas is 50km from Molina along a narrow gravel road. **Buses Hernández** (☎ 075-491-607, 491-179; Maipú 1723, Molina) goes to Parque Inglés (US$2, two hours) daily at 5:30pm (returning at 8:30am) all year; in January and February, there are

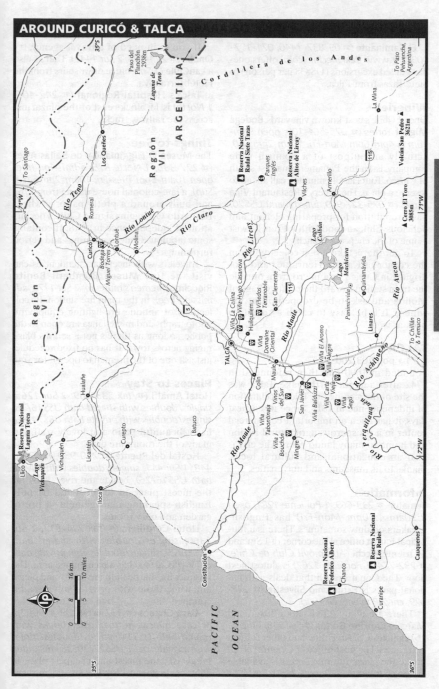

AROUND CURICÓ & TALCA

up to seven buses daily, some of them direct from Curicó.

El Caminante (☎ 09-837-1440, 071-197-0097; W www.trekkingchile.com) offers one-day guided excursions (US$38 per person) to Siete Tazas from Talca.

Wineries
One of Chile's best-known vineyards, **Bodega Miguel Torres** (☎ 075-564-100; open 9am-1pm & 4pm-6pm Mon-Fri, 10am-2pm Sat), actually an outpost of a Spanish wine company, is on the Panamericana just south of Curicó. Tours last 45 minutes; call ahead to reserve a place. The winery's **Restaurant Viña Torres** (☎ 075-327-949; lunch menú US$20) has a reputation for preparing elegant and delicious Chilean food with a French twist (some of the chefs are French).

To get there, take a taxi colectivo from the corner of Camilo Henríquez and Rodríguez in Curicó or a micro from outside the train station toward the pretty village of **Molina** and ask to be dropped off at the winery. It'll be easy to catch a colectivo back as well.

TALCA
☎ 71 • pop 203,200
Founded in 1690 and then refounded in 1742 after a major earthquake, Talca was the site of the signing of Chile's declaration of independence in 1818. Since its earliest days, it has been an important commercial center in a prosperous agricultural region and home to many landowners. The city is also an educational and cultural locus, thanks to its museums and universities.

Information
Sernatur (☎ 233-669; 1 Poniente 1281; open 8:30am-4:30pm Mon-Fri) has English-speakers on duty sometimes. There is a **municipal tourist office** at the corner of 1 Sur and 4 Oriente. **Acchi** (Automóvil Club de Chile; ☎ 232-774; 1 Poniente 1267) is almost next door. The Conaf branch that deals with national parks is **Patrimonio Silvestre** (☎ 228-029; cnr 2 Poniente & 3 Sur).

There are many ATMs along 1 Sur, and **Marcelo Cancino Cortés** (1 Sur 898, Oficina 15) changes US, Argentine and other foreign currencies. The **post office** (1 Oriente) is opposite the plaza. Internet access is available at **Zona 5 Internet** (7 Oriente 1180) for US$1

per hour. There's an **Entel** phone center at the corner of 1 Sur and 4 Oriente.

If you're in need of a travel agency, try **Onuba** (☎ 224-196; 2 Sur 1442). There's also a **LanChile** (1 Sur) office downstairs from the Hotel Terranova.

Talca's Hospital Regional (☎ 242-406; 1 Norte) is 11 blocks east of the plaza, just across the railway tracks.

Things to See
The **Museo O'Higginiano y de Bellas Artes** (☎ 227-330; 1 Norte 875; admission free; open 10am-6pm Tues-Fri, 10am-2pm Sat & Sun), a late-colonial house dating from 1762 and built around a pretty patio, is where Bernardo O'Higgins signed Chile's declaration of independence in 1818. It contains some fabulous Chilean paintings and period furnishings.

Travelers with incendiary tendencies can visit the tiny **Museo Bomberil Benito Riquelme** (firemen's museum; 2 Sur 1172; admission free), in the main fire station. Its collections of antique fire-fighting equipment, photographs and miscellanea are open to the public, so long as there's not a serious blaze raging across town. It has no fixed schedule; just ask one of the firemen to open it for you.

Places to Stay
Hotel Amalfi (☎/fax 233-389; 2 Sur 1265; singles/doubles with shared bath US$16/28, singles/doubles with private bath US$24/36) has a beautiful patio and lovely staff, but many of the rooms are drab.

Hostal del Puente (☎ 220-930, fax 225-448; 1 Sur 411; singles/doubles with private bath US$16/26), beside the river, is by far the nicest place in town. It has friendly English-speaking management, a pretty garden and cozy rooms.

Hotel Cordillera (☎/fax 221-817; 2 Sur 1360; singles/doubles with shared bath US$16/29, singles/doubles with private bath & TV US$28/43) has a nice lounge area. The rooms with shared bath are sunny and pleasant, while those with private bath are a bit cramped.

Casa Chueca (☎ 197-0096, 09-4190625; e casachueca@hotmail.com; bunks with shared bath US$11, singles/doubles/triples with private bath US$22/30/36, including breakfast), the nicest and cheapest place in Talca, is on its outskirts. Guests stay in rustic cabañas set amid beautifully landscaped gardens with a view of the Río Lircay and surrounding countryside. There's a cozy dining room that's a great place to meet other travelers, and a pool. It's also a fine place to gather information about the region; the friendly, knowledgable owners lead hiking trips in the mountains and can organize all kinds of activities.

Hotel Napoli (*☎ 227-373; 2 Sur 1314; singles/doubles US$33/49 with private bath, TV & breakfast*) has a pleasant patio and simply decorated, comfortable rooms (the doubles are nicer than the singles).

Hotel Terranova (*☎ 239-608; 1 Sur 1026; singles/doubles US$38/51 including breakfast*) is central and has pleasant but overpriced rooms.

Hotel Marcos Gamero (*☎ 223-388, fax 224-400; 1 Oriente 1070; singles/doubles US$40/50*) is a bit claustrophobic despite the ample array of multilevel lounge areas filled with boofy cushions. Anyone with a fascination for '70s décor should take a peek.

Hotel Terrabella (*☎/fax 226-555; 1 Sur 641; singles/doubles US$50/64 including*

breakfast) has a sunny breakfast room overlooking a gorgeous garden with a well-groomed lawn, mature trees and a swimming pool. The rooms are a little bit pink for all tastes, but they're comfortable enough.

Hotel Plaza (*☎ 226-150; 1 Poniente 1141; singles/doubles with breakfast from US$55/78*) has an exterior that's seen better days, but hidden inside is a grand and elegant salon and spacious rooms overlooking tranquil Plaza de Armas.

Places to Eat

For bargain-basement grub, head to the **completos stands** on 5 Oriente – a huge hotdog and soft drink will set you back only US$0.80.

Mercado Central, bounded by 1 Norte, 5 Oriente, 1 Sur and 4 Oriente, has a few incredibly cute cocinerías serving cheap meals.

Ibiza (*1 Sur 1168*) dispatches rotisserie chicken (US$4) and other grills.

Kebabs House (*☎ 225-504; 6 Oriente*) has sandwiches and snacks and is the only place open on Sundays.

El Gobelino (*1 Sur & 1 Oriente*) serves up reliable standard fare.

MIDDLE CHILE

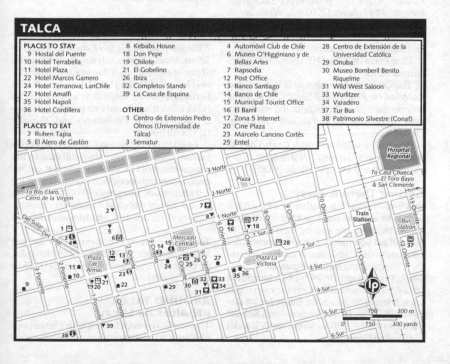

TALCA

PLACES TO STAY
9 Hostal del Puente
10 Hotel Terrabella
11 Hotel Plaza
22 Hotel Marcos Gamero
24 Hotel Terranova; LanChile
27 Hotel Amalfi
35 Hotel Napoli
36 Hotel Cordillera

PLACES TO EAT
2 Ruben Tapia
5 El Alero de Gastón

8 Kebabs House
18 Don Pepe
19 Chilote
21 El Gobelino
26 Ibiza
32 Completos Stands
39 La Casa de Esquina

OTHER
1 Centro de Extensión Pedro Olmos (Universidad de Talca)
3 Sernatur

4 Automóvil Club de Chile
6 Museo O'Higginiano y de Bellas Artes
7 Rapsodia
12 Post Office
13 Banco Santiago
14 Banco de Chile
15 Municipal Tourist Office
16 El Barril
17 Zona 5 Internet
20 Cine Plaza
23 Marcelo Cancino Cortés
25 Entel

28 Centro de Extensión de la Universidad Católica
29 Onuba
30 Museo Bomberil Benito Riquelme
31 Wild West Saloon
33 Wurlitzer
34 Varadero
37 Tur Bus
38 Patrimonio Silvestre (Conaf)

Chilote (☎ 215-267; 1 Sur 706) specializes in seafood.

La Casa de Esquina (☎ 237-073; 1 Poniente 898; open dinner only; mains US$5-8) has exciting Spanish food and tapas, with house specialties such as calamari in ink (US$6) and Galician-style octopus (US$6).

El Alero de Gastón (☎ 233-785; 2 Norte 858; lunch menú US$4) features a broad range of Chilean and Spanish dishes on its menu. It's known for its fine service and elegant surroundings; it also has an extensive wine list. The lunch menu is quite a bargain.

Rubin Tapia (☎ 237-875; 2 Oriente 379) has great regional dishes (including fried frogs!); it also features a large selection of wines.

El Toro Bayo (☎ 247-643; Camino Las Rostras), 2.5km outside Talca, serves excellent food in an old colonial house.

For coffee, head to **Don Pepe** (cnr 7 Oriente & 1 Sur).

Entertainment

Talca's pub gulch is on and near 5 Oriente, close to the corner of 2 Sur. The most well-known places are **Wild West Saloon** (5 Oriente 1191; beers US$0.80); **Wurlitzer** (5 Oriente); **Varadero** (5 Oriente 932); **El Barril** (1 Norte), which sometimes has live music; and **Rapsodia** (6 Oriente).

Cine Plaza (☎ 232-310; 1 Sur 770) shows current films.

The **Centro de Extensión de la Universidad Católica** (☎ 226-303; 2 Sur 1525) screens independent films throughout the university year, beginning in March and ending in December.

The Universidad de Talca's **Centro de Extensión Pedro Olmos** (2 Norte 685) hosts various cultural events, including films.

Getting There & Away

Bus Talca's main bus station (☎ 243-270; 2 Sur 1920) is across the tracks but not directly accessible from the nearby train station (1 Sur will get you there). Domestic companies with northbound and southbound services on the Panamericana include **Buses Lit** (☎ 242-048); **Tas Choapa** (☎ 243-334); **Varmontt** (☎ 242-120), which is good for overnight trips; **Intersur** (☎ 245-920); **Buses Jac** (☎ 02-776-1582) – as far as Temuco – and **Sol del Pacífico** (☎ 244-199) to Valparaíso/Viña del Mar and to Concepción.

Pullman del Sur (☎ 244-039) goes to the coastal resort of Constitución. **Buses Vilches** (☎ 243-366) leaves three times daily, at 7am, 1pm and 4:50pm, for the village of Vilches and beyond, turning around at the entrance to Reserva Nacional Altos del Lircay.

Tur Bus (☎ 241-748; 3 Sur 1960), utilizing a separate terminal one block south, travels north and south on the Panamericana. **Buses Biotal** (☎ 223-727) is the agent for **Transporte Pehuenche** (☎ 073-212-322, in Linares), a minibus service that crosses the spectacular 2553m Paso Pehuenche to the Argentine cities of Malargüe and San Rafael in the summertime.

Sample fares and journey times follow:

destination	duration in hours	cost
Chillán	4	US$6
Constitución	2	US$2
Malargüe (Ar)	8	US$40
Puerto Montt	11	US$18
San Rafael (Ar)	10	US$60
Santiago	4	US$6
Temuco	6	US$13
Valparaíso/Viña del Mar	6	US$13

Train The train station (☎ 226-254; 11 Oriente 1000) is at the eastern end of 2 Sur. All trains from Santiago's Estación Central to Temuco and points south stop here en route. There are five trains a day to Chillán (US$3, two hours), Curicó (US$2, one hour), San Fernando (US$3, 1½ hours) and Rancagua (US$4, 2¼ hours), and one per day to Concepción (US$5, 5½ hours) and Temuco (US$8, 10 hours).

In addition to the long-distance service, a narrow-gauge passenger train still runs to the coastal resort of Constitución, where there are impressive sand dunes. Well worth a detour for rail aficionados, this service (US$2, 2½ hours) runs at 7:30am daily and 4:10pm weekdays, returning at 7:15am daily and 4pm weekdays.

Taxi For impeccable service, call Sergio Medel Gonzales (☎ 09-315-2136). He'll pick up promptly and charge a fair price (US$5 to Casa Chueca).

AROUND TALCA
RN Altos de Lircay

This southern beech habitat with a large population of screechy tricahues and other native parrots is one of Chile's most important ecosystems. The park (admission US$2.50) occupies 12,163 hectares in the Andean foothills east of Talca. The deciduous forest is spectacular in autumn.

The park is a favorite hiking and horse-trekking area, and Conaf's helpful Centro de Información Ambiental, near the park entrance, has excellent displays on local natural and cultural history (there have been four sequential Indian occupations).

Hiking Within the park, it's possible to camp in the upper basin of the Río Lircay and to make hiking excursions to the basaltic plateau of **El Enladrillado**, to **Laguna El Alto** and **Laguna Tomate**, and up the canyon of the Valle del Venado. Well-organized trekkers can loop across the drainage of the Río Claro to exit at Reserva Nacional Radal Siete Tazas. Since the trail is not always obvious, it's advisable to hire a local guide.

Probably the best single hike between Santiago and Temuco, El Enladrillado offers tiring but exhilarating hiking crowned by top-of-the-world views from this unique columnar basalt plateau. About one hour's walk above the entrance station, a signed lateral follows an abandoned logging road for about half an hour to an ill-marked junction (look for an 'E' and an arrow carved in a tree at a small clearing). This is where the trail proper begins, just before the logging road begins to drop.

From this junction, the trail climbs steeply through dense forest, zigzagging for about an hour before leveling off and winding around various volcanic outcrops. The trail finally emerges onto El Enladrillado, a site where it seems as if a mad gardener has placed massive flagstones for an immense patio and planted prostrate shrubs among them. The views from here to the Río Claro canyon are breathtaking.

From the park entrance, figure about five hours up and 3½ hours down for this strenuous but rewarding hike, and allow at least an hour on top. There are two or three potable springs before the trail emerges above treeline, but carry as much water as possible. Close gates to keep livestock from the upper reaches of the trail.

Trekkers can also choose to descend the valley of the Río Lircay, where backcountry camping is possible, and continue north to Radal Siete Tazas, in the Río Claro drainage, but a guide is needed, as the trail is not marked. **El Caminante** (☎ 09-837-1440, 071-197-0097; ⓦ www.trekkingchile.com) has years of experience and can organize guided hikes.

Horseback Riding Good but inexpensive rental horses are available just outside the park entrance. These are a good alternative for visitors with little time to explore the park, and you can also travel to Laguna de Alto (two days), El Endrillado and Siete Tazas (four days) or Descabezado Grande (five days).

Danilo 'El Pollo' Contreras (☎ 09-266-9246) is a locally famous guide. He charges US$13 per horse plus US$17 for guidance.

Places to Stay & Eat The **Conaf campground** (US$13 for up to 5 people), within the reserve but a one-hour hike from the bus stop, is not bad; you can also camp at backcountry sites.

Don Tito's Coca Cola shack in Vilches is your last chance for a coffee, soft drink or sandwich. Don Tito is a mountain guide and has a CB radio if you need to call for help.

Getting There & Away Altos del Lircay is 65km from Talca via paved Chile 115 and a lateral is one of the dustiest roads in all of Chile. From Talca, **Buses Vilches** goes directly to the park entrance at 7:10am, returning at 4:45pm daily, though the schedule is subject to change. The fare is US$1.50.

Huilquilemu

Once an important fundo (farm), this complex of restored 19th-century buildings, 10km east of Talca on the San Clemente highway, houses museums, chapels and the swanky **Maule Valley Enoteca** (see Ruta del Vino boxed text). The surrounding gardens are lovely, with mature sequoias, araucarias, magnolias, palms and oaks. There is also a **restaurant** on site.

Admission to the **Museo Obispo Manuel Larraín**, a religious museum with religious artifacts and paintings in a beautiful hall, is included in the entrance fee to **Villa Cultural Huilquilemu** (☎ 071-242-474; adult/child US$0.85/0.30; open 9am-1pm & 3pm-6:30pm Tues-Fri, 4pm-6:30pm Sat, 11am-2pm Sun).

You'll also gain entry to a rather melo-dramatic **Sala Annunciation**, which comes complete with a sound-and-light show, and a room with historic local handicrafts (some made of horsehair) and household items, including llama saddles and a very interesting antique clothes drier.

All San Clemente micros departing from Talca's bus station pass Huilquilemu and will stop there.

San Javier

About 19km south of Talca, the Panamer-icana passes the **Puente Maule**, an impressive, 442m-long iron bridge, dating from 1885, spanning the canyon of the Río Maule. About 2km farther south, a lateral road leads to San Javier, where you'll find **Viña Balduzzi** and a number of other wineries (see the 'Ruta del Vino Valle del Maule' boxed text for more information).

Ruta del Vino Valle del Maule

The Maule Valley is Chile's biggest wine-producing region and is responsible for half of the country's export wine.

Local wineries have banded together to establish a Ruta del Vino (not to be confused with the similar set-up in the Colchagua Valley), with its headquarters at the stylish new **Maule Valley Enoteca** (☎ 071-246-460; ⍵ www.chilewineroute.com; open 9am-1pm & 3pm-6:30pm Tues-Fri, 11am-6:30pm Sat & Sun) in the old villa at Huilquilemu. You can taste and buy all Maule wines at the enoteca.

The Ruta del Vino offers a range of tours. A half-day (US$22, 2-person minimum; US$10 without transport) tour includes guided visits to two wineries with tastings. A full-day (US$54, 2-person minimum) is similar but includes lunch and a visit to the Villa Cultural Huilquilemu. There are two weekend-long tours (US$120, cheaper without transport, 2-person minimum), both including guided visits to two wineries with tastings, two lunches and accommodations in a double room with breakfast. One of the tours includes a guided walk through native forest at Altos del Lircay, while the alternative involves visits to the lovely colonial towns of Villa Alegre and Yerbas Buenas. Reservations should be made 48 hours in advance.

It's also possible to visit the wineries independently, mostly with advance notice. Eleven wineries are involved in the Ruta del Vino Valle del Maule, all offering tastings for US$1.60. See the Around Curicó & Talca map for locations.

Viña Balduzzi (☎ 073-322-138; Av Balmaceda 1189; open 9am-6pm Mon-Sat) is a boutique winery set among spacious gardens and well-kept colonial buildings near San Javier. Other wineries near San Javier include **Viña J Bouchón** (☎ 073-372-708; Ⓔ julio@jbouchon.cl; Fundo Santa María de Mingre, Camino Constitución Km 26; open 9am-5pm Sat), **Viña Segú** (☎ 073-210-078; Ⓔ vinosegu@entelchile.net; Fundo Mirador, Km 10 Melozal; open 9am-5pm Mon-Sat; call ahead), **Viña Tabontinaja** (☎ 073-375-539; Ⓔ tabontinaja@gillmore.cl; Camino Constitución Km 20; open 9am-5pm Mon-Sat; call ahead) and **Vinos del Sur** (☎ 02-240-0410; Ⓔ vinsur@entelchile.net; Fundo Las Cañas, Camino El Morro Km 8; call ahead).

Viña Hugo Casanova (☎ 071-266-540; Ⓔ hcasanov@ctcinternet.cl; Fundo Purísima, Camino Las Ratras Km 8; open 2:30pm-6pm Mon-Fri; call ahead) is a small fourth-generation family winery with beautiful colonial buildings and good visitor facilities near Talca. Other wineries near Talca include: **Viña La Calina** (☎ 071-263-126; Ⓔ vinos@calina.cl; Fundo El Maitén, Camino Las Rastras Km 7; tours & tastings 11am-5pm Sat & Sun) and **Viña Domaine Oriental** (☎ 071-242-506; Ⓔ courrier@domaineoriental.cl; Fundo La Oriental, Camino Palmira Km 3.5; open 8am-6pm Mon-Fri).

Viña Carta Vieja (☎ 073-381-612; Ⓔ vocar@ctc-mundo.net; Av Francisco Antonio Encina 231; open 2:30pm-6pm Mon-Wed; call ahead) and **Viña El Aromo** (☎ 071-242-438; Fundo El Trapiche, Km 4.6 Villa Alegre; call ahead) are both near Villa Alegre, while **Viñedos Terranoble** (☎ 071-231-800; Ⓔ terranob@ctcreuna.cl; Fundo Santa Camilla, sector casas viejas, Camino Santa Elena Km 7) is close to San Clemente.

There's no public transport to the wineries, but if you're staying at Casa Chueca, near Talca, it's possible to visit many of them by bicycle, which are loaned free of charge.

Taking in the view of the Santiago skyline from the Cerro Santa Lucía

Mementos at the Confitería Las Torres

Plaza de Armas: reflecting history

Santiago's grand 16th-century architecture

Andean peaks beckoning east of Santiago

Artists lending color to the cityscape in the Plaza de Armas

Harvesting grapes near the capital

Buses to San Javier run frequently from Talca's bus station.

The nearby village of **Villa Alegre** is a delightful colonial town with orange trees lining the streets; the road into town is bordered by plane trees and vineyards and is a spectacular sight in autumn.

CHILLÁN

☎ 42 • pop 163,000

Birthplace of Chilean liberator Bernardo O'Higgins, the market city of Chillán marks the northern border of La Frontera, that area over which Spain – and Chile – never really exercised effective control until the state finally subdued the Mapuche in the late 19th century. Founded in 1565 as a military outpost, then destroyed and refounded several times after earthquakes and Mapuche sieges, it moved to its present site in 1835. The old city, nearby Chillán Viejo, has never really died.

In addition to its colorful market, perhaps Chile's finest, Chillán has several notable museums and landmark works by the famous Mexican muralist David Alfaro Siqueiros and his colleague Xavier Guerrero. Thanks to this combination of attractions, Chillán is the best stopover of all the cities along the Panamericana between Santiago and Temuco.

Orientation

Chillán sits on an alluvial plain between the Río Ñuble and its smaller southern tributary, the Río Chillán. The city's heart is an area 12 blocks square, bounded by the divided, tree-lined Avs Ecuador, Brasil, Collín and Argentina. The center proper is the Plaza de Armas, bounded by Av Libertad, 18 de Septiembre, Constitución and Arauco.

Av O'Higgins leads north to the Panamericana (which passes northwest of the city) and south to the suburb of Chillán Viejo.

Information

Sernatur (☎/fax 223-272; 18 de Septiembre 455; open 8:30am-7:30pm Mon-Fri year-round, plus 10am-2pm Sat & Sun mid-Dec–Feb) is half a block north of the plaza. There's also a small **information kiosk** at the María Teresa bus terminal (see Getting There & Around).

There are many ATMs, including one at **Banco Concepción** (Constitución 550).

There's a **post office** (Libertad 505). **Telefónica (CTC)** (Arauco 625) has a long-distance office. Next door is **Entel** (Arauco 623), and there's also **Chilexpress** (18 de Septiembre 490, Local 201). Phone facilities are also available at the Terminal María Teresa. **Planet Cybercafe** (Arauco; $1.30/hr) has lots of computers.

Chillán's has quite a few travel agencies; try **Centrotur** (☎ 221-306; w www.centrotur.cl; 18 de Septiembre 656).

For laundry services, head to **Lava Matic** (Arturo Prat 357-B).

Chillán's **Hospital Herminda Martín** (☎ 212-345; cnr Constitución & Av Argentina) is six blocks east of the Plaza de Armas.

Escuela México

After a 1939 earthquake devastated Chillán, the Mexican government of President Lázaro Cárdenas donated to the city a new school, Escuela México (O'Higgins 250; donations welcome; open 10am-12:30pm & 3pm-6pm daily). Before its completion, at the urging of Pablo Neruda, Mexican muralist David Alfaro Siqueiros decorated the library with spectacular murals honoring both indigenous and post-Columbian figures from each country's history – the northern wall devoted to Mexico and the southern wall to Chile.

Among the Mexican figures depicted on Siqueiros' murals, which bear the title Muerte al Invasor (Death to the Invader), are the Aztec emperor Cuauhtémoc and his Spanish nemesis Hernán Cortés; revolutionary priest Miguel Hidalgo and his contemporary ally José María Morelos; the Zapotec Indian and President Benito Juárez; agrarian rebel Emiliano Zapata; and reformist President Cárdenas and his successor Manuel Avila Camacho. Chilean figures represented on the murals include the Mapuche resistance leaders Caupolicán, Lautaro and Galvarino; independence hero Bernardo O'Higgins; anticlerical writer Francisco Bilbao; and reformist presidents José Manuel Balmaceda and Pedro Aguirre Cerda.

Siqueiros' countryman Xavier Guerrero also participated in the project. His own simple but powerful murals, Hermanos

Mexicanos (Mexican Brothers), flank the library staircase. Unfortunately, the murals' state of preservation is declining.

Although the Escuela México is a functioning school rather than a museum, the staff welcomes visitors to the library at O'Higgins 250, between Gamero and Vega de Saldías.

Feria de Chillán

Chillán's open-air market *(Plaza de la Merced; open daily)*, one of Chile's most colorful, is a sprawling affair with a superb selection of local crafts and mountains of fresh produce. Especially lively on Saturday, the market occupies the entire Plaza de la Merced, bounded by Maipón, 5 de Abril, Arturo Prat and Isabel Riquelme, but spills over into adjacent streets as well.

Museo Franciscano

Chillán's Franciscan museum *(☎ 237-606; Sargento Aldea; admission free; open 9am-1pm & 3pm-6pm Tues-Sat, 1pm-2pm Sun)* displays historical materials of the missionary order that, from 1585, proselytized among the Mapuche in 15 settlements, from Chillán in the north to Río Bueno in the south. The museum is in the church opposite Plaza General Lagos.

Parque Monumental Bernardo O'Higgins

In Chillán Viejo, only a short bus or cab ride from downtown, a tiled mural 60m long and 6m high marks O'Higgins's birthplace and illustrates scenes from his life.

Places to Stay

Hospedaje Sonia Segui *(☎ 214-879; Itata 288; per person US$6)* is no great shakes but is run by friendly folk, and a good, generous breakfast is included.

Centrally located **Hostal Canadá** *(☎ 221-263; Av Libertad 269; per person US$6)* has pleasant, cozy rooms with shared bath.

Residencial 18 *(☎ 211-102; 18 de Septiembre 317; per person US$7)* is a lovely, central place with pool tables.

Residencial Su Casa *(☎ 223-931; Cocharcas 555; per person US$9)* is a cramped but characterful place run by a friendly señora.

Hotel Libertador *(☎ 223-255; Av Libertad 85; singles/doubles with shared bath US$11/20, with private bath US$17/25)* is family run and close to the bus station;

make sure you ask for an upstairs room – they're much nicer.

Hotel Rukalef *(☎ 233-366, fax 230-393; e hotel@rukalef.cl; Arauco 740; singles/doubles US$26/33)* is a clean and central option with friendly staff; rates include breakfast, parking, cable and private bathroom.

Hotel Nevado *(☎ 237-788; Av Libertad 219; singles/doubles US$37/47 including breakfast)* is a professionally run, clean and spacious place with lots of modern conveniences; definitely the pick of this car-parts neighborhood.

Hotel Las Terrazas *(☎ 227-000, fax 227-001; Constitución 664, 5th floor; singles/doubles US$46/55 including breakfast)* has small but fancy rooms with a good view over town; there's also a nice sunny breakfast area.

Gran Hotel Isabel Riquelme *(☎ 213-663, fax 211-541; Arauco 600; singles/doubles US$48/64 including breakfast)* is a little tatty around the edges, but its spacious rooms are comfortable and have a nice view over Plaza de Armas, and the staff are polite and accommodating. It's probably not the best option for anyone sensitive to street noise though.

Places to Eat

Mercado Central *(Maipón)*, between 5 de Abril and Isabel Riquelme, contains simple but excellent and reasonably priced cocinerías that prepare local specialties. The *longaniza* sausage is the thing to try.

Fuente Alemana *(☎ 212-720; Arauco 661)* is a fine choice for sandwiches and küchen.

Centro Español *(☎ 216-212; Arauco 555)* has excellent Spanish-Chilean food and service.

Casino Cuerpo de Bomberos *(El Roble & 18 de Septiembre)* is, like its counterparts in other Chilean cities, a reliable place for traditional Chilean cuisine.

Trienta y Tantos, in Chillán Viejo, has 30 varieties of empanadas and great pisco sours; ask a local for its location.

Kuranepe *(☎ 221-409; O'Higgins 0420)*, north of the bus terminal, is also worth a try.

Café Paris *(☎ 225-495; Arauco 660)* is open 24 hours and has good sandwiches, coffee, and beer on tap.

Entertainment

Restaurant Pub Santos Pescadores *(☎ 274-302; Av Vicente Méndez 275; open 10pm)* is a big, late-night place with candles on the tables; order a *tabla* and drink the night away. To get there, follow Av Ecuador east until you reach Av Vicente Méndez, and then continue north.

There are a few pub-discos west of the center, including **La Bohemia** (*Claudio Arau 462*) and **La Kassa** (*Claudio Arau 470*).

Pan de Azúcar (*cnr 18 de Septiembre & Maipón; open till 5am*) is a happening spot with three floors of dancing.

Teatro Municipal (*18 de Septiembre 580, 3rd floor*) screens art films and also host concerts and plays.

Shopping

Chillán is one of central Chile's major artisan zones, and the Feria de Chillán is the best place to look. Especially good are ceramics from the nearby villages of Quinchamalí, Paine and Florida. In addition you'll see leatherwork, basketry, horse gear, weavings and the typical straw hats called *chupallas*. Chillán's main shopping district for clothes is north of the market, along El Roble.

Getting There & Around

Chillán's modern bus station, **Terminal María Teresa** (☎ 272-149; Av O'Higgins 010), is just north of Av Ecuador. A few companies, specifically identified below, still sell tickets and leave from the old **Terminal de Buses Interregionales** (☎ 221-014; Constitución 01), at the corner of Av Brasil. Unless otherwise indicated, buses use the Terminal María Teresa.

CHILLÁN

Tur Bus (☎ *212-502; Interregionales & María Teresa*) runs numerous northbound buses to Talca and Santiago; southbound, it leaves twice daily for Concepción and Los Angeles, and daily for Angol, Temuco, Valdivia, Osorno and Puerto Montt. Its office on Av Libertad sells tickets.

Línea Azul (☎ *211-192*) has many buses that go to Concepción, plus two daily to Santiago; it also travels to Valle Los Trancas each morning (returning at 4pm), continuing to Termas de Chillán in summer.

Buses Jota Be (☎ *215-862*) makes seven journeys daily to Salto del Laja and Los Angeles, with additional services to Angol. **Biotal** (☎ *213-223*) service includes three to Los Angeles, four to Concepción and seven to Talca. **Cinta Azul** (☎ *212-505; Constitución 85*) goes to Concepción and Santiago.

Tas Choapa (☎ *223-062*) provides regular service north and south along the Panamericana, direct service to Valparaíso-Viña del Mar and Mendoza, Argentina (US$15). It also offers direct service to Bariloche, Argentina, daily (US$24).

Sol del Sur (☎ *041-313-841*) and **Sol del Pacífico** (☎ *056-752-008*) also go to Santiago, Viña and Valparaíso. **Buses Lit** (☎ *222-960*) runs similar routes and also goes to Concepción, Temuco and other points south. Other companies covering the Panamericana include **Buses Jac** (☎ *042-273-581*), between Temuco and Santiago; **Tramaca** (☎ *226-922*), from Santiago south to Villarrica and Pucón; **Via Tur** (☎ *02-779-5433*), to Santiago, Temuco and Valdivia; and **Inter Sur** (☎ *071-245-920*), to Santiago.

For local and regional services, the **Terminal de Buses Rurales** (☎ *223-606; Sargento Aldea*) is south of Maipón.

Typical fares and journey times from Chillán are as follows:

destination	duration in hours	cost
Angol	3	US$4.30
Concepción	1½	US$3
Los Angeles	1½	US$3
Puerto Montt	9	US$12
Santiago	6	US$9
Talca	3	US$4
Temuco	5	US$6
Valdivia	6	US$8.50
Valparaíso/Viña del Mar	8	US$12

Trains between Santiago and Temuco arrive and depart from the **train station** (☎ *222-424; Av Brasil*), at the west end of Libertad. There are three daily to Santiago (five hours), two to Temuco (6½ hours) and one to Concepción (3½ hours).

If you prefer to drive, try **Jorge Ibáñez Méndez** (☎ *211-218; 18 de Septiembre 380*).

AROUND CHILLÁN
Termas de Chillán

Long renowned for its **thermal baths** (*adult/child US$20/16; open year-round*), Termas de Chillán has more recently become celebrated for its **skiing**, on the southern slopes of 3122m Volcán Chillán. The 28 runs vary from 90m to 1100m in vertical drop, and from 400m to 2500m in length; there are 11 lifts. Some of the runs at Termas de Chillán are through forest. The season ranges from mid-May to mid-October; in summer, the peak is a walk-up, with no special equipment necessary.

Gran Hotel Termas de Chillán (*3-day stay per person US$351-US$870*) is the most luxurious hotel at Termas. Rates, which vary depending on season and type of room, include breakfast, dinner, lift tickets, babysitter and transfer from Chillán or Concepción.

Nuevo Hotel Pirigallo (*3-day stay per person US$285-US$846*) has some bunk rooms and is less exclusive than the Gran Hotel. Rates, which vary depending on season and type of room, include breakfast, dinner, lift tickets, babysitter and transfer from Chillán or Concepción.

Reservations can be made at **Centro de Ski Termas de Chillán** (☎ *042-223-887, fax 042-223-576, 02-233-1313;* e *ventachi@ termachillan.cl; Av Libertad 1042, Chillán*).

Cabañas Rucahue (☎ *042-220-817;* w *www.rucahueescalador.cl; US$10 per person; open year-round*), in Valle Las Trancas, in the mountains 7km before Termas de Chillán, offers cute-as-pie cabins in the woods. The cabins are fully equipped with kitchen, heating and TV, and there's a swimming pool and restaurant on site. The owners can organize trekking, excursions and transport to Termas; they also rent ski equipment.

The bus company **Línea Azul** (☎ *042-211-192*), in Chillán, goes to Valle Las Trancas year-round at 8am (returning at 4pm) and continues to Termas in summer.

Ninhue

Arturo Prat, the naval officer who tried to sink a Peruvian ironclad with his sword in Iquique harbor, was born in this village, 40km northwest of Chillán via the Panamericana and another good paved road. Honoring the local hero is **Santuario Cuna de Prat** (adult/child US$1.60/0.80; open 10am-6pm Tues-Sun), a lovely old homestead with an interesting museum filled with household items from Prat's era.

Agroturismo Lo Vliches de Ñuble, just off the road from Ninhue to Chillán, is a working farm that's open to the public. Horseback-riding is possible, but a stop for a meal (US$5 for a huge and succulent parrilla with salad, appetizers and dessert) is definitely worthwhile.

Via Itata buses to Ninhue (US$1, one hour) leave from Chillán's Terminal de Buses Rurales, on Sargento Aldea (see the Chillán section, earlier).

Coastal Towns

Northwest of Chillán there are some interesting remote coastal villages. **Cobquecura**, a quiet little town with picturesque houses and dry walls made from the local slate, has a long, wide beach with wild surf. About 50m offshore a rocky outcrop known as **Piedra de la Lobería** is home to large colony of noisy sea lions. Just north of town, 5km along the coast road, the exquisite **Iglesia de Piedra** (Church of Stone) is a massive monolith containing huge caves that open to the sea, one containing an image of the Virgin. The light inside the caves is magical, as is the lush vegetation clinging the rock.

Buchupureo, situated in a fertile valley 13km north of Cobquecura, is a tranquil village popular with surfers. It has a tropical air to it, and papayas are a major crop (as are potatoes, which many claim are the best in the country). Despite an influx of surfers, the traditional ways carry on here; it's one of the few places in Chile where you'll see oxen yoked together by their horns and pulling carts. It's also a famous fishing spot – corvina apparently jump onto any hook dangled off the beach.

Buchupureo has some nice, laid-back places to stay. **La Joya del Mar Cabañas** (☎ 042-197-1733; 4-person cabin with kitchen US$50), run by a friendly young Californian couple, has dreamy two-story cabins set in a tropical garden overlooking the sea.

Restaurant El Puerto (☎ 042-197-1608; 3-person cabins US$16/25 low/high season) has basic but comfortable cabins without cooking facilities, but if you provide food, the cook at the restaurant will prepare it for you at no extra charge. The restaurant itself is a pleasant sunny place with cheap hearty lunches (US$1.60 if you're staying in the cabins, US$3 if you're not). The owners also organise outings that combine horseback-riding in the pretty backcountry with visits to traditional farms and houses (US$20, including lunch) that allow a peek at local culture; this excursion is most interesting during the late-summer wheat harvest.

If you have your own transport, it's worth checking out the nice beaches south of Cobquecura. **El Rinconada**, 6km south, is a favorite surf spot where fisherfolk sell crabs, sea urchins and abalone, and oxen drag carts and boats up the beach.

CONCEPCIÓN

☎ 41 • pop 214,500

Industry, convenient energy resources, port facilities and universities have combined to make Concepción the second most important city in Chile after Santiago. Concepción is not a particularly scenic city, but it's infused with a comforting hustle and bustle, and there are pleasant plazas, pedestrian malls and galerías. Signs of the large student presence are everywhere and add a youthful vibe.

The inhabitants of Concepción are known as Penquistas after the city's original site at the nearby town of Penco.

History

Founded in 1551 by Pedro de Valdivia, menaced constantly by Mapuches and devastated by earthquakes in 1730 and 1751, Concepción moved several times before settling at its present site in 1764. After a major Mapuche uprising in 1598, Spain never again seriously contested Mapuche control of the area south of the Biobío, and Concepción remained one of the empire's southernmost fortified outposts.

After independence, Concepción's isolation from Santiago, coupled with the presence of lignite (brown coal) near Lota, a coastal town south of Concepción, fomented an autonomous industrial tradition. The

MIDDLE CHILE

export of wheat for the California gold-rush market further spurred the area's economic growth. The railway reached Concepción in 1872 and, after the Mapuche threat receded, the government bridged the Biobío to improve access to the mines and give the city a strategic role in the colonization of La Frontera, the present-day lakes region.

Despite Concepción's industrial importance, wages and living standards are relatively low. This, coupled with activism at the Universidad de Concepción, made the city and its industrial hinterland the locus of a highly politicized labor movement that was a bulwark of support for Salvador Allende and the Unidad Popular. As a center of leftist opposition, the area suffered more than other regions under the military dictatorship of 1973–89.

Orientation

Concepción sits on the north bank of the Río Biobío, Chile's only significant navigable waterway. Cerro Caracol, a scenic overlook, blocks any eastward expansion so that Concepción and its port of Talcahuano, 15km

northwest on the sheltered Bahía de Concepción, are rapidly growing together.

Concepción's standard grid centers on Plaza Independencia, a pleasantly landscaped and bustling space. Barros Arana and Aníbal Pinto have lively pedestrian malls leading two or three blocks to the north and west of the plaza.

Information

Sernatur (☎ 227-976; e serna08@entelchile .net; Aníbal Pinto 460; open 8:30am-8pm daily in summer, 8:30am-1pm & 3pm-6pm Mon-Fri rest of year) is well stocked with maps and brochures and has helpful, well-informed staff. In summer there's usually an English-speaker on hand. For information on national parks go to **Conaf** (☎ 220-094; Barros Arana 215).

Acchi (Automóvil Club de Chile; ☎ 311-968; Freire 1867) is also a good source of information.

To change traveler's checks, try **Afex** (Barros Arana 565, Local 57). There are numerous downtown ATMs, including a **Banco de Chile** (O'Higgins & Caupolicán).

CONCEPCIÓN

PLACES TO STAY	PLACES TO EAT	OTHER
9 Hotel El Araucano; Café Caribe; La Gruta	6 El Rancho de Julio	1 Feria Artesanal
12 Hostal Antuco; Residencial San Sebastián	7 Chela's	2 El Medio Toro
21 Hotel El Dorado	11 Café Haití	3 Mezcal
23 Residencial Metro	16 China Town	4 Choripan
25 Hotel San Sebastián	18 Arcolris	
35 Hotel Alonso de Ercilla	19 Chung-Hwa	
	24 Café Montreal	5 Conaf
	28 Di Marco; EFE Venta de Pasajes	8 Entel
	37 Café Creación	10 Afex
	40 Verde Quete Quiero Verde	13 Cyberc@fé
		14 LanChile
		15 Tur Bus
		17 Treinta y Tanto
		20 Cine Regina
		22 Casa Loosli
		26 Iglesia Catedral
		27 LanChile
		29 Sernatur
		30 Post Office
		31 Banco de Chile
		32 Portal
		33 Laverap
		34 Cine de Concepción
		36 Hospital Regional
		38 EconoRent
		39 Casa del Arte
		41 Avis Rent a Car
		42 Galería de la Historia

There's a **post office** (*O'Higgins 799*) at the corner of Colo Colo. Phone centers include **Entel** (*Barros Arana 541, Local 2*), but others are dotted around town.

The **CyberC@fé** (☎ *253-992; Portales 530; US$1.50/hr*) offers Internet access, as does **Portal** (*Caupolicán 314; US$1/hr*).

For fast laundry services, try **Laverap** (*Caupolicán 334*).

Concepción's **Hospital Regional** (☎ *237-445; San Martín & Av Roosevelt*) is eight blocks north of Plaza Independencia.

Galería de la Historia

Vivid dioramas of local and regional history are the strongpoint of this fine museum (☎ *231-830; Av Lamas & Lincoyán; admission free; open 3pm-6:30pm Mon, 10am-1:30pm & 3pm-6:30pm Tues-Fri, 10am-2pm & 3pm-7pm Sat & Sun*) on the edge of Parque Ecuador, near Cerro Caracol. Among the subjects are pre-Columbian Mapuche subsistence, the arrival of the Spaniards and battles between the two peoples (with fine representations of Mapuche battle tactics), construction of fortifications at Penco (the original site of Concepción), treaty signings, military and literary figure Alonso de Ercilla, Chile's declaration of independence, the 1851 battle of Loncomilla, the devastating 1939 earthquake (15,000 houses destroyed) and a finely detailed scale model of a local factory.

Upstairs there's an art gallery with temporary exhibits by local artists.

Casa del Arte

The highlight of this university art museum (☎ *204-126; Barrio Universitario, Chacabuco & Larenas; admission free; open 10am-6pm Tues-Fri, 10am-4pm Sat, 10am-1pm Sun*) is *La Presencia de América Latina*, a massive mural by Mexican artist Jorge González Camarena (a protégé of José Clemente Orozco). The museum also contains two rooms of landscapes and portraits.

Special Events

Organized by the universities, Concepción's **Fiesta de la Primavera** (Festival of Spring), commemorating the founding of the city, lasts an entire week in early October.

Places to Stay

Residencial Metro (☎ *225-305; Barros Arana 464; singles/doubles US$10/16 including breakfast*) has spacious rooms with high ceilings and nicely faded, homey décor.

Hostal Antuco (☎ *235-485; Barros Arana 741, Departamento 33; singles/doubles US$12/22 with shared bath & breakfast*) has decent rooms above an arcade. Ring the buzzer at the gate to the stairs just inside the entrance to the arcade.

Residencial San Sebastián (☎ *242-710, fax 243-412; Barros Arana 741, Departamento 35; singles/doubles with private bath US$12/20 with shared bath & breakfast*) is virtually identical to Residencial Antuco but has slightly nicer rooms. Like the Antuco (earlier), you'll need to ring the buzzer to get in here too.

Hotel San Sebastián (☎/fax *910-270; Rengo 463; singles/doubles US$26/33 with shared bath, US$36/43 with private bath, all rates include breakfast*) is sparkling clean, central and friendly.

Hotel Alonso de Ercilla (☎ *227-984, fax 230-053; Colo Colo 334; singles/doubles US$33/55 including breakfast*) is clean and comfortable with nice woody '70s décor, good heating and English-speaking staff. Rates include a top-notch breakfast.

Hotel El Araucano (☎ *740-606, fax 740-690; Caupolicán 521; rooms US$42/53 Sat & Sun/Mon-Fri*) is swish. The staff are friendly, and rooms have a great view of the city lights.

Hotel El Dorado (☎ *229-400, fax 231-018; Barros Arana 348; singles/doubles US$50/54*) is quite luxurious and a bit of a bargain; the bathrooms have a big tub.

Places to Eat

Concepción's **Mercado Central**, with its pickled onions, strings of red chilies and bundles of seaweed, has a multitude of cheap and excellent eateries. Waitresses literally drag customers into their venues. There's not much difference among these places in price, quality or décor, so just follow your nose.

Fuente Alemana (☎ *228-307; O'Higgins 513*) serves reliably good sandwiches.

Arcolris (☎ *520-300; Barros Arana 244*) offers healthy vegetarian fare in spacious, airy surrounds.

Café Creación (☎ *981-128; San Martín 756*) is a sunny little café serving real coffee, cakes and snacks, including vegetarian options. The lunch menu is only US$2.25.

MIDDLE CHILE

Chela's (☎ 243-367; Barros Arana 405) is a popular and cheap lunch spot; try the fried fish with salad (US$3) or the *cazuela de ave* (US$1.75).

Verde Quete Quiero Verde (☎ 250-291, Colo Colo 174) is the nicest place to eat in all of Concepción. It serves inspiring vegetarian food, which is just the ticket after a spell in meat-mad Chile. You can choose from inventive juices (apple and mint US$2), unusual salads (US$3-5), pastas (US$6), hearty sandwiches (US$3) and more. The interior is simple, bright and uncluttered, and the staff are so friendly that they'll bring you something to read if you're sitting alone. There's a gallery adjacent to the dining room, and artists' studios are out the back and upstairs; on Friday nights (9pm onward), the studios are open to anyone who cares to visit.

El Rancho de Julio (☎ 228-207; Barros Arana 337) is the kind of place where solo men go to eat steak, and it's not cheap. If you go, be hungry.

For Chinese food, visit **Chung-Hwa** (☎ 229-539; Barros Arana 262) or **China Town** (☎ 233-218; Barros Arana 1115).

Penquistas seem to have an inordinate fondness for *onces* – there are cafés and salones de té everywhere you look, always packed with locals gossiping over küchen and coffee.

Café Haití (☎ 230-755; Caupolicán 511, Local 7) has a lovely upstairs area that looks out over the street – perfect for people-watching.

Café Caribe (☎ 241-937; Caupolicán 521, Local 34), in the same building as the Araucano hotel, is slightly more hip than Haití.

Other spots worth a try are **Di Marco**, in the arcade next to Sernatur, and **Café Montreal** (☎ 214-770, Barros Arana 526).

Entertainment

West of Plaza Independencia, across from the train station, the area known as Barrio Estación is home to several popular pub-restaurants. **Treinta y Tanto** (☎ 240-451; Prat 404; open dinner only), which has outstanding empanadas (over 30 varieties) and *vino navegado* (mulled wine), is the most notable place. Other choices for bar-hoppers include the **Comanche Pub** (Prat 442), **Mezcal** (Prat 532), **Choripan** (Prat 546) and **El Medio Toro** (Prat 592), but there are many more.

Concepción has a couple decent movie theaters: the **Cine de Concepción** (☎ 227-193; O'Higgins 650) and the **Cine Regina** (☎ 225-904; Barros Arana 340). **Casa del Arte** (☎ 234-985; Chacabuco & Larenas), in the Barrio Universitario, screens films and puts on plays.

Shopping

Many of Concepción's shops are in galerías, and the main shopping street is Barros Arana. Local and regional crafts are sold at the **Mercado Central**, **Feria Artesanal** (Freire 757) and at **La Gruta** (Caupolicán 521, Local 64). The best things to look for are woolens, basketry, ceramics, wood carvings and leather goods. Knitters will notice an abundance of shops selling yarn (sometimes alpaca). **Casa Loosli** (Barros Arana 466) sells traditional-looking parchment lampshades.

Getting There & Away

Air Chile's airline, **LanChile** (☎ 229-138; Barros Arana 600 • ☎ 521-092; Colo Colo 550), has up to eight flights daily to Santiago (US$117), four to Punta Arenas (US$250, via Santiago), and one to Valdivia (US$70).

Bus Concepción has two long-distance bus terminals. Almost all carriers leave from **Terminal de Buses Collao** (as known as Puchacay; ☎ 316-666; Tegualda 860), on the outskirts of town near the highway to Chillán, but some companies use the separate **Terminal Chillancito** (☎ 315-036; Camilo Henríquez 2565), the northward extension of Bulnes. Unless otherwise indicated, the following companies use Terminal Collao. Micros, taxi colectivos and taxis (US$4) connect downtown with both the Chillancito and Collao bus terminals.

Tur Bus (☎ 315-555; Tucapel 530), **Sol del Pacífico**, **Buses Lit** (☎ 230-722), **Tas Choapa** (☎ 312-639), **Pullman Sur** (☎ 314-912), **Sol del Sur** (☎ 313-841), **Estrella del Sur** (☎ 321-383), **Via Costa** (☎ 221-914), **Transtur**, **Intersur** and many other companies run frequent buses daily to Santiago, Valparaíso-Viña del Mar.

Pullman Sur also goes to Talca, as does **Via Costa**, which stops at Curicó and Rancagua as well.

Línea Azul (☎ 311-126) travels to Chillán, Valles Las Trancas and Termas de Chillán.

Tas Choapa (☎ 312-639) provides excellent connections to northern Chile and Argentina.

Companies travelling southbound to Temuco, Valdivia and Puerto Montt include Tur Bus (see earlier), **Varmontt** (☎ 314-010), **Igi Llaima** (☎ 312-498 and **Cruz del Sur** (☎ 314-372).

Frequent services to Los Angeles, Angol and Salto del Laja are provided by **Jota Be** (☎ 312-652), **Buses Biobío** (☎ 310-764) and Igi Llaima (see earlier).

For services down the coast to Coronel, Lota, Arauco, Lebú, Cañete and Contulmo, try **Buses Los Alces** (☎ 240-855) or **Buses Jota Ewert** (☎ 229-212), but there are also micros from the corner of Tucapel and Ave Los Carrera.

Typical fares and journey times from Concepción are as follows:

destination	duration in hours	cost
Angol	1½	US$4
Chillán	2	US$3
Los Angeles	2	US$3
Puerto Montt	7	US$13
Santiago	7	US$7-15
Talca	4	US$8
Temuco	4	US$6
Valdivia	6	US$10
Valparaíso/Viña del Mar	9	US$13

Train Concepción's **train station** (☎ 227-777; *Arturo Prat)* is at the end of Barros Arana, but there's also an **EFE venta de pasajes** *(ticket office; ☎ 225-286; Aníbal Pinto 478, Local 3)* right near Di Marco (see Places to Eat). Trains to Santiago (US$13/34 salón/ cama baja) leave nightly at 10pm, arriving at approximately 6:30am.

Getting Around

To/From the Airport Aeropuerto Carriel Sur is 5km northwest of downtown, on the road to Talcahuano. Several companies run airport minibuses for about US$3, including **Airport Express** (☎ 236-444), **Turismo Ritz** (☎ 237-637) and **Taxivan** (☎ 248-748). All three connect with flights in front of LanChile offices but will also pick up passengers at hotels.

Micro Micros from the bus station run constantly to the center of town along San Martín; the fare is US$0.40. There are also micros to Lota (US$0.60) every 15 minutes or so from the corner of Tucapel and Av Los Carrera, while micros to Talcahuano run continuously down O'Higgins and San Martín.

Train Concepción's has a limited network of suburban trains known as Bio-Trén. The new **Bio-Trén station** is behind the monolithic Líder supermarket, at the end of Freire. There are departures every half-hour to Talcahuano Puerto, Hualqui and other places within the greater metropolitan area.

Car Concepción has several rental agencies to choose among, including **EconoRent** (☎ 225-377; Castellón 134) and **Avis** (☎ 235-837; Chacabuco 726).

AROUND CONCEPCIÓN
Buque Huáscar

Built in Birkenhead, England, in 1865, captured from the Peruvian navy in 1879 and now on display in Talcahuano, the Buque Huáscar (☎ 041-745-715; adult/child US$1.60/0.80; open 9:30am-12:30pm & 1:30pm-5pm Tues-Sun) was one of the world's earliest ironclad battleships. It owes its remarkable state of preservation to the labor of naval conscripts, whose spit-and-polish maintenance work never ends.

From Concepción, take any 'Galaxias' bus that has 'Base Naval' on its placard along San Martín to the Apostadero Naval, beyond Talcahuano's Club de Yates on Av Villaroel. You'll be required to leave your passport at the gate. Photography is permitted, but only with the port of Talcahuano or the open sea as background – do *not* photograph other naval vessels or any part of the base itself.

La Costa del Carbón

As an advertising slogan, the 'Coast of Coal' may sound improbable, but substantial crowds are drawn south of the Río Biobío to and around Coronel, Lota, Arauco and Península Lebú. The best excursion is to **Lota**, a hilly town that was once the center of Chile's coal industry. The mines closed in 1997, and the town, which smells hauntingly of coal, is now trying to promote itself as a tourist destination. There is some interesting old company-town architecture, as well as bleak but eye-opening shantytown architecture – visitors should be prepared to see some quite confronting poverty.

On a more positive note, Lota is the site of the 14-hectare **Parque Botánico**

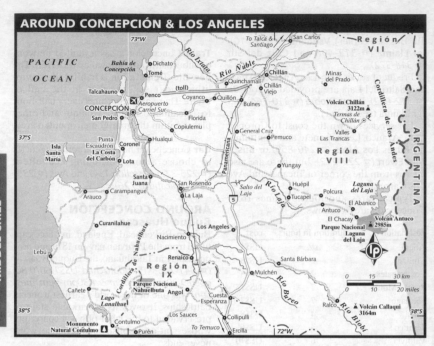

AROUND CONCEPCIÓN & LOS ANGELES

Isidora Cousiño (☎ 041-871-549; adult/child US$2.70/2; open 9am-8pm daily), a cacophonous mix of palms, pines, clipped hedges, ponds and aviaries. The park is a remarkable demonstration of the resilient survival of cultivated beauty alongside massive slag heaps and shantytowns; its western end affords superb views over the bay, which must have once been very pretty.

Just before the park is the **Museo Histórico del Carbón** (☎ 041-871-549; Carlos Cousiño; entry included in park admission fee; open 9am-8pm daily). It contains displays on the history of coal mining in the region, as well as fine ceramics and bricks that were once produced in Lota.

Since the demise of the local coal industry, part of the government's response to worsening economic conditions has been to train former miners as guides to the **Mina Chiflón Carlos** (45-min descent US$6; open 9am-7:30pm daily), in the coast range behind Lota. Reservations are essential for visits to the mine; contact the **Fundación de Chile** (☎ 041-871-459).

Nearby, **Chiflón del Diablo** (Devil's Whistle; ☎ 041-871-565; open 9am-6:30pm daily) was a working mine until 1976, but now, laid-off coal miners take tourists through the mine (US$7 to US$14 depending on length – and depth – of tour; arrive before 4pm if taking the long tour). Ask the microbus driver to drop you off at Parada Calero. Go down street Bajada Defensa Niño, and you'll see a long wall with the name.

The town of **Coronel**, just north of Lota, holds a **Muestra Cultural de Folklore** (folklore festival) in early February.

Micros to Lota (US$0.60) and other Costa del Carbón destinations depart from Concepción every 15 minutes or so from the corner of Tucapel and Av Los Carrera.

Cañete

At Cañete, 135km south of Concepción, Mapuche resistance led to the death of Pedro de Valdivia in 1553. The **Museo Mapuche de Cañete** (☎ 041-611-093; admission US$1; open 9:30am-5:50pm Mon-Fri, 11am-7pm Sat & Sun) has some good exhibits on Mapuche funerary customs, musical instruments, textiles and silverwork.

SALTO DEL LAJA

On the Panamericana, 25km north of Los Angeles en route to Chillán, the Río Laja plunges nearly 50m over a steep escarpment to form a miniature Iguazú Falls before joining the Biobío at La Laja, 40km to the west. Salto del Laja is a popular recreation area, perhaps as much for its accessibility as its scenery. The falls are hardly worth more than a quick stop, and it's an easy excursion from Los Angeles, but camping grounds, cabañas and hotels abound.

El Rinconcito (☎ *043-328-095; sites US$10, cabañas US$25, rooms from US$30),* by the bridge, offers year-round camping, as well as cabins and rooms.

Hostería Salto del Laja (☎ *043-321-706, fax 313-996;* e *saltodellaja@entel.net; singles/doubles start at US$33/42 including breakfast)* is a nice place.

Fundo Curanilahue (☎ *043-197-2819;* e *jacksonmay@entelchile.net; US$150 per person with full board)* is just north of Salto del Laja and 3km east of the Panamericana. It's a pleasant working farm that offers accommodations on a call-ahead basis only. Horseback-riding, a heated swimming pool, tennis, motor boat trips up the river, and laundry service are included in the rates.

Hospedaje El Rincón (☎ *09-441-5019;* e *interbruna@entelchile.net; bargain single US$6, regular singles/doubles US$12/24 with shared bath, US$15/30 with private bath, breakfast included in rates)* is a lovely German-run lodge. English, German and French are spoken, and the proprietors also offer excursions to the Alto Biobío, Laguna del Laja, Parque Nacional Nahuelbuta, Termas de Chillán and the Concepción coastline. Weeklong intensive Spanish courses (five hours daily) are also available (US$180). Call to arrange pickup from Los Angeles or from Cruce La Mona if coming from the north.

To get to Salto del Laja take one of the hourly Jota Be buses from Los Angeles' Terminal Vega Techada; buses to and from Concepción also pass through Salto del Lajas.

PN LAGUNA DEL LAJA

The lake from which this park takes its name was formed when lava from 2985m Volcán Antuco dammed the Río Laja. The park protects the mountain cypress (*Austrocedrus chilensis)* and the monkey-puzzle tree at the northern limit of its distribution, as well as other uncommon tree species. Mammals are rare, though pumas, foxes and vizcachas do exist in the park. Nearly 50 bird species inhabit the area, including the Andean condor.

The lake is so modified by hydroelectric projects, including tunnels and dams, that it more closely resembles a reservoir. The park itself, however, is a mountainous area ranging from 1000m to nearly 3000m above sea level. Its most striking feature is Antuco's symmetrical cone, but the higher Sierra Velluda to the southwest, beyond the park boundaries, offers a series of impressive glaciers. The volcano may seem quiet, but it is not extinct; volcanic activity was last recorded about 70 years ago.

Laguna del Laja has trails suitable for day hikes as well as for longer excursions; the best is the circuit around Volcán Antuco, which provides views of both the Sierra Velluda and the lake.

Places to Stay

Hotel Malalcura (☎ *043-313-183; Abanico),* 9km west of the park entrance, is the closest hotel to the park.

Refugio Digeder (☎ *041-229-054; beds US$10; open winter only)* is operated by Concepción's Dirección General de Deportes y Recreación, at the base of Volcán Antuco.

Getting There & Away

From Los Angeles' Terminal Santa Rita at the corner of Villagrán and Rengo, **ERS** (☎ *043-322-356)* buses go to the villages of Antuco and Abanico, gateways to Parque Nacional Laguna del Laja, seven times daily on weekends, three times daily on weekdays. The trip takes about 1½ hours, but it takes another several hours to walk the 11km to Chacay, where Conaf maintains administrative offices and a small visitor center. Hitchhiking is possible, but vehicles are a rare sight on weekends.

LOS ANGELES

☎ 43 • pop 164,500

Founded in 1739 as a bulwark against the Mapuche, Los Angeles is an unprepossessing agricultural and industrial service center 110km south of Chillán. While not terribly interesting in itself, Los Angeles does make a good base for forays into the upper reaches of the Río Biobío and Parque Nacional Laguna del Laja (see that section, later), which includes 2985m Volcán Antuco.

Information

Perhaps the best source of information is the **Automóvil Club de Chile** (☎ 314-209; Caupolicán 201).

LanChile (☎ 600-661-3000; Lautaro 551 • Lautaro 186) has two offices.

Inter Bruna (☎ 313-812; Caupolicán 350) changes money, and there are numerous ATMs in town.

The **post office** (Caupolicán) is on the south side of the Plaza de Armas. Telefónica long-distance offices are at the long-distance bus terminal. **Entel** (Colo Colo 489, Local 1) has public phones.

Los Angeles' **Hospital Regional** (☎ 321-456; Av Ricardo Vicuña) is just east of Los Carrera.

Museo de la Alta Frontera

Los Angeles' municipal museum (Caupolicán & Colón, 2nd floor; admission free; 8:15am-2pm & 2:45pm-6:45pm Mon-Fri) has an extraordinary collection of Mapuche silverwork, masks and headdresses. The museum is at the southeast corner of the Plaza de Armas, in the same building as the tourist office.

Places to Stay

Los Angeles differs from many other Chilean cities in that many of its accommodations are along the Panamericana rather than in the city itself, because of the Salto del Laja, the area's biggest nearby attraction. Nevertheless, the most reasonable options are in town.

Residencial El Angelino (☎ 325-627; Colo Colo 335; US$10 per person with shared bath) is a great place with very clean, cheerful rooms.

Hotel Oceano (☎ 341-694; Colo Colo 327; singles/doubles US$18/35 with private bath & breakfast) has simple unadorned rooms and is a reasonable option.

Hotel Villena (☎ 321-643; Lautaro 579; rooms US$20 with private bath & breakfast), dating from 1907, is a fantastic, rambling place that's well kept. It also has a wonderful restaurant (see Places to Eat).

Gran Hotel Muso (☎ 313-183; Valdivia 222; singles/doubles US$43/57) has an intriguingly funky facade and a foyer with orange and blue plastic bubble windows in the floor, but it all stops there – the rooms are surprisingly drab.

Hotel Mariscal Alcázar (☎ 311-725; Lautaro 385; singles/doubles from US$52/65) is Los Angeles' flashest joint. Despite its airs and spacious lounge areas, the rooms are small and fairly ordinary.

Places to Eat

Café Prymos (☎ 323-731; Colón 400) is an excellent choice for breakfast, coffee or sandwiches.

Café Suizo (☎ 340-515; Lautaro 346) is another good place for coffee, juices, cakes and sandwiches.

Restaurant de Villena (☎ 321-643; Lautaro 579) has superb, cheap homestyle cooking and is a local favorite. Try the mariscal caliente (US$4) or the congrio (US$5). There are lunch menus for US$2.25 and US$3.

Julio's Pizza (☎ 314-530; Colón 452) is part of a small Argentinian chain and has good pizza, pasta and meat dishes.

Bavaria (☎ 315-531; Colón 357) serves reliable meals and sandwiches.

El Alero (☎ 312-899; Colo Colo 235) is a popular parrilla joint, with salty food and cheesy karaoke-type live entertainment.

For something posher, try the **Club de la Unión** (☎ 322-218; Colón 261), which serves classy Chilean fare.

Getting There & Away

There's a **First Rent a Car** (☎ 313-812; Caupolicán 350) in the center of town.

Long-distance buses leave from Los Angeles' **Terminal Santa María** (Av Sor Vicenta 2051), on the northeast outskirts of town, most easily reached via Av Villagrán.

There are frequent buses between Los Angeles and Concepción with **Biobío** (☎ 314-621), **Igi Llaima** (☎ 321-666), **Los Alces** and **Jota Be** (☎ 363-037), which also runs to Angol, the gateway to Parque Nacional Nahuelbuta, via Renaico (US$2, 1½ hours). Most buses to Concepción stop at Salto del Laja.

Other Los Angeles bus companies running north-south services along the Panamericana are **Biotal** (☎ 317-357), **Cruz del Sur** (☎ 317-630), **Fénix Pullman Norte** (☎ 322-502),

Buses Jac (☎ 317-469), Buses Laja (☎ 316-729), Tas Choapa (☎ 322-266), Unión del Sur (☎ 316-891) and Tur Bus (☎ 328-062).

From Terminal Santa Rita, at the corner of Villagrán and Rengo, ERS (☎ 322-356) goes to the village of Antuco, gateway to Parque Nacional Laguna del Laja, seven times daily on weekends, three times daily on weekdays. Other rural buses, including hourly Jota Be buses to Salto del Laja, leave from the Terminal Vega Techada, at the corner of Villagrán and Tucapel. Confusingly, a few rural buses leave from the other side of the river, across the pedestrian bridge.

Sample fares and journey times include the following:

destination	duration in hours	cost
Angol	1	US$1
Chillán	1½	US$3
Concepción	2	US$3
Temuco	4	US$6
Puerto Montt	8	US$13
Santiago	8	US$12
Salto del Laja	¾	US$1

ANGOL
☎ 45 • pop 49,000

Founded in 1553 by Pedro de Valdivia as a strategic frontier outpost – and destroyed half a dozen times over three centuries in the Mapuche wars – Angol de los Confines finally survived the Indian resistance after 1862. Easily reached by southbound travelers from Los Angeles, as well as from Temuco, it provides the best access into mountainous Parque Nacional Nahuelbuta, a forest reserve that protects the largest remaining coastal stands of araucaria pines.

Angol straddles the Río Vergara, an upper tributary of the Biobío formed by the confluence of the Ríos Picoiquén and Rehue. The city's older core, centered on a particularly attractive Plaza de Armas (bounded by Lautaro, Prat, Bunster and Chorrillos) lies west of the river.

Information
Angol's Oficina Municipal de Turismo (☎ 201-556, fax 201-571; open 9am-1pm & 3pm-7pm Mon-Fri year-round, plus 9am-1pm Sat in summer) is just east of the bridge across the Río Vergara. It has few maps and brochures but boasts a hard-working, well-informed staff.

Angol has no formal cambios, but Boutique Boston (☎ 713-946; Sepúlveda 3-A), between Prat and Lautaro, changes US cash 9am to 1pm and 3pm to 7pm weekdays. You can also try the travel agencies Turismo Christopher (☎ 715-156; Ilabaca 421) or Nahuel Tour (☎ 715-457; Pedro Aguirre Cerda 307). There's a Banco de Chile (Lautaro 2) and other ATMs near the square.

The post office (Lautaro & Chorrillos) is at the northeast corner of the Plaza de Armas. Telefónica (CTC) (O'Higgins 297) has long-distance offices west of the river.

Things to See & Do
Built in 1863, Convento San Buenaventura (Covadonga), between Vergara and Dieciocho, a Franciscan convent, is the region's oldest church and is well worth a visit.

If you're interested in architecture, check out the wacky Jardín Infantil Espignita (Prat 499). This pink and blue, twin-turreted affair flanked by palms is now a private childcare center, but its exterior is worth a look.

Developed as both a plant nursery and gardens by Anglo-Chilean Manuel Bunster in the 19th century, then acquired by Methodist missionaries in 1920, the Escuela Agrícola El Vergel (grounds open 8:30am-noon & 2:30pm-6pm daily) is an agricultural college. Its Museo Bullock (☎ 711-142; adult/child US$0.75/0.40; open 9am-1pm & 3pm-6:30pm daily), which houses a fine collection of natural-history specimens and archaeological artifacts, is the legacy of North American Methodist Dillman S Bullock, who spent nearly 70 years in Chile learning the Mapuche language and publishing articles on the region's biology, natural history and archaeology. El Vergel is 5km east of Angol but is easily reached by taxi colectivo No 2 from the Plaza de Armas.

Angol is renowned for fine (though somewhat tacky) ceramics. Cerámica Serra (Bunster 153) and Cerámica Lablé (Purén 864) are both small factories open to the public.

Special Events
In the second week of January, the Municipalidad de Angol sponsors Brotes de Chile, a folksong festival with prizes ranging up to US$3000. One of Chile's most important festivals for more than a decade, it features music, dance, food and crafts.

MIDDLE CHILE

MIDDLE CHILE

Places to Stay & Eat

Residencial Olimpia (☎ 711-162; Caupolicán 625; singles/doubles US$12/22) is a five-minute walk from the bus station in a pleasant residential area.

Hotel Millaray (☎ 711-570; Prat 420; singles/doubles with shared bath US$12/20, with private bath US$21/27) is a solid clean place with pleasant rooms one block from the plaza.

Hotel Club Social (☎ 711-103; Caupolicán 498; singles/doubles with private bath US$27/33), a couple of blocks from the bus station, has huge, nicely decorated apartmentlike rooms. There's also a pool, bar and good restaurant; it's best to call ahead.

Sparlatto Pizza (Lautaro 418) is popular and cozy.

The **Club Social** (Caupolicán 498) is a classy place with a good selection of dishes.

Lomitón (Lautaro 145) is a fast-food outlet with reliable sandwiches.

Café La Ruequa, on Lautaro, is about the only place you'll find espresso.

Getting There & Away

For long-distance services, Angol's **Terminal Buses Thiele** (Caupolicán 200) is a block north of the plaza. **Buses Biobío** (☎ 711-777) has buses every half-hour to Temuco (US$3, two hours) and to Concepción (US$4). Most buses to Santiago depart around 10pm. **Tur Bus** (☎ 711-655) and **Trans Tur** have morning and evening departures for Santiago (US$8 to US$18, eight hours). **Igi Llaima** (☎ 711-920) goes to Los Angeles and Concepción twice daily and to Santiago nightly.

Buses Thiele (☎ 711-110) has extensive regional services, connecting Angol to the Costa del Carbón via Contulmo, Cañete and Lebú (US$4), and to Concepción via Nacimiento and Santa Juana. **Jota Be** (☎ 712-262) has 22 buses daily to Los Angeles (US$1) via Renaico.

The **Terminal Rural** (☎ 712-021; Ilabaca 422), for local and regional services, is at the corner of Lautaro. **Buses Angol** (☎ 712-021) goes from Angol to Vegas Blancas (US$1.70), 7km from the entrance to Parque Nacional Nahuelbuta, Monday, Wednesday and Friday at 6:45am and 4pm, returning at 9am and 6pm. **Buses Nahuelbuta** (☎ 715-611) travels to the Vegas Blancas Tuesday, Thursday and Saturday at 6:45am, returning at 4pm, from the corner of Ilabaca and

Caupolican. For details on park tours, see the following section.

PN NAHUELBUTA

Between Angol and the Pacific, covered with araucaria pines, the coastal range rises to nearly 1600m in Parque Nacional Nahuelbuta (admission US$3). Created in 1939 to protect one of the last non-Andean refuges of the pehuen (monkey-puzzle tree), whose largest specimens can reach 50m in height and 2m in diameter, this 6832-hectare park also features stands of Nothofagus (southern beech). Occasional sightings of rare mammals such as puma, culpeo (Chiloé fox) and the miniature Chilean deer known as the pudú have been known to happen. The park is also a favorite UFO-spotting zone.

On the road from Angol, Conaf maintains a **Centro de Informaciones Ecológicas**, with a small museum, where rangers offer audiovisual presentations about the local environment.

The park enjoys warm, dry summers, but snow sometimes falls at higher elevations in

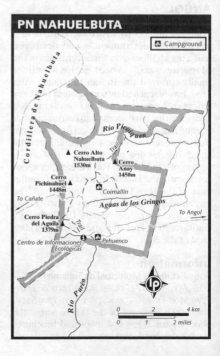

PN NAHUELBUTA

🏕 Campground

winter. November to April is the best time for a visit.

Things to See & Do

Nahuelbuta has 30km of roads and 15km of footpaths, so car-touring, camping and hiking are all possible. From Pehuenco, a 4km trail winds through pehuen forests, with occasional springs, to the granite outcrop of **Piedra del Aguila**, a 1379m overlook with views from the Andes to the Pacific except to the north-northeast, where the forest crown blocks the view. To the southeast, the entire string of Andean volcanoes – from Antuco, east of Chillán, to Villarrica and Lanín, east of Pucón – is visible; on a really clear day, even Osorno may appear on the southern horizon.

Piedra del Aguila is only an 800m hike from a shorter approach accessible by car, but it's possible, and more interesting, to loop back to Pehuenco via the valley of the Estero Cabrería to the south via a trail that starts beneath the west side of Piedra del Aguila.

Cerro Anay, 1450m above sea level, has similar views; the trail itself, reached via Coimallín, is relatively short and has countless wildflowers and huge stands of araucarias.

Places to Stay

Camping Pehuenco (sites US$9), 5km from the park entrance and near park headquar-

ters, has 11 sites available in shady forest clearings with picnic tables and bathrooms with flush toilets and cold showers.

Camping Coimallín (sites US$9), 5km north of Pehuenco, has four sites. The Coimallín is more rustic and lacks running water.

Getting There & Away

See Angol's Getting There & Away section for information on buses. Motorists with low-clearance vehicles may find the steep and dusty road difficult in spots. Few mountain bikers will be able to do the ride without dismounting and walking at least part of the time, and water is hard to find.

MONUMENTO NATURAL CONTULMO

A worthwhile stop for travelers passing through en route to Angol and Los Angeles, Monumento Natural Contulmo is a small (84-hectare) forest corridor abutting the highway. An 8km trail leads through woods as dense and verdant as a tropical rainforest; plaques identify major tree species, but the giant ferns and climbing vines are just as intriguing. There is a picnic area, but the nearest camping facilities are at Lago Lanalhue, a few kilometers to the west, at **Camping Municipal** (☎ 041-611-237; sites US$1 per person).

Norte Grande

Norte Grande features the Pacific Ocean, the starkly desolate but unique Atacama Desert with its deeply incised canyons, and the Andean altiplano (steppe) with its volcanic summits. The region's great mineral wealth has given it a special role in Chilean history; most cities in the Atacama, such as Iquique and Antofagasta, owe their existence to nitrates and copper.

The Atacama is the most 'perfect' of deserts; some coastal stations have never recorded measurable rainfall, although infrequent 'El Niño' events can bring brief but phenomenal downpours in other places. Otherwise, the only precipitation comes from the convective fogs known as *camanchaca* or *garúa*, which condense at higher elevations and support scattered vegetation on the *lomas* (coastal hills). In all the Norte Grande, the meandering Río Loa, which cuts through Calama, is the only river whose flow consistently reaches the Pacific.

Rainfall and vegetation increase with elevation and distance from the sea. In the precordillera, or foothills, Aymara farmers still cultivate the manmade terraces designed for soil conservation and irrigation that have covered the hillsides for millennia, although alfalfa has largely replaced quinoa (a native Andean grain) and the myriad varieties of potato. Cultivation reaches as high as 4000m. Above this level, the Aymara pasture llamas, alpacas and a few sheep on the grasslands of the puna (highlands). In the very high, arid Puna de Atacama, there is too little moisture to support any permanent human habitation – even the 5916m peak of Licancábur has no permanent snow cover.

Norte Grande consists of Región I (Tarapacá), Región II (Antofagasta) and the northernmost part of Región III (Atacama).

History

The sea was the main source of subsistence for the Chango Indians, who populated the coast in pre-Columbian times, fishing from sealskin canoes and hunting guanaco in coastal-range pastures. Coastal people also exchanged products such as fish and guano for maize and *charqui* (sun-dried llama or alpaca meat) with their Andean kin.

The interior of the Norte Grande was more closely linked to the Andean highlands than to coastal areas. Although the landscape was utterly barren for nearly 200km to the east,

Highlights

- Seeking out endangered vicuñas, flashy flamingos and lonesome desert cemeteries at Parque Nacional Lauca
- Prowling the desolate ruins of Humberstone, a mining ghost town
- Gaping 850m deep into the world's largest open-pit copper mine, at Chuquicamata
- Sauntering around the desert oasis of San Pedro de Atacama
- Watching the sun set over multicolored sand at Valle de la Luna
- Boiling eggs for breakfast in the El Tatio Geysers

Chile 11 & PN Lauca
page 187

Arica
page 180

Iquique
page 197

Around Calama &
San Pedro de Atacama
page 213

Calama
page 209

San Pedro
de Atacama
page 215

Antofagasta
page 223

OTHER MAPS
Norte Grande page 177

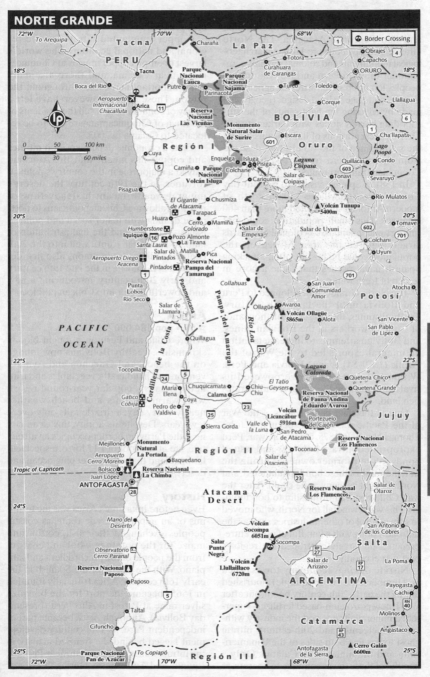

irrigated agriculture sustained relatively dense sedentary populations in oases like Calama and San Pedro de Atacama. The Norte Grande's conspicuous pre-Hispanic archaeological monuments and colonial remains complement those in Peru and Bolivia. Indian peoples left impressive fortresses, agricultural terraces and huge stylized designs (geoglyphs) made by covering the light sands of the surrounding barren slopes with darker stones. Their representations of llama trains depict the significance of the valleys that descend from the cordillera to the coast as pre-Columbian transport routes.

In 1581, a Spanish visitor to present-day Cobija, a coastal village 130km north of modern Antofagasta, counted more than 400 Changos. This small population could not support encomiendas, so colonial Spaniards largely ignored the area. Moreover, the population could be hostile, often attacking Spanish naval parties that came ashore in search of fresh water.

The Norte Grande area belonged to Peru and Bolivia until the late 19th century. Treaty disputes, the presence of thousands of Chilean workers in the Bolivian mines, and Bolivian attempts to increase taxation on mineral exports led to the War of the Pacific (1879–84) against Bolivia and Peru. Within five years, Chile overpowered its rivals and annexed the copper- and nitrate-rich land.

One of the chief beneficiaries of the War of the Pacific was British speculator John Thomas North. In 1875, before the war, Peru expropriated nitrate holdings and issued bonds to their former owners. During the war, the value of these bonds plummeted, and North bought as many as he could. After the war, Chile restored ownership to bondholders. This was a windfall for North, who moved to gain control of other industries, such as the railroad. Along with a handful of other entrepreneurs, he largely controlled the region's post-war economy.

Nitrate *oficinas* (company towns) such as Humberstone (near Iquique) flourished during the early-20th-century boom, but after WWI, new petroleum-based fertilizers superseded mineral nitrates, and the industry withered. Nineteenth- and 20th-century nitrate ghost towns line both sides of the Panamericana and the highway to Calama. Only a handful of these towns continue to operate, as newer methods make processing lower-grade ores profitable.

Copper supplanted nitrates in the regional and national economy. The world's largest open-pit copper mine is at Chuquicamata, near Calama, and there are many other important new mines throughout the region. These mines, however, have left a legacy of contamination – all the residents of the town of Chuquicamata are due to be relocated to Calama in 2003.

Chile's economic dependence on nitrates and copper has meant that the Atacama played a major role in the country's political fortunes. In the 19th century, the desert's mineral wealth meant a steady flow of revenue, allowing Chilean politicians to postpone dealing with major social and political issues – taxation and the maldistribution of land, in particular – until well into the 20th century. Militant trade unions also first developed in the north, in the late 19th century and early 20th century, introducing a new and powerful factor into Chilean politics.

ARICA
☎ 58 • pop 184,000
Where Chile and Peru once fought bloody skirmishes, wealthy Bolivians now lounge on the beach, and Quechua and Aymara vendors sell handicrafts, vegetables and trinkets. Arica is a popular year-round resort, with warm currents and beach weather nearly every day; a drizzle falls only every few years. Despite its aridity, this clean city near the Peruvian border occupies an attractive site at the foot of El Morro, a spectacular headland that offers sweeping ocean and desert views.

History
Even before Inka times, Arica was the terminus of an important trade route, as coastal peoples exchanged their fish, cotton and maize for the potatoes, wool and charqui from the people of the precordillera and altiplano. With the arrival of the Spanish in the early 16th century, Arica (officially founded in 1565) became the port for the bonanza silver mine at Potosí in Alto Peru (present-day Bolivia). Although Arica became part of independent Peru, its 19th-century development lagged behind the frenzied activity in the nitrate mines farther south, near Pisagua, Iquique and Antofagasta. During the War of

the Pacific, Arica became de facto Chilean territory, an arrangement formalized in 1929.

The War of the Pacific left Bolivia completely landlocked. Chile has periodically proposed territorial compensation to provide Bolivia sea access; however, offers of a narrow strip between the Lluta valley and the Peruvian border for a Bolivian corridor to the sea have proved unacceptable to Peru.

In the 1960s, Chile made a conscious effort to industrialize the region around the city by offering tax incentives to automobile and electronics industries to set up shop, powered by diverting the eastward-flowing Río Lauca to a hydroelectric facility in the precordillera. Industrialization failed, but by the 1970s, Arica had become a city of 120,000 (a sixfold increase in less than two decades) because of international trade and the active promotion of the area as a customs-free zone.

Bolivia's exports have traditionally passed through Arica, but Peru's grant of free port rights to Bolivia at Ilo have affected Arica's economy. The Chilean government proposed a number of tax- and duty-free incentives to encourage investment in the provinces of Arica and Parinacota (around PN Lauca), but this has met opposition from authorities in Iquique, whose *zona franca* (duty-free area) has also faltered in recent years. Unemployment in Arica has exceeded 10% in recent years.

Orientation

Arica lies at the northeastern base of El Morro, which rises dramatically out of the Pacific. Between El Morro and the Río San José (which rarely has any surface flow), the city center is a slightly irregular grid. The main shopping street, 21 de Mayo, has a pleasant pedestrian mall running between Prat and Patricio Lynch.

At the foot of El Morro are the manicured gardens of Plaza Vicuña Mackenna, from which Av Comandante San Martín (do not confuse with Calle San Martín, east of downtown) snakes west and south towards the city's most popular beaches. In the other direction, Av Máximo Lira swerves sharply at sprawling Parque Brasil to become Av General Velásquez, leading to the Panamericana Norte and the Peruvian border, 20km to the north. To get to the Panamericana Sur, toward Iquique, take either 18 de Septiembre or 21 de Mayo eastbound.

Information

Tourist Offices If arriving from Peru or Bolivia, a good place to orient yourself is the local office of **Sernatur** (☎ 252-054, fax 254-506; San Marcos 101; open 8:30am-7pm Mon-Sat & 10am-2pm Sun Dec-Feb; 8:30am-5:20pm Mon-Fri Mar-Nov). It has friendly, helpful staff who distribute a useful city map plus a few brochures on Tarapacá and other Chilean regions.

The **Automóvil Club de Chile** (☎ 252-678; Chacabuco 460; open 9am-1pm & 3pm-7pm Mon-Fri, 9am-1pm Sat) sells highway maps.

Conaf (☎ 250-207, 250-570; Vicuña Mackenna 820; open 8:30am-5:15pm Mon-Fri) has spotty information on Región I (Tarapacá) national parks. To get there, take bus No 12 from downtown (US$0.40).

Visas To replace a lost tourist card or renew a visa, go to the **Departamento de Extranjería** (☎ 250-377; Angamos 990; open 8:30am-12:30pm & 3:30pm-6pm Mon-Fri). However, given high Chilean visa-renewal charges, it would be cheaper to make a day trip to Tacna (Peru) or to go to La Paz (Bolivia) for a couple days.

Arica has diplomatic missions for several countries, including the **Bolivian consulate** (☎ 231-030; Patricio Lynch 292; open 9am-2pm Mon-Fri) and the **Peruvian consulate** (☎ 231-020; San Martín 234; open 8:30am-1pm Mon-Fri).

Money Arica enjoys the best rates and least bureaucracy for changing money north of Santiago, and there are several 24-hour ATMs along the pedestrian mall (21 de Mayo).

Casas de cambio on 21 de Mayo change US cash, Peruvian, Bolivian and Argentine currency, and euros. **Cambio Yanulaque** (21 de Mayo 175) has decent rates. You could also try **Turismo Sol y Mar** (☎ 224-678; Colón 610) or, if you're game, the street changers at the corner of 21 de Mayo and Colón.

Post & Communications The post office (Prat 305; open 8:30am-1:30pm & 3pm-6:30pm Mon-Fri, 9am-12:30pm Sat) is on a walkway between Pedro Montt and Prat. There are numerous public payphones along 21 de Mayo, or you can go to **Entel** (21 de Mayo 372; open 9am-1:30pm & 3pm-7:30pm Mon-Fri) or **Telefónica (CTC)** (Colón

ARICA

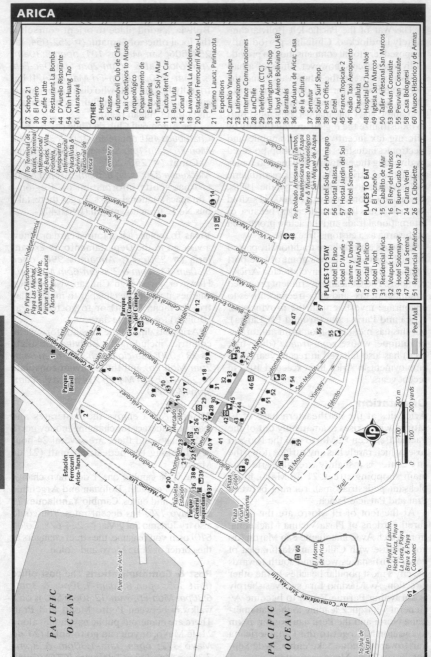

OTHER

27	Schop 21
30	El Arriero
40	Caffe Latte
44	Restaurant La Bomba
44	D'Aurelio Ristorante
54	Chin Huang Tao
61	Maracuyá
3	Hertz
5	Klasse
6	Automóvil Club de Chile
7	Taxi Colectivos to Museo Arqueológico
8	Departamento de Extranjería
10	Turismo Sol y Mar
11	Cactus Rent A Car
13	Bus Lluta
14	Conaf
18	Lavandería La Moderna
20	Estación Ferrocarril Arica-La Paz
21	Turismo Lauca; Parinacota Expeditions
22	Cambio Yanulaque
23	Latinorizons
25	Interface Comunicaciones
28	LanChile
29	Telefónica (CTC)
33	Huntington Surf Shop
34	Lloyd Aéreo Boliviano (LAB)
35	Barrabás
36	Ex-Aduana de Arica; Casa de la Cultura
37	Sernatur
38	Solari Surf Shop
39	Post Office
42	Entel
45	France Tropicale 2
46	Radio Taxi Aeropuerto Chacalluta
48	Hospital Dr Juan Noé
49	Iglesia San Marcos
50	Taller Artesanal San Marcos
53	Bolívian Consulate
55	Peruvian Consulate
58	Casa Bolognesi
60	Museo Histórico y de Armas

PLACES TO STAY

1	Hotel El Paso
4	Hotel D'Marie - Jeanne y David
9	Hotel Mar Azul
12	Hostal Pacífico
19	Hotel Lynch
31	Residencial Arica
32	Volapük Hotel
43	Hotel Sotomayor
47	Hostal La Serena
51	Residencial América
52	Hotel Solar de Almagro
56	Hostal Raissa
57	Hostal Jardín del Sol
59	Hotel Savona

PLACES TO EAT

2	El Tacneño
15	Caballito de Mar
16	El Rey del Marisco
17	Buen Gusto No 2
24	Canta Verdi
26	La Ciboulette

Ped Mall

476). Throughout the city, there are also many **Centros de Llamados**, which tend to be cheaper than the major companies, but line quality may not be as good.

Several Internet cafés can be found along and around 21 de Mayo, with rates starting at less than US$1 per hour. **Interface Comunicaciones** *(open 10am-11pm Mon-Sat, 3pm-10pm Sun; US$0.80/hr, minimum US$0.45),* at Thompson and Bolognesi, is one of the quieter, smaller ones.

Laundry Lavandería La Moderna *(☎ 232-006; 18 de Septiembre 457; open 9:30am-1:30pm & 4:30pm-9pm Mon-Fri, 9:30am-2pm Sat)* has good drop-off service, though it's not cheap (US$3 per kilogram, or about US$6 for a small load).

Medical Services Hospital Dr Juan Noé *(☎ 229-200; 18 de Septiembre 1000)* is a short distance east of downtown.

Things to See & Do
Overlooking the city, with panoramic views of the port and the Pacific Ocean, the 110m headland known as **El Morro de Arica** is also a historical monument whose open-air **Museo Histórico y de Armas** *(☎ 255-416; adult/child US$0.80/0.45; open 8:30am-8pm daily)* commemorates a crucial battle between Chilean and Peruvian forces on June 7, 1880, about a year into the War of the Pacific. It's accessible by car or taxi (US$5 round trip), or by a footpath from the south end of Calle Colón. If you look up from the coastline south of El Morro at night, you'll see the lighted head and outstretched arms of a huge statue of Jesus peeking over the cliff's edge.

At the base of El Morro, one of downtown's most imposing buildings is the blue-and-white **Casa Bolognesi** *(cnr Colón & Yungay),* which was the command center for Peruvian forces in the War of the Pacific and later served as the Peruvian consulate for a time. It's not open to the public.

Famous for his Parisian tower, Alexandre Gustave Eiffel designed many prefabricated landmarks in Latin America, including the **Ex-Aduana de Arica** *(☎ 206-366; open 8:30am-8pm Mon-Fri, 9am-9pm Sat & Sun; admission free),* the former customhouse. Though it once fronted on the harbor, a century of landfill has left it about 200m inland, facing Parque General Baquedano.

Prefabricated in Paris, it was assembled on site in 1874, with walls made of blocks and bricks stacked between metallic supports. Restored as the city's **Casa de la Cultura**, it displays historical photographs and occasional art exhibitions on the 2nd floor, reached by a 32-step, wrought iron spiral staircase.

Arica's other Eiffel monument is the **Iglesia San Marcos** *(open 9am-2pm & 6pm-8pm daily),* opposite Plaza Colón. This church was prefabricated in Eiffel's Paris shop between 1871 and 1875 at the order of the Peruvian president; it was assembled on site, and opened in July 1876. Originally intended for the bathing resort of Ancón, north of Lima, the Gothic-style building (note the pointed arches) replaced a church destroyed by an earthquake in 1868. The entire structure is made of cast iron (including not only the pillars and beams but also the plates between them) laminated and painted to look less metallic; only the door is made of wood.

The 1924 German locomotive that once pulled trains on the Arica-La Paz line now stands in the **Plazoleta Estación** *(cnr 21 de Mayo & Pedro Montt),* part of Parque General Baquedano. On the north side of the Plazoleta, the **Estación Ferrocarril Arica-La Paz**, the train station, dates from 1913. Inside is the periodically open **Museo Ferroviario**, a small, free museum with railroad-related antiques and documents.

Beaches
Arica is one of Chile's best beach resorts, since the Pacific is warm enough for comfortable bathing, but all the beaches have strong ocean currents and may be dangerous, some more so than others.

The most frequented beaches are south of town, along Av Comandante San Martín, where there are a number of sheltered coves and seaside restaurants. The closest is **Playa El Laucho**, followed by **Playa La Lisera**, 2.5km south of downtown; both have calm surf and are suitable for swimming. Nearby, rougher **Playa Brava** is suitable for sunbathing only. About 10km south of town, **Playa Corazones** is the most southerly accessible beach. Bus No 8, which leaves from the northeast corner of General Velásquez and Chacabuco, serves this area.

Beaches along the Panamericana Norte, toward the Peruvian border, are cleaner than those to the south. **Playa Chinchorro**,

Eiffel Beyond the Tower

Few are aware that French engineer Alexandre Gustave Eiffel, so renowned for his tower in Paris, also played a significant role in the New World. New York's Statue of Liberty is his most prominent transatlantic landmark (he designed the steel framework inside it), but his designs also dot the Latin American landscape from Mexico to Chile. Arica's Iglesia San Marcos and restored Aduana (customhouse) are but two of many examples.

In 1868, in partnership with another engineer, Théophile Seyrig, Eiffel had formed G Eiffel et Compagnie, which later became the Compagnie des Etablissements Eiffel. While the bulk of its metal construction work took place in France and in French colonies, an aggressive Buenos Aires agent landed many contracts for South American public buildings. In addition to the Arica landmarks, Eiffel's notable creations include the gasworks of La Paz, Bolivia, and the railroad bridges of Oroya, Peru, but his work appears as far north as the Iglesia Santa Bárbara, in Santa Rosalía, in the Mexican state of Baja California Sur. Most of these were designed and built in Eiffel's workshops in the Parisian suburb of Levallois-Perret, then shipped abroad for assembly.

What might have been his greatest Latin American monument effectively ended his career. In the late 19th century, Eiffel had argued strongly in favor of a transoceanic canal across Nicaragua, but a few years later he obtained a contract to build the locks for Ferdinand de Lesseps' corruption-plagued French canal across Panama. Eiffel was indicted for the botched financial dealings but was eventually exonerated. He spent the remainder of his career performing studies on aerodynamics and wind resistance and designing wind tunnels and airplane wings.

— Wayne Bernhardson

2km north of downtown, is a very wide and popular beach, suitable for swimming and diving, although the discharge of silt from Río San José turns the water murky in February. **Playa Las Machas**, a few kilometers north, is too rough for swimming but ideal for surfing and fishing. Take bus No 12 or 18 from General Velásquez and Chacabuco.

Arica has several surf shops, including **Huntington Surf Shop** (21 de Mayo 493) and **Solari Surf Shop** (21 de Mayo 160). For fishing permits, contact the **Servicio Nacional de Pesca** (Sernap; ☎ 252-308; Shopping Center del Pacífico, Local 330; open 8am-1pm & 3pm-7pm Mon-Fri), next to the bus stations.

Poblado Artesanal

On the outskirts of Arica near the Panamericana Sur is this mock altiplano village (☎ 226-683; Hualles 2825; open 9:30am-1:30pm & 4pm-7:30pm Tues-Sun). Complete with church and bell tower, it's a good place to shop for ceramics, weavings, musical instruments, carvings and similar crafts, and has an excellent restaurant, El Tambo (see Places to Eat).

A peña folclórica (folk music and cultural club) meets here irregularly, usually on Saturday nights.

Taxi colectivos Nos 8, 13 and U pass near the entrance, as do buses Nos 2, 3, 7, 8 and 9.

Museo Arqueológico San Miguel de Azapa

In the Azapa Valley, the continually improving Museo Arqueológico (☎ 205-551; adult/child US$1.50/0.75; open 9am-8pm daily Jan & Feb, 10am-6pm daily Mar-Dec) displays a superb assemblage of exhibits on regional culture sequences from the 7th century BC to the Spanish invasion, in a building expressly designed for the purpose. It is also increasingly interactive, with computers on site, and the museum sells books, journals and artisanal goods. Well-written booklets in several languages are available.

The staff can point out nearby archaeological sites – ask about early geoglyphs at **Atoca**, Tiwanaku-era (AD 700–1000) fortifications at **Pukará San Lorenzo** and the Inkaic **Cerro Sagrado** (AD 1000–1400). Some Arica tour companies include the museum and other valley sites on their itineraries.

The museum is 12km east of Arica. From Parque General Carlos Ibañez del Campo in Arica, at the corner of Chacabuco and Patricio Lynch, taxi colectivos charge about US$1.25 to the front gate.

Organized Tours

Numerous travel agencies arrange trips around the city and to the Azapa Valley, the precordillera, Parque Nacional Lauca (see that section, later, for agencies) and other altiplano destinations; some run trips themselves, while others contract out. When booking a tour indirectly, confirm the operator's name.

Turismo Lauca (☎/fax 252-322; Arturo Prat 430, Local 10) gives city tours, as well as tours to other local destinations, including Parque Nacional Lauca (see that section, later).

Special Events

Arica's unpretentious Carnaval Ginga draws around 15,000 spectators during a three-day weekend in mid-February. During the festival, the Municipalidad blocks off Av Comandante San Martín near El Morro for a parade that features regional *comparsas* (groups of musicians and dancers) performing traditional dances. The music mostly consists of brass bands. It's worth a look for visitors who happen to be in town.

The biggest local event is early June's Semana Ariqueña (Arica Week), about the same time as the Concurso Nacional de Cueca, a folkloric dance festival in the Azapa Valley.

Places to Stay

Arica has abundant accommodations at reasonable prices; though many budget places are cramped and malodorous, and some lack hot water. Others are excellent. The places listed below were clean enough for the price during research.

Budget Arica usually has an inexpensive student **hostel** in January and February; ask at Sernatur for current information.

Playa Corazones, 8km south of Arica at the end of Av Comandante San Martín, has free camping, but sites are dirty and crowded, and there's no water.

Playa Las Machas, 5km north of Arica, allows camping free of charge, and the beach here is better than Playa Corazones.

El Refugio (☎ 227-545; sites US$14), in the Azapa Valley at Km 1.5, has campsites for up to five people.

Arica has numerous *residenciales*. The cheapest charge as little as US$4 per person but generally do not include breakfast.

Hostal Pacífico (☎ 251-616; General Lagos 672; singles/doubles with shared bath US$4/8, with private bath US$6/12), in a commercial neighborhood, is quiet. Rates do not include kitchen privileges.

Hostal La Serena (☎ 258-439; Sotomayor 757; singles/doubles US$5/10) is very friendly and has laundry, kitchen privileges and homemade bread.

Residencial Arica (☎ 255-399; 18 de Septiembre 466; singles/doubles US$6/12), near the bustling Mercado Colón, is clean and central and has huge shared bathrooms.

Hostal Jardín del Sol (☎ 232-795; Sotomayor 848; singles/doubles with private bath US$11/17) offers a peaceful, garden setting. Single rooms are small, but common areas are bright and airy. Rooms upstairs are better quality. Breakfast is included.

Residencial América (☎ 254-148; Sotomayor 430; singles/doubles US$12/18) is friendly and well located. Rooms are clean and have cable TV and private bath, but soft beds.

Hotel MarAzul (☎ 256-272; Colón 665; singles/doubles US$12/24) is one of the best deals in town, with clean rooms, private bath, decent breakfast, pet birds and a pool. They're often full.

Hostal Raissa (☎ 251-700; San Martín 281; per person US$12), on the edge of a quieter residential area, offers kitchen privileges, a community fridge and lots of caged, chirping birds. Mango and papaya trees decorate the pleasant courtyard. All rooms have private baths and cable TV, and rates include breakfast.

Hotel Lynch (☎/fax 231-581; Patricio Lynch 589; singles/doubles start at US$13/20) has simple but clean rooms with private bath built around a central courtyard.

Hotel D'Marie – Jeanne y David (☎/fax 258-231; Av General Velásquez 792; singles/doubles US$16/29), run by a superfriendly French/Chilean couple, is located on a busy roundabout, but the heavy concrete structure with thick walls helps cushion the traffic noise. The simple rooms include private bath, fans and TV. The rates include breakfast.

Mid-Range The friendly staff at **Hotel Solar de Almagro** (☎ 224-444; Sotomayor 490; singles/doubles US$27/32) offers large, bright and clean rooms with private bath and cable TV.

Hotel Sotomayor (☎ 232-970; e reservas@ hotelsotomayor.cl; Sotomayor 367; singles/ doubles/triples with breakfast US$30/37/42) is well located and friendly. All rooms have private bath, cable TV and air conditioning.

Hotel Savona (☎ 231-000; Yungay 380; singles/doubles US$35/49), in a relatively quiet residential area at the foot of El Morro, is built around a courtyard with attractive bougainvillea blooms. Rooms are modern but sparsely furnished. Rates include breakfast.

Casona Azul (☎/fax 216-491; e casonazul @hotmail.com; Libertador Sucre 65; doubles US$50), in Villa Frontera, between Arica and the airport and a half-mile from the Panamericana, is a new hotel in the restored administration house for the old railroad. This comfortable place has large rooms with private bath, high ceilings with fans, lovely wood furniture, a large porch overlooking a garden, and a large swimming pool. Rates include breakfast.

Volapuk Hotel (☎ 252-575, fax 251-168; 21 de Mayo 425; singles/doubles US$45/60), part of the Best Western chain, is conveniently located on the pedestrian mall. Rooms have air conditioning, cable TV, fridges, Internet connections and huge bathrooms. Standard rooms are small and unimpressive; some lack windows. Superior rooms (US$70) are larger and have a glassed-in balcony overlooking 21 de Mayo. Rates include parking.

Top End In the Azapa Valley, **Azapa Inn** (☎ 244-517, fax 225-191; Guillermo Sánchez 660; standard/superior/suites US$65/95/120) is only a short taxi ride from downtown (US$1.50). This inn is set on restful grounds with striking gardens. Amenities include a pool, basketball court, tennis court, bike rental and a restaurant. Standard rooms are unexciting modern hotel rooms; all rooms have air conditioning. Rates include buffet breakfast.

Hotel El Paso (☎ 230-808, fax 231-965; w www.hotelelpaso.cl; General Velásquez 1109; singles US$75-105, doubles US$85-130) is within walking distance of the waterfront. All rooms have air conditioning and refrigerators. The newer section is nicer and has suites overlooking the swimming pool; rooms are bright and airy but somewhat generic.

Hotel Arica (☎ 254-540, fax 231-133; Av Comandante San Martín 599; singles US$100-325, doubles US$115-300), next to Playa El Laucho at the southern end of town, has large, bright rooms, each with a patio that overlooks the sea.

Places to Eat

There are numerous cafés and restaurants along 21 de Mayo, 18 de Septiembre, Maipú, Bolognesi and Colón.

Buen Gusto No 2 (Baquedano 559; sandwiches US$2), a tiny snack bar near the market, serves hot-dog-and-coffee specials (US$0.50), sandwiches and fruit juices (US$1.25).

Schop 21 (☎ 232-126; 21 de Mayo 301; sandwiches US$2, main dishes US$3-5), at Colón, offers sandwiches, pizza, snacks, coffee and lager beer in a patio setting. Many foreign travelers congregate here.

Caffe Latte (21 de Mayo 248; sandwiches US$3-4, pizza US$4; open 9am-1am daily) is popular, with tables in the midst of the pedestrian mall; it serves huge sandwiches, pizza, salads, shakes, desserts and espresso drinks.

La Ciboulette (☎ 250-007; Thompson 238; set lunch US$3-4; open lunch only) stands out with economic meals and excellent food.

Restaurant La Bomba (☎ 255-626; Colón 357; meals US$3-6; open noon-midnight), inside the fire station, is the place to go for large, inexpensive lunches. If you can't find it, listen for its deafening siren at noon.

Canta Verdi (☎ 258-242; Bolognesi 453; sandwiches or small pizza US$4-6), a cozy restaurant which looks out onto the artisans' market, has a wide selection of sandwiches, pizzas, snacks (fluffy empanadas, quesadillas, chorizo), good juices and a full bar.

El Tacneño (Prat & Chacabuco; dishes US$3-5; open 10am-midnight daily) is out of the way but serves good Peruvian dishes and has friendly staff.

Caballito de Mar (Colón & Maipú; fish dishes US$3-5; open breakfast & lunch), within the bustling Mercado Colón, has well-prepared corvina, cojinova and other fish dinners; a set meal of fried fish is available for US$2.

El Rey del Marisco (☎ 229-232; Colón & Maipú; fish dishes US$5-7; open noon-1am daily), upstairs in Mercado Colón, is a more expensive but worthwhile alternative. From its 2nd floor, you can spy on the lively street scene below. Chicken and steak are also available.

D'Aurelio Ristorante (☎ 321-471; Baquedano 369; main dishes US$4-9) is a very good Italian restaurant with a bright and cheerful yet cozy atmosphere. It has a good selection of soups and salads and exceptionally tasty appetizers such as olives and pickled onions, as well as the classic pebre.

Chin Huang Tao (Patricio Lynch 224; dishes US$6) is a romantic chifa, but there's nothing here for vegetarians.

El Arriero (☎ 232-636; 21 de Mayo 385; main dishes plus 1 side US$5-9; open 10am-4pm & 7pm-11pm daily) is a fine parrilla with pleasant atmosphere and friendly service.

Maracuyá (☎ 227-600; Av Comandante San Martín 0321; dishes US$10-15; open 12:30pm-4pm & 8pm-1am daily), south of downtown next to Playa El Laucho, is an excellent seafood restaurant complete with bow-tie service and cloth napkins. Set above the seaside rocks, the patio provides a great view of an astounding sunset. The smoked salmon salad (US$5) with heart of palm and avocados is very tasty.

El Tambo (☎ 241-757; Hualles 2825; dishes US$4-8), inside the Poblado Artesanal, serves traditional food in agreeable surroundings.

Entertainment
Many places on 21 de Mayo are good for a cheap beer outside, next to the pedestrian mall.

France Tropicale 2 (☎ 257-217; 21 de Mayo 384, 2nd floor; pizza US$3-5, beer US$1.50) is a pleasant pub with plenty of drinks and great pizzas; it's very popular with travelers and quiet enough for conversation.

Barrabás (18 de Septiembre 520), a louder bar and disco, draws a young crowd and has strong drinks.

In the summer, bars and discos on the beach stay lively, including **Soho Discotheque** (Playa Chinchorro; cover US$5; open Fri & Sat nights) and the attached **Pub Drake**.

Shopping
A narrow passageway off Plaza Colón between Sotomayor and 21 de Mayo, Pasaje Bolognesi has a lively **artisans' market**. There are also many permanent shops along the walkway and along 21 de Mayo.

The **Taller Artesanal San Marcos** (☎ 203-405; Sotomayor & Baquedano; open 9am-

1pm & 3:30pm-6:30pm Mon-Fri), operated by the Gendarmería de Chile, sells prisoners' crafts, mostly leather purses and knitted cotton clothing. Where else can you get a handmade cotton bikini made by Chilean women prisoners for less than US$5?

See also Poblado Artesanal, earlier in the chapter.

Getting There & Away
From Arica, travelers can head north across the Peruvian border to Tacna and Lima, south toward Santiago or east to Bolivia.

Air About 18km north of Arica is **Aeropuerto Internacional Chacalluta** (☎ 211-116). Santiago-bound passengers should sit on the left side of the plane for awesome views of the Andes and the interminable brownness of the Atacama Desert.

LanChile (☎ 252-600; 21 de Mayo 345) has seven daily flights to Santiago (US$225) via Iquique (US$25). LanChile has one flight daily to La Paz, Bolivia (US$120 one-way). **Lloyd Aéreo Boliviano** (☎ 251-919; Patricio Lynch 298) flies to Bolivia: La Paz (US$100), Santa Cruz (US$155) and Cochabamba (US$130).

Bus Arica has two main bus terminals: the **Terminal Rodoviario de Arica** (Terminal de Buses; ☎ 241-390; Diego Portales 948) houses most companies traveling south to other destinations in Chile. Next door, the **Terminal Internacional de Buses** (☎ 248-709; Diego Portales 1002) handles international and some regional destinations. The area is notorious for petty thievery, so keep an eye on your luggage at all times. To reach the terminals, take colectivo No 1, 4 or 11 from Maipú.

More than a dozen companies have offices in the Terminal Rodoviario and ply destinations toward the south, from Iquique to Santiago. Some major ones include the following:

Buses Pullman Santa Rosa	☎ 241-029
Pullman Carmelita	☎ 241-591
Ramos Cholele	☎ 221-029
Pullman Bus	☎ 223-837
Pullman San Andrés	☎ 242-933
Flota Barrios	☎ 223 587
Tur Bus	☎ 222-217
Fénix Pullman	☎ 222-457

A schedule board inside the terminal makes it easy to find the next bus headed to where you want to go (but it's not always accurate). Buses on Sunday run less often and can fill up.

Some of the standard destinations and fares are shown in the following table. More comfortable *cama* or *semi-cama* buses cost a bit more.

destination	duration in hours	cost
Antofagasta	12	US$13
Calama	11	US$12
Copiapó	18	US$27
Iquique	4	US$6
La Serena	19	US$32
Santiago	26	US$38

Faster taxi colectivos charge US$13 to Iquique.

Bus Lluta (*Chacabuco & Vicuña Mackenna*) goes to Poconchile and Lluta five times daily (US$1; one hour).

Buses La Paloma (☎ *222-710; Germán Riesco 2071*) travels to the Belén precordillera villages of Socoroma on Tuesday and Saturday (US$3), Belén on Tuesday and Friday (US$3) and to Putre daily (US$3); all depart Arica at 6:30am. To reach the terminal, take bus No 7 to Germán Riesco, about 12 blocks east of the hospital, or arrange for their special taxibus (US$0.50) to come to your hotel. La Paloma also goes to the precordillera villages of Tignamar and Codpa Monday and Friday at 8am (US$3; three hours), returning at 5pm. It's possible to make a loop on public transportation, but it's not particularly convenient. You would have to walk or hitchhike (with very few vehicles on the dry and dusty road) the 13km between Belén and Tignamar. Lonely Planet does not recommend hitchhiking.

For Parinacota (US$7) and Putre (US$6), look for **Buses Martínez, Agencia de Buses Humire** (☎ *260-164*) and **Trans Cali Internacional** (☎ *261-068*), all in the international terminal. Most trips depart on Tuesdays and Fridays.

For Tacna, Peru, **Adsubliata** buses leaves the international terminal every half hour (US$2); colectivos charge US$3. Give the colectivo driver your passport – he'll deal with the border crossing. No produce is allowed across the border. **Tas-Choapa** (☎ *222-817; international bus terminal*) operates services

to Lima, Peru (US$45; 20 hours), but it's cheaper to take local transportation to Tacna and then buy a separate ticket to Lima or elsewhere in Peru.

To get to La Paz, Bolivia (US$15-24, nine hours), **Buses Humire, Chile Bus, Buses Litoral, Pullman Zuleta** and **Buses Géminis** (the most comfortable), all in the international bus terminal, have morning departures (8am to 10am). Buses on this route will drop passengers in Parque Nacional Lauca, but expect to pay full fare to La Paz.

Getting Around

To/From the Airport The **Aeropuerto Internacional Chacalluta** (☎ *211-116*) is 18km north of Arica, near the Peruvian border. Several taxi stands charge the same: US$4 for a shared taxi or US$9 for an individual taxi to Arica, or US$26 to Tacna, Peru (rates to Peru are much lower using shared taxis from the bus station). In town, call **Radio Taxi Aeropuerto Chacalluta** (☎ *254-812; Patricio Lynch 371*).

Bus Local buses and taxi colectivos connect downtown with the main bus terminal. Taxi colectivos, only slightly more expensive than buses, are faster and more frequent. Destinations are clearly marked on an illuminated sign atop the cab.

Car Rental cars are available from **Hertz** (☎ *231-487; Baquedano 999*), but they are cheaper at **Klasse** (☎ *254-498; Av General Velásquez 762, Local 25*) and **Cactus Rent a Car** (☎ *257-430;* e *cactusrent@latinmail .com; Baquedano 635, Local 36*). Rates start at US$33/day.

Bicycle You can rent mountain bikes at **Parinacota Expeditions** (☎/*fax 256-227; Arturo Prat 430, Local 5*) or **Cactus Rent a Car** (*see Car, above*) for US$4/12 per hour/day.

CHILE 11 HIGHWAY

About 10km north of Arica, the Panamericana intersects paved Chile 11, which leads east up the valley of the Río Lluta to Poconchile and on to Parque Nacional Lauca (see the Chile 11 & PN Lauca Area map). Although the national park is the premier attraction of the area, ancient ruins, colonial churches, and mountain villages are also worthy stops.

Lluta Geoglyphs

A short distance inland from the intersection of the Panamericana and Chile 11, a series of restored pre-Columbian geoglyphs cover an otherwise barren slope on the right. These figures, made by grouping dark stones over light-colored soil, include representations of llamas and recall the importance of pre-Columbian pack trains on the route to Tiahuanaco, a traffic which only recently disappeared with the construction of good motor roads.

Poconchile

Built in the 17th century, reconstructed in the 19th century and restored in the 20th century, Poconchile's **Iglesia de San Gerónimo** is one of the oldest churches in the country. Behind the church is a desolate **cemetery** set against the stark brown landscape. Free **camping** is possible along the Río Lluta.

On Chile 11 about 8km beyond Poconchile is **Km 38½**, an excellent restaurant offering traditional regional dishes made from alpaca, and vegetarian plates (US$2.50)

with local corn and goat cheese. The friendly owners are knowledgeable about local sites.

To get to Poconchile, 35km from Arica, take Bus Lluta (see Getting There & Away for Arica, earlier) to the end of the line at the *carabineros* (police) checkpoint.

Pukará de Copaquilla

As Chile 11 zigzags up the desolate mountainside, there are exceptional views of the upper Lluta valley. Along the route, the very appropriately named *cactus candelabro* ('candle-holder' cactus, or *Browningia candelaris*) grows just 5mm to 7mm a year and flowers once a year for only 24 hours. These cacti and other plants absorb moisture from the *camanchaca* (fog) that penetrates inland.

Near Copaquilla, overlooking a spectacular canyon, the partially restored 12th-century fortress Pukará de Copaquilla was built to protect Indian farmlands below – notice the abandoned terraces, evidence of a much larger pre-Columbian population. Tours from Arica to Parque Nacional Lauca normally make a brief stop here.

NORTE GRANDE

CHILE 11 & PN LAUCA

Along the highway just west of Copaquilla, the eccentric **Posada Pueblo Maiko** is a surviving remnant of 1994's eclipse mania and a good spot to stop for fresh bread and a drink (including *mate de coca*, from the fresh coca leaf). A windmill charges a bank of batteries, the stove is solar powered, and the German embassy has provided funding to create a center for renewable energy here. **Camping** is available at a reasonable cost, as is guide service to local *pukarás* (fortresses) and cave paintings. Any highway bus will drop you off and pick you up here.

Socoroma

On the colonial pack route between Arica and Potosí, Socoroma – 5km along a rough road from Chile 11 – is an Aymara farming village featuring cobbled streets, the 17th-century **Iglesia de San Francisco**, other colonial remains, and terraced hills of oregano.

Emilia Humire has a simple **hospedaje** (three beds) and also offers excellent home-cooked **traditional meals**. See the Getting There & Away entry for Arica for transportation details.

Belén Precordillera

At Zapahuira, a gravel road leaves the international highway and heads south through a series of villages in an area showcasing numerous archaeological sites, including pre-Columbian fortresses and agricultural terraces, as well as colonial relics comparable to those in many parts of Peru. The highlights are the *pukarás* (pre-Hispanic fortifications) of **Belén**, **Lupica** and **Saxamar**, and there are also colonial churches at Belén and **Tignamar Viejo**.

This route makes an excellent day trip from Arica for travelers with vehicles, but tourist services are rare: in Belén, María Martínez offers a simple **hospedaje** (two beds) for less than US$10 and also serves **meals**. **Hostería Codpa** (☎ *212-423; doubles US$26*) requires a 10-day advance notice. A new **residencial** (*beds US$9*) run by Alberto Roco is also available; reservations can be made through the *defensa civil* (☎ *058-221-100*) in Arica. Alberto arranges **horseback trips** (*US$15-20 per day*) with local guides to nearby archeological sites and cave paintings.

South of Tignamar, the road deteriorates through a narrow and dusty canyon, but improves beyond the turnoff to Timar and

Codpa, where it becomes a wide, smooth dirt road that rejoins the Panamericana 21km south of Arica. At the junction with the Panamericana, the state arts agency Fondart has sponsored a series of desert sculptures known as **Presencias Tutelares** (guardian spirits).

See Getting There & Away for Arica, earlier for information on traveling to and from these parts.

Putre

☎ 58 • pop 2200

Placed on the international travel map due to the total solar eclipse of 1994, Putre is an appealing Aymara village in the precordillera, 150km from Arica, 5km from Chile 11 and 3500m above sea level. Many visitors spend at least a night acclimatizing here before proceeding to Parque Nacional Lauca, on the altiplano. Originally a 16th-century *reducción* (settlement), established by the Spaniards to facilitate control of the native population, Putre retains many houses with late-colonial elements. In the surrounding hills, local farmers raise alfalfa for llamas, sheep and cattle on extensive stone-faced agricultural terraces of even greater antiquity.

Dating from 1670, the adobe **Iglesia de Putre**, on the north side of the Plaza de Armas, was restored two centuries later. To visit its interior, which contains valuable colonial artifacts, ask for the keys and leave a small donation.

Putre's February **Carnaval** is an informal, spontaneous affair in which visitors may be either willing or unwilling participants – fortunately, the locals fill their balloons with flour rather than water, and cover onlookers with *chaya* (multicolored paper dots) rather than fresh fruit. Two noncompetitive groups, the older *banda* and the younger *tarqueada*, provide the music. The event ends with the burning of the *momo*, a figure symbolizing the frivolity of Carnaval.

Information There is a **post office** (*Carrera & Prat; open 9am-1pm Mon-Fri, 10am-2pm Sat*). **Entel** (*open 9am-1pm & 4pm-8pm daily*) is on the south side of the Plaza de Armas.

Organized Tours The warmly recommended **Alto Andino Nature Tours** (☎ *messages 300-013, fax 222-735;* Ⓦ *www.birdingalto*

NORTE GRANDE

andino.com; Baquedano 299) is run by Alaskan biologist Barbara Knapton, who offers private birding and natural-history excursions. All tours are in English (unless Spanish is preferred). Destinations include Parque Nacional Lauca, Salar de Surire, Parque Nacional Volcán Isluga, spots throughout the Atacama Desert and marine-mammal colonies. Trips last from one to seven days. Costs are highly dependent on the type of tour and the guide specialization required, and Barbara herself leads all birding and specialized nature trips. Oxygen, binoculars, spotting scopes and (if necessary) sleeping bags are provided for all tours. Make reservations well in advance.

Alto Andino also has contact details for **Freddy Torrejón**, a great guide for hikes to cave paintings and other nearby sights, as well as for reliable guide **Valentina Alave**, a young Aymara woman who provides guide services in the area. These make good excursions while you're acclimatizing to the altitude.

Places to Stay & Eat The **Residencial La Paloma** *(Baquedano s/n; beds per person US$6)* has hot showers, clean, spacious rooms and good beds, but the thin walls mean it's noisy sometimes, and it does get cold at night.

Hostal Cali *(Baquedano s/n; per person with shared/private bath US$6/11)*, across from La Paloma, is spotless and friendly and has excellent rooms.

Refugio Putre *(O'Higgins s/n; per person US$11)*, opposite the army camp, offers comfy dorm-style lodging when space permits. There are six beds, hot showers and cooking facilities.

Casa Barbarita *(☎ messages 300-013, fax 222-735; w www.birdingaltoandino.com; Baquedano 299; house rental for 2/4 people US$45/65)*, the site of Alto Andino Nature Tours (see Organized Tours, earlier), is a rental house complete with kitchen, hot showers, and use of a naturalist library. The house is available only by advance reservations.

Hostería Las Vicuñas *(☎ 224-466; doubles with breakfast & dinner US$85)*, at the approach to town, was originally built for mining interests.

Kuchu-Marka *(Baquedano)* is a cozy restaurant that stays open late, serving up good food, drinks and atmosphere.

Restaurant La Paloma *(Baquedano s/n)* is bright and cheerful, with decent food and excellent corn soup.

Restaurant Rosamel *(Cochrane s/n; dinner US$3)* provides modest accommodations and serves lunch to Lauca tour groups. The slightly more expensive set meals are also a good value.

Getting There & Away Putre is 150km east of Arica via paved Chile 11, the international highway to Bolivia. **Buses La Paloma** *(☎ 222-710; Germán Riesco 2071, Arica)* serves Putre daily, departing Arica at 6:30am, returning in the early afternoon. Buses to Parinacota, in Parque Nacional Lauca (see below), pass the turnoff to Putre, which is 5km from the main highway.

PN LAUCA

Situated 160km northeast of Arica, near the Bolivian border, Parque Nacional Lauca comprises 138,000 hectares of altiplano (between 3000m and 6300m above sea level). Contiguous to the park, but more difficult to access, are Reserva Nacional Las Vicuñas and Monumento Natural Salar de Surire (see South of PN Lauca, later). Once part of the park, they now constitute technically separate units but are still managed by Conaf.

Among the park's spectacular features is Lago Chungará, one of the world's highest lakes, at the foot of the dormant twin Payachata volcanoes (Volcán Pomerape and Volcán Parinacota). Slightly to the south, Volcán Guallatire smokes ominously.

The park's altitude, well above 4000m in most parts, requires the visitor to adapt gradually. Do not exert yourself at first, and eat and drink moderately; if you suffer anyway, try a cup of tea made from the common Aymara herbal remedy *chachacoma*, readily gathered around the settlements, or *mate de coca*. Keep water at your side, as the throat desiccates rapidly in the arid climate, and wear sunblock – tropical rays can be truly brutal at this elevation.

Lauca is currently under siege from mining interests who, with support from some regional officials, have formed a coalition that threatens to amputate the park's western third for a speculative, unquestionably destructive, gold-seeking venture. An even greater threat to the altiplano is the potential draining of the aquifer for agricultural use in Arica. At the same time, courts have ruled that roughly 80% of the park belongs not to the state, but to Aymara residents, some of whose titles date from the days of Peruvian sovereignty. The next few years are likely to see continuing struggles over control of the land.

Geography & Climate

Beyond Copaquilla, paved Chile 11 climbs steadily but gradually through the precordillera to the park entrance at Las Cuevas, where the altiplano proper begins. Rainfall and vegetation increase with altitude and distance from the coast; it can snow during the summer rainy season, known as *invierno boliviano* (Bolivian winter), when heavy fog often covers the precordillera approaches to the park.

Flora & Fauna

Parque Nacional Lauca is a World Biosphere Reserve harboring vicuña, the mountain viscacha *(Lagidium viscacia,* a wild Andean relative of the domestic chinchilla) and more than 150 bird species (including condor and rhea), plus cultural and archaeological landmarks and Aymara herders of llamas and alpacas. Lago Chungará is home to abundant, unusual bird life, including the Chilean flamingo *(Phoenicopterus chilensis),* the *tagua gigante* or giant coot *(Fulica gigantea),* and the Andean gull *(Larus serranus).* Around Surire, vicuña, *ñandú* (rhea) and three species of flamingo are often seen.

Along the highway and at Las Cuevas (the entrance and information center), vicuña *(Vicugna vicugna),* a wild relative of the llama, are living advertisements for a major Chilean wildlife conservation success story. Their numbers have increased from barely a thousand in the early 1970s to nearly 25,000 today. Over the past decade of protection, they have also become exceptionally tame.

Pay special attention to the ground-hugging, bright green *llareta (Laretia compacta),* a densely growing shrub with a cushionlike appearance that belies the fact that it's nearly as hard as rock – the Aymara need a pick or mattock to break open dead llareta, which they collect for fuel.

The Aymara pasture their llamas and alpacas on verdant *bofedales* (swampy alluvial grasslands) and the lower slopes of the surrounding mountains, and sell handicrafts woven from the animals' wool in the village of Parinacota and at Lago Chungará.

Information

The park is administered from the refugio at Parinacota. Otherwise, rangers at the Las Cuevas entrance (see next) and at Lago Chungará are available for consultation.

Organized Tours

Many agencies offer one-day blitzes from sea-level Arica to 4515m Lago Chungará in Parque Nacional Lauca – a sure-fire method to get *soroche* (altitude sickness). These tours cost about US$20 to US$25 (including a late lunch in Putre) and leave around 7:30am, returning about 8:30pm. Verify whether the operator carries oxygen on the bus – this is not a minor issue, as many people become very sick at high altitudes. Avoid overeating, smoking and alcohol consumption.

Tours lasting 1½ days include a night in Putre, allowing more time to acclimatize to the altitude; they cost around US$55-60. A 2½-day tour to Lauca and the Monumento Natural Salar de Surire costs about US$120-130; a three-day circuit to Lauca, Surire, Parque Nacional Volcán Isluga and Iquique, returning to Arica late the third night, costs US$200.

English-speaking tour guides are rare, although with extra time and money you can eventually find one. Many operators only have limited departures, so a certain amount of flexibility and shoe leather are helpful, especially if you are traveling solo or in a small group. The Sernatur office occasionally has warnings on operators against whom they have received a lot of complaints (including Ecotour when this book was researched, although this list can always change).

The following agencies are all located in Arica.

Turismo Lauca *(☎/fax 252-322; Arturo Prat 430, Local 10)* is the most traditional operator, with the biggest buses. It's the most likely company to have daily departures for the one-day trip.

Latinorizons *(☎/fax 250-007;* |e| *latinor@ entelchile.net; Bolognesi 449)* is reliable and Belgian-run. If this office is closed, check around the corner at Thompson 236 (Hostal Chez Charlie).

Parinacota Expeditions *(☎/fax 256-227;* |e| *aqueveque_horiols@hotmail.com; Arturo*

Prat 430, Local 5) is a small operation (two owners/guides) that focuses on longer trips. In addition to the standard 1½-day to 3-day options, they offer volcano ascents and tours where you can descend by bike from 4500m to 1500m along llama trails.

Vicuña Tours (☎/fax 228916; **e** victours@ terra.cl) offers tours with multilingual guides knowledgeable in Aymara culture and archaeology, but these tours require advance arrangements.

Las Cuevas

At the park's western entrance, Las Cuevas has a permanent ranger station that is a good source of information and an excellent place to view and photograph the vicuña. Look for curious viscacha scrambling amongst the rocks and posing for tourists. Rustic **thermal baths** are nearby, where **camping** may be possible.

Just beyond Las Cuevas, Conaf has built a new overlook, **Mirador Pampa Chucuyo**, featuring a massive, out-of-place sculpture in orange, blue and yellow that partly resembles the Andean *zampoña* (panpipes).

Bofedal de Parinacota

On the north side of Chile 11, between the tiny settlements of Chucuyo and Parinacota, *guallatas* (Andean geese) and ducks drift on the Río Lauca and nest on the shore, while the viscacha peeks out from numerous rockeries that rise above the swampy sediments of the park's largest *bofedal*.

Most of the Aymaras' domestic livestock (eg, alpaca, llamas) also graze the *ciénegas* (swamps), which shelter some interesting cultural relics – there's a **colonial chapel** just below Restaurant Matilde at Chucuyo, and another about half an hour's walk from Parinacota. Some stores in Chucoyo sell locally made woolen items.

Parinacota

Five kilometers off the international highway and 46km from Putre, Parinacota is a picturesque but nearly depopulated pastoral village whose 17th-century **colonial church**, reconstructed in 1789, contains surrealistic murals, the work of artists from the Cuzco school. The murals recall Hieronymus Bosch's *Sinners in the Hands of an Angry God*, but note also the depiction of the soldiers bearing Christ to the cross as Spaniards. According to

local legend, the small table chained to the wall used to leave the church at night in search of spirits. To visit the church, ask caretaker Cipriano Morales for the key and leave a small donation. Vendors sell **woven goods** around the plaza.

Conaf has a refugio at Parinacota, built originally for a high-altitude genetic research project (see Places to Stay & Eat, later in this section). Ask rangers for information on surrounding sights, such as Laguna Cotacotani and Cerro Guane Guane (next).

Laguna Cotacotani

This lake feeds the Río Lauca, but unfortunate diversions by the privatized national electric company have caused fluctuations in lake levels that undermine its ecological integrity. Still, along its shores, at the foot of sprawling lava flows and cinder cones, you will see diverse bird life and scattered groves of *queñoa (Polylepis tarapacana)*, one of the world's highest-elevation trees, reaching about 5m in height. Though puma are rarely seen, tracks are not unusual, and foxes are fairly common. Follow the road along the south bank of the Río Lauca from Parinacota.

Cerro Guane Guane

Immediately north of Parinacota, Guane Guane is a 5096m peak with extraordinary panoramic views of the park and beyond. From the village, it's climbable along its eastern shoulder in about four hours, but the last 500m in particular are a difficult slog through porous volcanic sand – one step forward, two steps back. Ask advice from Conaf's rangers, and do not attempt to climb in threatening weather, since there is no shelter from lightning.

Lago Chungará

More than 4500m above sea level and 192km from Arica, Lago Chungará is a shallow body of water formed when a lava flow dammed the snowmelt stream from 6350m Volcán Parinacota, which dominates the lake to the north. You can reach the west end of the lake from Parinacota on foot in about two hours. But most of the wildlife is more distant, near the Conaf ranger station on Chile 11 and the Chilean customs post near the border, so you may want to drive to one of these spots and then hike.

NORTE GRANDE

Because of Arica's increasing consumption of hydroelectricity and the Azapa Valley's insatiable thirst, the electric company has built an intricate system of pumps and canals that constitute a continuing menace to Lago Chungará's ecological integrity, though they are unused at present. Since the lake is so shallow, any lowering of its level would dramatically reduce its overall surface area and impinge on those parts where wading birds such as the **flamingo and giant coot** feed and nest.

Woolens and other crafts are sold in the parking lot at the Conaf refugio, but much of the merchandise here comes from Bolivia; for locally made goods, try the stores in Parinacota or Chucuyo.

At the east end of Lago Chungará, the border post of Tambo Quemado is also the site of a colorful **international market** (feria) on alternate Fridays.

Places to Stay & Eat

While the Parque Nacional Lauca has no formal accommodations, there are several reasonable alternatives.

Refugio Las Cuevas, run by Conaf at the park entrance, may offer a bed in a pinch.

Restaurant Matilde, in Chucuyo, directly on the highway to Bolivia near the junction to Parinacota, usually has an extra bed at a very reasonable price. Matilde Morales prepares alpaca steaks and other simple meals, and there are two other inexpensive restaurants. Limited supplies, including food, are available, but it's cheaper and more convenient to bring them from Arica.

Refugio Parinacota (beds US$7; campsites US$10), 3km from Chucuyo, is spacious but sparsely furnished; bring your own sleeping bag. The availability of hot showers depends on the sporadic arrival of gas canisters from Arica. Two small tent campsites are available nearby.

Hostal Terán (☎ 058-228-761; e leonel_teran@yahoo.com; US$4 per person), opposite the church in Parinacota, offers simple rooms with kitchen privileges.

Camping Chungará, at the lake, has picnic tables and 1.2m-high stone walls for shelter from the wind. At 4500m above sea level, it gets frigid at night.

Refugio Chungará (beds US$7) is lakeside and has four beds. Bring your own food and water.

South of PN Lauca

RN Las Vicuñas Directly south of Lauca, Reserva Nacional Las Vicuñas is well off the beaten path to Parque Nacional Lauca. The reserve consists of 210,000 sparsely inhabited hectares surrounded by sky-hugging volcanoes, where the endangered vicuña has proliferated.

At the base of smoking Volcán Guallatire, 60km from Parinacota via a roundabout route, the village of Guallatire features a 17th-century **church**. Also in Guallatire, Conaf's **Refugio Guallatire** (beds US$9 per person) is not always staffed (ask in Arica, Las Cuevas or Parinacota). South of Guallatire, on the Surire road, are ruins of a colonial **silver mill**.

Farther south, new bridges cross the Río Viluvio, a tributary of the Lauca, but the road can still be impassable during summer rains, even with 4WD. Carabineros at Guallatire and Chilcaya (farther south) have 4WD vehicles and *may* be able to help vehicles in distress.

Monumento Natural Salar de Surire En route to Surire, 126km from Putre and 108km from Parinacota, vicuña and flocks of the sprinting ñandú (the ostrich-like rhea, *Pterocnemia pennata*) dot the countryside. Formed in 1983, when the Chilean government reduced the size of Parque Nacional Lauca, the monument itself comprises 11,300 hectares around a sprawling salt lake with breeding colonies of three species of flamingos, including the rare James flamingo (*parina chica* or *Phoenicoparrus jamesi*), which are present from December to April. In 1989, the outgoing military dictatorship gave 4560 hectares to the mining company Quiborax.

Again, there is no public transportation. Lonely Planet doesn't recommend hitching a ride, but it may be possible to hitchhike with trucks from the nearby borax mine or with Conaf, whose **Refugio Surire** has four beds for US$11; check with Conaf in Arica first. **Camping** is possible at Polloquere, where there are rustic **thermal baths**, but no toilet facilities.

Although most visitors return to Putre and Arica, it's possible to make a southerly circuit through Parque Nacional Volcán Isluga and back to Arica via Camiña or Huara. Do not attempt this without consulting either Conaf or the *carabineros*. The

Ascensor Artilleria, a Valparaíso funicular

Pilgrims celebrating in Lo Vásquez

Standing guard over Viña del Mar's Palacio Vergara

Sun setting over the coast near Valparaíso

Mighty cascades at PN Laguna del Laja

Soaking up the sun on the beach at Viña del Mar

route is particularly iffy during the summer rainy season.

Getting There & Away

Parque Nacional Lauca straddles Chile 11, the Arica-La Paz highway, which is paved all the way to La Paz; the trip from Arica takes about three hours. From Arica, there is regular passenger service with **Buses Martínez** (☎ 058-232-265; international terminal) or **Transportes Humire** (☎ 058-253-497; international terminal). Martínez leaves Tuesday and Friday at 10am; Humire departs at 10pm the same days. Fares to Parinacota are about US$7. Other bus companies with daily service to La Paz, Bolivia (see Getting There & Away in the Arica section) will drop you off in the park, but you might have to pay the full fare.

Several travel agencies in Arica offer tours to the park – for details, see Organized Tours in the PN Lauca section, earlier. Although tours provide a good introduction, you spend most of the time in transit, so to see more of the park, try to arrange a longer stay at Chucuyo, Parinacota or Chungará. One alternative is renting a car in Arica and driving to the park, providing access to more remote sites like Guallatire, Caquena and the Salar de Surire (the latter only with a high-clearance vehicle, since it involves fording several watercourses). Carry extra fuel in cans – most rental agencies will provide them – but fuel is available from Empresa de Comercio Agrícola (ECA) in Putre and perhaps from Matilde Morales in Chucuyo. Do not forget warm clothing and sleeping gear, and take time to acclimatize.

PISAGUA
☎ 57 • pop 150

The isolated coastal village of Pisagua – 240km south of Arica and 120km north of Iquique – has a long, sometimes inglorious history. One of Chile's largest 19th-century nitrate ports, Pisagua became a penal colony after the decline of the nitrate industry. It acquired true notoriety as a prison camp for the military dictatorship of 1973–89. After the return to democracy, the discovery of unmarked mass graves in the local cemetery caused an international scandal.

Pisagua occupies a narrow shelf at the foot of the coastal range, which rises almost vertically from the shore. There are good free **campsites** and beaches at the north end of town, as well as several surviving architectural landmarks. Visitors not deterred by the town's grim history will find much of interest and, as work proceeds on a road north toward Arica, this stretch of coastline may become more popular.

An **information kiosk** is across from the Teatro Municipal.

Things to See & Do

On a hillock overlooking the town, Pisagua's brightly painted **Torre Reloj** (clock tower) is a national monument dating from the nitrate glory days, when the port had a population of several thousand.

North of the palm-shaded Plaza de Armas, the surf laps at the foundations of the **Teatro Municipal**, a once-lavish theater with a broad stage, opera-style boxes, and ceiling murals of cherubim. The building's northern half, which once held dressing rooms, municipal offices and a market, is also worth exploring, but be cautious – one 2nd-story door plunges directly into the ocean. To enter the theater, stop by the information kiosk across the street; if no one's there, use the phone at the kiosk to call for a key (the number is posted).

A half-block inland from the plaza, the **Colonia Penal Pisagua** (US$1) was a conventional prison and not the primary site for incarceration of political prisoners after the military coup of 1973. Now the town's only hotel, it features a few portraits of leftist icons such as poet Pablo Neruda and folksinger Violeta Parra.

Just beyond the police station, the **abandoned train station** recalls the time when Pisagua was the northern terminus of El Longino, the longitudinal railway that connected the nitrate mines with the ports of the Norte Grande. Just outside town and off the road to the north, the **Monolito Centenario** commemorates a local battle during the War of the Pacific.

A 30-minute hike or 10-minute boat ride south of town will take you to a colony of **sea lions**.

About 2km north of town, the faded wooden crosses at Pisagua's **cemetery** mark tombs from the town's historic past; this was also the notorious site of a mass grave of victims of the Pinochet dictatorship. A memorial plaque proclaims that 'Although the tracks may touch this site for a thousand years, they will not cover the blood of those who fell here.'

Beyond the cemetery, the road continues to **Pisagua Vieja**, with a handful of adobe ruins, scattered, mummified human remains from a pre-Columbian cemetery, and a broad sandy beach. From here, a rough road (appropriate only for 4WD vehicles) continues up the Quebrada de Tana to Hacienda Tiliviche, a 19th-century British-nitrate family's house. The nearby British cemetery and Geoglifos de Tiliviche are worthwhile to visit. Summer rains can create dangerous washouts.

Places to Stay & Eat

Camping Municipal *(free)*, with clean toilets and showers, is basically a large parking lot at Playa Seis, a small but fine sandy beach just beyond the ruins of the former fish pro

cessing factory that once incarcerated political prisoners. You can also camp north of town at **Playa Blanca**, beneath the Monolito Centenario, but there are no facilities.

Hotel Pisagua (☎ 731-509, ☎ 09-510-8017; Videla s/n; per person US$9; meals US$5) is in the former jail, with simple rooms, shared bathrooms, and breakfast included. The guest rooms remain labeled for their original institutional occupants – the warden, guards and other prison personnel. Visitors can dine among banana trees and gardenias on the patio. In addition to superb pisco sours, ping-pong and billiard tables provide amusement.

Getting There & Away

Pisagua is 40km west of the Panamericana by a paved but potholed road from a turnoff 85km south of the *carabineros* checkpoint at Cuya and 47km north of Huara. There is no public transportation directly to the town. To

---

The New World Camelids

The Western Hemisphere had few grazing mammals after the Pleistocene, when mammoths, horses and other large herbivores disappeared, possibly due to hunting by the earliest inhabitants of the plains and pampas of North and South America. For millennia, however, Andean peoples have relied on the New World camels – the wild guanaco and vicuña; the domesticated llama and alpaca – for food and fiber.

The range of the **guanaco** (*Lama guanicoe*) extends from the central Andes to Tierra del Fuego, at elevations from sea level up to 4000m or more. In the central Andes, where the human population is small and widely dispersed but domestic livestock are numerous, its numbers are small, but on the plains of Argentine Patagonia and in reserves such as southern Chile's Parque Nacional Torres del Paine, herds of rust-colored guanaco are still a common sight. Native hunters ate its meat and dressed in its skins.

Guanaco

By contrast, the **vicuña** (*Vicugna vicugna*) occupies a much smaller geographical range, high above 4000m, in the puna and altiplano, and spanning from southcentral Peru to northwestern Argentina. While not so numerous as the guanaco, this animal played a critical role in the cultural life of pre-Columbian Peru; its very fine golden wool was the exclusive property of the Inka kings. Strict Inka authority protected the vicuña, but the Spanish invasion

Vicuña

arrange to be picked up from the shadeless junction of the Pisagua road with the Panamericana, call Hotel Pisagua. Be sure to leave enough time in the day to flag down a return bus should your ride not show up.

IQUIQUE
☎ 57 • pop 215,000

Iquique's 19th-century mining boom is still evident in its preserved Georgian mansions, the Victorian clock tower on Plaza Prat, and Corinthian theater. Some architecture has been surprisingly preserved, but the town's focus is now on its new glitzy casino and mall, port and chaotic duty-free shopping center *(zona franca)*, which uses the ominous sandy hills behind the town as an outlandish nighttime billboard.

The city is 1853km north of Santiago by a combination of the Panamericana and Ruta 1, and is a roundabout 315km from Arica via the Panamericana and paved Ruta 16,

which passes through the spreading hilltop suburb of Alto Hospicio.

History

Prior to the Spanish invasion, Iquique was a minor concentration of coastal Chango Indians who traded fish and guano from offshore islands for maize, potatoes and other products of the precordillera and the altiplano. During the colonial era, guano grew in importance, but the region's real wealth stemmed from the Huantajaya silver mine in the coast range, second only to the bonanza vein at Potosí.

During the 19th century, Tarapacá's minerals and nitrates were shipped by narrow-gauge railways through ports such as Iquique, once little more than a collection of shanties at the base of the barren headlands. As the nitrate industry grew, so did Iquique's population – exceeding 40,000 by the end of the 19th century. Mining barons

The New World Camelids

destroyed that authority and made the species vulnerable to hunting pressure. By the middle of this century, poaching reduced its numbers from two million to perhaps 10,000 and put it on the endangered-species list. But conservation programs such as those in northern Chile's Parque Nacional Lauca have achieved an impressive recovery. In Lauca and surrounding areas, vicuña numbers grew from barely a thousand in the early 1970s to more than 24,000 nearly three decades later. In Santiago, legal purchases of vicuña wool may be possible at **Casimiro Castrodonoso** (☎ 695-4091; *Moneda 950, Central • ☎ 233-4/89; Bucarest 25, Providencia).*

The communities of the puna and altiplano (in northern Chile, mostly Aymara

Llama

Indians) still depend on llamas and alpacas for their livelihood. While the two species appear similar, they differ in several important respects.

The taller, rangier and hardier **llama** *(Lama glama)* is a pack animal whose relatively coarse wool serves for blankets, ropes and other household goods (llama trains are rare in Chile since good roads penetrated the altiplano). It can survive – even flourish – on poor, dry pastures.

The smaller, more delicate **alpaca** *(Lama pacos)* is not a pack animal and requires well-watered, sometimes irrigated grasslands in order to produce its much finer wool, which has great commercial value.

Alpaca

NORTE GRANDE

built opulent mansions, while authorities piped in water from the distant cordillera and imported topsoil for public plazas and private gardens. Downtown Iquique reflects this 19th-century boom; nearby ghost towns such as Humberstone and Santa Laura, with their rusting machinery, recall the source of this wealth.

The nitrate era also made Iquique the site of one of the most notorious episodes in Chilean labor history: In 1907, nearly 8500 strikers gathered in and around the Escuela Santa María to protest unemployment and unfair treatment in the *salitreras* (nitrate mines), and to agitate for improved benefits. When they refused to abandon the school, the police and military fired machine guns upon the unarmed strikers, killing hundreds and wounding many more. The Chilean folk group Quilapayún immortalized the incident in their record *Cantata Popular Santa María de Iquique*.

Iquique is still one of Norte Grande's largest ports, but fishing has supplanted mining as its primary industry – Iquique ships more fishmeal than any other port in the world. Establishment of the *zona franca* (duty-free zone) in 1975 has made it one of Chile's most prosperous cities, and the paving of Ruta 1 to Antofagasta is bringing larger numbers of visitors.

Downtown retains the atmosphere of a 19th-century port, with ramshackle wooden houses, sailors' bars and street life, but the city is spreading south along the coast, where many houses are built on sand and, consequently, vulnerable to the area's frequent earthquakes. New high-rise apartment blocks and hotels along the beach remind some visitors of Miami Beach, on a lesser scale. On the desert plain high above Iquique, toward the Panamericana, new housing developments are making the once tiny community of Alto Hospicio an integral part of the city. Alto Hospicio is also home to burgeoning shantytowns of low-skilled, low-wage workers who can no longer afford to live in Iquique proper.

Orientation

Iquique sits on a narrow terrace at the foot of the coastal range, which abruptly rises 600m above the city. Blocked by the mountains, it has sprawled north and, especially, south along the coast.

The city's focus is Plaza Prat. Av Baquedano, which runs north-south along the east side of the plaza, is the main thoroughfare; the section near Plaza Prat is being converted to a pedestrian mall. Calle Tarapacá runs east four blocks to Plaza Condell, a pleasant park with shaded benches and surrounded by a secondary center of downtown activity. Most points of interest are within a roughly rectangular area marked by Sotomayor to the north, Av Costanera to the west, Amunátegui to the east, and Manuel Bulnes to the south. The main beaches are south of downtown, along Av Arturo Prat.

Information

Iquique's **Sernatur** (☎ 312-238; *Anibal Pinto 436; open 9am-8pm Mon-Sat, 9am-1pm Sun Jan & Feb; 8:30am-1pm & 3pm-5pm Mon-Fri Mar-Dec)* provides a free city map and brochures, plus information on the region, but is less well stocked than its counterparts in other Chilean cities. The **Automóvil Club de Chile** (☎ 413-206; *Serrano 154)* sells maps.

Iquique has diplomatic missions for several countries, including the **Bolivian consulate** (☎ 421-777; *Gorostiaga 215, Dept E)* and the **Peruvian consulate** (☎ 411-584; *Zegers 570, 2nd floor).*

Afex (*Serrano 396; open 8:30am-6:30pm Mon-Fri, 10am-1:30pm Sat)* changes foreign currency and traveler's checks, and there are many ATMs downtown and at the *zona franca* (where there are also cambios).

There is a **post office** (*Bolívar 458; open 8:30am-12:30pm & 3pm-7pm Mon-Fri, 9am-1pm Sat).*

Iquique has several telephone offices, including **Telefónica (CTC)** (*Ramírez 587 • zona franca, Módulo 212, 2nd level)* and **Entel** (*Gorostiaga 251).*

Centro Internet (☎ 416-370; *Serrano & Obispo Labbé; US$1.25/hr; open 9am-11pm daily)* is centrally located.

The Swiss-run **Academia de Idiomas del Norte** (☎ 411-827, fax 429-343; [w] *www .languages.cl; Ramírez 1345)* provides Spanish-language instruction and has been in business since 1980. Classes typically are small (one to four students) and cost about US$340 (four hours per day) to US$410 (five hours per day) per week.

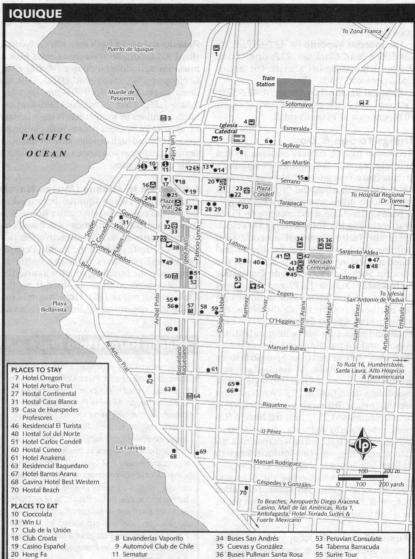

IQUIQUE

PLACES TO STAY
7 Hotel Oregon
24 Hotel Arturo Prat
27 Hostal Continental
31 Hostal Casa Blanca
39 Casa de Huespedes
   Profesores
46 Residencial El Turista
48 Hostal Sol del Norte
51 Hotel Carlos Condell
60 Hostal Cuneo
61 Hotel Anakena
63 Residencial Baquedano
67 Hotel Barros Arana
68 Gavina Hotel Best Western
70 Hostal Beach

PLACES TO EAT
10 Cioccolata
13 Win Li
17 Club de la Unión
18 Club Croata
19 Casino Español
20 Hong Fa
30 Supermercado Rossi
32 La Protectora
49 Bavaria

OTHER
1 Terminal Rodoviario
2 Chile Bus
3 Edificio de la Aduana;
   Museo Naval
4 Tur Bus
5 Post Office
6 Civet Adventure

8 Lavanderías Vaporito
9 Automóvil Club de Chile
11 Sernatur
12 Afex
14 Lloyd Aéreo Boliviano (LAB)
15 Procar
16 Radiotaxi Aeropuerto
21 Centro Internet
22 Solari y Compañía
23 Telefónica (CTC)
25 Torre Reloj
26 Taxis Aeropuerto
28 TAM
29 LanChile
33 Teatro Municipal

34 Buses San Andrés
35 Cuevas y González
36 Buses Pullman Santa Rosa
37 Entel
38 Bolivian Consulate
40 Feria Artesanal de Iquique
41 Taxitur
42 Buses Carmelita
43 Ramos Cholele
44 Taxis Tamarugal
45 Turismo Mamiña
47 Lavanderías Vaporito
50 Museo Regional
   (ex-Tribunales de Justicia)
52 Coki Tour

53 Peruvian Consulate
54 Taberna Barracuda
55 Surire Tour
56 Mane Tour
57 Palacio Astoreca (Centro
   de Cultura)
58 Nippan Rent-a-Car
59 Econorent Car Rental
62 Hertz
64 Museo Histórico Militar
   Primer Cuerpo de Ejército
65 Books and Bits
66 Academia de Idiomas del
   Norte
69 Iquique English College

NORTE GRANDE

Next door to the language school, **Books and Bits** (Ramírez 1341) is an all-English bookstore.

Lavanderías Vaporito (☎ 421-652; Bolívar 505 • Juan Martínez 832; open until 9:30pm) has drop-off service for about US$6 per small load.

Hospital Regional Dr Torres (☎ 422-370; Tarapacá & Av Héroes de la Concepción) is 10 blocks east of Plaza Condell.

Things to See & Do

Because of its 19th-century heritage, rooted in foreign exploitation of nitrates, Iquique's architecture resembles that of few other Latin American cities, and fire is a constant hazard to its distinctive wooden buildings.

Many interesting structures are on Plaza Prat, including the **Torre Reloj** (1877) clock tower; the **Teatro Municipal**, a neoclassical building that has hosted opera, theater and other cultural activities since 1890; and the adjacent **Sociedad Protectora de Empleados de Tarapacá** (1913), or 'La Protectora,' one of the country's first labor union buildings. At the northeast corner, facing the plaza, the Moorish-style **Casino Español** (1904) is now a club and restaurant whose interior features murals and oil paintings based on themes from *Don Quixote* and from Spanish history.

South of the plaza, Av Baquedano is a preservation zone for Georgian-style buildings dating from 1880 to 1930. Among them are the former **Tribunales de Justicia** (law courts; Baquedano 951), now the Museo Regional; the **Palacio Astoreca** (Baquedano & O'Higgins), a nitrate baron's mansion that's also a museum; and the **Iquique English College** (Av Arturo Prat & Patricio Lynch).

About five blocks east of the Mercado Centenario, the **Iglesia San Antonio de Padua** (Latorre & 21 de Mayo) is worth a visit for its twin bell towers.

Museo Regional Occupying Iquique's former courthouse, the regional museum (☎ 411-214; Baquedano 951; adult/child US$0.60/0.30; open 8:30am-4pm Mon-Fri, 10:30am-1pm Sat) features a mock altiplano village with adobe houses and mannequins in Aymara dress, plus a large collection of pre-Columbian artifacts, including raft and canoe paddles, fish hooks, harpoons, arrows and quivers made from animal hide. There's also an exhibition of Indian ceramics and weaving, photos of Iquique's early days and a fascinating display on the nitrate industry.

Palacio Astoreca Built for a nitrate tycoon, this 1904 Georgian-style mansion is now a museum and cultural center (☎ 425-600; O'Higgins 350; adult/child US$0.70/0.35; open 10am-1pm & 4pm-7:30pm Tues-Fri, 10am-1:30pm Sat, 11am-2pm Sun) that exhibits paintings by local artists. It has a fantastic interior of opulent rooms with elaborate woodwork and high ceilings, massive chandeliers, stained-glass windows, a gigantic billiard table and balconies.

Edificio de la Aduana (Museo Naval) Built in 1871 (when Iquique belonged to Peru), the colonial-style customhouse is a two-story structure with meter-thick walls, an octagonal tower and an attractive interior patio. During the War of the Pacific, Peru incarcerated prisoners from the battle of Iquique in the building, which was also the site of armed confrontations during the Chilean civil war of 1891. Unfortunately, the Aduana is deteriorating, and only its naval

---

Chilean Hero Arturo Prat

While other Latin American cities have their Avenidas Bolívar and Plaza Colón, Northern Chile has Arturo Prat – nearly every city here, it seems, has an Avenida Prat or a Plaza Prat. There's a university, and even an Antarctic research station named Arturo Prat. Pretty soon, even the most incurious traveler starts to wonder, well, who was this guy?

Agustín Arturo Prat Chacón (1848–79) was a naval officer, government spy and legal scholar who was killed in one of the early battles of the War of the Pacific. In May 1879, Prat captained one of two small ships blockading Iquique. Vastly overpowered by ironclad Peruvian warships, Prat gave a stirring speech to his crew aboard the *Esmeralda*, swearing to die in battle and hoping his officers would 'know their duty.' He promptly died, shot while boarding the deck of the enemy ship. Chile lost the battle but went on to win the war, inspired, sources say, by widely published accounts of Prat's heroism.

— Rina Saperstein

museum (☎ 402-121; Esmeralda 250; admission US$0.50; open 9:30am-12:30pm & 3pm-6pm Tues-Sat, 10am-1pm Sun) is open to the public; it contains artifacts salvaged from the sunken Esmeralda and biographical material on Arturo Prat (see the boxed text).

Muelle de Pasajeros Just west of the Edificio de la Aduana, Iquique's passenger pier dates from 1901. Harbor tours (US$2.50) leave from here, passing the buoy that marks the site of the Esmeralda and approaching the colony of sea lions that cover the nearby rocks. Depending on the tide, more or fewer of the interestingly constructed steps are exposed to view.

About 10 minutes from the pier by launch, in the middle of Iquique harbor, the **Boya Conmemorativa del Combate de Iquique** is a buoy marking the spot where Arturo Prat's ship Esmeralda sank in a confrontation with the Peruvian ironclad Huáscar in the War of the Pacific.

Museo Histórico Militar Primer Cuerpo de Ejército In the historic district, the Chilean army's military museum (☎ 431-555; Baquedano 1396; donation requested; open 10am-1:15pm & 4:15pm-7:15pm Mon, Tues, Thur & Fri, 10am-1:30pm Wed) features articles from the War of the Pacific.

Zona Franca (Zofri)
Created in 1975, this massive monument to uncontrolled consumption is the reason most Chileans visit Iquique, and why many have moved here. The entire region of Tarapacá is legally a customs-free zone, but its nucleus is this sprawling shopping center for imported electronics, clothing, automobiles and almost anything else.

The **Zofri** (☎ 214-129; open 11am-9pm Mon-Sat), as it is commonly known, employs more than 10,000 workers in 1500 different companies, helping make Iquique's unemployment rate the lowest in the country. Also benefiting from its proximity to Peru, Bolivia and Argentina, the Zofri turns over around US$3 billion in merchandise per annum.

Iquiqueños and tourists agree that the prices aren't that much better than what you can buy with a lot less hassle in Santiago. But if you want to shop, take any northbound taxi colectivo from downtown.

Beaches
Playa Cavancha, beginning at the intersection of Av Arturo Prat and Amunátegui, is Iquique's most popular beach. It's good for swimming and surfing but is sometimes crowded. There's also a playground for children.

Farther south, crashing waves and rip currents at scenic **Playa Brava** make it too rough to go in the water, but it's fine for sunbathing. Toward the hills, look for the massive dunes of Cerro Dragón, which looks like a set for a science-fiction film. The easiest way to Playa Brava is by taxi colectivo from downtown – look for the destination on the sign atop the cab.

There are scores of sandy beaches to the south, but they aren't as deserted and pristine as they used to be. The best way to get there is by renting a car or taking a taxi.

Surfing
Surfing is best in winter, when swells come from the north, but it is possible at any time of year. Chilean surfers, mostly bodyboarders, sleep late, so there's less competition for early morning waves at Playa Cavancha. Playa Huaiquique, on the southern outskirts of town, is also a good choice, but the sea is warmer farther north near Arica.

Solari y Compañía (Tarapacá & Obispo Labbé) sells, but doesn't rent, surfboards.

Paragliding
Iquique's unique geography – with its steep coastal escarpment, rising air currents and the soft, extensive dunes of Cerro Dragón – makes it ideal for parapente (paragliding), an activity that involves jumping off a cliff to get airborne. It's theoretically possible to glide all the way to Tocopilla, 240km to the south – but that's not for novices. See the website w www.parapenteiquique.cl for general Iquique parasailing information.

Altazor Skysports (☎/fax 437-437, ☎/fax 431-382; e altazor@entelchile.net; Av Diego Portales 920, 1502A), in the 15-story Edificio Arrecife at Playa Cavancha, offers paragliding courses and guidance, charging about US$60 per person per day, including all equipment and transportation. An introductory tandem flight costs US$40; a complete 14-day course, US$500. Rental equipment and repair is available for experienced paragliders. Altazor Skysports also offers 'kitebuggying' and 'kitesurfing.' Owner Philip Maltry speaks German, Spanish, English, Portuguese and French.

The French-run **Escuela de Parapente Manutara** (☎/fax 418-280; e *manutarachile@ hotmail.com; 18 de Septiembre 1512*) offers short introductory flights for about US$40, with three-day courses available for US$135 and 10- to 12-day courses to become a licensed paraglider pilot for US$400.

Organized Tours

Public transportation to many nearby areas is difficult, so tours are worth considering. Before taking any tour, ask for a detailed explanation to be sure that your expectations coincide with the tour operator's.

Traditional 12-hour excursions take in the nitrate ruins at Humberstone, geoglyph sites at Cerro Unita and Pintados and oases at Pica and Matilla for US$25 per person. Three-hour city tours cost around US$15; 10-hour coastal excursions toward the Río Loa are about US$25; the Tarapacá Valley is US$30; and the Gigante de Atacama and Pisagua (14 hours) costs US$35. Most trips require a four-person minimum. English-speaking guides sometimes are available for an extra charge and with advance reservations.

Coki Tour (☎/fax 428-984; e *cokitouriqq@ terra.cl; Baquedano 982*) offers tours in Spanish but also English, French or German by prior arrangement. Other agencies to try include **Mane Tour** (☎ 473-032; w *www.iqq.cl/manetour; Baquedano 1067*) and **Surire Tour** (☎/fax 411-795; *Baquedano 1035, Local 8*).

Civet Adventure (☎/fax 428-483; e *civet cor@ctcinternet.cl; Bolívar 684*) organizes small, all-equipped 4WD or bicycle adventure tours to altiplano destinations for three or more days, as well as landsailing in the Atacama Desert, with all equipment and instruction provided. German and English are spoken. Note that during summer, continuous rain makes some roads in the altiplano impassable.

Places to Stay

Budget North of Iquique, wild **camping** is possible free of charge on the beaches near Pisagua and Cuya.

Hostal Sol del Norte (☎ 421-546; *Juan Martínez 852; rooms with shared/private bath US$5/18*) has some of the cheapest rooms.

Casa de Huespedes Profesores (☎/fax 475-175; e *anitainostroza@hotmail.com; Ramírez 839; rooms with shared/private bath per person US$6/8*) is a simple family-run place two blocks from Mercado Centenario.

Residencial El Turista (☎ 422-245; *Juan Martínez 857; singles/doubles US$6/10*) is spotless.

Residencial Baquedano (☎ 422-990; *Baquedano 1315; per person US$8*) has small, clean singles without breakfast; ask for hot water.

Hostal Cuneo (☎ 428-654; *Baquedano 1175; per person with shared bath US$8, singles/doubles with private bath US$12/20*) is a fine place on historic Baquedano a few blocks south of the plaza, but some interior rooms lack windows. It's decorated with photos of old Iquique. Breakfast is included.

Hostal Beach (☎ 429-653; *Vivar 1707; singles/doubles US$10/20*) is a decent and clean place on a busy street but within sight of the beach.

Hostal Continental (☎ 429-145; *Patricio Lynch 679; per person with private bath US$10*), on a busy street, is nondescript but passable.

Hotel Oregon (☎ 410-959, *San Martín 294; per person US$9*) is centrally located and is next to a pool hall. It has high ceilings and is clean but needs maintenance.

Hostal Casa Blanca (☎ 420-007; *Gorostiaga 127; singles/doubles US$16/25*) is a good deal in a decent area.

Mid-Range Overlooking the new pedestrian mall, **Hotel Carlos Condell** (☎/fax 313-027; e *hotel-carlos-condell@entelchile.net; Baquedano 964; singles/doubles/triples US$23/36/49*) is a historic renovation. More attention to maintenance, cleanliness and service would make this a top choice in its price range, given its location and character.

Hotel Anakena (☎ 510-182; *Orella 456; singles/doubles/triples US$29/36/47*) is a very appealing historic restoration but is often full.

Hotel Barros Arana (☎/fax 412-840; *Barros Arana 1302; singles/doubles/triples US$31-37/37-46/49-59*) is less central than others but closer to the beach. Standard rooms are nice but small; superior rooms are large, with portable fans, refrigerators and cable TV. The hotel has a relaxing pool. Breakfast is included.

Top End At Playa Cavancha, **Gavina Hotel Best Western** (☎ 413-030; ⓦ www.gavina.cl; Av Arturo Prat 1497; singles/doubles US$120/138) is a multistory hotel with large rooms, all of which have a view of the sea. Rates include a large breakfast buffet.

Hotel Arturo Prat (☎ 427-000; ⓦ www .hotelarturoprat.cl; Aníbal Pinto 695; singles/doubles/triples US$48-65/53-74/66-95), one of Iquique's traditional favorites, is opposite Plaza Prat, but its central location also means some rooms can be noisy. The cheaper 'classic' rooms overlook the plaza but are smaller. 'Superior' rooms overlook a quieter, uninteresting street but are larger and have air conditioning. The hotel has a swimming pool and bar.

Hotel Terrado Suites (☎ 488-000; ⓦ www .terradohoteles.co.cl; Los Rieles 126; singles/doubles US$80-115/95-130), near Playa Cavancha, is a high-rise hotel with a pool and gym. The smaller rooms have a view of the city; superior rooms have a view of the sea. All rooms have air conditioning.

Places to Eat
The cheapest place to go for a meal is the **Mercado Centenario** (Barros Arana) between Sargento Aldea and Latorre, where upstairs cocinerías offer varied seafood.

Supermercado Rossi (Tarapacá; open 9am-10pm Mon-Sat, 10am-2pm Sun), between Labbé and Ramírez, has decent variety and fresh produce.

Cioccolata (☎ 413-010; Aníbal Pinto 487; fixed menú US$5, sandwiches US$4; open 8:30am-10pm Mon-Sat) is a comfortable cafeteria offering decent breakfasts, sandwiches, desserts, espresso, juices and ice cream.

Bavaria (☎ 427-888; Aníbal Pinto 930; fixed meals US$4, main dishes US$5-7) is the local outlet of the popular nationwide chain; simpler fare is served downstairs, and it also has a delicatessen with good take-out food. It's a familiar-feeling place, with attentive service and schnitzel.

La Protectora (☎ 421-923; Thompson 207; fixed lunch US$5, main dishes US$5-10), whose full name is Sociedad Protectora de Empleados de Tarapacá, on the plaza, offers economical fixed-price lunches with Old World charm. The restaurant serves seafood, fish, chicken, meat and pastas. Prices include one drink.

Club Croata (☎ 427-412; Plaza Prat 310; fixed menú US$4, main dishes US$4-11; open noon-3:30pm & 8:30pm-midnight Mon-Sat, 8:30pm-midnight Sun), with a good view of the plaza, has popular fixed lunches but tends to be deserted at night. The menu includes pasta, chicken, seafood and omelets.

Club de la Unión (☎ 413-236; Plaza Prat 278, 4th floor; set menú US$5, main dishes US$5-9; open 1pm-4pm & 8:30pm-midnight Mon-Sat, 1pm-4pm Sun) also has reasonable lunches and a great view of the plaza.

Casino Español (☎ 423-284; Plaza Prat 584; main dishes US$7-11; open 1pm-3:30pm & 8:30pm-11:30pm Mon-Sat, 1pm-3:30pm Sun) is not to be missed for its Moorish interior and ornate artwork. Even if you don't eat here, give yourself a tour. Oh yeah, it has food, too, including fish, omelets, and many flambé dishes and desserts (peach flambé, US$6). The leisurely service is not especially designed for the single traveler uninterested in sitting around for two hours, having a conversation with himself.

Chinese restaurants are abundant – including the inexpensive **Win Li** (☎ 425-942; San Martín 439; main dishes US$3-5, combos US$2-3; open 11:30am-4pm & 7pm-1am daily), a simple place with uninteresting atmosphere, and **Hong Fa** (☎ 422-319; Serrano 489; main dishes US$4-9; open 11am-4pm & 7pm-midnight daily), which is better but more expensive.

Locals enjoy Mexican food at **Santa Fe**, in the Mall de las Américas, and at more expensive **Fuerte Mexicano** (Av Playa Brava 3118; main dishes US$7-9), which has excellent food and plenty of atmosphere.

Entertainment
Taberna Barracuda (☎ 427-969; Gorostiaga 601) is a lively gathering spot with a happy hour from 8pm to 10pm. South of Playa Brava, on Av Costanera, are kitschy discos **Pharo's**, which is larger and draws a younger crowd, and **Kamikaze**, often packed with a gyrating 'older' (late-20s/30s) crowd. Nothing much starts until 1am. Many Iquiqueños head to Mall de las Américas, which has a multiplex cinema, stores and a host of restaurants.

Shopping
Most Chilean shoppers swarm to the zona franca (see that section, earlier), but for regional arts and crafts, **Feria Artesanal de**

NORTE GRANDE

Iquique (*Vivar & Latorre*) has a variety of artisan shops.

Getting There & Away

Air The local airport, **Aeropuerto Diego Aracena**, is 41km south of downtown via Ruta 1.

LanChile (☎ 427-600; Tarapacá 465; open 9am-1:30pm & 4pm-8pm Mon-Fri, 9:30am-1pm Sat) flies four or five times daily to Arica (US$36 one way; 40 minutes), once daily to Antofagasta (US$45 one way; 45 minutes), about seven times per day to Santiago (US$130 one way; 2½ hours), and once daily to La Paz, Bolivia (US$180 one way; two hours).

Lloyd Aéreo Boliviano (*LAB;* ☎ 426-750, 423-587; Serrano 442) flies Monday, Wednesday and Friday to Santiago and Santa Cruz, Bolivia.

TAM (☎ 390-600; Tarapacá 451) flies on Monday, Wednesday and Friday to Asunción, Paraguay (US$350 roundtrip), and offers decent deals to/from Miami, Florida (USA) and Paris, France.

Bus The bus station, **Terminal Rodoviario** (☎ 416-315), is at the north end of Patricio Lynch, but it's easier and safer to catch buses at the many company ticket offices concentrated on Sargento Aldea and Barros Arana, near the Mercado Centenario. Services north (to Arica) and south are frequent, but nearly all southbound services now use Ruta 1, the coastal highway to Tocopilla (for connections to Calama) and Antofagasta (for Panamericana connections to Copiapó, La Serena and Santiago).

Several major bus companies travel north to Arica and south as far as Santiago, including **Tur Bus** (☎ 421-702; W www.turbus.cl; Esmeralda 594), **Buses Carmelita** (☎ 413-227; Barros Arana 841) and **Ramos Cholele** (☎ 411-650; Barros Arana 851).

Sample fares are the following:

destination	duration in hours	cost
Antofagasta	8	US$10
Arica	5	US$5
Calama	7	US$9
Copiapó	14	US$19
La Serena	18	US$24
Santiago	26	US$25
Tocopilla	3½	US$5

Faster taxi colectivos to Arica charge about US$13 per person with **Taxis Tamarugal** (☎ 419-288; Barros Arana 897-B) and **Taxitur** (☎ 114-815; Sargento Aldea 791). More expensive *cama* services cost around US$40 to Santiago.

Buses San Andrés (☎ 413-953; Sargento Aldeo & Barros Arana) and **Buses Pullman Santa Rosa** (☎ 428-126; Barros Arana 777) both go daily to Pica. Also near Mercado Centenario are many taxi colectivo agencies and tour operators running transportation and tours to Pica and Mamiña.

Turismo Mamiña (☎ 420-330; Latorre 779) runs tours to Pica for US$26 and to Mamiña for US$32. **Taxitur** (☎ 414-875; Sargento Aldea 791) has taxi colectivos to Mamiña (US$15) and Pica (US$10). **Taxis Tamarugal** offers tours to Santa Laura, Humberstone, Pozo Almonte, La Tirana and Pica, leaving daily at 9am and returning at 5pm; and daily departures for Mamiña. Taxi colectivos to Pozo Almonte (US$2) and La Tirana (US$4) leave from the north side of the Mercado Centenario.

To get to La Paz, Bolivia, **Cuevas y González** (☎ 412-471; Sargento Aldea 850) leaves Monday through Saturday at 11pm (US$18; 13 hours). **Ramos Cholele** (☎ 411-650; Barros Arana 851) leaves at 2am; it offers direct service to Oruro (US$35) and La Paz (US$38; 24 hours). **Chile Bus** (☎ 474-363; Esmeralda 978) also serves Oruro and La Paz; prices are similar to those of Ramos Cholele.

To Jujuy and Salta, Argentina, **Buses Tramacá**, at the bus station, leaves Monday and Thursday night via Calama (US$70).

Getting Around

As in Arica, taxi colectivos are the easiest way to get around town. Destinations are clearly marked on an illuminated sign on top of the cab.

To/From the Airport Iquique's Aeropuerto Diego Aracena is 41km south of town on Ruta 1; for about US$10, it's easy to find a taxi colectivo on Plaza Prat to connect with your flight. Try **Taxis Aeropuerto** (☎ 413-368) on the plaza. For door-to-door transportation, contact **Radiotaxi Aeropuerto** (☎ 415-036; Aníbal Pinto 595).

Car For rental vehicles, try **Procar** (☎/fax 413-470; Serrano 796 • airport), **Hertz** (☎ 510-

432; Aníbal Pinto 1303), **Nippan Rent-a-Car**
(☎ *470-998; O'Higgins 410)* or **Econorent
Car Rental** (☎ *417-091;* e *reservas@econo
rent.net; Obispo Labbé 1089)*. Cars start at
US$43 per day. Note that local agencies often
require an international driver's license.

EAST OF IQUIQUE
☎ 57

The inland area east of Iquique consists of
sparsely populated desert, with a number of
interesting sites, most of which can be made
as day trips from Iquique. Ghost towns are
forlorn reminders of the importance that
nitrates once played in the area, and numerous geoglyphs recall the presence of inhabitants from a much earlier age. Several
precordillera hot-spring villages provide a
respite for modern-day workers and travelers, and there are a few natural attractions
and altiplano settlements as well.

Humberstone & Santa Laura
The eerie ghost town of Humberstone was
once a flourishing nitrate company town of
4000 workers. It was established in 1872 and
reached its pinnacle in 1940, but it declined
rapidly with the collapse of the nitrate industry after World War II. Around its central Plaza de Armas, nearly all the original
buildings, such as the theater, church and
market, are still standing. Some are starting
to crumble, but others, including the church,
have undergone restoration.

The area is dotted with interesting remnants from the era, such as a now-faded sign
reminding miners that 'One accident could
destroy all your hopes.' Another warns that
workers' contracts prohibit sheltering anyone
not associated with the company.

Humberstone was in some ways a model
company town. The company provided
housing, health care, food and merchandise
(goods were normally purchased only with
fichas, tokens that took the place of cash and
were worthless elsewhere). Also on offer
were amenities such as tennis and basketball
courts. The most impressive recreational
feature is the now-empty, enormous swimming pool, built of cast iron from a shipwreck
in Iquique harbor. At the west end of town,
the electrical power plant still stands, along
with the remains of the narrow-gauge railway
to the older but less well-preserved *Oficina*
Santa Laura, easily visible across the highway.

Most of Humberstone's amenities date
from the 1930s. The collapse of the nitrate-
mining industry after the introduction of
synthetic nitrates forced forced the *oficina's*
closure by 1960, leaving 3000 workers un-
employed. (Not surprisingly, union organiz-
ers were never welcomed.)

The remaining buildings were acquired by
the Andía family, who paid for the property
partly by dismantling it, and the place became
a historical monument – largely a symbolic
measure – in 1970. Andía's bankruptcy placed
the site in legal limbo, and it has recently
become vulnerable to vandalism and unau-
thorized salvage. Given the nebulous legal situation, Humberstone (and nearby Santa
Laura) are open to the public without charge,
but the Andía family, who have a caretaker
on site, request donations at the entry kiosk
for routine maintenance. The kiosk also has
maps and souvenirs for sale.

The most accessible of the former mining
settlements, Humberstone sits less than 1km
off the Panamericana, about 45km due east
of Iquique. Any eastbound bus from Iquique
will drop you off there, and it is easy to catch
a return bus. Tours and taxis are available
from Iquique. Take food, water and a camera,
since it is easy to spend many hours exploring
the town, but modest supplies are available.
Early morning hours are the best time
for wandering around, although afternoon
breezes often moderate the midday heat.

El Gigante de Atacama
The Giant of the Atacama, a geoglyph 14km
east of Huara on the southern slope of Cerro
Unita, is the largest archaeological representation of a human figure in the world – a
massive 86m high.

From the figure's rectangular head, supported by a pencil-thin neck, emanate a
dozen rays – four from the top and four from
each side. The eyes and mouth are square, the
torso long and narrow, the arms bent (one
hand appears to be an arrowhead). The size
of the feet suggest the figure is wearing boots,
and there are odd protrusions from the knees
and thighs. Alongside the giant is another odd
creature with what appears to be a tail –
perhaps a monkey, although a reptile seems
likelier in the desert environment.

The two figures are set amidst a small
complex of lines and circles, and on one side
of the hill (facing the Huara-Chusmiza road,

visible as you approach the hill) are a number of enormous clearings. The entire Gigante is visible if you stand several hundred meters back from the base of the isolated hill. Don't climb the hill; this damages the site.

The Huara-Colchane road, the main Iquique-Bolivia route, is paved as far as the village of Chusmiza; only the very short stretch (about 1km) from the paved road to the hill itself crosses the unpaved desert. The best way to visit the site is to rent a car or taxi, or take a tour (which can be arranged by agencies in Iquique).

Tarapacá
In colonial and early republican times, San Lorenzo de Tarapacá was one of Peru's most important settlements. But then the nitrate boom spurred the growth of nearby Iquique. The Battle of Tarapacá, during the War of the Pacific, marked the town's eclipse. Today, although its 18th-century **Iglesia San Lorenzo** is being restored, other adobe buildings are crumbling, and the handful of remaining residents are nearly all elderly.

About 5km east of Cerro Unita, a paved lateral drops into the Quebrada de Tarapacá to the still-irrigated but nearly depopulated valley. At the entrance to town, a monument displays a map of the Battle of Tarapacá, which took place on November 27, 1879, and marks the spot where Chilean military hero Eleuterio Ramírez lost his life.

To visit the church, ask for the key at the store at the southeast corner of the Plaza de Armas. Tarapacá has neither accommodations nor a restaurant, so bring food.

Chusmiza
At 3200m in the Quebrada de Tarapacá, 106km from Iquique, Chusmiza is a thermal-springs resort. It's known both for bottling a popular brand of mineral water and because it is the site of extensive, well-kept pre-Columbian terraces. Accommodations may be obtainable at **Hostería Chusmiza** (☎ 422-179 in Iquique). Buses from Iquique pass the turnoff to Chusmiza, which is another 6km from the highway.

PN Volcán Isluga
This national park's 175,000 hectares contain natural and cultural features similar to those of Parque Nacional Lauca (see that section, earlier in this chapter), but this more isolated

area, home to some of Chile's most traditional peoples, is much less visited than park areas farther north.

Parque Nacional Volcán Isluga is 250km from Iquique and 6km west of the village of Isluga, the main gateway to the park. Entrance is free. At Colchane, 3750m above sea level on the Bolivian border, it's also possible to cross the border and catch a truck or bus to the city of Oruro, in Bolivia.

Refugio Enquelga (dorm beds per person US$7) is in Enquelga.

Camping Aguas Calientes (free), 2km south of Enquelga, has thermal baths.

From Isluga, it's possible to travel north to the Salar de Surire and Parque Nacional Lauca and west to Arica, but inquire about the state of roads, especially in the summer rainy season, and do not attempt the trip without a high-clearance vehicle.

Pozo Almonte
Only a few kilometers south of the junction of the Panamericana and Ruta 16 to Iquique is the former nitrate service town of Pozo Almonte. The place, which got its name from a freshwater well used by local *hacendados* (landowners) during colonial times, is booming again due to its proximity to the paved highways that lead northeast to the copper mine at Cerro Colorado and the hot-springs resort of Mamiña, and southeast to the massive new copper mine at Collahuasi.

Pozo Almonte is not exactly a tourist hot spot, but it does acknowledge its past through the modest **Museo Histórico Salitrero** (admission US$0.25; open 9am-1pm & 4pm-7:30pm Tues-Sat), which is on the south side of the Plaza de Armas.

Mamiña
☎ 57 • pop 450
This dusty town 73km east of Pozo Almonte features hot-spring baths of marginal quality favored mainly by workers from the nearby mines. Winter is the peak season because of its dry, clear weather, though nights can be very chilly.

Orientation & Information The village of Mamiña divides conveniently into upper and lower sectors, the former clustered around the bedrock outcrop where the church stands, while the latter lies in the valley at the foot of Cerro Ipla, just to the south. A handful of hotels and services are in the upper sector, but most hotels and baths are in the valley below. The best view of the town and its surroundings is from the hilltop cemetery.

There's a **public telephone office** on the plaza opposite the church.

Things to See & Do The **Pukará del Cerro Inca** (*Cerro Ipla*) is a pre-Hispanic fortress 3km east of town, while the **Iglesia de Nuestra Señora del Rosario**, near the town's entrance, is a national historical monument dating from 1632. Its twin bell tower is unique in Andean Chile, but the rest of the building has undergone substantial modifications. The **Centro Cultural Kespikala** (*☎ 425-810 in Iquique*) is a gathering place for Aymara artists and artisans.

'Resort' facilities include **Barros Chinos**, 1km from the entrance, with restorative mud treatments (sit in a flimsy lawn chair and get plastered with the stuff) for US$1.50; **Baños Ipla**, where US$1.40 buys a 20-minute soak in tiny tubs; and, in better condition, **Baños Rosario**, below Refugio del Salitre.

Places to Stay & Eat Mamiña has plenty of accommodations in all price ranges; note that most of the telephone contacts below are in Iquique, and that street addresses, while indicated here, don't mean much in village context.

Cerro Morado (*sites US$10*) serves up fixed-price lunches and offers camping in the backyard.

Residencial Cholele (*☎ 09-281-1148; Ipla s/n; per person US$11, with full board US$20*) is a friendly place with a few comfortable rooms. Rates include breakfast.

Hotel Llama Inn (*☎ 419-893; Ipla s/n; singles/doubles US$32/36*) is pleasant, and rates include breakfast. Come for the US$5 fixed-price lunch and use the pool for free.

Hotel La Coruña (*☎ 09-543-0370; Santa Rosa 687; singles/doubles US$30/60*) has a thermal pool, thermal baths in rooms, and an attractive bar-restaurant; breakfast is included in the room price.

Hotel Los Cardenales (*☎ 09-545-1091; per person with full board US$50*), set among beautiful gardens, is friendly and Lithuanian-run. It has kitschy décor, each room has a whirlpool tub, and there's a large covered pool.

El Refugio del Salitre (*☎ 751-203; Mamiña s/n; singles/doubles with full board*

US$60/105) is a nitrate-era relic; some parts of the building are run-down compared with other nearby places. For nonguests, breakfast costs US$5; lunch or dinner, US$10.

Getting There & Away Buses and taxi colectivos from Iquique stop in the plaza opposite the church. See the Iquique section for transportation options.

La Tirana

In mid-July, up to 80,000 pilgrims overrun the village of La Tirana (permanent population 600) to pay homage to the Virgin of Carmen by dancing in the streets with spectacular masks and costumes in a Carnaval-like atmosphere. One of Chile's most important religious shrines, La Tirana is 72km from Iquique at the north end of the Salar de Pintados, in the Pampa del Tamarugal.

The **Santuario de La Tirana** (see the boxed text 'The Legend of La Tirana') consists of a broad ceremonial plaza graced by one of the country's most unusual, even eccentric, churches. Although several restaurants surround the plaza, there are no accommodations – pilgrims camp in the open spaces east

---

The Legend of La Tirana

According to legend, an Inkan princess accompanied Diego de Almagro in his foray into Chile in 1535. The princess, however, despised the Spanish and escaped at Pica with 100 Inka warriors. Her band of soldiers fought the Spanish invaders, killing any of them she found, as well as any Indians they had baptized. She became known as La Tirana – 'The Tyrant.' In 1544, her followers captured a Portuguese miner fighting for the Spanish. The princess fell in love with the soldier and tried to protect him from execution, earning her the suspicion of her army. As the miner was baptizing her with a pitcher of water so that they could be forever together in heaven, they were slain by arrows from her followers. Ten years later, a traveling evangelist discovered a cross in the middle of the woods, supposedly marking the lovers' grave, and built a chapel. This structure was eventually replaced by a larger building, and the legend of La Tirana fluorished.

of town. Have a glance at the one-room **Museo Regional del Salitre** *(free)* on the north side of the plaza, which has a wild, haphazard assortment of artifacts from the nitrate *oficinas.*

RN Pampa del Tamarugal

The desolate pampas of the Atacama seem an improbable site for extensive forests, but the dense groves on both sides of the Panamericana, south of Pozo Almonte, are no mirage. Although not a natural forest, the trees are in fact a native species – the tamarugo *(Prosopis tamarugo)*, which covered thousands of square kilometers of the Pampa del Tamarugal until the species nearly disappeared under the pressures of woodcutting for the nitrate mines of the Norte Grande.

Managed by Conaf, the 108,000-hectare Reserva Nacional Pampa del Tamarugal has restored much of this forest, which survives despite excessively saline soils, providing fuelwood for local people and fodder for livestock. Although there is no surface water, seedlings are planted in holes dug through the salt hardpan; after a few months' irrigation, they can reach groundwater that has seeped westward from the Andean foothills. Unfortunately, wells dug to supply the city of Iquique have lowered the regional water table from 4m to about 15m, desiccating many of the trees within the reserve.

The reserve consists of several discrete sectors, the most interesting of which is Pintados. Conaf's **Centro de Información Ambiental** *(☎ 751-055; open 8:30am-6pm daily)* is 24km south of Pozo Almonte, on the east side of the Panamericana, with excellent exhibits on the biology and ecology of the tamarugo and the pampas.

Places to Stay On the west side of the Panamericana, opposite the Centro de Información Ambiental, Conaf maintains a **campground** *(sites US$7, guesthouse beds US$10)*. There are shaded sites with tables and benches, as well as a limited number of beds in the guesthouse. Despite the highway that bisects the reserve, it's a pleasant, restful stopover, with extraordinary views of the southern night sky.

Pintados

At Pintados, one of the world's most elaborate archaeological sites, 355 individual geoglyphs blanket a large hillside in the coast range. From close up, it's difficult to discern what most of them represent, but from a distance, the outlines of human figures (121), animals (97), and various geometric designs (137) become apparent. Most of them date from between AD 500 and AD 1450, and they are believed to either mark trade routes, indicate the presence of water, identify ethnic groups or express religious meaning.

A derelict nitrate rail yard with a number of ruined buildings and rusting rolling stock, the village of Pintados lies 7km west of the Panamericana via a gravel road 45km south of Pozo Almonte, nearly opposite the eastward turnoff to Pica.

Pica
☎ 57 • pop 1500

From a distance, Pica appears as a painter's splotch of green on a lifeless brown canvas. This desert oasis is well known for limes, a key ingredient in any decent pisco sour. Chileans come here to cool off in the attractive freshwater pool and to sip on the plethora of fresh fruit drinks.

History Spanish conquistador Diego de Almagro skirmished with local Indians near Pica on his expedition to Chile in 1535, but in later colonial times, this agreeable oasis became famous for its wines and fruits. In the 19th century, it supplied wheat, wine, figs, raisins and alfalfa to the nitrate mines of the pampas, then became a sort of 'hill station' for the nitrate barons.

The Spaniards developed an elaborate system of more than 15km of tunnels to carry groundwater to the village. When Iquique boomed with nitrate exports, the Tarapacá Water Company then piped water from Pica, 119km to the southeast, to the coast to accommodate the city's growth.

Only 42km from La Tirana by an excellent paved road, Pica, which has several hotels and restaurants, has become a more democratic destination (no longer a preserve of the nitrate barons) and is popular on the weekends.

Things to See & Do Many visitors take advantage of the small freshwater pool at **Cocha Resbaladero** *(admission US$2)*, at the upper end of General Ibáñez. Expect a crowd. There are bathrooms, changing rooms and a snack bar. An information kiosk near the entrance distributes a town map.

The 19th-century **Iglesia de San Andrés**, opposite the Plaza de Armas, replaced two earlier churches destroyed by earthquakes. The last two days of November, Pica celebrates the **Fiesta de San Andrés**, a religious festival that includes traditional dances and fireworks.

In the adjacent village of **Matilla**, 3km west, the **Iglesia de San Antonio** is a national monument dating from 1887 but built on 17th-century foundations. More interesting is the **Lagar Siglo XVIII Museo de Sitio**, an on-site museum with an inoperative colonial winepress made from a large tree trunk. It's opened to the public sporadically by a guide, who collects tips.

Places to Stay & Eat The nearly shadeless **Camping Miraflores** (☎ 741-338; Miraflores s/n; sites per person US$2) still gets crowded, especially weekends.

El Tambo (☎ 741-041; General Ibáñez 68; per person US$5, cabañas US$27), a rickety 1906 building opposite the Resbaladero pool, has simple but airy rooms with shared bath and equipped cabañas for four. Meals are also available.

Hotel San Andrés (☎ 741-319; Balmaceda 197; per person US$9) is a friendly place with spacious rooms, including private bath and breakfast, as well as a good-quality restaurant with cheap, filling lunches.

There are several inexpensive restaurants near the Plaza de Armas, on Balmaceda, but nothing really special.

Stop by the locally famous **Alfajores 'Rah,'** on Balmaceda across from the church, for the best alfajores (two crackers with sweetened condensed milk in the middle, rolled in shredded coconut) and local honey; the treats cost a mere US$1 for eight.

El Edén de Pica (☎ 741-332; Riquelme 12; main dishes US$6-11), half a block off the Plaza de Armas, has pleasant patio dining. The menu features Chilean dishes with seafood, meat and chicken.

Getting There & Away Buses, taxi colectivos and tours operate between Iquique and Pica; see the Iquique section for details.

TOCOPILLA
☎ 55 • pop 25,000

Desolate Tocopilla is an unattractive port for the remaining nitrate oficinas of Pedro de Valdivia and María Elena, and is the site of Codelco's thermoelectric plant for Chuquicamata. Fishing is also a significant industry. There's nothing much of interest here, but if you want to avoid the scramble of Antofagasta, this smaller town offers transportation connections and acceptable accommodations.

Ruta 1, the paved highway between Iquique and Tocopilla (Región II), has largely superseded the older Panamericana for southbound travelers. There is spectacular coastal desert scenery, but heavy truck traffic has damaged a highway originally intended for recreational traffic, and improved access has also meant that careless campers are rapidly despoiling the beaches with trash.

While most of the beaches south of Iquique are too rocky for surfing, the beach near the customs post at the Río Loa, on the border between Regiones I and II, is a good choice. At Río Seco, 96km south of Iquique, there's a private open-air **Museo Parque** with good artifacts from pre-Columbian Chango fishermen as well as from the nitrate era.

Orientation & Information

The main thoroughfare is the north-south Arturo Prat, while the main commercial street is 21 de Mayo, one block east. Most services are a few blocks either north or south from Plaza Condell, at the corner of 21 de Mayo and Aníbal Pinto.

Like other northern coastal towns, Tocopilla's smattering of wooden buildings, mostly along Prat and 21 de Mayo, give it a turn-of-the-20th-century atmosphere. The **Torre Reloj** (clock tower; Prat & Baquedano) was relocated intact from the nitrate oficina of Coya, near María Elena. **Playa El Salitre**, reached by a staircase from Calle Colón, is the best spot for sunbathing, but the water is too contaminated for swimming.

There is a **post office** (21 de Mayo & Aníbal Pinto), an **Entel** (21 de Mayo 2066) and **Telefónica (CTC)** (Manuel Rodríguez 1337).

Tocopilla's **hospital** (☎ 821-839; Santa Rosa & Matta) is a few blocks northeast of downtown.

NORTE GRANDE

Places to Stay & Eat
Residencial Alvarez (☎ 811-578; Serrano
1234; rooms per person US$8) is amiable
and has spacious, well-kept rooms with high
ceilings, all set around an attractive patio.

Hostería Bolívar (☎ 812-783; Bolívar
1332; rooms per person US$10) is friendly
and also a good value; rooms have shared
bath. It has a restaurant.

Hotel Colonial (☎ 811-621, fax 811-940;
21 de Mayo 1717; doubles US$20), near
the central plaza, has friendly hosts, huge
breakfasts and private parking.

Hotel Vucina (☎ 812-155; 21 de Mayo
2069; singles/doubles US$24/32) includes
cable TV and breakfast.

Club de la Unión (☎ 813-198; Prat 1354;
4-course lunch US$6), Tocopilla's top
restaurant, is reasonably priced. It has good
four-course Sunday lunches, including a
tasty pisco sour.

Getting There & Away
Buses between Iquique and Antofagasta
stop here, and eastbound taxi colectivos
to Chuquicamata and Calama (US$6) leave
from Iquique at the corner of 21 de Mayo
and Manuel Rodríguez.

GATICO & COBIJA
Only a few kilometers apart, 130km north of
Antofagasta and 60km south of Tocopilla,
Gatico and Cobija are coastal ghost towns
where a few families eke out a living by
fishing and collecting seaweed. In the early
19th century though, flourishing Cobija was
Bolivia's outlet to the Pacific, serving the
mines of the altiplano despite a precarious
water supply, whose distribution reflected
the early republican hierarchy. After an
earthquake and tsunami nearly obliterated
the town in 1877, Cobija's population declined rapidly; by 1907, it had only 35 inhabitants, and now there are even fewer.

If you visit Cobija or Gatico, bring your
own supplies. You may be able to purchase
fish, but everything else is at a premium –
except for free **camping** among the atmospheric adobe walls overlooking the sea. In a
few places, such as the plaza, the church and
the cemetery (with its wooden fences and
crosses, and a few crumbling adobe crypts),
the ruins are obvious. But for the most part,
visitors must guess the past identity of any
given building.

MARÍA ELENA
☎ 55 • pop 7500
Near the junction of the Panamericana and
the Tocopilla-Chuquicamata highway, sleepy
María Elena is one of the last functioning
oficinas, with a street plan patterned after
the British Union Jack. There are traveler's
services here, including a **residencial** and
camping, as well as a **Museo Arqueológico e
Histórico** (☎ 632-935; Ignacio Carrera Pinto;
open 9am-1pm & 4pm-7pm Mon-Sat,
10am-1pm & 5pm-8pm Sun). Swimming is
not advisable in the heavily polluted river.

There are dozens of nitrate ghost towns
in the Antofagasta region, lining both sides
of the highway between Baquedano and
Calama, and along the Panamericana north
of the Tocopilla-Chuquicamata highway.
The best preserved is **Oficina Chacabuco**, a
national monument just north of the junction between the two highways, that also
served as a prison during the military dictatorship of 1973–89.

CALAMA
☎ 55 • pop 137,000
Calama is not an especially interesting city
for travelers, but it has many services. It's
also the gateway to Chuquicamata and
backpacker mecca San Pedro de Atacama.

Well-heeled businessmen mix with a
growing population of out-of-work youth in
this bustling town. Indicative of its macho
mining culture, streets are lined with schops
con piernas – which are the same idea as the
cafés con piernas (see the Santiago chapter),
but with beer.

It's a measure of Calama's own brief
history that the city did not acquire its **Iglesia
Catedral San Juan Bautista** until 1906 – until
then, it was ecclesiastically subordinate to tiny
Chiu Chiu. Major changes are in store,
though: By 2003 the entire population of
heavily polluted Chuquicamata will relocate
to Calama. Improvements are under way and
the city is becoming a livelier place. But most
visitors will use the city as a brief stopover en
route to the sights of the Atacama outback.

Orientation
Calama sits on the north bank of the Río
Loa, 220km from Antofagasta and 2250m
above sea level. Though the city has sprawled
with the influx of laborers from Chuquicamata, its central core is still pedestrian-

friendly. Calle Ramírez between Abaroa and Vivar is an attractive pedestrian mall. Named for the date of Calama's occupation by Chile in the War of the Pacific, the modest Plaza 23 de Marzo is the focus of downtown activity.

Information

The **Oficina Municipal de Información Turística** (☎ 345-345; **e** calamainfotour@entel chile.net; Latorre 1689; open 8:30am-1pm & 3pm-7pm Mon-Thur, 8:30am-1pm & 3pm-6pm Fri) has a friendly, helpful staff. You can store your luggage here for US$0.50 per bag.

Marbumor Money Exchange (☎ 341-595; Sotomayor 1837) pays good rates, with no commission for traveler's checks.

There's a **post office** (Vicuña Mackenna 2167; open 9am-1:30pm & 3:30pm-7pm Mon-Fri, 9am-1pm Sat). There are pay phones throughout the pedestrian mall, or more private but expensive service is provided by **Telefónica (CTC)** (Abaroa 1756) and **Entel** (Sotomayor 2027).

Cybernet (Calle Vargas; open 9am-midnight; US$1.25/hr) has Internet access. **Cyber Café Machi** (Vivar between Vargas &

Ramírez; open 10am-11pm Mon-Sat, 5pm-10:30pm Sun) also serves coffee and snacks but is more expensive.

Lavexpress (☎ 313-361; Sotomayor 1887; open 9am-9pm Mon-Sat) has excellent drop-off laundry service for US$2/kg.

Hospital Carlos Cisterna (☎ 342-347; Av Granaderos) is near the corner with Cisterna, five blocks north of Plaza 23 de Marzo.

There's a **Bolivian consulate** (☎ 344-413; Vicuña Mackenna 1984; open 9am-1pm Mon-Fri) if you need to get a visa for Bolivia.

Parque El Loa

At the south end of Av O'Higgins, this rather drab park features a riverside swimming pool and a scale model of the famous church at Chiu Chiu, with its twin bell towers. In the park you'll also find Calama's **Museo Arqueológico y Etnológico** (☎ 316-400; adult/child US$0.50/0.25; open 10am-1pm & 3pm-7:30pm Tues-Fri, 3pm-8:30pm Sat & Sun), with exhibits on the peoples of the Atacama, a decent collection of artifacts, and good models. There's also the **Museo de Historia Natural** (☎ 349-103; adult/child

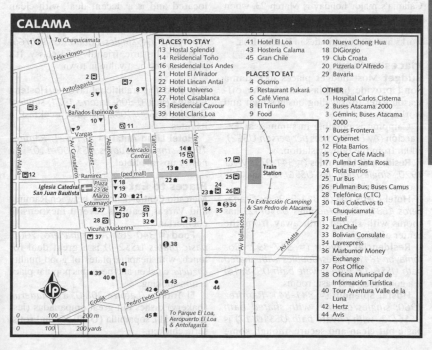

CALAMA

PLACES TO STAY
13 Hostal Splendid
14 Residencial Toño
16 Residencial Los Andes
21 Hotel El Mirador
22 Hotel Lincan Antai
23 Hotel Universo
27 Hotel Casablanca
35 Residencial Cavour
39 Hotel Claris Loa
41 Hotel El Loa
43 Hostería Calama
45 Gran Chile

PLACES TO EAT
4 Osorno
5 Restaurant Pukará
6 Café Viena
8 El Triunfo
9 Food

10 Nueva Chong Hua
18 DiGiorgio
19 Club Croata
20 Pizzería D'Alfredo
29 Bavaria

OTHER
1 Hospital Carlos Cisterna
2 Buses Atacama 2000
3 Géminis; Buses Atacama 2000
7 Buses Frontera
11 Cybernet
12 Flota Barrios
15 Cyber Café Machi
17 Pullman Santa Rosa
24 Flota Barrios
25 Tur Bus
26 Pullman Bus; Buses Camus
28 Telefónica (CTC)
30 Taxi Colectivos to Chuquicamata
31 Entel
32 LanChile
33 Bolivian Consulate
34 Lavexpress
36 Marbumor Money Exchange
37 Post Office
38 Oficina Municipal de Información Turística
40 Tour Aventura Valle de la Luna
42 Hertz
44 Avis

To Chuquicamata
Félix Hoyos
Antofagasta
Bañados Espinoza
Vargas
Av Granaderos
Velásquez
Abaroa
Santa María
Ramírez
Mercado Central
(ped mall)
Iglesia Catedral San Juan Bautista
Plaza 23 de Marzo
Sotomayor
Vicuña Mackenna
Latorre
Vivar
Train Station
To Extracción (Camping) & San Pedro de Atacama
Av Balmaceda
Av Matta
Cobija
Pedro León Gallo
To Parque El Loa, Aeropuerto El Loa & Antofagasta

0   100   200 m
0   100   200 yards

US$0.50/0.25), which has the same hours as Museo Arqueológico y Etnológico.

Organized Tours

The **Corporación Cultural y Turismo** (☎ 364-176) leads trips around the city and to outlying areas, but they need a minimum of 10 people for the city tour and four people for other tours. Excursions include the half-day city tour (US$4); half-day tour to Pukará de Lasana and Chiu Chiu (US$20); full-day tour to the El Tatio Geysers, Caspana, Lasana and Chiu Chiu (US$70); and a full-day tour to San Pedro de Atacama, Toconao, and Valle de la Luna (US$70). For reservations, you have to visit the municipal tourist office (see Information, earlier).

Calama also has a few travel agencies that arrange excursions to more remote parts of the desert – though some of these trips can be arranged more easily and cheaply from San Pedro de Atacama because of the much higher tourist traffic there. Among the Calama agencies is **Tour Aventura Valle de la Luna** (☎/fax 310-720; Abaroa 1620).

Special Events

Calama's major holiday is March 23, when the city celebrates the arrival of Chilean troops during the War of the Pacific with fireworks and other festivities in Parque Loa.

Places to Stay

Budget Most budget places in Calama don't provide breakfast and in the off-season cater to traveling businessmen and workers.

Camping is possible in summer at **Extracción** (Av La Paz; sites per person US$2), 500m from the railway station.

Residencial Los Andes (☎ 341-073; Vivar 1920; singles/doubles US$6/12) has tidy rooms with shared bath.

Hotel Claris Loa (☎ 311-939; Av Granaderos 1631; singles/doubles US$6/12) has rooms with shared bath away from the center of things.

Residencial Cavour (☎ 317-392; Sotomayor 1841; singles/doubles with shared bath US$6/12, with private bath US$8/16) is a good deal with basic rooms.

Hostal Splendid (☎ 341-841; Ramírez 1960; singles/doubles with shared bath US$6/12, with private bath US$10/17) is basic but clean and secure, though some rooms are small and have no exterior windows. The management is helpful.

Residencial Toño (☎ 341-185; Vivar 1970; singles/doubles with shared bath US$8/15, with private bath US$15/25), long popular with foreign visitors, is fairly tranquil, has clean sheets and provides plenty of blankets, but you might find some of the beds uncomfortable.

Hotel El Loa (☎ 341-963; Abaroa 1617; singles/doubles US$10/20) is a friendly place that offers spotless rooms with shared bath, although the front rooms can be noisy.

Gran Chile (☎ 317-455; Latorre 1474; per person US$12) is quiet and clean.

Mid-Range Mid-range accommodations are relatively scarce in Calama, but there are a few choices.

Hotel Casablanca (☎ 341-938; Sotomayor 2161; singles/doubles US$26/33), opposite Plaza 23 de Marzo, is a worn Art Deco–style place in need of maintenance, but it's still appealing for its clean, spacious rooms; avoid the small, gloomy single rooms.

Hotel Universo (☎ 361-640; Sotomayor 1822; singles/doubles US$30/36) is well located and is a decent deal, with clean rooms, pleasant staff and breakfast included.

Hotel El Mirador (☎/fax 340-329; Sotomayor 2064; singles/doubles US$55/65) is stylish, historic, friendly and classy. It's probably the best value in town.

Top End The traditional favorite, **Hostería Calama** (☎ 310-306; Latorre 1521; singles/doubles US$80/105), includes breakfast in its rates.

Hotel Lican Antai (☎ 341-621; Ramírez 1937; singles/doubles US$100/110) is a newer upscale hotel.

Places to Eat

Mercado Central (Latorre), between Ramírez and Vargas, features several inexpensive cocinerías.

Food (☎ 340-269; Av Granaderos 2005; basic plates US$2-4) is a great deal for lunch, with heaping plates of good-quality cazuela, chicken and beef; this popular place is nonsmoking.

El Triunfo (Latorre 2084), a panadería, (bakery) dishes out great empanadas (less than US$1), sopaipilla (US$0.25) and rotisserie chicken.

Café Viena *(Abaroa 2023; dishes US$2-4)* has a decent selection of salads (US$2.50) and sandwiches (US$1-3).

DiGiorgio *(Ramírez 2099)* is the best place for cold beers, ice cream and snacks, if you need a quick bite.

Club Croata, facing Plaza 23 de Marzo, is an upscale spot but features good fixed-price lunches.

Restaurant Pukará *(Abaroa 2051-B; fixed menú US$2.50, main dishes US$4-6)* is small and dark but cozy and friendly, and is known for its Chilean specialties. The *menú* of the day is a good deal.

Osorno *(☎ 341-035; Bañados Espinoza 2198; set lunches US$3)* is inexpensive and is also a peña at night.

Bavaria *(☎ 341-371; Sotomayor 2095; fixed menú US$5, main dishes US$5-8)* is part of a comfortable nationwide chain with passable sandwiches (US$3-4).

Pizzería D'Alfredo *(☎ 319-440; Abaroa 1835; individual pizza US$5, sandwiches US$3)* is the local branch of a reliable regional chain; the rather small pizzas are good but could use more sauce. Caffeine addicts will find cappuccino and espresso here.

Nueva Chong Hua *(☎ 313-387; Abaroa 2008)* has Chinese fixed-price meals but also a diverse à la carte menu.

Getting There & Away

From Calama, travelers can head north to Iquique and Arica, southwest to Antofagasta, west to Tocopilla, northeast by train to Bolivia, or east by bus to San Pedro de Atacama and to Salta, in Argentina.

Air LanChile *(☎ 341-394; Latorre 1726)* flies to Antofagasta (US$25 one way) and Santiago (starting at US$100 one way) five times daily.

Bus Calama has no central bus terminal, but most bus companies are fairly central, within a few blocks of each other. Companies with services north- and southbound on the Panamericana include: **Tur Bus** *(☎ 316-699; Ramírez 1802)*; **Pullman Bus** *(☎ 341-282; Balmaceda 1802)*; **Pullman Santa Rosa** *(☎ 363-080; Balmaceda 1902)*; **Flota Barrios** *(☎ 341-497; Ramírez 2298 • Sotomayor 1812-A)*; and **Géminis** *(☎ 341-993; Antofagasta 2239)*.

Sample fares from Calama include:

destination	duration in hours	cost
Antofagasta	3	US$4
Arica	9	US$12
Iquique	6	US$14
La Serena	16	US$23
Santiago	7	US$25

Buses Frontera *(☎ 346-005; Antofagasta 2041)* provides the most departures per day to San Pedro de Atacama (US$2.50), Toconao (US$3), Peine (US$4) and Socaire (US$5). **Buses Atacama 2000** *(☎ 341-993; Antofagasta 2238 • Abaroa 2105B)* also serves San Pedro and Toconao; Tur Bus (see earlier) provides services to San Pedro.

Linea 80 *(☎ 362-523)* provides taxi colectivo service to Chiu Chiu.

Buses Camus *(☎ 342-800; Balmaceda 1802)* serves Tocopilla.

International buses are invariably full, so make reservations as far in advance as possible. **Buses Manchego** *(☎ 316-612; Alonso de Ercilla 2142)* has buses to Uyuni, Bolivia, on Wednesdays and Sundays at midnight (US$12; 15 hours); the office is open the day before departure for ticket purchases. Service to Salta and Jujuy, Argentina, is provided by Tur Bus on Wednesday mornings (US$39; 12 hours), and also by Géminis on Wednesday and Sunday mornings (US$35; 12 hours).

Train The only active passenger train service in the north operates between Calama and Ollagüe, on the Bolivian border, with connections to Uyuni (US$12; 24 hours) and Oruro (US$18; 30 hours). The train leaves every Wednesday at 11pm. Tickets are available at **Estación de Ferrocarril** *(train station; ☎ 342-004; Balmaceda 1777)*. Tickets should be purchased by the Saturday prior to departure. The ride passes through the altiplano, with wonderful views, but is basic and tough, and there can be long complications at the border.

Show your passport when buying tickets, and obtain a Bolivian visa if you need one (see Information, earlier). Temperatures can drop well below freezing on this route, so bring warm clothing and sleeping gear.

Getting Around

Aeropuerto El Loa *(☎ 312-348)* is only a short cab ride south of Calama (US$2.50

NORTE GRANDE

per person for a colectivo, US$3 total for a private cab). Colectivos (US$5 per person) and taxis (US$30 total) also go to San Pedro de Atacama.

Frequent taxi colectivos to Chuquicamata leave from Abaroa, a block from Plaza 23 de Marzo, between Vicuña Mackenna and Sotomayor. The fare is about US$0.75.

Calama car rental agencies include **Hertz** (☎ 340-018; Latorre 1510) and **Avis** (☎ 319-797; Pedro León Gallo 1883). To visit the geysers at El Tatio, rent a 4WD or pickup truck – ordinary passenger cars lack sufficient clearance for the area's rugged roads and may get stuck in the mud at river fords.

AROUND CALAMA
Chuquicamata

The seemingly inexhaustible reserves at Chuquicamata (or just Chuqui), 16km north of Calama, have made Chile the world's greatest copper producer. Foreign capital originally financed the exploitation of its relatively low-grade ores, with open-pit techniques initially developed in the USA. Today, it's the world's largest open-pit copper mine and the largest single supplier of copper, producing 600,000 tons annually. Despite Chile's attempts at economic diversification, Chuqui still provides about 43% of the country's total copper output and around 17% of annual export income. In total, copper accounts for nearly 40% of Chilean exports.

Chuqui's perpetual plume of eastward-blowing dust and smoke gives away its location from a great distance in the cloudless desert, but everything here dwarfs the human scale, from the fleet of 115 massive diesel trucks that carry 170- to 330-ton loads on tires more than 3m high (and that cost US$12,000 each), to the towering mountains of *tortas* (tailings, some of which are being reprocessed) that have accumulated over eight decades. The mine complex's single most impressive feature, though, is the massive open pit, 4.3km long, 3km wide and 850m deep, from which the ore comes. Much of the time on two-hour tours is spent simply gazing into the depths of this immense excavation.

The town of Chuquicamata proper was once a clean, well-ordered company town whose landscape is a constant reminder of its history. Because of persistent environmental problems and copper reserves beneath the town, the entire population will relocate to Calama during the year 2003.

History Prospectors first discovered the Chuquicamata deposits in 1911, and the US Anaconda Copper Mining Company began excavations in 1915. Out of nothing, the company created a city, with housing, schools, cinemas, shops, a hospital and many other amenities, although many Chileans accused the company of taking out more than it put back into the country. At the same time, labor unrest added to the resentment felt toward the huge, powerful corporation.

By the 1960s, Chile's three largest mines (the other two were Anaconda's El Salvador, in Región III of Atacama, and Kennecott's El Teniente, in Región VI of Rancagua) accounted for more than 80% of copper production, 60% of total exports and 80% of tax revenues. Anaconda, although it paid a greater percentage of its profits in taxes than other mining companies, became the target of those who advocated nationalization of the industry.

Congressional leftists had introduced nationalization bills since the early 1950s, but support for nationalization grew even among the Christian Democrats and other centrists. During the Christian Democratic govern-

Copper Processing

Given Chuquicamata's low-grade ore, only large quantities make production practical. The ore is quarried by blasting and power shovels; at the mining stage, material is classified as ore or waste, depending on its copper content. Sufficiently rich material is dumped into a crusher, which reduces it to fine particles. The metal is then removed from the rock by a flotation process in which the copper is separated and concentrated through chemically induced differences in surface tension. It is carried to the surface of pools of water – the large pools of blue solution at the processing works are the concentrators where this process takes place. The copper concentrate becomes a thick slurry, from which the final product is extracted by smelting.

—Wayne Bernhardson

ment of President Eduardo Frei Montalva in the late 1960s, Chile gained a majority shareholding in the Chilean assets of Anaconda and Kennecott, partly because the companies feared expropriation under a future leftist regime.

In 1971 Congress approved nationalization of the industry by a large majority that included rightist elements. After 1973, the new military junta agreed to compensate companies for loss of assets, but retained ownership through the Corporación del Cobre de Chile (Codelco), although it has encouraged the return of foreign capital. In early 1996 there was a brief but contentious strike, revealing factionalism in the local labor movement. Some conservative legislators are urging privatization of Codelco.

Organized Tours Chuquicamata's **Oficina de Relaciones Públicas** *(public relations office;* ☎ *321-861)* offers tours seven days a week, in both English and Spanish, to nearly 40,000 people each year. Report to the Oficina Ayuda a la Infancia at the top of Av JM Carrera, by 9am or earlier, bringing your passport for identification and making a modest donation of about US$2.50. Tours are ostensibly limited to the first 40 arrivals, but if there are at least 15 more visitors, they'll add a second bus. Demand is high in January and February, so get there early, but if demand is sufficient there may be afternoon tours as well. Children under age 12 are not permitted.

The two- to three-hour tours begin at 9:30am with a 10-minute video shown in

AROUND CALAMA & SAN PEDRO DE ATACAMA

NORTE GRANDE

RNLF   Reserva Nacional Los Flamencos

Spanish; on completion, those who understand Spanish go directly to the tour bus, while others sit through the English-language version. Visitors should wear sturdy footwear (no open sandals), long pants and long sleeves; photos are allowed. Do not arrange the tour through agencies in Calama, which may charge more than Codelco's nominal fee.

Getting There & Away From Calama, taxi colectivos (about US$1.50) leave from Abaroa between Vicuña Mackenna and Sotomayor, just south of Plaza 23 de Marzo.

Geoglifos Chug Chug

About 15km west of Chuquicamata, on the paved highway to Tocopilla, a dirt road leads north to Chug Chug, a hillside whose restored geoglyphs are mostly geometric rhomboids; one resembles a pre-Columbian surfer. Some date from the Tiwanaku culture (AD 500 to AD 1000), which was centered around Bolivia and Peru, while other geoglyphs are regional (dating from about 1100–1450), and the remainder Inkaic (1450–1530).

SAN PEDRO DE ATACAMA
☎ 55 • pop 4900

Sleepy, laid-back San Pedro de Atacama is the gringo gathering spot of northern Chile, where Spanish-speaking locals are frequently outnumbered by German, French and English-speaking travelers. After days of watching brown desert roll by from bus windows, this oasis village offers a delightful bit of green, an addicting feel of laziness, and plenty of options to keep you longer than planned. Situated at the north end of the Salar de Atacama, a vast saline lake, San Pedro is the base for one-day and multiday trips to sites around the desert.

San Pedro was once a major pre-Columbian stop on the trading route from the highlands to the coast. It was visited by Pedro de Valdivia in 1540, and the town later became a major stop on early-20th-century cattle drives from the Argentine province of Salta to the nitrate *oficinas* of the desert. The town declined when railroad construction across the Andes made stock drives obsolete.

No longer on the cattle trail, San Pedro has become a popular stop on the gringo trail, though many young Chileans also spend their holidays here. San Pedro, with its small adobe houses, pleasant tree-lined plaza and postcard-perfect church, relies heavily on tourism, which also jeopardizes its sublime tranquility. High season brings in thousands of tourists and stresses the sensitive balance with the locals. Some restaurants have started hustling on the streets, trying to attract customers with annoying patter.

Besides tourism, the other main source of local employment is irrigated farming by the surrounding indigenous communities *(ayllus)*, pronounced 'a-EE-oos.' East of the Salar rise immense volcanoes, some active but mostly extinct. Symmetrical Licancábur, at 5916m, is one of the most conspicuous. Near San Pedro, the colorful Valle de la Luna (Valley of the Moon), one of the Atacama's most scenic areas, is part of Conaf's Reserva Nacional Los Flamencos.

Travelers to and from Argentina and Bolivia clear immigration with the Policía Internacional, as well as customs and agricultural inspections, just outside of town to the east.

Local residents, especially the indigenous Atacameño peoples, are sensitive to what they perceive as an overwhelming presence of outsiders. Make a special effort to behave appropriately and blend in as best you can.

San Pedro's water is not potable. Bottled water is readily available in all stores. Water is scarce (obviously), so refrain from long soaks in the shower.

The town electricity and lights go out about 1am each night; an hour later on the weekend. If you're planning to be out and about after then, you'll need a flashlight.

Orientation

San Pedro, 2440m above sea level, is some 106km southeast of Calama via paved Chile 23. The village itself is small and compact, with almost everything of interest within easy walking distance of the Plaza de Armas.

Many buildings have recently been given street numbers, although many still do without. The main commercial street is Caracoles, south of the Plaza de Armas. The street name Antofagasta has been changed to Gustavo Le Paige, although the old name appears on old maps and even a modern street sign or two.

Information

San Pedro's helpful, knowledgeable **Oficina de Información Turística** *(no phone; Toconao*

& Gustavo Le Paige; open 9:30am-1pm &
3pm-7pm Fri-Wed, till 8pm in summer) is
on the east side of the Plaza de Armas. The
Conaf information center (open 10am-1pm
& 2:30pm-4:30pm daily) is at Solcor, about
2km past San Pedro's customs and immigration
post on the Toconao road.

The excellent JLM map of San Pedro and
surroundings is a worthwhile investment, especially
if you're exploring without organized
tours. It's available at Azimut 360 (see
Organized Tours, later) and other agencies.

Change money at the unimaginatively
named **Money Exchange** (Toconao 492) or at
Apacheta Café (Toconao s/n), at the southeast
corner of the plaza. Don't expect good
rates for traveler's checks. There are no

ATMs in town, to the surprise and alarm of
many travelers who have to bus back to
Calama for cash. Many hotels, restaurants
and tour agencies take credit cards, but some
still prefer the real stuff. It's best to bring a
suitable cash supply with you.

The **post office** (Gustavo Le Paige; open
9am-12:30pm & 2:30pm-6pm Mon-Fri, 9am-
noon Sat) is opposite the archeology museum.
Entel (open 8:30am-10pm Mon-Fri, 9am-
9pm Sat & Sun) is at the southwest corner of
the plaza; **Telefónica (CTC)** (Caracoles; open
8:30am-10pm Mon-Fri, 10am-10pm Sat &
Sun) is half a block south of the plaza.

Internet service is offered at **Café Etnico**
(Tocopilla s/n) and **El Adobe** (Caracoles s/n)
for about US$2.50/hour. At Apacheta Café

SAN PEDRO DE ATACAMA

PLACES TO STAY
5 Hostal/Café Sonchek
7 Residencial Rayco
9 Residencial Chiloé
10 Hotel Tambillo
12 Hostal Katarpe
17 Hotel Terrantai
29 Hostal Nuevo Porvenir
32 Hostal/Camping Takha
   Takha
34 Hotel Kimal
46 Hotel Licancábur
48 Camping Los Perales
49 Camping Éden

PLACES TO EAT
1 Quitor
22 Restaurant Juanita
30 Café Export
36 Casa Piedra
37 El Adobe
39 La Estaka
40 Todo Natural
44 Petro Pizza

OTHER
2 Tur Bus
3 Buses Frontera
4 Buses Atacama 2000
6 Tour Operador Internacional
8 Tara Expediciones
11 Cactus Tour
13 Laundry Alana
14 Turismo Colque
15 Flota Barrios; Licancábur Tours
16 Cordillera Traveller
18 Café Etnico
19 Iglesia San Pedro
20 Telefónica (CTC)
21 Entel
23 Apacheta Café
24 Oficina de Información Turística
25 Posta Médica
26 Atacama Inca Tour
27 Casa Incaica
28 Géminis
31 Post Office
33 Southern Cross Adventures
35 Azimut 360
38 Cosmo Andino
42 Money Exchange
45 Pamela Tours
47 La Marca

To Pukará Quitor & Catarpe

To Calama

To Camping Oasis Alberto Terrazas,
Pozo 3, Toconao, Peine,
Customs & Immigration &
Conaf Information Center

Cemetery

Licancábur

Paseo Artesanal (ped mall)

Museo Gustavo
Le Paige

Gustavo Le Paige

Plaza de Armas

Tocopilla (ped mall)

Toconao

Domingo Atienza

Calama

Caracoles

To Camping Buenas
Peras & Hotel
La Aldea

Solcor

Palpana

To Yaye & Sequitor

To Hostal Quinta
Adela, Solcor & Solor

NORTE GRANDE

0   50   100 m
0   50   100 yards

(mentioned earlier), you can change money, use the Internet, and drink coffee.

Laundry Alana (*Caracoles 162-B*) has drop-off service for US$2.50/kg.

The **Posta Médica** (☎ 851-010; *Toconao*), at the east side of the plaza, is the local clinic.

Things to See & Do

On the east side of the plaza stands the restored adobe **Casa Incaica**, ostensibly built in 1540 for Valdivia, but it might be safer to say that Valdivia slept here. Since it's private property, visits are not possible. On the west side stands the **Iglesia San Pedro**, a colonial church built with indigenous or artisanal materials – adobe, wood from the *cardón* cactus (*Cereus atacamensis*) and, in lieu of nails, large leather straps. It dates from the 17th century, though its present walls were built in 1745, and the bell tower was added in 1890.

Museo Gustavo Le Paige

Half a block northeast of the plaza is the must-see Museo Gustavo Le Paige (☎ 851-002; *Gustavo Le Paige; adult/student US$2/1; open 9am-noon & 2pm-6pm Mon-Fri, 10am-noon & 2pm-6pm Sat & Sun*).

The Atacama is nirvana for archeologists because of its nearly rainless environment, which preserves artifacts and other materials for millennia. In 1955, a Belgian priest and archaeologist, Gustavo Le Paige, assisted by the villagers of San Pedro and the Universidad Católica del Norte in Antofagasta, began to organize one of South America's finest museums, offering an overview of this region's cultural evolution through an extraordinary collection of pre-Columbian artifacts. Though primarily an archaeological museum – its explanatory panels on stone tool making are outstanding – it also includes exhibits on the Inka conquest and the Spanish invasion.

Among the traditional displays are Paleo-Indian mummies, including a child buried in a pottery urn, and skulls that show deliberate malformation. Most of the bodies have been replaced with replicas, in conformity with current anthropological practice respecting indigenous burial practices. There are also fragments of ancient weavings, pottery, tools, jewelry and paraphernalia for preparing, ingesting and smoking hallucinogenic plants.

Organized Tours

An exhausting number of tour operators compete for clients to take on half-day to two-day tours of nearby sites. The quality of the tours has become somewhat lax, and travelers complain of operators who cancel abruptly or run unsafe vehicles. Tour leaders are often merely drivers rather than trained guides. Many tour agencies contract out to independent drivers, many of whom work for different companies, so the quality of your driver on any given day is really just the luck of the draw. You may find that the agency to which you paid your money is not the same agency that picks you up. Some agencies offer tours in English, German or Dutch, but these tours may require advance notice or a premium payment. Competition keeps prices down, and operators come and go year to year, but ask yourself whether you can realistically expect a conscientious driver; four-star chef; English-speaking, professional naturalist guide; a luxurious and well-maintained 4WD vehicle *and* a foot massage for only US$20 a day.

That being said, don't unfairly dismiss local, Spanish-speaking drivers – many of them are perfectly courteous and acceptably knowledgeable, and they can provide an insider's viewpoint better than a well-trained outsider.

The Tourist Information Office has a helpful, entertaining and occasionally terrifying book of complaints on various tour agencies; the problem is that nearly every agency is featured at least once, and by the time you read about unlicensed or drunken drivers over the passes to Bolivia, you may decide to do nothing but write postcards from the safety of your hostel, which would be a tragic mistake in such a beautiful area. Nevertheless, when choosing an operator, ask lots of questions, talk to other travelers, trust your judgment, and try to be flexible.

Some of the routinely offered tours are the following (see the Around San Pedro section below for descriptions of the areas):

El Tatio Geysers (US$16-20). Typically leaves San Pedro at 4am in order to see the geysers at sunrise, returning at noon. Includes thermal baths and breakfast. This hugely popular tour features a long line of vans crawling up the mountain; don't expect the geysers to yourself.

Valle de la Luna (US$5-8). Leaves San Pedro around 4:30pm to catch the sunset over the valley, returning at 8:30pm. Includes visits to the Valle de Marte, overlook of the Salar de Atacama, Valle de la Muerte, and Tres Marías.

Altiplano lakes (US$26-36). Leaves San Pedro around 7am to see flamingos at Laguna Chaxa in the Salar de Atacama, town of Socaire, Lagunas Miñiques and Miscanti, Toconao and the Quebrada de Jerez, returning about 5pm.

Geysers and pueblos (US$33-42). Leaves at 4am for the geysers, then visits Caspana, the Pukará de Lasana and Chiu-Chiu, ending up in Calama at 5pm, or returning to San Pedro by 6pm.

Uyuni, Bolivia (see boxed text 'Excursion to Uyuni, Bolivia'). Very popular three-day, 4WD tour of the remote and beautiful *salar* region. It costs US$70, plus an additional US$30 to return on the fourth day, including all meals and basic accommodations.

Cactus Tour (☎ *851-534;* e *cactustour@ hotmail.com; Domingo Atienza 419*), a relatively new addition to the scene, has polite, Spanish-speaking guides, comfortable vehicles (all seats face forward) and good food.

Cosmo Andino (☎/fax *851-069;* e *cosmo andino@entelchile.net; Caracoles s/n*) is Dutch-run and one of the best-established, if most expensive, agencies.

Southern Cross Adventure (☎ *851-416;* w *www.scadventure.com; Caracoles 119*) is recommended and offers the standard tours, plus alluring one- to three-day volcano-climbing trips (about US$50 per day),

trekking, sport climbing, and mountain biking (they carry you up, so the ride is flat or downhill; about US$40).

Others to try include **Atacama Inca Tour** (☎ *851-034; Toconao*), **Azimut 360** (☎ *851-469; Caracoles s/n*) and **Tara Expediciones** (☎ *851-228; Gustavo Le Paige s/n*).

In addition to bus tours, there are mountain bike, horseback and sandboarding tours (see Getting Around, later).

Special Events

In the first days of February, San Pedro celebrates the **Fiesta de Nuestra Señora de la Candelaria** with religious dances. **Carnaval** takes place in February or March, depending on the date of Easter. June 29 marks the local **Fiesta de San Pedro y San Pablo**, celebrated with folkdancing groups, a Mass, a very impressive procession of statues through the streets, a rodeo and modern dancing that can get rowdy by midnight. (The statues, incidentally, are replicas made by local artisans, after the originals were burned by arsonists in February 2000.)

August's **Limpia de Canales** is the resurrection of an old tradition of the cleaning of San Pedro's irrigation canals prior to the upcoming agricultural season. On August 30, the **Fiesta de Santa Rosa de Lima** is a traditional religious festival.

Excursion to Uyuni, Bolivia

An increasing number of tour operators are offering 4WD trips through the remote and beautiful *salar* region east of San Pedro. The three-day trips cross the Bolivian border at Portezuelo del Cajón, go to Laguna Colorada and then continue to the Salar de Uyuni before ending in the town of Uyuni.

The going rate of US$70 includes transportation in crowded 4WD jeeps, very basic accommodations and food; an extra US$30 will get you back to San Pedro on the fourth day (some tour operators drive through the third night). Bring your own water, drinks and snacks. It can get very cold in the mountains, especially in winter, so bring a sleeping bag if you have it. Travelers clear Chilean immigration at San Pedro and Bolivian immigration on arrival at Uyuni. Some operators have had problems with Bolivian authorities at this legally ambiguous border crossing.

Turismo Colque (☎ *055-851-109; Caracoles s/n*) remains the biggest and most popular company with the most departures to Uyuni, although the quality of the trip depends in part on the contracted driver you get. The agency has drawn broth praise and dire warnings from travelers (see the comment book at the tourist-information office for horror stories). They accept credit cards. Other operators offering similar trips include **Tour Operador Internacional** (☎ *055-851-285; Gustavo Le Paige & Calama*), **Cordillera Traveller** (☎ *055-851-111;* e *ctraveler@123mail.cl; Tocopilla s/n*), **Pamela Tours** (☎ *09-676-6841; Toconao 522*), and **Licancábur Tours** (☎ *851-081; Calama 402*).

NORTE GRANDE

Places to Stay

Budget accommodations can be scarce, especially in the summer and around holiday periods. Most budget places will request that solo travelers share a room, and few include breakfast in the price. Consider whether it's wise to share rooms when half the group is leaving at 4am for a geyser tour.

Budget About 1.5km from the plaza, **Camping Buenas Peras** (*Ckilapana 688; sites per person US$2.50*) offers sites in the pear orchard; bathrooms are available, but no kitchen.

Camping Los Perales (☎ *851-114; Tocopilla 481; sites per person US$5*) is large, friendly and cheap, and has a place to wash clothes.

Camping Edén (☎ *851-154; Toconao 592; sites per person US$3.50*) has a large, dusty camping area with dirty shared bathrooms.

Camping Oasis Alberto Terrazas (☎ *851-042; sites per person US$4*) is 3km east of San Pedro, and rates include access to pools (which may not be filled off-season).

Hostal/Camping Takha Takha (☎ *851-038; Caracoles 101-B; sites per person US$6, singles with shared bath US$11, singles/doubles with private bath start at US$32/42*) has plain but comfortable rooms set among pleasant gardens shared with campers.

Hotel Licancábur (☎ *851-007; Toconao s/n; rooms with shared/private bath US$10/20*) enjoys a friendly family atmosphere with a laundry area, a restaurant and Internet service.

Residencial Rayco (☎ *851-008; Gustavo Le Paige 202; per person US$7, doubles with shared/private bath US$17/34*) is rustic and has a peaceful interior patio, but it sometimes lacks hot water, and some of the bathroom locks are broken.

Residencial Chiloé (☎ *851-017; Domingo Atienza s/n; per person US$8*) is cheap and clean but unimpressive.

Hostal Sonchek (☎ *851-112;* e *soncheksp @hotmail.com; Calama 370; dorm beds US$9*), run by Slovenian immigrants, is artsy, cool and always full, if a bit abrasive to some. Guests can use the kitchen.

Hostal Katarpe (☎/fax *851-033;* e *katarpe@galeon.com; Domingo Atienza 441; doubles with shared/private bath US$20/42*) has clean and comfortable rooms, a relaxing courtyard and solar-powered lights.

Mid-Range Five minutes south of the plaza, **Hostal Quinta Adela** (☎ *851-272; Toconao 624; doubles start at US$33*) moves at a slow pace. The hostel is on a family orchard, with large rooms in an old hacienda building in need of some maintenance.

Hostal Nuevo Porvenir (☎/fax *851-076; Toconao 441-C; singles/doubles US33/42*), half a block south of the plaza, is clean and agreeable, although the outside décor isn't much to look at.

Hotel Tambillo (☎ *851-078; Gustavo Le Paige s/n; singles/doubles US$38/50*) has pseudomodern clean rooms facing an inner breezeway, a pleasant and shady courtyard, and solar lights.

Top End A nice place away from town, **Hotel La Aldea** (☎ *851-149;* e *reservas@ hotelaldea.cl; Ckilapana 69 B; singles/doubles US$61/81*) has cool adobe cabins in tranquil surroundings. Amenities include a large swimming pool, restaurant, bar, bicycle rental and Internet access.

Hotel Kimal (☎ *851-152;* e *kimal@entel chile.net; Domingo Atienza 452; singles/doubles US$62/85*) sports large, comfortable rooms with sensible portable fans. Rates include continental breakfast. It's attractively landscaped.

Hotel Terrantai (☎ *851-045;* e *info@ terrantai.com; Tocopilla 411; singles/doubles US$100/112*) has large, bright rooms with ceiling fans and telephones, a tiny but refreshing pool and a pleasant courtyard. The hotel only offers packages of two or more nights and caters mostly to groups.

Places to Eat

A word of warning: While San Pedro restaurants do offer welcomed variety, especially for vegetarians, the prices don't necessarily reflect quality.

Quitor (☎ *851-190; Licancábur & Domingo Atienza; meals about US$4*), one of the few places where local residents outnumber gringos, prepares simple and cheap but nourishing meals.

Restaurant Juanita (*Plaza de Armas; lunch US$3, dinner US$4*) has similar, traditional meals (excellent soup).

Café Sonchek (*Calama s/n; breakfast US$2-3, set menú US$4.50, main dishes US$3; closed Sun*), at Hostal Sonchek, draws high praise for veggie meals and great breakfasts.

NORTE GRANDE

Todo Natural *(Caracoles s/n; breakfast US$3-4, empanadas US$2, pizza US$3)* is a tiny place where you can watch the owner make large and tasty empanadas, refreshing fruit juices, and a good selection of vegetarian and breakfast options.

Petro Pizza *(☎ 851-373; Toconao 446; pizzas US$2-3)* serves up fine wood-fired pizzas.

Café Export *(Toconao & Caracoles; dishes US$5, including a drink)* serves up strong coffee drinks, homemade pasta and decent pizzas in a cool subterranean atmosphere with loud music.

La Estaka *(☎ 851-038; Caracoles s/n; dishes US$6-7)* has a range of excellent food. Steak, crepes and good vegetarian options are served in a funky, cavelike atmosphere with a fireplace. The touts are a turnoff, though.

El Adobe *(☎ 851-089; Caracoles s/n; breakfast US$4, lunch & dinner US$6-8)* gets more points for style than for food, though it's always popular with travelers. Also featured are an Internet café, one of the few places that serves breakfast *before* 9am, a cozy but polluting fire in the middle of the outside dining room, and an especially obnoxious brand of street hustling.

Casa Piedra *(☎ 851-271; Caracoles 225; set menú US$6, main dishes US$6-10)*, popular with tour groups, offers enjoyable pasta dishes and Chilean specialties, although it's more expensive than others.

Entertainment
Establishments that sell only alcohol were outlawed a couple of years ago, and local police started cracking down on public drinking.

Locals head to Calama for the disco scene. Currently, there are no places to catch live music. Nevertheless, travelers congregate in many of the restaurant bars at night. Especially popular are El Adobe with its open fire, La Estaka with its happy hour, and Café Export, with intimate tables and loud music (the back is quieter).

Shopping
The **Paseo Artesanal**, a shaded alley running north from the plaza, is a good place to look for *cardón* (cactus-wood) carvings, llama and alpaca woolens, and other souvenirs, but much of the stuff is imported from

Bolivia. Other artisanal outlets are scattered throughout town.

Getting There & Away
Buses Atacama 2000 *(Licancábur & Paseo Artesanal)* has daily buses to Calama (US$2), Toconao (US$1) and Peine (US$2.25). **Buses Frontera** *(☎ 851-117; Licancábur)* serves the same destinations, plus Socaire.

Tur Bus *(☎ 851-549; Licancábur 11)* has daily buses to Calama and from there onward to Arica and Antofagasta (US$7). **Flota Barrios** *(Calama 402)*, in the same office as Licancábur Tours, has one bus per day to Calama.

Géminis *(Toconao s/n)* serves Salta and Jujuy, Argentina, at 11pm on Wednesday, Friday and Sunday (US$33; 12 hours).

Getting Around
Mountain bikes are a good way to get around San Pedro and vicinity. Be sure to carry water and sunblock.

Vulcano *(☎ 851-373; Caracoles 329)* rents Trek bikes (US$5/9 per half/full day) and sandboards.

Rental horses are available at **La Marca** *(☎ 09-470-7248; Domingo Atienza 560; US$5/hr)*. There's a minimum of four to six people for trips with a guide; the recommended tour to Valle de la Muerte takes four to five hours.

AROUND SAN PEDRO DE ATACAMA
Most of San Pedro's attractions are more than walking distance from town, and public transportation is limited. Options include renting a car (in Calama), renting a bike or taking a tour. Luckily, heavy competition among numerous operators keeps tours reasonably priced. See Organized Tours in the San Pedro de Atacama section for specific tours and operators.

Pukará de Quitor & Catarpe
Just 3km northwest of San Pedro, on a promontory overlooking the Río San Pedro, are the ruins of a 12th-century Indian *pukará*. From the top of the fortifications, part of the last bastion against Pedro de Valdivia and the Spanish, you can see the entire oasis. Archaeologists have reconstructed portions of its ruined walls. Three kilometers farther north, on the east side of the

NORTE GRANDE

river, are the ruins of Catarpe, a former Inka administrative center.

Termas de Puritama

These volcanic hot springs (admission US$10), in a box canyon about 30km north of San Pedro en route to El Tatio, are maintained by the Explora company. Tours rarely stop here because of the hefty admission charged. Should you decide Puritama is worth the price, it's a 20-minute walk from the junction (where there's an ample parking lot) along an obvious gravel track. The temperature of the springs is about 33°C, and there are several falls and pools. Bring food and water.

RN LOS FLAMENCOS

Reserva Nacional Los Flamencos consists of seven geographically distinct sectors, totaling about 74,000 hectares, mostly to the south and east of San Pedro de Atacama. Its varied environments range from the Valle de la Luna and the Salar de Atacama (where Laguna Chaxa is home to breeding colonies of three species of flamingos) to high-altitude salt lakes toward the Argentine border. As the highway to Argentina improves in the coming years, this latter area is likely to become more easily accessible.

Conaf maintains a **Centro de Información Ambiental** (open 10am-1pm & 2:30pm-4:30pm daily) at the ayllu (hamlet) of Solcor, about 2km past San Pedro de Atacama's customs and immigration post on the road to Toconao. There's another Conaf office on the southern outskirts of Toconao, and a ranger station at Laguna Chaxa.

Valle de la Luna

Latin Americans call every place where flood and wind have left oddly shaped polychrome desert landforms the 'Valley of the Moon' – there are others in Bolivia and Argentina. This one, 15km west of San Pedro de Atacama and part of Reserva Nacional Los Flamencos, definitely deserves a visit. At the northern end of the Cordillera de la Sal, it's one of San Pedro's most popular attractions and cheapest organized tour options.

Tours from San Pedro typically leave about 4:30pm and include a sunset view over the colorful valley. This involves a long slog up a sand dune, rewarded with views of the amazing, multicolored geology. If you want to avoid loads of tourist vans, all taking the same route and making the same stops, pick an alternative time.

Mountain biking is an excellent exploration option (see the San Pedro section for bicycle-rental details), but keep to the roads and trails. If driving, you can leave the highway to explore the dirt roads and box canyons to the north; take care not to get stuck in the sand. Park only on the shoulder or at other designated areas – do not tear up the fragile desert with tire tracks.

Note that camping is not permitted in this part of Los Flamencos.

Laguna Chaxa

In the midst of the Salar de Atacama, about 25km southwest of the village of Toconao, 65km from San Pedro, Laguna Chaxa (adult/child US$3/1) is the reserve's most easily accessible flamingo breeding site. Besides the operator's tour fees, rangers collect an admission charge. Three of the five known species of flamingos can be seen here. Sunrise is feeding time for the birds and is best time to see them.

Laguna Miñiques

From a junction 3km south of Toconao, Ruta 23 heads 46km south toward the village of Socaire (which features an attractive colonial church with a roof made of cactus wood, and a remarkable density of Inkan terraces on relatively gentle slopes), then climbs another 18km to an eastbound turnoff leading to Laguna Miñiques and the smaller Laguna Miscanti, a high-Andean flamingo breeding site. This area is a good place for a picnic. Rejoining Ruta 23 about 15km south of the turnoff, the road heads eastward past several other impressive salt lakes, most notably Laguna Tuyajto, and continues to the Argentine border at 4079m Paso de Lago Sico. Many high-country tours take this route. Socaire is 100km from San Pedro, and the lagunas are 120km distant.

EL TATIO GEYSERS

At 4300m above sea level, the world's highest geyser field is less dramatic than the intermittent explosions of Yellowstone, but the visual impact of its steaming fumaroles at sunrise in the azure clarity of the altiplano is unforgettable, and the individual structures formed when the boiling water evaporates and leaves behind dissolved minerals are strikingly beautiful. The geysers are 95km north of San Pedro de Atacama. Entrance is free.

Early morning, about 6am, is the best time to see the geysers, and every tour agency in San Pedro will have several vans departing at 4am to deliver hundreds of tourists at the appointed hour. After about 8:30am, morning winds disperse the steam, although most tours leave by that hour and you can enjoy the large thermal pool in virtual privacy. Watch your step – in some places, visitors have fallen through the thin crust into underlying pools of scalding water and suffered severe burns. Dress in layers – it's freezing cold at sunbreak, but you'll bake in the van on the way back down.

Places to Stay

Corfo, the state development agency, has a free **refugio** about 2km before the geysers – very run-down, but better than being outside. It's also possible to **camp**, but heavy frosts are nightly events at this elevation. Campers should bring plenty of food and water, since nothing is available on site.

Getting There & Away

Tours from San Pedro (see Around San Pedro de Atacama, earlier in the chapter) include breakfast, often with fresh eggs boiled in geyser pools.

If driving, leave San Pedro no later than 4am to reach the geysers by sunrise. The route north from San Pedro is signed, but some drivers prefer to follow tour agencies' jeeps and minibuses in the dark (tour drivers do not appreciate this, however). Do not attempt this road – which is very rough in spots and has some difficult stream fords – without a high-clearance pickup or jeep, preferably one with 4WD.

If you have rented a vehicle in Calama, it's possible to return via the picturesque villages of Caspana, Toconce, Ayquina and Chiu Chiu (see the Upper Loa & Its Tributaries, next) rather than via San Pedro, on much improved roads. Some tours from Calama and San Pedro take this route as well.

The Upper Loa & Its Tributaries

North of San Pedro de Atacama and east of Calama, a string of typically Andean villages and archaeological monuments dot the landscape of the upper Río Loa and its eastern tributaries. A few tour operators from San Pedro visit these villages after the early morning spectacle of watching El Tatio Geysers; tours departing from Calama also visit this area. Visitors should be aware that the drinking water of Chiu Chiu and Caspana is contaminated with arsenic. Although this danger may be alleviated by a new treatment plant, at present it's better to stick to bottled water.

From the geysers, it's 46km along some switchbacks to **Caspana**, a real gem. Nestled in its namesake valley, it's exactly what an Andean village is supposed to look like – verdant terraces, thatched roofs, the colonial **Iglesia de San Lucas** and a **museum** (admission US$1), organized by Maltese anthropologist George Serracino, that would be the pride of many larger communities.

Heading north you'll come to **Ayquina**, an agricultural village in the Río Caspana Valley, best known for the **Museo Votivo de Ayquina** (open 9am-1pm & 2pm-5:30pm Tues-Sun), which emphasizes religious artifacts and folkloric dance groups. A few kilometers north of here is the **Vegas de Turi**, a thermal spring whose flow, unfortunately, is declining because of water extraction for mining and use by inhabitants of Calama. Toward the east is **Toconce**, known for a church and extensive agricultural terraces.

Heading west toward Calama along the upper of two gravel roads, you'll come to the reconstructed **Pukará de Lasana** (entrance US$1), an extensive fortress originally dating from the 12th century. Closest to Calama is **Chiu Chiu**, 33km away via paved Ruta 21. Chiu Chiu boasts the **Iglesia de San Francisco** (a national monument) and the modest **Hotel Tujina** (☎ 326-386; Esmeralda s/n). Try **Restaurant Muley** (3-course lunch US$3.50) for local food.

Several companies in San Pedro de Atacama and Calama offer organized tours to this area.

TOCONAO

Known for finely hewn volcanic stone houses and an intricate irrigation system, the village of Toconao is about 40km south of San Pedro. Its **Iglesia de San Lucas**, with a separate bell tower, dates from the mid-18th century.

Toconao farmers produce almonds, grapes, pomegranates, apples and herbs. Most of their orchards and fields are near the

Quebrada de Jerez *(admission US$1)*, a delightful place for a walk or a wade in the stream (the name translates as 'stream of sherry wine.' Its water is of such high quality that, in the early 20th century, affluent families from San Pedro sent peons with mules to Toconao to fetch casks of drinking water. This oasis is full of the white-trunked *higera* trees, as well as *membrillo* (quince), pear, and plum trees (which you're not allowed to eat).

In the village proper, local women sell fine llama wool products, including ponchos, pullovers, gloves and socks, as well as souvenirs cut from local stone.

Toconao has several inexpensive residenciales and restaurants near the plaza. **Residencial y Restaurant Valle de Toconao** *(Calle Lascar)* is a few blocks from the plaza.

Buses Frontera and Buses Atacama 2000 have bus service daily to and from San Pedro.

MEJILLONES
☎ 55 • pop 8400

This small port town, 60km north of Antofagasta, used to be a key Bolivian port. Mejillones first thrived off guano and then nitrate, but for decades, it's been a weekend beach resort for Antofagasta residents. Construction of a huge thermoelectric plant and a new megaport project seem to be putting the town back on the economic map – perhaps at the cost of its relative tranquillity.

Mejillones' main drag is the beachfront Av San Martín. Its historic landmarks are mostly relics of Bolivian sovereignty and the nitrate era. The oldest is the U-shaped 1866 **Aduana** *(customhouse; Francisco Antonio Pinto 110)*, which now holds the **Museo de Mejillones** *(☎ 621-289; adult/child US$0.50/free; open 10:30am-2pm & 5pm-9pm Tues-Sun Dec-Feb, 10:30am-2pm & 5pm-7:30pm Mar-Nov)*.

At the foot of Av Manuel Rodríguez, overlooking the Plaza Fuerza Aérea, the 1876 **Capitanía del Puerto** *(port authority)* is a French-style building with a lighthouse tower. The **Iglesia Corazón de María** *(Latorre & Almirante Castillo)* is a striking wooden building that dates from 1906.

Bus companies and taxi colectivos serve Mejillones from Antofagasta.

ANTOFAGASTA
☎ 55 • pop 298,000

Chile's second-largest city is considered by many travelers to be too chaotic and more trouble than it's worth. Indeed, most travelers heading to San Pedro de Atacama, Iquique or Arica can rest up in Calama instead. Although Antofagasta does have a few pleasant places, this is a working town, short on tourist attractions.

The port of Antofagasta handles most of the minerals from the Atacama, especially the copper from Chuquicamata, and is still a major import-export node for Bolivia, which lost the region to Chile during the War of the Pacific. The city's distinctive architecture, resembling Iquique's, dates from the nitrate era.

Like the rest of the coastal Norte Grande, Antofagasta rarely receives rainfall, but infrequent meteorological events can be catastrophic. In general, though, the city has an ideal climate, clear and dry, neither too hot nor too cold at any time of year.

History

Founded in 1870, the city earned its importance by offering the easiest route to the nitrate mines of the interior. By 1877, the railroad reached halfway to Calama, but it was not completed as far as Oruro until after the War of the Pacific, when Chile acquired the territory.

After the war, Antofagasta exported tin and silver from Bolivia, borax from the Salar de Ascotán, and nitrates from the pampas. After the turn of the century, when Antofagasta's port proved to be inadequate for the expanded nitrate trade, the nearby harbor of Mejillones took up much of the slack. Later, however, infrastructural improvements restored Antofagasta's preeminence, and it came to handle the highest tonnage of any South American Pacific port.

Orientation

Like Iquique, Antofagasta sits on a terrace at the foot of the coastal range, some 1350km north of Santiago and 700km south of Arica. The north-south Panamericana passes inland, about 15km east of the city, but there are paved northern and southern access roads.

Downtown's western boundary is north-south Av Balmaceda, immediately east of the modern port; Balmaceda veers northeast at Uribe and eventually becomes Aníbal Pinto; to the south, it becomes Av Grecia. Streets run southwest to northeast in this central grid, bounded also by Bolívar and JS Ossa. Refurbished Plaza Colón, bounded by Sucre,

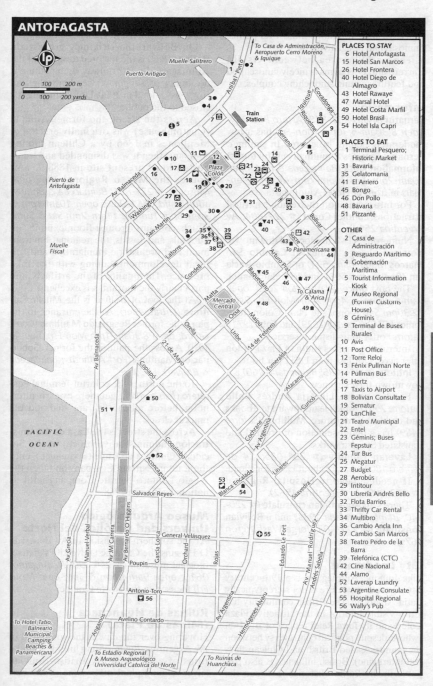

ANTOFAGASTA

PLACES TO STAY
6 Hotel Antofagasta
15 Hotel San Marcos
26 Hotel Frontera
40 Hotel Diego de
   Almagro
43 Hotel Rawaye
47 Marsal Hotel
49 Hotel Costa Marfil
50 Hotel Brasil
54 Hotel Isla Capri

PLACES TO EAT
1 Terminal Pesquero;
   Historic Market
31 Bavaria
35 Gelatomania
41 El Arriero
45 Bongo
46 Don Pollo
48 Bavaria
51 Pizzanté

OTHER
2 Casa de
   Administración
3 Resguardo Marítimo
4 Gobernación
   Marítima
5 Tourist Information
   Kiosk
7 Museo Regional
   (Former Customs
   House)
8 Géminis
9 Terminal de Buses
   Rurales
10 Avis
11 Post Office
12 Torre Reloj
13 Fénix Pullman Norte
14 Pullman Bus
16 Hertz
17 Taxis to Airport
18 Bolivian Consulate
19 Sernatur
20 LanChile
21 Teatro Municipal
22 Entel
23 Géminis; Buses
   Fepstur
24 Tur Bus
25 Megatur
27 Budget
28 Aerobús
29 Intitour
30 Librería Andrés Bello
32 Flota Barrios
33 Thrifty Car Rental
34 Multibro
36 Cambio Ancla Inn
37 Cambio San Marcos
38 Teatro Pedro de la
   Barra
39 Telefónica (CTC)
42 Cine Nacional
44 Alamo
52 Laverap Laundry
53 Argentine Consulate
55 Hospital Regional
56 Wally's Pub

Washington, San Martín and Arturo Prat, sports rushing fountains amidst its palms, mimosas and bougainvilleas.

The parklike area between Avs JM Carrera and O'Higgins is nicely landscaped and features young smooching couples.

Information

Sernatur *(☎/fax 451-818; Arturo Prat 384; open 8:30am-5:30pm Mon-Fri)* has a few moderately helpful brochures. In summer, Sernatur operates a minimally useful **tourist information kiosk** *(Balmaceda & Prat; open 10am-2pm & 3:30pm-7pm Mon-Fri Jan-Mar)* in front of Hotel Antofagasta.

For information on the region's natural attractions, contact **Conaf** *(☎ 227-804; Av Argentina 2510)*.

Numerous ATMs are located downtown. You can change money at **Cambio San Marcos** *(Baquedano 524)* or **Cambio Ancla Inn** *(Baquedano 508)*, inside Gelatomania.

The **post office** *(Washington 2623; open 9am-1:30pm & 4pm-7pm Mon-Fri, 9am-12:30pm Sat)* is opposite Plaza Colón. **Telefónica (CTC)** *(Condell 2529)* and **Entel** *(2713 Latorre)* offer long-distance services.

Internet businesses south of Plaza Colón offer access for less than US$1 per hour.

Intitour *(☎ 266-185; Baquedano 460)* is a downtown travel agency.

For books, try **Librería Andrés Bello** *(Latorre 2551)*, which leans toward textbooks and children's literature. **Multibro** *(Latorre 2489)* has a better selection of original and translated Spanish works.

Laverap Laundry *(☎ 251-085; 14 de Febrero 1802)* charges about US$6 for a load.

If needed, head to **Hospital Regional** *(☎ 269-009; Av Argentina 1962)*.

There's an **Argentinian consulate** *(☎ 220-440; Blanco Encalada 1933)* and a **Bolivian consulate** *(☎ 221-403; Jorge Washington 2675)*.

City Landmarks

Like Iquique, Antofagasta is a 19th-century city whose architecture is not stereotypically Latin American. The British community has left a visible imprint in the attractive **Plaza Colón** and its **Torre Reloj** replica of Big Ben (where, despite political controversy between the countries, tiled British and Chilean flags still intertwine). British influence is also palpable in the **Barrio Histórico**, between the

plaza and the old port, which features many wooden Victorian and Georgian buildings.

On Bolívar, the strikingly green **train station** (1887) is the restored terminus of the Antofagasta-La Paz railway, though there is no longer passenger service here; the 2nd story was added in 1900. Unfortunately, it's closed to the public.

Across the street, the former Aduana (Customhouse) was originally erected in Mejillones in 1866 by a Chilean mining company; then it was dismantled and transported to its present site in 1888. It now houses the **Museo Regional** *(Regional Museum; ☎ 221-836; Balmaceda & Bolívar; adult/child US$1/0.50; open 10am-1pm & 3pm-6pm Tue-Fri, 11am-2pm Sat & Sun)*, which contains ground-floor exhibits on minerals and fossils, the regional environment and prehistoric immigration and cultural development, ending with the Inka presence. The quality of the artifacts, and particularly the dioramas, is excellent.

At the foot of Bolívar is the **Muelle Salitrero** *(Nitrate Pier)*. At the entrance to the pier is the former **Resguardo Marítimo** *(Coast Guard; open 8:30am-1pm Mon-Fri)*, built in 1910. Across the patio is the former **Gobernación Marítima** *(Port Authority; Balmaceda & Bolívar)*.

To the north is the colorful **Terminal Pesquero** *(fish market)*; get there by early afternoon, before all the fish are sold and the market closes.

Across the street is the **Casa de Administración** (administrative office) of the Sociedad Química de Chile (Soquimich), once the Lautaro Nitrate Company and then the Anglo Lautaro Nitrate Company until its nationalization in 1968.

Museo Arqueológico Universidad Católica del Norte

At the southern extension of Av Bernardo O'Higgins, the Catholic University's archaeological museum *(☎ 255-090; Av Angamos 0610; open 9am-noon & 3pm-6pm Mon-Fri)* focuses on the Norte Grande.

Ruinas de Huanchaca (Minas de Plata)

Hovering over the city, at the south end of Av Argentina, the imposing hillside foundations of a 19th-century British-Bolivian silver-refining plant offer some of the best

Dramatic desertscape at Valle de la Luna, near San Pedro de Atacama

Parading through the streets in Antofagasta

Plunging headfirst into soccer

One of the most popular spots in Norte Grande: Monumento Natural La Portada

DAVID RYAN

Geoglyphs, an Indian art form, on the hills along the Panamericana

DAVID RYAN

Colorful scene in an Antofagasta harbor

TOM COCKREM

El Tatio geysers letting off steam in the Atacama Desert

panoramas of the city. From downtown, take colectivo No 3 and ask for Minas de Plata.

Special Events
February 14, the anniversary of the founding of the city, is a major local holiday. There are fireworks at the Balneario Municipal at the south end of Av Grecia.

Places to Stay
Budget About 6km south of town on the coast road is **Camping Las Garumas** (☎ 247-763; Anexo 42; camp sites for up to 4 people US$8).

Camping Rucamóvil (☎ 223-929; Km 11; site per person US$4), also south of town, is another option.

Hotel Rawaye (☎ 225-399; Sucre 762; singles/doubles US$7/10) is decent and cheap. Rooms have shared bath.

Hotel Isla Capri (☎ 263-703; Copiapó 1208; singles/doubles with shared bath US$8/16, with private bath US$12/24), near the university, is a good value, with immaculate rooms and breakfast included in the rates.

Hotel Brasil (☎ 267-268; JS Ossa 1978; singles/doubles with shared bath US$9/13, doubles with private bath US$20) is a good value, with clean, spacious rooms. The upstairs rooms are older and cheaper but still good.

Hotel Frontera (☎ 281-219; Bolívar 558; singles/doubles with shared bath US$11/16, doubles with private bath US$21) is popular, central and has a few cheaper rooms with shared bath, but most come with private bath. Breakfast costs US$2 extra.

Mid-Range The **Hotel Costa Marfil** (☎ 225-569; Arturo Prat 950; singles/doubles from US$21/28) has small rooms but decent beds.

Hotel San Marcos (☎ 251-763; Latorre 2946; singles/doubles with private bath US$24/34) is boxy and bleak but tidy and quiet. The hotel has a restaurant, and breakfast is included.

Marsal Hotel (☎ 268-063; Arturo Prat 867; singles/doubles US$36/43) has nice, modern rooms with cable TV, portable fans, breakfast and unimpressive views of the parking lot.

Hotel Diego de Almagro (☎ 268-331; Condell 2624; singles/doubles US$38/53) is centrally located and well kept but not very friendly. Rooms are large and comfortable. Rates include breakfast.

Top End South of downtown, **Hotel Tatio** (☎ 419-111; Av Grecia 1000; singles/doubles US$48/57) has comfortable, bright rooms. Some rooms have views of the sea, but these also get traffic noise from Av Grecia.

Hotel Antofagasta (☎ 228-811; Balmaceda 2575; singles/doubles start at US$80/105), on the waterfront, is a grand hotel acknowledged as the city's best. It's the largest in town and has a pool. Larger rooms with a view of the city are available for singles/doubles US$126/154, and with a view of the sea for US$145/170. Room rates include a buffet breakfast.

Places to Eat
At the unpretentious **Terminal Pesquero**, at the north end of the old port, a collection of inexpensive stands peddle tasty fresh shellfish. It's especially lively on Saturday mornings, but even if you find raw sea urchins unpalatable, the pelicans that crowd the pier for scraps are always amusing. Similar fare is available at the **Mercado Central** (JS Ossa), between Maipú and Uribe.

Don Pollo (☎ 263-361; JS Ossa 2594; chicken US$2.50) is inexpensive and always crowded. It specializes in grilled chicken and has outdoor seating.

Bongo (☎ 263-697; Baquedano 743; fixed menú US$2.50) is suitable for sandwiches and draft beer.

Pizzanté (☎ 223-344; Av JM Carrera 1857; pizza US$4-7, sandwiches US$2.50-5), is Antofagasta's best pizzería, with large portions, reasonable prices, good service, a large nonsmoking section and pleasant ambience. Pizzas are eccentrically decorated with oddities such as corn, asparagus and string beans, which don't quite live up to the promise of the concept (the veggies are canned). There is also a wide array of appealing sandwiches, including a good vegetarian selection, and desserts.

Bavaria (☎ 259-373; Latorre 2618 • ☎ 266-567; JS Ossa 2424; fixed menú US$5, main dishes US$5-7) is part of a reliable but uninspired chain.

El Arriero (☎ 264-371; Condell 2644; fixed menú US$5, main dishes US$6-10) is a fine parrilla. Carnivores will find large portions, attentive service, classic décor and (less appealingly) crashing piano duets.

Gelatomania (Baquedano & Latorre) has more than three dozen flavors of ice creams, tasty cakes and less tasteful music.

NORTE GRANDE

Entertainment

For theater and other performing arts, check **Teatro Pedro de la Barra** (☎ 263-400; Condell 2495) or the **Teatro Municipal** (☎ 264-919; Sucre 433).

Wally's Pub (☎ 223-697; Antonino Toro 982; open from 6pm Mon-Sat) is a British-style pub with outside seating; it also serves meals.

Cine Nacional (☎ 269-166; Sucre 735) shows recent films.

Shopping

There's a good informal market for historical items like banknotes, coins, fichas from nitrate oficinas and other odds and ends at the foot of the Terminal Pesquero, on the west side of Aníbal Pinto, north of downtown.

Getting There & Away

Air Tickets can be purchased at **LanChile** (☎/fax 265-151; Arturo Prat 445), with seven to 12 daily flights to Santiago (US$60-90 one way, two hours), as well as direct daily flights to Iquique (US$25, 45 minutes), Calama (US$20, 35 minutes), Copiapó (US$30, one hour) and La Serena (US$60, 1½ hours).

Bus Most bus companies operate out of their own terminals near downtown. A few long-distance and most locally based companies use the **Terminal de Buses Rurales** (Riquelme 513).

Nearly all northbound services now use coastal Ruta 1, via Tocopilla, en route to Iquique and Arica. Companies that ply the north-south routes include **Fénix Pullman Norte** (☎ 268-896; San Martín 2717), **Flota Barrios** (☎ 268-559; Condell 2764), **Géminis** (☎ 263-968, Latorre 3055 • ☎ 497-404, Latorre 2715), **Buses Pullman Santa Rosa** (☎ 282-763; Terminal de Buses Rurales), **Pullman Bus** (☎ 268-838; Latorre 2805) and **Tur Bus** (☎ 264-487; Latorre 2751).

Typical rates are the following:

destination	duration in hours	cost
Arica	11	US$12
Calama	3	US$4
Copiapó	7	US$12
Iquique	6	US$10
La Serena	12	US$18
Santiago	19	US$23
Tocopilla	3	US$5

Megatur (☎ 452-292; Latorre) has taxi colectivos to Mejillones every half hour (US$1.75, one hour). **Buses Fepstur** (☎ 251-176; Latorre 2715 • Terminal de Buses Rurales) and **Buses Biaggini** (☎ 623-451; Terminal de Buses Rurales) provide slightly cheaper bus service (US$1.25) to Mejillones.

Géminis (mentioned earlier) goes to Salta & Jujuy, Argentina on Wednesday and Sunday at 7:30am (US$36; 14 hours).

Getting Around

To/From the Airport Antofagasta's Aeropuerto Cerro Moreno is 25km north of the city, at the south end of Península Mejillones. From the Terminal Pesquero, local bus No 15 goes to the airport for US$0.50, but only every two hours or so from 7:30am to 10:30pm.

Shared taxis leave from the stand on Washington half a block from Plaza Colón for US$3 per person, but **Aerobús** (☎ 262-727; Baquedano 328) provides door-to-door service for US$6.

Car Rentals are available from **Avis** (☎/fax 221-073; Av Balmaceda 2556), **Hertz** (☎ 269-043; Av Balmaceda 2492), **Budget** (☎ 452-132; Baquedano 300), Thrifty Car Rental (☎ 225-777; Bolívar 623) and **Alamo** (☎ 261-864; Av Argentina 2779).

AROUND ANTOFAGASTA

A rather desolate area, the Antofagasta area has little to offer except small, forgotten seaside port towns and eerie ghost towns that line both sides of the Baquedano-Calama Road and the Panamericana north of the Tocopilla-Chuquicamata highway, all easily appreciated from inside a speeding, air-conditioned bus.

RN La Chimba

In the coastal range, 15km northeast of Antofagasta, 2583-hectare Reserva Nacional La Chimba consists of several tributary canyons, moistened by the *camanchaca* fog. This supports a surprisingly varied flora and fauna, the latter including foxes, guanacos, reptiles and many bird species.

Unfortunately, sprawling Antofagasta is encroaching on the reserve, which is presently closed to public access. For the latest information, however, contact the Conaf office in Antofagasta (see that section, earlier).

NORTE GRANDE

Monumento Natural La Portada

Probably the most photographed sight on the Norte Grande coastline, 31-hectare La Portada's centerpiece is an offshore stack of marine sediments, which have been eroded into a natural arch by the stormy Pacific, upon a volcanic base. About 25km north of Antofagasta, on a short westbound lateral off the highway south of Aeropuerto Cerro Moreno, it's a pleasant spot for a relaxing beach afternoon. Take micro No 15 from Antofagasta's Terminal Pesquero to the junction at La Portada, then walk 3km to the arch. If driving, leave belongings in the trunk and lock your car; break-ins have occurred at the lot.

Juan López & Bolsico

At the south end of Península Mejillones, just north of La Portada, a paved road leads west to the beach villages of Juan López (take the left fork at Km 11) and Bolsico (take the right fork gravel road). The latter route passes offshore Isla Santa María, a site with several impressive ocean blowholes.

Check with Sernatur in Antofagasta for information on taxi colectivos to Juan López (about US$2).

SOUTH OF ANTOFAGASTA

The Panamericana south of Antofagasta continues its trip through the dry Atacama Desert, where water, people – and tourist attractions – are scarce.

Mano del Desierto

About 45km south of the junction of the Panamericana and Ruta 28 (the lateral to Antofagasta), an eerie hand rises out of the pampa. This *mano del desierto* was built in 1992 by Antofagasta sculptor Mario Irrarrázaval. Bus travelers should look to the west side of the highway.

Observatorio Cerro Paranal

Just south of the Mano del Desierto, an ill-marked lateral leaves the Panamericana to follow a steep, dusty mountain road southwest to a wild desert coast comparable to the route between Tocopilla and Iquique. The latter route hits the coast at Caleta El Cobre and eventually ends up at the former nitrate port of Taltal, but the alternative inland route leads past 2664m Cerro Paranal, a major new astronomical facility of the European Space

Organization (ESO), about 120km south of Antofagasta.

The observatory has a Very Large Telescope (VLT) consisting of an array for four 8m telescopes. Free visits are allowed the last two weekends of every month, except in December, beginning at 2pm and ending at 4pm. You'll need to schedule months in advance, and you'll also need your own vehicle to get there. Check the observatory's website or the Antofagasta office (☎ 260-032, fax 260-081; W www.eso.org/paranal; Balmaceda 2536, Oficina 504) for updates.

From Paranal, it's possible to continue to **Taltal**, another 120km south, on a good dirt road before descending the Quebrada de Despoblado to the coastal fish camp of **Paposo**.

RN Paposo

About 30km north of Taltal, the coastal range reaches well over 2000m in places, dropping abruptly to the coast, where deep canyons such as **Quebrada El Médano** contain rock-art sites between 500 and 1000 years old, and the *camanchaca* supports a surprisingly varied flora. Access to this 13,000-hectare reserve, which is surrounded by a 30,000-hectare private buffer zone, is still difficult, but it may become easier as the highway improves and as Conaf provides more information and assistance. Ask for details in Antofagasta before making the trip here.

Taltal

☎ 55 • pop 11,000

About 300km south of Antofagasta and 115km north of Chañaral (see the Norte Chico chapter, next), the Panamericana veers inland but passes near Taltal, a simple fishing port and modest beach town with a decaying cluster of period architecture from its nitrate export heyday (when its population was 20,000). The population shrank as the *oficinas* closed (between 1940 and 1960).

From an intersection on the Panamericana, a paved lateral heads northwest to Taltal. The main commercial street of Arturo Prat leads to the central Plaza Arturo Prat. Most of the town's historic monuments are east of O'Higgins.

During the nitrate era, this was the headquarters of the **Taltal Railway Company**, whose restored narrow-gauge **Locomotora No 59** (locomotive) sits on the east side of O'Higgins, between Esmeralda and Prat. The

NORTE GRANDE

rusting crane on the **Muelle Salitrero** (nitrate pier) dates from 1903. Pick your way carefully out onto the pier, watching your step to avoid falling through the huge gaps into the sea. Taltalinos come here to fish at sunset.

Downtown monuments of the nitrate era include the wooden **Iglesia San Francisco Javier** (1897) and **Teatro Alhambra** (1921), both opposite Plaza Prat. The **Museo Augusto Capteville** *(Prat 642)* is the modest municipal museum, with a fine selection of Andean ceramics. On Esmeralda, between Torreblanca and Ramírez, **Plaza Riquelme** overlooks the **Balneario Municipal**, the city beach.

Taltal has plenty of hotels, and restaurants are easy to find.

Hotel San Martín *(☎ 611-088; Martínez 279; singles/doubles with shared bath US$9/17, doubles with private bath US$31)* is basic and is the cheapest lodging in town.

Hotel Verdy *(☎ 611-105; Ramírez 345; per person with shared bath US$9, doubles with private bath US$28)* includes breakfast in its rates.

Hostería del Taltal *(☎ 611-173; Esmeralda 671; singles US$23-38, doubles US$29-40)*, on the beachfront, is Taltal's best. Rates include private bath and breakfast.

Several companies provide bus services north and south on the Panamericana, including **Tur Bus** *(☎ 611-426; Prat 63)*.

Cifuncho

Midway between Taltal and the Panamericana, a gravel lateral heads southwest to Cifuncho, a tiny fishing camp that's also one of the most popular beaches in the area. En route to Cifuncho, a track suitable only for 4WD vehicles heads northwest to isolated **Las Tórtolas**, an even more attractive area.

Norte Chico

South of the Atacama Desert, Norte Chico (Little North) is a semiarid transition zone to the central valley's Mediterranean-like climate. Formerly known as the 'region of 10,000 mines,' this once-great silver mining area is still an important global source of copper and iron. Several notable rivers make irrigated agriculture productive, although the region contains only a small percentage of Chile's total arable land.

Geographically, Norte Chico's northern boundary lies just beyond Copiapó, at about 27°S, while its approximate southern boundary is the Río Aconcagua at about 33°S. Politically, it comprises Región III of Atacama (capital Copiapó) and Región IV of Coquimbo (capital La Serena).

Norte Chico's major attractions are its balmy coastal climate, pleasant beaches and colonial-style cities, such as La Serena. Off the beaten track of the Panamericana, there are intriguing villages and spectacular mountain scenery in areas where foreign travelers are still a novelty. Not far off the Panamericana there are two increasingly popular national parks, Pan de Azúcar and Fray Jorge. Only a handful of people visit newer, more remote reserves such as Parque Nacional Llanos de Challe, on the coast north of Huasco, and Parque Nacional Nevado Tres Cruces, northeast of Copiapó, an area that seems likely to gain popularity in the coming years.

One of the Norte Chico's ephemeral charms is the *desierto florido*, the 'flowering desert' that appears when dormant wildflower seeds sprout in years of sudden, heavy rains. Llanos de Challe is reportedly one of the best places to see this phenomenon, but the region's erratic rainfall patterns make it difficult to predict the best sites in any given year.

History

In pre-Columbian times, coastal Norte Chico, like Norte Grande, was home to Chango fisherfolk. Sedentary Diaguita farmers inhabited the fertile river valleys farther inland and even parts of the less-fertile uplands. The Diaguita, who crossed the Andes from what is now Argentina, cultivated and irrigated maize. They also raised some complementary

Highlights

- Pursuing the perfect pisco sour and absorbing New Age energy vibes in the Elqui Valley

- Horse trekking or hiking through cactus-covered hills at Hacienda Los Andes, followed by a refreshing dip in the creek

- Escaping into wonderful wildlife near the world's highest active volcano in Parque Nacional Nevado Tres Cruces

- Spying on nesting Humboldt penguins, cormorants, gulls, boobies, sea lions and dolphins at Reserva Nacional Pingüino de Humboldt

- Exploring the beaches, churches and neocolonial architecture of La Serena, one of Chile's oldest cities

- Celebrating the Milky Way, the Southern Cross and millions more stars in perfectly clear night skies

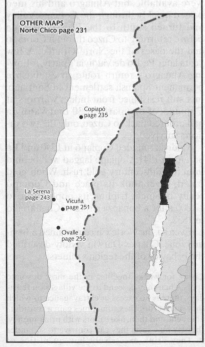

OTHER MAPS
Norte Chico page 231

Copiapó
page 235

La Serena
page 243

Vicuña
page 251

Ovalle
page 255

NORTE CHICO

229

crops such as potatoes, beans, squash and quinoa, and they probably herded llamas. While their numbers were smaller and their political organization less complex than those of the major civilizations of Peru and Bolivia, the Diaguita were able to mobilize sufficient labor to build agricultural terraces and military fortifications. Some decades before the European invasion, the Inka Empire began to expand its influence among the Diaguita and other southern Andean peoples, but the area remained peripheral to the Central Andean civilizations.

Europeans first saw the region in 1535, when Diego de Almagro's expedition crossed the Paso San Francisco from Salta (now Argentina). Surviving phenomenal hardship, a member of Almagro's party left a graphic, gruesome account of the group's miserable 800km march over the Puna de Atacama (which took 20 days in the best of times), reporting that men and horses froze to death and that members of later expeditions, finding the undecomposed horses, 'were glad to eat them.'

In the lowlands, at least food and water were available, but Almagro and his men passed quickly through the Copiapó Valley and turned south to the Río Aconcagua before returning to Cuzco through Copiapó and the oases of the Norte Grande. A few years later Pedro de Valdivia's party, following Almagro's return route to establish a permanent Spanish settlement at Santiago, met stiff resistance from Indian warriors at Copiapó; of one party of 30 that Valdivia had ordered back to Cuzco, only the two officers survived.

Valdivia founded Copiapó in 1540 and La Serena in 1541; Copiapó lagged well behind until its 18th-century gold rush. When gold failed, silver took its place and Copiapó really boomed, tripling its population to 12,000 after a bonanza strike at Chañarcillo in 1832.

Even so, the Norte Chico remained a frontier zone. Charles Darwin vividly described the behavior of the region's miners:

Living for weeks together in the most desolate spots, when they descend to the villages on feast-days, there is no excess or extravagance to which they do not run. They sometimes gain a considerable sum, and then, like sailors with prize-money, they try how soon they can contrive to squander it. They drink excessively, buy quantities of clothes, and in a few days return penniless to their miserable abodes, there to work harder than beasts of burden.

Silver mining declined by the late 19th century, but copper mining soon replaced it. The area around La Serena and the northern sector around Bahía Inglesa have undergone tourist booms (La Serena has overtaken traditional holiday destinations such as Viña del Mar), but mining continues to be significant.

Irrigated agriculture has always been important, but in recent years the Copiapó, Huasco and Elqui Valleys have become major contributors to Chile's booming fruit exports. Their vineyards are notable for producing *pisco,* Chile's potent grape brandy.

The region is also significant in Chilean cultural life – Nobel Prize–winning poet Gabriela Mistral, for instance, was a native of the Elqui Valley, east of La Serena.

CHAÑARAL
☎ 52 • pop 14,000

Near the boundary between Regions II and III, Chañaral is a dilapidated but intriguing mining and fishing port set among the rugged headlands of the Sierra de las Animas. The town dates from 1833, almost a decade after Diego de Almeyda discovered the nearby Las Animas copper reserves; the area's economic powerhouse is the huge copper mine at El Salvador, in the mountains to the east.

For the people of Chañaral, El Salvador has been a mixed blessing – providing their economic livelihood but also polluting the town they call home. Chile's Environmental Health Service is considering moving the entire town a few dozen kilometers away to escape the arsenic-contaminated beach and polluted air.

Just north of Chañaral, the coastal Parque Nacional Pan de Azúcar (see later in this chapter) straddles the regional border. This increasingly popular, scenic destination, which offers excellent camping, is the best reason for a stopover in the area.

Orientation & Information
About 165km northwest of Copiapó and 400km south of Antofagasta, Chañaral has two distinct sections: the industrial port sprawling along the shoreline and the Panamericana, and a residential zone scaling the hills south of the highway.

NORTE CHICO

PACIFIC OCEAN

Región II

To Antofagasta

Paposo
Taltal
Cifuncho
Las Bombas
Parque Nacional
Pan de Azúcar
Sierra Colorada
El Salvador
Chañaral
Diego de
Almagro
Porterillos
Salar de
Pedernales

Cordillera de los Andes

Cerro Galán
6600m ▲
Antofagasta
de la Sierra

Catamarca

Río Salado

Región III

Santuario
de la Naturaleza
Granito Orbicular

Cerros
Tres
Cruces
6330m
Laguna
Verde
Paso de San
Francisco
4727m

Caldera
Bahía Inglesa
Río Copiapó
COPIAPÓ
Tierra Amarilla
Mina El Tránsito
Nantoco
Pabellón
Los Loros
Chañarcillo

Laguna
Santa Rosa

Parque Nacional
Nevado Tres
Cruces

Laguna
del Negro
Francisco

Ojos del
Salado 6893m
Palo Blanco

RN
60

Belén

Carrizal Bajo

Parque Nacional
Llanos de Challe

Huasco
Freirina
Vallenar
Alto del Carmen
San Félix

▲Cerro Pissis
6779m

▲Cerro
Bonito
Chico
6850m

Tinogasta

San Blas

La Rioja

RN
40

Reserva Nacional
Pingüino de Humboldt

Domeyko

Observatorio
Las Campanas

Observatorio
La Silla

Vinchina

ARGENTINA

Chilecito

Caleta de Choros
Choros

Caleta Hornos
Observatorio
Cerro
Mamalluca

Chapilca

LA SERENA
Coquimbo
Observatorio
Cerro Tololo
Tongoy
Guanaqueros

Paihuano
Vicuña
Pisco Elqui
Cochiguaz

Monte Grande

Hurtado

Paso del
Agua Negra
4765m

Villa Unión

RP
26

RN
74

RN
150

Región IV

Ovalle
Valle del
Encanto
Termas
de Socos

Pismanta
San José
de Jáchal

San Juan

San Agustín
de Valle Fértil

RP
510

Parque Nacional
Fray Jorge

Tulahuén

Combarbalá

RP
436

RP
12

SAN JUAN

Panamericana

Illapel
Salamanca

Los Vilos

Pichidangui

RP
39

Cerro Mercedario
▲6770m

RN
141

RN
20

Papudo
Zapallar

La Ligua

Cerro Aconcagua
▲6960m

San Felipe

Quintero

Región V

San Antonio

VALPARAÍSO
Viña del Mar

Colina

SANTIAGO

Las Cuevas

RN
7

MENDOZA

Mendoza

San Luis

Río Desaguadero

RN
40

RN
7

Cordillera de los Andes

Río Blanco

Río Copiapó

0   50   100 km
0   30   60 miles

72°W   70°W   68°W

26°S
28°S
30°S
32°S

NORTE CHICO

Chañaral's **tourist office** (cnr Merino Jarpa & Conchuelas) is half a block northeast of the bus terminal; the office schedule is erratic.

The **post office** (Comercio) is at the west end of town. The **Telefónica (CTC)** (Los Carrera 618) has a long-distance telephone office, as does **Entel** (Merino Jarpa 1197).

Places to Stay & Eat

Accommodations are limited.

Hotel La Marina (Merino Jarpa 562; singles/doubles US$5/9) offers basic rooms.

Hostería de Chañaral (☎ 480-050; Miller 268; singles/doubles start at US$35/40) is appealing and the best in town.

Nuria (Yungay 434), facing the Plaza de Armas, offers well-prepared, reasonably priced seafood, salads and snacks, with friendly, attentive service.

San Pedro, below Aliccinto at La Caleta, serves humble but good fish dishes.

Getting There & Around

Chañaral has a **main bus terminal** (Merino Jarpa 854), with **Tur Bus** (Merino Jarpa 858) next door. Other companies with offices in town are **Flota Barrios** (Merino Jarpa 567) and **Pullman Bus** (Merino Jarpa & Los Baños), which also serves Diego de Almagro and El Salvador.

Chango Turismo (☎ 480-484; Panamericana Norte s/n), opposite the Pullman Bus station, has daily departures to Parque Nacional Pan de Azúcar in summer, less frequently the rest of the year.

PN PAN DE AZÚCAR

Only 30km north of Chañaral, Parque Nacional Pan de Azúcar comprises 43,754 hectares of coastal desert and cordillera, with sheltered coves, white sandy beaches, stony headlands, abundant wildlife and unique flora. Humboldt penguins nest on an island offshore. There's excellent camping in some coastal areas, and the park is becoming an increasingly popular and crowded summer destination.

Park altitudes range from sea level to 900m. The park has a humid coastal desert climate with abundant fog and cloud cover, which usually burns off in the afternoon. The mean annual temperature is about 16°C.

In the coastal zone, the cool Humboldt Current supports a variety of marine life, such as otters and sea lions, and many birds, including pelicans, cormorants and the Humboldt penguin. At higher elevations, moisture from the *camanchaca* (fog) nurtures a unique collection of more than 20 species of cacti and succulents. Farther inland, guanacos and foxes are common sights.

Information

Conaf's **Centro de Información Ambiental** (Caleta Pan de Azúcar; adult/child US$4/2; open 8:30am-12:30pm & 2pm-6pm daily) offers slide presentations about the park's environment and also has a cactarium. At the southern entrance, rangers collect the admission charge.

Isla Pan de Azúcar

About 2000 Humboldt penguins, plus other seabirds, nest on the island of Pan de Azúcar, which seems to float on the ocean as the camanchaca advances inland at twilight. The island is a restricted area, but the birds are visible from the shore with binoculars. Local fishermen also approach the 100-hectare island by boat for better views.

Launches charge about US$7 per person for a minimum of six people from Caleta Pan de Azúcar; a roundtrip takes about 1½ hours. **Pingüi Tour** (☎ 09-743-0011; [W] www.galeon.com/pinguitour), opposite the Conaf office, has regularly scheduled departures.

Places to Stay

Camping (sites without/with shade canopies US$5/10) is available at Playa Piqueros (25 sites), Playa El Soldado (12 sites) and Caleta Pan de Azúcar (6 sites). Facilities include toilets, water, picnic tables and showers (no hot water). There are also two **cabañas** (up to 6 people US$60), with kitchens, solar electricity and hot water; bring your own sheets. Make camping and cabin reservations at Conaf's Copiapó office, especially in January and February and on weekends.

A small market at Caleta Pan de Azúcar has limited supplies, and fresh fish is also available from local residents, but supplies are cheaper and more abundant in the nearby town of Chañaral.

Getting There & Away

Pan de Azúcar is 30km north of Chañaral by a smooth but unpaved road. For public transportation to and from the park, see Getting There & Around under Chañaral earlier in this chapter. It's also possible to hire a taxi from Chañaral.

If you're driving and approaching from the north, there are also two poorly marked park entrances between Sierro Colorado and Las Bombas, about 45km north of Chañaral on the Panamericana, where good roads descend Quebrada Pan de Azúcar to the coast.

CALDERA
☎ 52 • pop 14,000

Once a beach resort for nearby Copiapó's well-heeled residents, Caldera is quiet most of the year, but gets crowded in the January-February season. The weather is just as good or better in the off-season, when it's cheaper and more pleasant, though perhaps *too* quiet. Along with nearby Bahía Inglesa, Caldera is Región III's most popular beach resort. Bahía Inglesa's beaches are more sheltered and attractive, but Caldera is livelier and cheaper.

In addition to tourism, the area's economy depends on fishing and mining. Locally cultivated scallops, oysters and seaweed are exported, although some are consumed locally.

Orientation & Information
Caldera is on the south shore of the Bahía de Caldera, 75km west of Copiapó and just west of the Panamericana. Av Diego de Almeyda, which links Caldera with the Panamericana, continues south as Av Carvallo to nearby Bahía Inglesa, on the north shore of the bay of the same name.

For tourist information, try the summer **tourist office** *(Vallejos & Gallo)* in the bus terminal; it's not always staffed.

Mail your letters at the **post office** *(Edwards 325)*. **Telefónica (CTC)** *(Edwards 360)* has a long-distance telephone office, as does **Entel** *(Tocornal 383)*.

The travel agency **Turismo Tour Mar** *(☎ 316-671, fax 316-126; Diego de Almeyda 904)* arranges coastal tours.

Things to See & Do
At the eastern approach to town, the **Cementerio Laico** *(Av Diego de Almeyda)* was Chile's first non-Catholic cemetery. Note the forged ironwork. There are a few older tombs belonging to English, Welsh, Scots and German immigrants, as well as one or two Chinese sepulchers.

Around the plaza and toward the colorful **Muelle Pesquero** (fishing jetty), the many distinctive 19th-century buildings include the **Iglesia San Vicente** (1862) with its gothic tower; the **Estación de Ferrocarril** (the 1850 train station); and several private houses. The **Municipalidad** *(Gana & Wheelwright)*, once the Aduana (customshouse), now houses the Centro de Desarollo Cultural and the local **museum**.

Nearby **Bahía Inglesa** takes its name from the British privateers who took refuge here in colonial times. In addition to swimming and sunbathing, windsurfing is a popular pastime; rental equipment is not available, so you must bring your own.

Places to Stay
Outside the peak summer season, prices drop considerably.

Camping Bahía Inglesa *(☎ 315-424; Playa Las Machas; sites high season US$30, cabañas with shared bath US$40, with private bath US$60-70)*, just south of Bahía Inglesa, has good camping facilities but costs are high during the season. All cabins have kitchenettes and sleep up to six people.

Residencial Millaray *(☎ 315-528; Cousiño 331; per person US$7)*, across from the Caldera plaza, is simple and one of the cheapest options, with clean, comfortable rooms and shared bath.

Residencial Palermo *(☎ 315-847; Cifuentes 150; singles/doubles US$14/21)* is small, funky and a bit too pricey; it has shared baths only.

Hotel Montecarlo *(☎ 315-388; Av Carvallo 627; doubles US$30)* provides good service and quality rooms, with private baths and laundry.

Hostería Puerta del Sol *(☎ 315-205; Wheelwright 750; singles/doubles US$30/50)* has private baths and a kid's pool.

Hotel Rocas de Bahía *(☎/fax 316-005; El Morro 888; singles/doubles US$98/112)* is in Bahía Inglesa proper. This four-star hotel has a restaurant and swimming pool.

Places to Eat
Seafood is the only reasonable choice when dining out.

The popular **New Charles** *(☎ 315-348; Ossa Cerda 350)*, despite its anglophone name, specializes in Chilean cuisine, including seafood empanadas.

El Coral (☎ 315-331; El Morro 564), in Bahía Inglesa, is upscale and offers superb seafood, including local scallops. It's expensive, but if you choose your meal wisely, you can eat here without shattering your budget.

Getting There & Around
The bus terminals are in Caldera, including separate terminals for **Pullman** (Gallo & Vallejos) and **Tur Bus** (Gallo 149). **Buses Recabarren** (Cousiño 260) serves Copiapó (US$2.50, one hour). Buses and taxi colectivos run to/from Caldera and Bahía Inglesa for US$1.

AROUND CALDERA
On the scenic coastline about 12km north of Caldera along the Panamericana, **Santuario de la Naturaleza Granito Orbicular** is a geological oddity that consists of a number of irregularly shaped mineral conglomerates. It is not part of Conaf's wildlands system, but instead is under the administration of the education ministry. About a mile or two away there's an offshore sea lion colony.

COPIAPÓ
☎ 52 • pop 128,000
Copiapó is a pleasant town and a point of departure for treks to Argentine peaks, Laguna Verde and Parque Nacional Nevado Tres Cruces. Founded in the mid-18th century, the town lagged behind other cities until an 18th-century gold boom, and then it really took off after the discovery of silver at nearby Chañarcillo in 1832. This provided Copiapó with several firsts: South America's first railroad (completed in 1852 to the port of Caldera), Chile's first telegraph and telephone lines, and the first gas works.

Copiapó's population has fluctuated with the mining industry, but the city retains its clean streets, historic buildings and businesslike atmosphere. Its pleasant climate and historical interest make it a worthwhile stopover on the Panamericana between La Serena and Antofagasta, and it's a suitable base for exploring the remote mountains near the Argentine border.

Orientation
Copiapó nestles in the narrow valley floor on the north bank of Río Copiapó, 330km north of La Serena, 800km north of Santiago and 565km south of Antofagasta. Three blocks north of Av Copayapu (the Panamericana), shaded by massive pepper trees, pleasant Plaza Prat marks the city's historical center. Watch out for the roving fortune-tellers, though once they get started, you'll have a hard time getting away without aspersions on your sexuality.

Most areas of interest to the visitor are in or near a roughly rectangular area bounded by Calle Manuel Rodríguez to the north, the Alameda Manuel Antonio Matta to the west, Av Henríquez to the east and the Río Copiapó to the south. Overlooking town from the northwest is the landmark Cerro La Cruz.

Information
Sernatur (☎ 212-838, fax 217-248; e info atacama@sernatur.cl; Los Carrera 691; open 8:30am-5:30pm Mon-Fri Mar-Dec; 8:30am-8pm Mon-Fri, 10am-2pm & 4pm-8pm Sat, and 10am-2pm Sun Jan & Feb) occupies a concrete bunker on the northeast side of Plaza Prat. The staff are congenial, helpful and well informed, and they can provide a list of accommodations, an excellent free map and many brochures.

Conaf (☎ 210-282, fax 239-067; Juan Martínez 55; open 8:30am-5:30pm Mon-Thur, 8:30am-4:30pm Fri) has limited information on regional parks, including Parque Nacional Pan de Azúcar and Parque Nacional Nevado Tres Cruces.

Numerous 24-hour ATMs are located at banks around the plaza. Change money at **Cambio Fides** (Centro Comercial Coimbra, Atacama 541, Office 3, 2nd floor; open 10:30am-2pm & 4:30pm-6:30pm Mon-Fri, 10am-2pm Sat).

The **post office** (Intendencia Regional, Los Carrera 691; open 9am-7pm Mon-Fri, 9:30am-1pm Sat) is behind the Sernatur office. **Telefónica (CTC)** (cnr Los Carrera & Chacabuco; open 8am-11pm Mon-Sat) has long-distance telephone offices opposite Plaza Prat. **Entel** (Colipí 484) is opposite the northeast corner of the plaza.

Cyber Chat (Vallejos between O'Higgins & Carrera; open 9am-midnight daily) offers Internet service.

Turismo Atacama (☎ 212-712, fax 217-357; e viajes_atacama@entelchile.net; Los Carrera 716) is a travel agency a block southeast of Plaza Prat. It also arranges tours through Peruvian Tours (see Organized Tours later in this section).

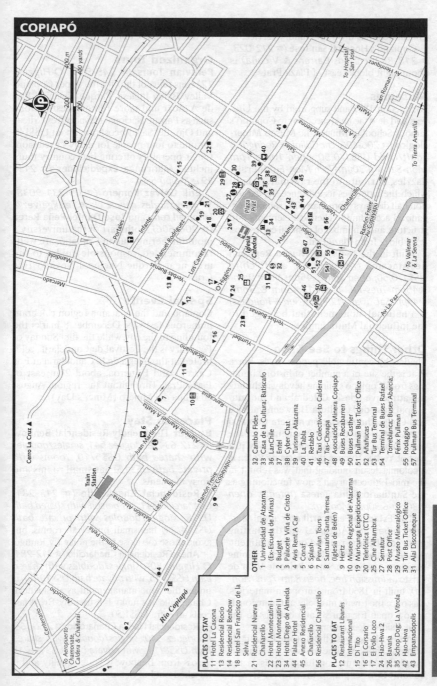

COPIAPÓ

400 m
400 yards

0   200
0   200

Cerro La Cruz ▲

To Aeropuerto
Chamonate,
Caldera & Chañaral

To Hospital
San José

To Tierra Amarilla

To Vallenar
& La Serena

Plaza Prat

Iglesia
Catedral

Río Copiapó

Train
Station

PLACES TO STAY
11 Hotel La Casona
13 Residencial Rocío
14 Residencial Benbow
18 Hotel San Francisco de la
    Selva
21 Residencial Nueva
    Chañarcillo
22 Hotel Montecatini I
23 Hotel Montecatini II
34 Hotel Diego de Almeida
44 Palace Hotel
45 Anexo Residencial
    Chañarcillo
56 Residencial Chañarcillo

PLACES TO EAT
12 Restaurant Libanés
    Internacional
15 Di Tito
16 El Corsario
17 El Pollo Loco
24 Hao-Hwa 2
26 Bavaria
35 Schop Dog; La Vítrola
42 Hao-Hwa
43 Empanadopolis

OTHER
1   Universidad de Atacama
    (Ex-Escuela de Minas)
2   Budget
3   Palacete Viña de Cristo
4   Avis Rent A Car
5   Conaf
6   Splash
7   Peruvian Tours
8   Santuario Santa Teresa
    (Iglesia de Belén)
9   Hertz
10 Museo Regional de Atacama
19 Maricunga Expediciones
20 Telefónica (CTC)
25 Cine Alhambra
27 Sernatur
28 Post Office
29 Museo Mineralógico
30 Tur Bus Ticket Office
31 Alai Discotheque
32 Cambio Fides
33 Casa de la Cultura; Batiscafo
36 LanChile
37 Entel
38 Cyber Chat
39 Turismo Atacama
40 La Tabla
41 Retablo
46 Taxi Colectivos to Caldera
47 Tas-Choapa
48 Asociación Minera Copiapó
49 Buses Recabarren
50 Buses Casther
51 Pullman Bus Ticket Office
52 Tur Bus Terminal
53 Añañucas
54 Terminal de Buses Rafael
    Torreblanca; Buses Abarcía;
    Fénix Pullman
55 Rodaggio
57 Pullman Bus Terminal

Añañucas (☎ 218-877; Chañarcillo near Chacabuco) has drop-off laundry service.

Copiapó's **Hospital San José** (☎ 212-023, ☎ 218-833; cnr Los Carrera & Vicuña) is about eight blocks east of Plaza Prat.

Museums

Founded in 1857 and supported by the Universidad de Atacama (successor to Copiapó's famous School of Mines), the **Museo Mineralógico** (☎ 206-606; cnr Colipí & Rodríguez; adult/child US$1/0.50; open 10am-1pm Mon-Sat & 3:30pm-7pm Mon-Fri) literally dazzles, a tribute to the raw materials to which the city owes its existence. Its exhibition hall displays more than 2000 samples, organized according to chemical elements and structure, and a number of mineral curiosities. It's a block from Plaza Prat.

Built in the 1840s, the **Museo Regional de Atacama** (Atacama 98; adult/child US$1/0.50; open 2pm-5:45pm Mon, 9am-5:45pm Tues-Fri, 10am-12:45pm & 3pm-5:45pm Sat, 10am-12:45pm Sun & holidays) is a national monument that belonged to the influential Matta family.

Other Things to See & Do

Shaded by century-old pepper trees, Plaza Prat is the site of a number of historic buildings from Copiapó's mining heyday, including the attractive **Iglesia Catedral** and the municipal **Casa de la Cultura**. Between Vallejos and Colipí, the **Asociación Minera Copiapó** (Atacama) is a national monument from the early mining days. A little out of the way, just east of Yerbas Buenas, the **Iglesia de Belén** is a colonial Jesuit building that was rebuilt in the mid-19th century; it's now functioning as the **Santuario Santa Teresa** (Infante; open 4:30pm-6:30pm Mon-Fri).

The **Estación Ferrocarril** (cnr Juan Martínez & Batallón Atacama) was the starting point for the first railroad on the continent. At the southern end of Rómulo Peña, mining magnate Apolinario Soto's **Palacete Viña de Cristo** (admission free; open 8am-7pm Mon-Fri), built in 1860 from European materials, was once the town's most elegant mansion. It is now open for tourists and belongs to the Universidad de Atacama.

A few blocks west, the historic **Escuela de Minas** (School of Mines) is now the Universidad de Atacama; on its grounds is the **Locomotora Copiapó**, the Norris Brothers locomotive that was the first to operate on the Caldera-Copiapó line.

Organized Tours

Peruvian Tours (☎ 249-995; O'Higgins 12) runs tours of the city, the upper Copiapó Valley, Bahía Inglesa, Parque Nacional Pan de Azúcar and more remote destinations such as Parque Nacional Nevado Tres Cruces and Ojos del Salado; costs are about US$140 for one to four people for a day's excursion. Other operators offering backcountry tours include **Maricunga Expediciones** (☎ 211-191; Maipú 580).

Erik Galvez Romero (☎ 05-231-9038; w www.andes-galvez.cl; e erikgalvez@latinmail.com) and **José Daniel Peña Pérez** (☎ 206-606), both part of the university's mountaineering club in Copiapó, are well-recommended, responsible guides to the area near Parque Nacional Nevado Tres Cruces.

Special Events

Copiapó and the Atacama region celebrate numerous festivals. December 8 marks the founding of the city, while the first Sunday of February is the Festival de Candelaria, celebrated at the Iglesia de la Candelaria at Los Carrera and Figueroa, about 2km east of Plaza Prat. Throughout the region, August 10 is Día del Minero (Miner's Day).

Places to Stay

Budget The friendly **Residencial Benbow** (☎ 217-634; Rodríguez 541; singles/doubles with shared bath US$5/10, rooms with private bath US$15) has small rooms and noisy moments.

Residencial Chañarcillo (☎ 213-281; Chañarcillo 741; per person with shared bath US$8, singles/doubles with private bath US$14/24) has small but clean rooms, but avoid those too close to the noisy TV lounge.

Anexo Residencial Chañarcillo (☎ 212-284; O'Higgins 804; singles/doubles with shared bath US$8/15, with private bath US$10/20) is under the same management as Residencial Chañarcillo; it's funky but friendly. Breakfast costs an extra US$1.50.

Residencial Nueva Chañarcillo (☎ 212-368; Rodríguez 540; singles/doubles with shared bath US$8/14, with private bath US$15/21), across from Benbow, is better quality and is kitsched-out but clean.

Residencial Rocio (☎ 215-360; Yerbas Buenas 581; singles/doubles US$7/12) is a cool spot, frequented by travelers, with decent basic rooms with shared bath.

Mid-Range One of Copiapó's best values, **Palace Hotel** (☎ 212-852; Atacama 741; singles/doubles US$21/31) has attractive rooms with private bath around a delightful patio. The staff are very friendly – the kind of people who will climb through your tiny bathroom window without complaining when you've locked your keys inside your room.

Hotel Montecatini I (☎ 211-363, fax 217-021; Infante 766; singles/doubles standard US$21/29, superior US$28/40) is very fine and in a quiet area with a peaceful interior patio, attractive gardens and a pool. The more expensive rooms, which are large and have cable TV, are worth the extra price.

Under the same management is **Hotel Montecatini II** (☎ 211-516, fax 214-773; Atacama 374; singles/doubles US$35/45).

Top End The colonial-style **Hotel La Casona** (☎/fax 217-278; O'Higgins 150; singles/doubles start at US$40/47) offers outstanding accommodations in a lovely garden setting; its restaurant serves fine food. The cheapest rooms are near the street. Rates include breakfast.

Hotel San Francisco de la Selva (☎ 217-013; Los Carrera 525; singles/doubles US$45/54) has modern and pleasant rooms, but those near the street are extremely noisy; ask for a room in the back. A few economy rooms (US$38) are available, but they are very small.

Hotel Diego de Almeida (☎ 212-075, fax 218-688; O'Higgins 656; singles/doubles start at US$52/62) is a pleasant business-class hotel with a swimming pool, bar and restaurant. Some rooms face Plaza Prat and can be noisy.

Places to Eat
Empanadopolis (☎ 240-798; Colipí 320; empanadas US$0.50-1.25; open lunch only) gets kudos for a bewildering variety of mouthwatering and cheap empanadas.

El Pollo Loco (O'Higgins 461; lunch specials US$2.50, half chicken US$2) has inexpensive grilled chicken.

SchopDog (Plaza Real, 2nd floor; plates US$2.50) is popular, with cheap and forgettable hot dogs and such, but memorable

views of the plaza. **La Vitrola,** in the same center, is a bar and gelateria where Copiapinos congregate for after-work drinks.

Bavaria (☎ 217-160; Chacabuco 487; fixed lunch US$5, dishes US$5-9), part of a popular chain, has decent sandwiches (US$2-4). The door closest to the corner leads to the main restaurant (no sandwiches), and the door farther away from the corner on Chacabuco leads to the simpler and cheaper cafeteria.

Di Tito (☎ 212-386; Chacabuco 710; dishes US$5-6) is a moderately priced pizzeria with friendly staff, pizza (large US$5) and Italian dishes.

El Corsario (☎ 215-374; Atacama 245; dishes US$4-7), occupying an older house with pleasant patio seating, serves varied Chilean food, including rabbit.

Restaurant Libanés Internacional (☎ 212-939; Los Carrera 350; dishes US$5-7) serves Middle Eastern food in an intimate setting.

Hao-Hwa (☎ 213-261; Colipí 340 • ☎ 215-484; Yerbas Buenas 334; lunch specials US$4, main dishes US$4-6) is one of northern Chile's better Chinese restaurants, with good food and pleasant ambience.

Batiscafo (O'Higgins 610), in the Casa de la Cultura, is a pleasant and cool spot for juices and decent coffee.

Entertainment
La Tabla (cnr Los Carrera & Vallejos) is worth a stop for a drink.

Copiapó has two downtown dance clubs: **Splash** (Juan Martínez 46) and **Alai Discotheque** (Maipú 279).

Cine Alhambra (☎ 212-187; Atacama 455) shows recent films.

Getting There & Away
Air Aeropuerto Chamonate (☎ 214-360) is 15km west of Copiapó, just north of the Panamericana. **LanChile** (☎ 213-512; Colipí 484; open 9am-1:30pm & 3pm-7pm Mon-Fri; 10am-1pm Sat) flies daily to Antofagasta (US$30 one-way, one hour), La Serena (US$40, 45 minutes) and Santiago (US$45, 1½ hours).

Bus Copiapó's main **Terminal de Buses Rafael Torreblanca** (☎ 212-577; Chacabuco 112) is three blocks south of Plaza Prat and just north of the river. Virtually all north-south buses stop here, as do many bound for the interior. Most bus companies have offices at the terminal, while others have offices and/or terminals nearby. **Pullman Bus** (☎ 212-977; Colipí 109) has a terminal near the main bus station and a ticket office at the corner of Chacabuco and Colipí. **Tur Bus** (☎ 238-612; Chañarcillo 680) has a terminal nearby and a ticket office downtown (Colipí 510). Many buses to northern, desert destinations leave at night.

Some of the standard destinations and fares are shown in the following table:

destination	duration in hours	cost
Antofagasta	8	US$12
Arica	18	US$21
Calama	11	US$18
Iquique	14	US$20
La Serena	5	US$5
Santiago	12	US$10
Vallenar	2	US$4

To get to Caldera (US$2.50), taxi colectivos leave from Buena Esperanza, a half block from the bus terminal. Across the street, **Buses Recabarren** (☎ 216-991; Buena Esperanza 557) costs less (US$1.75) but has fewer departures.

Buses Abarcia (☎ 212-483; main terminal) has service to towns along the Río Copiapó, including Los Loros and Lautaro, as do **Buses Casther** (☎ 218-889; Buena Esperanza 557) and Buses Recabarren (from the main terminal).

Tas-Choapa (☎ 238-066; Chañarcillo 631) has service to Mendoza and Cordoba, Argentina. **Fénix Pullman** (☎ 214-929; main terminal) has a direct bus to Mendoza and Buenos Aires.

Getting Around

To/From the Airport Taxis to the airport, 15km west of Copiapó, depart from in front of the Iglesia Catedral for US$5-8 per person, or try **Radio Taxi San Francisco** (☎ 218-788).

Car Copiapó's car rental agencies include **Hertz** (☎ 213-522; Av Copayapu 173 • airport); **Avis** (☎ 213-966; e copiapo@avis chile.cl; Rómulo Peña 102 • airport), southwest of the train station; **Budget** (☎ 218-802; Ramón Freire 466 • airport); **Rodaggio** (☎ 212-153; w www.rodaggio.cl; Colipí 127); and **Retablo** (☎ 214-427; Los Carrera 955).

Rodaggio has the cheapest unlimited mileage rates, at US$30 per day plus 18% IVA for a small car, but pickup trucks, suitable for exploring the backcountry, cost at least US$55 per day, and 4WDs cost at least US$80.

AROUND COPIAPÓ

Up the valley of the Río Copiapó, southeast of the city, many worthwhile sights are accessible by public transportation. At nearby Tierra Amarilla, the **Iglesia Nuestra Señora de Loreto** (1898) is the work of Spanish architect José Miguel Retornano. The municipal **Casa de Cultura** (☎ 320-098, ask for Alejandro Aracena Siares) arranges visits to **Mina El Tránsito**, a former gold mine in the Sierra de Ojancos. Dating from 1743 but reaching its peak in the early 19th century, El Tránsito was once a substantial community as well as a work site, but only the administrator's house, now partly a museum, remains in anything approximating its original condition. Some machinery is still standing, and there are open shafts.

About 23km from Copiapó, flood-prone **Nantoco** is the site of a colonial church, a 19th-century silver and copper smelter, and the former hacienda of Apolinario Soto, dating from 1870. At Km 34, **Hacienda Jotabeche** belonged to the notable Chilean essayist José Joaquín Vallejo. Better known by his pseudonym, Jotabeche, Vallejo was a pioneer of Chilean literature and a keen observer of his country's customs.

Los Loros, 64km from Copiapó, is a picturesque village in a rich agricultural zone that yields excellent grapes, watermelons, citrus and other fruits. **Viña del Cerro,** an archaeological monument on a spur off the main valley road, consists of the restored remains of a Diaguita-Inka copper foundry, with associated houses and other constructions, including more than 30 ovens.

Several bus companies run buses up the valley from Copiapó.

Chañarcillo

Juan Godoy found silver at Chañarcillo on May 16, 1832. The town that grew up alongside the mine reached a maximum population of about 7000 before declining at the end of the 19th century, when water flooded the mines, rendering them unusable. Now it's a ghost town. Foxes scurry among its remaining stone and adobe ruins, including public offices, the police station and jail, a theater, a hospital and the cemetery. Most of these are now difficult to distinguish, though the cumulative impact of the site makes it worth a visit. One interesting recognizable ruin is the rustic, still-functioning water well.

To reach Chañarcillo, take the Panamericana south to Km 59, where a dusty but excellent eastbound lateral goes toward Mina Bandurrias, a contemporary mine. The road continues east over scenic desert mountains and through deep canyons before intersecting the paved highway in the upper Río Copiapó, near Nantoco and Pabellón. This very interesting route is inadvisable in a vehicle without high clearance, and 4WD is desirable. There's an interesting detour that dead-ends at **Mina Tres Marías,** an abandoned ridge-top mine with exceptional panoramas.

PN NEVADO TRES CRUCES

A worthy attraction for adventurous travelers, Parque Nacional Nevado Tres Cruces (*admission US$6*) protects about 61,000 hectares in two separate sectors of the high Andes east of Copiapó along Ruta 31, the international highway to Argentina via Paso de San Francisco. Flamingos spend the summer season here; the park is also home to vicuñas, guanacos, giant and horned coots, Andean geese and gulls, pumas and other species.

The larger **Sector Laguna Santa Rosa** comprises 49,000 hectares surrounding the lake of the same name, but also includes the Salar de Maricunga to the north. The smaller **Sector Laguna del Negro Francisco** consists of 12,000 hectares surrounding its namesake lake. While flamingos do not nest in the park, the shallow waters (barely a meter deep in most places) are ideal for the 8000 birds that summer here. About 56% are Andean flamingos, 40% are Chilean flamingos, and the remaining 4% are rare James flamingos. The highest quantity of birds is present from December through February.

Laguna del Negro Francisco itself consists of two ecologically distinct areas. A peninsula separates the upper Laguna Dulce, whose less saline waters supply plankton to the flamingos' diet. In the lower, saltier Laguna Salada, crustaceans are the main food source.

For more information, contact Sernatur or Conaf in Copiapó, or check in at the Laguna Negro Francisco ranger station (no phone). Overnight visitors should be self-sufficient.

Outside the park boundaries proper, 6893m **Ojos del Salado** is Chile's highest peak (almost, but not quite, measuring up to South America's highest peak – 6962m Aconcagua in Argentina). It is the highest active volcano in the world, with the most recent eruptions in 1937 and 1956. At the 5100m level, the Universidad de Atacama maintains the rustic **Refugio UDA** that can shelter four to six climbers; at 5700m, **Refugio César Tejos** has a capacity of 12. The mountain can be climbed between October and April; allow seven days. The climb only becomes technical in the last 50m or so.

Because Ojos del Salado straddles the border, climbers must obtain authorization from Chile's **Dirección de Fronteras y Límites** (*Difrol;* ☎ *02-671-4110, fax 02-697-1909;* ⓦ *www.difrol.cl; Bandera 52, 5th floor, Santiago*), which oversees border area activities. It's possible to request permission prior to arriving in Chile through the website.

Places to Stay

Refugio Laguna del Negro Francisco (*dorm beds US$10*) is Conaf's cozy refuge, with beds, cooking facilities, electricity, flush toilets and hot showers. Bring your own bed linen, drinking water and cooking gas. **Laguna Santa Rosa** has a tiny, free refugio, with space to sleep and eat out of the wind and cold. You can also set up a tent outside the refugios.

Getting There & Away

Sector Laguna Santa Rosa is 146km east of Copiapó via Ruta 31 and another road that climbs up the scenic Quebrada de Paipote. Sector Laguna del Negro Francisco is another 85km south via a roundabout road that passes Mina Marte, a defunct gold mine, and drops into the valley of the Río Astaburuaga to arrive at the lake. Note that the road that passes directly west from the Conaf refugio to Mina Aldabarán to Quebrada San Miguel is not passable.

There is no regularly scheduled public transportation to the park; visitors should ask Conaf or Sernatur in Copiapó about current alternatives. For tours of the area, see the Organized Tours heading in the Copiapó section.

VALLENAR

☎ 51 • pop 48,000

In the valley of the Río Huasco, roughly midway between Copiapó and La Serena, Vallenar is a center of mining and agriculture for the province of Huasco; olives and the sweet wine known as *parajete* are regional specialties. Vallenar is also a point of departure for Parque Nacional Llanos de Challe.

The town dates from the late 18th century, when colonial governor Ambrosio O'Higgins applied the name of his native Ballenagh, Ireland, to the area – 'Ballenagh' became 'Vallenar.' Charles Darwin later visited the area on horseback. After serious earthquake damage in 1922, Vallenar was rebuilt with wood instead of adobe, but the city's buildings still rest on unconsolidated sediments.

Orientation & Information

Motorists often bypass Vallenar, which is 145km south of Copiapó and 190km north of La Serena, because Puente Huasco (Huasco Bridge), which spans the valley here, does not drop down into the town, readily visible below. At the south end of the bridge, the Vallenar-Huasco highway leads east into town, crossing the river via Puente Brasil. Everything in Vallenar is within easy walking distance of the central Plaza O'Higgins, at the intersection of Prat and Vallejos.

Municipal authorities have turned part of the northern riverbank, from Vallejos eastward across Av Brasil, into an attractive park. Prat has become a semi-peatonal, a wide sidewalk with a single automobile lane, east of Plaza O'Higgins.

Regular travel facilities – an occasionally open tourist kiosk, banks, post office and long-distance telephone offices – are available around the plaza and at the corner of Brasil and Prat.

Things to See & Do

Vallenar's **Iglesia Parroquial**, on the east side of Plaza O'Higgins, is notable for the copper dome on its wooden tower.

The historic **Museo del Huasco** (☎ 611-320; Sargento Aldea 742; admission free; open 3pm-6pm Tues-Fri) has a modest collection of local artifacts and materials, including an excellent photo collection.

Special Events

January 5 is a local holiday celebrating the founding of the city; the local songfest, Festival Vallenar Canta, takes place later in the month. In the village of San Félix, 58km up the valley of the Río Huasco, the annual grape harvest in February is celebrated with the Festival de la Vendimia.

Places to Stay & Eat

Residencial Oriental (☎ 613-889; Serrano 720; singles/doubles with shared bath US$6/12, with private bath US$11/20) has the cheapest accommodations. Rooms are set around an attractive patio.

Hotel Viña del Mar (☎ 611-478; Serrano 611; singles/doubles US13/23) is cheerful, family-run and Vallenar's best value; rooms have private bath.

Hostal Camino del Rey (☎ 613-184; Merced 943; singles/doubles with shared bath US$13/21, with private bath US$21/30) fills up fast.

Hostería de Vallenar (☎ 614-379, fax 614-538; Alonso de Ercilla 848; singles/doubles US$64/75) is the finest in town; it also has a top-notch restaurant.

For basic, inexpensive meals, try the cocinerías in the **Mercado Municipal** (municipal market; cnr Serrano & Santiago).

Il Bocatto (☎ 619-482; Prat 750) has small but good pizzas and snacks.

Getting There & Away

Vallenar's **Terminal de Buses** (cnr Prat & Av Matta) is at the west end of town, but several companies have downtown ticket offices, including **Pullman** (☎ 612-461; Serrano 551). **Tur Bus** (☎ 611-738), with its own terminal on Prat opposite the main terminal, has extensive north- and southbound routes.

AROUND VALLENAR
Huasco

An hour west of Vallenar by paved highway, the picturesque fishing port of Huasco is a pleasant surprise, with good beaches, decent hotels and fine seafood. En route to Huasco, the village of Freirina is worth a stop to see its **Iglesia Santa Rosa de Lima** (1869), a wooden church with an impressive bell tower.

Hostal San Fernando (☎/fax 531-726; Pedro de Valdivia 176; rooms with shared bath US$9, doubles with private bath US$20) has a spacious older section and an equally roomy newer section.

Hostería Huasco (☎ 531-026; Ignacio Carrera Pinto 110; singles/doubles US$32/42) is an older but still pleasant facility with private bath and sea views.

Buses to Huasco depart from the main Vallenar terminal.

Carrizal Bajo

From the farming village of Huasco Bajo, at the eastern approach to Huasco, a paved northbound road soon turns into a good but sandy coastal road that continues to Carrizal Bajo, a quasi-ghost town where, on summer weekends, up to 3000 people come to camp on the beach and among abandoned buildings. Concrete buttresses support the crumbling adobe walls of its landmark church, a national monument.

Carrizal Bajo gained a certain fame (or notoriety) in 1986, when the leftist Frente Patriótico Manuel Rodríguez (FPMR) chose the deserted port to smuggle in a large cache of weapons to aid its armed struggle against the Pinochet dictatorship – the same year the FPMR made an attempt on General Pinochet's life in the Cajón del Maipo.

PN Llanos de Challe

Designated a national park in 1994 for its unique flora, most notably the endemic *Garra de León* (an endangered species that is possibly Chile's rarest and most beautiful flower), Parque Nacional Llanos de Challe (admission US$6) comprises 45,000 hectares of coastal desert, 50km north of Huasco. During wet years, it's one of the best places to see the wildflower display of the *desierto florido*; there is also a selection of cacti to be seen, as well as guanacos and foxes (despite continued poaching in the northern part of the park).

Accessible only by private vehicle, Llanos de Challe consists of a coastal sector south of Carrizal Bajo around Punta Los Pozos, where Conaf plans to install a campground, and an inland sector along the Quebrada Carrizal, 15km southeast of Carrizal Bajo. In addition to the road north from Huasco Bajo, a slightly shorter route to Llanos de Challe leaves the Panamericana 15km north of Vallenar. For more information, contact Sernatur or Conaf in Copiapó.

RN PINGÜINO DE HUMBOLDT

Several offshore islands on the border between Regions III and IV make up the 860-hectare Reserva Nacional Pingüino de Humboldt (adult/child US$3/1), one of the best excursions in Norte Chico. It is most easily reached from La Serena. The reserve takes its name from the nesting Humboldt penguin, but there are also remarkable numbers of cormorants, gulls and boobies, as well as marine mammals such as sea lions, dolphins and otters.

Orientation & Information

From a turnoff on the Panamericana, about 78km north of La Serena, a rough gravel road passes through **Choros**, an oasis of olive trees that was one of Spain's earliest (1605) settlements in the area, and continues to Caleta de Choros (123km from La Serena), site of Conaf's small but outstanding Centro de Información Ambiental, where visitors pay the park admission charge. Sernatur and Conaf in La Serena can also provide more information.

At Caleta de Choros, it's possible to hire a launch to Isla Damas and around Isla Choros (where landing is not permitted). Isla Chañaral, the largest and most northerly of the three islands comprising the reserve, is less easily accessible, but its wildlife is similar to that around Isla Choros.

Things to See & Do

Hired launches from Caleta de Choros, charging around US$70 total for up to seven people, carry passengers along the east coast of 320-hectare **Isla Choros**, which has it all – pods of bottle-nosed dolphins that dive and surface alongside the boat, a large sea lion colony, groups of otters and Humboldt penguins, and massive rookeries of cormorants, gulls and boobies.

Isla Damas, a 60-hectare metamorphic outcrop capped by a low granite summit, is usually visited on the return from Isla Choros. It has two main beaches: **Playa La Poza** at the landing point, and the attractive white-sand **Playa Tijeras**, roughly a 1km walk.

Limited climbing is possible on the granite heights of Damas, but none of the faces is big enough to be really challenging.

Places to Stay & Eat

Camping (sites US$20) is available on the Playa La Poza. Conaf's campground has clean toilets but no potable water, so bring your own water and food (it's also possible to buy fresh fish from the nearby fishermen's camp). Isla Damas is crowded in summer and on weekends (although most visitors are day-trippers); on weekdays and in the off-season it's pretty deserted. Campers must bring bags to pack out trash.

Getting There & Away

While there is no regular public transportation to Caleta de Choros, several travel agencies in La Serena offer visits to Isla Choros and Isla Damas as day trips. Be aware, though, that the one-way, 123-km distance means a lot of time in transit. It's possible to leave one day and return another after camping on Isla Damas, but this is more difficult outside the peak season, when demand for tours is lower.

LA SERENA

☎ 51 • pop 159,000

Peaceful most of the year, pretty La Serena is a trendy beach resort in summer. Founded in 1544, the city sports a good deal of interesting architecture: some of it is original colonial (this is Chile's second-oldest city), but most is neocolonial – the product of Serena-born President Gabriel González Videla's 'Plan Serena' of the late 1940s. There's also an impressive array of 29 churches. La Serena is the capital of Región IV.

Besides its beaches, La Serena has numerous attractions in the surrounding countryside, including quaint villages such as Vicuña (home to Nobel Prize–winning poet Gabriela Mistral), with its nearby vineyards, and several international astronomical observatories, which take advantage of the region's exceptional atmospheric conditions and dark skies. Many tours leave from here.

Success comes with a price. Recent upscale developments are rapidly overshadowing the city's historical legacy. High-rises along the beach make access easy but mar the view. Water shortages remains a serious concern in this semidesert area. An astounding and disappointing amount of graffiti stands out against the white colonial buildings.

History

Encomendero Juan Bohón, Pedro de Valdivia's lieutenant, founded La Serena in 1544, but after Bohón died in an Indian uprising, his successor Francisco de Aguirre refounded the city in 1549. Following Chilean independence, silver and copper became the backbone of its economy, supported and supplemented by irrigated agriculture in the Elqui Valley. Silver discoveries were so significant that the Chilean government created an independent mint in the city.

Orientation

La Serena lies on the south bank of the Río Elqui, about 2km above its outlet to the Pacific, 470km north of Santiago. The Panamericana, known as Av Juan Bohón, skirts the western edge of town.

Centered on the Plaza de Armas, the city plan is a regular grid, complicated by a few diagonals toward the east, but orientation is easy. Most areas of interest fall within a rectangular area marked by Av Bohón and Parque Pedro de Valdivia to the west, the Río Elqui to the north, Calle Benavente to the east and Av Francisco de Aguirre to the south.

Information

Tourist Offices The **Sernatur office** (☎ 213-956, ☎/fax 225-199; e infocoquimbo@ sernatur.cl; Matta 405; open 8:45am-6pm daily Jan & Feb, 8:45am-6pm Mon-Fri the rest of the year) is on the west side of the plaza, just south of the post office.

La Serena's minimalist **Cámara de Turismo kiosk** (cnr Prat & Balmaceda; hours vary) is in front of Iglesia La Merced.

For information on Región IV's national parks and other reserves, visit **Conaf** (☎ 225-685; Cordovez 281; open 8:30am-2pm Mon-Fri).

Money Both US cash and traveler's checks, as well as Argentine pesos, are easily negotiated at any of La Serena's cambios. Try **Gira Tour** (Prat 689) or **Cambios Inter** (☎ 224-673; Eduardo de la Barra 435). Banks with 24-hour ATMs are readily available in the blocks around the plaza.

Post & Communications The **post office** (cnr Matta & Prat; open 8:30am-6:30pm Mon-Fri, 9:30am-1pm Sat) is on the west side of the Plaza de Armas. **Entel** (Prat 571) has a long-distance telephone office.

The **Net Café** (☎ 212-187; Cordovez 285; open 9am-dusk Mon-Sat, noon-10pm Sun) has pricey Internet access (US$3 per hour),

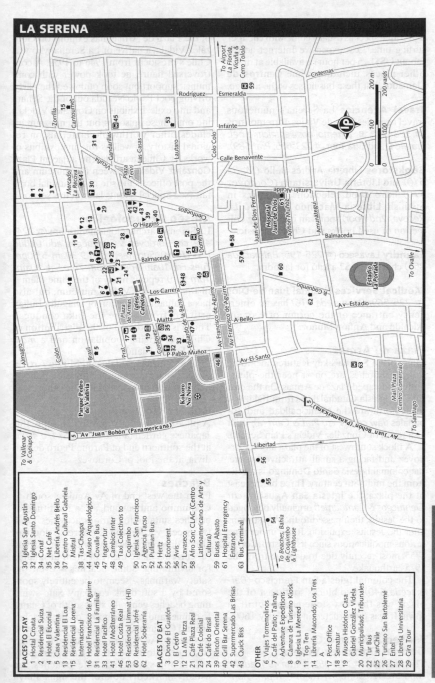

LA SERENA

PLACES TO STAY
1 Hostal Croata
2 Residencial Suiza
4 Hotel El Escorial
5 Casa Valentina
13 Residencial El Loa
15 Residencial Lorena Internacional
16 Hotel Francisco de Aguirre
31 Residencial La Familiar
33 Hotel Pacífico
41 Hotel Mediterráneo
46 Hotel Costa Real
53 Residencial Limmat (HJ)
62 Hotel Soberanía

PLACES TO EAT
3 Donde El Guatón
10 El Cedro
12 La Mía Pizza
21 Café Plaza Real
23 Café Colonial
24 Café do Brasil
39 Rincón Oriental
40 Grill Bar Serena
42 Supermercado Las Brisas
43 Quick Biss

30 Iglesia San Agustín
32 Iglesia Santo Domingo
34 Conaf
35 Net Café
36 Librería Andrés Bello
37 Centro Cultural Gabriela Mistral
38 Tas-Choapa
44 Museo Arqueológico
45 Covalle Bus
48 Ingservtur
49 Taxi Colectivos to Coquimbo
50 Iglesia San Francisco
51 Agencia Tacso
52 Pullman Bus
54 Hertz
55 Econorent
56 Avis
57 Lavaseco
58 Afro Son; CLAC (Centro Latinoamericano de Arte y Cultura)
59 Buses Abasto
59 Hospital Emergency Entrance
63 Bus Terminal

OTHER
6 Viajes Torremolinos
7 Café del Patio; Talinay Adventure Expeditions
8 Cámara de Turismo Kiosk
9 Iglesia La Merced
11 Top Ten
14 Librería Macondo; Los Tres A
17 Post Office
18 Sernatur
19 Museo Histórico Casa Gabriel González Videla
20 Municipalidad; Tribunales
22 Tur Bus
25 LanChile
26 Turismo San Bartolemé
27 Entel
28 Librería Universitaria
29 Gira Tour

but a bewildering array of sandwich, snack and coffee specials usually come with cheaper surfing time. Less expensive Internet access (about US$1.25 per hour) is available at many other places, including some **Centros de Llamados**, but these businesses come and go.

Travel Agencies La Serena's numerous travel agencies include **Viajes Torremolinos** (☎ 228-061; e torremolinos@entelchile.net; Prat 464) and **Gira Tour** (☎ 223-535; Prat 689).

Bookstores Librería Andrés Bello (Matta 510) and **Librería Universitaria** (Cordovez 470) have good selections of books in Spanish. **Librería Macondo** (Mercado La Recova, 2nd floor) sports an interesting collection of used books and Chilean music.

Laundry Lavaseco (☎ 225-195; Balmaceda 851) charges US$2 a kilo for laundry.

Medical Services Hospital Juan de Diós (☎ 225-569; Balmaceda 916) has an emergency entrance at the corner of Larraín Alcalde and Anfión Muñoz.

Plaza de Armas

Many of La Serena's key features, including several churches, are on or near the pleasantly landscaped Plaza de Armas. On the east side, the **Iglesia Catedral** dates from 1844. Just to its north are the **Municipalidad** and **Tribunales** (law courts; cnr Prat & Carrera), built as a result of González Videla's Plan Serena.

A block southwest of the plaza along Cordovez and facing a small, attractive square, the colonial **Iglesia Santo Domingo** is a relic from the mid-18th century. Three blocks east of the plaza, the **Iglesia San Agustín** (cnr Cienfuegos & Cantournet) originally belonged to the Jesuits, then passed to the Agustinians after the Jesuits' expulsion. It has undergone serious modifications since its construction in 1755, most recently due to damage from the 1975 earthquake.

The colonial **Iglesia San Francisco** (Balmaceda 640), two blocks southeast of the plaza, was the first stone church built in town. It was constructed in the early 1600s.

Museo Histórico Casa Gabriel González Videla

This museum (☎ 215-082; Matta 495; adult/ child US$1/0.50; open 10am-6:10pm Mon-Fri, 10am-1pm Sat), at the southwest corner of the Plaza de Armas, has exhibits on González Videla, a native of La Serena who was Chile's president from 1946 to 1952. A controversial figure, he took power with communist support but soon outlawed the party, driving poet Pablo Neruda out of the Senate and into exile. Exhibits on González Videla's life omit these episodes, but the museum includes other worthwhile materials on regional history, as well as rotating exhibits of works by Chilean artists. The adjacent **Plaza González Videla**, between the museum and the post office, is the site of the annual book fair (see Special Events later in this section).

Museo Arqueológico

La Serena's archaeological museum (☎ 224-492; cnr Cordovez & Cienfuegos; adult/child US$1/0.50, Sun free; open 9:30am-5:50pm Tues-Fri, 10am-1pm & 4pm-7pm Sat, 10am-1pm Sun) repeats many of the same themes of the González Videla museum, but also has a valuable collection of Diaguita Indian artifacts from before the Inka conquest. There is a good map of the distribution of Chile's aboriginal population and a *moai* from Easter Island.

The González Videla and Museo Arqueológico share a common admission policy – admission to one is valid for the other.

Kokoro No Niwa

A pleasant respite from sun and sand, this Japanese garden (adult/child US$1/0.40) is at the southern end of Parque Pedro de Valdivia, at the foot of Cordovez.

Beaches

From the west end of Av Aguirre, south to Coquimbo and beyond, are a multitude of beaches suitable for various activities. On a two-week vacation in La Serena, you can visit a different beach every day, but strong rip currents make many of them unsuitable for swimming. Some beaches – even the safety warnings – seem to be entirely sponsored by a soft drink company. Safe swimming beaches generally start south of Cuatro Esquinas and include most of the beaches around Coquimbo. The beaches between the west end of Av Aquirre and Cuatro Esquinas (ie, those closest to town) are generally unsafe for swimming. Safe beaches are usually marked: Look for the signs 'Playa

Apta' (meaning beach safe for swimming) and 'Playa No Apta' (meaning beach not safe for swimming).

The bus line Antena Lianco Compañías heads down Av Francisco de Aguirre to Playa El Faro in January and February only. The taxi colectivo line Vista Hermosa serves the Playa Cuatro Esquinas area. There is no direct service the remainder of the year. The bus line Liserco travels the Panamericana between La Serena and Coquimbo, and can let you off at Av Cuatro Esquinas, which leads to the beach.

Besides swimming and sunbathing, other popular activities include sailing (if you make friends with a member of the yacht club), surfing (Playa El Faro is a favorite with body-boarders) and windsurfing. Windsurfers who do not respect the rights of swimmers within 200m of the beach may run afoul of the naval Gobernación Marítima. Playa Totoralillo, south of Coquimbo, is good for surfing and windsurfing.

Organized Tours

Numerous agencies offer a variety of excursions from La Serena, ranging from conventional city tours to visits to nearby national parks, nighttime astronomical trips and even New Age trips to Cochiguaz. Traditional excursions include half-day city tours (around US$10), full-day trips to various destinations in the Elqui Valley (US$25-35), Parque Nacional Fray Jorge (US$25), and Isla Damas in the Parque Nacional Pingü'ino de Humboldt (US$40). These agencies also provide transportation to the observatories and to Mamalluca in Vicuña (US$20). The minimum number of passengers typically ranges from two to six, with destinations closer to La Serena having lower minimums.

Ingservtur (☎/fax 220-165; ⓦ www .ingservtur.cl; Matta 611) has friendly English-speaking staff, and provides English- or German-speaking guides for about 20% more than the standard prices. The company may add a trip to less-visited Hurtado in the future.

Turismo San Bartolomé (☎/fax 221-992; ⓦ www.angelfire.com/home/turismo sanbartolome; Galería Buale, Cordovez 540, Local 114) also offers the standard tours.

Talinay Adventure Expeditions (☎/fax 218-658; ⓔ talinay@turismoaventura.com; Prat 470) has bilingual guides. In addition to the standard tours, Talinay offers more adventur-

ous options, including mountain biking, diving, horseback riding and sandboarding trips. They also rent bikes (US$2/8/13 per hour/half day/full day).

Special Events

In the second week of January, the city hosts the **Jornadas Musicales de La Serena,** a series of musical events that has been held for nearly 20 years.

In the first fortnight of February, the **Feria Internacional del Libro de La Serena,** the annual book fair, displays the latest works from national and foreign publishing houses. Many prominent Chilean authors visit the city and give public readings during this time. This is followed in the second fortnight of February by an artisan's fair. Both events take place on the Plaza Gabriel González Videla, next to the historical museum.

Places to Stay

Many families who house students from the university during the school year (March to December) also rent to tourists in the summer, but some may have a spare bed at other times (contact Sernatur for details). Seasonal price differentials in La Serena are substantial; the prices below are high-season (January and February). Off-season prices may be significantly lower.

Budget Residencial La Familiar (☎ 215-927; Infante 435; rooms US$8) provides basic rooms with shared bath, and it has a delightful, thatched-roof dining area.

Residencial El Loa (☎ 210-304; O'Higgins 362; per person US$8.50) has some dark rooms, but others are fine. Rooms have shared bath.

Residencial Lorena Internacional (☎ 223-380; Cantournet 950; rooms US$9) has spacious rooms with shared bath and kitchen; during the school year, university students occupy most of the generally quieter rooms at the back.

Residencial Limmat (☎ 211-373; Lautaro 914; dorm beds US$10) is the local HI affiliate, with spotless rooms (some of them small), attractive common spaces and shared baths.

Casa Valentina (☎ 223-142; ⓦ www .angelfire.com/va3/casavalentina; Brasil 271; per person US$9) is a hostel that opened in 2000 in a colonial house with nice high ceilings and a pleasant common area. Most rooms have shared bath, although one room has private bath (US$11). Solo travelers may have to share. Breakfast is not available, but guests can use the family kitchen. Laundry, haircuts and even Spanish lessons are offered for extra cost. German and English are spoken.

Residencial Jofré (☎ 222-335; e hostaljofre @hotmail.com; Regimiento Coquimbo 964; per person US$9), on a quiet street close to the bus terminal, has rooms with private bath. Rates include breakfast and kitchen privileges; Internet access is also available.

Hostal Croata (☎ 224-997; Cienfuegos 248; singles/doubles US$13/20) is central and family-run, with bright clean rooms, private bath, bike rental and Internet access. They'll also do your laundry for a reasonable fee.

Mid-Range On a relatively quiet street, **Hotel Pacífico** (☎ 225-674; Eduardo de la Barra 252; doubles with shared/private bath US$20/26) has friendly staff. Some rooms are a bit rundown and musty. Try for a room upstairs, where the rooms are larger and brighter.

Hotel Soberanía (☎ 227-672; Regimiento Coquimbo 1049; singles/doubles US$20/35) is a colonial-style family hotel on a quiet street; some rooms are a little cramped. Breakfast costs an extra US$2.50.

Residencial Suiza (☎ 216-092; Cienfuegos 250; singles/doubles US$21/38), though not really Swiss, is friendly and tidy.

Hotel El Escorial (☎ 215-193, fax 221-433; Brasil 476; singles/doubles US$25/33) is in an older building with a functional open courtyard. The newer rooms are decent and cheerful with large windows. Rates include breakfast. Laundry service is available.

A mass of cabañas operates along the beach in the summertime. **Cabañas Norero** (☎/fax 226-999; Av Del Mar 1000; cabins for up to 3/5/7 people US$45/55/65), about 600m from the lighthouse, is eccentrically operated, with pleasant three-bedroom, fully equipped cabins. It would be quiet here except for all the dogs. The cabins are actually on a side street off Av Del Mar; turn down Amunategui.

Top End Built in 1998, **Hotel Costa Real** (☎ 221-010, fax 221-122; Av Francisco de Aguirre 170; singles/doubles US$95/115) is tasteful and one of La Serena's more appealing places, with large rooms and windows.

Amenities include a swimming pool and a full restaurant with sushi. Significant discounts may be available through tourist agencies.

Hotel Mediterráneo (☎/fax 225-837; Cienfuegos 509; singles/doubles US$52/66) is very central but at the intersection of two noisy streets. Rooms are only so-so for the price; those facing the front and side are brighter but noisier.

Hotel Francisco de Aguirre (☎ 222-991; Cordovez 210; singles/doubles start at US$72/88) is handsome, but guests who are not early risers may be disturbed by the bells at the nearby Iglesia Santo Domingo. The room rate includes breakfast.

Places to Eat

Upstairs from the **Mercado La Recova** (Cienfuegos & Cantournet) are lots of good seafood restaurants; **Los Tres A** is a favorite.

Quick Biss (☎ 226-300; Cienfuegos 545, 2nd floor; self-serve lunch dishes US$2, dinner dishes US$4-5) is the best fast-food choice, with a wide selection of surprisingly good cafeteria fare at low prices. It also has a separate smoke-free area.

Café do Brasil (Balmaceda 461; sandwiches US$2-3) serves coffee, snacks and sandwiches, and has inside and outside seating.

Café Plaza Real (☎ 217-166; Prat 465; lunch dishes US$3-5) has good breakfasts and fixed-price lunches.

La Mía Pizza (O'Higgins 360; pizzas US$4) is popular and has a decent vegetarian pizza, in addition to breakfast, onces, ice cream, drinks and basic pastas.

Café Colonial (☎ 216-373; Balmaceda 475; breakfast US$3-4, fixed lunch menú US$4, pizza US$6; open 9am-'late') has good breakfast options (croissants, pancakes, omelets), sandwiches, burgers, pizza and good-looking desserts, with a plan to add more Chilean food. This comfortable, tourist-oriented café has inside and outside seating, and plays jazz music rather than the usual American pop. Live music is featured on Friday and Saturday nights starting about 10pm.

Grill Bar Serena (Eduardo de la Barra 614; fixed lunch menú US$2.50, dishes US$4-7) serves cheap seafood and plentiful desserts, and is popular.

El Cedro (☎ 221-427; Prat 572; fixed lunch menú US$4.50, main dishes US$5-8) is a pleasant, though pricey, Chilean–Middle Eastern restaurant.

Donde El Guatón (☎ 211-519; Brasil 750; dishes US$4-10) has good beef and chicken but snooty service.

Rincón Oriental (O'Higgins 570; main dishes US$4-6) is one of La Serena's better Chinese restaurants.

There are also many places to eat along the beach, heading south from the lighthouse toward Peñuelas.

Supermercado Las Brisas (Cienfuegos 545) is a large, bright supermarket.

Entertainment

Top Ten (O'Higgins 327) is an often-crowded pool hall where the sharks shoot.

Centro Cultural Gabriela Mistral (Cordovez 399) hosts local music acts and theater.

Café del Patio (Prat 470 • Av del Mar 5700; fixed lunch menú US$3-4, main dishes US$4-7) is a small café that turns into a lively jazz and blues venue and offers good bar food on Friday and Saturday nights, although it keeps long hours every day of the week. In summer, some of Santiago's best musicians play the club; the local bands that play the rest of the year are still worth hearing. Its lunch is also worthwhile.

Afro Son (☎ 229-344; Balmaceda 824), in a 130-year-old house, is part of the Centro Latinoamericano de Arte y Cultura and has live Chilean folk music on Friday and Saturday nights, typically starting at midnight. Latin cinema is usually shown once a week around 9pm.

Cine Mark (Av Albert Solari 1490), in the Mall Plaza near the bus terminal, shows big-name movies.

Shopping

Check **Mercado La Recova** (cnr Cienfuegos & Cantournet) if you want to shop for musical instruments, woolens and dried fruits from the Elqui Valley.

Getting There & Away

Air La Serena's **Aeropuerto La Florida** (Hwy 41) is a short distance east of downtown. **LanChile** (☎ 221-531; Balmaceda 406; open 9am-1:30pm & 3pm-7pm Mon-Fri, 10am-1pm Sat) flies three to five times daily to Santiago (US$30 one-way, 50 minutes), twice a day to Copiapó (US$25, 45 minutes) and once on most days to Antofagasta (US$60). The Mall Plaza office has longer

hours (10am-2pm & 4pm-9pm Mon-Fri, 10am-9pm Sat & Sun).

Bus La Serena's **Terminal de Buses** (☎ 224-573; cnr Amunátegui & Av El Santo) is southwest of downtown. Many carriers ply the long-distance Panamericana routes, from Santiago north to Arica, including the major carriers **Tur Bus** (☎ 215-953; main terminal • Balmaceda 437), **Pullman Bus** (☎ 225-152; main terminal • ☎ 225-284; Domeyko), **Pullman Carmelita** (main terminal), and **Flota Barrios** (main terminal).

Typical destinations and fares are:

destination	duration in hours	cost
Antofagasta	13	US$16
Arica	23	US$24
Calama	16	US$22
Copiapó	5	US$6
Iquique	19	US$24
Santiago	7	US$6
Vallenar	3	US$4

To get to Vicuña (US$2, one hour), look for Buses Serenamar, Pullman Carmelita and Los Diamontes de Elqui in the main terminal, or **Buses Abasto** (Pení & Esmeralda). For Ovalle (US$2.50), try Elqui Bus, Buses Serenamar, Los Diamontes de Elqui, Lasval or Liktur in the main terminal.

Buses Abasto also has the most departures for Pisco Elqui (US$3, two hours) and Monte Grande (US$3, two hours), departing every half-hour to one and a half hours between 7am and 10:30pm. Buses Serenamar runs several buses a day to Guanaqueros, Tongoy and Andacollo.

For Argentine destinations, **Covalle Bus** (☎ 213-127; Infante 538) goes to Mendoza (US$33; 12 hours) and San Juan (US$35; 14 hours) via the Libertadores pass on Tuesday, Thursday, and Sunday at 11pm. **Tas-Choapa** (☎ 613-822; main terminal • cnr La Barra & O'Higgins) also goes to Mendoza, but via Santiago.

Taxi Colectivo Many regional destinations are more frequently and rapidly served by taxi colectivo. Colectivos to Coquimbo leave from Av Francisco de Aguirre between Balmaceda and Los Carrera. **Agencia Tacso** (☎ 227-379; Domeyko 589) goes to Ovalle (US$3), Vicuña (US$2.50) and Andacollo (US$2.50), and you can also hire the taxi for the day to tour Valle de Elqui for about US$50. Other colectivo agencies on this street also serve Ovalle, Vicuña and Andacollo.

Getting Around

Cabs to La Serena's Aeropuerto La Florida, a short distance east of downtown on Chile 41, the route to Vicuña and the Elqui Valley, cost only US$3 to US$4. There's a taxi stand on the southeast corner of Balmaceda and La Barra.

For rental cars, try **Avis** (☎ 227-049; Av Aguirre 063 • airport), **Hertz** (☎ 225-471; Av Aguirre 0225), **Flota Verschae** (☎ 227-645; Balmaceda 3856), south of Cuatro Esquinas, or **Econorent** (Av Aguirre 0135).

AROUND LA SERENA
Caleta Hornos

About 25km north of La Serena, directly on the Panamericana, this small fishing settlement is known for its good, inexpensive seafood picadas, most notably **Brisas Marinas**, that serve the catch fresh off the boat.

Observatorio Cerro Tololo

Operated by the Tucson-based Association of Universities for Research in Astronomy (Aura; a group of about 25 institutions including the Universidad de Chile), Observatorio Interamericano Cerro Tololo sits 2200m above sea level, 88km southeast of La Serena. Its 4m telescope, once the Southern Hemisphere's largest, has since been superseded by 8m giants at Cerro Paranal, south of Antofagasta, but it is still a popular excursion for visitors to the Norte Chico, thanks to guided tours led by knowledgeable staff, all of whom speak English (although most visitors are Chilean). Telescopes measuring 8m and 4.2m are under construction on Cerro Pachón nearby.

Tours of Cerro Tololo, a futuristic-looking multidomed campus on a hill, take place Saturday only and are free of charge. They feature visits to two of the main telescopes, including the 4m giant, and an audiovisual program with images of some of the observatory's 'stellar' discoveries of the past decade or so. It's a daytime visit – even the astronomers don't peer through the actual telescopes. Instead, all the data is fed into computers and re-sorted into monitor images that the human eye can handle. Nevertheless, Tololo is still a worthwhile excursion. To see the nighttime skies, try a visit to Mamalluca near Vicuña (see Around Vicuña later in this chapter).

To visit Cerro Tololo, make reservations by contacting **Aura** (☎ 205-200; **w** www.ctio .noao.edu; **e** ctiorecp@noao.edu). Tours are at 9am and 1pm on Saturday and are limited to 40 people each, so make reservations as far in advance as you can; the observatory suggests at least one month in the high season. Many visitors who show up without reservations are disappointed. There is no public transportation to the observatory, so renting a car, hiring a taxi or arranging with a tour operator are pretty much the only options. (Even if you make arrangements with a tour operator, you *still* must make your own reservations with the observatory directly.) The well-marked, gated turnoff to Tololo is 52km east of La Serena via Ruta 41, where people who have contracted tours ascend the smooth but winding gravel road in a caravan of vehicles.

COQUIMBO

☎ 51 • pop 163,000

In the rocky hills of Península Coquimbo, between the Bahía de Coquimbo and the smaller Bahía Herradura de Guayacán, the bustling port of Coquimbo takes its name from a Diaguita word meaning 'place of calm waters.' Though a less attractive place to stay than La Serena, the town does have an appealing plaza, an authentic working harbor and good beaches nearby.

The **Casa de la Cultura y Turismo** (☎ 313-971; cnr Freire & Av Costanera; open 8:30am-5:30pm daily Mar-Dec) doles out tourist information. In summer, tourist information is given out at the modest **Museo de Sitio** (Calle Aldunate; open 9:30am-8:30pm Mon-Sat, 9:30am-2pm Sun Jan & Feb), site of a pre-Columbian graveyard discovered serendipitously when clearing a lot for expanding the Plaza de Armas. It dates from Las Animas cultural complex, AD 900–1100, which predated the Diaguita.

Coquimbo's newest tourist attraction is the **Cruz del Tercer Milenio** (Cross of the Third Millennium; Cerro El Vigía; general admission US$1; open 10am-7pm Mon-Fri, 11am-8pm Sat & Sun), a cross between a holy pilgrimage site and touristy kitsch, where you're likely to meet families running around in short pants dodging nuns at mass. This astounding 96m-high concrete cross, il-

The Starry Southern Skies

Inland from the perpetually fogbound coast, in the western foothills of the Andes, Norte Chico hosts the most important cluster of astronomical observatories in the Southern Hemisphere. Within 150km of La Serena are three major facilities: above the Elqui Valley is the Cerro Tololo Interamerican Observatory (CTIO); at La Silla, the European Southern Observatory (ESO); and the Carnegie Institution's Observatorio Las Campanas. The last two are east of the Panamericana on the border between Regions III and IV.

Plans for new telescopes will only increase Chile's astronomical importance. Currently, the Southern Hemisphere's largest telescope is the cluster of four 8.2m trapezoidal Very Large Telescopes (VLTs) at ESO's Cerro Paranal observatory, 120km south of Antofagasta in Region II. At Las Campanas, the Carnegie Institution will be adding two 6.5m VLTs.

Even more massive is the planned Atacama Large Millimeter Array (ALMA), which will consist of 64 12m radio telescopes or antennas spread over a 10km area on the Llano de Chajnantor, 5000m above sea level and 40km east of San Pedro de Atacama in Region II. Part of the US National Science Foundation's Project Gemini, it will complement a similar facility on Hawaii's Mt Mauna Kea. In what sounds like a case of celestial hubris, the area may also be the site for an Overwhelmingly Large Telescope (OWT), budgeted at US$1 billion (perhaps the next step is the ILT – Impossibly Large Telescope).

In addition to encouraging research by foreign institutions, Chile hopes to foment more local participation, and Chile's small community of 30 or so astronomers will be guaranteed a certain amount of research time on the facilities.

One problem that concerns astronomers is the urbanization of Chile's northern deserts. Once-remote areas such as Cerro Tololo are now vulnerable to light pollution from growing towns and cities such as Vicuña and La Serena. To ensure Chile's astronomical future, a 1998 law sets standards for lighting fixtures in the Norte Chico and Norte Grande. The observatories also work with neighboring towns to reduce light pollution. For example, the Cerro Tololo Observatory helped Vicuña make changes to their street lighting, resulting in an increase in ground-level illumination while cutting light emissions to the sky by 95% *and* cutting the town's lighting bill in half. To recognize the town's efforts, the US National Science Foundation donated a 12-inch telescope to the town, now featured at the Observatorio Comunal Cerro Mamalluca outside Vicuña.

—Wayne Bernhardson

luminated at night, can be seen from the beaches of La Serena. The site includes a museum, praying rooms and an elevator ride to the top (US$2), where visitors get a dizzying but good view of the bay. Mass is held every Sunday. The first level is free.

Half-hour boat tours (US$3) of the harbor depart from Av Costanera daily between 10am and 9pm in January and February, weekends only the rest of the year. There are very popular beaches along the Bahía Herradura de Guayacán, easily reached from either Coquimbo or La Serena.

Places to Stay & Eat
Hotel Iberia (☎ 312-141; Lastra 400; singles/doubles US$12/22), a block from the main commercial street (Calle Aldunate), offers excellent budget accommodations. Rooms have private bath.

The market, a block east of Calle Aldunate, is a good place to look for great seafood, especially La Maria, with plentiful and delicious seafood dishes. The Terminal Pesquero (fish market) along the bay offers cheaper but still tasty fish options.

Entertainment
Nightlife options in Coquimbo tend to be seedier than in La Serena, with a notable exception being the Club de Jazz (Aldunate 739; cover US$5), in an old house with marble stairs. The club has live music on weekends starting at 11pm.

Getting There & Away
Coquimbo's Terminal de Buses (Varela) is between Borgoño and Barriga. Long-distance services are similar to those to and from La Serena; many local buses and

taxi colectivos also link the two cities (US$0.50 bus; US$5 private taxi).

GUANAQUEROS

At the south end of Bahía Guanaqueros, 30km south of Coquimbo and 5km west of the Panamericana, Guanaqueros' long, white, sandy beach makes it one of the area's most popular resorts. It's suitable for a day trip.

Hotel La Bahía *(☎ 395-107; Arturo Prat 058)* is open all year.

El Pequeño Restaurant *(☎ 391-341; Av Costanera 306)* has traditionally been a favorite for Chilean food, and it has a terrace with a view of the sea.

Buses and taxi colectivos run frequently from Coquimbo and La Serena and continue to Tongoy; see La Serena earlier in this chapter and Tongoy below for more information.

TONGOY

On a rocky peninsula 58km south of La Serena lies the lively beach resort of Tongoy, with an artisans market, family-oriented beachfront restaurants and souvenir shops. The moderately priced *marisquerías* (seafood restaurants) along the south side of Playa Grande are enjoyable places to spend the afternoon and watch the action. Playa Socos, on the north side of the peninsula, is more sheltered and popular for bathing.

Residencial D'Pardo *(Fundición Norte 668; per person US$10)* is friendly and has plain rooms with shared bath set among pleasant gardens.

Hostería Tongoy *(☎ 391-203; Costanera 10; doubles US$66)* is an upscale choice with a good restaurant.

From the La Serena bus terminal, Buses Serenamar runs several buses a day to Tongoy (US$2). From Coquimbo's bus terminal, Alfamar taxi colectivos reach Tongoy in about 45 minutes (US$2).

VICUÑA

☎ 51 • pop 24,000

In the upper Elqui Valley, logos bearing the names of piscos Capel, Control and Tres Erres are as conspicuous as international soft-drink billboards in the rest of the country. Vicuña, 62km east of La Serena, is a quiet village of adobe houses in an area that grows avocados, papayas and other fruits, but most notably provides the raw grapes that

local distilleries transform into Chile's powerful brandy. Vicuña holds its annual grape harvest festival, **Festival de la Vendimia**, in February; it ends February 22, the anniversary of the city's founding. Suitable either for a day trip or a few days' stay, Vicuña and its surrounding communities have also acquired a reputation for attracting oddballs, which began with the arrival of several groups convinced that UFOs frequent the area, most notably in nearby Cochiguaz.

From Vicuña, eastbound Ruta 41 leads over the Andes to Argentina. A rugged, dusty secondary road leads south to the town of Hurtado, the modest petrified forest of Monumento Natural Pichasca and the city of Ovalle.

Orientation & Information

On the north bank of the Río Elqui, across a narrow bridge from Ruta 41, Vicuña has a geometric town plan centered on the wooded Plaza de Armas. Av Gabriela Mistral, running east-west off the plaza, is the main commercial street. Every important service or feature is within easy walking distance.

The Municipalidad's **Oficina de Información Turística** *(☎ 209-125; Torre Bauer, Plaza de Armas; open 8:30am-8:30pm daily Jan & Feb; 8:30am-5:30pm Mon-Fri, 9am-1pm & 2pm-5:30pm Sat & Sun Mar-Dec)* is moderately helpful.

Banks changing cash or traveler's checks and universal ATMs are in short supply; it's better to change money in La Serena.

The **post office** *(cnr Mistral & San Martín)* is in the Municipalidad. **Telefónica (CTC)** *(Prat 378)* and **Entel** *(Gabriela Mistral 351)* have long-distance telephone offices. Internet service is offered by **Mami Sabina** *(cnr Mistral & Infante)*.

Hospital San Juan de Dios *(☎ 411-263; cnr Independencia & Prat)* is a few blocks north of the plaza.

Things to See & Do

Built by a former German mayor, the **Torre Bauer** (1905), an unusual clock tower on the west side of the Plaza de Armas, resembles a castle with wooden battlements. The **Iglesia de la Inmaculada Concepción** (1909), opposite the northwest corner of the plaza, has a few ceiling paintings and an image of the Virgen del Carmen carried by Chilean troops during the War of the Pacific.

On the south side of the plaza, the **Museo Entomológico y de Historia Natural** (☎ 411-283; Chacabuco 334; adult/child US$0.75/0.35; open 10:30am-2:30pm & 3:30pm-7pm daily) specializes in insects.

Dating from 1875, the **Casa de los Madariaga** (☎ 411-220; Gabriela Mistral 683; adult/child US$1/0.50; open 10am-1pm & 3pm-7pm daily Jan-Mar, 11am-1pm & 2:30pm-5:30pm daily Apr-Dec) contains furnishings and artifacts from an influential family. The **Museo Histórico de Elqui** (☎ 09-351-8554; Prat 90; adult/child US$0.75/0.25; open 10am-4pm daily) has Diaguita artifacts.

The hike up **Cerro de la Virgen**, just north of town, offers vast panoramas of the entire Elqui Valley, but it's hot and exposed – bring plenty of water and snacks. There's a road most of the way to the summit, less than an hour's walk from the Plaza de Armas.

Museo Gabriela Mistral Vicuña's landmark museum (☎ 411-223; Av Gabriela Mistral; adult/child US$1/0.50; open 10am-7pm Mon-Sat, 10am-6pm Sun Jan & Feb; open 10am-1pm & 2:30pm-5:45pm Mon-Fri, 10am-1pm & 3pm-5:45pm Sat, 10am-1pm Sun Mar-Dec), between Riquelme and Baquedano, is a tangible eulogy to one of Chile's most famous literary figures. Gabriela Mistral was born Lucila Godoy Alcayaga in 1889 in the nearby village of Monte Grande. Museum exhibits include a handsomely presented photographic history of her life (including a picture of a sculpted bust that makes her seem a particularly strict and severe schoolmarm), modest personal artifacts such as her desk and a bookcase, and a replica of her adobe birthplace. Her family tree indicates Spanish, Indian and African ancestry. Like Pablo Neruda, she served in the Chilean diplomatic corps.

Planta Capel Capel, a pisco cooperative with member growers throughout the Norte Chico from Copiapó to Illapel, distills some of its product at this facility, where grapes arrive in vehicles ranging from tractors and pickups to 18-wheelers. The cooperative also has its only bottling plant here, with 36 million bottles per year shipped to imbibing consumers. Fermentation takes 10 to 21 days,

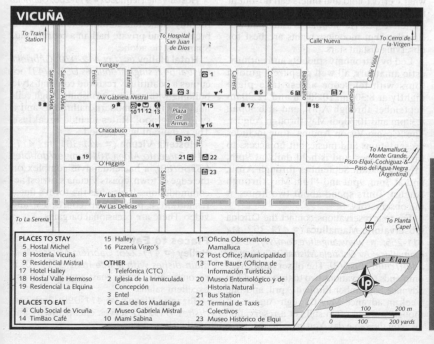

VICUÑA

To Train Station
To Hospital San Juan de Dios
Calle Nueva
To Cerro de la Virgen

Yungay
Sargento Aldea
Sargento Aldea
Frere
Infante
Carrera
Condell
Baquedano
Calle Viola

Av Gabriela Mistral
8
9
10 11 12 13
Plaza de Armas
14
15
16
17
18
Riquelme

Chacabuco
O'Higgins
Prat
San Martín
19
20
21
22
23

To Mamalluca, Monte Grande, Pisco Elqui, Cochiguaz & Paso del Agua Negra (Argentina)

Av Las Delicias
Av Las Delicias
To La Serena
To Planta Capel
41
Río Elqui

0   100   200 m
0   100   200 yards

distillation 10 hours, and the brew is then aged for five months to two years before it is bottled for consumption.

Across the bridge from Vicuña, free tours take place about every half-hour from 10am to 6pm daily in January and February, and from 10am to 12:30pm and 2:30pm to 6pm the rest of the year. Mornings are less crowded, and there is no minimum attendance required – guides literally provide individual attention if only one person shows up. Free but miniscule samples are served on conclusion. Presentations are generally bilingual (Spanish and English). In addition to pisco, the sales room offers *pajarete*, the region's delicious dessert wine.

Be forewarned that tours are only 20 minutes long, so it takes more time to get to the plant than to take the tour. Up to 2000 people tramp through the place in summer.

Observatorio Comunal Cerro Mamalluca Vicuña's charming municipal facility 9km outside of town allows visitors to view the southern night skies through a 12-inch telescope, magnifying selected stars such as Alpha Centauri up to 140 times – not nearly what Cerro Tololo and others can do, but at those observatories you can't look through the telescopes. The weather is usually almost cloudless, but moonless nights are best for observing distant stars.

Led by astronomy students and enthusiastic amateurs, all well prepared, guided tours with telescope access take place nightly at 8:30pm, 10:30pm and 12:30am September through April, and at 6:30pm, 8:30pm and 10:30pm May through August. The 'Cosmo Visión Andina' tour includes presentations and music, but no access to the telescopes, and is held daily at 9pm, 11pm, and 1am September through April, and at 7pm, 9pm and 11pm May through August. Tours spend about two hours at the observatory.

For tour reservations, contact the **Oficina Observatorio Mamalluca** (☎ 411-352, fax 411-255; [W] www.angelfire.com/wy/observ-mamalluca; Av Gabriela Mistral 260, Vicuña; adult/child US$6/3). The observatory recommends reservations two to three weeks in advance September through April, and one week in advance May through August, although you can often still get a reservation even on the same day. You can also reserve a tour by calling or visiting the tourist office in Vicuña.

There is no public transportation, although a small minivan can take up to six people from the Vicuña office (reserve in advance). Some La Serena tour agencies arrange trips (see Organized Tours under La Serena earlier in this chapter); it's also possible to hire a cab in Vicuña. Vehicles go by convoy to the site, which is difficult to find if you don't know the route, as it climbs a dark, winding mountain road.

Places to Stay

Residencial Mistral (☎ 411-278; Gabriela Mistral 180; per person US$6) is clean and friendly; rooms have shared bath. There is also a popular restaurant.

Hostal Michel (☎ 411-060; Gabriela Mistral 573; rooms US$8) is plain but spacious, with private bath but no breakfast.

Residencial La Elquina (☎ 411-317; O'Higgins 65; singles/doubles with shared bath US$10/18, with private bath US$18/30), on a quiet street a few blocks from the center, is an attractive house with lush gardens and fruit trees. Though La Elquina is warmly recommended, some rooms are cramped.

Hostal Valle Hermoso (☎ 411-206; Gabriela Mistral 706; singles/doubles US$11/20) is friendly and offers comfortable rooms with breakfast and private bath in a century-old, Spanish-style adobe.

Hotel Halley (☎/fax 412-070; Gabriela Mistral 542; singles/doubles US$25/43) occupies a beautifully restored colonial-style building with antique furnishings, high ceilings, airy rooms, modern bathrooms and a swimming pool. Rates include breakfast. The restaurant here is good.

Hostería Vicuña (☎ 411-301, fax 411-144; Sargento Aldea 101; singles/doubles US$66/89), a hacienda-style complex on the edge of town, boasts Vicuña's ritziest accommodations. It also has the town's finest restaurant, a pool, tennis courts, TV and video. There are occasional bargains.

Places to Eat

Halley (☎ 411-225; Gabriela Mistral 404; main dishes with a side item US$4-10) is recommended for its roast goat (US$7) and excellent salads.

Pizzería Virgo's (☎ 411-090; Prat 234; dishes US$2-3) serves cheap pizzas and sandwiches.

TimBao Café *(San Martín 203; set lunch menú US$3, sandwiches US$2-3)* is centrally located.

Club Social de Vicuña *(411-853; Gabriela Mistral 445; sandwiches US$2-3, main dishes US$4-8)* is relatively expensive but has a good menu of Chilean food in an attractive setting.

Solar Villaseca *(☎ 412-189; daily menú US$4)*, 6km from Vicuña, is highly praised for its solar-cooked organic dishes. It's reasonably priced (the daily *menú* includes two courses, a dessert and drink) and very popular, so reservations are a must during summer.

Getting There & Away

The **bus terminal** *(Prat & O'Higgins)* is a block south of the plaza, from which there are many buses to La Serena, Coquimbo and Pisco Elqui (US$2). Some companies also have service to Santiago. There is a wider choice of destinations, especially northbound, in La Serena; fares are only a couple of dollars higher than those from La Serena.

Across Prat from the bus terminal is the separate **Terminal de Taxis Colectivos**, the departure point for shared taxis to La Serena (US$3), Monte Grande (US$1.50) and Paihuano (US$1).

MONTE GRANDE

This small town of 4000 is Gabriela Mistral's birthplace. Her burial site, on a nearby hillside, is the destination of many Chilean and literary pilgrims. She received her primary schooling at the Casa Escuela y Correo, where there's a modest **museum** *(adult/child US$0.50/0.25; open 10am-1pm & 3pm-6pm Tues-Sun)*.

Monte Grande has no accommodations itself, but there are hotels in Pisco Elqui, just up the valley, and several cabañas in the nearby village of Cochiguaz (see below). Monte Grande's restaurant **Mesón del Fraile**, opposite the Casa Escuela y Correo, is worth stopping at for a meal.

Local buses and taxi colectivos provide regular service from Vicuña.

COCHIGUAZ

Considered a significant location by New Age adherents, Cochiguaz is, according to one brochure, a 'place among the mountains that concentrates cosmic energy.' But you needn't be a believer to enjoy the secluded valley,

which is also the starting point for hikes and horseback rides in the backcountry.

Camping Cochiguaz *(☎ 327-046; sites up to 4 persons US$16)* has campsites available.

Casa del Agua *(☎/fax 293-798; ☒ www .valledeelqui.cl/maincasadelagua.htm; 4-person cabins US$75)*, 13km north of Monte Grande, offers fully equipped cabins with a view of the valley and surrounding mountains. There's a bar, restaurant (breakfast US$3, lunch and dinner US$8), natural pools, mountain bike rental and walking paths. It also offers tours from US$20.

PISCO ELQUI
☎ 51

Renamed to publicize the area's most famous product, the former village of La Unión is a placid community in the upper drainage area of the Río Claro, a tributary of the Elqui. Its main attraction, the **Solar de Pisco Elqui**, produces the premium Tres Erres brand; there are no scheduled tours, but it's a nice place to taste free samples and inspect the antique machinery of the old distillery and bodegas. Horseback rides around the hills may be available – look for horses near the plaza, or inquire at Hotel Elqui.

According to local legend, former Chilean President Gabriel González Videla personally changed La Unión's original name to undermine Peruvian claims of having originated the beverage (the provincial city of Pisco, in the valley of the same name south of Lima, also produces the drink). Despite producers' complaints of competition from foreign imports such as whiskey, acreage planted to grapes seems to have skyrocketed over the past decade – an apparent pisco boom.

From Vicuña, frequent taxi colectivos go to Pisco Elqui.

Places to Stay & Eat

Camping El Olivo *(☎ 451-790 in Vicuña; campsites US$7)* is north of the plaza and has a simple restaurant. Rates include pool access.

Hostería de Don Juan *(☎ 451-087; Arturo Prat s/n; rooms per person US$7)*, in a dilapidated, mysterious old mansion, is creaky but congenial.

Hotel Elqui *(☎ 198-2523; O'Higgins s/n; rooms per person US$13)* is quaint and friendly; rates include breakfast and use of the pool. Lunches are reasonably priced (about US$6).

El Tesoro de Elqui (☎ 198-2609; e tesoro@ pisco.de; Prat s/n; singles US$12-19, doubles US$19-38), a delightful oasis, is a German-run place that has attractive cabañas with shared bath, a common kitchen and a pool. Breakfast is included, and there is a great restaurant.

Opposite the Plaza de Armas, shady **Jugos Naturales** serves huge fresh juices from oranges, papayas, pineapples and apricots.

PASO DEL AGUA NEGRA

East of Vicuña, Ruta 41 climbs the valley of the Río Turbio to the Chilean customs and immigration post at Juntas del Toro. It then continues south along the Río de La Laguna before switchbacking steeply northeast to 4765m Paso del Agua Negra, one of the highest Andean passes between Chile and Argentina. Once mined by the Argentine military during tensions over the Beagle Channel in 1978, the route is usually open to vehicular traffic from mid-November to mid-March or April, and a fair number of cyclists enjoy this steep, difficult route for its spectacular mountain scenery. The road is passable for any passenger vehicle in good condition.

Leading to the hot springs resort of Termas de Pismanta in Argentina, and to the provincial capital of San Juan, Agua Negra is one of the best areas to see the frozen snow formations known as *penitentes*, so called because they resemble a line of monks garbed in tunics. There are also accessible glaciers on both the Chilean and Argentine sides.

OVALLE

☎ 53 • pop 97,000

Founded as a satellite of older La Serena in early republican times, Ovalle is the spotlessly clean capital of the prosperous agricultural province of Limarí. Although the city is half an hour east of the Panamericana, many north-south buses pass through here. Ovalle is a pleasant stop if you are planning trips to Parque Nacional Fray Jorge or Valle del Encanto.

Orientation & Information

Ovalle sits on the north bank of the Río Limarí, 90km south of La Serena and 30km east of the Panamericana. Everything of interest is within easy walking distance of the Plaza de Armas, which is beautifully landscaped and partially shaded.

There's a **tourist kiosk** (Benavente) in Parque Alameda, with minimal information. **Limtur** (☎/fax 630-057; Vicuña Mackenna 370, office 9A), in front of Plaza del Armas, also has information and can arrange tours to nearby attractions. There's also a **Conaf office** (☎ 620-058; Covarrubias 75).

It's better to change money in a larger town, but try **Tres Valles Turismo** (☎ 629-650; cnr Carmen & Libertad) for exchanging US cash only. There are ATMs around the plaza.

The **post office** (Vicuña Mackenna; open 8:30am-6pm Mon-Fri, 9am-12:30pm Sat) is opposite the plaza. Long-distance calls can be made at **Telefónica (CTC)** (Ariztía Oriente 234) and **Entel** (Vicuña Mackenna 115). **Sky Internet** (Vicuña Mackenna near Carmen; open 9am-7:30pm Mon-Fri, 10am-1pm Sat) has Internet access (US$2 per hour); some of the Centros de Llamados have longer hours.

For medical attention, go to **Hospital Dr Antonio Tirado** (☎ 620-042; Ariztía Poniente & Socos).

Museo del Limarí

Ovalle's archaeological museum (☎ 620-029; cnr Covarrubias & Antofagasta; adult/child US$1/0.40, Wed free; open 9am-1pm & 3pm-7pm Tues-Fri, 10am-1pm Sat & Sun), part of the Centro Cultural Guillermo Durruty Alvarez, is a modest but worthwhile endeavor stressing the trans-Andean links between the Diaguita peoples of coastal Chile and northwest Argentina. There are also pieces from the earlier Huentelauquén and El Molle cultures. Some of the larger ceramics are in excellent condition.

Places to Stay & Eat

Hotel Roxy (☎ 620-080; Libertad 155; singles/doubles with shared bath US$10/16, with private bath US$14/21) has a pleasant sun-drenched patio and is a great value despite soft beds.

Hotel Turismo (☎ 623-258; Victoria 295; singles/doubles US$32/46) is a modern hotel with pleasant and comfortable rooms. It's conveniently located on the plaza, yet still quiet.

There are many moderately priced places to eat along Calle Independencia, near the Mercado Municipal.

For good fixed-price lunches, try the **Club Comercial** (*Aguirre 244; set lunch US$2.50, main dishes US$3-5*).

Club Social Arabe (*☎ 620-015; Arauco 255; set menús US$2-3, main dishes US$3.50-6*) offers Chilean dishes and Middle Eastern specialties such as stuffed grape leaves; they offer vegetarian preparations as well.

El Quijote (*Arauco 295; sandwiches US$1.25-2, main dishes US$3-4*), dark and musty, pays homage to Latin American literary and political figures and serves up OK meals with friendly service. More a pub than a restaurant, this is also a good place to grab a beer.

Feria Modelo de Ovalle (*open 8am-4pm Mon, Wed, Fri & Sat*), the town's lively fruit and vegetable market, is also a good place to look for crafts. It's east on Av Benavente (which is Vicuña Mackenna west of Ariztía), in the former repair facilities of the railroad.

Getting There & Away

The **bus terminal** (*cnr Maestranza & Balmaceda*) has plenty of buses to La Serena, Santiago and other points north and south.

All the standard companies are represented. Regional companies provide service to more out-of-the-way destinations such as Combarbalá, Quilitapia, Tulahuén, and Manquehua. **Los Molinos** (*☎ 629-578; Ariztía Poniente 387*) provides service to Punitaqui.

Taxi colectivos to La Serena and Coquimbo leave from Poniente between Socos and Libertad.

AROUND OVALLE

The area around Ovalle has a few worthwhile attractions – toward the Panamericana to the west and more remotely in the valley of Río Hurtado to the northeast, a less-explored and less-crowded alternative to the Elqui Valley. If you have your own transportation, you can also make a loop from La Serena to Vicuña, Hurtado and Ovalle, then back to La Serena. The 43km gravel road from Vicuña to Hurtado is usually manageable in a regular car, but a 4WD or high-clearance vehicle would be less terrifying; pisco trucks have damaged the road. The drive is through beautiful, sometimes steep, desert scenery, with cacti, multicolored rocks, plenty of birds and

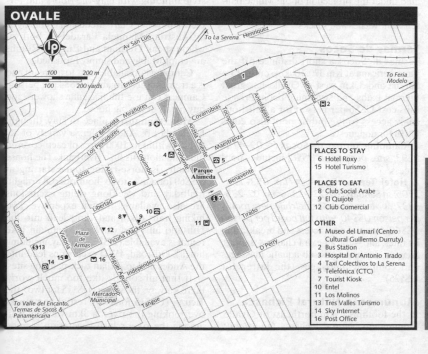

OVALLE

To La Serena

To Feria Modelo

To Valle del Encanto, Termas de Socos & Panamericana

PLACES TO STAY
6   Hotel Roxy
15 Hotel Turismo

PLACES TO EAT
8   Club Social Arabe
9   El Quijote
12 Club Comercial

OTHER
1   Museo del Limarí (Centro Cultural Guillermo Durruty)
2   Bus Station
3   Hospital Dr Antonio Tirado
4   Taxi Colectivos to La Serena
5   Telefónica (CTC)
7   Tourist Kiosk
10 Entel
11 Los Molinos
13 Tres Valles Turismo
14 Sky Internet
16 Post Office

good views. Public transportation from Ovalle goes as far as Hurtado, but there is no direct connection to Vicuña.

Valle del Encanto

Monumento Arqueológico Valle del Encanto (*adult/child US$1/0.50; open 9am-4:30pm daily*), a rocky tributary canyon of the Río Limarí, contains a remarkable density of Indian petroglyphs, pictographs and mortars from El Molle culture, which inhabited the area from the second to the seventh century AD. The rock art is best viewed in the early afternoon, when shadows are fewer, but it can be very hot at that time of day. A lot of families come here on weekends.

Both picnicking and camping are possible at Valle del Encanto, 19km west of Ovalle. To get there, take any westbound bus out of Ovalle toward Termas de Socos and disembark at the highway marker; Valle del Encanto is an easy 5km walk along a clearly marked gravel road, but with luck, someone will offer you a lift. Bring water for the hike, although there is potable water in the canyon itself. Roundtrip by taxi costs about US$25.

The Monumento Arqueológico is operated under the protection of the Municipalidad of Ovalle. On weekends, a concessionaire sells sandwiches and snacks.

Termas de Socos

Termas de Socos, a short distance off the Panamericana at Km 370, 100km south of La Serena and 33km west of Ovalle, has great thermal baths and swimming pools. Private tubs cost US$6 per person for a half-hour soak; access to the public pool also costs US$6 for nonguests.

Camping Termas de Socos (*☎ 09-418-0293; sites per person US$8*) includes pool access.

Hotel Termas Socos (*☎/fax 053-198-2505; in Santiago 02-236-3336, fax 02-236-3337; e termasocos@entelchile.net; rooms per person US$40, with full board per person US$60*) includes pool access and breakfast in its rates, and – for an extra charge – saunas, Jacuzzis, dry massages, sub-aquatic massages and complete massages (the latter for US$25).

Monumento Natural Pichasca

In the foothills 45km northeast of Ovalle, Monumento Natural Pichasca (*adult/child US$2.50/1; open 9am-5pm daily*) guards 128 hectares of petrified araucaria forest along the Río Hurtado. Sadly, so many fossil trees were carted away before the area acquired Conaf protection that it's barely worth a detour for anyone expecting to see a large petrified forest. Also within the monument, a natural overhang known as **Casa de Piedra** has a smattering of pre-Columbian Molle rock art, but smoke from decades of campfires lit by stock drivers who camped here has damaged the paintings.

Local buses from Ovalle's Feria Modelo go as far as Hurtado, passing the lateral to Pichasca, a 2km uphill walk in the summer heat. Motorists can take the dusty, winding gravel road north or south, to or from Vicuña.

About 1km north of the monument is the perfect small town of Pichasca, with an adobe church painted blue.

Hacienda Los Andes

Overlooking the banks of Río Hurtado, Hacienda Los Andes (*☎ 53-691-822; w www.haciendalosandes.com; singles/doubles start at US$32/40*) is the kind of place that's hard to leave. The hacienda is a beautiful, colonial-style building with clay-tile floors and terracotta roof tiles, designed and built by German owner Clark Stede and comanaged by Austrian Manuela Paradeiser, both of whom speak German and English. Rooms are comfortable and simply furnished.

Camping is available next to a stream and is a tremendous bargain at US$4 per person. Campers can use the hacienda showers and buy meals at the big house.

More than just a place to stay, though, Hacienda Los Andes offers a variety of activities within its 1000 acres of cacti-covered hills and along its lush riverbank. The house specialty is horse-riding tours, starting at US$60 for a five- to six-hour ride. Overnight, multiday and weeklong riding excursions are also available, though expensive. Two hiking trails (4km and 7km) lead into the Hurtado hills and canyons. Mountain bike rental is available (US$25 per day, including lunch). Off-road, 4WD excursions lead into the Andes and to Indian rock-painting sites.

If that all sounds like too much work, there's always the sauna (US$15 for two), the Jacuzzi (US$15 for two), restful hammocks overlooking the river, a 3km walking trail among the river's lush vegetation, a nude beach at a secluded spot in the middle of the creek, and the dark night sky above.

Meals (breakfast US$7, lunch $10, dinner $10) are created using local fruits, cheese and vegetables from small farmers in the Hurtado valley.

In nearby Hurtado, **Restaurant Penita** is a cheaper, friendly place with freshly prepared meals. Don't expect fast food here.

To reach the hacienda, you can drive or take the daily bus from Ovalle to Hurtado; the hacienda is 3km before Hurtado, just before the bridge. Or, the hacienda provides pickup service from Ovalle and Vicuña (each US$35 per person) and from La Serena (US$60 per person). The hacienda is 46km from Vicuña via gravel mountain road, and 97km from Ovalle (the road is paved as far as Samo Alto).

PN FRAY JORGE

Moistened by the Pacific Ocean camanchaca, Parque Nacional Fray Jorge is an ecological island of Valdivian cloud forest (a type of rainforest found around Valdivia, several hundred kilometers south) in an otherwise semiarid region, 110km south of La Serena and 82km west of Ovalle. Illapel, for instance, gets only about 150mm of rainfall per annum, but Fray Jorge, 140km north, receives up to 10 times that, supporting vegetation that is more like the verdant forests of southern Chile than the Mediterranean scrub that covers most of Norte Chico. Elevations range from sea level to 600m.

Of Fray Jorge's 10,000 hectares, there remain only 400 hectares of this truly unique vegetation – enough, though, to make it a Unesco World Biosphere Reserve. Some scientists believe this relict vegetation is evidence of dramatic climate change, but others argue that humans are responsible for the destruction of these forests, using them for fuel, farming and timber.

The effect of the ocean fog is most pronounced at elevations above 450m; here there are stands of *olivillo (Aetoxicon punctatum), arrayán* (myrtle; *Myrceugenia correaeifolia*) and *canelo (Drimys winteri)*, plus countless other shrubs and epiphytes. The few mammals include two species of fox *(Dusicyon culpaeus* and *Dusicyon griseus)*, skunks and sea otters. There are some 80 bird species, including the occasional Andean condor.

The park is named after the first recorded European visitor, a Franciscan priest named Fray Jorge, in 1672. Camping and limited hiking are available in the park.

Information

Fray Jorge *(adult/child US$3/1; open 9am-4:30pm Fri-Sun Dec 15-Mar 15, open Sat & Sun only rest of year)* has staff limitations, and the gated road may be locked outside opening hours. The **Centro de Información** is about 1km past the entrance and has information and interesting photographic displays. Contact Conaf or Sernatur in La Serena for more information.

Activities

In late afternoon, the rising camanchaca moistens the dense vegetation at **Sendero El Bosque**, a 1km trail that runs along the ridge above the ocean. The best time to appreciate the forest's ecological characteristics is early morning, when condensation from the fog leaves the plants dripping with moisture.

A short distance inland from the main forest, contrasting with the parched semi-desert of the surrounding hills, discontinuous patches of green suggest that the forest at one time must have been far more extensive. The trail is at the end of the road from the Panamericana, 7km from the campground at El Arrayancito. Hikers will find the last segment of the road to the trailhead very steep and dusty.

With permission from Conaf, it's possible to walk down the fire trail from the ridge to the coast. Three kilometers from the Centro de Información is the park Administración, a historic building that was once the *casco* (big house) for a local hacienda. From there it's possible to walk 15km to a beach campsite, but Conaf discourages hikers from taking this route because part of it goes through private property.

Places to Stay

El Arrayancito *(sites US$10)* is a sheltered camp 3km from the visitor center and 7km west of El Bosque. Each of its 13 sites has a firepit (firewood is available), a picnic table, potable water, clean toilets, cold showers and plenty of annoying bugs. Bring your own food.

Conaf also offers a **cabin** *(☎ 51-272-798/799; up to 5 people US$35)*. The **Casa de Administración** may have food service

(US$7), but verify this is still an option in La Serena or Ovalle before you show up in the park without food.

Getting There & Away

Reach the park by taking a westward lateral off the Panamericana, about 20km north of the Ovalle junction. There's no public transportation, but several agencies in La Serena and Ovalle offer tours. A taxi from Ovalle will cost about US$40.

LOS VILOS

☎ 53 • pop 17,000

In the peak summer season, up to 20,000 visitors jam the working-class beach resort of Los Vilos. Midway between Santiago and La Serena, it has plenty of inexpensive accommodations and fine seafood, and it is especially lively Sunday mornings when the Caleta San Pedro market offers live fresh crab, dozens of kinds of fish, a roving hurdy-gurdy man and thousands of colorful balloons.

In addition to the usual beach activities, local launches approach seabird colonies at Isla de Huevos (US$2 per person) and the 1400-strong sea lion colony of Isla de Lobos (US$10 per person), from 9am to 7pm daily.

According to local legend, the name Los Vilos is a corruption of *Lord Willow*, a British privateer that shipwrecked nearby. An alternative explanation is that it comes from the Araucanian *vilú*, a term that means serpent or snake and is common elsewhere in the region.

Held the second week of February, **Semana Vileña** (Vilos Week) is the town's biggest celebration of the year.

Orientation & Information

Los Vilos consists of two distinct areas, an older part with a regular grid west of the railroad tracks, and a newer, less regular section between the tracks and the Panamericana. Av Costanera, leading to the beach, is more of a focus of activity than the Plaza de Armas. Most hotels and restaurants are along Av Caupolicán, which links the town with the Panamericana.

In January and February, Sernatur sponsors a tourist representative at the municipal **Corporación Cultural** (*Caupolicán 278; open 10am-2:30pm & 4pm-8pm daily*).

It's best to exchange money in Santiago or La Serena.

The **post office** (*cnr Lincoyán & Galvarino*) is opposite the plaza. On Caupolicán, both **Telefónica (CTC)** and **Entel** have long-distance telephone offices.

Hospital San Pedro (☎ 541-061; Lincoyán & Arauco) is two blocks south of the plaza.

Places to Stay

Residencial Yeko's (*Purén 168; per person US$7*) is friendly and has a restaurant and spacious rooms (with shared bath) in an attractive garden setting, but it lacks hot water.

Hotel Bellavista (☎ 541-073; Rengo 020; per person with shared bath US$8, with private bath US$12.50) is popular and central, and rates include breakfast.

Residencial Turismo (☎ 541-176; Caupolicán 437; singles/doubles US$13/25) has rooms with shared bath and a laundry.

Residencial Vienesa (☎ 541-143; Av Los Vilos 11; per person US$12.50) is friendly and appealing, but is often full.

American Motel (☎ 541-020, fax 541-163; Panamericana Km 224; singles/doubles US$50/69), in shady grounds at the junction of Caupolicán and the highway, is excellent.

Places to Eat

Hotel Bellavista has a fine restaurant overlooking the sea and serving huge portions.

El Faro (☎ 541-190; Colipí 224) has attentive service, large portions and good fish.

Beachfront cafés along Av Costanera are cheap and good, especially **El Refugio del Pescador**, at Caleta San Pedro, and across the street, **Costanera** (☎ 541-010) and **Internacional**, both facing the beach.

Getting There & Away

Los Vilos has remade the former railroad station, at the west end of Caupolicán, into its **Terminal de Buses**, but some companies also maintain separate offices on Caupolicán. Buses depart to most north-south destinations, including Santiago (US$5, three hours) and La Serena (US$5, four hours).

La Araucanía & the Lakes District

Few landscapes surpass the beauty of this region, where volcanic cones, blanketed by glaciers, tower above deep blue lakes, ancient forests and verdant farmland. Dive into this kaleidoscope of green by getting off the Ruta 5 and following bumpy dirt roads into the wild and undeveloped countryside. There's a little bit of everything: from rafting to climbing, from hiking to hot-springs hopping, from taking *onces* in colonial towns to sharing a mate with the local huasos. Along the way, the warmth and hospitality of the *sureños* (southerners) and the region's magic are sure to enrapture you, beckoning you to stay just a few days (or weeks) longer.

The region's most important cities are Temuco, Valdivia, Osorno and Puerto Montt, but half the region's population lives in the countryside, where logging, cereal production, dairy farming and livestock raising are important industries.

This section takes in Temuco and its surrounding Andean parks down to Puerto Montt.

History

South of Concepción, Spanish conquistadors found small quantities of precious metals, good farmland and a large potential Indian workforce. Despite the optimism of the conquistadors, this area was a dangerous frontier, and its settlements were constantly under threat from Mapuche attack or natural hazards, such as volcanoes, earthquakes and floods. The Mapuche constantly besieged settlements such as Osorno and Valdivia, especially in the general rebellion of 1598. By the mid-17th century, the Spaniards had abandoned most of the area except for a resettled and heavily fortified Valdivia; another century passed before they reclaimed settlements south of the Biobío.

Even after Chilean independence from Spain, growth was slow, as Mapuche control of the countryside made overland communications difficult and dangerous.

Since the mid-19th century, Germans have been the most influential immigrant group, and they have left their mark on the region, particularly in architecture, food, manufacturing and dairy farming.

Today, several hundred thousand Mapuche remain in the provinces between the Biobío and the Río Tóltén, still commonly known as 'La Frontera.' Deprived of land by colonial

Highlights

- Trekking across Sahara-like dunes in search of riverside hot springs at Parque Nacional Puyehue
- Rafting on Río Petrohué and recounting highlights over beers at Barómetro in Puerto Varas
- Climbing Volcán Villarrica one day, rafting the next day and hiking to the araucarias the next – all easily accessible from Pucón.
- Trekking or horse riding through the Cochamó Valley, southeast of Lago Llanguihue
- Pitching fish to the sea lions at Valdivia's market

Temuco
page 263

Around Pucón
page 281

Villarrica
page 273

Pucón
page 276

Valdivia
page 288

Osorno
page 296

Frutillar
page 304

Puerto Varas
page 306

Puerto Montt
pages 318-319

OTHER MAPS
La Araucanía &
the Lakes District pages 260-261
PN Puyehue page 300
PN Vicente Pérez Rosales page 313

LA ARAUCANÍA

LA ARAUCANÍA & THE LAKES DISTRICT

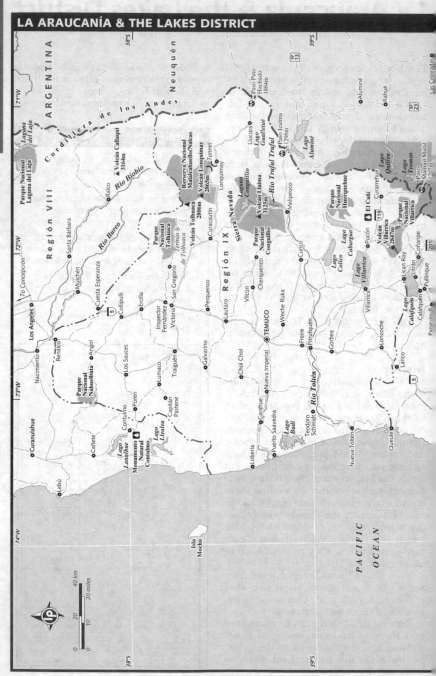

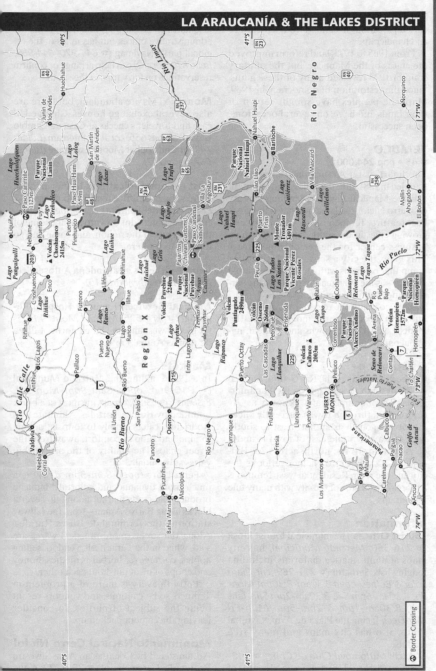

Border Crossing

Spaniards and republican Chileans, they now earn a precarious livelihood from agriculture and handicrafts.

From 1965 to 1973, land reform improved the status of the Mapuche, but the military coup of 1973 reversed many of these gains. Since the restoration of democracy in 1989, Mapuche peoples have sought return of their lands and have, on several occasions, been successful.

TEMUCO
☎ 45 • pop 244,000

The heart of La Araucanía, Temuco was founded in 1881 after the Chilean government and the Mapuche signed a landmark treaty on Cerro Ñielol, the large hill that is the city's best feature. Temuco is one of the fastest-growing cities in the south, and it's the main business center for the region's industries. This gives the city a sense of white-collar pomp that contrasts with its other traditional identity – as the main market town for the surrounding Mapuche community.

Temuco is also the regional transportation hub, with links to nearby indigenous settlements, Lakes District towns and Andean national parks.

Orientation

On the north bank of the Río Cautín, Temuco is 675km south of Santiago via the Panamericana. The Panamericana (known as Av Caupolicán through town) currently slices the city diagonally from northeast to southwest, but a new route east of town is under construction. To the north, across Av Balmaceda, historic Cerro Ñielol overlooks the city and the river. Residential west Temuco is a more relaxed area of the city with many fine restaurants.

Information

Tourist Offices The municipal **tourist kiosk** (☎ 216-360; Mercado Municipal) has city maps and informative materials, including lodging lists. **Sernatur** (☎ 211-969; cnr Claro Solar & Bulnes; open 8:30am-8:30pm Mon-Fri, 8:30am-6pm Sat, 8:30am-2pm Sun Jan-Feb; 8:30am-1pm & 2pm-5pm Mon-Fri Mar-Dec), facing the Plaza de Armas Aníbal Pinto, also has city maps and many free leaflets.

Acchi (Automóvil Club de Chile; ☎ 248-903; San Martín 0278) is also a good source of

information. **Conaf** (☎ 298-100; e temuco @conaf.cl; Av Bilbao 931, 2nd floor) is mainly administrative offices, but has maps of the regional parks. **Navimag** (☎ 644-970, 644-969; Bello 870, Local 2) can help arrange or confirm reservations on ferry trips in the south.

Money ATMs are abundant, but there are also several exchange houses. Change US cash and traveler's checks at **Casa de Cambio Global** (Bulnes 655, Local 1), **Intercam** (Bulnes 743) or **Christopher Money Exchange** (Bulnes 667, Local 202).

Post & Communications To stay in touch there's the **post office** (cnr Diego Portales & Prat) and **Entel** (cnr Prat & Manuel Montt). Internet centers dot downtown, are some of the cheapest in the region, and come and go too fast to list here.

Laundry There's a **Lavandería Autoservicio Marva** (Manuel Montt 415).

Medical Services Temuco's **Hospital Regional** (☎ 212-525; Manuel Montt 115) is six blocks west and one block north of Plaza de Armas Aníbal Pinto.

Markets

In a 1929 building, the **Mercado Municipal** (☎ 210-964; open 8am-8pm Mon-Sat, 8:30am-3pm Sun), occupying most of a block bounded by Bulnes, Portales, Aldunate and Rodríguez, caters mainly to tourists looking to dine and shop in comfort, away from the street chaos. The quality of the artisanship varies substantially.

Feria Libre (open 8am-5pm daily) is a much more dynamic and colorful Mapuche produce and crafts market taking up several blocks along Barros Arana – from the railway station to the Terminal de Buses Rurales. Along the streets, more practical wares are sold, while in the Feria itself, vendors selling apples, cochayuyo, herbal remedies, honey and chops of meat outshout each other.

Petty thievery is more of a problem in Temuco, so be cautious, and vendors resent being the subject of photos, so consider leaving the camera packed up.

Monumento Natural Cerro Ñielol

Administered by Conaf as an Area Silvestre Protegida, Cerro Ñielol (☎ 298-222; Calle

TEMUCO

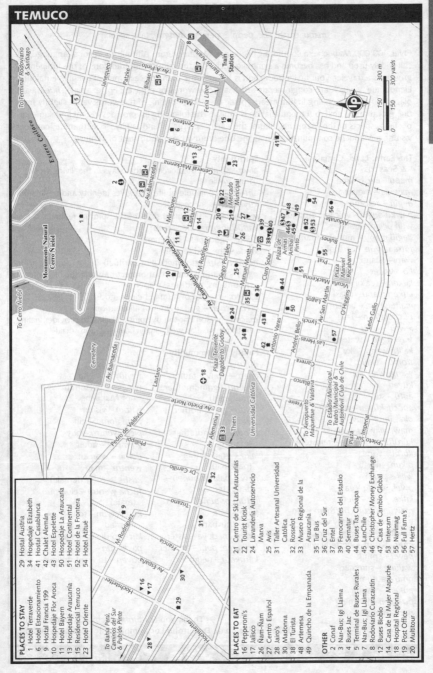

Mapudungun, the Mapuche Language

mapu, earth; *che*, people, person; *dungun*, talk, speech

Over 400,000 Mapuche in southern Chile speak Mapudungun. Although a second language, it's still widely used and has become a symbolic anchor to the culture and traditions of this indigenous group. As a traveler, your first introduction is through the many place names – Puyehue, Futaleufú, Llanquihue – which are conglomerates of Mapuche words or phrases. For example, *hue* means place, so anything ending in hue means 'place of...' The spelling of the words varies slightly from one group to the next, but pronunciation is similar. The following list provides insight into some important aspects of the Mapuche culture: the earth, spirituality and family. To learn more, consider visiting a Mapuche community, such as the one around Lago Budi, west of Temuco.

The Earth: Land, Climate & Seasons

mapu – earth, land
mawida – mountain
degiñ – volcano
pawkü degiñ – volcanic eruption
wün pillan – crater
degiñ mapu – mountain range
fütra nüyün – earthquake
wapi – island
ko – water
lafken – sea or lake
lafken mapu – coast
inaltulafken – beach
püchülafken – lake
lewfü – river
trayengko – waterfall
kallfü wenu – sky
tromü – cloud
wangülen – star
küyen – moon
antü – sun
apochi küyen – full moon
pire, üni – snow
maw, mawün – rain
kürüftuku mawün – rainstorm
kürüf – wind
pikun – north
willi – south
pwel, wente – east
lafken, nag – west
mawün kürüf – northern wind
waywen – southerly wind
pwelche – easterly winds
nagpa kürüf – westerly winds
pewü – spring
walüng – summer
rimü – autumn
pukem – winter
pu liwen – morning
pun – night

Spirituality

alwe – spirit of the deceased that stays in the 'living world' for a while
am – soul; principle of life that gives identity and perfection
kuyfikeche – ancestors
wenumapu – the dimensions of the spiritual realm
kalfüdungun – the sacred
küme – goodness, in general
weda – the bad or evil
newen – strength (mental or spiritual)
ngen – spiritual forces that protect natural aspects: water, mountains, medicinal plants
Elchen – creator of human beings; god
Ngünechen – god, owner of all creation
machi – person chosen by spiritual being to provide healing, both physical as well as psychological and social

Family & Community

ñuke – mother
chao – chaw – father
chuchu – grandmother (maternal)
kuku – grandmother (paternal)
chedki – grandfather (maternal)
laku – grandfather (paternal)
ñawe, palu or püñeñ – daughter
fotüm or püñeñ – son
kure – wife
füta – husband
lamngen, deya – sister
lamngen, peñi – brother
karukatu – neighbor

üñam – lover
wenüy – friend
wingka – person that is not Mapuche
witran – visitor
pichi domo – girl
pichi wentru – boy
yremche – adult
domo – woman
wentru – man
kushe – elder (female)
fücha wentru – elder (male)
kureyewün – to get married
lan – to die (general)
piwkeyün – to love
poyen – to want, to love

— Thank you *(caltumay)* Pablo Calfuqueo Lefio, of the Fundación de Desarrollo Local Impulsa, for this contribution.

Prat; adult/child US$1.25/0.30; open 8:30am-10pm daily) encompasses 89 hectares of native forests. Chile's national flower, the copihue (*Lapageria rosea*), grows here in abundance, flowering from March to July. The monument is also of historical importance, since it was here, in 1881, at the tree-shaded site known as **La Patagua** that Mapuche leaders ceded land to the colonists to found Temuco. Whether or not the actual papers were signed on the hill is up for debate. The park has picnic sites, a small lagoon, footpaths and an environmental information center.

Museo Regional de La Araucanía

Housed in a handsome frontier-style building dating from 1924, this regional museum (☎ 730-006; Av Alemania 084; admission US$1, Sun free; open 9am-5pm Mon-Fri, 11am-2:30pm Sat, 11am-2pm Sun) has permanent exhibits recounting the history of the Araucanian peoples before, during and since the Spanish invasion.

A display on Mapuche resistance to the Spaniards illustrates native weapons, but overlooks the Mapuche's effective guerrilla tactics.

There's a good photographic display of early Temuco, including buildings destroyed in the earthquake of 1960. Everything is well presented, but labeled in Spanish only. The 5000-volume library emphasizes Mapuche culture.

Bus No 9 runs from downtown to Av Alemania, but it's also reasonable walking distance.

Organized Tours

Caminos del Sur (☎ 09-593-4754, fax 321-857; bus terminal, office No 14; e info@ caminosdelsur.cl; Gerona 670) organizes tours with an emphasis on rural communities, such as the Mapuche. **Multitour** (☎ 237-913, fax 233-536; Bulnes 307, Oficina 203) does city tours and more traditional destinations.

Places to Stay

Patience and tolerance are required to find decent accommodations in Temuco. The area around the train station and Feria Libre has the cheapest but least reputable places, while the neighborhood between the plaza and the university has some of the better budget options, especially for women. Budget places rarely include breakfast in the price (usually US$2.50 extra). Around the plaza, mid-range hotels cater to the business crowd.

Budget The HI affiliate, **Residencial Temuco** (☎ 233-721; Rodríguez 1341, 2nd floor; dorm beds US$8.50) has a friendly staff, but it's small and the beds squeak enough to challenge a good night's rest. For HI members, room rates include breakfast.

Hospedaje La Araucaría (☎ 322-820; Antonio Varas 568; per person US$8.50) is one of the better options, with clean ample rooms and firm beds in an old home, plus a large independent kitchen and eating area overlooking the back garden.

Hospedaje Flor Aroca (☎ 234-205; Lautaro 591; per person US$7) is just off Caupolicán enough to not be too bothered by street traffic. Rooms are cheerful and spacious, although the place could use another bathroom. The owner doesn't offer kitchen privileges, but can serve up a breakfast for US$1.50.

Hospedaje Araucanía (☎ 219-089; General Mackenna 151; per person US$7), family-oriented and right in the heart of downtown, offers quiet upstairs rooms in a grand old wooden house with plenty of character.

Hospedaje Elizabeth (☎ 323-192; Las Heras 560; per person US$8.50) is a worthwhile budget choice, often full with students. Breakfast may be included.

Hostal Casablanca (☎/fax 212-740; Manuel Montt 1306; singles with shared/private bath US$10/16) can be seen much sooner than you can hear the noise coming from the busy intersection. In a rambling old white building, Casablanca requires earplugs, but offers breakfast, and rooms with private bath have cable TV.

Hotel Oriente (☎ 233-232; Manuel Rodríguez 1146; singles/doubles with shared bath US$12/21, with private bath US$15/26) offers rooms with views of a busy street and others with no windows at all. Bathrooms are decent; breakfast costs an additional US$2.50.

Mid-Range In west Temuco, **Hostal Austria** (☎/fax 247-169; e hostalaustria@terra.cl; Hochstetter 599; per person US$20-35) is an outstanding choice for its friendly, peaceful, nonsmoking environment. The very comfortable rooms have cozy duvets and cable TV, and the bathrooms are clean, large and have plenty of hot water. Breakfasts are equally impressive, disrupted only by a very protective and spoiled house dog.

Hostal Francia 199 (☎ 235-594; *Francia 199; per person with shared/private bath US$15/20*) is also in west Temuco, but lacks a sense of hospitality.

Somewhat charming, **Hotel Espelette** (☎ 234-805; *Claro Solar 492; per person with shared bath US$11, singles/doubles with private bath US$25/35*) has florist shops out front and artwork inside. While the upstairs rooms aren't up to snuff, management does provide great towels and is professional. Downstairs rooms, with private bath, are much larger, but face right onto the streets and common TV room. Dowdy breakfasts cost US$1.50 more.

Chalet Alemán (☎ 212-818; *Antonio Varas 349; singles/doubles US$25/41*) is an attractive home on a quiet street with lots of garden space. Upstairs rooms have high slanted ceilings and lots of room; one room even sports a balcony. Breakfast is extra, making this a bit overpriced in summer, but the rest of the year it could be a good deal.

Hotel Estacionamiento (☎ 215-503; *Balmaceda 1246; doubles/triples US$20-25/30*) is applauded for its tacky décor: some rooms sport tamale-red Jacuzzi baths, plastic plants, mirrors and hard-foam double beds covered in canary-yellow satin bedspreads. Other rooms aren't quite so, well, sensuous. Aim for a room away from the neighboring cabaret.

Hotel Continental (☎ 238-973, fax 233-830; *Antonio Varas 709; singles/doubles with bath down the hall US$12/21, with shared bath for two rooms US$20/26, with private bath US$23/33*) has hosted such preeminent guests as poets Gabriela Mistral and Pablo Neruda and presidents Pedro Aguirre Cerda and Salvador Allende. While the walls have history, the rooms have been modernized with good beds and fixtures. Even if you don't stay, you can enjoy a lunch in its classic dining room or a drink at its equally classic bar.

Top End In the city center, **Hotel de la Frontera** (☎/fax 200-400; e *reservas@hotelfrontera.cl; Bulnes 733; singles or doubles US$65*) is the main business hotel, with conference facilities attached. The room rate includes transfers to/from the airport, a morning paper and buffet breakfast. The dining room offers a generous buffet lunch for US$8.

Hotel Bayern (☎ 276-000, fax 212-291; e *hotelbayern@tie.cl; Prat 146; singles/doubles/triples US$37/50/60*) is a good option for people with vehicles. Rooms are well furnished with cable TV, and many are protected from street noise. Staff are professional and courteous.

Hotel Aitué (☎ 211-917, fax 212-608; *Antonio Varas 1048; singles/doubles US$37/43*) is a surprisingly good value. Financial newspapers in the lobby show they cater heavily to the business set, but the rooms are equally appealing to a traveler; they even have hairdryers for those missing theirs back home. Some rooms have the unfortunate view of an auto body shop, but most are quiet; 3rd-floor rooms are the better option.

Hotel Terraverde (☎ 239-999, fax 239-455; e *resterra@panamericanahoteles.cl; Prat 0220; singles/doubles US$70/86*) is a luxury seven-story high-rise near Cerro Ñielol. Rooms are well appointed with plush fabrics, carpet and blindingly white bathrooms, while the lobby sports a mini-grand piano and a petting zoo of puffed-up couches.

Places to Eat

Cheap eats can be found at the **Feria Libre**, where vendors cut, dice, boil and fry fresh produce, fish and meat into tasty stews and dishes at many stalls. You could get away with a decent lunch for about US$3 here.

Restaurants at the Mercado Municipal are another decent option, if touristy. Best choices are seafood dishes, especially the soups (*caldillos*). **El Caribe** (*Puesto 45; mains US$4*) specializes in *lomo a lo pobre*, served up with lots of fries. **El Turista** (*Puesto 32; mains US$4-8*) serves a bounty of seafood dishes to be shared, as well as *pastel del choclo*. **El Criollito** (*Puestos 38-39; mains US$6-10*) has similar fare served with a heavier dose of pretension. Market restaurants close early, around 7pm.

Student-oriented **Ñam Ñam** (*Diego Portales 802 & 855; sandwiches US$3-6*) offers heaping sandwiches and draft beer and provides a nonsmoking section. **Quincho de la Empanada** (☎ 216-307; *Aldunate 698; empanadas US$1-2*) sells empanadas, with a variety of fillings, including vegetarian.

Artemesa (☎ 730-758; *Aldunate 620, Local 801; mains US$4-8*) is Temuco's vegetarian restaurant, open for both lunch and dinner.

El Turista (☎ 237-238; Claro Solar 839; coffee & pastry US$1.50-3) is a chocolatería with a lacy-quaint café on the second floor where good coffees can be enjoyed with butter-rich cookies and a heavy dose of Temucian pomp and gossip. Do try such specialties as the hot chocolate with raspberry liqueur.

Centro Español (☎ 741-440; Bulnes 483; lunch US$5.50; closed Sun) fills up with the business set at lunch, creating a more formal ambience. And the food, Mediterranean in focus, is worth checking out.

Madonna (☎ 329-393; Av Alemania 0660; individual/shared pizzas US$5/8-12, pastas US$6-8) is Temuco's top spot for pizza and pasta, with almost 30 different pies to choose from plus mix-and-match pasta and salsas. It's a fun, informal spot with good hearty Italian fare.

With a lively atmosphere, **Pepperoni's** (☎ 261-271; Hochstetter 425; mains US$5-10) is another good choice for pasta, as well as salads and pizza.

Bahía Perú (☎ 268-700; Av Alemania cnr Recreo; mains US$8-11) brings Peruvian spice to town with enormous platters of salmon or shrimp with veggies, choritos a la chalaca or a tasty ceviche with just a splash of Pernod.

Jairo's (☎ 248-849; Av Alemania 0830; mains US$7.50-8) is the city's top and fanciest seafood restaurant with an intimate and formal dining room and delectable dishes. Try ostiones a la crema (scallops in cream sauce) or a cocktail of erizos (sea urchins) followed by your choice of fish in Jairo's sauce of shrimp, mushrooms, tarragon and chive.

Entertainment

Besides hanging out in the old bar of Hotel Continental, most of the nightlife is in west Temuco. **Bahía Perú**, **Pepperoni's** (for both, see Places to Eat above) and **Jalisco** (☎ 243-254; Hochstetter 435), a Tex-Mex theme restaurant, all pack in the weekend crowds. Nearby **Pub de Pinte** (☎ 245-431; cnr Recreo & Alessandri) is a more tranquil affair, with lots of wood, candles, good music and draft beer in an attractively revamped house.

Teatro Municipal (☎ 265-858; Av Pablo Neruda cnr Olimpia) hosts symphony, opera and ballet performances throughout the year.

Shopping

One of Temuco's saving graces is that it's a good spot to shop for Mapuche woolen goods (ponchos, blankets and pullovers), pottery and musical instruments, such as zampoñas (pan pipes) and drums. Shops also sell difficult-to-find copies of Mapuche jewelry. The **Mercado Municipal** has the most in one place, along with a fair amount of kitsch.

Run by a cooperative of women, the **Casa de la Mujer Mapuche** (☎ 233-886; Prat 283; open 9am-1pm & 3pm-6pm Mon-Fri) sells a wide selection of traditional indigenous crafts, most notably textiles and ceramics. Profits benefit members of the cooperative.

The **Taller Artesanal Universidad Católica** (Av Alemania 0422; open 9am-1pm & 3pm-7pm Mon-Fri) sells quality silver reproductions of Mapuche jewelry, created by artisans and local students.

Getting There & Away

Air LanChile (☎ 272-138, 213-180; Bulnes 687) has plenty of flights to Santiago (US$157), and daily flights to Puerto Montt (US$60) and Punta Arenas (US$220).

Bus Most long-haul buses use **Terminal Rodoviario** (☎ 255-005; Pérez Rosales 01609), at the northern approach to town. Companies have ticket offices around downtown. Times and frequencies vary throughout the year, with fewer buses in winter.

Bus lines serving main cities along the Panamericana include **Tur Bus** (☎ 278-161; cnr Lagos & Montt), which has the most frequent service to Santiago; **Tas Choapa** (☎ 212-422; Varas 609), which serves northern destinations up to Antofagasta; **Cruz del Sur** (☎ 730-320; Claro Solar 599), which also serves the island of Chiloé; and **Igi Llaima** (☎ 407-700; Balmaceda 995).

Argentina is more easily accessed from Osorno or Santiago. Cruz del Sur has service to Bariloche via Paso Cardenal Samoré east of Osorno at 2:45am; however, the Thursday and Sunday 8am departure is more time efficient. Tas Choapa has similar service. Igi Llaima's other terminal (☎ 210-364; Miraflores 1535) also has service to Zapala and Neuquén daily at 3am, but has received complaints from travelers.

The **Terminal de Buses Rurales** (☎ 210-494; Balmaceda & Pinto) serves local and regional destinations. Buses to Chol Chol leave about every hour, while those to Melipeuco leave five times daily before noon. **Buses Jac** (☎ 231-340; cnr Balmaceda & Aldunate), with its own terminal, offers the most frequent service to Villarrica and Pucón, plus service to Santiago, Lican Ray and Coñaripe.

Buses Biobío (☎ 210-599; Lautaro 853) runs frequent services to Angol, Los Angeles and Concepción. **Nar-Bus** (☎ 407-700; Balmaceda 995 • Miraflores 1535) services Victoria and Cunco from where transfers can be made to Melipeuco. The **Rodoviario Curacautín** (Barros Arana 191) is the departure point for buses to Curacautín, Lonquimay and the upper Biobío.

Sample travel times and costs are as follows:

destination	duration in hours	cost
Ancud	7	US$11
Angol	2	US$3.50
Bariloche (Ar)	10½–12	US$18
Castro	8	US$14
Chillán	4	US$6.50
Coñaripe	2½	US$4
Concepción	4½	US$5
Cunco	1½	US$1.20
Curacautín	1½	US$3
Osorno	3	US$5
Pucón	1	US$3.50
Puerto Montt/Puerto Varas	5	US$7
Santiago	8	US$15-30
Valdivia	3	US$3
Valparaíso-Viña del Mar	10	US$18-20
Victoria	1	US$1.50
Villarrica	1	US$3.50
Zapala and Neuquén (Ar)	10	US$30

Train The train from Temuco goes north to Santiago (about 11½ hours) at 10:30pm nightly, stopping at various stations en route. Buy tickets either at the **Estación de Ferrocarril** (☎ 233-416; Av Barros Arana), eight blocks east of Plaza de Armas Aníbal Pinto, or at the downtown office of **Ferrocarriles del Estado** (EFE; ☎ 233-522; Bulnes 582). Fares to Santiago are US$11 económica, US$14 turista, US$19 salón, US$26 cama alta and US$35 cama baja. As of September 2003 high-speed trains are to be in operation, so expect schedule and rate changes.

Getting Around

Bus No 1 runs from downtown to the train station. Colectivos 11P and 25A leave from downtown (Claro Solar) to the bus terminal.

Temuco's Aeropuerto Maquehue is 6km south of town, just off the Panamericana. Taxis leaving from the west side of the Plaza de Armas take passengers for US$5. Car rental is available at **Automóvil Club de Chile** (☎ 215-132; San Martín 0278), **Rosselot** (☎ 952-525; Av Alemania 0180), **Hertz** (☎ 235-385; Las Heras 999), **Avis** (☎ 238-013; Vicuña Mackenna 448) and **Full Fama's** (☎/fax 215-420; Andrés Bello 1096).

AROUND TEMUCO

Visiting the small Mapuche communities around Temuco provides a glimpse into the lives of this strong indigenous group. **Weche Ruka** (☎ 09-669-3178, 319-382), some 20km southeast of Temuco, past Comuna de Padre Las Casas, is a community of about 35 families, about a third of whom practice 'ethnic tourism.' They provide a range of services to tourists: You can have just a chat (US$5.50); stay for a full day, with lunch and music and dance workshops (US$20); a full day, plus a home stay (US$25); and have a meeting with a machi, or spiritual leader (US$6.50). Micro No 3, which leaves from General Mackenna, takes you within 2km of the community or hop on buses heading to Cunco and ask to be dropped off at the intersection.

At the coast, 80km west of Temuco, **Puerto Saavedra** is a dusty stretch of town. The municipality, next to the Banco de Estado at the plaza, has tourist information. Camping is possible at the exposed and ugly **Camping Los Cisnes** at the southern end of town, where there are also two hosterías. Better accommodations can be found just south of town at **Boca Budi**. Ten kilometers south is **Lago Budi**, a saltwater lagoon with good bird-watching (about 135 species recorded) and a network of Mapuche communities offering ethnic tourism. In Puerto Saavedra, María Ester (☎ 197-5764; e mllanceleo@lagobudi.cl; 8 de Octubre 102) runs a small taller (workshop) and distributes information about the communities. Some offer camping (US$8 per site; bring your own tent), but most are artisan shops or places to organize boating or horse rides with the locals. Authentic rukas are on the south side of the lake at Ina Lafken Ruka and Llaguepulli.

Chol Chol, 29km northwest of Temuco, is a Mapuche village of wooden, tin-roofed bungalows with a few traditional *rukas* on its outskirts. Buses to Chol Chol leave from Temuco's Terminal de Buses Rurales (US$1, 1½ hours).

PN TOLHUACA

Nestled in the precordillera northeast of Temuco, on the north bank of the Río Malleco, 6400-hectare Parque Nacional Tolhuaca *(admission US$2.50)* is one of the park system's best-kept secrets, mainly because it's harder to get to than nearby Conguillío. Tragically, in 2002, a forest fire consumed some 4200 hectares of the western sector, plus half of the adjacent RN Malleco, but the areas most attractive to travelers were not affected. Within the park, elevations range from 850m around Laguna Malleco to 1830m on the summit of Cerro Colomahuida; 2806m Volcán Tolhuaca is beyond the park boundaries. Rainfall reaches 3000mm per year, but summer is relatively dry. For more information, contact Conaf in Temuco.

Hiking

Shallow **Laguna Malleco,** a good spot for waterfowl watching, has a signed nature trail along the north shore leading through dense forest of raulí, coigue (both species of southern beech), quila and araucaria to its outlet. Here, the **Salto Malleco** tumbles 50m over resistant columnar basalt into a deep pool, surrounded by massive nalcas and water-loving ferns and mosses. The trail continues down to the river, through even denser vegetation.

Also from the north shore, another trail climbs steeply to the **Prados de Mesacura** and continues east to **Lagunillas** through an araucaria forest with outstanding panoramas. Water is scarce on this trail, which is a full-day excursion.

The park's best trip goes to **Laguna Verde,** reached via a trailhead about 5km east of Laguna Malleco, on the road to Termas de Tolhuaca. The trail crosses the Río Malleco and passes several waterfalls.

Places to Stay

Camping Inalaufquén *(sites US$12),* on the southeastern shore of Laguna Malleco, has secluded woodsy sites, including running water, firepits, picnic tables and immaculate toilets with cold showers. Backpackers may negotiate a better per person charge.

Getting There & Away

There is no direct public transportation from Temuco. From Victoria, buses leave weekdays for San Gregorio, from where it's a 19km walk to the campground at Laguna Malleco. Beyond San Gregorio, the road narrows rapidly and deadfalls may be a problem after storms, but any carefully driven passenger car can pass in good weather. This would be an ideal mountain-bike route, as it climbs gradually into the precordillera.

From the town of Curacautín, north of Parque Nacional Conguillío, taxi colectivos access the hot springs resort of Termas de Tolhuaca (see below) near the eastern entrance, from where it's feasible to hike the 10km to the campground. The road to Laguna Malleco is now acceptable for ordinary passenger cars.

TERMAS DE TOLHUACA

Easily accessed from the eastern sector of Parque Nacional Tolhuaca and 35km north of Curacautín, Termas de Tolhuaca (☎ 045-881-211; **w** *www.termasdetolhuaca.co.cl; Calama 240, Curacautín; day use US$10)* has some very hot baths in attractive outdoor settings, plus an array of spa services – massage, mud wraps etc. **Camping** *(up to 6 people US$14)* does not include day use of the baths, while rooms at **Hotel Termas de Tolhuaca** *(per person US$60)* include full board.

PN CONGUILLÍO

Created in 1950 primarily to preserve the distinctive araucaria, or monkey-puzzle tree, and a Unesco Biosphere Reserve, Conguillío shelters 60,835 hectares of alpine lakes, deep canyons and native forests surrounding the smoldering, snow-covered Volcán Llaima (3125m). Since 1640, Llaima has experienced 34 violent eruptions, most recently in 1957. Around 2000 years ago, a lava flow off Llaima's northern flank dammed the Río Truful-Truful to form Laguna Conguillío, Laguna Arco Iris and Laguna Verde. Forest fires in 2002 burned 1633 hectares of the seldom-visited eastern section of the park.

The glaciated peaks of the Sierra Nevada, north of Laguna Conguillío, consistently exceed 2500m.

Orientation & Information

You can access PN Conguillío from three directions. The first and shortest (80km) is directly east of Temuco via Vilcún and Cherquenco; this accesses the ski resorts at Sector Los Paraguas, but doesn't access (by road, anyway) the campgrounds, main visitor center and trailheads. All of those are best reached by taking the more northern route from Temuco (120km) via Curacautín. The park's southern entrance, also 120km from Temuco, is accessed via Melipeuco. From here a road heads north through the park to the northern entrance, also accessing the trailheads and campgrounds.

Conaf's **Centro de Información Ambiental** (*Laguna Conguillío;* **w** *www.parquenacional conguillio.cl; open 10am-1pm & 3pm-7:30pm daily*) offers a variety of programs mainly in January and February, including slide shows and ecology talks, hikes to the Sierra Nevada, outings for children and boat excursions on the lake. Good trail maps with basic topographic information and trail descriptions are sold for a small fee. Climbers can apply for permits here.

Hiking

One of Chile's finest short hikes, the **Sierra Nevada trail** (10km, three hours one-way) to the base of the Sierra Nevada leaves from the small parking lot at Playa Linda, at the east end of Laguna Conguillío. Climbing steadily northeast through dense coigue forests, the trail passes a pair of lake overlooks; from the second and more scenic, you can see solid stands of araucarias begin to supplant coigues on the ridge top.

Continuing along the ridge top, keep an eye open for the abundant *lagartija,* a tiny lizard, and the rosette succulent *añañisca,* which grows where fallen ñire leaves have begun to mix with volcanic ash to form humus, or an incipient soil.

Conaf discourages all but the most experienced, well-prepared hikers from continuing north on the **Travesía Río Blanco** (5km, five hours one-way), an excursion detailed in *Trekking in the Patagonian Andes.*

Near the visitors center, the **Sendero Araucarias** (0.8km, 45 minutes) meanders through a verdant rainforest. At **Laguna Verde**, a short trail goes to La Ensenada, a peaceful beach area. The **Cañadon Truful-Truful trail** (0.8km, 30 minutes) passes through the canyon, where

the colorful strata, exposed by the rushing waters of Río Truful-Truful, are a vivid record of Llaima's numerous eruptions. The nearby **Los Vertientes** trail (0.8km, 30 minutes) leads to an open spot among rushing springs.

The newest addition to the trail system is the **Sendero de Chile** (18km, six hours one-way), which links Laguna Captrén with Guardaría Truful-Truful. Also at Laguna Captrén, **Los Carpinteros** (8km, 2½ hours one way) passes through habitat of the *carpintero negro* (black woodpecker) and to the 1800-year-old Araucaría Madre; with a width of 3m, it is considered the largest tree in the park.

Climbing

Experienced climbers can tackle Volcán Llaima from **Sector Los Paraguas** on the west side of the park, where there is a refugio on the road from Cherquenco, or from Captrén on the north side. Before climbing, get permission from Conaf in Temuco or at the Centro de Información Ambiental. To avoid waiting, Conaf recommends emailing the request to the Temuco office one month in advance.

Skiing

The **Centro de Ski Las Araucarias** (☎ 562-313; 274-141; Bulnes 351, Oficina 47, Temuco), at Sector Los Paraguas, has just three ski runs, but much more scenery than many of Chile's ski spots. Lift tickets cost US$15/17.50 for a half/full day, while ski/snowboard rental costs US$16/22 per day.

Places to Stay & Eat

Backcountry camping is not permitted. Campgrounds **Los Ñirres** (44 sites), **El Estero** (10 sites), **Los Carpinteros** (12 sites) and **La Caseta** (12 sites), which are on or near the south shore of Laguna Conguillío, are all managed by concession. From January to early May these are expensive at US$22 for two tents with up to five people; the rest of the year, they are US$13. Conaf reserves a limited number of backpacker sites for US$5 per person at **El Estero**, specifically for those arriving on foot or bicycle. At **Laguna Captrén**, at the north entrance to the park, sites are available for US$25 from mid-January to the end of February; they go for only US$10 the rest of the year.

Cabañas Conguillío (☎ 214-363, 211-493 in Temuco; 4-person cabañas US$58, 8-

person US$83), at the southwest end of Laguna Conguillío, also has a restaurant and a small store that are open from mid-December to early March.

Centro de Ski Las Araucarias (☎ 045-562-313; *dorm beds without/with bedding US$10/12, 5-bed apartments US$120*) is the most convenient place to stay for the skiing crowd, but bring your own sleeping bag.

La Baita (☎ 730-138 in Temuco; 09-733-2442; w *www.labaitaconguillo.cl; 4-8 person cabins US$60-85*) is just outside the park's southern boundary, but it is definitely worth consideration for its location and efforts toward environmental conservation. Well spaced amid pristine forest, the six attractive cabins come fully equipped and have slow-burning furnaces, limited electricity and hot water. In high season, meals, excursions and a small store are available. Discounts are available in the low season and for stays of three or more nights. La Baita is 15km from Melipeuco and 60km from Curacautín.

Getting There & Away

To reach Sector Los Paraguas, **Buses Flota Erbuc** (☎ 272-204), at Temuco's Terminal de Buses Rurales, runs a dozen times daily to Cherquenco (US$2), from where it's a 17km walk or hitchhike to the ski lodge at Los Paraguas.

For the northern entrance, Buses Flota Erbuc has regular service to Curacautín, from where a shuttle (US$1) runs to the park border at Guardería Captrén Monday to Friday. From December to March, if conditions allow, it continues to Laguna Captrén. In heavy rain, ordinary passenger vehicles may not be able to pass the road between Laguna Conguillío and Laguna Captrén.

For the southern entrance, **Nar-Bus** (☎ 211-611) in Temuco runs seven buses daily to Melipeuco (US$2.50), where Hostería Huentelén (see Melipeuco later in this chapter) can arrange a cab to park headquarters. Travelers who can afford to rent a car can combine these two routes in a loop trip from Temuco.

CURACAUTÍN

☎ 45 • pop 16,900

Curacautín is the northern gateway to Parque Nacional Conguillío. The **tourist office** (☎ 882-560; *Plaza de Armas*) has brochures and information on the park and lodging in town.

Lodging options include **Hostal Rayén** (☎ 881-262; *Manuel Rodríguez 140; per person US$10*), a family-run place with comfortable rooms and excellent showers; and **Hotel Plaza** (☎ 881-256; *Yungay 157; per person US$13*), in front of the plaza in a colonial-style house, which includes breakfast in the rates and has a restaurant.

The **bus terminal** (*Arica & Manuel Rodríguez*) is directly on the highway to Lonquimay. Buses Flota Erbuc connects the town to Lonquimay and Temuco (US$3) six times daily via Victoria, and four times via Lautaro. For transportation details to PN Conguillío, see that section above.

RN MALALCAHUELLO/NALCAS

Off the track of the main park circuit, this combined reserve of 30,300 hectares is just north of the town of Malalcahuello, en route to Lonquimay, and extends almost to the border of PN Tolhuaca. Nalca's western boundary abuts Volcán Tolhuaca, while Volcán Longuimay marks the division between the two reserves. In Nalcas, **Sendero Tolhuaca** (40km, 24 hours one-way) is accessible only from **Sendero Laguna Blanca** (40km, two days one-way), which traverses the western flank of Volcán Lonquimay. However, an old logging road connects the trail west to Termas de Tolhuaca and Laguna Verde in PN Tolhuaca (trails may be hard to find; guides recommended).

Less-ambitious hikes can be found near Cráter Navidad, which last blew on December 25, 1988. The most easily accessible trail is **Piedra Santa** (7.5km, five hours), which is the beginning stretch of the longer Laguna Blanca trail. From Piedra Santa, **El Raleo** (3.5km, two hours) branches off and leads through coigue forest and introduced pine. The trail starts near the small Conaf office near the road to the hamlet of Malacahuello along the highway to Lonquimay. Wild camping is permissible along the trails.

At the foot of the 2865m Volcán Lonquimay is the drab **Centro de Esquí Lonquimay** (☎ 045-881-106), a ski center accessed from a steep and dusty road to Lonquimay.

Places to Stay

Suizandina (☎ 09-884-9541, fax 045-881-892; w *www.suizandina.com; camping per person US$4, dorm beds US$8-10, cabañas* for 2 people US$22, per person with private bath US$22), at Km 28 on the road to Lonquimay, has become as much a destination for travelers as the parks that surround it. Run by a young Swiss family, this is a smart place to hang the pack and explore the nearby trails. The owners organize treks and horse rides in PN Conguillío or around Volcán Lonquimay. Evening meals may include Swiss specialties such as raclette or fondue. A hearty breakfast is included.

UPPER BIOBÍO

East of Malalcahuello, the road passes through the intriguing drippy, mossy Túnel Las Raíces, a converted railway tunnel, which emerges into the drainage of the upper Biobío. The road forks north to the town of **Lonquimay**, with an unusual oval street plan and basic tourist services (most shut down out of season). **Hostería Follil Pewenche** (☎/fax 045-891-110; e quimque@entelchile .net; Ignacio Carrera Pinto 110) has lodging, a restaurant with Mapuche cuisine, laundry, and organizes hiking and horse treks around the area and to Lago Galletué. At the lake, there's a **campground** with hot-water showers and farm produce for sale.

Continuing east, the road reaches 1884m Paso Pino Hachado, a border crossing that leads to the Argentine cities of Zapala and Neuquén.

MELIPEUCO

☎ 45 • pop 5600

Melipeuco, the southern gateway to Parque Nacional Conguillío, is 90km east of Temuco via Cunco. It has a summer-only **tourist office** (Pedro Aguirre Cerda) but little to offer.

Hostería Huetelén (☎ 581-005; Pedro Aguirre Cerda 1; singles with breakfast/full pension US$16/25, 3-person cabins US$25) offers reasonable accommodations with private bath and heat in a new home with a roaring fireplace. Or try **Hospedaje Icalma** (☎ 581-108; Pedro Aguirre Cerda 729; per person US$8), with room for just two or three, and breakfast included.

Along the International Hwy toward the border crossing at Paso Icalma, **Santa Elvira de Tracura** (☎ 171-2-1968-503; Km 18; per person US$8) is a recommended place to stay, especially for small groups looking to get off the beaten track. There are three fully equipped cabins; breakfast is included; they

will prepare homemade lunches (US$5); and horse rentals are available for day treks (or longer).

From Temuco's Terminal de Buses Rurales, Nar-Bus has seven buses daily to Melipeuco. A taxi from Melipeuco to PN Conguillío should cost about US$15.

VILLARRICA

☎ 45 • pop 45,350

On the southwest shore of Lago Villarrica, and 86km southwest of Temuco, Villarrica is one of Chile's oldest cities, a fact that is hard to fathom when walking through the cramped commercial downtown. Founded in 1552 by Gerónimo de Alderete, Santa María Magdalena de Villarrica was repeatedly attacked by Mapuche during colonial times. In 1576, just 800 Spanish held Villarrica's fort against 12,000 indigenous fighters. In 1602, Cacique Cuminaguel took control of the city and destroyed it. Not until 1883 did the Mapuche toqui Epuléf allow the Chilean state to maintain a permanent presence. Villarrica grew as a lake resort and commerce center for nearby hamlets. While its 'resort' status has been lost to nearby Pucón, it is a much more tranquil and cheaper place to stay than its neighbor.

Information

The municipal **Oficina de Turismo** (☎ 206-619; e turis@entelchile.net; Pedro de Valdivia 1070; open 8:30am-11pm daily Jan-Mar, 8:30am-1pm & 2:30pm-6pm Mon-Fri Apr-Dec) has helpful staff and provides many useful leaflets. The **Cámara de Turismo** (☎ 415-057; cnr General Urrutia & A Bello) lists hospedajes.

Banks with ATMs are plentiful, especially near the corner of Alderete and Pedro de Valdivia, including **Banco Santander** and **Banco de Chile. Turcamb** (Pedro de Valdivia 1061) exchanges US cash.

To stay in contact, there's the **post office** (Anfión Muñoz 315), **Entel** (Henríquez 446) and **Telefónica (CTC)** (Henríquez 544).

Todo Lavado (☎ 414-452; General Urrutia 699, Local 7) has efficient same-day laundry services.

For medical care, go to **Hospital Villarrica** (☎ 411-169; San Martín 460).

Things to See & Do

Mapuche artifacts – including jewelry, musical instruments and roughly hewn wooden masks – are the focus of the **Museo Histórico y Arqueológico** (☎ 413-445; Pedro de Valdivia 1050; admission US$0.50; open 9am-1pm & 3pm-7:30pm Mon-Fri), alongside the tourist office. Gracing the grounds is a Mapuche ruka, oblong with thatched walls and roof, traditionally built by four men in four days under a reciprocal labor system known as *minga*. Reeds from the lake provide the thatch, which is so skillfully intertwined that water cannot penetrate even in this very damp climate.

Local fishing is good, especially on the Río Toltén, but first obtain a license from the **Municipalidad** (Municipality; ☎ 206-500; cnr Pedro Montt & Pedro de Valdivia). The season runs from the second week of

November to the second week of May. Fly-fishing operators include **Süd Explorer**, next to the tourist office. **Gastón Balboa** (San Martín 348) is a knowledgeable fishing guide.

Many of the same tours organized in Pucón can be arranged here; try the agency **Politur** (☎ 414-547; Henríquez 475) and the operators working out of **Touring** (see Places to Eat later in this section). For a description of activities, see Pucón later in this chapter.

Special Events
The annual Muestra Cultural Mapuche, in January and February, has exhibits of local artisans, indigenous music and ritual dance.

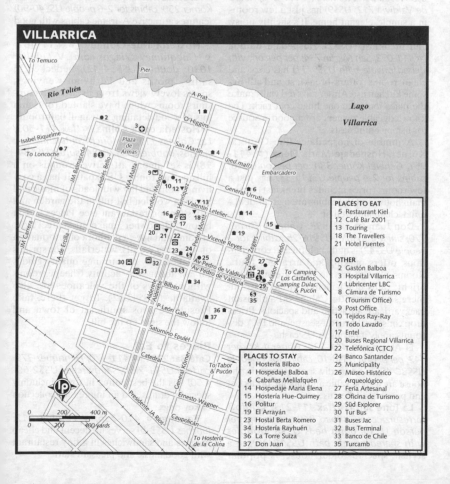

VILLARRICA

To Temuco
Pier
Río Toltén
A Prat
Lago
Villarrica
Isabel Riquelme
To Loncoche
Plaza de Armas
O'Higgins
San Martín
(ped mall)
Embarcadero
General Urrutia
Valentín Letelier
Camilo Henríquez
Pedro Montt
Vicente Reyes
Julio Zegers
Aviador Acevedo
Av Pedro de Valdivia
Av Pedro de Valdivia
To Camping Los Castaños, Camping Dulac & Pucón
Alderete
Bilbao
P. León Gallo
Saturnino Epuléf
To Tabor & Pucón
Catedral
General Körner
Ernesto Wagner
Presidente JA Ríos
Caupolicán
To Hostería de la Colina

0   200   400 m
0   200   490 yards

PLACES TO EAT
5 Restaurant Kiel
12 Café Bar 2001
13 Touring
18 The Travellers
21 Hotel Fuentes

OTHER
2 Gastón Balboa
3 Hospital Villarrica
7 Lubricenter LBC
8 Cámara de Turismo (Tourism Office)
9 Post Office
10 Tejidos Ray-Ray
11 Todo Lavado
17 Entel
20 Buses Regional Villarrica
22 Telefónica (CTC)
24 Banco Santander
25 Municipality
26 Museo Histórico Arqueológico
27 Feria Artesanal
28 Oficina de Turismo
29 Süd Explorer
30 Tur Bus
31 Buses Jac
32 Bus Terminal
33 Banco de Chile
35 Turcamb

PLACES TO STAY
1 Hostería Bilbao
4 Hospedaje Balboa
6 Cabañas Melilafquén
14 Hospedaje María Elena
15 Hostería Hue-Quimey
16 Politur
21 El Arrayán
23 Hostal Berta Romero
34 Hostería Rayhuén
36 La Torre Suiza
37 Don Juan

Places to Stay

Prices for lodging vary considerably throughout the year, the peak summer months and the ski season being the highest. The rest of the year prices are very reasonable.

Budget More than half a dozen campgrounds dot the road between Villarrica and Pucón, but recommended are **Camping Los Castaños** (☎ 412-330; sites US$16), 1km east of town, and **Camping Dulac** (☎ 412-097; sites US$19), 2km east, both with reasonably private, shady sites and hot showers.

In the center, the adventure agency **Politur** (see Things to See & Do above; per person US$6) runs a small hospedaje with kitchen use. **Hostal Berta Romero** (☎ 411-276; Pedro de Valdivia 712; US$9) has just a few rooms in a simple, elegant home. It's slightly noisy, but an excellent value, including kitchen use and breakfast (US$2). **Hospedaje Balboa** (☎ 411-098; San Martín 734; per person with shared/private bath US$9/11) has cozy and clean rooms, offers breakfast and allows some kitchen use. Antler-covered walls make the place look like one huge coat rack. The knowledgeable owners are a good resource for fishing enthusiasts.

A jumble of hospedajes line General Körner. **Hospedaje Maria Elena** (☎ 411-951, General Körner 380; per person US$8; cabins for 2-4 people US$15-33) has just a few rooms (price includes breakfast) in the main house, but the cabins are a great deal – quiet, clean and well lit.

Don Juan (☎ 411-833; General Körner 770; singles/doubles US$16/25, cabins for 2 people US$42) is quite helpful and conscientious, offers parking and arranges tours. Rooms, all with private bath, are small but bright; rates don't include breakfast, but there's a kitchenette. Cabins, off a pleasant backyard, are attractive and spacious. Prices drop considerably in off-season, and IVA discounts apply if paying in US cash.

El Arrayán (☎ 411-235; General Körner 442; per person US$8-10; cabins for 4 people US$36-40) is a friendly spot. Rooms in the house are a good value and include breakfast and possible kitchen use.

La Torre Suiza (☎/fax 411-213; e info@ torresuiza.com; Bilbao 969; camping per person US$5, dorm beds US$8, doubles with shared/private bath US$18/25), in a stylish, spacious older house, is popular with European travelers. Garden campers have use of indoor facilities, breakfast is included, and there's a fully equipped kitchen, laundry, bike rental, Internet access and lots of area information.

Mid-Range & Top End **Hostería Rayhuén** (☎ 411-571; Pedro Montt 668; singles/doubles US$23/35) is a charming place with hot showers, well-heated rooms and a fine restaurant. Rates include an abundant breakfast.

Hostería Bilbao (☎ 411-186; Henríquez 43; singles/doubles US$30/40) is quieter and well protected by nice gardens, and it has cordial staff.

Cabañas Melilafquén (☎ 411-562; General Körner 250; cabins for 2-6 people US$40-90) features attractive A-frame cabins with good amenities.

Hostería Hue-Quimey (☎ 411-462; e Huequimey@7lagos.com; V Letelier 1030; doubles US$34-42), bedecked in sailing motifs and Peruvian weavings, sports lovely views from its attractive upstairs rooms, which have slanted roofs and lots of wood detailing but small bathrooms.

Hostería de la Colina (☎/fax 411-503; Las Colinas 115; e aldrich@entelchile.net; singles/doubles US$70/84, suites US$84-98) is set among attractive grounds on a hillside and run by US expats. It has a cozy living room and bar with loads of music and books, a wooden hot tub in the garden and a destination restaurant (see Places to Eat below). The owners make guests feel right at home and have a plethora of information on the area's trails, waterfalls, hot springs and lakes; they can arrange quality guides for just about every activity. Cheaper rooms without views of the volcanoes are also available (US$42/62). To get there, take Presidente Ríos southeast of town and follow the signs up the hill.

Places to Eat

Café Bar 2001 (☎ 411-470; Henríquez 379; coffees US$1-2.50; sandwiches US$2.50-4.50) has the best coffee in town, including specialty drinks, and an impressive collection of key rings.

Touring (☎ 410-735; V Letelier 712; lunches US$3-5) serves up decent and cheap lunches and sandwiches in a tiny restaurant with good music and pleasant staff.

Hotel Fuentes (☎ 411-595; Vicente Reyes 665; lunches US$4) is a noisy, crowded, popular spot dishing out consistently good and filling meals of cazuela and steak, all under the hum of a large-screen TV.

The Travellers (☎ 412-830; V Letelier 753; mains US$4-8) has an ambitious menu of Chilean, Chinese, Thai and Mexican dishes, some of which are disappointing. The array of breakfasts, from wonton soup to oatmeal, is impressive. Still, the best bet might be to enjoy the fun surroundings at night when the place turns into a jazz club.

Restaurant Kiel (☎ 411-631; General Körner 153; mains US$9-14) enjoys formal dining around a roaring fireplace and views of the lake. Try the baked trout stuffed with veggies and crabmeat or the lomo yachting, a choice pork chop with grilled tomatoes and cheese served with Arabian rice.

Tabor (☎ 411-901; Epuléf 1187; mains US$8-13) isn't in a great location, but is highly regarded for its fish and seafood specialties, served in a whimsical dining room.

The restaurant at **Hostería de la Colina** (see Places to Stay above) is a worthwhile trek for anyone. A range of creative soups (US$3) – such as gazpacho, chestnut, and Chinese carrot – and mains (US$6-8) – try lasagna, pot roast or any Chilean-inspired plate – are filling and bursting with flavor. Leave room, though, for their famous handmade, hand-cranked ice cream.

Shopping

Directly behind and next to the tourist office, Villarrica's **Feria Artesanal** (artisans market) has Mapuche silverwork, baskets, woolens and carvings and traditional Mapuche food. **Tejidos Ray-Ray** (☎ 412-006; Anfión Muñoz 386) sells sweaters and brightly colored wool yarn by the kilo.

Getting There & Around

Villarrica has a main **bus terminal** (Pedro de Valdivia 621), though a few companies have separate offices nearby. Long-distance fares are similar to those from Temuco (an hour away), which has more choices for southbound travel.

Buses Jac (Bilbao 610), goes to Pucón (US$0.60), Temuco (US$3) and Lican Ray (US$0.60) every thirty minutes, and to Coñaripe (US$1.25) eight times daily. **Buses**

Regional Villarrica (Vicente Reyes 619) also has frequent buses to Pucón.

To Santiago, nightly service is provided by buses leaving the main bus terminal, as well as Buses Jac and **Tur Bus** (Anfión Muñoz 657) (US$10-38).

Other destinations include Valdivia (US$3.50), Los Ángeles (US$6), Concepción (US$7.50) and Puerto Montt (US$7).

For Argentine destinations, **Igi Llaima** leaves at 6:45am Monday, Wednesday and Friday for San Martín de los Andes (US$23), Zapala and Neuquén (US$35, 16 hours) via Paso Mamuil Malal. **Buses San Martín** has similar service, and both leave from the main bus terminal.

Lubricenter LBC (☎ 411-333; JM Carrera 366) rents cars.

PUCÓN
☎ 45 • pop 21,000

A hot spot for vacationing Santiaguinos and a must-stop on the gringo trail, this is the most touristy place in southern Chile. While that can repel some, it can also be an advantage – Pucón does have all the services a tourist could want, plus some excellent food (a variety of cuisine, por fin). The city is growing at a rapid pace, with more condo construction along the beach and seemingly not a care in the world that a smoldering volcano is the next-door neighbor. The adventure travel business grows at a similar pace, with agencies appearing and disappearing from season to season, while at the same time, environmental activism continues to gain strength and recognition. All of this makes for a fun dynamic, a mix of geared-up adrenaline junkies and sunbathing casino-going lazies who never even see what makes Pucón really attractive: everything outside of town.

Summer and Easter vacations in Pucón are jam-packed, the lodging expensive and service staff at times quite rude. Pucón is a worthwhile winter option, when days can be filled with skiing followed by long soaks at the hot springs.

Orientation

Pucón is 25km from Villarrica at the east end of Lago Villarrica, between the estuary of the Río Pucón to the north and Volcán Villarrica to the south. Structured along a conventional grid system, this very compact town is bounded by the lake to the north, the Costanera Roberto Geis to the west, the flanks of the volcano to the south, and Av Colo Colo to the east. To the northwest, a wooded peninsula (now under private hands) juts into the lake, forming the sheltered inlet La Poza at the west end of Av Libertador Bernardo O'Higgins (often called just Av O'Higgins), the main commercial street and thoroughfare.

Information

Tourist Offices The **Oficina de Turismo** (☎ 293-002; O'Higgins & Palguín; open 8:30am-10pm daily summer, to 7pm in winter) has stacks of brochures and usually an English speaker on staff. They can help with some details but don't recommend businesses. **Sernatur** (cnr Brasil & Caupolicán) has similar info, but isn't as helpful. **Conaf** (☎ 443-781; Lincoyán 336) has information on the nearby national parks and is developing a Centro de Información about the area ecology.

Money Exchange rates are better in Santiago and Temuco. Cambios include **Turismo Christopher** (O'Higgins 335) and **TravelSur** (Fresia 285). **Supermercado Elitt** (O'Higgins 336) will change US cash and has an ATM.

Post & Communications The post office (Fresia 183) and **Entel** (Ansorena 299) have offices. For Internet services, **Café Brinck** (Ansorena 243) is one of the better places.

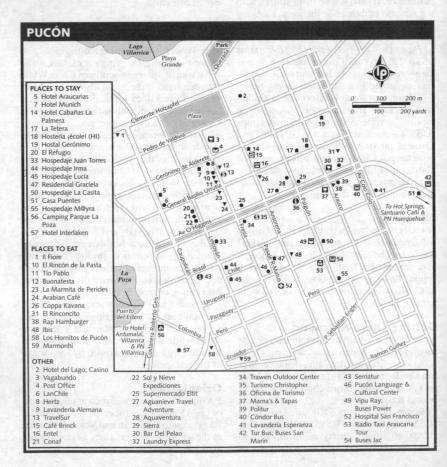

PUCÓN

PLACES TO STAY
5 Hotel Araucarias
7 Hotel Munich
14 Hotel Cabañas La Palmera
17 La Tetera
18 Hostería ¡école! (HI)
19 Hostal Gerónimo
20 El Refugio
33 Hospedaje Juan Torres
44 Hospedaje Irma
45 Hospedaje Lucía
47 Residencial Graciela
50 Hospedaje La Casita
51 Casa Puentes
55 Hospedaje M@yra
56 Camping Parque La Poza
57 Hotel Interlaken

PLACES TO EAT
1 Il Fiore
10 El Rincón de la Pasta
11 Tío Pablo
12 Buonatesta
23 La Marmita de Pericles
24 Arabian Café
26 Coppa Kavana
31 El Rinconcito
38 Rap Hamburger
48 Ibis
58 Los Hornitos de Pucón
59 Marmonhi

OTHER
2 Hotel del Lago; Casino
3 Vagabundo
4 Post Office
6 LanChile
8 Hertz
9 Lavandería Alemana
13 TravelSur
15 Café Brinck
16 Entel
21 Conaf
22 Sol y Nieve Expediciones
25 Supermercado Elitt
27 Aguanieve Travel Adventure
28 Aquaventura
29 Sierra
30 Bar Del Pelao
32 Laundry Express
34 Trawen Outdoor Center
35 Turismo Christopher
36 Oficina de Turismo
37 Mama's & Tapas
39 Politur
40 Cóndor Bus
41 Lavandería Esperanza
42 Tur Bus; Buses San Marín
43 Sernatur
46 Pucón Language & Cultural Center
49 Vipu Ray; Buses Power
52 Hospital San Francisco
53 Radio Taxi Araucaria Tour
54 Buses Jac

Language Courses A number of lodging options also provide quality Spanish-language classes. Contact **Hostería ¡ecole!**, **La Tetera** and **Hospedaje La Casita** *(see Places to Stay later in this section)*. **Pucón Language & Cultural Center** *(☎ 443-315, 09-935-9417; Uruguay 306)* is another option, and like the others, interweaves learning with cultural and outdoor activities around the area, structured in short- and long-term courses.

Laundry There's **Lavandería Alemana** *(☎ 441-106; Fresia 224)*, **Laundry Express** *(O'Higgins 660, Local 2)* and **Lavandería Esperanza** *(☎ 441-379; Colo Colo 475)*.

Medical Services For medical care, head to **Hospital San Francisco** *(☎ 441-177; Uruguay 325)*.

Activities & Organized Tours

It's easy to get overwhelmed by all the tour operators and taxi companies along O'Higgins offering access to the bounty of activities that surrounds Pucón. Sorting out what to do, when to do it and with whom is all part of the experience. The standards – climbing Villarrica and rafting Río Trancura – are on offer by many, but keep your eyes open for activities that take you away from the swells of adrenaline-seeking tourists, such as horseback riding or renting a bike to explore on your own. Whatever the choosing, you won't be disappointed, whether it's sloshing down a river or swooshing down the slopes.

Climbing The hike up Volcán Villarrica is a full-day excursion (US$45-60), leaving around 7:30am. All equipment can be rented, but use your own boots if they fit the crampons, and take along extra snacks and water. Note that organized ascents may be delayed for days, cancelled due to bad weather, or required to turn back halfway up. Check cancellation policies carefully. Some people prefer to take a taxi to the cafetería at the base of the volcano, where you can rent all the necessary equipment and tackle the volcano without a tour. This shouldn't be done alone and should only be done under the best of conditions. There's a climbing wall at the corner of Colo Colo & O'Higgins for anyone thinking the ascent was a 'climb.' (For more information, see PN Villarrica later in this chapter.)

Rafting & Kayaking Trip durations include transportation, not just the time spent on the water. On offer are 2½-hour rafting trips down the lower Río Trancura (US$10-15), or three-hour trips on the more rugged (Class IV) upper Trancura (US$25-35). Kayaking trips take in Río Liucura (US$13-17, three hours to half day) and Río Caburgua (US$18, four hours).

Mountain Biking The most popular route takes cyclists to Ojos de Caburgua. Take the turnoff to the airport about 4km east of town and across Río Trancura. Rental agencies worth their salt should supply a route map.

Horseback Riding Excellent options for horse treks abound in this region. A half-day ride ranges from US$23 to US$35 depending on the grade of difficulty. Previous riding experience is best, but recommended outfitters offer first-time instruction; see the list below. Most rides take in various environments and may include stopovers so riders can meet with local huasos or Mapuche communities.

Outfitters Most of the tour operators are on Av O'Higgins or within a half block. Prices are similar, but quality of service can vary. In summer, seasonal operators pop up on all corners, but are not as established as those listed below. Many hospedajes also run their own operations; use your judgment. For outfitters outside of Pucón center, make reservations by phone or website or through other agencies, such as Hostería École.

Aguanieve Travel Adventure *(☎ 443-690; O'Higgins 448-B)*; small, but sound

Aquaventura *(☎ 444-246; Palguín 336)*; good bet for rafting and kayaking, also does rappeling and canyoning, snowshoeing in winter; arranges trips to El Cañi

Campo Antilco *(☎ 09-713-9758; w www.antilco .com)*, 15km east of Pucón on Río Liucura; recommended outfitter for half- to five-day horse treks in Liucura Valley and the cordillera, and for half-day and two-day kayaking trips, designed for both beginners and experts, with English-speaking guides

Centro Ecuestre Huepil-Malal *(☎ 09-643-3204; w www.huepil-malal.cl)*, Km 27 on Camino Pucón-Huife; reputable equestrian center with half-day to multiday treks in the cordillera, run by a charming couple

Hostería École (*see Places to Stay below*); arranges transportation to just about everyplace and works with other outfitters; organizes excursions to farther Chilean destinations; for information, contact **École Adventures International** (☎ 800-447-1483 in the USA, ☎/fax 707-923-3001; Box 2453, Redway, CA 95560)

Politur (☎ 441-373; O'Higgins 635); well established and straightforward

Rancho de Caballos (☎ 441-575), Palguín Alto; three-hour to six-day horseback treks near PN Villarrica

Sol y Nieve Expediciones (☎/fax 441-070; e sol nieve@entelchile.net; O'Higgins 192); well known for the Villarrica ascent and after-rafting *asados*

Trawen Outdoor Center (☎ 442-024; O'Higgins 311, Local 5); fun youthful guides leading a number of activities

Special Events

Mid-January's Jornadas Musicales de Pucón is an annual musical festival. The first week of February the town fills with the überathletes competing in the Triatlón Internacional de Pucón (Pucón International Triathlon).

Places to Stay

While Pucón has plenty of places to stay, prices are higher than in other cities (even for the budget options) and few places include breakfast. In the low season, rates are about 20% less. Whenever you come, reservations are advisable. The Oficina de Turismo (see Tourist Offices earlier in this section) has a list of mid-range to top-end places and may be able to help find vacancies.

Budget Camping Parque La Poza (☎ 441-435; Costanera Roberto Geis 769; per person US$4) has about 80 sites on shady grounds, and a fair amount of noise from the busy road. It's a car camping facility with a place to cook, lockers to store your stuff and hot water.

Budget accommodations start around US$10, usually with breakfast or kitchen privileges, at such places as **Hospedaje La Casita** (☎ 441-712; Palguín 555), a quaint place near bus transportation that organizes Spanish classes, but doesn't have many single rooms; **Hospedaje Juan Torres** (☎ 441-248; Lincoyán 445), which is quiet and friendly, with overflowing flower gardens, kitchen use and laundry; **Hospedaje Lucía** (☎ 441-271; Lincoyán 565), with a friendly owner who allows use of the kitchen and organizes fishing trips; **Hospedaje Irma** (☎ 442-

226; Lincoyán 545), with kitchen privileges, laundry and good common areas; **El Refugio** (☎ 441-347; Lincoyán 348), which has small but pleasant rooms above a restaurant; and **Residencial Graciela** (☎ 441-494; Roland Matus 521), which allows use of the kitchen and has a distracted staff and tidy rooms (no singles), many of which look out onto the central corridor.

Hostería École (☎/fax 441-675; e ecole@ entelchile.net; Urrutia 592; dorm bed US$4.50, shared rooms US$12.50, singles/ doubles with private bath US$25/31, 4-person room US$38), an HI affiliate, is as much an attitude as an accommodation. Artistic and laidback, it's *the* place to meet others, enjoy vegetarian food and plan excursions. A backyard garden may be used for tai chi or yoga classes, and there's a plethora of information on conservation issues. One of the few places with dorm beds, it's a good option for solo travelers. Rooms with private bath have very thin walls, but some have volcano views.

Hospedaje M@yra (☎ 442-745; Palguín 695; per person US$10), right by the bus station, has comfortable common areas, Internet and kitchen use, some cozy rooms and congenial owners.

Casa Puentes (☎ 441-613; O'Higgins 831-B; US$9), across from the Tur Bus station, is a basic place that fits five people, with kitchen access. It's a good choice for early-morning or late-night buses.

La Tetera (☎ 441-462; Urrutia 580; e info@ tetera.cl; rooms US$17-35) has a small range of cozy, tidy and well-heated rooms with shared or private bath. The back of the house has an attractive deck, and one double room sports a balcony. Prices include breakfast: You get to choose what kind. The owners are multilingual (as is their book exchange), and they can help arrange tours or transportation to areas of interest.

Hostal Gerónimo (☎ 443-762; Alderete 665; singles/doubles US$25/40) is another reputable spot worth checking out.

Mid-Range & Top End Hotel Cabañas **La Palmera** (☎/fax 441-083; Ansorena 221; singles/doubles US$50/61, cabins US$41-58) gives you the choice of hotel or cabin atmosphere. In the hotel, suites have better beds and nicer bathrooms, while first-floor rooms are a tad dark and have softer beds.

Cabins, for two to six people, are fully equipped – with microwave, even – and are the better deal of the two choices.

Hotel Interlaken (☎ 441-276, fax 441-242; Caupolicán 720; singles US$50-57, doubles US$58-66, chalet doubles US$76-117) provides a medley of swanky 'chalets' amid nice gardens. Its most intriguing feature is the glasshouse lounge area near the entrance. Cheaper chalets have the same amenities – heat, TV, hair dryer, comfort – but get the road noise. This is a good choice for families.

Hotel Araucarias (☎ 441-963; e hotel@araucarias.cl; Caupolicán 243; singles/doubles/triples US$50/75/100) has solid rooms and smart efficient service. Triples look out onto a pleasant garden. It's a decent place away from the ruckus of town, and it has a pool-and-sauna spa attached (open to the public; US$9 per day).

Hotel Munich (☎ 444-595; e munich@pucon.com; Alderete 275; singles/doubles US$67/76) has very attractive rooms, some with balconies, others with volcano views, and all with fabulous beds, heated floors and top-notch bathrooms. An ample breakfast is included. Artwork by Chilean artists decorates the hotel, which has helpful English- and German-speaking staff.

Hotel Antumalal (☎ 441-011/2, fax 441-013; e antumalal@entelchile.net; singles/doubles US$153/212, off-season US$120/140), at Km 2 on the road to Villarrica, offers one of the most luxurious and personalized stays in the Lakes District. Bauhaus in design (with a bow to organic architecture), by Chilean architect Jorge Elton, the hotel's lounge areas recall retro-swank James Bond digs, while each of the 16 rooms, occupying two wings, has an enormous picture window with lake views and a fireplace. Around the hotel and sweeping down to the water's edge are eight acres of expertly maintained hillside gardens with flower beds, winding stone paths, waterfalls, magnificent arrayanes and other native tree species. Choosing where to relax is each day's dilemma – shall it be the garden patio, the heated pool, the private beach, the lookout, the spacious lounge or the intimate bar?

Places to Eat

One of Pucón's saving graces is the variety of cuisine available, including the most vegetarian options in Chile.

For a quick bite, try **Los Hornitos de Pucón** (Caupolicán 710) for empanadas (weekends only); **Tío Pablo** (☎ 441-333; Urrutia 215; US$2.50) for filling fries and cazuela; and **Rap Hamburger** (O'Higgins & Arauco; US$1.50) for late-night cheeseburgers.

Economic restaurants, serving sandwiches and OK fixed-price lunches, include **Coppa Kavana** (☎ 449-033; Urrutia 407; US$2.50-5) and **El Rinconcito** (☎ 443-680, O'Higgins 660; US$2.50).

Hostería École (see Places to Stay above; mains US$4-7) is a Pucón institution serving hearty vegetarian food, including soups, crepes, lasagna and fabulous bread, plus a few fish specials. Service is a bit slow, but the wait is worth it.

La Tetera (see Places to Stay above) has the best breakfasts in town, plus economic spaghetti lunches, raclette (US$33 for four people) and afternoon tea.

Trawen (☎ 442-024; O'Higgins 311; mains US$3-7) is a hip adventure outfitter that doubles as a vegetarian haven, with huge bowls of soup, overstuffed empanadas, fresh juices and fixed-price meals.

Marmonhi (☎ 441-972; Ecuador 175; mains US$4-6) specializes in regional cuisine, including empanadas and humitas, and offers large, but not super cheap, fixed-price lunches.

Il Fiore (☎ 441-565; Holzapfel 83; steaks US$7-12) will tempt steak lovers with generous cuts plus rich sauces to be enjoyed on a shady outdoor terrace away from the town's chaos. The owner puts on parrillas at

---

Rural Rest Spots

Want to flee town lodging and support the rural way of life? **Turismo Rural Folil Mapu** (w www.folilmapu.cl) is a network of campgrounds and home stays around Pucón. En route to Lago Caburgua are a number of places to pitch the tent and explore the area for about US$9 per site. En route to Curarrehue, **Kila Leufu** (☎ 09-711-8064; singles/doubles US$10/23) is a much-praised home stay choice in a bucolic farmland setting. Check the website for a list of participants and contact details. In Pucón, the tourist office may have copies of the brochures.

times, and the homemade pastas are another house specialty.

Buonatesta (☎ 441-434; Fresia 243; pizzas US$5-8) makes pizza the crispy thin-crust way. They're big and have a variety of toppings – ordering a half portion is quite acceptable.

El Rincón de la Pasta (☎ 444-258; Fresia 284; pasta US$6-8.50) has the best pasta dishes in town, all homemade, fresh, accompanied by a range of sauces (even the veggie options are good) and served up with swift efficiency.

La Marmita de Pericles (☎ 442-431; Fresia 300; fondue for 2 US$26) makes you feel so, well, Alpine. Fondues – steak, fish, or cheese – plus crepes are the specialties, all well prepared and served in a fun-loving, informal, gingham and candle-lit space.

El Refugio (see Places to Stay above; mains US$4-10) serves up vegetarian plates, including a soyburger big enough to share but too dry, plus crepes.

Arabian Café (☎ 443-469; Fresia 354; mains US$5-8) shows its authenticity by considering lomo a lo pobre an 'alternative dish.' Expect Arabian delights from falafel and stuffed eggplant to sweet meats. Service is a bit distracted, the lights too bright, but where else can you find baba ganoush?

Ibis (☎ 444-770; Ansorena 555; mains US$7-10), a Puerto Varas original, specializes in well-prepared fish dishes, plus a good variety of meat, served in a more formal setting.

Entertainment

Pucón's nightlife has a similar scene as its big-city counterparts, and an attitude to match.

Vagabundo (☎ 444-691; Fresia 135) mixes a good selection of drinks, from mojitos to margaritas, in this small, vibrant bar-café that gets packed with a fun-loving sporty crew. Come earlier for quiche.

Bar Del Pelao (O'Higgins & Arauco) is a large and not terribly attractive place where the goals are to drink till drunk and dance till dawn; both are easily attained.

Mama's & Tapas (☎ 449-002; O'Higgins 587) has a more sophisticated edge. Push through the enormous door into the cool, mood-lit round bar with all-in-black bar staff and ambient beats. Yes, they do serve tapas (unimpressive) and have a weekday happy hour until 10pm.

Hotel del Lago (☎ 291-000; Ansorena 23), the ostentatious lux hotel taking up a whole block, is ridiculously overpriced for a night's stay, but it has two venues that entertain: a movie salon showing somewhat recently released movies and the dizzyingly glitzy, light-blaring casino, where you can enjoy the adventure of watching people lose their pesos or saddle up to a machine to try your own luck.

Getting There & Away

LanChile (☎ 443-516, 443-522; Urrutia 102) has occasional summer flights to Santiago (US$180), but normally flies out of Temuco (they sometimes provide the transfer).

Bus transportation to/from Santiago (US$13-27) is with **Tur Bus** (☎ 443-328) east of town on O'Higgins, **Buses Jac** (☎ 443-693; cnr Uruguay & Palguín), **Cóndor Bus** (Colo Colo 430) and **Buses Power** (☎ 444-507; Palguín 550), the cheapest (and least comfortable) option.

Tur Bus also goes to Puerto Montt daily (US$9, five hours). For Temuco, Tur Bus leaves every hour and Buses Jac every half-hour (US$3.50). For Valdivia, Jac has five daily buses (US$3.50, three hours). Buses Jac and **Minibuses Vipu Ray** (Palguín 550) have continuous service to Villarrica and Curarrehue. Buses Jac also has service to Caburgua, Paillaco and PN Huerquehue. For San Martín de los Andes, Argentina, **Buses San Martín** (☎ 441-965; Tur Bus terminal) has six weekly departures (US$16, five hours) stopping in Junín on the way.

Getting Around

A number of travel agencies rent cars and prices can be competitive, especially in the off-season; also consider renting in Temuco. Daily rates range from US$46 for passenger cars to US$70 for 4WD pickups. Try **Sierra Nevada** (☎ 444-210, O'Higgins 524A), which also rents bikes (US$10 per day), **Pucón Rent a Car** (☎ 441-922, Camino Internacional 1395) or **Hertz** (☎ 441-664; cnr Alderete & Fresia). If renting long-term, ask about drop-off charges.

Around town, taxi companies will try to take you somewhere, and their service is a viable option to get to the parks and hot springs resorts. Recommended **Radio Taxi Araucaria Tour** (☎ 442-323, Palguín & Uruguay) charges, for a maximum of four passengers, US$12 roundtrip to Ojos del Caburgua,

US$26 roundtrip to Termas Los Pozones (both with a two-hour wait), and US$16 one-way to either PN Huerquehue or Villarrica.

RÍO LIUCURA VALLEY

Heading east out of Pucón, take the Camino Pucón-Huife to access myriad hot springs, El Cañi nature sanctuary and views of the silver-ribbon Río Liucura that cuts through this richly verdant valley. Kilometer markings mentioned below refer to the Camino Pucón-Huife and are well marked along the road.

El Cañi

Chile's first conservation success story, **El Cañi** *(Km 21; entrance without/with guide US$5/10)* protects some 400 hectares of ancient araucaria forest. When logging interests threatened the area in 1991, Fundación Lahuen, just a small cluster of concerned folks with start-up funding from Ancient Forests International, formed to purchase the land and develop a park with an emphasis on education and scientific research.

A **hiking trail** (9km, three hours) ascends the steep terrain (the first 3km very steep) of lenga and araucaria to arrive at Laguna Negra. On clear days, the lookout – another 40 minutes – allows for spectacular views of the area's volcanoes. Except in summer when the trail is easier to find, all hikers must go with a guide. An alternative route, which detours the steepest part, starts along the road to Cailaco; a guide is required.

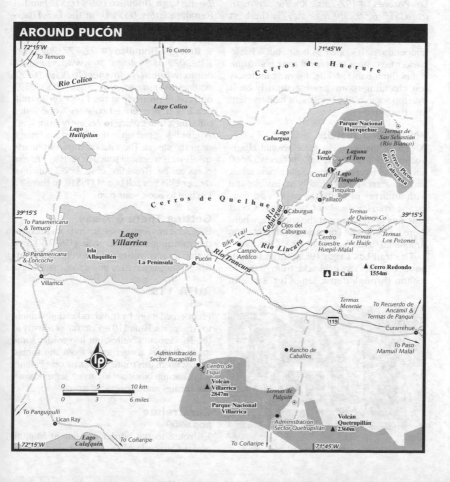

AROUND PUCÓN

Make arrangements to visit El Cañi at the park entrance or through Hostería École or Aquaventura (see Pucón earlier in this chapter).

Hot Springs

A casual resort, **Termas de Quimey-Co** (☎ 443-544, Km 30; day use US$5.50; camping/cabins per person US$7.50/13; open till 9pm) has two small pools by the river, an unimpressive restaurant and a few walking trails. **Termas de Huife** (☎ 441-222; Km 33; day use US$9; doubles US$120) is a large upscale locale, popular with busloads of more mature travelers. Three attractive pools of different temperatures line the river's edge. An assortment of spa services is available. **Termas Los Pozones** (☎ 197-2350; Km 36; day/night use US$5/6.50; 3hr max stay) is the best choice on this route: the six natural stone pools are spaced apart and have a variety of temperatures. It's open 24 hours, but a backpacker favorite is to come during nighttime hours (8pm-6am) and light some candles. A few changing rooms are ingeniously built overtop some of the pools with ladders right into the water.

PN HUERQUEHUE

A gem of the area, Parque Nacional Huerquehue (admission US$3.50) protects 12,500 hectares of rivers and waterfalls, alpine lakes, and araucaria forests. Easily accessible and with an array of trails, the park is an easy escape from Pucón, about 35km away. Conaf sells decent trail maps at the entrance, where there's a **Centro de Educación e Intepretación Ambiental** (open 8am-8pm Jan-Mar).

The trail **Los Lagos** (9km, three to four hours one-way) switchbacks from 700m to 1300m through dense lenga forests with

Countryside architecture east of Pucón

rushing waterfalls, then enters solid stands of araucaria surrounding a cluster of pristine and placid lakes. Most hikers turn back at Lago Verde and Laguna el Toro, the largest of the cluster, but continuing on the northern loop to Lago Los Patos and Laguna Huerquehue will treat you to some of the best scenery on the hike. At Laguna Huerquehue, the trail **Los Huerquenes** (two days) continues north then east to cross the park and access **Termas de San Sebastián (Río Blanco)** (☎ 045-341-961), just east of the park boundary. From there a gravel road connects to the north end of Lago Caburgua and Cunco.

Places to Stay

Camping options are at Conaf-managed 24-site **Lago Tinquilco** (sites US$14) and at **Renahue** (sites US$14) on the Los Huerquenes trail. Conaf may install rustic refugios on the longer routes.

Refugio Tinquilco (☎ 02-777-7673, fax 735-3079 in Santiago; W www.tinquilco.cl; bunks without/with sheets US$9/10.50, doubles with shared/private bath US$31/39), on private property at the Lago Verde trailhead, is an attractive two-story wood lodge offering a quiet place to get away from it all. After hiking, rest up in the downstairs lounge or in the sauna. The kitchen turns out hearty meals with welcome touches, such as French-press coffee. Breakfast costs US$2, lunch or dinner US$5 or full board US$10, or there's a kitchen to cook your own.

Getting There & Away

Buses Jac has regular service to/from Pucón in the morning and afternoon (US$2.50, one hour); reserve your spot beforehand. Otherwise outfitters have excursions, or share a taxi.

RUTA 119
☎ 45

Frequented more by travelers heading straight to Argentina, Ruta 119 isn't as full of activity as the Río Liucura Valley, but it provides some great chances to get away from the tourist frenzy. From this route, you can access Palguín Alto, Parque Nacional Villarrica, lesser known hot springs and slow-paced towns.

Curarrehue
pop 6800

En route to the border crossing at Mamuil Malal, Curarrehue is a quiet but colorful little town with a Mapuche cultural influence and a few places to stay. The **tourist office** (☎ 197-1573; *Plaza*) has some info on activities in the area, but across the street, the *carabineros* know everyone in town and may have better contacts for horse treks and hiking guides. For a chance to learn about Mapuche culture, **Aldea Trawu Peyüm** is a cultural center–museum offering traditional food.

Camping is available at the **Municipal Camping** (*Cruce a Panqui*) while a few hospedajes are in town, such as the attractive **Hospedaje La Mamy** (*O'Higgins 973*), offering breakfast in an old frontier-style house, and **Hospedaje Ulloa** (☎ 351-511; *O'Higgins 984*).

Buses have multiple departures daily to Curarrehue from Pucón (US$1.20) and Villarrica (US$2). There is also service to San Martín de los Andes. For Argentine-bound buses, see Pucón earlier in this chapter.

Hot Springs
Only 5km northeast of Curarrehue, quiet and rustic **Recuerdo de Ancamil** (☎ 351-587) on the banks of Río Maichín has eight natural pools, including one in a grotto. There's camping and a few cabins are available.

Another 10km farther, in a gorgeous location, **Termas de Panqui** (☎ 442-039, *reservations O'Higgins 555, Pucón; day use US$10; vegetarian meals US$5-7.50; tepee/hotel per person US$15/20*) is well known but not always for the best of reasons. Clients have complained of the expensive and rigid pricing structure, and women cite inappropriate behavior. Priding itself as a spiritual retreat, it's got the drum-beating, watsu-massaging, medicine-wheel-twirling 'om' about it, but whether or not one can truly relax here is questionable. Panqui is some 58km east of Pucón, with the last few kilometers passable only by high-clearance vehicles. The owner can arrange transportation here, but might not be as helpful arranging transportation back.

Taking the access road to PN Villarrica and Coñaripe leads you past **Termas de Palguín** (☎/fax 441-968; *day use US$6.50; singles/doubles US$50/90*), 30km southeast of Pucón. With serene paths through stands of quila and past sulfuric thermal sources, it is one of the best settings on the Río Palguín, but it offers only unimpressive common pools and a variety of very hot private indoor baths. Perhaps its most impressive feature is the old-

style but effective hydroelectric system, viewed from some hotel rooms.

Note that while the access road to PN Villarrica is in fine condition, crossing the park requires 4WD.

PN VILLARRICA
Established in 1940, Parque Nacional Villarrica protects 60,000 hectares of remarkable volcanic scenery and the dragons that made it that way: 2847m Villarrica, 2360m Quetrupillán and, along the Argentine border, a section of 3746m Lanín. (The rest of Lanín is protected in an equally impressive park in Argentina, from where it may be climbed.) Its enormity is broken into three sectors and has an array of trails for day-trippers and traversers.

In 1971, Volcán Villarrica had a major eruption that opened a 4km-wide fracture, which in turn emitted 30 million cubic meters of lava and displaced several rivers. One flow, down the Río Challupén, was 14km long, 200m wide and 5m high. Wow.

Hiking
The most accessible sector of the park **Rucapillán**, is directly south of Pucón along a well-maintained road and takes in the most popular hikes up and around Villarrica. The popular climb to the sulfur-smoky summit is physically but not technically demanding, requiring equipment and either experience or a guide, usually with a group tour. However, Conaf will let you go it alone if you show you know what you're doing and have the proper equipment. (For more climb details and outfitters, see Pucón earlier in this chapter.)

The trail **Challupen Chinay** (*23km, 12 hours*) rounds the volcano's southern side crossing through a variety of scenery to end at the entrance to the **Quetrupillán** sector. This sector is easily accessed via the passable road that goes to Termas de Palguín. However, if you plan to continue through to Coñaripe, the road south through the park requires 4WD even in good weather. A 32km combination of hikes, with a couple of camping areas, links to the **Puesco** sector, near the Argentine border, where there is public transportation back to Curarrehue and Pucón (or make connections to carry on to Argentina).

Skiing
Centro de Esquí Villarrica (☎ 441-001; *Gran Hotel Pucón, Holzapfel 190*) has five lifts

leading to slopes of varying difficulty all on the volcano's north face. The views can't be beat, and it gives you the rare chance to cut powder on an active volcano. Lift tickets run about US$23 to US$27 per day, and rentals are available. The season runs from June until late September.

Getting There & Away

Taxis, your own car or a tour are the only ways to get to the Rucapillán sector. For details, see Pucón earlier in this chapter. Buses Regional Villarrica run between the Puesco sector and Pucón (see Villarrica earlier in this chapter).

LICAN RAY

☎ 45 • pop 4000

On the north shore of island-studded Lago Calafquén, Lican Ray (30km south of Villarrica) boasts a long black-sand beach that attracts the summer vacationers like a high-powered magnet. The town itself is tiny, packed with cabins along its streets and grandiose front-yard gardens (Lican Ray draws its name from a Mapuche phrase meaning 'flower among the stones'). Its only paved street is Av General Urrutia, lined with restaurants, cafés and artisan markets. Off-season, Lican Ray is so quiet you can almost hear the chilco blossoms drop.

Information

The **Oficina de Turismo** (☎ 431-516; General Urrutia 310; open 9am-11pm daily in summer, limited hours rest of year), directly on the Plaza de Armas, distributes maps and brochures and has a list of accommodations. The **post office** is in the same spot. Bring cash with you. **Call centers** can be found near the plaza, on Huenumán.

Places to Stay & Eat

A lot of places close up when the last tour bus leaves. These listed are open year-round (with the exception, possibly, of the campgrounds). Note that there are tons more options in the summer. Within 5km on either side of Lican Ray are lakeside campgrounds charging US$16-20 per site, for up to six people.

Residencial Temuco (☎ 431-130; Gabriela Mistral 515; per person US$8) is fairly basic, with uncomfortable bumpy beds. **Residencial Nadime Munre** (☎ 431-093; Catriñi 140; per person US$9; 5-person cabins US$40) is

woodsy and friendly with limited in-house lodging (but with kitchen use) and some rundown but large cabins set away from the street.

Hostal Hofmann (☎ 431-109; Camino Coñripe 100; per person US$20), on the main road leading out of town, is the best option any time of year. The attractive shingled home, surrounded by abundant flower gardens, has just a few rooms (all with private bath), allowing for comfort and personalized attention. Feather down pillows, strong hot showers and a filling breakfast, including excellent *küchen*, help reenergize. Area hiking trails start right from the premises.

Hotel Refugio Inaltulafquén (☎ 412-543; Punulef 510; per person US$17.50), fronting Playa Grande, is an attractive choice with cozy rooms, shared baths and breakfast. The restaurant is also one of the better places to eat in town.

Los Ñaños (Urrutia 105) serves overpriced Chilean specialties; best bets are the oven-baked empanadas on the weekends.

Getting There & Away

Buses Jac (Urrutia & Marichanquín), goes often to Villarrica (45 minutes) and Coñaripe (30 minutes). Other buses leave from the corner of Urrutia and Huenumán. Every morning at 7:30am, a local bus goes to Panguipulli (US$2, two hours) via back roads.

COÑARIPE

☎ 63

Twenty-two kilometers east of Lican Ray and overshadowed by its more touristy neighbors, Coñaripe maintains the sense of a regular town, but its black-sand beaches also attract the summer crowds. At the east end of town, the main drag, Av Guido Beck Ramberga, intersects Ruta 201, the international highway to Junín de los Andes, Argentina; the westbound fork leads to Panguipulli and the southeast to Termas de Coñaripe, Liquiñe and the border crossing at Paso Carririñe. The road north of town leads to a number of rustic hot springs and the southern boundary of Parque Nacional Villarrica. The road can be muddy, but it is passable to high-clearance vehicles up until the park, where 4WD is a must. A small **tourist kiosk** (☎ 317-403; Plaza de Armas) has some basic information. **Turismo Aventura Chumay** (☎ 317-287; e excursioneschumay@hotmail

.com; Las Tepas 201) is the best source of information on the area and organizes trips to the nearby parks and rivers. Daily rates run about US$16 per person for transportation and guide. Ask about its thermal-spring base camp and horse-trekking options.

Places to Stay & Eat

Campgrounds by the lake are mostly small lots with cramped spaces charging a negotiable US$13-17 per site. Try **Millaray** (☎ 317-210) or **Rucahue** (☎ 317-210).

Hospedaje Plaza (☎ 317-227; Beck Ramberga 458; per person US$9) is a simple and quaint option that includes breakfast.

Hostal Chumay (☎ 317-287; Las Tepas 201; per person with shared bath US$10, doubles with private bath US$25), behind the plaza, is a great deal, not just for the lodgings (which come with breakfast), but for the restaurant, which is one of the best in town. The fixed-price menú (US$4) can include a superb trout dish.

Hotel Entre Montañas (☎ 317-298; Beck Ramberga 496; doubles/triples US$24/27.50), opposite the plaza, provides clean but rather dark and small rooms. Beds are large, though, breakfast is included, and the downstairs restaurant is a decent choice.

Getting There & Away

Buses Jac has several buses daily from Villarrica to Coñaripe via Lican Ray (US$2). From the main **bus terminal** (Beck Ramberga), there's several daily departures to Villarrica, Liquiñe and Panguipulli (all about US$1.20). There are no buses on Sunday, and departures are more limited in the off-season.

AROUND COÑARIPE

The isolated road north to Parque Nacional Villarrica accesses a few remote, unique and very rustic hot springs, including **Termas Vergara** (Km 14; day use US$3.50; camping US$1.50), which has wooden-box-style private baths, lots of concrete minipools, exposed but decent campsites and good bathrooms. Five kilometers farther north is **El Rincón** (Km 19; day use US$3.50; rooms per person US$8.50), with a quila- and fern-covered very rustic spring at the base of a beautiful waterfall. The owners provide some campsites and lodging in their charming rustic home perched on a hill. They can arrange horse treks to Laguna Azul and

Volcán Quetrupillán. The southern entrance to PN Villarrica is another 4km north.

About 15km southeast of Coñaripe, on Ruta 201 to Liquiñe, **Termas Coñaripe** (☎ 063-317-330 or 045-431-407; day use US$9-15) is a high-end resort featuring poshly designed stone pools within a red-brick complex of hotel rooms and a restaurant. Its most unusual feature is the on-premises trout farm.

At the same turnoff, the very exposed **EcoTermas Pellaifa** (day use US$3) may be the only place where you may have to walk through a herd of sheep to get to a thermal bath; the place gets points for using what they've got. Camping may be possible, and there's a café.

LIQUIÑE
☎ 63

Liquiñe, along its namesake river and 31km southeast of Coñaripe via Ruta 201, is a secluded town with an impressive number of hot springs: several posh ones are in town, and numerous rustic ones are nestled in the nearby hills. Artesans' kiosks line the town's entrance selling attractive wooden bowls and plates made of raulí. There is a single public telephone (☎/fax 063-311-060), where messages can be left for accommodations that do not have extensions.

Hot springs around town include **Termas Manquecura** (day use US$4; camping free, 2-5 person cabins US$21-42), which has an attractive stone pool, tubs, a mud bath and beautiful views of the valley and Salto Liquiñe. Down the road is **Termas Punulaf** (day use US$2.50; sites US$11, 6-person cabins US$29), featuring a large round pool and shadier campsites. Better yet, head 8km toward Paso Carirriñe to **Termas Hipolito Muñoz** (day use US$2.50; camping per person/site US$3/7, 4-person cabins US$15), which has a hot and sulfur-smelly pool right by the river, plus a rather inventive steam bath. Their cabins, however, are best described as shacks. Of all of them, Manquecura has the best campsites and Punulaf the best cabins.

Residencial La Frontera (singles with shared/private bath US$6/10), managed by a vivacious woman, mainly has bunk beds, but one nicer room has a private bath. Breakfast is US$2.50 extra, and kitchen use is possible.

Hospedaje La Casona (per person US$11) has annex rooms that can be a bit musty, while the couple of rooms in the main building share a bath but are nicer. Lunches cost US$5.

Termas Río Liquiñe (*☎ 230-004; rooms without/with full board US$20/44*) offers rustically deluxe cabañas, manicured lawns around the large warm pool and a well-regarded restaurant.

There's regular bus service to Panguipulli (except on Sunday) and to Coñaripe, Lican Ray, and Villarrica (on Sunday one bus at 5pm).

LAGO PANGUIPULLI
☎ 63 • pop 32,000

At the northwest end of Lago Panguipulli, the town of **Panguipulli** is a quiet spot with awkward beach access and a surprising number of restaurants. Most travelers come here just to make transportation connections. The **tourist office** (*☎ 311-311, anexo 731; open 8:30am-9pm daily Dec–mid-Mar, until 8pm the rest of the year*), across from Plaza Arturo Prat, has lots of listings for the area and helpful staff. The regular assortment of traveler services can be found up and down the main road, Martínez de Rozsa, leading toward the lake.

Little more than two streets at the east end of Lago Panguipulli, the cute hamlet **Choshuenco** has a sweeping beach with views that are a study in serenity, scripted with crystal waters and rolling hills of green. It's a relaxing base for hikes, or a good place to rest before or after the Lago Pirihueico crossing to Argentina. The old passenger barge rusting on the beach used to make the long miserable trip across the lake to Panguipulli back in the roadless days.

Just south, near the very isolated Lago Riñihue, is Enco, the access point to 2415m **Volcán Choshuenco**, which has two tops – the higher conical peak and Mocho Choshuenco, a tableau-shaped peak. Mocho offers the more accessible hiking. Local guide Luis Méndez (*☎ 318-223*) can arrange transportation and lead climbs. **Ruca Pillán Expediciones** (*☎ 318-220;* **W** *www.rucapillan.cl; San Martín 85, Choshuenco*) also leads treks to Mocho and plans to start rafting down the Río Fuy.

Places to Stay & Eat
Panguipulli has the most selection of accommodations and restaurants. **Camping El Bosque** (*☎ 311-489; sites per person US$4.50*), only 200m north of Plaza Prat, has 15 tent sites (no drive-in sites) and hot showers. **Playa Chauquén**, south of town, has more variety of camping. In summer a shuttle runs to and from the beach twice daily. **Hospedaje Berrocal** (*☎ 311-812; Portales 72; per person US$8-10*) is an excellent place to stay – simple, but personable and with good home-made meals. **Hotel Central** (*☎ 09-319-5640; Pedro de Valdivia 115; per person US$11*) is friendly, with airy rooms and clean bathrooms with hot water (and even bathtubs); upstairs rooms are quieter and larger. **Hostal España** (*☎ 311-166; O'Higgins 790; singles/doubles US$20/33*) has rooms with private bath and breakfast in homey surroundings.

Of the plethora of restaurants on the main strip in Panguipulli, the following two stand out; both have fixed-price lunches for about US$3.50: **Girasol** (*Martínez de Rozas 664*) has an attractive upstairs dining room and pastel de choclo; and **Gardylafquen** (*☎ 311-887; Martínez de Rozas 722*) offers inviting options like stuffed zucchini and olive oil for your salad.

What Choshuenco lacks in quantity it makes up for in location. **Camping Choshuenco** (*☎ 318-220; US$5 per tent; open Dec-Mar*) has beachfront sites.

Hotel Rucapillán (*☎ 318-220;* **e** *rucapi@telsur.cl; San Martín 85; doubles with shared/private bath US$20/23*) is the best choice in town – tidy and well heated, with a good restaurant, hot showers and friendly staff. An abundant lunch costs only US$6.

Hostería Pulmahue (*☎ 318-224; doubles with private bath US$30-40; cabins US$58-75*) sits among gardens overlooking the lake. The cabins, nestled in a labyrinth of forest and stone walkways, are the best bet. Or come enjoy the coziest of lounges with over 40 years of memories and the wise owners who made them.

Getting There & Away
Panguipulli's main **Terminal de Buses** (*☎ 311-055; Gabriela Mistral 100*) at the corner of Diego Portales, has regular departures Monday to Saturday to Liquiñe, Coñaripe and Lican Ray; to Choshuenco, Neltume and Puerto Fuy; and to Valdivia and Temuco. Buses from Panguipulli to Puerto Fuy (two hours) pass through Choshuenco and return to Panguipulli early the following morning.

LAGO PIRIHUEICO

The road to Puerto Fuy on Lago Pirihueico parallels Río Huilo Huilo, which tumbles and falls through awe-inspiring scenery. **Huilo Huilo** (☎ 02-334-4565; w *www.huilo huilo.cl; admission US$1.50*), encompassing 60,000 hectares of private land, plans to open up this treasure to its abundant adventurous potential. For now, old logging tracks lead to viewpoints of the river and a few impressive waterfalls, and you can meander through some incredible terrain strewn with coipihue flowers. Keep an eye out for *chucaos*, flightless red-breasted birds with a sing-song call.

From Puerto Fuy, the ferry *Hua-Hum* (☎ *063-311-334 in Panguipulli*) carries passengers and vehicles to and from Puerto Pirehueico (1½ hours) January to mid-March twice daily in each direction, and from mid-March to January once daily.

Automobiles pay US$16; jeeps and pickups US$25. Pedestrians pay only US$1, bicycle US$3. The *Hua-Hum* can fit 30 vehicles, so make reservations.

VALDIVIA

☎ 63 • pop 137,000

With a lively university scene, a strong emphasis on the arts and plenty of history – and surrounded in natural beauty – Valdivia just may be Chile's most attractive and enjoyable city. Called *Ciudad de los Ríos* (City of the Rivers), it has that vibe found in many river cities, where crew teams stream back and forth, birds frolic, and tour boats chug along calling out points of interest.

Three rivers, the Calle Calle, Cau Cau and Cruces, converge here and open to the ocean. Such a strategic transportation and military position was not overlooked by the Spanish, who took possession of the area in 1544, only to have their town obliterated by the original dwellers, the Mapuche, some 55 years later. The Dutch soon after attempted to occupy the area, the act of which spurred the Spaniards to fortify their city from any further attack with a wall encompassing the city and forts on the strategic points of Corral, Niebla and Mancera, creating the largest Spanish fortification in South America. However, in 1820, Chilean patriots launched a surprise attack on Spanish loyalists at Corral.

The influential immigration of Germans in the mid-19th-century led to the creation of grandiose mansions and industries. But the disastrous 1960 earthquake crumbled many buildings and reshaped Valdivia's river banks. Still, along General Lagos, near the riverfront, one can find several European-style buildings and mansions.

Orientation

Valdivia, 160km southwest of Temuco and 45km west of the Panamericana, sits on the south bank of the Río Calle Calle where it becomes Río Valdivia. Av Costanera Arturo Prat (known simply as Prat) is a major focus of activity, but most important public buildings are on Plaza de la República. From the Panamericana, Av Ramón Picarte is the main eastern approach. To the west, the Puente Pedro de Valdivia crosses the river to Isla Teja, a leafy suburb that is the site of the Universidad Austral.

Information

Sernatur (☎ *213-596; Prat 555; open 8:30am-5:30pm Mon-Fri Mar-Dec, daily Jan & Feb*) is on the riverfront. There is also an **Oficina de Informaciones** (☎ *212-212*) at the bus terminal at Prat and Muñoz.

To change money, try **Cambio Arauco** (*Arauco 331, Local 24*), open on Saturday, or **Cambio La Reconquista** (*Carampangue 329*). Downtown ATMs are abundant, including those at **Banco de Chile** (*Independencia & Chacabuco*).

There is a **post office** (*O'Higgins 575*). Call centers include **Telefónica (CTC)** (*Valdés & Picarte*) and **Entel** (*Pérez Rosales 601*). The best place for Internet and long-distance rates is **Café Phonet** (*Libertad 127*).

Travel agencies include **Turismo Cochrane** (☎ *212-213; Arauco 435*) and **Turismo Paraty** (☎ *215-585; Independencia 640*).

Laundry services are at **Lavandería Manantial** (*Henríquez 809*) and **Supermatic Lavandería** (*Henríquez 316*).

The **Hospital Regional** (☎ *214-066; Bueras 1003*) is south of town, near Aníbal Pinto.

Museo Histórico y Arqueológico

Housed in a fine riverfront mansion on Isla Teja, this museum (☎ *212-872; Los Laureles 47; adult/child US$1.25/0.50; open 9am-1pm & 2:30pm-6pm Dec-Mar, 10am-1pm & 2pm-6pm Apr-Nov*) is one of Chile's most beautiful. It features a large, well-labeled collection from pre-Columbian times to the

VALDIVIA

PLACES TO STAY
1   Hotel Isla Teja
2   Hotel Pedro de Valdivia
3   Hostal Donde Marcelo
4   Hotel Prat
10 Hotel Palace
19 Hotel Casa Grande
30 Residencial Germania (HI)
31 Hotel Regional
41 Hostal Internacional
42 Hospedaje Ríos
46 Hostal Esmeralda
49 Hostal Torreón
54 Hostal Villa Paulina

PLACES TO EAT
7   Café Hausmann
20 Shanghai
27 Club de la Unión
29 Bar La Bomba
37 Entrelagos
48 La Calesa
50 La Última Frontera
51 CasAbuela

11 Feria Fluvial
12 Feria Artesanal Camino de
    Luna
13 Banco de Chile
14 Tur Bus
15 Telefónica (CTC)
16 Hertz
17 Automóvil Club de Chile
18 Anticura Expediciones
21 Museo de Arte
    Contemporáneo
22 Sernatur
23 Café Phonet
24 Church
25 Post Office
26 LanChile/LanExpress
28 Galería Artesanal Arauco
32 Torreón del Barro
33 Museo Histórico y
    Arqueológico
34 Puerto Fluvial
35 Turismo Paraty
36 Entel
38 Cambio Arauco
39 Cubana Club
40 Turismo Cochrane
43 Centro Cultural El Austral
44 Arte-Bar
45 AutoVald
47 El Legado
52 Artesanía Ruca Indiana
53 Torreón de los Canelos
55 Lavandería Manantial

OTHER
5   Coalición para la
    Conservación de la
    Cordillera de la Costa
6   Cine Cervantes
8   Pub en el Clavo
9   Cambio La Reconquista;
    Supermatic Lavandería

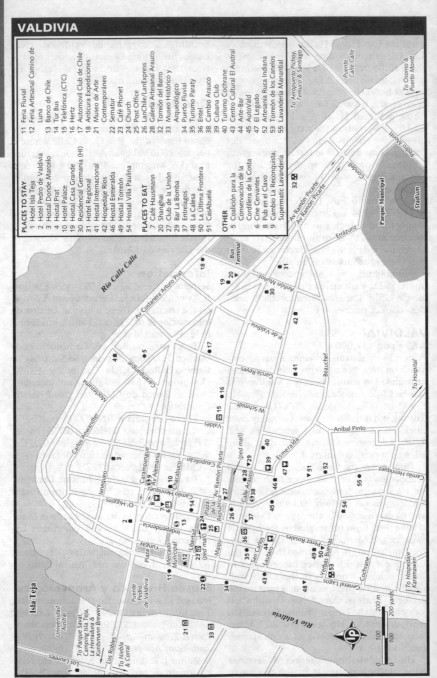

present, with particularly fine displays of Mapuche Indian artifacts and household items from early German settlements.

Take the bridge across the Río Valdivia, turn left at the first intersection and walk about 200m; the entrance is on the left (east) side.

Museo de Arte Contemporáneo

Valdivia's modern art museum (☎ 221-968; adult/child US$1/0.50; open 10am-1pm & 3pm-7pm Tues-Sun), almost alongside the archaeological museum, sits atop the foundations of the former Cervecería Anwandter, the onetime brewery that tumbled during the 1960 earthquake. The museum has fine views across the river to the city.

Other Things to See & Do

Valdivia's Feria Fluvial is a lively riverside market south of the Valdivia bridge, where vendors sell fresh fish, meat and produce. Rolly sea lions, not the least bit shy, come right up to the edge grunting for handouts. The Centro Cultural El Austral (☎ 213-658; Yungay 733) hosts impressive visual arts and music events. Parque Saval on Isla Teja has a riverside beach and a pleasant trail that follows the shoreline of Laguna de los Lotos, covered with lily pads. It's a good place for bird-watching.

A couple of turrets can be seen around town: East of the bus terminal, the Torreón del Barro is from a Spanish fort built in 1774, while the Torreón de los Canelos (cnr Yerbas Buenas & General Lagos) dates from the 17th century.

Organized Tours

Valdivia's main and traditional tourist attraction is the boat cruises (US$22-26; 6½ hours) that ply the rivers to visit the different forts (for descriptions, see Corral, Niebla & Isla Mancera later in this chapter). Each tour says it's different, but most take the same route, stopping at Corral and Isla Mancera for 45 minutes to one hour each, and all include lunch and onces. Outfitters include the large Neptuno (☎ 218-952), which entertains its audience with a live music show, and the smaller Reina Sofía (☎ 207-120) with less pretensions. All cruises leave from Puerto Fluvial, at the base of Arauco.

Cruises north to the Río de Cruces Santuario de la Naturaleza take 3½ hours; they go

slowly through the habitat of 16,000 black-necked swans to the confluence of the three rivers. Then they make a mandatory stop at the Huilliche village of Punucapa, where one delights in the ecotourism movement while sipping apple cider below flapping Pepsi flags. Cruises include Bahía (☎ 224-680), which provides knowledgeable guides, binoculars and cramped but practical inside seating.

Anticura Expediciones (☎ 212-630; W www .anticura.com; Anfión Muñoz 327) specializes in arranging trekking and climbing trips in remote areas of the region, tailored to individual skill levels. Hostal Internacional (see Places to Stay later in this section) organizes jeep trips up to Parque Oncol, with side trips to secluded beach areas (6½ hours; per person US$22, three-person minimum). Bring your own lunch and snacks.

Fundo Teja Norte (☎ 221-956), accessed from the road to Parque Saval, organizes horse-riding trips near the Río de Cruces Santuario de la Naturaleza.

Special Events

The largest happening is Noche de Valdivia, the third Saturday in February, which features decorated riverboats and fireworks.

Places to Stay

For most of the year, students from the Universidad Austral monopolize the cheapest lodging, but many of these same places vigorously court travelers in summer.

You'll find a number of hospedajes near the bus terminal along Av Ramón Picarte and Carlos Anwandter, but only a handful stand out as being acceptable and of decent value. Sernatur keeps a roster of seasonal accommodations, which change from year to year.

Budget A half hour's walk across Puente Pedro de Valdivia, Camping Isla Teja (☎ 225-855; Los Cipreses 1125; campsites US$10-15) is at the end of Calle Los Robles and Los Cipreses. It has good facilities, a riverside beach and sites in a pleasant apple orchard – with free apples in late summer. Take Bus No 9 from the Mercado Municipal.

Residencial Germania (☎ 212-405; Picarte 873; per person with/without HI card US$8.50/15), the current HI affiliate, offers clean rooms with hot showers.

Hotel Regional (☎ 216-027; Picarte 1005; singles with shared bath US$6, doubles with private bath US$20) is friendly, plain and clean.

Hospedaje Karamawen (General Lagos 1334; per person US$10), south of the city center, provides an artistic ambience mixed with generous hospitality. Artwork from contemporary Valdivian artists accompany the fading floral wallpaper throughout the house. On sunny weekends, the abundant breakfast may be served in the backyard. English, French and Swedish are spoken.

Hospedaje Ríos (Arauco 869; per person US$8) has been praised by readers for informative, friendly owners who offer kitchen use and breakfast.

Hostal Esmeralda (☎ 215-659; Esmeralda 651; per person US$11) is in a rambling old building near many of the nightclubs.

Hospedaje Internacional (☎ 212-015; García Reyes 660; singles with shared/private bath US$10/20-25, doubles US$19/26-30) is a popular spot with backpackers for its hospitable German- and English-speaking owners, organized tours, relaxing common spaces and backyard, which is great for cookouts.

Hostal Donde Marcelo (☎/fax 205-295; Janequeo 355; singles/doubles US$20/30), well located and inviting, has good rooms with smallish beds and private baths, and rates include breakfast and cable TV.

A top choice, **Hostal Prat** (☎ 22-020; Prat 575; singles/doubles US$20/27) is attractively furnished with wood paneling, and rooms have private baths with good showers.

Hostal Casa Grande (☎ 202-035; Anwandter 880; singles/doubles US$17/26), near the bus terminal, has spacious but thin-walled rooms, private baths and a good breakfast served in a bright, river-view room.

Mid-Range & Top End Complejo Turístico Isla Teja (see Camping Isla Teja above; doubles with private bath US$20-30; cabins US$40-50) provides some cozy rooms with picture-view windows of the river and gardens. The cabins are built close together but are well equipped and clean. In the off-season, this is a marvelously tranquil spot.

Hostal Torreón (☎ 212-622; Pérez Rosales 783; singles/doubles US$29/50) is a smart choice. It has comfortable rooms with private bath in an elegant old home, and it is managed by superb people. The breakfast spread is more than generous.

Hotel Palace (☎ 213-319, fax 219-133; Chacabuco 308; singles/doubles US$37/42) is a good choice for its very central location. Rooms get lots of light, but also a fair degree of street noise. IVA discounts given if paying in US dollars cash.

Hostal Villa Paulina (☎ 212-445, fax 216-372; Yerbas Buenas 389; singles/doubles US$40/54) is a charming option with personalized service.

Hotel Isla Teja (☎ 215-014, fax 214-911; Las Encinas 220; singles/doubles start at US$49/59), just across Puente Pedro de Valdivia, has a tranquil setting. The standard rooms and small bathrooms are unimpressive, but it's still a decent value. It's used mainly for academic conferences.

Hotel Pedro de Valdivia (☎/fax 212-931; Carampangue 190; singles/doubles US$87/114) is the city's classic hotel, a pink monster walled in by a garden of trees and a manicured lawn. Rooms are quiet and attractive with views of the river, and the breakfast is buffet style. Pay in pesos for a better rate.

Places to Eat
For inexpensive seafood, visit any of the several restaurants at the renovated **Mercado Central**, bounded by Chacabuco, Yungay, Libertad and Prat.

La Última Frontera (☎ 235-363; Pérez Rosales 787; mains US$3-6) serves up some of the best sandwiches, including veggie options, huge beers and fruit drinks in a hip, artistic restored mansion that brims with good vibes day and night.

Café Hausmann (☎ 213-878; O'Higgins 394; US$1.50-3) is a must stop for any visitor to Valdivia. It's a tiny place, very historic and charming, and the plates to order are cruditos (carpaccio, basically), strudel and küchen.

CasAbuela (☎ 218-807; Camilo Henríquez 746; lunches US$5, US$8-10) packs in hungry folks eager to fill up on Valdivia's best home-style Chilean cooking, including pastel de choclo and pastel de jaivas. In summer, ask for the English-language menu featuring a variety of typical dishes.

Club de la Unión (☎ 213-377; Camilo Henríquez 540; fixed price lunches US$6), opposite the plaza, offers filling, well-prepared, three-course meals.

Bar La Bomba (☎ 213-317; Caupolicán 594; fixed-price lunches US$6) is another good lunch choice in a locally popular spot. Order some grilled fish and tune into the soccer game.

Shanghai *(☎ 212-577; Anwandter 898; family-style meal for 2 people US$10)* serves decent and rather authentic Chinese food, also available for take-away.

La Calesa *(☎ 213-712; Yungay 735; dinner with drinks US$12)* serves high-end Peruvian dinners, such as shellfish with rice, garlic roasted chicken and pork chops with onion and tomato. Vegetarians might try a vegetable curry. Finish off with tiramisu or a lemon mousse.

Entrelagos *(☎ 218-333; Pérez Rosales 640; cake & coffee US$3)* is Valdivia's favorite for fancy coffees and cakes served with formality. Next door is the tad touristy chocolate emporium, filled with sumptuous morsels.

Kunstmann Brewery *(☎ 292-969; pitchers US$5; meals with drinks US$12-15)*, on Isla Teja at Km 5 on the road to Niebla, is a large brewpub and beer museum. In the evening, the hearty German fare includes lots of pork chops, späetzle, sauerkraut, apple sauce and spuds. For the truly thirsty, order a *columana*, a long tube filled with 2.5 liters of beer. Any bus or colectivo to Isla Teja (US$0.50) can drop you off.

Entertainment

Befitting the vibrant city that it is, Valdivia has a great assortment of night spots. For those planning to party it up all night, make sure you're staying in a place that doesn't lock up early. For the 'now' hot spots, ask local university students.

Arte-Bar *(San Carlos 169)* hosts live music (bossa nova, classic rock) and literary readings in intimate, mellow surroundings.

Pub en el Clavo *(☎ 211-229; Av Alemania 290)* is your typical drinking spot.

Cubana Club *(☎ 256-969; Esmeralda 680)* shimmies with salsa and merengue, while across the street, **El Legado** *(☎ 207-546; Esmeralda 657)* simmers in a more sedate and trendy atmosphere.

Cine Cervantes *(Chacabuco 210)* shows first-run movies.

Shopping

Feria Artesanal Camino de Luna *(Mercado Municipal)* is a good spot to pick up a wooden rolling pin or napkin holder. There's also some woolen goods. Also check out **Galería**

Artesanal Arauco *(☎ 251-412; Arauco 340)* and, for Mapuche crafts, **Artesanía Ruca Indiana** *(Camilo Henríquez 772)*.

Getting There & Away

Air Aeropuerto Pichoy is north of the city via the Puente Calle Calle. LanChile *(☎ 258-840, 258-844; Maipú 271)* flies a couple of times a week to Temuco (US$30) and twice daily to Concepción (US$70) and Santiago (US$157).

Bus Valdivia's **Terminal de Buses** *(☎ 212-212; Anfión Muñoz 360)* has frequent buses to destinations on or near the Panamericana between Puerto Montt and Santiago. Companies include **Tur Bus** *(☎ 226-010; ticket office ☎ 342-710; O'Higgins 460)*, **Tas Choapa** *(☎ 213-124)*, **Andesmar** *(☎ 224-665)*, **Buses Norte** *(☎ 212-800)*, **Igi Llaima** *(☎ 213-542)*, **Buses Lit** *(☎ 212-835)* and **Cruz del Sur** *(☎ 213-840)*, with service to the island of Chiloé. Prices to Santiago fluctuate according to demand; long haul buses north normally leave in early morning and late evening.

Regional carriers include **Pirehueico** and **Sur Express** to Panguipulli; **Bus Futrono** *(☎ 202-225)* to Futrono once in the evening; **Buses Jac** *(☎ 212-925)* to Villarrica, Pucón and Temuco; and **Buses Cordillera Sur** *(☎ 229-533)* to other interior Lakes District destinations.

Tas Choapa and Andesmar go to Bariloche, Argentina. Igi Llaima goes to San Martín de los Andes and Neuquén once daily.

destination	duration in hours	cost
Ancud	5½	US$9
Bariloche (Ar)	5	US$16.50
Castro	7	US$10
Futrono	1½	US$1.50
Lago Ranco	2	US$1.50
Mehuin/Queule	1½	US$1.50
Neuquén (Ar)	14	US$25
Osorno	1½	US$2
Panguipulli	2½	US$1.75
Pucón	3	US$3.50
Puerto Montt	3½	US$4.50
Riñihue	2½	US$2.50
San Martín de los Andes (Ar)	8	US$17.50
Santiago	10	US$13-36
Temuco	3	US$3.50

Getting Around

From the bus terminal, any bus marked 'Plaza' will take you to Plaza de la República. There are also taxi colectivos around town.

To/from the airport, **Transfer Aeropuerto Valdivia** (☎ 204-111) provides on-demand minibus service (US$3.50). **Autovald** (☎ 212-786; Henríquez 610) or **Hertz** (☎ 218-317; Picarte 640) rent vehicles. **Automovil Club de Chile** (☎ 212-376; Garcia Reyes 440) is also helpful.

CORRAL, NIEBLA & ISLA MANCERA

Southwest of Valdivia, where the Río Valdivia and the Río Tornagaleones join the Pacific, there are 17th-century Spanish fortifications at Corral, Niebla and Isla Mancera. Largest and most intact is the **Castillo de Corral**, consisting of the Castillo San Sebastián de la Cruz (1645), the gun emplacements of the Batería de la Argolla (1764)

and the Batería de la Cortina (1767). Nearby **Fuerte Castillo de Amargos**, a half-hour walk north of Corral, lurks on a crag above a small fishing village.

On the north side of the river, **Fuerte Niebla** (1645) allowed Spanish forces to catch potential invaders in a crossfire. However, the broken ramparts of **Castillo de la Pura y Limpia Concepción de Monfort de Lemus** (1671) are the oldest remaining ruins. Isla Mancera's **Castillo San Pedro de Alcántara** (1645) guarded the confluence of the Valdivia and the Tornagaleones Rivers; later it became the residence of the military governor.

In summer, Spanish military maneuvers are reenacted at Corral.

Consider camping or bunkering down in Niebla's lodging. **La Herradura** (☎ 204-123; Km 8; sites US$17), en route to Niebla, is a forest-shaded place along the Río Valdivia. **Cabañas Fischer** (☎ 282-007; Del Castillo 1115; cabins for 2/5 people US$21/46) has

Paving Paradise – the Coastal Highway

While the Andes Mountains draw in travelers with their abrupt majesty, the much older Coastal Range remains relatively unknown. Huilliche communities live peacefully within the old-growth temperate coastal forest, thick in olivillo and alerces. The shoreline provides shelter for dolphins and whales and is lined with stunningly pristine beaches.

Over the millennia, the forests of the Coastal Range have remained separate from those to the east, where shifting plates and melting glaciers created valleys and lakes. As a consequence, it has a high percentage of endemic species, most notably the *monito de monte*, a miniature marsupial that is the oldest recorded species of marsupial. Other endemic species include the *huillín*, a large river otter, and the *huet huet*, an understory bird. The endangered *pudú*, the world's smallest deer, also lives within the forests.

Between Valdivia and Osorno, some 450,000 hectares of forest remain untouched – at least for now. Hunger for fast-growing wood has meant that pine and eucalyptus plantations are overtaking native forest, and the construction of a coastal highway threatens even more native forest.

Construction of the Coastal Highway began in 1994 with the objectives to link coastal villages from Puerto Montt to Arica, provide an alternative to Ruta 5 and give commercial interests access to unexploited forest and fishing areas. No stretch of this master plan has been more controversial than the 200km swath being cut through the Valdivian temperate rainforest. Clearing land and construction began before proper environmental impact studies were performed, and crews have strategically focused on building bridges first in order to justify continuing the roadwork, again without performing the proper studies. Huilliche communities are threatened, and Chile is in danger of losing one of its most important ecosystems and a potential ecotourism highlight.

Indeed, hiking in this prized section of Chile is an unforgettable experience. Huilliche guides lead you through days of pristine forest and to remote beaches where there is no one else, the only sounds those of birdsong and breezes. Trails are hard to follow, however, and the best way to arrange a multiday trek is through the nonprofit organization working to protect the forests, the **Coalición para la Conservación de la Cordillera de la Costa** (☎ 063-257-673; **w** www.ccc.terra.cl; Carlos Anwandter 624, Casa 4, Valdivia).

attractive log cabins with stunning views of the water, and it offers camping. At Niebla's port, **Canto del Agua** (☎ 282-019; US$5-10) gets the fish right off the boat, then serves it up as part of a hearty economic lunch or as more elaborate entrees. **Los Molinos**, a beach spot north of Niebla, has a few over-priced restaurants worth going to for the view more than the food.

Getting There & Away

The tours that leave from the Puerto Fluvial in Valdivia would like you to believe they are the only way to get to the fortifications, but there's a much more economic alterna-tive: **Colectivos** (cnr Chacabuco & Yungay; US$0.75) to Niebla, marked either 'T-350' or yellow, leave from the Mercado Municipal, as do town buses (US$0.50), which take longer. From Niebla, ferries jot back and forth between Isla Teja, Corral, Isla Mencera and Isla del Rey every 20 to 30 minutes. The ferries run between 8:15am and 8:30pm, and each leg is US$1.

LAGO RANCO

☎ 63

Off the Lakes District tourist track, Lago Ranco, 124km from Valdivia, is an out-of-the-way gem. In one circuit around this lake of crystalline waters you can enjoy majestic views of the Andes, simple working towns, high-end fishing resorts and Mapuche com-munities. This section takes you clockwise from Futrono to the town of Lago Ranco, the two most accessible towns on the lake.

Futrono

pop 14,000

On the north shore of Lago Ranco, 102km from Valdivia via Paillaco, dusty Futrono is the main service center for the Mapuche community on Isla Huapi. Beach access is awkward, but it may be improved in the future. Nearby Bahía Coique has a public beach with views that will beckon you to dive in and swim your way there.

The **Oficina de Turismo** (☎ 482-636; O'Hig-gins & Balmaceda) is at the western approach to town. **Barcaza Guapi** (US$1.50; 1¼ hrs), takes day-trippers to Isla Huapi on Friday at 9:30am, returning at 3pm. Regular service, for the islanders, is Monday, Wednesday and Friday to Futrono at 7am; to Isla Huapi at 4pm. **Turismo Kintumapu** (☎ 482-599; Bal-

maceda 210; day trips US$10-15) organizes trips around the lake and to out-of-the-way thermals, community stays at Lago Maihue, and horse treks, among other excursions.

For those interested in rural communities, Futrono also has a network of rural tourism, **Futronhué** (☎ 481-060; Sector Diolon). It will help you organize home stays or rent cabins, where you can enjoy hearty farm food and engage with locals; most lodgings are in Caunahue, about 15km east of Futrono. It's a satisfying way to experience the land, and it helps the local communities.

Places to Stay & Eat Hospedaje Futronhué (☎ 481-265; Balmaceda 90; singles/doubles with shared bath US$9/15; doubles with private bath US$20) is the most reasonable choice, with friendly management, clean rooms with good beds and hot showers. Breakfast is extra (US$1.50). The best meals in town are at **Don Floro** (☎ 481-271; Bal-maceda 114; lunches US$3.50), where sizes are enormous without compromising flavor.

On Isla Huapi, camping is possible, and locals prepare typical dishes and sell produce. Ask around for lodging options.

Llifén

For now, Llifén, at the east side of Lago Ranco, is difficult to access, which suits sport-fishing enthusiasts just fine. Road improvements, however, may expose this expensive and secluded fishing resort snuggled in the Andes. Of the resorts, try **Hostería Lican** (☎ 215-757, fax 213-155; doubles US$30) and **Hostería Chollinco** (☎ 197-1979; campsites US$30, per person US$40), a short distance up the road to Lago Maihue. Part of the rural tourism network, **Hospedaje Rural Chollinco** (☎ 197-1929), 1km from the road to Chollinco, is an intriguing alternative to these fancy fish retreats.

Riñinahue
This hamlet doesn't have much to offer, except access to **Saltos de Nilahue** (entrance US$0.75; camping per site US$7.50), an impressive waterfall on private land. Campsites have cold-water showers. Other camping spots around town include **Camping Arenal** and **Quichel** (per site US$8.50). Riñinahue is also the northern end of the Volcán Puyehue trek (for details, see El Caulle later in this chapter). However, some hikers report that the trail here is difficult to follow, and that they have been charged to cross private land to reach the park boundary. Unlike the southern approach, land owners don't maintain the trails.

Lago Ranco
pop 10,000
On the south shore, modest Lago Ranco is a terraced town brimming with flowers and shade trees with a long accessible beach. A bumpy dirt road continues west and north, crossing over Río Bueno and accessing beaches and angler's lodges; eventually it joins up with the main road, which leads west to Paillaco and Ruta 5 and east to Futrono. The **tourist office** (☎ 491-212; Av Concepción & Linares) and the **municipality** distribute area information.

Places to Stay & Eat Camping Municipal (☎ 491-254; sites US$10) is on a crowded lakefront site with limited shade and limited hot showers. **Camping Las Bandurrias** (☎ 491-420; Valparaiso 207; per person US$3.50) is another option.

Hospedaje Los Pinos (☎ 491-329; Valparaiso 537; per person US$7.50) is a decent choice.

A cheerful place on the lakefront, **Casona Italiana** (☎ 491-225; Viña del Mar 367; per person US$10, cabins for 2/3 people US$36/45) has in-house lodging and breakfast in the off-season only.

Hostería Phoenix (☎ 491-226; Viña del Mar 359; per person US$12) is a delightful spot despite leaky bathrooms and distracted service. Many rooms have a bit of a lake view. Rates include an ample breakfast. Other meals, meticulously prepared and served, are available.

Parque Thule (☎ 491-293; Camino a Puerto Lapi Km 2; singles/doubles US$58/90), set within sweeping lawns and overlooking the lake, may be a bit too luxurious, but consider coming here to sip a cocktail on the porch and soak in the breathtaking view. The rooms are grandiose and a bit heavy on the chrome and marble. Pay in US cash to get the IVA discount. To get here, head west from Lago Ranco toward Puerto Lapi; a taxi ride is about US$3.50.

Getting There & Away
There is bus service daily to both Futrono and Lago Ranco from Valdivia (US$2.50-3, 2½ hours) and to Lago Ranco from Osorno (US$2, two hours), but you could also catch a bus to the town of Río Bueno and transfer there. From Futrono, Buses Cordillera Sur goes to Llifén, continuing to Riñinahue (a bridge over Río Calcurrupe facilitating the trip). From Lago Ranco, buses go to Llifén at noon and 9pm, continuing to Futrono, and about five times daily to Riñinahue. Only the western edge of the lake currently is not accessible by bus. The crossing at Puerto Lapi is a manually operated barge, run on demand.

OSORNO
☎ 64 • pop 142,000
A commercial center for this agricultural zone, Osorno, 910km south of Santiago and 110km north of Puerto Montt via the Panamericana, is often a must-stop for transportation transfers. There is little of interest here besides a few historic houses in ill-repair. Osorno's most useful feature just might be its supersize supermarkets, where you can stock up before getting out of town.

Information
Sernatur (☎ 237-575; O'Higgins 667; open 8:30am-6:30pm daily in summer, 8:30am-1pm & 2pm-5pm Mon-Fri rest of year) is on the west side of the Plaza de Armas.

There's also a **tourist booth** (open until 11pm) at the bus station with details on lodging. From mid-December through March, look for a **tourist kiosk** at the northwest corner of the plaza. **Conaf** (☎ 234-393; Martínez de Rosas) has details on Parque Nacional Puyehue.

Change money at **Turismo Frontera** (☎ 236-394; Ramírez 959, Local 12), or at **Cambiotur** (☎ 234-846; Juan Mackenna 1004, Local B).

There is a **post office** (O'Higgins 645), and you'll also find an **Entel** (Ramírez 1107).

Aventura (☎ 238-860; Bilbao 997) is a travel agency. Laundry facilities are at **Lavandería Limpec** (Prat 678). The **Hospital Base** (☎ 235-572; Av Bühler) is on the southward extension of Arturo Prat.

Things to See & Do
Osorno's well-arranged **Museo Histórico Municipal** (☎ 238-615; Matta 809; admission free; open 10am-12:30pm & 2:30pm-5pm Mon-Fri; plus 11am-1pm & 4pm-7pm Sat in summer) includes exhibits on Mapuche culture, the city's shaky colonial origins, German colonization and 19th-century development, all in an impressive neocolonial building dating from 1929.

Between the Plaza de Armas and the dilapidated 1912 **Estación de Ferrocarril**, Osorno's **Distrito Histórico** (historic district) is threatened by new construction. Among the deteriorating but intriguing buildings are obsolete factories and weathered Victorian houses.

From 1876, the **Casa Mohr Pérez** (Mackenna 949), a private home, is Osorno's oldest surviving Germanic construction. The 1000 block of Mackenna, between Cochrane and Freire, also preserves a solid row of early Germanic houses.

Places to Stay
Budget Camping Olegario Mohr (☎ 204-860; sites US$8.50), on the south bank of the Río Damas just off the Panamericana, is a shady municipal site, with picnic tables, firepits, cold showers and limited toilets. Any taxi colectivo going to Av Buschmann will drop you at the Panamericana, within a few minutes' walk of the site.

Near the bus terminal are a bunch of budget hostels. **Hospedaje Sánchez** (☎ 232-560; Los Carrera 1595; per person US$8.50) is run by a delightful couple who provide

breakfast and kitchen privileges with grandmotherly charm.

Hospedaje San Diego (☎ 237-208; Los Carrera 1551; per person US$7.50) is equally charming, offers breakfast and kitchen use, and has friendly owners, but the rooms lack ventilation, as most windows open to the interior.

Hospedaje Webar (☎ 319-034; Los Carrera 872; per person US$8.50) is the most charming of the bunch. In an old house with fading wallpaper and lots of artistic expression, high-ceiling rooms are adequate with so-so mattresses and no outside windows, but the rates include breakfast and there are lots of bathrooms, on the plus side.

Residencial Ortega (☎ 232-592; Colón 602; per person US$9) is a backpacker's favorite and gets a bit too crowded, but it has a large eating area, and even the smallest of rooms has cable TV. There's also secure parking.

Residencial Alemana (☎ 250-588; Colón 666; per person US$11) is a great choice for comfortable and quiet rooms with either shared or private bath, parking, and a large breakfast.

Mid-Range A great value, **Hotel Villa Eduviges** (☎/fax 235-023; Eduviges 856; singles/doubles US$23/36) is in a more residential area south of the bus terminal. It has spacious rooms with large beds, loads of plants, pink floral wallpaper and kind management. Rates include breakfast. The rooms in back have larger bathrooms, and there's secure parking.

Hotel Rucaitué (☎ 239-922; Freire 546; singles/doubles US$23/37), in the center of town, has large bright rooms with little details that make stays worthwhile, like chocolates on the pillow. All rooms have TV and private bath and include breakfast.

Hostal Bilbao Express (☎/fax 262-200; Francisco Bilbao 1019; singles/doubles US$15/20) has all the same fixings as its more expensive sister hotel, **Residencial Bilbao** (☎ 264-444; Juan Mackenna 1205; singles/doubles US$20/28), the latter with large lounge areas overlooking the neighborhood. Rooms at both hotels have private bath and include breakfast.

Top End Hotel Pumalal (☎/fax 242-477; Bulnes 630; singles/doubles US$27/37) is

OSORNO

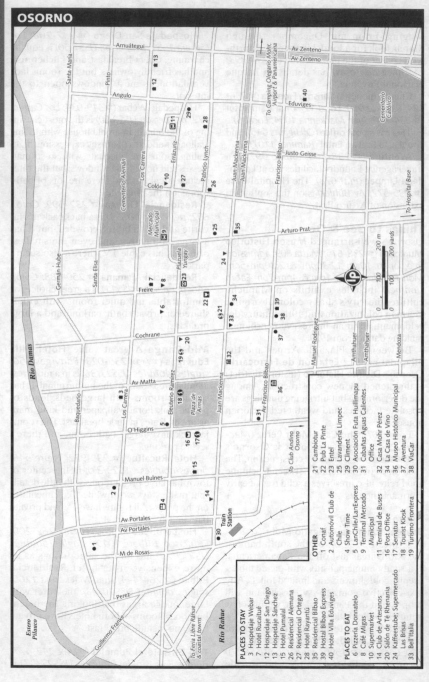

PLACES TO STAY
3 Hospedaje Webar
7 Hotel Rucatué
12 Hospedaje San Diego
13 Hospedaje Sánchez
15 Hotel Pumalal
26 Residencial Alemana
27 Residencial Ortega
28 Hotel Rayantú
35 Residencial Bilbao
39 Hostal Bilbao Express
40 Hotel Villa Eduviges

PLACES TO EAT
6 Pizzería Donnatelo
8 Café Migas
10 Supermarket
14 Club de Artesanos
20 Salón de Té Rhenania
24 Kaffeestube; Supermercado
33 Bell'Italia

OTHER
1 Conaf
2 Automóvil Club de Chile
4 Show Time
5 LanChile/LanExpress
9 Terminal Mercado Municipal
11 Terminal de Buses
16 Post Office
17 Sernatur
18 Tourist Kiosk
19 Turismo Frontera
21 Cambiotur
22 Pub La Pinte
23 Entel
25 Lavandería Limpec
29 Climent
30 Asociación Futa Huillimapu Office
31 Cabañas Aguas Calientes
32 Casa Mohr Pérez
34 La Casa de Vino
36 Museo Histórico Municipal
37 Aventura
38 ViaCar

a modern, light hotel in a quieter location. It's a great choice, and even has a Jacuzzi and sauna.

Hotel Rayantú (☎ 238-114, fax 238-116; Patricio Lynch 1462; singles/doubles US$30/42) caters to the business set offering more posh surroundings and fine customer service.

Places to Eat

Mercado Municipal (cnr Prat & Errázuriz) has an array of cocinerías serving good and inexpensive food. Within the old butchers' row, try **Entre Amigos** (☎ 252-001; Local 2; plates US$1.50-4), where you can choose among lots of seafood dishes, ranging from caldillos to chupe de jaivas.

Kaffeestube (☎ 230-262; Mackenna 1150; sandwiches US$3-6), in the Supermercado Las Brisas, gets filled with local workers and exhausted grocery shoppers. It's a fine spot for a quick coffee and something sweet (lots of choices), but the mains are a bit overpriced.

Salón de Té Rhenania (☎ 235-457; Ramírez 977; snacks US$1-3; closed Sunday), a bright and breezy eatery above one of the town's best bakeries, serves up a variety of empanadas, most fried, but all absolutely enormous. Sandwiches are equally good and large.

Café Migas (☎ 235-541; Freire 584) serves empanadas, pizzas and cakes, plus a US$3 lunch special, in a cozy gingham café. Best of all, the owner speaks English and enjoys helping travelers enjoy the Osorno area.

Pizzería Donnatelo (Cochrane & Ramírez), on a side alley off Cochrane, is a bit hard to find and open only for dinner, but locals claim it has the best pizza in town.

Bell'Italia (☎ 233-693; Mackenna 1027; pastas and pizzas US$6-9), part of an Italian culinary arts school housed in an attractive colonial mansion, has a tantalizing variety of pastas and sauces, plus daily specials.

Club de Artesanos (☎ 230-307; Mackenna 634; mains US$2.50-7) is a union house that's been converted into the most alluring place to put away a pint or pastel del choclo. It is also one of few places that serve local homebrew Märzen. Chilean specialties are the rule, and portions are ample. Try lomo a lo pobre or a cazuela. The bar,

perhaps the most interesting place in town, stays open until 11pm.

Entertainment

Late-night munchies and drinks can be had at **Pub La Pinte** (Freire 677). **Show Time** (☎ 233-890; Ramírez 650) is Osorno's two-screen movie house.

Shopping

Asociación Futa Huillimapu (Mackenna & Portales) sells quality woven and wooden goods, supporting an association of indigenous women. **La Casa de Vino** (☎ 207-576; Mackenna 1071) has an impressive collection of Chilean wines to choose from, plus knowledgeable owners to help make your selections.

Climent (☎/fax 233-248; Angulo 603) sells camping supplies.

Getting There & Away

Air Osorno's **Aeropuerto Carlos Hott Siebert** (also known as Cañal Bajo) is 7km east of downtown, across the Panamericana via Av Buschmann. **LanChile** (☎ 314-949; Ramíréz 802) flies twice daily to Santiago (US$157).

Bus Long-distance and Argentine-bound buses use the **main terminal** (☎ 234-149; Av Errázuriz 1400), near Angulo.

Bus companies include **Tas Choapa** (☎ 233-933), **Tur Bus** (☎ 234-170), **Buses Lit** (☎ 237-048), **Intersur** (☎ 231-325), **Igi Llaima** (☎ 234-371), **Buses Norte** (☎ 236-076), **Transaustral** (☎ 233-633), **Turibús** (☎ 233-633) and **Cruz del Sur** (☎ 232-777).

Most service going north on the Panamericana starts in Puerto Montt, departing about every hour, with mainly overnight service to Santiago. Buses to destinations in Argentina and Chilean Patagonia, such as Coyhaique, Punta Arenas and Puerto Natales go via Ruta 215 and Paso Cardenal Antonio Samoré.

Transaustral heads to Coyhaique once weekly, as does Buses Lit, and Turibús to Punta Arenas. Igi Llaima goes to Zapala and Neuquén on weekdays, while Tas Choapa and Buses Norte have daily service to Bariloche. Many but not all of these services also originate in Puerto Montt; for more details, see Getting There & Away in Puerto Montt later in this chapter.

Sample travel times and fares follow:

destination	duration in hours	cost
Ancud	3½	US$6
Bariloche (Ar)	5	US$13
Concepción	9	US$13
Coyhaique	22	US$30
Puerto Montt	1½	US$2
Punta Arenas	28	US$41
Santiago	12	US$21-40
Temuco	3	US$5
Valdivia	1½	US$2.50
Valparaíso/Viña del Mar	16	US$21
Zapala-Neuquén (Ar)	17	US$28

Also from the main bus terminal is service to Río Bueno, with connections to Lago Ranco, to Panguipulli (via Valdivia), and many departures daily to locations around Lago Llanquihue at the foot of Volcán Osorno. Other local and regional destinations leave from the **Terminal Mercado Municipal** (☎ 201-237; cnr Errázuriz & Prat) in the Mercado Municipal. Destinations include Entre Lagos (US$1, leaves from front of market), Termas Puyehue/ Aguas Calientes (US$1.50, leaves from back of market), Anticura (US$3, 1½ hours), Pajaritos (Customs; US$3) and Río Negro (US$1). Taxi colectivos go to Entre Lagos all year, and to Aguas Calientes in summer only.

To get to Bahía Mansa (US$2, two hours), Pucatrihue and Maicolpué on the coast, cross the Río Rahue to the bus stops at Feria Libre Rahue (☎ 269-704). Better yet, catch a colectivo on the corner of República and Victoria.

Getting Around
Osorno's **Aeropuerto Carlos Hott Siebert** (or Cañal Bajo) is 7km east of downtown, across the Panamericana via Av Buschmann. An airport cab costs about US$3.50. **Automóvil Club de Chile** (☎ 255-555; Bulnes 463) rents jeeps and cars. **ViaCar** (☎ 252-000; Bilbao 1011) also has decent rates.

SAN JUAN DE LA COSTA
☎ 64 • pop 8800
The area west of Osorno, San Juan de la Costa, is rich in Mapuche-Huilliche culture; 70% of the sector's residents are of indigenous origin. Its tranquil seaside fishing villages are bordered by a vast native forest, both of which will soon be considerably altered when the controversial coastal highway is completed (see the boxed text 'Paving Paradise – the Coastal Highway' earlier in this chapter). Some 64km from Osorno, the coastal area has three inlets: Bahía Mansa, the most accessible but least alluring; Maicolpué, just to the south on the same road; and Pucatrihue, accessed from a fork in the road a few kilometers before Bahía Mansa.

Maicolpué
Maicolpué is a treat: it encompasses two beaches of crashing surf separated by a marshy brook, stands of native olivillo trees, pastel-colored cabins on stilts, and serenity... at least on weekdays and in the off-season. For the more adventurous, trails lead past the southern edge of town along the coastline toward Tril Tril. **Campsites** (per tent US$1.50) are available at the southern section of town, but expect rusticity. Get details at Supermercado Pacífico. **Cabañas Rosenburg** (per person US$6.50), accessed from a side road before coming down the hill, has gnome-like, wood-shingled A-frames with views of town and the coastline. The kindly owner allows kitchen use in the main house.

Hostería Miller (☎ 197-5360; rooms/ cabins per person US$15/17; open year-round) provides pleasant lodging, with shared bath, and breakfast included. Most rooms have at least partial ocean view, and a fire in the lobby keeps the place cozy on foggy days.

La Pica del Bigote, across from the beach parking lot, serves up carefully prepared fish and greasy-good empanadas stuffed with potatoes, locos, cheese and cream. A dozen goes for US$5.

Pucatrihue
Accessed from the fork in the road before Bahía Mansa, 63km from Osorno, less-touristy Pucatrihue is a Huilliche community and fishing village where locals eke out a living from fishing and cochayuyo (kelp) harvesting. The long stretch of coastline, ranging from sand dune to rocky tide pool, is impressive, as is the drive in, but the town itself lacks a sense of place. In the northern sector, **Camping Licarayen** offers exposed sites near a lagoon and sand dunes. You can rent horses here to explore farther north to Caleta Manzano. The eatery **El Gigante,** accessed from hillside steps, specializes in fried fish (US$4-6), served in the slightly ramshackle dining hall or outside on the terrace; it's open year-round.

Trafunco-Los Vados

Trafunco-Los Vados is a Huilliche community located in 12,500 hectares of native forest. From the village of Pilfuco, accessed by horseback from Punotro (about 50km northwest of Osorno), you can depart on hikes from four hours to two days, winding through the forests and accessing beaches. All hikes are guided by members of the community. Daily rates for guide/horse/camping are US$8/25/3. For more details contact ☎ 09-569-3566, or the Coalición Costanera (see the boxed text 'Paving Paradise – the Coastal Highway' earlier in this chapter).

Getting There & Away

The best option is to have your own transportation, but there are many departures in summer and one to two daily the rest of the year between Maicolpué, Pucatrihue and Punotro and Osorno's Feria Libre Ráhue (US$1.50). Taxi colectivos make runs from the beach towns to Osorno.

ENTRE LAGOS
☎ 64

Entre Lagos is an unpretentious beach town 50km east of Osorno on Ruta 215, on the southwest shore of Lago Puyehue. It's a good alternative to Osorno, especially as a halfway point before going to PN Puyehue or embarking on the Puyehue traverse from El Caulle. The town is split into two; the western entrance being more commercial (with post office and ATM), and the eastern leading to more lodging choices and the beach.

Places to Stay & Eat

Camping No Me Olvides (☎ 371-633; sites for 5 people US$25, per person US$5; cabins per person US$13-17), 6km east of town on Ruta 215, is a topnotch campground with large garden sites divided by pruned hedges. There's abundant firewood, excellent showers and a kiosk selling breads and cakes in the summer. Cabins fronting the lake are creatively designed, while smaller ones are closer to the road but are warmer. An on-premises *quincho* makes hearty economic lunches for lodgers.

Hospedaje Panorama (☎ 371-398; General Lagos 687; per person US$7.50) is a busy spot brimming with fruit trees, friendly German shepherds and a lively family. Beds have wool duvets, and the excellent breakfasts, including

delicious apple pie, can be enjoyed on the back porch.

Hostal Millaray (☎ 371-251; per person US$10) is a quieter choice run by retired teachers who are great sources of information about the area.

Hostería Entre Lagos (☎ 371-225; Ramírez 65; singles/doubles US$16/25) was built by the proprietor, Sofia Garcia, then rebuilt after the 1960 earthquake. Rooms on the top wing have the best views, but the bottom wing is a bit newer. All the rooms are spacious, simple and comfortable.

Al Fin (☎ 371-509; Las Dalias 123; mains US$3-5) is a small place overlooking the town's *plazoleta*. The chef, once of Termas de Puyehue, makes carefully prepared plates and specializes in the sauces.

Getting There & Away

Buses between Osorno and Aguas Calientes (US$1) stop in town at the Casa de Deportes on O'Higgins every half-hour. There's also continuous service to/from Osorno (US$1). Colectivos to Osorno cost US$2.50, to Aguas Calientes US$11.

TERMAS DE PUYEHUE

Just off Ruta 215, 76km east of Osorno, is one of Chile's most famous hot springs resorts, Termas de Puyehue (☎ 064-232-157, fax 02-283-1010 in Santiago; e puyehue@ ctcreuna.cl; day use US$7.50-12.50; singles/ doubles US$65/100). This baronial resort, set on elegant grounds, defines luxury with echo-chamber slate foyers, wide hallways and never-ending staircases. The spa, with its own set of hallways, has an outdoor pool, an indoor pool with jets and Jacuzzis, and bath treatments with mud, seaweed, salts, essential oils, herbs, sulfur, or just about any combination thereof. Rooms are attractively furnished; pay 30% more for a view or a TV.

From the resort the north fork of 215 goes to Anticura and the Argentine border, while the southern lateral leads to Aguas Calientes and Antillanca in Parque Nacional Puyehue.

PN PUYEHUE

Volcán Puyehue, 2240m tall, blew its top the day after the earthquake in 1960, turning a large chunk of dense humid evergreen forest into a stark landscape of sand dunes and lava rivers. Today, Parque Nacional Puyehue (admission US$1.20; e parquepuyehue@ terra.cl) protects 107,000 hectares of this contrasting environment, and it is one of the more 'developed' of the national parks, with a large ski resort and hot springs resort within its boundaries. There are also a number of hikes that explore more pristine areas. Aguas Calientes is the main sector of the park, with the hot springs resort and a Conaf information center. Park fees are usually paid here. Closer to the Argentine border is Anticura, where you can also find Conaf park rangers and campsites, but the visitor center remains closed.

Up to 4000mm of rain falls at Aguas Calientes, with winter temperatures as low as 5°C and summer averaging about 14°C.

Conaf's **Centro de Información Ambiental** (Aguas Calientes; open 9am-7pm daily in summer, 9am-1pm & 2pm-8:30pm rest of the year) has an informative display on Puyehue's natural history and geomorphology.

The park's western border is about 75km east of Osorno via the paved Ruta 215, which continues through the park, following the course of the Río Golgol to the Argentine border.

Aguas Calientes

An unpretentious hot springs resort (day use US$2-4.50), Aguas Calientes is popular with vacationing families and gets crowded in the summer months. On offer are typical spa services, individual tubs, a very hot indoor

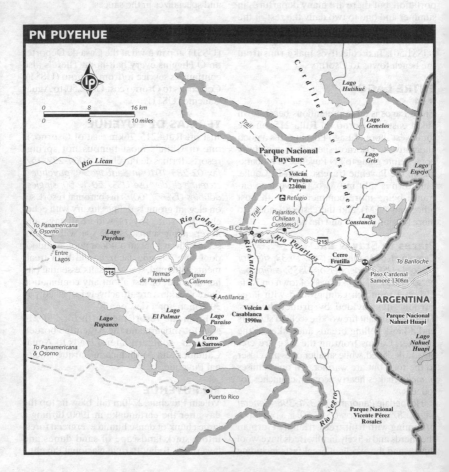

PN PUYEHUE

pool and a large shallow cement pool by the side of the river. Cross the footbridge to access rustic hot springs on the riverbank. Another way to get your heart rate up is to hike the enjoyable **Sendero El Pionero,** a steep 1800m nature trail that ends with splendid views of Lago Puyehue, the valley of the Río Golgol and Volcán Puyehue.

An easier nature trail is the **Sendero Rápidos del Chanleufú,** which follows the river for 1200m. For a longer excursion, take the 11km trail to **Lago Bertín.** Past the lake the trail continues over Cerro Haique to access Centro de Ski Antillanca. In summer, Conaf organizes thrice weekly 10pm **night-time walks** to observe the park's many nocturnal creatures.

Down the street from the resort facilities, **Camping Chanleufú** *(☎ 064-236-988 in Osorno; 4-person sites US$20)* has pretty, well-spaced sites, some near the river. It doesn't have hot showers, but fees entitle you to use the outside pool and facilities. Nearby, open only in summer, **Camping Los Derrumbes** *(4-person sites US$13)* heats its own water. In January and February, both campsites fill to maximum capacity, obstructing any sense of natural serenity.

Cabañas Aguas Calientes *(☎ 064-236-988; O'Higgins 784, Osorno; 4-10 person cabins US$100-200)* is the only lodging option. Its A-frame cabins are stacked up along the hillside like a cute well-planned village, and they are remarkably comfortable, with plush beds, full kitchens, hot showers (of course) and wood stoves. Rates include spa facilities and a filling breakfast. The **restaurant** *(fixed-price meals US$8-11)* may have resort prices, but the service is exceptional and the menu offers a diverse selection of dishes. In summer, there's also a **quincho** and a small store.

Antillanca

At the foot of Volcán Casablanca (1990m), Antillanca is a popular ski resort 18km beyond Aguas Calientes. The road up to the resort twists and turns through scenic areas and past glassy lakes. During the no-snow months, Antillanca is rather drab and unattractive, and the resort's appeal rests with its trails, especially the walk or drive (per vehicle US$8) to the crater lookout, where you can drink in a spectacular view of the surrounding mountain range. Mountain bikes and canoes can be rented. The ski season runs from early

June to late October; full-day lift tickets cost US$24, and rentals US$18-23. The ski area has three surface lifts, 460m of vertical drop and a friendly, clublike atmosphere. For details on ski packages, contact the **Club Andino Osorno** *(☎ 064-232-297, fax 238-877; Casilla 765, O'Higgins 1073, Osorno).*

Hotel Antillanca *(☎ 064-235-114; singles/ doubles in refugio US$18/26; in hotel US$30/43)* has all the typical ski resort trimmings: a gym, sauna, disco, boutique and shops, all of which seem horribly out of place here. Rates, which double during ski season, include breakfast.

Anticura

Anticura, on Ruta 215 17km northwest of the Aguas Calientes turnoff, is the best base for exploring the park's wilder sectors. Short hikes from the often-closed visitor center include **Salto de Princesa, Salto del Indio** (where, according to legend, a lone Mapuche hid to escape encomienda service in a nearby Spanish gold mine), and **Repucura,** which ends back up on Ruta 215 (buses come careening down the highway; walk on the opposite side). There's also a 4km steep hike up to a lookout point. At the same trailhead, the trail to Sector Último Puesto begins. This is a new addition, so check with the rangers first. To hike the Pampa Frutilla, where a poorly marked trail accesses the small Laguna Los Monos and wild camping is possible, you need permission from international police.

Camping Catrué *(2-person sites US$6.50, 2/4 person cabins US$46/63)* has 10 woodsy, well-spaced, level sites with tree-trunk picnic tables, limited electricity and decent bathrooms. The cabins are fully equipped. This is a better option to the often full and noisy Aguas Calientes sites.

El Caulle

Two kilometers west of Anticura, **El Caulle** *(☎ 09-641-2000; w www.elcaulle.cbj.net; one-time fee US$11)* is the southern entrance for the trek across the magnificently desolate plateau at the western base of Volcán Puyehue. While officially within park boundaries, the access land is privately owned. The admission fee is steep, but funds are used to maintain the refugio and the trails, to put up signs and to provide emergency assistance. Trekkers can stash extra gear at the entrance. The **Puyehue Traverse** (three to four days) starts with a steep hike through lenga forest and loose volcanic soil to a campsite and refugio with a woodstove and water (most of the time). From there, you can trudge up to the top of the crater or continue four hours through a moonscape of massive lava flows and dunes to Los Baños, a series of riverbank thermal baths. The trail continues to an impressive field of geysers. From there either head back or continue north to Riñinahue, at the south end of Lago Ranco, although trails north are not maintained and may be difficult to follow. (Hikers report being charged to cross private land leaving the park as well.) Another hike, **Ruta de los Americanos** (six to eight days) branches off the Los Baños trail and loops around the eastern side of the volcano. Wild camping is possible. **Horse trekking** *(per person daily, all inclusive US$120),* organized with El Caulle, is a fun and faster way to explore the area.

Getting There & Away
Buses and taxi colectivos from Osorno's **Mercado Municipal** *(cnr Errázuriz & Prat)* go to Termas de Puyehue, Aguas Calientes, Anticura and Chilean customs and immigration at Pajaritos. Any bus heading to Anticura can drop off trekkers at El Caulle. In winter, there may be a shuttle to the ski lodge at Antillanca; contact the **Club Andino Osorno** *(☎ 064-232-297; O'Higgins 1073, Osorno).* Otherwise, you'll need to arrange your own transportation.

PUERTO OCTAY
☎ 64 • pop 10,000
In the early days of German settlement, when poor roads made water transportation critically important, the Lago Llanquihue harbor of Puerto Octay, 50km from Osorno at the north end of the lake, was a key transportation link between Puerto Montt and Osorno. Today, the village is a charming alternative to the lake's more touristy towns, and it contains an impressive assortment of original German buildings.

Puerto Octay's **tourist office** *(☎ 391-750; Esperanza 555; open 8:30am-8pm Nov-Mar)* is on the east side of the Plaza de Armas. Ask for the map of the town's historic houses.

February is the month for the Festival de Canción Salmon de Oro and also crew competitions on the lake.

Museo El Colono
Puerto Octay's excellent museum *(☎ 391-523; cnr Independencia & Esperanza; admission US$0.75; open 10am-1pm & 3pm-7pm; off-season ask in the library)* includes displays on German colonization, relevant and well-labeled historical photographs and local architecture, all curated with elegance and intelligence.

Places to Stay & Eat
Camping Centinela *(Península Centinela; sites up to 7 people US$13)* does offer discounts for just two. It's a shady spot right near the lakeshore.

Zapato Amarillo *(☎/fax 391-575; dorm beds/doubles US$9/21; lunch or dinner US$5),* about 2km north of town on the road to Osorno, is a favorite with the backpacker set, due in large part to the hospitality of the Chilean-Swiss owners. On a small farm, it's a tranquil spot with dorm beds wrapped in terry bedcovers, the common spaces are comfortable and nonsmoking, and the meals are prepared using homegrown veggies. There's a separate kitchen for lodgers. Excursions around the area and transportation to Volcán Osorno can be arranged, or you can rent a bike for your own exploring.

Hospedaje Costanera *(☎ 391-329; Pedro Montt 306; per person US$9)* has adequate lodging. Ask at the downstairs supermarket.

Hospedaje Barrientos *(☎ 391-381; Independencia 488; per person US$8)* is a rickety old house up on a hill with loads of rose bushes and character, but the mattresses might be as old as the house, and the matrons running the place seem equally tired. Downstairs rooms lock, upstairs ones don't.

Hostería La Baja *(☎ 09-444-6884; Península Centinela; rooms with shared/private bath US$9/10),* a few kilometers south of town, comes praised by readers. The view of Puerto Octay and its colorful houses is quite lovely. Rates include breakfast.

The **Hotel Centinela** *(☎/fax 391-326; e hcentinela@telsur.cl; Andrés Schmoelz s/n; doubles with lake/forest view US$78/70),* a massive chalet at the end of the peninsula, is considered one of the most romantic hotels in the region (possibly because there's not much more to do than enjoy the bedrooms). The older downstairs rooms have more charm, with wood-paneling, rustic furniture and grandiose doors.

Baviera *(☎ 391-460; Germán Wulf 582; lunches US$2.50)* usually just offers the daily special to order – some meat with a side dish. It's plain but filling, and exceptions can be made for vegetarians.

El Fogón de Anita *(☎ 391-455; US$6-15)*, 1km along the road to Osorno, has *parrillada* and onces.

Tante Valy *(☎ 391-461; Km 3, Frutillar Hwy; onces US$6)* offers a worthwhile and less touristy option for afternoon tea (onces). One order is easily shared by two, since the bread rolls and coffee (Nescafé or regular) are limitless and the cake sizes enormous. Look for the dark shingled house surrounded in flower gardens en route to Frutillar.

Getting There & Away

Puerto Octay's **bus terminal** *(Balmaceda & Esperanza)* has regular service to Osorno, Frutillar, Puerto Varas, Puerto Montt and Cruce de Rupanco, from where Osorno–Las Cascadas buses can be picked up. Alternatively, for Las Cascadas there's one bus at 5pm weekdays.

LAS CASCADAS

On the eastern shore of Lago Llanquihue, Las Cascadas is a tiny settlement fronting on a black-sand beach. For those looking for less touristy spots, this is a good option, but transportation in and out is a bit more complicated. The town's supermarket has maps with hikes in the area, including nearby waterfalls. The bus ride from Puerto Octay offers grand views of Volcán Osorno as you pass through dairy country, which is dotted with small farms and tiny, shingled churches with corrugated metal roofs. The road south to Ensenada is a popular bicycle route, but it's very exposed and cyclists are vulnerable to the irritating, biting *tábanos*.

Places to Stay & Eat

Hostería Irma *(☎ 396-227; per person US$10)*, 1km south of town on the road to Ensenada, is a slanting ranch-style home with rooms off the main terrace overlooking a delightful flower garden. Rates include breakfast. Opposite the hostería, alongside the lake, is a peaceful, quiet and free campsite with few facilities.

Camping Las Cañitas *(☎ 09-643-4295; sites up to 6 people US$17.50, 6-person cabins US$48)*, 5km down the Ensenada

road, is a well-run spot. The campsites are clustered together, so there's not much privacy, but the cabins are decent if very thin-walled. Prices plunge in the off-season.

Donde 'Don Pancho' *(☎ 396-229; Vicente Pérez Rosales 210; per person US$7)*, is right in the heart of Las Cascadas, offering acceptable beds with shared bath. The dinette below has a limited, inexpensive menu with US$2.50 breakfasts and US$1.50 hamburgers.

Getting There & Away

Buses Cordillera runs direct to/from Osorno three times daily. From Puerto Octay, there's a 5pm bus each weekday, leaving Las Cascadas at 7:30am.

FRUTILLAR

☎ 65 • pop 15,000

Frutillar, 70km south of Osorno and 40km north of Puerto Montt, is one of Chile's most popular lake resorts. Founded in 1856, it is known for its meticulously preserved German architecture and its annual music festival. While its scenery and the quality of travelers' services are high, Frutillar may be just a little too perfect and orderly for some. Quite unfortunately, the new concert venue – more aptly the 'concrete' venue, a stone-and-copper monstrosity of a music hall – is being built smack-dab in the middle of a perfect half-moon bay. The town is actually split in two: the resort area by the lake is Frutillar Bajo (Lower Frutillar), while the commercial section near the Panamericana is Frutillar Alto (Upper Frutillar), about 2km west.

Frutillar is an easy day trip from Puerto Octay or Puerto Varas, but evening tranquility and decent lodging options make it an attractive place to overnight, especially in the off-season.

Information

Frutillar's municipal **tourist kiosk** *(☎ 421-198; Av Philippi; open 10am-9pm Dec-Mar)* is just south of the municipality, between San Martín and O'Higgins. Around the municipality, you can find the regular banks, post office and call centers.

Lavandería Frutillar *(☎ 421-555; Carlos Richter 335)* is in Frutillar Alto.

You can shower for US$0.50 at the municipal **Baños Públicos** *(public baths; O'Higgins; open Dec-Mar)*, between Philippi and Pérez Rosales.

Museo Histórico Colonial Alemán

Built with assistance from the Federal Republic of Germany and managed by the Universidad Austral, Frutillar's museum (☎ 421-142; *Pérez Rosales & Prat; US$1.50; open 10am-2pm & 3pm-6pm Tues-Sun*) features nearly perfect reconstructions of a water-powered mill, a smithy and a mansion set among manicured gardens.

Centro Forestal Edmundo Winkler

Possibly the best thing to do in Frutillar is escape to this 33-hectare forest reserve (☎ 422-307; *Calle Caupolicán*) on the spit of land north of town. Managed by the Universidad de Chile, the reserve has an 800-meter loop trail along which species of trees are identified. Pick up a brochure (Spanish only) that describes other interesting natural facts. Thank Mr Winkler for donating his property in 1959 with the intention that it be used to study native plants, rather than letting it be clear cut for grazing animals like much of the surrounding area.

Special Events

For 10 days from late January to early February, the Semana Musical de Frutillar showcases a variety of musical styles, from chamber music to jazz, with informal daytime shows and more formal evening performances. Some symphony and ballet tickets are relatively costly (US$10-plus), but midday concerts are cheaper.

Places to Stay

Hotel Posada Campesina (☎ 339-123; *sites for up to 6 people US$17, rooms per person US$13*), on a small peninsula at the south end of Frutillar Bajo, is a tourist complex, with restaurant, boat dock and hotel. The 50 campsites are well distributed with enough dividing bushes. It's got all the amenities: hot showers, electricity and firepits.

Playa Maqui (☎ 339-139; *Km 6 toward Puerto Octay; sites US$13-18*) is another big campsite, but farther away from the downtown bustle.

Hospedaje Kaiserseehaus (☎ 421-387; *Philippi 1333; per person with shared/private bath US$7.50/10*) might look closed, but it is still running, and with more character each year. Creaky hallways and staircases lead to upstairs chambers with slanted ceilings and

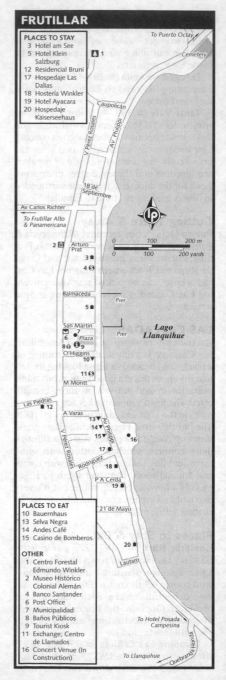

FRUTILLAR

PLACES TO STAY
3 Hotel am See
5 Hotel Klein Salzburg
12 Residencial Bruni
17 Hospedaje Las Dalias
18 Hostería Winkler
19 Hotel Ayacara
20 Hospedaje Kaiserseehaus

Lago Llanquihue

PLACES TO EAT
10 Bauernhaus
13 Selva Negra
14 Andes Café
15 Casino de Bomberos

OTHER
1 Centro Forestal Edmundo Winkler
2 Museo Histórico Colonial Alemán
4 Banco Santander
6 Post Office
7 Municipalidad
8 Baños Públicos
9 Tourist Kiosk
11 Exchange; Centro de Llamados
16 Concert Venue (In Construction)

To Puerto Octay
Cemetery
Caupolicán
V Pérez Rosales
Av Philippi
18 de Septiembre
Av Carlos Richter
To Frutillar Alto & Panamericana
Arturo Prat
Balmaceda
Pier
San Martín
Plaza
O'Higgins
M Montt
Las Piedras
A Varas
V Pérez Rosales
Av Philippi
Rodríguez
P A Cerda
21 de Mayo
Lautaro
To Hotel Posada Campesina
To Llanquihue
Quebrada Honda

some picturesque views. Mornings are a bonus, with one of the best breakfast spreads in the area.

Hostería Winkler *(☎ 421-388; Philippi 1155; dorm beds (HI only) US$10, rooms US$26)* opens up annex rooms to share for HI affiliates. Otherwise, you stay in regular hotel rooms with sometimes bothered service.

Residencial Bruni *(☎ 421-309; Las Piedras 60; per person US$10)*, away from the lakeshore, is open only in summer. Rooms have shared bath.

Hospedaje Las Dalias *(☎ 421-393; Philippi 1095; singles/doubles with private bath US$30/40)*, in front of the new concert venue, is a decent choice with a kindly owner who is not alone in bemoaning the construction going on out front.

Hotel am See *(☎ 421-539; Philippi 539; singles/doubles with private bath US$25/33)* keeps clients content with plenty of homemade breads and cakes, which, along with cozy woolen goods, are also for sale in the lobby.

Hotel Klein Salzburg *(☎ 421-201, fax 421-750; Philippi 663; singles/doubles with private bath US$21/38)* satisfies the need to sleep in a pristine and perfect colonial building, detailed in slate blue and white. The restaurant is a favorite for meals and onces.

The **Hotel Ayacara** *(☎/fax 421-550; e hayacara@telsur.cl; Philippi 1215; doubles with private bath US$47-58)* occupies a remodeled 1910 house originally owned by the Lutheran pastor and redesigned by architect Eduardo Roja. Streams of light flow through the inviting living areas, and upstairs front-facing rooms get a spectacular volcano view. This is Frutillar's most attractive option, with high standards, loads of hospitality and a sense of comfort without a twee overdose.

Places to Eat

Bauernhaus *(O'Higgins & Philippi)* is mainly a souvenir store, but it sells slices of some very rich cakes that can be enjoyed on uncomfortable seats in the back.

Hotel Klein Salzburg *(see Places to Stay above)*, dolled out in doilies, is considered one of the better places in town for that afternoon cholesterol intake called onces.

Casino de Bomberos *(☎ 421-588; Philippi 1065; 4-course lunch US$5)* is Frutillar's best value. Filling lunches and saucy fish and meat dishes are served with formality in its lackluster dining room.

Andes Café *(Philippi 1057; sandwiches US$3, parrillada for 2 US$14)* considers itself mainly a parrilla, but it also has OK sandwiches, espresso coffee and onces.

Selva Negra *(☎ 421-164; Antonio Varas 24; mains US$7.50)* is a fun, intimate place in the shape of a quincho, with witches of all sorts swinging from the ceiling. Try the pork medallions in port wine sauce, but save room for the delectable desserts.

Getting There & Around

All transportation leaves from Frutillar Alto. **Cruz del Sur** *(Alessandri 360)* has the most frequent services from Osorno or Puerto Montt, plus three daily departures to Chiloé. **Tur Bus** *(Diego Portales 150)* also provides long-distance services. At the Alessandri terminal, **Thaebus** goes to Puerto Octay, and **Buses Fierro** goes to Puerto Varas, Puerto Montt and Osorno.

Inexpensive taxi colectivos shuttle the short distance of Av Carlos Richter between Frutillar Alto and Frutillar Bajo.

PUERTO VARAS
☎ 65 • pop 33,000

Puerto Varas is no longer the working-class lake port of yesteryear. Today, the growing town attracts well-heeled weekenders heading to the ostentatious casino or dropping by en route to Bariloche, Argentina, and it is becoming a leading destination for hardcore climbers, kayakers and anglers, who relish in the myriad activities around town. While it has started to attract the Pucón set, the town itself – with perhaps the best-preserved concentration of Middle European architecture in the entire country, plus a strong, friendly community – is considerably more interesting and laid-back.

Orientation

On the southern shore of Lago Llanquihue, Puerto Varas is only 20km north of Puerto Montt. Most services are within a small grid bounded by Portales, San Bernardo, Del Salvador and the lakeshore.

Av Costanera, an eastward extension of Del Salvador, becomes paved Chile 225 to Ensenada, Petrohué, and Lago Todos Los Santos.

PUERTO VARAS

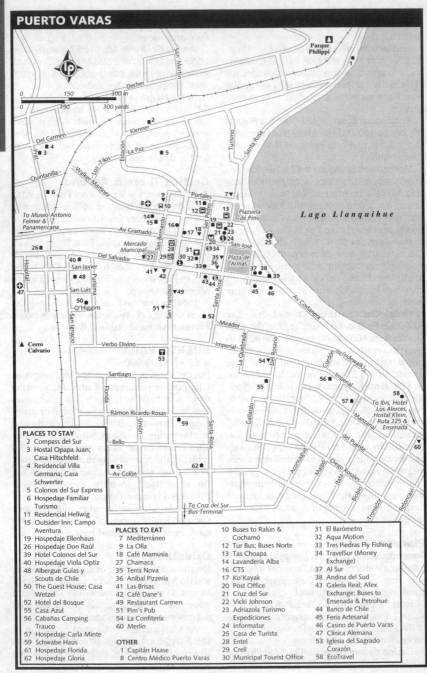

0   150   300 m
0   150   300 yards

PLACES TO STAY
2 Compass del Sur
3 Hostal Opapa Juan; Casa Hitschfeld
4 Residencial Villa Germana; Casa Schwerter
5 Colonos del Sur Express
6 Hospedaje Familiar Turismo
11 Residencial Hellwig
15 Outsider Inn; Campo Aventura
19 Hospedaje Ellenhaus
26 Hospedaje Don Raúl
39 Hotel Colonos del Sur
40 Hospedaje Viola Optiz
48 Albergue Guías y Scouts de Chile
50 The Guest House; Casa Wetzel
52 Hotel del Bosque
55 Casa Azul
56 Cabañas Camping Trauco
57 Hospedaje Carla Minte
59 Schwabe Haus
61 Hospedaje Florida
62 Hospedaje Gloria

PLACES TO EAT
7 Mediterráneo
9 La Olla
18 Café Mamusia
27 Chamaca
35 Terra Nova
36 Aníbal Pizzería
41 Las Brisas
42 Café Dane's
49 Restaurant Carmen
51 Pim's Pub
54 La Confitería
60 Merlín

OTHER
1 Capitán Haase
8 Centro Médico Puerto Varas
10 Buses to Ralún & Cochamó
12 Tur Bus; Buses Norte
13 Tas Choapa
14 Lavandería Alba
16 CTS
17 Ko'Kayak
20 Post Office
21 Cruz del Sur
22 Vicki Johnson
23 Adriazola Turismo Expediciones
24 Informatur
25 Casa de Turista
28 Entel
29 Crell
30 Municipal Tourist Office
31 El Barómetro
32 Aqua Motion
33 Tres Piedras Fly Fishing
34 TravelSur (Money Exchange)
37 Al Sur
38 Andina del Sud
43 Galería Real; Afex Exchange; Buses to Ensenada & Petrohué
44 Banco de Chile
45 Feria Artesanal
46 Casino de Puerto Varas
47 Clínica Alemana
53 Iglesia del Sagrado Corazón
58 EcoTravel

Information

Tourist Offices Puerto Varas' **Casa del Turista** (☎ 237-956; W www.puertovaras.org; Av Costanera; open 9am-10pm daily in high season, 9am-7pm Mon-Fri low season) is a privately run tourist center with energetic staff and good information, which focuses on the organization's members. **Informatur** (☎ 338-542; cnr San José & Santa Rosa; open 8am-midnight daily in summer, 10am-7pm daily rest of the year) has helpful staff with smart lists of hospedajes around town. The municipality's **tourist office** (☎ 232-437; San Francisco 431; open 9am-9pm daily in summer, 10am-2pm & 4pm-6pm rest of the year) has basic brochures and free maps of the area.

Money There are numerous downtown ATMs, including **Banco de Chile** (cnr Del Salvador & Santa Rosa). Change cash and traveler's checks at **Afex Exchange** (Del Salvador 257, Local 8), in Galería Real, or at **TravelSur** (☎ 236-000; San Pedro 451, Local 4).

Post & Communications There's a **post office** (cnr San Pedro & San José) and an **Entel** (San José 413). **Crell** (San Francisco 430) is the best bet for Internet access with fast connections; computers are upstairs from the call center.

Travel Agencies CTS (☎ 237-330; San Francisco 320; e ctsptv@telsur.cl) comes well recommended for personalized service and knowledgeable staff. It can help with the basic stuff like plane tickets and car rental and also arrange regional tours. **TravelSur** (☎ 236-000; San Pedro 451, Local 4) offers similar services.

Laundry Many of the hospedajes offer laundry service at cost, but there's also **Lavandería Alba** (☎ 232-908; Walker Martínez 511).

Medical Services Puerto Varas' **Clínica Alemana** (☎ 232-336; Hospital 810, Cerro Calvario) is near Del Salvador's southwest exit from town. There's also the **Centro Médico Puerto Varas** (☎ 232-792; Walker Martínez 576).

Historic Buildings

Puerto Varas' well-maintained German colonial architecture gives the town a distinctive middle European ambience. The imposing and colorful 1915 **Iglesia del Sagrado Corazón** (cnr San Francisco & Verbo Divino), overlooking downtown from a promontory, is based on the Marienkirche of Black Forest, Germany. Other notable constructions are private houses from the early twentieth century. Ask at the tourist offices for the brochure *Paseo Patrimonial*, which suggests a walking tour of 28 different houses, or the brochure *Monumentos Nacionales*. Several of these houses serve as hospedajes, including the 1941–42 **Casa Schwerter** (Del Carmen 873), the 1930 **Casa Hitschfeld** (Arturo Prat 107) and the 1930 **Casa Wetzel** (O'Higgins 608).

Museo Antonio Felmer

Museo Antonio Felmer (☎ 338-831; Fundo Bellavista, Nueva Braunau; open 10am-1pm & 3pm-8pm Tues-Sun), 8km west of town past the Panamericana cloverleaf, exhibits a collection of colonial knickknacks, including cuckoo clocks and gramophones, some of which were originally in the Frutillar museum. And, of course, there's a café to enjoy some küchen and coffee.

Activities & Organized Tours

Nearby lakes, mountains, rivers and fjords provide variety enough for a week's worth of activities. For information on climbing and skiing on Volcán Osorno, see PN Vicente Pérez Rosales later in this chapter.

Day Tours Easy day tours include visits to Puerto Montt (US$13), Frutillar (US$15), Saltos del Petrohué (US$10) and around the lake; for operators, ask at the travel agencies listed earlier in this section, at Ellenhaus (see Places to Stay later in this section) and Andina del Sud (see Getting There & Away later in this section). Day tours to Chiloé are also offered, but most of your tour is spent in transport, and you do not get a quality experience of the island. **EcoTravel** (☎ 233-222; e ecotrvel@entelchile.net; Costanera s/n) organizes outings with an emphasis on ecology and culture, with trips to PN Alerce Andino and to the archaeological site of Monte Verde.

Rafting & Kayaking Opportunities abound for great rafting and kayaking. Río Petrohué's diamond-blue waters churn up Class III and IV rapids. Rafting trips range from US$30 (5½ hours total, two hours river time) to US$70, which includes some canyoning. All-day kayaking on Lago Todos Los Santos is about US$50. **Ko'Kayak** (☎ 346-433; ⓦ www.paddlechile.com; San José 320) has French-speaking, careful and fun-loving guides. **Al Sur** (☎/fax 232-300; ⓔ alsur@telsur.cl; Del Salvador 100) is a larger outfitter with higher-end tours, including kayaking trips within the fjords of Parque Pumalín (see the Aisén & the Carretera Austral chapter).

Sailing & Cruising With such a huge lake as a playground, there's a surprising absence of sailboats. But **Capitán Haase** (☎ 232-747, 09-810-7665; 'La Rada,' Santa Rosa 132; adults/children US$30/20) offers fun and relaxing sunset cruises on a 65-foot splendor of a sailboat from late October to mid-April. Cruises around Chiloé and Parque Pumalín aboard *Cahuella* can be organized from Puerto Varas at Campo Aventura (see Horse Trekking later in this section).

Many travelers enjoy the scenery around Lago Todos Los Santos, which can be crossed either as a day tour or as part of the bus-boat excursion across the Andes to Bariloche, Argentina. If the weather is clear, it's a pleasant tour, but otherwise it can be quite frustrating.

Only one company, Cruce de Lagos, does the trip; reservations are made through **Andina del Sud** (☎/fax 232-511; Del Salvador 72). See the boxed text 'Crossing the Lakes' later in this section.

Fly-Fishing There are loads of places to cast a line, but knowing just where the best spots are will require some local knowledge. **Adriazola Turismo Expediciones** (☎ 233-477; Santa Rosa 340) is a worthwhile outfitter. A day of fishing, including guide, gear and meals is about US$180 per person. Other recommended outfitters are **Gray Fly Fishing** (☎ 232-136) and **Tres Piedras** (☎ 346-452). For an independent guide with a wealth of information and expertise, call John Joy at the **Tres Ríos al Mar Lodge** (☎ 09-792-8376).

Horse Trekking The best spot for a horse trek is farther southeast in the Cochamó Valley (see Cochamó later in this chapter). **Campo Aventura** (☎/fax 232-910; ⓔ outsider @telsur.cl; San Bernardo 318) offers single- to multiday treks, often in conjunction with some hiking, rafting or kayaking. English and German are spoken.

Females Fly-Fish, Too

The lakes and rivers of Chile's Región X boast beauty, abundance and big fish, making this area a mecca for fly fishermen from around the world. Even if you haven't come to fish, if you're here between mid-November and early May, you'll run into those who have – men with crazed visions of bubbas, logs, trunks and pigs (that is, fat brown and rainbow trout, as well as Chinook, Coho and Atlantic salmon).

I arrive in Puerto Varas, located near the Petrohué, Puelo and Cochamó Rivers, hooked on such fish tales. A woman in waders is a strange sight for the average Chilean man, but my guide doesn't bat an eye as I approach. He begins with a lesson on tying the fly and then a riverbank crash course on casting. After initial tangles, I get the line out of the trees and into the water.

Sufficiently primed, I move out into the river, begin to cast and fall into a meditative state…until I feel the tug on the line. I slowly bring in a beautiful rainbow trout. Ringing in at about two pounds, she's no bubba, but she's good enough for me. I admire her spectacular rainbow flank, then drop her back in: fishing here is catch and release.

Back in Puerto Varas, I meet a local gentleman walking home with his fishing pole. Feeling like part of a new society, I stop to ask him about his day. He looks at me inquiringly. 'You fish?' he asks, shocked. With one river under my belt, I boldly respond in the affirmative. 'Perhaps love would last longer if more women fished,' he muses. 'Forget those fancy flies,' he continues. 'I've got something you can throw together with pantyhose, fish eggs and dental floss that will land you *el grandote* in a snap.'

Perhaps next year, the bubba will bring me back.

— **Kishma Patnaik**

Special Events

The city celebrates its 1854 founding the last week of January and the first week of February. In the second week of February, the annual Concurso de Pintura El Color del Sur attracts painters from throughout the country.

Places to Stay

Puerto Varas' many hospedajes fill up fast in the high season; it's better to phone ahead. For more camping, head to Ensenada (see later in this chapter).

Budget With an artistic ambience, **Cabañas Camping Trauco** (☎ 233-325; Imperial 433; campsites US$7, cabins US$14) offers pleasant but cramped garden camping and rickety '70s-style cabins (with parking).

Open only in January and February, **Albergue Guías y Scouts de Chile** (☎ 232-774; San Ignacio 879; dorm beds US$5) offers hot showers, meals and kitchen privileges with its accommodations.

Residencial Hellwig (☎ 232-472; San Pedro 210; per person with shared bath US$8), in a 1915 German house, is the oldest residencial in the town; it's also where some long-distance bus companies drop off and pick up. Inside, it's spacious but rather gloomy, with sagging beds and small bathrooms. Breakfast is not included. Rooms facing Portales have less bus noise.

Compass del Sur (☎ 232-044; Klenner 467; per person US$14), in a colonial house with Scandinavian touches, gets warm praise for its lodging, including Internet access, a garden, kitchen for lodgers and comfortable beds. Breakfast is US$4 more.

Hospedaje Florida (☎ 233-387; Florida 1361; per person US$7) is a friendly place in a suburban area, with kitchen use but no breakfast.

Hospedaje Don Raúl (☎ 310-897; Del Salvador 928; per person US$7) offers kitchen privileges and breakfast.

Hospedaje Ellenhaus (☎ 233-577; Walker Martínez 239; per person US$9) is a great find. It has small but very clean upstairs rooms with fluffy duvets, large bathrooms, a kitchen just for travelers and breakfast included. The vivacious owner also runs tours around the area.

Hostal Klein (☎/fax 233-109; Ramírez 1255; per person US$11) is a great deal, not only for the fabulous quirky character and

the matronly owner, but for its decent rooms with private bath (even if the beds are sad). The huge breakfast (US$3) includes chicken salad and some of the best cake in town. Dinners cost US$6.

Many hospedajes line Colón between San Francisco and Del Rosario. Try **Hospedaje Gloria** (☎ 233-664; Colón 348; per person with shared/private bath US$12/9), which is a good value with breakfast.

Hospedaje Viola Optiz (☎ 232-890; Del Salvador 408, Depto 302; per person US$10) keeps receiving loads of praise for its attentive owner and comfortable old house.

Hospedaje Familiar Turismo (☎ 232-339; Arturo Prat 273; per person US$10) offers grandmotherly charm in a quiet house. The beds aren't the best, but some of the views are quite nice, and breakfast is included.

Casa Azul (☎ 232-904; e casaazul@ telsur.cl; Manzanal 66 & Del Rosario; per person with shared/private bath US$10/13) is a consistent favorite with backpackers. It has cozy well-heated rooms, a kitchen for travelers and a large garden to kick back in. The congenial owners speak German and English. Breakfast (US$3) includes home-made muesli and yogurt.

Schwabe Haus (☎ 233-165; Rosas 361; per person US$10), open only in January and February, is a sweet place with large bathrooms, uncluttered rooms with washbasins, and breakfast included.

Hospedaje Carla Minte (☎ 232-880; Maipó 1010; per person US$14), on a quiet street up from the lake, provides comfort, tranquility, küchen and good breakfasts.

Mid-Range Some of the best mid-range options are in historic houses.

Residencial Villa Germana (☎ 233-162; Del Carmen 873; per person US$11), in the Casa Schwerter, has rooms with TV and private bath (small showers); the upstairs rooms are loaded with floral décor. Breakfast (US$5) is only offered in summer months.

Hostal Opapa Juan (☎ 232-234; Arturo Prat 107; singles/doubles US$23/33), in the Casa Hitschfeld, has loads of historic character. The comfortable rooms are plain but have some nice views of the lake. German is spoken, and breakfast is included and abundant, of course, with homemade black bread.

The Guest House (☎ 231-521; e vjohnson @telsur.cl; O'Higgins 608; singles/doubles/

triples US$40/60/80), in Casa Wetzel, provides an informally elegant stay with unique extras, such as morning yoga classes and a masseuse. The bright rooms, all with high ceilings, are attractively appointed and have great showers. Large breakfasts are included and often come with real coffee, bran muffins or hearty breads. A cheaper rate not including breakfast may be available for backpackers.

Outsider Inn (☎ 232-910; San Bernardo 318; singles/doubles US$25/40) is a stylish, gaucho-themed inn with warm, carpeted rooms and private baths. Breakfast is included, is brought to your room and comes with whole wheat bread and homemade jams.

Hotel del Bosque (☎ 232-897, fax 233-085; e travelsur@travelsur.com; Santa Rosa 714; singles/doubles US$30/40) offers views of town and Lago Llanquihue from most of its rooms, which come with private bath and comfortable beds. Service is attentive and the breakfast continental.

Top End With its growing reputation as a resort destination, Puerto Varas has its share of top spots, but none really stands out. Rooms are heavily discounted in the off-season.

Colonos del Sur Express (☎ 235-555; Av La Paz 507; singles/doubles US$60/65), a sister hotel to the lakeside original, is a three-story building (no elevators) above town. It's quite attractive and sports clean, spacious, if slightly boring rooms, all outfitted in yellow and amber with bright gray bathrooms and unique window fixings.

Hotel Colonos del Sur (☎ 233-369; e reservas@colonosdelsur.cl; Del Salvador 24; singles/doubles US$90/105), across from the casino, offers the luxurious details of a classy hotel, such as heated towel racks, business services, sauna, soft beds and very spacious suites with lake views. Some rooms face the hotel's interior; try for a discount if you get one of these.

Hotel Los Alerces (☎ 235-985, fax 236-212; e cabanaslosalerces@entelchile.net; Pérez Rosales 1251; singles/doubles/triples US$85/90/110, cabins US$150) is a boutique hotel with cabins in front that are good deals for small groups (up to six people), while some hotel rooms have four-poster beds and more cushions and frillies than really fit. Plush couches make the bars attractive rest spots, or head to the very hot pool and hot tub.

Places to Eat

Café Dane's (☎ 232-371; Del Salvador 441; sandwiches US$2-5) has excellent cakes, juices, coffees and sandwiches, and it stays open late. It could use some fans to kick out the cigarette smoke.

Café Mamusia (☎ 233-343; San José 316; fixed lunch US$5, cakes US$1.50) has an array of cakes, all fresh, good and not overly sweet. The regular menu has a good mix of Chilean specialties and sandwiches, all served in the usual doily and floral décor.

La Confitería (☎ 338-188; cnr Imperial & Del Rosario; cakes US$1.50-2, onces US$6) raises cholesterol levels with delicious, enormous slices of pies and cakes, such as the mixta naranja, a mix of merengue, custard, cake, wafers and a heavy dose of orange flavoring. Berry pies are equally good.

Aníbal Pizzeria (☎ 235-222; Del Salvador & Santa Rosa; pizzas US$3-6) is a popular spot for varied Argentine-style pizza and pasta dishes.

Terra Nova (☎ 310-822; Santa Rosa 580; crepes US$2.50-4), tiny but active, serves savory and sweet crepes. Or just come in for one of the many cocktails the French waiters can prepare.

Restaurant Carmen (☎ 346-469; San Francisco 669; sandwiches US$2-3) sports Cristal posters, rollicking Latino music and a typical Chilean diner feel, offering a break from the Euro-influence. Huge platos combinados and cheap sandwiches are the best bets, enjoyed with cheap pitchers of beer.

Serving the best seafood in town, **La Olla** (☎ 234-605; San Bernardo 240; mains US$4-8) packs in locals and tourists alike. The ceviche caribeño, with salmon and congrio, is a meal in itself, as is the caldillo. Don't pass up the cilantro and garlic bread spread.

Chamaca Inn (☎ 232-876; Del Salvador, above the market; mains US$4-8) is similar to La Olla (two sisters run the two places) with well-prepared huge portions. It's a bright and busy place, though it doesn't quite match La Olla's fame. Best bet is the caldillo.

Mediterráneo (☎ 237-268; Santa Rosa 068; dinners US$7-15), with a great outdoor deck, cooks up tapas of all sorts, including a good variety of veggie options, and heaping, flavorful pasta dishes. It's a popular and fun spot, with erratic service at times.

Pim's Pub (☎ 233-998; San Francisco 712; mains US$5-10) serves up Tex-Mex in a typical

US-style restaurant. Salads are large and decent, and the ice cream is some of the best.

Ibis (☎ 232-017; Pérez Rosales 1117; mains US$7-10) is considered one of the better fine-dining options. The menu is quite extensive, but the best option is fish with one of the many sauces – such as fine herbs, cognac and butter, or the chef's specialty of a scallop, shrimp and king crab medley (and that's just the sauce).

Merlín (☎ 233-105; Imperial 0605; dinners US$16-20) creates culinary delicacies that wake up the palate. Redefining Chilean cuisine, the chef and his crew conjure such originals as smoked scallops with peach, tomato and basil and seared salmon with just a hint of papaya. Try the rabbit liver sautéed with roasted peppers and a touch of port, or a filet mignon with oysters and glazed green onions. Whatever the choosing, a frambuesa sour, made with home-distilled raspberry wine, is a fine way to start the experience.

Las Brisas (Del Salvador & San Berardo) is a large supermarket with good variety, but you may have better luck with fruits and veggies at the stands behind the Mercado Municipal.

Entertainment

El Barómetro (☎ 236-371; San Pedro 418) intentionally makes itself divey, which works well if you want to pound a few pitchers and swap tales of adventure.

Pim's Pub (see Places to Eat above) gets hopping into the late hours as the plethora of powerful drinks keep pouring.

Kamikaze (☎ 237-230) is the favorite area dance club; it's outside of town en route to Puerto Montt.

Casino de Puerto Varas (☎ 346-600; Del Salvador 21) has a large top-floor terrace bar with views of the lake and reasonably priced drinks. Inside this posh new spectacle are two large floors of glittery slot machines, card tables and large windows with views of the lake and Volcán Osorno. As far as Chilean casinos go, this one is attractive, but being mesmerized by a sunset over the volcano will always be a better gamble.

Shopping

The local **Feria Artesanal** (Plazuela del Vino), near the lakefront, sells handicrafts from around the region, but it doesn't have the variety of Puerto Montt. **Vicki Johnson**

(☎ 232-240; Santa Rosa 318) sells Puerto Varas' finest chocolates and top-quality wood and wool products.

Getting There & Around

Most long-distance bus services from Puerto Varas originate in Puerto Montt; for fares and trip duration information, see Puerto Montt later in this chapter. Buses leave from individual offices around downtown. For Osorno, Valdivia and Temuco, **Cruz del Sur** (terminal: San Francisco 1317; office: Walker Martínez 230), has eight departures daily; it also goes to Chiloé and Punta Arenas (departures Tuesday, Thursday and Saturday). Also check out **Tur Bus** (San Pedro 210). For Santiago, Tur Bus, **Tas Choapa** (Walker Martínez 227), and **Buses Norte** (San Pedro 210), have nightly departures.

For Bariloche, Argentina, Tas Choapa leaves Monday and Saturday, while Cruz del Sur leaves every day. For information on the popular bus/boat combination to Bariloche, see the boxed text 'Crossing the Lakes.'

Minibuses to/from Ensenada (US$1.25) and Petrohué (US$2.50) leave frequently in summer and thrice daily in the off-season in front of Galería Real, at Del Salvador and San Pedro, or at other stops along Del Salvador. Minibuses leave for Puerto Montt (US$0.75), Frutillar and Puerto Octay frequently; catch the bus along San José between the plaza and San Francisco. To get to Ralún and Cochamó, minibuses leave from the corner of Walker Martínez and San Bernardo.

From the Puerto Montt airport, taxis cost US$18, while a door-to-door shuttle costs US$13.

ENSENADA
☎ 65

The road between Puerto Varas and Ensenada to the east is lined with stalls and off-road farms selling fresh jams, küchen, honey, homemade cheese and smoked salmon. If on a bike or in your own car, indulge in some stop-and-go grazing, pick up some delicacies for later, then head to the beaches of Ensenada, a tranquil stopover on Ruta 225 to Petrohué and Lago Todos Los Santos, at the base of Volcán Osorno. To the south is the jagged crater of Volcán Calbuco, which blew its top during the Pleistocene.

Crossing the Lakes

One of the most popular excursions in the Lakes District is the Cruce de Lagos bus-and-boat crossing from Puerto Montt and Puerto Varas to the Argentine city of San Carlos de Bariloche. Tickets can be purchased through the Chilean representative, **Andina del Sud** in Puerto Varas (☎ 232-511; e adspuerto.varas@andinadelsud.cl; Del Salvador 72) and in Puerto Montt (☎ 257-797; A Varas 437). Reservations for the whole excursion must be made two days in advance; however, if you're only going as far as Peulla, tickets can be purchased at the Petrohué dock.

From September to March, departures are regular, but are fewer in the off-season. Bring your own food for the first part of the trip, since meals aboard the 300-passenger catamaran to Peulla and in Peulla are expensive and dull.

leg	duration in hours	cost	transportation
Puerto Montt – Petrohué	2	US$7	bus
Petrohué – Peulla	1¾	US$32	boat
Peulla – Puerto Frías, Argentina	2	US$70	bus
Puerto Frías – Puerto Blest	¾	US$12	boat & bus
Puerto Blest – Puerto Pañuelo	1	US$14	boat
Puerto Pañuelo – Bariloche	½	US$5	bus

The total fare from Puerto Montt or Puerto Varas to Bariloche is US$140. Discounts may apply for students with valid ID cards.

Places to Stay & Eat

Caleta Trauco Camping (☎ 212-033; Km 43; sites US$4-7) offers camping in a fun, artsy atmosphere; sites closest to the water cost the most. There's hot water and fireplaces. **Camping Montaña** (☎ 235-285; sites US$8), in front of the police station, is a viable alternative. **Escala Dos** (☎ 212-075; Km 40.5; sites/rooms per person US$3.50/US$12) is a hospedaje where, in summer, you can camp in the backyard or have a room with breakfast.

Hospedaje Ensenada (☎ 212-050; Km 43; per person US$13-17) provides a great option in a large immaculate house. The place is tranquil (except for the doorbell), with a yard large enough for a volleyball game, a patio just begging for loungers and beach access. Rooms have private bath, and breakfast is included. It's open only December to late April/ early May.

Hotel Ensenada (☎ 212-028/017; singles/ doubles US$60/80) is the first large building on the road to Las Cascadas and Puerto Octay, beyond the Petrohué turnoff. Old-time details, like claw-foot tubs and lavendar bouquets, add to this top-notch place. The large restaurant and living room are full of enough odd bits of ironwork and machinery to keep one amused for hours. If you can peel yourself away from the yellowing magazines and

antiquities, bikes are available, and there's a sweet, private beach across the road.

Getting There & Away

Minibuses frequently shuttle between Puerto Montt or Puerto Varas and Ensenada. There is no public transportation between Ensenada and Las Cascadas, a distance of 22km on the road to Puerto Octay. Pedestrians and cyclists should beware that this is a hot, exposed route infested with tábanos from December to the end of February.

PN VICENTE PÉREZ ROSALES

☎ 65

Beneath the flawless cone of snow-capped, 2660m Volcán Osorno, Lago Todos Los Santos is the centerpiece of Parque Nacional Vicente Pérez Rosales and the jewel of Chile's southern mainland lakes. A glacial basin scoured between densely forested ridges, the lake offers dramatic views of the volcano, at least when the clouds clear. Lava flows from Volcán Osorno blocked Río Petrohué's former westward drainage into Lago Llanquihue, detouring the river to flow south into the Golfo de Reloncaví. The needle point of Volcán Puntiagudo (2490m) lurks to the north; to the east, craggy Monte Tronador (3491m) marks the Argentine border.

In pre-Columbian times, Mapuche traveled the 'Camino de Vuriloche,' a major trans-Andean route they managed to conceal from the Spaniards for more than a century after the 1599 uprising. Jesuit missionaries traveled from Chiloé, continuing up the Estuario de Reloncaví and crossing the pass south of Tronador to Lago Nahuel Huapi, avoiding the riskiest crossings of the region's lakes and rivers.

The park experiences more than 200 days of rain annually, with an average rainfall of 2500mm near Ensenada, and about 4000mm (most snow) at higher altitudes. The summers are the driest months, with average temperatures about 16°C, falling to 6.5°C in winter.

Established in 1926, 251,000-hectare Pérez Rosales is Chile's first national park,

about 50km east of Puerto Varas via paved Ruta 225.

Conaf has small offices at Centro de Esqui La Burbuja at Volcán Osorno and at Saltos de Petrohué, where they collect an admission fee (US$2). The park is open year-round, depending on weather conditions.

Volcán Osorno

Adventure travel companies in Puerto Varas offer guided **climbing** trips up Volcán Osorno, which require snow and ice-climbing gear and cost around US$150 per person in groups of three, or US$200 for solo climbers, including all equipment. The trip lasts 12 hours, leaving at 5am. If weather turns and the trip is aborted before leaving, agencies will refund a

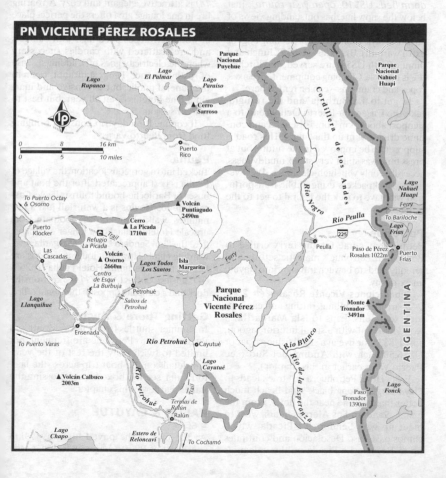

PN VICENTE PÉREZ ROSALES

percentage of the cost. Trips up Volcán Calbuco (2003m) range from US$65 to US$90. Contact **Aqua Motion** (*☎/fax 232-747;* e *info@aquamotion.cl; San Pedro 422*) or Al Sur (see Puerto Varas earlier in this chapter). Independent climbers must obtain Conaf permission, providing detailed personal qualifications as well as lists of equipment and intended routes.

The once-abandoned ski slopes of **Centro de Esquí La Burbuja** (*adults/children US$16/13*) have been newly renovated and are open for skiers to enjoy. Two chairlifts lead to seven different runs with spectacular views, one specifically for beginners. Rentals are available. Just downhill from the ski slopes, the rustic **Refugio Teski Ski Club** (*☎ 212-012; dorm beds US$10; open year-round*), just below the snow line, has outstanding views of Lago Llanquihue. Beds are in small but pleasant dorm-style rooms (bring a sleeping bag for extra warmth). Breakfast (US$5), lunch and dinner (both US$9) are served, and kitchen use is possible. Climbing equipment – ice axes, ropes and crampons – can be rented here.

To get to 'La Burbuja' and the refugio, take the Ensenada-Puerto Octay road to a signpost about 3km from Ensenada and continue driving 9km up the lateral. This road is supposed to be improved in the future, but at press time was still a very steep, muddy mess, accessible only with high-clearance, 4WD vehicles. Backpackers using public transportation will have to trek the lateral to get to the refugio.

Petrohué

People may come for the ferry cruise to Peulla, but Petrohué's majestic setting and serenity tends to bewitch travelers into staying an extra day.

Expediciones Vicente Rosales (*☎ 258-042*) arranges climbing, rafting and canyoning excursions. Trips to **Isla Margarita**, a wooded island with a small interior lagoon, cost US$35 for five in a small fishing boat or US$6.50 each with Andina del Sud (see Puerto Varas earlier in this chapter).

From Hotel Petrohué, a dirt track leads to **Playa Larga,** a long black-sand beach much better than the one near the hotel. From the beach, **Sendero Los Alerces** heads west to meet up with **Sendero La Picada**, which climbs past Paso Desolación and continues on to Refugio La Picada on the volcano's

north side. Alternatively, follow Los Alerces back to the hotel. Six kilometers southwest of Petrohué, the **Saltos del Petrohué** (*admission US$2*) is a booming, frothing waterfall over basalt columns. Anyone wondering why the rafting trips don't start from the lake will find the answer here, although experienced kayakers have been known to take it on.

Places to Stay & Eat Hospedaje Küschel (*campsites/rooms per person US$5/10*) is across the river and reached by rowboat (US$0.50). It has basic farmhouse rooms with breakfast included, or you can camp with the cows. Try their home-smoked trout at lunch.

Hotel Petrohué (*☎/fax 258-042; singles US$44-55, doubles US$67-82; lunch US$10-14*) is attractive, elegant and cozy. A roaring fire in one lounge area offers the perfect place to warm up and read a book, while rooms, rich in wood, have beds piled high with blankets and are scattered with candles (necessary when the electricity goes off), adding a sense of rustic romance. The restaurant is open to the general public, but expensive and marginal. The hotel is open all year, but best to visit off-season.

If coming for a daytrip, consider bringing food from Puerto Varas.

Peulla

Tucked into a gorgeous location, the village of Peulla is best appreciated after the boat and buses of Bariloche-bound tourists leave. **Cascada de los Novios** is a waterfall just a few minutes' walk along an easy footpath from upscale Hotel Peulla. For a longer excursion, take the 8km **Sendero Laguna Margarita**, a rewarding climb. However, lodging options are limited to the declining **Hotel Peulla** (*☎ 258-041; singles/doubles US$75/114*), 1km from the dock and a **campsite** opposite the Conaf office.

Getting There & Away

In summer, shuttles from Puerto Montt and Puerto Varas to Petrohué are frequent, but limited to twice daily the rest of the year. For details on the boat trip across the lake to Peulla, see the boxed text 'Crossing the Lakes' earlier in this chapter.

RALÚN & CAYUTUÉ

☎ 65

At the end of the paved highway, 79km southeast of Puerto Varas, is Ralún, easily missed with the blink of an eye. Here, the Río Petrohué discharges into the Seno de Reloncaví. The main attraction is rustic **Termas de Ralún** along the river's opposite bank. Rowboats shuttle bathers across the swift river (US$1.20-1.75 roundtrip) to the five holes of different temperatures. When the river level is too high, however, they fill with cold water. On the same side of the river are some **cabins** *(up to 6 people US$33)* with kitchens; enquire about vacancy at the cabins here called Puerto Viejo. On the highway side of the river, there's a **campsite** *(per person US$4)* with shady willow trees and some rain protection but poorly maintained bathrooms.

Los Ulmos de Ralún *(☎ 243-644;* e *los ulmos@telsur.cl; cabins per person US$16)* is mainly a fishing lodge, but offers nonanglers lodging in quaint, simple cabins with good kitchens and wood stoves. People looking for little-known hikes in the area would do well to stay here and talk with the owner. Rates include breakfast; full board is available. A fly-fishing package costs US$250 for two people, all inclusive except the rods.

From Ralún, it's possible to hike to **Cayutué**, on the southern arm of Lago Todos Los Santos. It's a five-hour hike on an easily followed trail to Lago Cayutué (excellent camping) and another four hours to Cayutué. If you want to continue on to Petrohué, you must hire a fisherman's launch for the 45-minute trip. Since these usually originate in Petrohué, doing this trek in reverse may be easier to organize.

COCHAMÓ
☎ 65 • pop 4400

Beyond Ralún, a decent gravel road leads another 16km south to the village of Cochamó. The Chilote-style, alerce-shingled **Iglesia Parroquial María Inmaculada** stands proudly against a backdrop of milky blue water, one of the most picturesque spots in this region. This is the gateway to the spectacular upper Río Cochamó Valley, whose Yosemite-like granite domes rise above the verdant rainforest.

Tourism has not yet overwhelmed the area, and a long day's trek to the valley affords brilliant isolation in fantastic scenery. The initial part of the route into the valley follows a 19th-century log road, built for oxcarts, which carried seafood to Argentina and beef back to Chile. La Junta, 17km from Cochamó,

surrounded in native forest, is a good base for climbers attracted to the impressive granite walls. Beyond La Junta the route continues to Lago Vidal Gormaz, passing El Arco, where there's a rustic refugio. For those who take the trail, be prepared for rain and mud, and allot extra time should some of the rivers be too high to cross.

Campo Aventura (see Puerto Varas earlier in this chapter) is the most established outfitter in this area, organizing horseback trips from its base 5km south of the village to its camp at La Junta and through the Andes. Horse treks last from 1½ to 10 days (and cost from US$97 to US$1480), and meals and lodging are included. Treks often include meeting locals.

To explore the estuary, **Francisco Méndez** *(☎ 216-292; Juan Jesus Molina s/n; per hour US$9)* can motor people across the waters to Pocoihuén Alto, Baños Sotomó and, a bit farther south, the trailhead into Parque Nacional Alerce Andino.

The **municipal office** in town provides information on other horse trek outfitters, and **Avenco** *(☎ 216-260),* in the 'Pueblo Hundido' section of town, has loads of area information. At both places and in Puerto Varas, look for the very useful Cochamó hiking map and brochure.

Places to Stay & Eat
Campo Aventura *(campsite/dorm beds per person US$4/15; breakfast US$5-8, lunch US$10, dinner US$14; open October 1 to April 15)* has three splendid shared cabins, a kitchen and indoor and outdoor dining areas at its riverside camp at Cochamó. At its 80-hectare La Junta backcountry camp, it has three bedrooms – one with five bunks (comfortable but cramped) and the other two with double beds – wood-fired hot showers and a dining room with a cozy central woodstove. The major concession to rusticity is the outhouse 30m up the hill. The facilities are primarily for horseback-tour clients, but are open to the general public on a space-available basis. In La Junta, lunches and dinners for non–horse trekkers cost US$8. Wine and homemade bread are also available. For contact information, see Puerto Varas earlier in this chapter.

Within town, and both charging US$9 per person for adequate rooms with breakfast and shared bath, are **Hospedaje Edicar**

(☎ 216-256; Av Prat & Sargento Aldea), right on the Costanera with lovely views and a little balcony, and **Hospedaje Maura** (☎ 09-913-0106; J Molina 12) with charming owners, good beds and very low ceilings. The best bet for meals is with the hospedajes, or try **La Herradura** (Barrio Hundido; lunches US$5), about 200m from the town center in Pueblo Hundido.

Getting There & Away
There are five daily departures to/from Puerto Montt, stopping in Puerto Varas and Ensenada. Most buses continue to Río Puelo.

RÍO PUELO
☎ 65

The road from Cochamó continues another 31km through jaw-dropping scenery to reach Río Puelo, a little hamlet that's bound for growth as a new land-lake route into Argentina develops. The **tourist office** (☎ 255-474) has information on lodging. From the village, the road continues inland to Lago Tagua Tagua, where ferry service crosses the lake to the road's extension, which parallels the river to Llanada Grande. Also under construction is a hiking trail from the town of Río Puelo south to **Parque Nacional Hornopirén**. Hiking trails within this region are numerous, but potentially disorienting; hiring a local guide is recommended. Camping and supplies are on offer in the communities along the way. Buses from Puerto Montt, Puerto Varas and Cochamó make the journey to Río Puelo three to five times daily.

PUERTO MONTT
☎ 65 • pop 175,000

One of southern Chile's most important cities, and capital of Región X, Los Lagos, Puerto Montt may also lay claim to being the most chaotic city. Just about every parcel, person, car, bus, ship or plane heading south or north passes through; traffic is maddening, the street grid disorienting and the freneticism high. To some, it's a welcome change from the staid towns of the Lakes District, and it does have a spectacular setting – which can be appreciated when it's clear, anyway. Regardless of the weather, colorful fish markets and crafts markets are fun places to pick up a taste of this port city. Gateway to the southern lakes, Chiloé and Chilean Patagonia, Puerto Montt is the main transportation hub to virtually all directions.

Orientation
Puerto Montt is 1020km south of Santiago via the Panamericana, which skirts the northern edge of the city as it continues to Chiloé.

The city center occupies a narrow terrace, partly on landfill, behind which hills rise steeply. The waterfront Av Diego Portales turns into Av Angelmó as it heads west to the small fishing and ferry port of Angelmó. To the east, Av Soler Manfredini continues to the bathing resort of Pelluco, connecting with the Carretera Austral.

Information
Tourist Offices The municipal **tourist office** (☎ 261-700, ext 823; Varas & O'Higgins; open 9am-1pm & 3pm-6pm Mon-Fri, 9am-1pm Sat Mar-Dec; 9am-9pm daily Jan-Feb), in a kiosk across from the plaza, is more helpful than **Sernatur** (☎ 252-720; open 8am-4:30pm Mon-Fri, 9:30am-6:30pm Sat & Sun Nov-Mar 15), on the west side of the Plaza de Armas.

Sernatur's **administrative office** (☎ 254-580; Av X Región 480, 2nd floor; open 8:30am-1pm & 1:30pm-5:45pm Mon-Fri) also provides information. It's a stiff climb from the waterfront. **Conaf** (☎ 290-711; Amunátegui 500) can provide details on nearby national parks.

Puerto Montt contains an **Argentine consulate** (☎ 253-996; Cauquenes 94, 2nd floor).

Money There's no shortage of casas de cambio. Try **Exchange** (Talca 84), **Afex** (Portales 516) or **Eureka Tour** (Antonio Varas 445). For ATM transactions, try **Banco de Chile** (Pedro Montt & Diego Portales).

Post & Communications There's a **post office** (Rancagua 126) and **Entel** (cnr Rancagua & Urmeneta). Lots of Internet places line Av Angelmó, including **Latin Star** (Av Angelmó 1672), which also has a call center and book exchange.

Travel Agencies English-run **Travellers** (☎ 262-099, fax 258-555; e info@travellers .cl; Av Angelmó 2456) is a popular spot for gringos looking to book Navimag passage or get details on what to do in the region, including organizing ascents for Volcán Osorno. **Travel & Adventure** (☎ 348-888; Av Angelmó

1760) is one of many all-services places, with Internet access, maps, money exchange and excursion planning. **Ace Lagos Andinos** (☎ 254-988; *Varas 445*) is another reputable travel agency that arranges excursions around the area. **Petrel Tours** (☎ 251-780; *Benavente 327*) has drawn praise for its individual attention arranging private day tours of the city or other regional destinations. English-speaking guides are extra.

Laundry For laundry service, **Full Fresh supermarket**, on Portales across from the bus terminal, has cheap rates. Also try **Arco Iris** (*San Martín 232*).

Bookstores **Sotavento Libros** (☎ 256-650; *Portales 580*) has a good selection of books on local history and literature, plus a small and expensive selection of new and used English-language mystery novels.

Medical Services Puerto Montt's **Hospital Regional** (☎ 261-134; *Seminario*) is near the intersection with Décima Región.

Things to See & Do
Built entirely of alerce in 1856, the **Iglesia Catedral** on the Plaza de Armas is the town's oldest building. The upstairs Sala Hardy Wistuba at the **Casa del Arte Diego Rivera** (☎ 261-817; *Quillota 116; admission free; open 10am-1pm & 3pm-9pm Mon-Fri, 10am-1pm Sat*), a joint Mexican-Chilean project finished in 1964, displays work by local and foreign artists and photographers. The downstairs Sala de Espectáculos offers theater, dance and films.

Puerto Montt's waterfront **Museo Juan Pablo II** (☎ 261-822; *Av Diego Portales 991; admission US$0.50; open 9am-7pm Mon-Fri, 10am-6pm Sat & Sun*) has displays on natural history, archaeology, the island of Chiloé, maritime history and weapons, religious iconography, German colonization and local urbanism.

Along busy, diesel-dusty Av Angelmó is a dizzying mix of street-side stalls selling artifacts, heaps of smoked mussels, cochayuyo and mysterious trinkets; crafts markets; and touristy seafood restaurants with croaking waiters beckoning you to a table. Enjoy the frenzy, but keep on going: The best quality both for crafts and food is found at the end of the road at the picturesque fishing port of **Angelmó**, 3km west of downtown. It's easily reached by frequent local buses and taxi colectivos.

Offshore **Isla Tenglo**, reached by inexpensive launches from the docks at Angelmó, is a favorite local beach spot.

Places to Stay
Perhaps because Puerto Montt draws a captive audience of travelers or because traditionally this is a business port town, not a tourist draw, the quality of lodging lags behind other nearby towns and cities; finding a decent spot can take time and patience.

When you arrive to Puerto Montt, a mob of hospedaje hawkers is bound to follow. Many of these represent 'pirate' operations, establishments that don't pay taxes and may not abide by certain standards. The city has tried to control this to some extent; there's a kiosk just outside the bus terminal at which licensed hospedajes can post and linger.

Budget Most of the budget places (except campgrounds) are within a few blocks of the bus station. If arriving at night, stay alert while walking; petty thievery does exist here. **Camping Los Paredes** (☎ 258-394; *sites US$14*), 6km west of town on the road to Chinquihue, has pleasant sites with hot showers; backpackers might get away as cheaply as US$3.50 per person. Local buses from the bus terminal will drop you at the entrance.

Camping Anderson (☎ 09-789-8998; *sites per person US$3*), farther out the road toward Panitao, on the shores of the Bahía de Huequillahue, is somewhat remote and inconvenient; sites include hot showers. Fresh provisions such as eggs, vegetables, cheese and bread are available on-site. Buses Bohle makes the 20km trip from Puerto Montt's bus terminal to Panitao six times daily except Sunday.

Residencial Independencia (☎ 277-949; *Independencia 167; per person US$6*) is the HI affiliate, but the quality of this tiny spot is marginal at best. Rates don't include breakfast, but there is a kitchen.

Near the bus terminal, a number of cheap spots line Av Juan Mira: **Hospedaje Anita** (☎ 315-479; *Mira 1094; per person US$8*) is decent with kitchen access, but bring your own padlock, and **San Sebastián** (☎ 257-719; *Mira 1096; US$5*) is rather bleak, but cheap. **Residencial Los Helechos** (☎ 259-525; *Chorrillos 1500; per person US$7*) charges slightly more with private bath, but is a good deal in a comfortable place. Breakfast costs US$2 more.

Hostería Casa Gladys *(☎ 260-247; Ancud 112; per person US$9)* is another decent spot, with conscientious owners and a very cool kitchen.

Hostal Sur *(☎ 292-535; Andrés Bello 973; per person US$10)* earns praise from readers for clean rooms with shared bath and cable TV.

Casa Almondacid *(☎ 257-565; Independencia 247; per person US$10)* is small, but a good alternative with breakfast and homemade goodies.

Hostal Marazul *(☎ 256-567; Ecuador 1558; rooms with shared/private bath US$7.50/10)* is convenient to the ferry port at Angelmó and includes breakfast.

Hostal Suizo *(☎ 252-640, 257-565; Independencia 231; rooms US$12.50-17)* is well known and quite original, with lots of artistic touches, though the owner/artist is known for a moody disposition. Some rooms have private bath.

Mid-Range Hotel Gamboa *(☎ 252-741; Pedro Montt 157; singles/doubles with shared bath US$13/26, with private bath US$17/30)* is surprisingly quiet for its location. The rooms are quite dark, and the bathrooms are awkward build-ins, but it's a helpful and charming spot and rates include breakfast.

Residencial Urmeneta *(☎ 253-262; Urmeneta 290, 2nd floor; singles/doubles with shared bath US$12.50/20, doubles with private bath US$28)* is a cozy spot with a lovely owner, clean rooms and firm beds. Some of the rooms are dark for lack of exterior windows. Rates include breakfast.

Hostal Pacífico *(☎ 256-229; Mira 1088; singles/doubles US$23/43)* provides one of the better choices, with clean rooms that are surprisingly quiet despite the noisy street. A large breakfast is part of the deal, and the staff is patient and helpful.

Residencial Millantú *(☎ 252-758, fax 263-550; Illapel 146; doubles/triples US$25/35)* is a decent choice with light, clean rooms, but it doesn't have singles. Try for rooms in the upper level.

Hotel Colina *(☎ 253-501, fax 259-331; Talca 81; doubles/triples US$26/33)* has decent accommodations with waterfront views and private bath. Staff are friendly

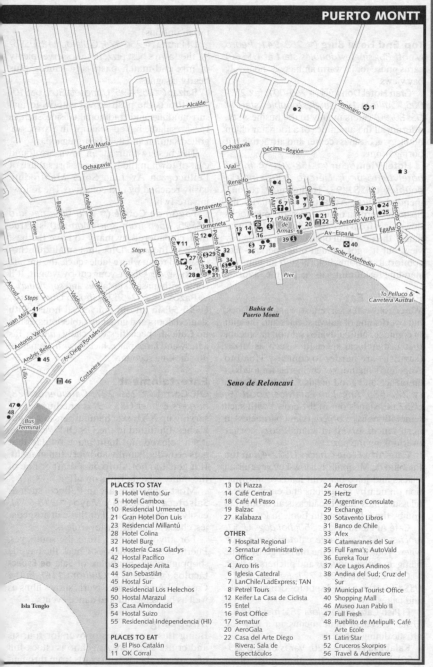

PUERTO MONTT

Alcalde

Seminario ● 1

● 2

Santa María

Ochagavía

Ochagavía

Vial

Décima–Región

Rengifo

● 3

Benavente

C Gallardo

Rancagua

San Martín

O'Higgins

Quillota

● 4

10

9

8

Serena

● 24
● 25

Serena

Illapel

San Felipe

● 23

Baquedano

Aníbal Pinto

Balmaceda

5 ●

Urmeneta

Talca

Pedro Montt

6 7

15

17 ●

13 14

16

19 20

18

21

22

Antonio Varas

Egaña

Ejército Copiapó

Freire

Plaza de Armas

Av-España

Av Soler Manfredini

Steps

Cauquenes

11

29

32

27

26

28

30

31

33

34

35

36

37 38

39 ●

40

Concepción

Chillán

Talcahuano

Pier

To Pelluco &
Carretera Austral

Ancud

Steps

Juan Mira

41 ●

Valdivia

Antonio Varas

Andrés Bello

45 ●

Lillo

Av Diego Portales

Costanera

46

**Bahía de
Puerto Montt**

Seno de Reloncaví

47 ●
48 ●

Bus
Terminal

Isla Tenglo

PLACES TO STAY
3 Hotel Viento Sur
5 Hotel Gamboa
10 Residencial Urmeneta
21 Gran Hotel Don Luis
23 Residencial Millantú
28 Hotel Colina
32 Hotel Burg
41 Hostería Casa Gladys
42 Hostal Pacífico
43 Hospedaje Anita
44 San Sebastián
45 Hostal Sur
49 Residencial Los Helechos
50 Hostal Marazul
53 Casa Almondacid
54 Hotel Suizo
55 Residencial Independencia (HI)

PLACES TO EAT
9 El Piso Catalán
11 OK Corral

13 Di Piazza
14 Café Central
18 Café Al Passo
19 Balzac
27 Kalabaza

OTHER
1 Hospital Regional
2 Sernatur Administrative
   Office
4 Arco Iris
6 Iglesia Catedral
7 LanChile/LadExpress; TAN
8 Petrel Tours
12 Keifer La Casa de Ciclista
15 Entel
16 Post Office
17 Sernatur
20 AeroGala
22 Casa del Arte Diego
   Rivera; Sala de
   Espectáculos

24 Aerosur
25 Hertz
26 Argentine Consulate
29 Exchange
30 Sotavento Libros
31 Banco de Chile
33 Afex
34 Catamaranes del Sur
35 Full Fama's; AutoVald
36 Eureka Tour
37 Ace Lagos Andinos
38 Andina del Sud; Cruz del
   Sur
39 Municipal Tourist Office
40 Shopping Mall
46 Museo Juan Pablo II
47 Full Fresh
48 Pueblito de Melipulli; Café
   Arte Ecole
51 Latin Star
52 Cruceros Skorpios
56 Travel & Adventure

and competent, but the walls are surprisingly thin.

Top End Hotel Burg (☎ 253-941; Pedro Montt 86; singles/doubles start at US$60) earns praise for its warm ambience and lovely bay views.

Gran Hotel Don Luis (☎ 259-001, fax 259-005; Quillota 146; singles/doubles start at US$80/90) caters mainly to the business set, offering all the amenities of a four-star chain hotel: gym, business center and attractive but boring rooms.

Hotel Viento Sur (☎ 258-701; e info@hotelvientosur.cl; Ejército 200; singles/doubles US$81/93) is the most recommended splurge. Attractive and well run, the Spanish/German designed 'castle' overlooks downtown from its east-end perch. Unfortunately, the new mall obstructs part of its bay view, but it's got enough other perks – like comfortable rooms, helpful staff and an outstanding restaurant – to keep it the favorite.

Places to Eat

Waterfront cafés serve tasty seafood dishes, but overfishing of native species and the glut of commercially cultivated salmon has meant that tastier local specialties such as *sierra* (sawfish) are harder to come by. Head to Angelmó's plethora of cocinerías for loads of ambience and good meals. Chilotito Marino (☎ 277-585; Angelmó Palafitos, Local 19; US$7.50) stands out in the crowd with such temptations as *picorocos* (giant barnacles) in herb sauce, served in a small cozy corner overlooking the port.

Café Arte Ecole (snacks US$2-4), in the Pueblito de Melipulli, is a low-key vegetarian snacks and juice bar with loads of information on nearby excursions and environmental issues, plus radio broadcasts, all brought to you by the folks who run École in Pucón.

Café Al Passo (Varas 350; hot dogs US$1, lunches US$3) is a large, cafeteria-style spot, where you can watch the masses go by while filling up with *completos* and pitchers of beer.

Café Central (☎ 254-721; Rancagua 117; US$1.50-4) is a good spot for drinks, snacks and cakes.

El Piso Catalán (Quillota 185; meals US$2-5) has excellent-value menus, in a low-key, artistic dining room.

Kalabaza (☎ 262-020; Varas 629; US$3-4.50) is more attractive than most other cafés in town, with sandwiches, Kuntsmann beer and fixed-price lunches (lots of vegetarian options).

Di Piazza (☎ 254-174; Gallardo 118; US$5-9), the town's best pizzeria, also serves plenty of mix-and-match pasta and sauces, plus hearty lasagnas.

Balzac (☎ 259-495; Urmeneta 305; US$10-15) attracts the posh crowd with its formal surroundings and traditional cuisine, such as caesar salads, baked scallops in parmesan, grilled salmon and beef bourguignon.

The best restaurants in town are found east of town in the bathing resort suburb of Pelluco, via Av Juan Soler Manfredini, easily reached by taxi colectivo. The following are two.

Fogón de Cotelé (☎ 278-000; per kilo US$25; open from 8pm Mon-Sat) is a true find, considered by many to have the best steak in the area. Dine in a small quincho-designed room where tables circle the fire and steaks sizzle. Order your cut by weight. It'll come with mashed potatoes and *sopaipillas*.

Pazos (☎ 252-552; Liborio Guerrero 1; US$5-9), in an old converted house with slanted floors and gingham tablecloths, dishes up Chilean specialties, especially *curanto*. It's a busy and large place, luckily with a separate no-smoking section.

Entertainment

OK Corral (☎ 266-287; Cauquenes 128; burgers & beer US$3-9) is one huge place serving up XXL-size hamburgers and sandwiches. Outfitted in the US Old West style, it's a relaxed and light place by day that gets crowded, smoky and very fun at night. If it gets too hot, slurp on a draft or one of the many mixed drinks on offer.

Most nightclubs are in Pelluco, such as Salsoteca Aquacero y Mayo (☎ 318-911), easily reached by taxi. For those in hospedajes, check what the curfew rule is.

For anyone coming from the south, yes, Puerto Montt has movies. Check the bayside shopping mall's multiplex, or Sala de Espectáculos (☎ 261-817; Quillota 116), in the Casa del Arte Diego Rivera, shows films as well as hosts theater and dance events.

Shopping

Being this a regular stopover for tourists and cruise ships, Av Angelmó is chock-full of souvenir stands, with crafts from throughout the country and an amazing amount of stuff from more northerly countries. Try the lively waterfront market **Pueblito de Melipulli**, opposite the bus terminal, or the crafts fair at Angelmó. Those along the street are exposed to dust and diesel all day long. Cyclists can stock up on parts at **Keifer La Casa de Ciclista** *(Montt 129)*.

Getting There & Away

Air LanChile *(☎ 253-315; O'Higgins 167, Local 1-B)* flies up to four times daily to Punta Arenas (US$200), three times daily to Balmaceda/Coyhaique (US$90) and up to eight times daily to Santiago (US$180).

TAN *(☎ 250-071; O'Higgins 167)* usually flies Tuesday and Friday mornings to the Argentine cities of Bariloche (US$73) and Neuquén (US$114); however service may have stopped due to Argentina's economic crisis.

Aerosur *(☎ 252-523; Urmeneta 149)* flies daily except Sunday to Chaitén on the Carretera Austral (US$50). **AeroGala** *(☎ 253-219; Quillota 127)* costs just slightly less, but isn't as established. Both include transfer to the airport.

Bus – Regional Puerto Montt's waterfront bus terminal *(☎ 253-143; Av Portales & Lillo)* is the main transportation hub for the region, and it gets busy and chaotic – watch your belongings or leave them with the *custodia* while sorting out travel plans. In summer, trips to Punta Arenas and Bariloche can sell out, so book in advance.

Minibuses to Puerto Varas (US$0.70), Frutillar (US$1.40) and Puerto Octay (US$1.70) leave frequently from the eastern side of the terminal. Buses leave for the villages of Ralún (US$4) and Cochamó (US$3.50, four hours) five times daily, three of which carry on to Río Puelo (US$5.50).

To get to Hornopirén, where there are summer ferry connections to Caleta Gonzalo, **Buses Fierro** has three daily departures (US$5, five hours). Public transportation is limited for the 56km between Caleta Gonzalo and the mainland port of Chaitén, which is more easily reached by ferry from Puerto Montt or from Quellón on Chiloé. Also note that off-season (mid-March to mid-December) bus transportation to Hornopirén and the upper Carretera Austral is very limited.

Buses Fierro also goes to Lenca, the turnoff for the southern approach to Parque Nacional Alerce Andino, and Chaica (US$1.50) five times daily. The coastal town of Maullín (US$1.25) is served by **Buses Bohle** and **ETM**, and the fishing village of Calbuco (US$1.50) by Bohle and **Buses Calbuco**.

Bus – Long-Distance Bus companies, all with offices at the bus terminal, include **Cruz del Sur** *(☎ 254-731; also Varas 437)*, with frequent services to Chiloé; **Tur Bus** *(☎ 253-329)*, with daily service to Valparaíso/Viña del Mar; **Igi Llaima** *(☎ 254-519)*; and **Buses Lit** *(☎ 254-011)*. All of them go to Santiago, stopping at various cities along the way; departures are usually around 10pm. For long-haul trips to Coyhaique and Punta Arenas via Argentina, try Cruz del Sur, **Queilen Bus** *(☎ 253-468)* or **Turibús** *(☎ 253-345)*.

For Bariloche, Argentina, **Tas Choapa** *(☎ 254-828)*, **Río de La Plata** *(☎ 253-841)* and Cruz del Sur travel daily via the Cardenal Samoré pass east of Osorno. **Andesmar** goes to Bariloche three times weekly. For information on the popular bus/boat combination trip to Bariloche, see the boxed text 'Crossing the Lakes' earlier in this chapter.

Sample travel times and costs are as follows:

destination	duration in hours	cost
Ancud	2½	US$4
Bariloche (Ar)	8	US$19
Castro	3½	US$6
Concepción	9	US$15
Osorno	1½	US$2
Pucón	6	US$7
Punta Arenas	30-36	US$50
Quellón	6	US$9
Santiago	13-16	US$11-23
Temuco	7	US$8
Valdivia	3½	US$5
Valparaíso/Viña del Mar	18	US$25

Boat At the **Terminal de Transbordadores** *(Av Angelmó 2187)* you can find ticket offices and waiting lounges for both **Navimag** *(☎ 253-318, fax 258-540)* and **Transmarchilay** *(☎ 270-416, fax 270-415)*, two cargo companies that offer maritime transportation. The former has done a better job of catering to the traveler, but keep in mind that the main source of income for both is cargo and local transportation; delays, because of rough seas, inclement weather or other undisclosed reasons, occur. On shorter journeys (12 hours or less) the lounge areas are not the most comfortable, and many passengers stay inside their vehicles. For longer trips, boats have been outfitted with more comfortable common areas and sleeping cabins.

Companies catering exclusively to passengers are **Cruceros Skorpios** (☎ 252-996; Av Angelmó 1660), offering traditional luxury cruises to Laguna San Rafael and the Chilean fjords, and **Catamaranes del Sur** (☎ 267-533; Diego Portales 510), focusing on shorter, faster trips and offering great service.

Chiloé Cruz del Sur operates auto-passenger ferries from Pargua, 60km southwest of Puerto Montt, to Chacao, on the northern tip of the Isla Grande de Chiloé (see the Chiloé chapter). Fares are about US$1 for passengers or US$12 per car, no matter how many passengers. There is no extra ferry charge for passengers on buses to Chiloé.

Chaitén Transmarchilay sails the ferry La Pincoya (10 hours) Monday, Tuesday, Thursday and Friday to Chaitén, with mostly evening departures (arriving in early morning) in high season; limited in off-season. Prices are US$26 per person, US$11 bicycle, US$23 motorcycle, US$100 car or pickup.

Navimag's M/N Alejandrina goes every Saturday at 10pm and costs US$20-25 per person, US$10 bicycle, US$20 motorcycle, US$100 car or pickup.

Catamaranes del Sur has the fastest and most comfortable service, taking four to five hours. The passenger-only (bicycles allowed) ferry leaves Monday, Wednesday and Friday and cost US$35 one-way, US$66 roundtrip.

For routes from Castro and Quellón to/from Chaitén, see those sections under Chiloé.

Puerto Chacabuco Navimag's M/N Puerto Edén sails to Puerto Chacabuco (18 hours) and costs from US$40 for a butaca (reclining chair) to US$297 for a dorm bed with shared bath per person, plus US$9 per bicycle, US$25 motorcycle, US$90 car or pickup. The M/N Evangelistas stops at Puerto Chacabuco en route to Laguna San Rafael; it runs every four or five days in summer, but only three or four times monthly the rest of the year. To Cha-

cobuco, it costs US$106 for bunks to US$283 for a cabin with private bath per person, plus US$16 bicycle, US$33 motorcycle, US$115 car or pickup.

Laguna San Rafael Catamaranes del Sur provides a three-day trip to Laguna San Rafael from Puerto Montt, costing US$605 per person. Its schedule allows for a daytime sail through the glorious fjords to the glacier. A day trip from Puerto Chacabuco costs US$286 per person.

Skorpios sails the elegant 125-person vessel M/V Skorpios III every Saturday from the Terminal Chinqüihue in high season for a seven-day roundtrip cruise, which also stops at its exclusive hot springs resort, Quitralco, and at towns in the Chiloé archipelago. Rates per person, based on double occupancy, range from US$1400 on the Atenas deck to US$2100 for a suite on the Athos deck. Rates include abundant buffets, open bar, and more bedroom detailing than most hotels.

Navimag's M/N Evangelistas leaves Puerto Montt for the glacier every four days in high season and about every six to eight days August to December. The boat stops in Puerto Chacabuco in either direction. Rates per person roundtrip range from US$533 in a double cabin, to US$358 for a dorm bed, to US$240 for a reclining chair; for those disembarking on the return at Puerto Chacabuco, rates are US$480/321/208. Students (with ID) can get a 10% discount, senior travelers 15%.

Puerto Natales Navimag's M/N Magallanes sails on Monday to Puerto Natales, a popular three-night journey through Chile's fjords; book passage at Navimag's Santiago offices (see the Getting Around chapter). You can also reserve via the website, but confirm with the Santiago office.

High season is December to February, midseason is September to November and March, and low season is April to August. Prices for the trip include scheduled meals. Per-person fares, which vary according to view and private or shared bath, are as follows:

class	high season	mid season	low season
AAA	US$792	US$738	US$228
AA	US$398	US$354	US$166
A	US$345	US$302	US$131
Berths	US$250	US$210	n/a

In addition, bicycles cost US$9 and motorcycles US$30; cars and pickups cost US$250 going from Puerto Montt to Puerto Natales, and US$200 the other way. Travelers prone to motion sickness should consider taking medication prior to crossing the Golfo de Penas, which is exposed to gut-wrenching Pacific swells.

Getting Around
ETM buses (US$1.50) go to **Aeropuerto El Tepual** (☎ 252-019), 16km west of town from the bus terminal; catch the bus 1½ hours before your flight's departure. Taxis to downtown cost US$10; door-to-door shuttles cost US$4.

Car rental agencies include **Acchi** (*Automóvil Club;* ☎ 252-968; *Esmeralda 70*), **Hertz** (☎ 259-585; *Varas 126*), **AutoVald** (☎ 313-158; *Portales 504*) and **Full Fama's** (☎ 258-060; *Portales 506*). These last two can help get permission to take rental vehicles into Argentina. Rates range from US$45 for a normal car to US$100 for a pickup or jeep.

AROUND PUERTO MONTT
☎ 65
En route to Chiloé, the archipelago of **Calbuco** (population 30,000) is 51km south of Puerto Montt and linked to the mainland by a causeway. It was founded in 1602 by Spanish survivors of the destruction of Osorno. The medley of islands, all dependent on the sea, offer some interesting architecture, pretty beaches and views of the area. The **tourist office** (☎ 461-807; *Av Los Héroes s/n*) has area information. **Costa Azul** (☎ 461-516; *Vicuña Mackenna 202*) is worth trying for seafood. There's regular transportation to/from Puerto Montt.

On the estuary of the Río Maullín, **Maullín** (population 15,000) is a small, sedate port dependent on fishing and algae harvesting. Boats trundle around the river and most people pass through en route to the beach communities farther south. The small **museum** explains the history of the town. **Residencial Toledo** (☎ 451-246; *21 de Mayo 147; per person US$7.50*) is a clean, decent spot to spend a night (breakfast US$1.50), and it has a restaurant. In the mercado central, track down **La Chilota** for tasty, greasy *empanadas de marisco.*

The seaside resort of **Pangal** is 5km west of Maullín. **Cabañas Pangal** (☎ 451-244; *sites* US$12.50, *4-bed cabañas US$63*) also has a well-regarded restaurant. Or try the municipal campground **Camping Punta Pangal** (☎ 451-242), which charges extra for hot showers.

At the end of a gravel road, 17km south of Maullín, **Carelmapu** is a scenic fishing village that remains rather tranquil for now: One of the new road improvements in the works will link Carelmapu to Pargua, which will most certainly increase traffic into this area. Lanchas can take you from the town's dock to some nice beaches at Quenvir (US$0.75). Camping is possible 2km from town at **Mar Brava**, on a cliff overlooking the Pacific. **Chamál** is a locally recommended restaurant, where US$4 gets you a mountain of seafood.

Among them, ETM, ETC and Carelmapu have about 30 buses daily from Puerto Montt (US$2) to and from Carelmapu via Maullín, between 7:30am and 8pm.

PN ALERCE ANDINO
Despite being only 40km from Puerto Montt, the mountainous 40,000-hectare Parque Nacional Alerce Andino *(admission US$2)* is little visited, though it offers some great hiking through old-growth alerce forest. The park was created in 1982 to protect some of the last remaining forests of alerce, found primarily 400m to 700m above sea level. Hikers can enjoy the lush evergreen forest, ranging from sea level to 900m, a thick twisting medley of coigue and ulmo, ferns, climbing vines and dense thickets of quila. Pumas, pudús, foxes and skunks are very occasionally seen, but you'll have better luck glimpsing condors, kingfishers and waterfowl. Up to 4500mm of rain a year can fall on the park. The average temperature is 15°C in January and 7°C in July.

The park consists of three main sectors: Sector Correntoso on the Río Chamiza at the northwestern end, Sector Lago Chapo only a few kilometers to the east and Sector Chaicas at the southwestern approach. The gate on the southwestern, Río Chaica side is open 9am to 5pm only, so visitors out for a long day's hike – and not planning an overnight stay – should park outside the gate, which is only half an hour's walk from the end of the road. Several agencies in Puerto Montt and Puerto Varas arrange hikes and tours of the park.

Hiking
A trail links the Correntoso and Río Chaica sectors, leading deep into the park to

Cargo Turned Cruiser: The Navimag Experience

The Navimag ferry ride between Puerto Montt and Puerto Natales through Chile's nearly uninhabited fjords has become one of the most popular backpacker trips in Chile. It's also the subject of much discussion among travelers, who either gush about each glorious day or grumble about unmet expectations and the boredom of rain. Either way, it has become as much a social experience as a sight-seeing tour, as strangers bond over beers and queasy stomachs and pledge to meet up along the Torres Circuit.

How did it all start? In the not-so-distant past, travelers begged passages in cramped bunks on rusty state-run freighters that carried cargo between Puerto Montt and Puerto Natales, or negotiated with truckers for a berth on ferries. Navimag caught on to the tourism potential and revamped their two ferries *Puerto Edén* and *Magallanes* to include tourist accommodations. Of the two ferries, *Magallanes* is the one currently sailing to Puerto Natales. Despite the glossy touristy adverts, the ferry is still predominantly cargo. Travelers bunking down in the dorm rooms are subject to the stench of cooped-up cows, sheep and horses. The common spaces lack comfort; all of the furniture is either cafeteria tables or plastic garden furniture. The crew do an impressive job of trying to entertain with games, slide shows, talent shows and disco nights, most of which take place in the common area called the 'pub.'

The sleeping areas are quite new and surprisingly comfortable. Dorm beds have curtains for some privacy, but lack sheets or towels, both of which can be rented. Each module has 20 beds, all with individual lockers, and about half with some windows. Both ferries have four-person cabins with private or shared bath with showers.

The 'mess hall' isn't large enough to fit everyone, so diners take shifts, which simply extends the amount of time you wait in line for meals that, while ample and varied, won't win culinary awards. Vegetarians need to request special meals in advance, but may also want to bring some backup. One vegetarian mentioned that eating three cold omelets a day just about did her in. Beer, wine, chocolates and snacks are available at the pub, but it's cheaper to bring your own.

Passengers staying in the higher-end, private, two-person cabins dine with the crew in the captain's dining room, with linen service but not much difference in quality.

And what about the truck drivers? Regular Navimag truckers share cabins on the same level as the high-end passengers and have their own dining room right across from the captain.

The Route – North to South The route stays in relatively sheltered waters such as Canal Moraleda before entering Aisén's maze of narrow channels. At the south end of Canal Errázuriz, the ferry heads west through the constricted Canal Chacabuco to enter the dreaded Golfo de Penas, where Pacific swells can make all but the most experienced sailors queasy.

The ferry then enters Canal Messier where, after navigating the Angostura Inglesa (a passage so confined that the ship seems to graze the shoreline on both sides), the boat passes Puerto Edén, a small fishing port and the last outpost of the region's Qawashqar Indians. To the south, the channels become narrower, the snow peaks get closer, and hundreds of waterfalls tumble from U-shaped glacial valleys before reaching Puerto Natales.

Practicalities If you're prone to seasickness, consider getting medication to buffer the queasiness of the rough Golfo de Penas crossing, and consider eating only lightly beforehand. Bring along your own entertainment, such as books, cards and heaps of postcards. Other extras to have on hand are ear plugs, extra camera film, flip flops and any special food items.

The *most* important practicality is planning. Because schedules change, it is essential that a trip itinerary take into consideration that you may have to wait an extra day (or two) for your ship to come in or leave. Don't arrange flights the day after a supposed arrival date. Despite reservation confirmations through the Santiago office, the offices in Puerto Montt or Puerto Natales occasionally mess up. While this may create confusion or complication, you'll still get on board, so bear with them.

experience the awesome alerce up close. For those with limited time and a private vehicle, or for the nontrekker, the entrance at Río Chaica is probably a better choice. From the campground at Río Chaica, there's a 4WD road to Laguna Chaiquenes, from where a two-hour hike leads to Laguna Triángulo. If dropped off at the entrance, it's still only 9.5km to the lake. Tábanos are a problem on the exposed parts of the trail in January and early February.

On the park's northern border, Lago Chapo, the largest of several glacial lakes, has been exploited for hydroelectricity and fish farming, since it is officially outside of park boundaries.

Places to Stay

Camping is the only option in the park proper. Conaf has a five-site campground (per site US$6.50) at Correntoso on the Río Chamiza at the northern end of the park, and another six-site campground near the head of the Río Chaica Valley. For trekkers, backcountry camping is another possibility, but Conaf also maintains rustic trailside refugios at Río Pangal, Laguna Sargazo and Laguna Fría.

Alerce Mountain Lodge (☎ 286-969; e smontt@telsur.cl; singles/doubles with full board US$265/460, cabins US$205), at Km 36 on Carretera Austral and set deep among alerce forests, offers serenity and comfort right by the edge of the park. Three- to five-day packages, which are much better value than a single night, are offered. Nightly rates include use of the sauna and hot tub, transportation and guided treks and excursions with bilingual guides. If you prefer using your own transportation, get directions from the lodge. The road getting there is hard to follow and requires 4WD or double traction.

Getting There & Away

To get there, take the Ruta 7, Carretera Austral, that runs to La Arena, on the Estero de Reloncaví. From Puerto Montt, Buses Fierro has four buses daily to the village of Correntoso, only 3km from the Río Chamiza entrance on the northern boundary of the park; this bus continues to Lago Chapo (US$1.75). Fierro also runs five buses daily to the crossroads at Lenca (US$1.50), on the Carretera Austral, where a narrow lateral road climbs 7km up the valley of the Río Chaica.

Chiloé

From the meat, potato and seafood stew *curanto* to the folkloric creature *Trauco*, from unique wood-shingled churches to stilted *palafitos* teetering on the edge of serene inlets, the Archipiélago de Chiloé has an identity all its own. About 180km long but only 50km wide, the Isla Grande de Chiloé, most easily accessed across the Canal de Chacao, is lush with undulating hills quilted in farm patterns to the north and blanketed in dense forest to the south. Smaller islands scattered along the Golfo de Ancud and the Golfo Corcovado are the most Chilote of all, holding strong to a self-sufficiency and lifestyle that all islanders take pride in. For much of the year, rain and mist obscure the sun, which when it finally breaks through reveals majestic panoramas across the Golfo de Ancud to the mainland's snow-capped volcanoes. For the best chance of a dry day, come in the summer months of January and February.

Darwin questioned whether the potato, which the Huilliche Indians cultivated prior to the Spaniards' arrival in the 16th century, might have originated in Chiloé. The Spaniards took possession of Chiloé in 1567, founding Castro the following year. During the wars of independence, Chiloé was a Spanish stronghold; the Spanish resisted criollo attacks in 1820 and 1824 from heavily fortified Ancud, until the final Spanish defeat in 1826. In 1843, the schooner *Ancud* left the shores of Chiloé full of islanders, who perservered four months of sailing to lay Chilean claim to Magallanes at Fuerte Bulnes. Chilote influence on the most southern corners of Chile is still very much felt.

Ancud and Castro are the only sizable towns. Some towns, most notably Castro, have picturesque neighborhoods of palafitos, rows of houses built on stilts over the water, where boats on a rising tide can anchor at the back door. The smaller villages provide the best insight into Chiloé's culture and the best examples of the island's unique architecture. Over 150 distinctive wooden churches, most up to two centuries old, dot the verdant hills; they are frequently a town's main focus. Several of the most impressive churches are now protected as an Unesco World Heritage Site. The churches and many of the wooden houses exhibit varied and sometimes unique shingle patterns, which turn a basic structure into a work of expression and even art.

Nearly all of Chiloé's 154,000 inhabitants live within sight of the sea. More than half make a living from subsistence agriculture,

Highlights

- Admiring shingle designs on Chiloé's quaint churches
- Slurping down the island's prized oysters either in style at Caulín or from a beach-side hammock at Curaco de Vélez
- Joining an 'agroturismo' excursion to visits locals' houses and participate in island farm life
- Hiking the windswept coastline and dense forest trails in Parque Nacional Chiloé
- Driving until you feel lost in time among the island's back roads and curious hamlets

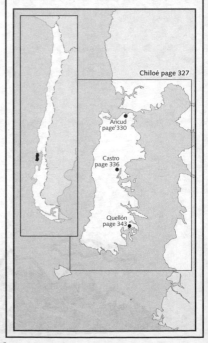

Chiloé page 327

Ancud page 330

Castro page 336

Quellón page 343

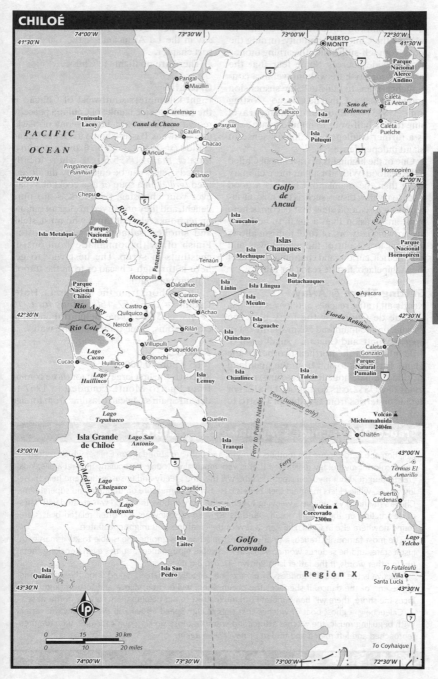

CHILOÉ

PACIFIC OCEAN

Península Lacuy

Pingüinera Punihuil

Chepu

Isla Metalqui

Parque Nacional Chiloé

Parque Nacional Chiloé

Río Anay

Río Cole Cole

Cucao

Lago Cucao

Lago Huillinco

Lago Tepuhueco

Isla Grande de Chiloé

Lago San Antonio

Lago Chaiguaco

Lago Chaiguata

Isla Quilán

Río Medina

Isla Laitec

Isla San Pedro

Pangal

Maullín

Carelmapu

Canal de Chacao

Caulín

Pargua

Chacao

Ancud

Linao

Calbuco

Isla Guar

Isla Puluqui

Seno de Reloncaví

Caleta La Arena

Caleta Puelche

Hornopirén

PUERTO MONTT

Parque Nacional Alerce Andino

Golfo de Ancud

Río Butalcura

Panamericana

Quemchi

Isla Caucahue

Islas Chauques

Isla Mechuque

Tenaún

Mocopulli

Dalcahue

Curaco de Vélez

Castro

Quilquico

Nercón

Rilán

Villupulli

Puqueldón

Chonchi

Huillinco

Isla Linlín

Achao

Isla Llingua

Isla Butachauques

Isla Meulín

Isla Caguache

Isla Quinchao

Isla Lemuy

Isla Chaulinec

Isla Talcán

Fiordo Reñihué

Ayacara

Parque Nacional Hornopirén

Caleta Gonzalo

Parque Natural Pumalín

Queilén

Isla Tranqui

Ferry to Puerto Natales

Ferry (summer only)

Volcán Michinmahuida 2404m

Chaitén

Termas El Amarillo

Región X

Quellón

Isla Cailín

Golfo Corcovado

Isla San Pedro

Volcán Corcovado 2300m

Ferry

Puerto Cárdenas

Lago Yelcho

To Futaleufú Villa Santa Lucía

To Coyhaique

0   15   30 km
0   10   20 miles

but many others depend on fishing. The growing salmon industry has begun to reshape the Chilote community, turning the focus from self-sufficiency to earning money from outside sources. Some fear that the fabric of society here will unravel as a consequence. Plans to build a 2.5km suspension bridge across the Canal de Chacao – costing some US$314 million and cutting travel time from a half-hour to minutes – are seen as a further challenge to Chiloé's sense of island independence.

One of the highlights of traveling in Chiloé is the seafood. With just a hint more culinary savvy than the mainland, Chiloé is a good place to try new dishes, such as the ubiquitous curanto – a seafood stew that becomes here more an occasion than a meal. In addition, the growing network of rural tourism allows travelers to get out of the main towns and into the rich, curious and charming corners of the archipelago. Just be ready for rain.

Getting There & Away

Nearly all traffic reaches and leaves the Isla Grande de Chiloé by the ferry between Pargua, on the mainland 56km southwest of Puerto Montt, and Chacao, a small town of little interest at the northeast corner of the island. Bus fares to and from the mainland include the half-hour ferry crossing; pedestrians pay US$2, cars cost about US$12. For details on ferries from Quellón or Castro to Chaitén, see those towns later in this section. For bus details from Puerto Montt, see that city in the La Araucanía & the Lakes District chapter.

There are no flights to Chiloé.

CAULÍN

Eight kilometers southwest of Chacao is the small bayside hamlet of **Caulín**, a peaceful retreat and home to a large colony of black-necked swans. It is also home to **Ostras Caulín Chiloé** (☎ 09-643-7005; e ostrascaulin@terra.cl; mains US$5.50-9), where locally farmed oysters can be enjoyed by the dozen, fried (grillé), in a soup or as a cocktail. Whatever your choosing, the morsels are pure delight, and they are served in elegant but unpretentious style. For those who must, steak and smoked salmon are also on offer. Finish off with homemade bonbons or chestnuts in syrup. The best way to get here is through Chacao or from the turnoff 3km farther south.

Downshore from the restaurant, **Hotel Caulín** (☎ 065-267-150; cabins for 6-10 people US$66-78) has delightful and spacious cabins, some quite near the water.

ANCUD

☎ 65 • pop 40,000

Ancud is the first large town for those coming from Puerto Montt. Founded in 1767 to defend Spain's Chilean coastline from foreign

---

Trauco Did It: Chiloé's Mythological Creatures

Isolation and hardship are the mothers of myth, and both are abundant on Chiloé, where centuries ago a colorful mythology developed that is very much alive today. Particularly in rural areas, kids are still taught about mythical creatures who will trick the greedy and unsuspecting and help those lost at sea, while elders maintain their beliefs based in equal measure on tradition and superstition. Chiloé's mythology is unique – weaving together the story of how the island was created with tales of destruction on the stormy ocean – and its 10 or so mischievous and often related beasts are found nowhere else in Chile. Here are a few of the creatures you might encounter:

The most famous is Trauco, a gnarly, strong, mischievous gnome. He is able to kill a man with just a stare, and he seduces women with his irresistible repugnance, at times even knocking them up. In other words, if the father isn't known, Trauco did it.

Pincoya is the beautiful goddess of plenty. She seductively dances naked upon the waves, and at the end of the dance, if she faces the ocean, there will be abundance and fertility, and if she faces the shore, there will be no more. Fishermen attest to her helping them survive storms at sea.

Caleuche is a ghost boat of witches that sails at high speed above and even below the water. With beguiling music, the witches attract and entrance those seeking quick fortune, who are then reproached and left ruined and foolish or never seen again.

intrusion, Ancud was once a rather wealthy town with gracious buildings, palafitos and a railway line. But the earthquake of 1960 reshaped the town, knocking down many of the buildings and letting the ocean reclaim a good 20m of shoreline, which wiped out the palafitos and covered the railway line. Today, Ancud boasts the best museum on the island, a bustling fish port and market and the ruins of Spain's last claim on Chilean soil. It's a great place to get a sense of the Chilote way of life, and with nearby penguin colonies and fabulously rugged beaches and sea kayaking spots, it's a good base for excursions.

Orientation & Information

Most points of interest are within a few blocks of the north-south Av Dr Salvador Allende, or Costanera, and the asymmetrical Plaza de Armas on the hill above it, around which is the modern-day cathedral and the Teatro Municipal. Calle Aníbal Pinto leads to the Panamericana.

Sernatur (☎ 622-800; Libertad 665; open 8:30am-8pm daily in summer, 8:30am-6pm Mon-Fri rest of the year), opposite the Plaza de Armas, is the only formal tourist office on the island. It has very helpful staff, brochures, town maps and lists of accommodations for the archipelago.

Change currency in Puerto Montt, where exchange rates are better; **Banco de Chile** and **Banco de Estado** have ATMs.

To keep in touch, there's the **post office** (cnr Pudeto & Blanco Encalada) and **Entel** (Pudeto 219), which also has Internet access. **Anay Libros** (Pudeto 353) has books and maps on Chile, some in English.

For laundry service, try **Clean Center** (☎ 623-838; Pudeto 45). The **Hospital de Ancud** (☎ 622-356; Almirante Latorre 405) is at the corner of Pedro Montt.

Museo Regional de Ancud

Colloquially known as the Museo Chilote (☎ 622-413; Libertad; adult/child US$1/0.25; open 10:30am-7:30pm daily Jan-Feb; 9:30am-5:30pm Mon-Fri, 10am-2pm Sat & Sun Mar-Dec), this fortress-style museum is a worthwhile stop. Superb displays track the history of the island, from the indigenous groups (with a large collection of household objects), to the Jesuits and their elaborate ways of converting the islanders, to the story of the Ancud, which sailed the treacherous

fjords of the Strait of Magellan to claim Chile's southernmost territories in the mid-19th century. Also look for the outstanding selection of photographs, a superb natural history display, interactive displays on the different styles of church architecture and a very fine three-dimensional relief map of Chiloé.

Fuerte San Antonio

At the northwest corner of town, late-colonial cannon emplacements still look down on the harbor from the early-19th-century remains of Fuerte San Antonio. During the wars of independence, this was Spain's last Chilean outpost.

Special Events

During the second week in January, Ancud observes the Semana Ancuditana (Ancud Week), which includes the annual Encuentro Folklórico de Chiloé, promoting the island's music, dance and cuisine.

Organized Tours

Austral Adventures (☎ 625-977; W www .austral-adventures.com; Lord Cochrane 432) provides a multiday 'immersion' tour that, depending on your interests, can include beach hiking, trips to the penguin colonies, kayaking, rural tourism home stays, and tours of the Unesco churches. A four-day excursion costs US$399 all inclusive. Day rates for hiking and penguin colonies are US$60, kayaking US$40. An added bonus is that the guides speak English. The owners operate the wooden motor cruiser Cahuella, which sails around the island and to Parque Nacional Pumalín; see Organized Tours in the Getting Around chapter. Excursions to farming communities and private homes that offer meals and lodging can be arranged through **Agro-turismo** (☎ 628-333; Ramírez 207) or at Residencial María Carolina.

Places to Stay

Ancud has a good variety of decent places to stay. Except at campsites, places usually include breakfast in the price; exceptions are noted below.

Budget With exquisite views, **Camping Arena Gruesa** (☎ 623-428; Av Costanera Norte 290, entrance on Hucke; camping per person US$3, rooms per person US$11) is a rolling lot of

ANCUD

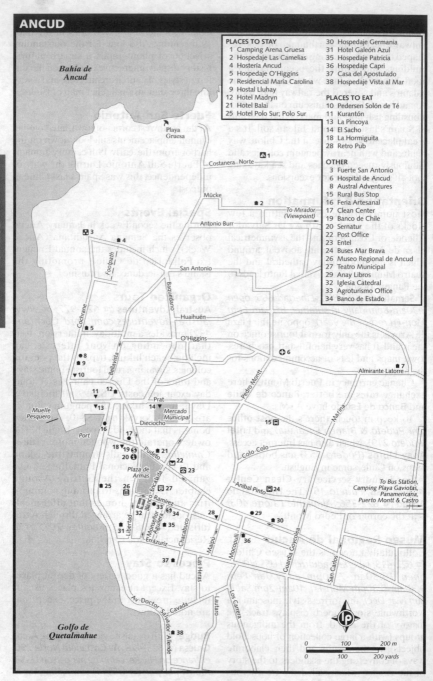

PLACES TO STAY
1 Camping Arena Gruesa
2 Hospedaje Las Camelias
4 Hostería Ancud
5 Hospedaje O'Higgins
7 Residencial María Carolina
9 Hostal Lluhay
12 Hotel Madryn
21 Hotel Balai
25 Hotel Polo Sur; Polo Sur
30 Hospedaje Germania
31 Hotel Galeón Azul
35 Hospedaje Patricia
36 Hospedaje Capri
37 Casa del Apostulado
38 Hospedaje Vista al Mar

PLACES TO EAT
10 Pedersen Solón de Té
11 Kurantón
13 La Pincoya
14 El Sacho
19 La Hormiguita
28 Retro Pub

OTHER
3 Fuerte San Antonio
6 Hospital de Ancud
8 Austral Adventures
15 Rural Bus Stop
16 Feria Artesanal
17 Clean Center
18 Banco de Chile
20 Sernatur
22 Post Office
23 Entel
24 Buses Mar Brava
26 Museo Regional de Ancud
27 Teatro Municipal
29 Anay Libros
32 Iglesia Catedral
33 Agroturismo Office
34 Banco de Estado

Bahía de
Ancud

Playa
Gruesa

Costanera Norte

Mücke

To Mirador
(Viewpoint)

Antonio Burr

San Antonio

Footpath

Cochrane

Baquedano

Huaihuén

O'Higgins

Bellavista

Almirante Latorre

Muelle
Pesquero

Prat

Pedro Montt

Marina

Mercado
Municipal

Dieciocho

Port

Pudeto

Plaza de
Armas

Banco Encalada

Colo-Colo

Ramirez

Aníbal Pinto

To Bus Station,
Camping Playa Gaviotas,
Panamericana,
Puerto Montt & Castro

Monseñor
Aguilera

Chacabuco

Errázuriz

Malipú

Mocopulli

Guardia Goycolea

San Carlos

Libertad

Las Heras

Los Carrera

Lautaro

Av. Doctor Salvador Allende

Cavada

Golfo de
Quetalmahue

CHILOÉ

0   100   200 m
0   100   200 yards

land right on the bluff. The sites are grassy and well maintained with electricity, hot water and a *refugio* for rainy nights, but they are pretty exposed to those strong ocean winds. Campers have access to a large independent kitchen in the main house, where there are decent rooms with shared bath.

Camping Playa Gaviotas (☎ 09-883-0489; *Ruta 5; sites for 2-6 people US$8-20),* 5km northeast of town, has similar facilities and good beach access, but little shade or shelter.

Casa del Apostulado (☎ 623-256; *Chacabuco 841; dorm beds US$3; open Dec-Mar),* at the end of the street, offers dorm-style rooms with flimsy beds. No smoking or alcohol are allowed. Other lodging is available the rest of the year at a different location; inquire within.

Hospedaje Vista al Mar (☎/fax 622-617; *Costanera 918; per person US$10, full cabin US$35)* has an annex cabin where HI members can shack up. It's a small spot – great for a small group – that has a decent kitchen and acceptable shared bathrooms.

Hospedaje Las Camelias (☎ 623-781; *J Mücke 190; per person US$6)* is tucked back in a residential area near the fort. The kind owners offer an intimate family-style place, with kitchen use, plenty of bathrooms and comfy beds. Breakfast is usually pretty filling, with eggs and homemade bread. It also has a minivan to make informal trips around the region.

Hospedaje Patricia (☎ 623-781; *Monseñor Aguilera 756; per person US$6)* offers cute rooms with good, firm beds and shared bath in a lively family environment. The room doors come with padlocks, but the owner recommends you bring your own.

Hospedaje O'Higgins (☎ 622-266; *O'Higgins 6; per person US$8.50)* is a spectacular mansion that's spacious and friendly.

Residencial María Carolina (☎ 622-458; *Almirante Latorre 558; per person US$10)* receives accolades for its quiet residential area, attractive common spaces and spacious gardens.

Hospedaje Capri (☎ 622-830; *Mocopulli 323; per person US$9),* above a restaurant, has basic rooms and is managed by a very caring matron.

Hospedaje Germania (☎ 622-214; *Pudeto 357; singles/doubles US$11/20)* is another good option; rooms are reasonable and the décor, all done by the owner, is attractive.

The many jigsaw puzzles speak of long winter days. Rooms with private bath are also available for US$6 more.

Hotel Madryn (☎ 622-128; *Bellavista 491; singles/doubles US$10/20)* comes well recommended for kind management and its tranquil atmosphere. Rooms upstairs are best, but all are good and come with private bath. Each room is slightly different.

Mid-Range Hostal Lluhay (☎ 622-656; *Cochrane 458; singles/doubles US$16/25)* is a top choice, not only for the comfortable rooms, but also for the very welcoming owners who make sure that you feel right at home, either enjoying *küchen* in the kitchen or sipping a drink by the roaring fireplace while they thump out a few tunes on the piano.

Hotel Polo Sur (☎ 622-200; *Costanera 630; singles/doubles US$16/23),* despite being on the waterfront, lacks ocean views from the rooms. It can get a bit noisy in summer due to a nearby discotheque.

Hotel Balai (☎ 622-541; *Pudeto 169; singles/doubles US$26/33)* provides a good deal of artistic creativity to go with its rooms, some of which could use a bit more light. Without being cluttered, this hotel has a great assortment of antique trinkets. Of note is an intricately carved alerce tabletop showing a flour-making *minga*.

Top End Hard to miss, **Hotel Galeón Azul** (☎ 622-543, fax 622-567; *Libertad 751; singles/doubles US$41/50)* has garish yellow and blue trimmings. Inside, the design allows for lots of light and great views of the harbor and the adjacent museum's garden, but the walls, some attractively shingled, are somewhat thin, and the bathrooms are small.

Hostería Ancud (☎ 622-340; ⓦ *www .hosteriancud.com; San Antonio 30; singles/doubles US$53/70)* is Ancud's top hotel, overlooking the sea and Fuerte San Antonio. Rooms are well appointed with bay views and sparkling clean bathrooms.

Places to Eat

Looking like a dark pub, **Retro Pub** (☎ 626-410; *Maipú 615; mains US$3-6)* whips up some tasty meals. There's something for everyone, including Tex-Mex, which is good but overpriced. Best value are the hamburgers and pastas. Retro is also a fun nightspot.

La Hormiguita (☎ 626-999; Pudeto 44; sandwiches US$2-4) is a bakery that serves pies and sandwiches (good veggie choices), fruit juices and real coffee.

El Sacho (☎ 622-260; Mercado Municipal; mains US$3-6), between Libertad and Blanco Encalada, is a basic comedor known mostly for heaping plates of seafood. The cazuela chilota, a tasty stew, or curanto are good options.

Polo Sur (☎ 622-200; Costanera 630; mains US$6-8), in its namesake hotel, satisfies patrons with large fish plates with a variety of sauces to choose from. Start off with machas a la parmesana and round it all out with a real espresso.

La Pincoya (☎ 622-613; Prat 61; mains US$6-9), most notable for its views, is a more formal affair serving the usual dishes.

Kurantón (☎ 622-216; Prat 94; curanto US$6.50) is the best place to go for its signature dish of curanto, served daily, but it also has a fair selection of fish and shellfish. The historic photos that cover the walls are worth a look.

Pedersen Salón de Té (☎ 622-642; Sargento Aldea 470; slice of cake US$1), overlooking the bustling port, makes one of the best raspberry cheesecakes in all of Chile. Pedersen is a great place to while away a rainy afternoon in Ancud.

Shopping
Crafts markets abound, and it's all decent quality. Try the stands around the Mercado Municipal, the seasonal Feria Artesanal set up along the Costanera, or the artisans at the museum. Woolens are the best bet.

Getting There & Away
The **Terminal de Buses** (☎ 624-017; Aníbal Pinto & Marcos Vera) is east of downtown. A taxi to or from the terminal to Av Costanera in downtown costs US$1.50.

Cruz del Sur (☎ 622-265) has the most departures to Chiloé's more southerly cities, with departures about every hour, and to cities on the Panamericana to the north, with three daily departures to Santiago. Many other bus companies have similar offerings. Queilén Bus goes to Punta Arenas every Tuesday morning at 8:30am. But travelers bound to most southerly regions beyond Chiloé and to Bariloche, Argentina, will do better to take buses from Puerto Montt.

Sample fares and times are as follows:

destination	duration in hours	cost
Concepción	6	US$21
Castro	1¼	US$2
Osorno	3½	US$6
Puerto Montt	2½	US$3.50
Punta Arenas	48	US$46
Quellón	2½	US$3.50
Santiago	16	US$27-50
Temuco	5	US$11
Valdivia	5	US$9

Chiloé's more rural destinations are serviced by buses that leave across the street from the Esso gas station about 100 meters from the corner of Montt and Prat. Buses Mar Brava, which leave from a desolate area of Anibal Pinto, has three buses weekly to Chepu, near the northern end of Parque Nacional Chiloé (US$1.25). There's service to Quemchi (US$1.50, 1½ hours), Linao and Tenuán.

PINGÜINERA PUÑIHUIL
Three islands off the coast of Puñihuil, on the Pacific Ocean, are breeding grounds for Magellanic and Humbolt penguins. These islands are now monitored by **Fundación Otway** (☎ 065-278-500; otway@telsur.cl), the non-profit organization managed by German volunteers that for years has protected the penguins north of Punta Arenas. Zodiac tours to get a closer glimpse of the birds cost US$6.50, or US$10 for an extended tour to also view sea lions. All-weather gear is provided. The small café and information center is a good place to warm up afterward. Many travel agencies in Ancud organize excursions to the site.

QUEMCHI
☎ 65
Often mist-covered, out-of-the-way Quemchi has a host of curious architecture and colorful skiffs silently bobbing in its protected inlet. The enclosed topography made this a favorite port for logging boats in bygone years. Now, in summer months, a **tourist kiosk** sets up on the plaza. Quemchi, founded in 1881, is 65km from Ancud and 67km from Castro.

Residencial Chiloé (☎ 691-220; Pedro Montt 241; per person US$4), in front of the fire station, is a cheap spot, so don't expect much; ask for rooms in the newer section.

Hospedaje Costanera (☎ *691-230; Diego Bahamonde 141; singles with shared/private bath US$6/9)* is an excellent deal, with comfortable beds, loads of light and views of the inlet. El Chejo (☎ *691-490; Diego Bahamonde 251)* has the best table in town for fish cooked to order, plus locally made fruit liqueurs.

Buses and *colectivos* make the trip to Ancud and Castro.

TENAÚN

Tiny Tenaún, founded in 1838 and 56km north of Castro, is little more than one main street paralleling a long rocky beach. But the unique architecture makes it worth the visit; the **church** (1842) steals the show, with three colorful blue towers and unique stars and trimmings.

Familia Vásquez Montaña (☎ *09-647-6750; lunches US$5, rooms US$10)*, part of the Agroturismo Network, is just past the church. An excellent cook, Mirella is serious about making sure her guests enjoy the multicourse meals she prepares. Call ahead.

Buses run between Castro or Ancud and Tenaún approximately three times daily (US$2, 1½ hours).

DALCAHUE

☎ 65 • pop 10,000

Artisans from offshore islands travel great distances for Dalcahue's Sunday morning **feria artesanal**, which is divided into stands of artisanship – woolens, wooden crafts and basketry – and a much larger representation of utilitarian clothing and kitchen gadgets. Traditionally the most important on Chiloé, the nonchalant market is the primary attraction of the small fishing port of Dalcahue, 20km northeast of Castro. The nearby **Museo Histórico** has a mishmash of artifacts – fossils, stuffed birds and antique household implements – that helps relate the anthropological history of the area, while the neoclassical **Iglesia Dalcahue** *(Plaza de Armas)*, with Doric columns, dates from 1858.

The town takes its name from the *dalca*, a type of canoe in which indigenous Chilotes went to sea. Dalcahue is the gateway to Isla Quinchao, one of archipelagic Chile's more accessible and interesting islands. The **tourist office**, a small storefront on the *costanera* alongside the Entel call center, keeps erratic hours.

Places to Stay & Eat

Residencial Playa (☎ *641-397; Rodríguez 009; per person US$5)* is the best budget choice. Some beds sag, but in general the simple rooms with shared bath are perfectly adequate and clean. The downstairs restaurant appears to be a local favorite; its basic menu includes curanto (US$5.50) and a plate of shellfish (US$3-5).

Residencial San Martín (☎ *641-207; San Martín 001; per person US$5)*, opposite the plaza, is another decent place. Most bedrooms have windows and small touches like lace-trimmed sheets, but some beds resemble hammocks. Check rooms first, and ask for hot water. Breakfast is an extra US$1.50.

Hospedaje Mary *(Teniente Merino 010; camping/rooms per person US$1.50/5)*, east of the church, may have backyard camping. Otherwise you can stay in the small and quiet home.

Hotel La Isla (☎ *641-241; Av Mocopulli 113; singles/doubles US$28/33)* is the fanciest place in town, but the service does not attest to its unearned three-star status.

Mercado Municipal *(mains US$3-5)* has simple *cocinerías* open everyday. These places are bigger on atmosphere than on quality; stout women pack folks in at wraparound tables that face cluttered kitchens full of curanto and steaming bowls of cazuela.

Dalca (☎ *641-222; US$3-7)*, above the boat dock and overlooking the main pier, puts the emphasis on quality, with large portions of well-prepared shellfish, or try a flavorful *caldillo*.

Getting There & Away

The main bus terminal is on Freire opposite O'Higgins, but buses also drop off and pick up at the market. **Dalcahue Expreso** *(Freire)*, between San Martín and Eugenio, has half-hourly buses to Castro (US$0.50) weekdays, but fewer on weekends. Taxi colectivos, leaving from Freire and O'Higgins, charge US$1 for the half-hour trip. **Cruz del Sur** *(San Martín 102)* runs buses to Puerto Montt twice daily (US$5).

The motor launch *Ultima Esperanza* connects Dalcahue with the outlying Islas Chauques at 2pm Tuesday and Friday. Ferries leave continuously to Isla Quinchao. Pedestrians go free (but take a bus to reach island destinations), and cars cost US$6 (roundtrip).

ISLA QUINCHAO
☎ 65

The elongated offshore island of Quinchao, easily accessed via a short ferry crossing from Dalcahue, is a hilly patchwork of pasturelands punctuated by small villages. A good road (paved in most parts) runs the length of the island. A good time to go is the first week of February to catch the **Encuentro Folklórico de las Islas del Archipiélago**, held in Achao and attracting musical groups from throughout the archipelago. Held simultaneously, the **Muestra Gastronómica y Artesanal** gives you a chance to taste traditional Chilote specialties and view demonstrations of antique machinery, like apple presses and grain mills.

Curaco de Vélez

Midway between Dalcahue and Achao, Curaco de Vélez dates from 1660, when a Jesuit mission was built there. The village is a treasure of vernacular Chilote architecture, including eight traditional water mills.

At the beach, look for signs to an **open-air restaurant** where oysters go for US$0.25 to US$0.50 each. Salmon, fresh bread and fries are also available, but most people come here to huddle around the large trunk tables and slurp down buckets of oysters with lemon and salt, followed with a good dent to a wine bottle and a long siesta on the hammocks.

Buses between Achao and Dalcahue stop in Curaco.

Achao

The village of Achao, 22km southeast of Dalcahue, is a charming destination with a landmark church, outstanding vernacular architecture and fine food and accommodations. People from nearby islands come to Achao to sell their wares and produce, creating quite a buzz of activity along its small jetty.

The small **tourist kiosk** (cnr Serrano & Ricardo Jara; open 9am to 8pm in the summer only) may help organize excursions to offshore Isla Llingua (see later in this section). The **post office** (Serrano) is between Ricardo Jara and Progreso, and there's a telephone office on Pasaje Freire, south of Pedro Montt. There's also a **hospital** (cnr Progreso & Riquelme).

Crowned by a 25m tower, sided with alerce shingles and held together with wooden pegs rather than nails, Achao's 18th-century Jesuit **Iglesia Santa María de Loreto de Achao**, on the south side of the Plaza de Armas, is now a national monument. Over the past few years, the church has been slowly restored with new wood juxtaposed to the old, but staying very truthful to the design. Open daily in the high season; in the off-season knock on the parochial door. Note the one pillar built on top of a boulder near the entrance.

The impressive little **Museo de Achao** (Delicias & Amunátegui; admission US$0.50; 10am-1pm & 2:30pm-6pm daily in summer only) highlights aspects of the Chono of Achao and other indigenous groups in Chiloé. Wood products, weavings, stones and plants used for tinting materials are all elegantly presented with informative material (Spanish only) including relevant vocabulary.

The **Grupo Artesanal Llingua**, artisans from the nearby Isla Llingua, have a well-stocked market of their crafts behind the tourist kiosk.

Places to Stay & Eat In the busy summer season, there's informal camping – for free or negligible cost – on Delicias between Sargento Aldea and Serrano.

Hospedaje São Paulo (☎ 661-245; Serrano 052; per person US$6.50) has the cheapest rooms, which are above a slightly divey restaurant. Service tends to be a bit apathetic, but it's cheap.

Hostal Plaza (☎ 661-283; Amunátegui 20; per person US$6.50), across from the plaza, is Achao's best budget spot. Rooms come with shared bath and breakfast, and the owner is helpful and kind.

Hospedaje Sol y Lluvias (☎ 253-996, 661-383; Gerónimo de Urmeneta 215; rooms with shared/private bath US$10/26) may be Achao's best choice. It's friendly, with comfortable, spotless rooms and a superb breakfast.

Hostería La Nave (☎ 661-219; Sargento Aldea 01; singles with shared bath US$9-13, doubles with private bath US$28) faces right onto the rocky beach. Rooms in the newer area of the hotel are better (and a bit pricier), although the bathrooms are rather tiny. Aim for a room with a bay view. The downstairs restaurant has an overly ambitious menu and service appears slow.

Mar y Velas (☎ 661-375; Serrano 02; mains US$5-8), at the foot of the pier, is always active with locals and visitors enjoying a bounty of outstanding seafood, efficient service and views of the activity below.

Getting There & Away The bus terminal is at the corner of Miraflores and Zañartu, a block south of the church. Buses run daily to Dalcahue and Castro every 15 to 20 minutes. There are also taxi colectivos to Castro.

Isla Llingua

Half an hour from Achao by launch, Isla Llingua is a small island whose century-old church is a local landmark (legend says that Chono Indians burned the first two churches on the site to get the nails). Well-trained local guides take visitors past Chono shell middens, into the church and its bell tower, and up the local mirador for a panorama of the tiny settlement. The island's artisans, who specialize in basketry, have moved most of their work to Achao.

CASTRO

☎ 65 • pop 39,000

Castro, 90km south of Ancud, is possibly the most popular destination in Chiloé, in large part due to the waterfront palafitos and the city's accessibility. The city also features the most colorful church on the island, the best crafts fair and a handful of decent museums. Founded in 1567 by Martín Ruiz de Gamboa, most of Castro sits on a bluff above its sheltered estuary. Castro is the capital of Chiloé province, and it is the island's transportation hub and largest city. On the other hand, for those looking to experience the quintessential Chilote lifestyle of small villages and pasturelands, Castro can feel a bit too much like any other mainland Chilean town.

Information

The small **tourist kiosk** (Plaza de Armas; open 9am-9pm daily in summer, 10am-6pm Mon-Sat rest of the year) distributes some moderately helpful brochures and maps and a limited list of lodging. **Conaf** (☎ 632-289; Gamboa 424) has details on Parque Nacional Chiloé.

For the best exchange rates, try **Julio Barrientos** (☎ 625-079; Chacabuco 286) or **Cambio de Monedas** (Gamboa 411). ATMs can be found at most banks around the Plaza de Armas, such as Banco de Chile.

The **post office** (O'Higgins 388) is on the west side of the Plaza de Armas. Place calls at **Entel** (O'Higgins 480). **Turismo Isla Grande** (☎ 632-384; Thompson 241) organizes excursions around the area and can help with

Historic wooden churches dot Chiloé.

Navimag bookings. **Turismo Pehuén** (☎ 632-361; W www.pehuentour.com; Blanco Encalada 299) comes recommended for well-organized tours to nearby islands and Parque Nacional Chiloé, plus some horse-riding tours.

Anay Libros (Serrano 357) has a selection of historical books.

To get the clothes cleaned, try **Lavandería Unic** (Gamboa 594) or **Clean Center** (Serrano 490).

The **Hospital de Castro** (☎ 632-445; Freire 852) is at the foot of Cerro Millantuy.

Iglesia San Francisco de Castro

Built in 1906 at the north end of the plaza, the Iglesia San Francisco assaults the vision with its gaudy exterior paint job – salmon with violet trim. The varnished-wood interior is more soothing, despite some gruesome portrayals of the crucifixion and other religious statuary. Termites and dry rot have begun to cause problems for this landmark wooden structure.

Locomotora Ancud-Castro

Near Hotel Unicornio Azul, you can take a look at the original, German-made locomotive (Av Pedro Montt) from the narrow-gauge railway that connected Castro with Ancud via Pupelde, Coquiao, Puntra, Butalcura,

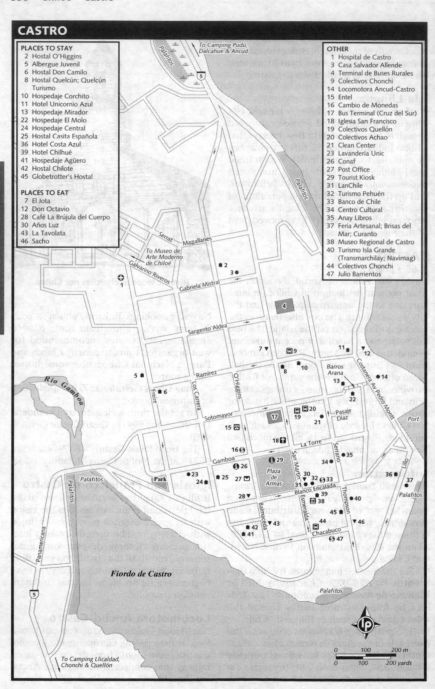

CASTRO

PLACES TO STAY
2 Hostal O'Higgins
5 Albergue Juvenil
6 Hostal Don Camilo
8 Hostal Quelcún; Quelcún Turismo
10 Hospedaje Corchito
11 Hotel Unicornio Azul
13 Hospedaje Mirador
22 Hospedaje El Molo
24 Hospedaje Central
25 Hostal Casita Española
36 Hotel Costa Azul
39 Hotel Chilhué
41 Hospedaje Agüero
42 Hostal Chilote
45 Globetrotter's Hostal

PLACES TO EAT
7 El Jota
12 Don Octavio
28 Café La Brújula del Cuerpo
30 Años Luz
43 La Tavolata
46 Sacho

OTHER
1 Hospital de Castro
3 Casa Salvador Allende
4 Terminal de Buses Rurales
9 Colectivos Chonchi
14 Locomotora Ancud-Castro
15 Entel
16 Cambio de Monedas
17 Bus Terminal (Cruz del Sur)
18 Iglesia San Francisco
19 Colectivos Quellón
20 Colectivos Achao
21 Clean Center
23 Lavandería Unic
26 Conaf
27 Post Office
29 Tourist Kiosk
31 LanChile
32 Turismo Pehuén
33 Banco de Chile
34 Centro Cultural
35 Anay Libros
37 Feria Artesanal; Brisas del Mar; Curanto
38 Museo Regional de Castro
40 Turismo Isla Grande (Transmarchilay; Navimag)
44 Colectivos Chonchi
47 Julio Barrientos

To Camping Pudú, Dalcahue & Ancud

Palafitos

To Museo de Arte Moderno de Chiloé

Río Gamboa

Palafitos

Park

Palafitos

Panamericana

5

Fiordo de Castro

Palafitos

To Camping Llicaldad, Chonchi & Quellón

Serrat
Magallanes
Gálvarino Riveros
Gabriela Mistral
Sargento Aldea
Ramírez
Los Carrera
Freire
O'Higgins
Sotomayor
San Martín
Gamboa
La Torre
Blanco Encalada
Esmeralda
Balmaceda
Chacabuco
Thompson
Serrano
Barros Arana
Costanera Av. Pedro Montt
Pasaje Díaz
Plaza de Armas
Port
Lillo

CHILOÉ

0   100   200 m
0   100   200 yards

Mocopulli and Pid Pid. According to legend, the only difference between 1st and 3rd class was that the conductor would order 3rd-class passengers off the train to help push the locomotive over the crest of even gentle slopes. Service on this line ended with the massive earthquake and tsunami of 1960.

Palafitos

All around Castro, shingled houses on stilts stretch out into estuaries and lagoons; at high tide, resident fishermen tie their boats to the stilts, but from the street these houses resemble any other in town. This truly singular architecture, now protected as a national historic monument, can be seen along Costanera Pedro Montt at the north end of town, at the *feria artesanal* on the south end (where some are restaurants) and at both ends of the bridge across the Río Gamboa, where the Panamericana heads south to Quellón.

Museo Regional de Castro

In attractive quarters half a block south of the Plaza de Armas, the regional museum (*Esmeralda; admission free; open 9:30am-8pm Mon-Sat, 10:30am-1pm Sun Jan-Feb, 9:30am-1pm & 3pm-6:30pm Mon-Sat, 10:30am-1pm Sun Mar-Dec*) houses an idiosyncratic but well-organized collection of Huilliche relics, traditional farm implements and exhibits on the evolution of Chilote urbanism. Its B&W photographs of the 1960 earthquake are remarkable.

Museo de Arte Moderno de Chiloé

Castro's spacious modern art museum (*☎ 635-454; Parque Municipal; open 10am-8pm daily in summer*), in an imaginatively recycled warehouse, features innovative works by contemporary Chilean artists, many of them Chilotes. The underfunded museum is located at the west end of Galvarino Riveros at the northwest end of town.

Feria Artesanal

Castro's waterfront market is open daily and has a fine selection of woolen ponchos and sweaters, caps, gloves and basketry. Note the bundles of dried seaweed and the rhubarblike *nalca*, both part of the local diet, and the blocks of peat used for fuel. The market contains several inexpensive seafood restaurants.

Special Events

In late January, the Festival de Huaso Chilote pays homage to local cowboys. And in mid-February, Castro celebrates the Festival Costumbrista, a weeklong party with folk music and dance and traditional foods.

Places to Stay

Budget Castro has an abundance of inexpensive hospedajes, mostly along San Martín and O'Higgins, and their immediate side streets.

Camping Llicaldad (*☎ 635-080; Fiordo de Castro; 4-person sites US$13*) is 5km south of town, off the Panamericana.

Camping Pudú (*☎ 632-268; 2-person sites US$9*), 10km north of Castro on the road to Dalcahue, has sites with reasonable facilities but is a bit far out of town.

Albergue Juvenil (*☎ 632-766; Freire 610; per person US$2.50; open summer only*), in the Gimnasio Fiscal, offers floor space; bring your sleeping bag.

The eastern end of Sotomayor turns into the wide concrete staircase Barros Arana, which could earn the moniker Steps of Home – just about every house along it has turned into a hospedaje. Rates are pretty much equal (around US$9 per person); only quality and vacancy vary. **Hospedaje Mirador** (*☎ 633-795; Barros Arana 127*) has some seaside views, great showers, large breakfasts and a warm atmosphere. **Hospedaje El Molo** (*☎ 635-026; Barros Arana 140*) is across the street from Mirador.

Hospedaje Central (*☎ 637-026; Los Carrera 316; per person US$7*) has spotless but small rooms with firm beds and shared bath, with breakfast included.

Globetrotter's Hostal (*☎ 09-310-1786; Thompson 262; dorm beds US$6-8*) provides the budget backpacker with the usual one-stop-spot: Kitchen, dorm beds, laundry and Internet are all offered in a tightly packed parcel.

Hospedaje Corchito (*☎ 632-806; Ramirez 251 & 240; singles with shared/private bath US$8/12*) provides comfortable rooms in secure grounds and amicable management. Breakfast, included, is marginal.

Hotel Costa Azul (*☎ 632-440; Lillo 67; per person US$8.50*), across from the Feria Artesanal, provides attractive views from its rooms, but the ocean breezes may make it damp and cold.

Hospedaje Agüero (☎ 635-735; Chacabuco 449; per person US$10) is recommended and enjoys a quiet location with views of the sea and Castro's southern palafitos. Rates include breakfast.

Hostal O'Higgins (☎ 632-016; O'Higgins 831 Interior; doubles US$20), set away from the road, has quiet, clean bedrooms and more than enough bathrooms to share. It's a great option and breakfast is included.

Hostal Chilote (☎ 635-021; Aldunate 456; singles with shared/private bath US$9/13) is a fun and lively spot managed by a lovely family. Rooms are spotless and spacious, and breakfast, served in the family kitchen and included in the rates, gets the morning going.

Mid-Range The friendly **Hostal Quelcún** (☎ 632-396; San Martín 581; singles with shared bath US$7.50, singles/doubles US$23/30) has some bargain rooms that are cramped but adequate. Behind the main house, the pricier rooms – with private bath and firm beds – are clustered around an interior rock garden and lack outside light.

Hostal Casita Española (☎ 635-186; Los Carrera 359; singles/doubles US$33/41) offers attractive rooms with private bath in a shady garden setting. The owners tender congeniality and are most helpful. Breakfast is included.

Hotel Chilhué (☎ 632-596; Blanco Encalada 278; singles/doubles with shared bath US$16/20, with private bath US$21/25) is a pleasant and central option. It doesn't have the most personality, but the service is efficient, and the rooms are comfortable and well maintained.

Hostal Don Camilo (☎ 632-180, fax 635-533; Ramírez 566; singles/doubles US$36/40) is a labyrinthine place with simple, standard rooms, all well maintained, that apparently attracts the visiting business set. They also have cheaper singles with shared bath (US$15). The adjacent restaurant is well known.

Five kilometers by boat from Castro, **Refugio Peuque** (☎ 631-600; e peuque@ chiloeweb.com; up to 6 people US$100) offers a singularly unique option – an ample, bayside, fully equipped cabin with its own beach that is surrounded by native trees. Get away from it all for a day or two. Boat transportation is arranged upon booking.

Top End On the waterfront, **Hotel Unicornio Azul** (☎ 632-359, fax 632-808; Pedro Montt 228; singles/doubles US$45/55) has Castro's best and most architecturally oddball accommodations. Chilco pink paint and unicorn art fill the common areas and the simple but attractive rooms, some of which have exceptional views.

Places to Eat
The palafito restaurants at the waterfront feria artesanal on the south end of town have the heartiest servings for the fewest pesos. **Brisas del Mar** and **Curanto** both have fixed-price lunches for about US$3.50, as well as more expensive specialties.

El Jota (☎ 633-873; San Martín 650; snacks US$0.50-1.50), near the bus terminal, is a local spot for a quick coffee and empanada or milcao breakfast.

Años Luz (☎ 532-700; San Martín 309; mains US$4.50-8; closed Sun) enlightens Castro's scene with an attractive bar made from a fishing boat, though it comes off as a little too hip and pretentious. With efficient service and creative, somewhat pricey cuisine – including exceptional salads, veggie entrées and tarte Tatin – it attracts a youthful gringo crowd.

Café La Brújula del Cuerpo (O'Higgins 308) always manages to be crowded, but the service is dreadful, the place smoky and its fast-food fixes not up to par. Best bet is an ice cream sundae.

La Tavolata (☎ 09-370-3880; Balmaceda 245; pastas/pizzas US$3-5) offers a great escape from fish: pizza and homemade pastas, all homemade and zesty. The owner also offers vegetarian raviolis and lasagna.

Sacho (☎ 632-079; Thompson 213; mains US$5-9) is considered one of the best restaurants on the island, and certainly it is one of the most formal and attractive, with crisp linens and sweeping views of the estuary. Its famous curanto – one serving easily feeds two – is available daily in summer; the rest of the year by request only. Fixed-price lunches are a good deal.

Don Octavio (☎ 632-855; Pedro Montt 261; mains US$6-9), across from the Hotel Unicornio Azul, is another rather pricey local favorite, in an attractive wooden circular palafito. The chefs here offer an extensive menu of consistently well-prepared seafood and main courses. It's a fine choice for a light appetizer and glass of chilled white wine.

Entertainment

Casa Salvador Allende (*Gabriela Mistral 357*) holds a Saturday night *peña* (folk music performance). **Centro Cultural** (*Serrano 320*) shows movies on the weekends.

Getting There & Around

Castro is the major hub for bus traffic on Chiloé. There are two main bus terminals: The municipal one, **Terminal de Buses Rurales** (*San Martín near Sargento Aldea*), has the most service to rural destinations around the island and some long-distance service. The second one, operated by **Cruz del Sur** (☎ *632-389; San Martín 486*), also houses Transchiloé and Turíbus and focuses on transportation to the main Chilote cities (Quellón and Ancud) and long-distance service, but Arriagada buses to Dalcahue and Isla Quinchao leave from here. From the municipal terminal, buses depart for Huillinco and Cucao, the entrance to Parque Nacional Chiloé on the west coast. Since most of these buses leave early in the morning and return in the early evening, it's possible to visit the park on a day trip. The fare is about US$2 one-way. Service is very limited off-season.

For those willing, you can get to Punta Arenas from Castro (via Puerto Montt and Argentina). Between Turíbus and Queilén, buses leave daily at 7 am, except on Sunday. For Bariloche, Argentina, Turíbus has twice-weekly departures. Sample fares and travel times are:

destination	duration in hours	cost
Ancud	1	US$2
Bariloche (Ar)	12	US$21
Concepción	12	US$23
Puerto Montt	3	US$5
Punta Arenas	36	US$46-80
Quellón	2	US$1.50
Santiago	19	US$29-48
Temuco	8	US$15

For nearby destinations, taxi colectivos provide a faster alternative. **Colectivos Chonchi** leave from Chacabuco near Esmeralda (US$1) as well as from Ramírez near San Martín. **Colectivos Quellón** leave from Sotomayor and San Martín (US$3), as do **Colectivos Achao** (US$1).

Catamaranes del Sur (☎ *267-533; Diego Portales 510, Puerto Montt*) has passenger-only ferries to Chaitén at 9am Tuesday and

Thursday in January and February only. One-way is US$20, roundtrip US$36. The ferry leaves from the port.

CHONCHI

☎ 65 • pop 12,000

Chonchi, 23km south of Castro and nestled on a hill above Canal Lemuy, was a pirates' delight and a port for the export of cypress. Founded in 1767, the town is known as the Ciudad de los Tres Pisos (City of Three Floors) for its abrupt topography, but its more colorful indigenous name literally means 'slippery earth.' It's a small spot, but with ferries to nearby islands and loads of charm, Chonchi makes it easy to stay longer than planned.

Most tourist services can be found along Centenario, including a **tourist office** (*cnr Sargento Candelaria & Centenario; open 9am-7pm daily Jan-Mar*).

The **Fiesta Criolla Chonchi**, in early February, has artisanship, culinary exhibits, music, folk dancing and sporting events.

Things to See & Do

Chonchi's landmark **Iglesia San Carlos de Chonchi**, with multiple arches, dates from the mid-19th century. Winds up to 60 km per hour knocked down the three-story tower in 2002, which will hopefully be restored to its previous elegance.

El Museo Viviente de las Tradiciones Chonchinas (☎ *671-214, Centenario 116; admission by donation; open 10am-6pm Oct-Mar*) exhibits an impressive collection of donations from Chonchi's citizens, smartly displayed to give a sense of a neoclassic Chilota household, including an original-style kitchen. Also of note is the collection of wooden door locks and a terrifying hair-curling machine.

Check in shop windows (strangely enough, often shoe stores) for signs of **'licor de oro'**; manufacturing this fermented cow milk liqueur is the town's cottage industry. Testing out different concoctions is a fun experience, but note that if you enter a store (or sometimes the store owner's house) and enjoy more than one tasting, you'll be expected to buy a bottle, even if you don't really like the stuff. You'll find a variety of tastes, created from infusing the liqueur with a variety of locally grown herbs. If you just want to taste and not run the risk of buying, try it out at a restaurant or bar.

CHILOÉ

Places to Stay & Eat

Camping los Manzanos (☎ 671-263; Pedro Aguirre Cerda 709; sites for up to 4 people US$9) has covered cooking areas and hot showers.

Hospedaje Guapi's (☎ 671-257; Andrade 297; per person US$6) offers very basic lodging with some sagging beds. When the kitchen isn't busy, lodgers can make simple meals. Breakfast is US$1; lunches cost US$3.50.

Hospedaje El Mirador (☎ 671-351; Ciriaco Alvaréz 198; per person US$7), in a white shingled house with kindly owners, has some rooms with bay views. It's an excellent value, with breakfast included.

Hospedaje La Esmeralda (☎ 671-954; e gredycel@entelchile.net; Irarrázabal s/n; bunks US$5.50, rooms per person US$7.50-10), on the beachfront, has become a destination all its own, thanks to Canadian expat Carl Gredy. The gregarious owner entertains with stories of Chonchi lore, organizes group dinners, will show you his mussel harvesting hobby, rents out fishing gear, loans out a small rowboat, suggests day trips, and knows heaps about the island and how to get around.

Hotel Huildín (☎ 671-388, fax 635-030; Centenario 102; singles with shared/private bath US$10/21) is a ho-hum labyrinthine place catering mainly to larger traveling groups. The somewhat dark rooms all open to a main hallway, and boxy bathrooms are awkwardly built into the rooms.

Hospedaje Chonchi (☎ 671-288; O'Higgins 379; singles with shared bath US$6.50, doubles with private bath US$20) has large rooms and extra blankets, but some beds sag and street noise seeps in. Rooms with private bath are off the common areas.

Posada El Antiguo Chalet (☎ 671-221; Irarrázaval s/n; singles/doubles with shared bath US$30/41, doubles with private bath US$50), dating from 1935 and built of native timber, is in a quiet location. Its cozy attic rooms have lots of woolen rugs and beds are piled high with Chilote woolen blankets. Even if the price doesn't suit the wallet, the attractive lobby and bar are fine places to relax and enjoy a small glass of some of the better licor de oro in town.

El Trébol (☎ 671-203; Irarrázaval 187; mains US$4-8) is considered the better place in town for basic fish and shellfish dishes. In the **mercado municipal**, try locally recommended cocinería No 3. **La Quila** (☎ 671-389; Andrade 183; lunch US$3.50) has fixed-price lunches and the usual fish-with-a-side-dish menu.

Getting There & Away

Opposite the Plaza de Armas, **Cruz del Sur** (☎ 671-218) and Transchiloé have several buses daily between Castro and Chonchi. Taxi colectivos (US$1) are also numerous and leave from around the plaza. To get to Quellón, you'll need to first go back to Castro and take a bus from there.

Surprisingly, considering what would seem like a very obvious route, getting to Parque Nacional Chiloé is not quite as structured. There is a bus service (US$2, 1½ hours), but it tends to be sporadic and may not run enough buses necessary to meet demand. Check around for the latest (for instance, at Hospedaje La Esmeralda, above).

There are free launches to the port of Ichuac on Isla Lemuy. The ferry *El Caleuche* leaves every half-hour between 8am and 8pm Monday to Saturday from Puerto Huichas, 5km to the south; on Sunday and in the off-season, service is hourly. The ferry lands at Chulchuy, with connections to Puqueldón.

PN CHILOÉ

Protecting extensive stands of native coniferous and evergreen forest, plus a long and almost pristine Pacific coastline, the 43,000-hectare Parque Nacional Chiloé (admission US$1.50) is about 30km west of Chonchi and 54km west of Castro. Within the park and along the eastern perimeter are a number of Huilliche communities, some of which manage campsites within the park. There are three sections: The northern sector, called Chepu and including Isla Metalqui (which has a sea lion colony) is less easily accessible without a car; in addition, Metalqui is highly restricted because of ecological concerns. The middle sector, Abtao, is restricted by Conaf and accessible only by an 18km hike from the Pichihué property. The southern sector, Chanquín, is the most accessible, and it is the starting point for the most popular hikes.

Chiloé's fox and the reclusive pudú, which inhabits the shadowy forests of the contorted *tepú* tree, live in the more inaccessible parts of the park. Sightings are slim but not improbable.

Visitors are at the mercy of Pacific storms, so expect rain and lots of it. The mean annual rainfall at Cucao is 2200mm, and anyone planning more than an hour-long walk should have water-resistant footwear and woolen socks. Insect repellent is also a good idea.

Sector Chanquín

About 1km past the bridge from Cucao, Conaf's **visitor center** (open 9am-7pm daily) has displays on local flora and fauna, the indigenous Huilliche peoples, the early mining industry and island folklore. The **Sendero Interpretivo El Tepual**, a short 1km nature trail built with tree trunks, branches and short footbridges, loops through dense, gloomy forest. At the *desavío* (Y intersection) near the end of the trail, one can branch off to meet 'el artesano' Don Aníbal, who sells wooden spoons, *pan amasado* (homemade bread) and *chicha* (apple cider) from his farmhouse. The **Sendero Dunas de Cucao** starts from the visitor center and heads 2km through a remnant of coastal forest to a series of dunes behind a long, white sandy beach. After the earthquake of 1960, a tsunami obliterated much of the coastal plant cover, and the dunes advanced for some years, but they have since stabilized. The beach is attractive, but the cold water and dangerous currents make swimming inadvisable.

Day hikers or trekkers can follow the coast north on a 3km trail to **Lago Huelde**. The most popular route is the **Sendero Chanquín-Cole Cole**, a 20km hike (about five hours) along the coast, past Lago Huelde to Río Cole Cole, where there's camping and a rustic refugio. Travelers report that the camping area gets infested with sand fleas; it is possible to do the hike there and back in one long day. The hike continues another 8km north to **Río Anay**, passing through a stand of arrayán to arrive at another rustic refugio in reasonable shape.

Organized Tours

Centro de Ecoturismo (Sector Chanquín; ☎ 09-919-1314; w www.parquechiloe.com) rents kayaks on Lago Cucao for US$5/hour. It organizes kayaking and trekking combos from Rancho Grande, near Río Cole Cole, to Laguna Huelde (US$50, five hours), horse treks to Río Cole Cole (US$45, eight hours) and to Punta Pirulil via the beach (US$41, six hours). More adventurous trekkers can arrange a one-week trek along Ruta Abtao, involving a number of river crossings.

Places to Stay & Eat

Local families run numerous camping sites in and around Cucao and across the bridge between Cucao and the park entrance; rates are about US$2 per person.

Within the park, **Camping Chanquín** (campsites per person US$5, cabins up to 7 people US$63), about 200m beyond Conaf's visitor center, has secluded sites with running water, firewood, hot showers and toilets. In case of rain, there is a *fogón* (a covered area for bonfires) that fits about 20 tightly. The cabins are spacious and fully equipped, and all have exceptional views. One of the cabins is kept available for individuals to share (per person US$9).

Just before the campground, **La Madrigüera** (breakfast US$1.50-3) is a small café that takes the rusticity out of camping with hot mugs of coffee and cocoa in the morning and drinks at night.

The community that runs the rustic campsite and refugio at **Cole Cole** charges US$1.50 per person for either floor space or a campsite; there are no kitchen facilities.

Cucao has a number of hospedajes within easy walking distance of the park entrance. All of them can be reached by calling their cell phone numbers, but should the number not work or there's no service, leave a message through Cucao's single **public telephone** (☎ 633-040). Half and full pension can be arranged ahead of time at most of them.

Hospedaje El Paraíso (☎ 09-296-5465; campsites per person US$1.50; rooms with shared bath US$9) is by far the best choice in Cucao, with an attentive owner, clean and cozy rooms and breakfast included. The camping, however, is exposed.

El Arrayán (☎ 09-219-3565; per person US$5) is across from the bus stop by the park entrance. Rooms in the main house are a bit better than those in the tight annex, which has its own wood stove. The cocinería serves sandwiches and basic meals, including breakfast (US$1.50).

Posada Cucao (☎ 09-219-3633; per person US$9), in a large rambling ranch house, lacks hospitality, the beds are flat, and the rooms are chilly. There's a small essentials market attached, and the breakfasts, included in the price, are a redeeming feature.

Getting There & Away

Cucao is 54km from Castro and 34km west of Chonchi via a bumpy gravel road, passable in all but the most inclement weather. There is regular bus transportation between Castro and Cucao. Schedules vary, but there are usually four to five buses daily (US$2.50). Service from Chonchi tends to be sporadic, but there's usually one bus per day in summer.

Buses Mar Brava has three buses weekly from Ancud to Chepu, at the northern end of the park (US$1.25).

QUELLÓN
☎ 65 • pop 21,000
The last outpost at the end of the Panamericana, 92km south of Castro, Quellón is, for travelers, most often a destination of necessity rather than desire. Personality it has, with piers full of activity – but some of it is unpleasant, as an unfortunate number of men drink too much and sack out on doorsteps. When the skies are clear, the best part of Quellón is the view of surrounding islands, including Cailín. For those who have been admiring Chilote vernacular architecture and churches, Quellón disappoints: The town began in 1905 as a logging port, so it doesn't have the style of Jesuit-founded towns.

Information
In summer, Quellón maintains an obliging **tourist kiosk** *(cnr Gómez García & Santos Vargas; open 9am-9pm daily Dec-Mar).*

Change money before coming to Quellón; **Banco del Estado** *(cnr Ladrilleros & Freire)* has an ATM. The **post office** *(22 de Mayo)* is between Ladrilleros and Santos Vargas. **Entel** *(cnr Ladrilleros & La Paz)* has long-distance service. **Ruck Zack** *(Ladrilleros 399)* is a laundry facility next to Los Suizos (see Places to Stay & Eat below). There's also the **Hospital de Quellón** *(☎ 681-443; Dr Ahués 305).*

Things to See & Do
Admiration for Chilote technological ingenuity, in the form of uniquely local artifacts fashioned with basic materials, is the rationale behind the **Museo Inchin Cuivi Ant (Nuestro Pasado)** *(Ladrilleros 225; admission US$1; open 9:30am-1:30pm & 2:30pm-8pm daily),* a surprisingly good museum. The outstanding explanatory panels are a bonus alongside displays of items like *cercos tejidos* (living fences; fences woven of living shrubs and trees), *bongos* (local watercraft resembling dalcas), flour mills, apple presses and sledges for moving heavy loads across soggy terrain.

The tourist kiosk has information on boats that go to the nearby islands. Boats leave from the pier farthest east of town to Cailín on Monday, Wednesday and Friday.

Places to Stay & Eat
Punta de Lapa, the spit of land southwest of downtown, has basic beach camping at **Centro Turístico Millaguén** *(☎ 681-166)* or 2km farther on at **Huillihuapi** *(☎ 09-527-3729).* Small shuttle buses access the area throughout the summer.

Club Deportivo Torino *(La Paz 316; per person US$1.50)* lets people sack out on its large wooden floor (bring your own pad) – it's a good spot when the rain kicks in.

Casa del Profesor *(☎ 681-516; La Paz & Santos Vargas; per person US$9)* is open summer months only, but is the best economy choice in town. It has quality mattresses, comfortable rooms and common areas, a laid-back environment and use of kitchen facilities. Run by a teacher's union, it gives priority to other teachers.

Hotel El Chico Leo *(☎ 681-567; Pedro Montt 325; singles with shared bath US$10; doubles with private bath US$30)* is an excellent choice with attentive staff, clean bright rooms and comfortable beds. It might get a bit loud from the popular and good restaurant below (lunches US$2.50-6), which specializes in all kinds of seafood and an impressive variety of sauces. A game of pool costs US$3 per hour.

Hotel Playa *(☎ 681-278; Pedro Montt 427; per person US$6),* on the waterfront, is the best budget hotel. The large rooms have wood paneling and clean shared bathrooms with hot water. Breakfast is not included.

Los Suizos *(☎ 681-787; e lossuizos@entel chile.net; Ladrilleros 399; singles/doubles US$20/25)* has comfortable and smartly decorated rooms, private bathrooms, heat and a Swiss-style breakfast. There's also laundry service and organized trips to neighboring islands in the summer. The equally cozy restaurant serves an intriguing variety of pasta dishes, Kashmir rice and other specialties (mains US$4-7).

Hostería Quellón & Melimoyu *(☎ 681-310; Pedro Montt 369; singles/doubles without view US$16/25, with view US$30/35)* are two moderate hotels joined together to create a rambling variety of rooms.

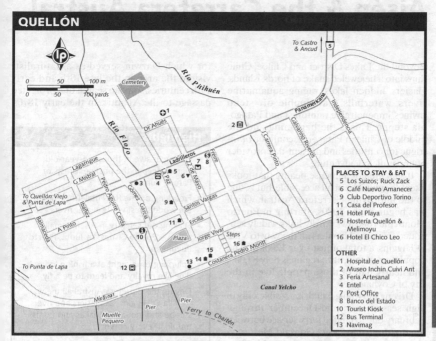

QUELLÓN

```
0    50    100 m
0    50    100 yards
```

To Castro & Ancud

Río Pitihuén

Río Flojo

Cemetery

Dr Ahués

Panamericana

Independencia

Calvarino Riveros

J. Carrera Pinto

Lagarrigue

G. Mistral

Pedro Aguirre Cerda

Ladrilleros

Freire

22 de Mayo

La Paz

Gómez Garcia

Ibañez

Balmaceda

A. Pinto

To Quellón Viejo & Punta de Lapa

Santos Vargas

Ercilla

Jorge Vivar

Steps

Plaza

Costanera Pedro Montt

To Punta de Lapa

Miramar

Pier

Pier

Muelle Pequeño

Ferry to Chaitén

Canal Yelcho

PLACES TO STAY & EAT
5 Los Suizos; Ruck Zack
6 Café Nuevo Amanecer
9 Club Deportivo Torino
11 Casa del Profesor
14 Hotel Playa
15 Hostería Quellón & Melimoyu
16 Hotel El Chico Leo

OTHER
1 Hospital de Quellón
2 Museo Inchin Cuivi Ant
3 Feria Artesanal
4 Entel
7 Post Office
8 Banco del Estado
10 Tourist Kiosk
12 Bus Terminal
13 Navimag

CHILOÉ

Café Nuevo Amanecer (☎ 682-026; 22 de Mayo 344; sandwiches US$3-5), with mirrored columns and a thumping stereo system, is more attractive as a nightspot, but it's still a decent place for an afternoon sandwich.

Getting There & Away

Buses to Castro (US$4, two hours) are frequent with Cruz del Sur and Transchiloé, which leave from the terminal at Aguirre Cerda and Miramar. There are also services to Puerto Montt (US$8, three hours) and taxi colectivos to Castro.

Navimag (Pedro Montt 457) sails *Alejandrina* to Chaitén Thursday at 3pm and Friday at 8am and midnight. Passenger rates for both are US$16 to US$21, bicycles US$10, motorcycles US$18, vehicles US$90.

Ferry schedules change seasonally, so you should verify departures at the Navimag office in Puerto Montt before planning your trip. Transmarchilay, which usually also operates a car ferry to Chaitén, suspended service at the end of 2002. Contact the Transmarchilay office in Puerto Montt for the current status of services.

Aisén & the Carretera Austral

Beyond the Lakes District and Chiloé, Chile thins into a bejeweled snake of fjords, islands, glaciers, hidden lakes, raging aquamarine rivers, waterfalls that tumble off steep ravines, impenetrable rainforest and Patagonia steppe. This is the beginning and the middle of Chilean Patagonia, conjurer of intrigue for centuries and present-day provider of unparalleled adventure.

It's an area of immense beauty that looks like it shouldn't be at all accessible, but is, due to the improving Carretera Austral, which was begun in the 1980s. Starting in Puerto Montt, the road awkwardly links widely separated towns and hamlets all the way to Villa O'Higgins, a total of just over 1200km. The population of the entire region is only 87,000, and nearly half of those people live in the city of Coyhaique.

Driving the whole length is possible only in high season from mid-December through February due to limited ferry service between Puerto Montt and Caleta Gonzalo. Most travelers opt to take a ferry from Puerto Montt or Chiloé to Chaitén or Puerto Chacabuco, fly to Chaitén or Coyhaique, or go overland via Argentina, accessing the region through Futaleufú. This section starts in Hornopirén and works down to Villa O'Higgins, offering routes both across and around Lago General Carrera.

History

For thousands of years, the Chonos and Alacalufes inhabited the intricate canals and islands, while their Tehuelche counterparts lived on the mainland steppes. The rugged geography of Aisén deterred European settlement for centuries – even after Francisco de Ulloa first set foot on the Península de Taitao in 1553. Fortune seekers believed the legendary 'City of the Caesars' to be in Trapananda, as Aisén was first known, but Jesuit missionaries from Chiloé were the first Europeans to explore the region intensively. In the late 17th century, Bartolomé Díaz Gallardo and Antonio de Vea came upon Laguna San Rafael and the Campo de Hielo Norte, the northern continental ice sheet.

A great many expeditions (including Captain Robert Fitzroy's British expedition

for which Darwin served as a naturalist) visited the area in the late 18th and early 19th centuries, some in search of a protected passage to the Atlantic. In the early 1870s,

Highlights

- Gazing in awe at thousand-year-old alerces deep in the pristine forests of Parque Pumalín

- Frolicking on the Río Futaleufú – one of the world's best white-water rivers

- Seeking out serenity in Aisén's small towns – Puerto Cisnes, La Junta, Puerto Puyuhuapi

- Splurging for a night at a fishing lodge to dine like royalty and learn to tie a fly

- Driving the Carretera Austral all the way to Villa O'Higgins, as glaciers and rivers, steppe and mountains, lakes and fjords unfold at every curve

OTHER MAPS
Aisén & the Carretera Austral
pages 346–347

Chaitén
page 351

Coyhaique
page 360

AISÉN

Chilean naval officer Enrique Simpson made the most thorough survey up to that time, mapping areas as far south as the Península de Taitao.

Not until the early 20th century did Chile actively promote colonization of the region, granting the Valparaíso-based Sociedad Industrial Aisén a long-term lease for exploitation of livestock and lumber. The company controlled nearly a million hectares in and around Coyhaique – and dominated the regional economy. Part of its legacy is the destruction of much of Aisén's native southern beech forest in a series of fires that raged for nearly a decade in the 1940s. Encouraged by a Chilean law that rewarded clearance with land titles, the company and colonists burned nearly three million hectares of lenga forest. While this burning was intentional, some fires raged out of control and the bleached trunks of downed trees now litter hillsides from Villa Mañihuales to Puerto Ibáñez.

Since the agrarian reform of the 1960s, the influence of the Sociedad and other large landowners has declined. The region is sparsely populated, most notably south of Coyhaique, an area that was devastated by the 1991 eruption of Volcán Hudson, which dumped tons of ash over thousands of square kilometers in both Chile and Argentina, ruining cropland and killing livestock by burying pasture grasses. Salmon farming has become a major economic activity, causing ecological disruption in some coastal areas, and the region's rivers are under threat from proposed hydroelectric projects on the Río Baker and the Río Futaleufú.

HORNOPIRÉN
☎ 65

Hornopirén, a dusty, humble outpost surrounded by brilliant scenery, is where the northernmost portion of Ruta 7 ends, making it the southern terminus of bus service from Puerto Montt. From here, a summer-only ferry operates to the ferry landing at Caleta Gonzalo in Parque Pumalín on Fiordo Reñihue, where the road continues south. A tranquil spot, Hornopirén is only slightly overrun by the obtrusive

---

Taking to the Highway, Austral-style

What cost an initial investment of US$300 million, took over 10 years to build and cost 11 workers their lives has become one of South America's best adventure road trips – the Carretera Austral, or Ruta 7. Part of the adventure is negotiating through the sometimes precarious parts of the road: Pinochet's plan to cut a highway through Aisén was not based on geographic common sense. To the north, ferry service is inadequate; through the middle, the harsh climate makes maintenance a nightmare (in Parque Nacional Queulat, a conspicuous road sign warns motorists not to stop for any reason in one 400m stretch where an ominous debris flow threatens to slither across the highway at any moment); while in the south, the road sits barely 1m above the flood-prone Río Baker, which carries the greatest flow of any Chilean river.

Trucks rumble up and down the road, forming in some places mogul-sized washboards, but increasingly the traffic seen kicking up dust is that of fishing lodge SUVs carrying determined anglers, adventure outfitters and pickups packed with backpackers. Each year sees more cyclists as well. While any economic benefit the road has brought to the area or the country is hard to gauge, the road has increased tourism to the region. It's a rollicking, rugged and fun road trip – just remember a few basics:

- Stop if someone looks like he or she might need help.
- Trucks tend to barrel past, almost knocking oncoming traffic off the road. Slow down until the dust clears and turn on the headlights.
- Always carry a spare tire (neumático) and make sure the vehicle has a car jack (una gata).
- Take extra water – for the vehicle and for you.
- Dependable petrol stations are in Hornopirén, Chaitén, Palena, La Junta, Puerto Puyuhuapi, Puerto Cisnes, Villa Mañihuales, Puerto Aisén, Puerto Chacabuco, Coyhaique, Puerto Guadal, Cochrane and Chile Chico. Fill up when you can, and carry extra if you'll be using lateral back roads.

AISÉN & THE CARRETERA AUSTRAL

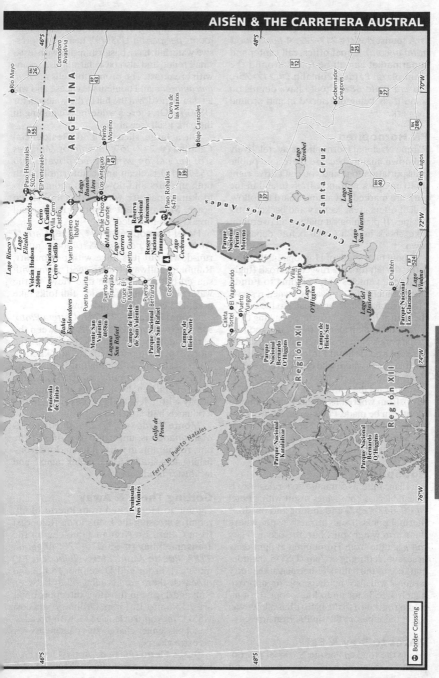

AISÉN & THE CARRETERA AUSTRAL

Salmon Multiexportador, and it's the closest entrance to Parque Nacional Hornopirén.

A **tourist kiosk** (☎ 217-222; e hualaihue@ hotmail.com), **Conaf office**, **call center** and **supermarket** can all be found around the main plaza. **Parque Pumalín** (☎ 217-256; Carrera Pinto 388) should have details on some trails being developed in and around the park.

PN Hornopirén

Parque Nacional Hornopirén stays relatively unknown, mainly because there's no public transportation to it, and you can't drive right up to any park entrance. Trails to and in the park are marked but at times hard to follow. Still, it offers great scenery and backcountry escapes. If planning on making an overnight hike, check in with Conaf before departing town.

About 6km south of Hornopirén, the road forks; the left fork is a rugged dirt road (high-clearance vehicles only) leading to Fundo Chaqueihua Alto, a privately owned reserve. (The right fork leads eventually to the end of the road at Pichanco.) Continue walking from here another 8km along a faintly marked trail to the park's entrance. Three kilometers from here is **Lago General Pinto Concha**, with a pristine beach where wild camping is possible. From there a poorly marked trail meanders north toward the town of Puelo (two to three days), from where bus connections to Puerto Montt can be made. Plans are in the works to connect Hornopirén with Parque Pumalín on the **Sendero Inexplorado**. Ask the Pumalín office for trail status.

Hot Springs

Isla Llancahué, a 45-minute boat ride away, is an established hot springs resort with a **hotel** (☎ 09-642-4857) and indoor and outdoor thermal pools. It's an attractive spot where the warm water spills into the ocean. They run a shuttle from Hornopirén at 3pm daily in season, returning at 7pm (US$15, includes entrance to the baths). Fishermen at the ferry terminal will also shuttle people for approximately US$35 for up to four people (not including entrance to the baths); this allows you to get there before the shuttle rush arrives.

Places to Stay & Eat

Along the road to Parque Nacional Horno-pirén are a number of campgrounds and cabins, a large site being at the Puente Horno-pirén. **Camping Vista Hermosa** (camping/ rooms per person US$5/9), near an impressive waterfall, has a basic campsite, with just a small toilet, and also basic farmhouse rooms with breakfast. The proprietor sells küchen, pan amasado and homemade cheese and will let you climb down the hill to the waterfall for US$0.75. Or, there's wilderness camping in the park itself (see above).

On a large slice of land, **Residencial Catalina** (☎ 217-359; Ingenieros Militares s/n; per person with shared/private bath US$10/15) is clean and comfortable, with both upstairs and downstairs rooms over-looking a pasture where cows and sheep graze. Management is very friendly, and breakfast is included.

Hotel Hornopirén (☎ 217-256; Carrera Pinto 388; per person US$10) looks rather run-down, but it is alive with personality. Rambling hallways lead to good rooms with shared bath, some with fine views of the water, and to outdoor patios. Tall folks take note: The ceilings are quite low.

Central Plaza (☎ 217-247; Carrera Pinto; 3-6 person cabins US$33-42), between the plaza and the water, rents decent cabins, the more expensive ones with TV and kitchen. The restaurant, with a fun outdoor seating area, serves up carne al disco (US$8): a large plate of chicken, lamb chops and sausages, or pay a little less and get only fish. There's a billiards hall attached.

Monte Verde (☎ 217-294; O'Higgins & Maldonado) is, unfortunately, one of the only restaurants in town. It has tacky décor – fishing nets, stuffed fish and pink lights – and lackluster food.

Getting There & Away

Getting to Hornopirén from Puerto Montt requires crossing the Estuario de Reloncaví from Caleta La Arena to Puelche on the **Transmarchilay** (☎ 65-270-420; Angelmó 2187, Puerto Montt) ferry Tehuelche (30 minutes). From mid-December to the end of March, there are 11 sailings daily between 8am and 11pm; in the other direction, times are 7:15am to 10:15pm. Ordinary cars cost US$11, pickup trucks US$13, with no additional passenger charge. Bus passengers pay no extra charge.

Buses Fierro (Plaza de Armas) has three buses daily to and from Puerto Montt (US$6, three hours), at 5:30am and 6:30am and 1:45pm.

Going south, Transmarchilay's ferry *Mailén* makes the six-hour trip to Caleta Gonzalo daily at 4pm; it operates in summer only – from the first week of January to the end of February. Other departures are sometimes scheduled, depending on demand. Passengers pay US$15, bicycles cost US$10, cars and pickups US$90 and motorcycles US$18.

PARQUE PUMALÍN
☎ 65

A remarkable forest conservation effort, Parque Pumalín protects 270,000 hectares of southern Chilean rainforest stretching from near Hornopirén in the north almost to Chaitén in the south. Chile's largest private park, Pumalín was established by US conservationist Douglas Tompkins, founder of Esprit clothing. During the 1960s Tompkins visited Patagonia often, and after cashing in his interest in Esprit, he started purchasing small *fundos*, or farms, the first being 17,000-hectare Fundo Reñihué to protect the Valdivian temperate rainforest from exploitation. Through the Conservation Land Trust, an entity he started through his California-based Foundation for Deep Ecology, he purchased more land in adjoining areas until he had amassed some 295,000 hectares, in two separate sections.

For one person, and a gringo at that, to own such a sweeping territory delimiting the Argentine border and stretching to the Pacific Coast, put politicians in a flurry and started all sorts of rumors over Tompkins' intentions. The fact that Tompkins declared that he wanted to donate the land to the Chilean government as a new national park did not mollify his detractors. However, once he realized that Conaf didn't have the resources to take on such a project, Tompkins decided to change his strategy. He is currently petitioning the government to declare the property a protected 'Nature Sanctuary,' and once this is done, he will have the Conservation Land Trust donate the land to a Chilean nonprofit, Fundación Pumalín.

While the controversy has died down and the park has become a popular destination for Chilenos as well as gringos, troubles still remain. As the government ponders granting the park Nature Sanctuary status, which would prioritize environmental protection

and nondevelopment, the public works department threatens to act on long-held plans to build a highway through parts of the property, a right the government has without having to offer due compensation to land owners. And in 2002, mayors within the Palena Province, in which Tompkins' total holdings of over 360,000 hectares take up almost a quarter of the entire province, demanded that he sell some of their land back.

The concept of the park is inspiring. Pumalín's staff participate in a variety of projects, from bee-keeping and organic farming to animal husbandry and ecotourism. Private fundos now within the park boundaries continue to operate with an emphasis on sustainable living. The park maintains a free *refugio* for the local workers, and it doesn't charge admission for visitors. Pumalíns goal is to allow visitors to immerse themselves in pristine nature and come out with a deeper appreciation for the natural environment that surrounds them.

Most people get to the park from Chaitén in the south. The 'center' of the park, where you'll find the visitors center, café and cabins, is at the small cove called Caleta Gonzalo, the landing for the ferry from Hornopirén.

Travelers who have grown accustomed to the minimalist aesthetic of Chilean parks may be impressed or taken aback by the Pumalín style: Along the well-maintained road, large, beautifully carved wooden signs indicate trailheads and campgrounds, the café would feel at home in a ritzy ski resort, and the information centers are heavier on glossy B&W photos than on dioramas or taxidermic displays.

Information
The **Centro de Visitantes** (*Caleta Gonzalo*) has brochures, photographs and environmental information on the park, and it also sells artisan goods from the region. If it's locked, ask someone at the café to open it for you. For more details before arriving contact its information centers in Puerto Montt (☎ 65-250-079; Buín 356), Chaitén or the USA (☎ 415-229-9339; ⓦ www.pumalinpark.org; Building 1062, Fort Cronkhite, Sausalito, CA 94965). The website has updated information.

Hiking
A number of the hikes shown on the park's brochure and website have yet to be created

or completed. Check with any information center before assuming your hiking plans.

If hiking here or in other southern Chilean rainforests, watch for tiny *sanguijuelas* (leeches), which are bothersome but not dangerous. Near the café at Caleta Gonzalo, the **Sendero Cascadas** (three hours roundtrip) is an undulating climb through dense forest that ends at a large waterfall. The river crossing about an hour into the hike can be dangerous to cross at high water.

About 12km south of Caleta Gonzalo, the marked route to **Laguna Tronador** is not so much a trail as it is – often literally – a staircase. Beginning as a boardwalk, it crosses a rushing stream on a *pasarela* (hanging bridge) before ascending a series of wooden stepladders where the soil is too steep and friable for anything else. After about an hour's climb, at the saddle, there's a mirador (platform) with fine views of Volcán Michinmahuida above the forest to the south. The trail then drops toward the lake, where there's a two-site campground with sturdy picnic tables (one set on a deck) and a latrine.

One kilometer farther south, only a few minutes off the highway to Chaitén, **Sendero los Alerces** crosses the river to a substantial grove of alerce trees, where interpretive signs along the way explain the importance of conserving these ancients. At **Cascadas Escondidas**, 14km south of Caleta Gonzalo, a one-hour trail leads from the campground to a series of waterfalls.

At **Michinmahuida**, 33km south of Caleta Gonzalo, a 12km trail is under construction to the base of the volcano. **Sendero Mirador**, another 12km trail located between the campgrounds at Leptepú and Pillán, is also being built. The trailhead is near the concrete bridge but is hard to find – ask for directions.

Other hiking trails are also still in development, including **Sendero Inexplorado**, a three- to four-day trek that links Pumalín with Parque Nacional Hornopirén, and **Lago Reñihué**, a 30km trek that can also be done on horseback.

Organized Tours

Currently, the only way to access some of the northern reaches of the park is by boat. Two operators organize boating and kayaking trips through the fjords and to otherwise inaccessible hot springs. Contact **Alsur** (☎ *065-287-628*; e *alsur@telsur.cl; Del Salvador 100, Puerto*

Varas) or **Austral Adventures** (☎/*fax 065-625-977;* w *www.austral-adventures.com; Lord Cochrane 432, Ancud, Chiloé*), which sails *Cahuella*, a 15m (50-foot) wooden motor cruiser, made in the traditional fishing boat style. Four- to seven-day sails around Chiloé's islands and through Pumalín's fjords range from US$775 to US$1600 per person. All sails include land transfers, accommodations, gourmet meals and daily stops to experience island culture and to hike, kayak, or soak in hot springs. Guides are knowledgeable and bilingual, and the atmosphere is fun, informal and personable.

Places to Stay & Eat

Campgrounds throughout the park cost US$2-3 per person, or US$9 for a covered site, some of which are on elevated platforms. Information centers and the website have details on all of the campgrounds, some of which are either at trailheads or at the end of a trail. The largest and most accessible is **Camping Río Gonzalo** (*Caleta Gonzalo; sites with firepit US$7*), on the shores of Fiordo Reñihué. This walk-in campground is surrounded by majestic stands of nalca, and it has a stylish shelter for cooking and bathrooms; cold showers only.

At Caleta Gonzalo, the **cabañas** (☎ *250-079 for reservations; singles/doubles US$50/70, extra person US$10*) remind one of a small gnome village, but they are incredibly cozy and overlook the fjord. They don't have kitchen facilities.

Café Caleta Gonzalo (*US$7-10*) is the only place to eat. They prepare tasty meals, but service can be slow and erratic.

Getting There & Away

Transmarchilay's summer-only ferry *Mailén* sails to Hornopirén (six hours) at 9am, leaving to return to Caleta Gonzalo at 4pm daily. For fares and full details, see Hornopirén earlier in this chapter. For transportation to and from Chaitén, see below.

CHAITÉN
☎ 65 • pop 3250; greater area 7000

As tourism to Parque Pumalín and the Carretera Austral increases, Chaitén's rough pioneer port feel is being scoured down and polished up with better traveler services and more of that Pumalín style. Even the gravel roads are getting paved. Still, isolation keeps this small outpost – little more than a six-block by eight-block grid between Bahía de Chaitén and Río Blanco – humble and peaceful. Though hugged by rugged hills and with spectacular views of 2404m Volcán Michimahuida to the northeast and 2300m Volcán Corcovado to the southwest, there's little to do in town. This is mainly a transportation stop for places farther along Carretera Austral and the access point for Parque Pumalín. Chaitén is 56km south of Caleta Gonzalo and 45km north of Puerto Cárdenas. The ferry port is about a 10-minute walk to the northwest.

Information

The municipal **tourist kiosk** (*Costanera & O'Higgins; open 9am-9pm daily Jan-Feb*) has a handful of leaflets and a list of *hospedajes*. **Pumalín Information Center** (*☎ 731-341; O'Higgins 62; open 9am-1:30pm, 3pm-7pm Mon-Sat, 10am-4pm Sun*) has lovely photo montages of the park, but lacks informative staff. Cabins in the park may be reserved here.

Banco del Estado (*cnr Libertad & O'Higgins*) may change US cash, but it gives poor rates and it does not exchange traveler's checks. It does, however, have an ATM, but don't bank on it having cash all the time.

The **post office** (*cnr Riveros & O'Higgins*) is opposite the plaza. To place calls, there's **Teléfonica del Sur** (*Costanera*) and **Entel**, on the east side of the Plaza de Armas.

Bellavista al Sur (*☎ 731-469; Riveros 479*) has Internet access, sells airline tickets, organizes rock-climbing trips and has local information.

Lavandería Masol (*☎ 731-566; Todesco 272, Local B*) offers laundry services.

The **Hospital de Chaitén** (*☎ 731-244; Av Ignacio Carrera Pinto*) is between Riveros and Portales.

Organized Tours

Chaitur (*☎ 731-429, fax 731-266; e nchaitur @hotmail.com; bus terminal*), possibly the best source of information in town, dispatches most of the buses and arranges trips with bilingual guides to Pumalín, the Yelcho glacier, Termas de Amarillo and beaches with sea lion colonies.

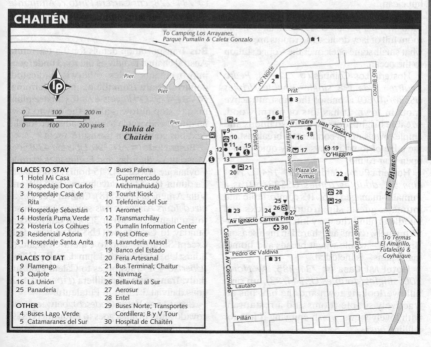

CHAITÉN

To Camping Los Arrayanes, Parque Pumalín & Caleta Gonzalo

Bahía de Chaitén

0   100   200 m
0   100   200 yards

Av Norte
Prat
Río Blanco
Av Padre Juan Todesco
Ercilla
Portales
Almirante Riveros
O'Higgins
Plaza de Armas
Pedro Aguirre Cerda
Av Ignacio Carrera Pinto
Costanera Av Corcovado
Pedro de Valdivia
Lautaro
Libertad
Pildó Pardo
Río Blanco
Pillán

To Termas El Amarillo, Futaleufú & Coyhaique

PLACES TO STAY	7	Buses Palena
1	Hotel Mi Casa			(Supermercado
2	Hospedaje Don Carlos			Michimahuida)
3	Hospedaje Casa de	8	Tourist Kiosk
	Rita	10	Teléfonica del Sur
6	Hospedaje Sebastián	11	Aeromet
14	Hostería Puma Verde	12	Transmarchilay
22	Hostería Los Coihues	15	Pumalín Information Center
23	Residencial Astoria	17	Post Office
31	Hospedaje Santa Anita	18	Lavandería Masol
		19	Banco del Estado
PLACES TO EAT	20	Feria Artesanal
9	Flamengo	21	Bus Terminal; Chaitur
13	Quijote	24	Navimag
16	La Unión	26	Bellavista al Sur
25	Panadería	27	Aerosur
		28	Entel
OTHER	29	Buses Norte; Transportes
4	Buses Lago Verde		Cordillera; B y V Tour
5	Catamaranes del Sur	30	Hospital de Chaitén

Places to Stay

With Chaitén's growing popularity, especially with the backpacking set, many homes turn into hospedajes in the summer months. The tourist kiosk has a list of all accommodations.

Los Arrayanes (☎ 218-202; sites per person US$2.50, plus per vehicle or tent US$0.60), the nearest campground, is 4km north of town. There are beachfront sites and hot showers.

Hospedaje Casa de Rita (cnr Almirante Riveros & Prat; per person US$6) is a basic family-run place; it's nonsmoking and quiet, and has kitchen access.

Hospedaje Don Carlos (☎ 731-287; Almirante Riveros 53; rooms with shared/private bath US$9/16) has a newer upstairs area with firm beds in cramped rooms. There's a patio to wash and dry clothes, breakfast is included, and the owners are helpful and friendly.

Hospedaje Sebastián (☎/fax 731-225; Todesco 188; rooms with shared/private bath US$9/23) is within a dimly lit older building.

Hospedaje Santa Anita (Pedro de Valdivia 129; rooms US$6.50) is a bit small and stuffy, but clean.

Residencial Astoria (☎ 731-263; Corcovado 442; per person US$9) has a large living room full of lacy doilies. The rooms are somewhat small; some peek over the Copec station to the ocean.

Hostería Los Coihues (☎ 731-461; Pedro Aguirre Cerda 398; singles/doubles/triples US$30/40/60) is one of the most attractive spots in town. It has lots of warm wood, sizeable bright rooms with crisp linens and ample towels, and a continental breakfast. At the edge of town, it stays plenty quiet and is open year-round.

Hostería Puma Verde (☎ 731-184; O'Higgins 54; doubles/triples US$33/50) is a Pumalín-managed spot. It's comfortable and intimate; guests slip around in socks and huddle around the cozy kitchen table. Unfortunately, rooms are shared in high season. Breakfast – whole wheat breads and homemade jams – is included.

Hotel Mi Casa (☎ 731-285; Av Norte 206; singles/doubles US$44/83), up on a hill overlooking town and the bay, has attractively simple rooms and a restaurant with lovely views, worth enjoying if just for a filling *onces*.

Places to Eat

Perhaps because few people stay in town for long, Chaitén's restaurant choices are limited. The best meals are most likely to be served in the place you're staying.

Flamengo (Corcovado 218; US$4.50-10) serves a hot and hearty bowl of *caldillo de congrio* plus fish plates that are easily shared.

Quijote (O'Higgins 42) seems to be Chaitén's favorite dive. Dark no matter the time of day, it's a better spot to enjoy a drink and local banter than to eat.

La Unión (Riveros 242; US$4) is a simple place with basic but filling cheap lunches. For a snack, there's the **panadería** (Riveros 453; US$1) with fresh empanadas and lemon pie.

Shopping

Both Hostería Puma Verde (see Places to Stay earlier in this section) and the feria artesanal, next to the bus terminal, have quality handicrafts, especially woolen hats, mittens and socks, plus homemade jams and honey.

Getting There & Away

Air Several air-taxi services fly to Puerto Montt (US$36 to US$43), including **Aerosur** (☎ 731-228; cnr Carrera Pinto & Almirante Riveros) and **Aeromet** (☎ 731-844; Costanera 243).

Bus Transportation details for the Carretera Austral change rapidly as the road undergoes improvements. Unless otherwise indicated, departures are from the main **bus terminal** (☎ 731-429; O'Higgins 67). If you are planning to stop at towns along the way to Coyhaique, it's advisable to pay in advance for the next bus going down to ensure a seat.

Buses Norte (☎ 731-390; Libertad 432) goes Monday, Wednesday and Friday at 9:30am to Coyhaique (US$25; 12-15 hours) stopping in La Junta (US$11), Puyuhuapi (US$13) and Villa Amengual (US$18). **Chaitur** (see Organized Tours earlier in this section) runs buses to Futaleufú (US$8) at 3:30pm daily except Sunday, to Coyhaique (US$25) at 9am daily except Saturday, and to Caleta Gonzalo (2 hours; US$5) at 7am and 5pm daily. **B y V Tour** (Libertad 432) runs buses to Caleta Gonzalo daily. **Transportes Cordillera** (Libertad 432) goes daily at 3:15pm to Futaleufú.

Buses Lago Verde (Todesco), between Corcovado and Portales, goes to La Junta (US$9) three times weekly.

Buses Palena *(cnr Corcovado & Todesco)* goes to Palena (US$8) thrice weekly from the Supermercado Michimahuida.

Boat Ferry schedules change, so confirm them at the relevant office before making plans. Please refer to Puerto Montt in the La Araucanía & the Lakes District chapter and to Quellón and Castro in the Chiloé chapter for rate information.

Catamaranes del Sur *(☎ 731-199; Juan Todesco 118)* sails passenger-only ferries to Puerto Montt Monday, Wednesday and Friday; and to Castro Tuesday and Thursday at 6pm.

Navimag *(☎ 731-570, fax 730-571; Ignacio Carrera Pinto 188)* sails the auto-passenger ferry *Alejandrina* to Quellón at 11pm Thursday, at 3pm Friday and at noon Sunday, and to Puerto Montt at 9am Saturday. **Transmarchilay** *(☎ 731-272; Corcovado 266)* sails the ferry *Pincoya* to Puerto Montt (10 hours) at midnight Monday and Wednesday, at 7am Friday and at 7pm Sunday; and to Quellón (five hours), at the south end of Chiloé, at 9am Wednesday and Saturday, and at 7pm Sunday.

Transmarchilay also has summer-only, daily ferry service from Caleta Gonzalo in Parque Pumalín to Hornopirén, where there are bus connections to Puerto Montt; see Hornopirén earlier in this chapter for details.

TERMAS EL AMARILLO
About 25km southeast of Chaitén, on a spur north off the Carretera Austral, Termas El Amarillo *(admission US$3; camping per tent US$5)* is a simple hot springs, with walk-in campsites (some on raised wooden platforms) in the damp, cool coigue forest. During the day, you can use two pools, a large one that's plenty hot in the morning and a smaller, hotter concrete tub overlooking Río Michinmahuida. The pools close at 9pm, but campers can access the riverside one for a starlight soak. The site is up for sale, however; it's simple rusticity might get a major overhaul.

Up the road 200m, **Hospedaje Los Mañíos** *(☎ 731-210 in Chaitén; rooms US$9, 4-6 person cabins US$50-70)* is a simple clapboard place with a few rooms and kitchen access, while the cabins are quite cozy and well equipped.

About 5km away, in the town of El Amarillo, **Residencial Marcela** *(☎ 065-264-422; per person US$9)* is a fun spot with friendly service. They can arrange, if you call in advance, all-day horse treks (per person US$40, three person minimum) that include lunch and transfers; the trips go to Volcán Michinmahuida.

LAGO YELCHO
Brilliantly blue and seemingly never-ending, 11,000 hectare Lago Yelcho is fed by the raging Río Futaleufú. Until the completion of the Carretera Austral, the only settlements were a number of small ports such as **Puerto Cárdenas**, which has some modest lodging choices, all open in summer only. **Residencial Puerto Cárdenas** *(☎ 065-264-429; Km 46; rooms with shared/private bath US$16/20)*, by the phone booth, is favored by anglers for its clean rooms, especially those in the back, which are warmer and have a lovely view. A large breakfast is included. Next door, **Hospedaje Lulu** is another possibility.

Approximately 5km south of Puerto Cardenas, along the lakeshore, **Yelcho en la Patagonia** *(☎ 065-731-337, 02-632-6117 in Santiago; e hotel@yelcho.cl; 4-person campsites US$32, singles/doubles US$54/74, 4-6 person cabins US$135-165; meals US$11)* is a fishing lodge and more. The main lodge, with a large shaded sun deck, is lakeside luxurious, while the modern-style cabins, with manicured lawns, are attractive but lack mature trees for privacy. Campsites have all the amenities that will be expected by those willing to pay top dollar to pitch a tent. Four- to seven-day all-inclusive fishing packages, based on double occupancy, cost US$340 to US$655. Bike and horse rental, excursions around the area and one-day fishing trips are also reasonable. Breakfast is included in regular rates; half-pension is available.

Farther on, only 15km south of Puerto Cárdenas, the Puente Ventisquero (Glacier Bridge) is the starting point for a hike to the **Ventisquero Yelcho**, a large hanging glacier. **Camping** is possible at the parking lot, where there is also a *quincho* and bathrooms. Just five minutes from the parking lot is a lookout of the glacier, but continue on about 50m for a better view. The trail continues 2½ hours along the river banks toward the glacier, but just one hour into the trail gives those short on time a place to stop and admire.

VILLA SANTA LUCÍA
The road to Futaleufú and Palena begins at the crossroads village of Villa Santa Lucia,

78km south of Chaitén, site of a large military compound and transfer point for buses. **Hospedaje San Antonio** (*rooms US$9*) provides those who get stuck here a few rooms with saggy beds and hot water, and it allows camping.

Where the road splits to Futaleufú (to the northeast) and to Palena (to the southeast) is **Puerto Ramírez** at the southeast corner of Lago Yelcho. **Hostería Verónica** (*rooms US$12*) offers shelter and breakfast, plus camping.

FUTALEUFÚ
☎ 65 • pop 1800

The 'Fu' or 'Futa' river, crystalline blue and impressively wild, has international fame as one of the best white-water runs and kayaking play rivers around. Year after year, more rafting enthusiasts and kayak-toting travelers make the journey to this hidden-away place, but whether or not the river will remain such a draw depends largely on plans to commit the environmental crime of damning it for a hydroelectricity project. The town of Futaleufú, a small 20-block spot of pastel-painted houses 155km southeast of Chaitén, is primarily a service center to the Argentine border, only 8km away, but it has grown up as the rapids-loving gringos descend upon it. For those not planning to run the river or continue on to the nearby Argentine towns of Trevelín and Esquel, and to Argentina's Parque Nacional Los Alerces, there's little to do in town but admire the incredible landscape. At the end of Piloto Carmona, past Laguna Espejo and the water tanks, is a staircase that leads to a **lookout** of the town.

Note that the Futaleufú border post, open 8am to 8pm daily, is far quicker and more efficient than the crossing at Palena (see later in this chapter), opposite the Argentine border town of Carrenleufú.

Information
The municipal **tourist office** (*O'Higgins 536*) is on the south side of the Plaza de Armas. The **post office** (*cnr Manuel Rodríguez*) is directly east. Bring all the money you'll need; **Banco del Estado** (*cnr O'Higgins & Manuel Rodríguez*) is the only choice for changing money.

White-Water Rafting & Kayaking
Several US rafting and kayaking outfitters operate in the area in summer; for details,

see Organized Tours in the Getting There & Away chapter. For Santiago-based operators, see the Getting Around chapter.

There are also local agencies that do the Río Espolón and segments of the more difficult Futaleufú, including **Centro Aventura Futaleufú** (☎ *721-320; O'Higgins 397*) at the Hostería Río Grande and **Club de Rafting y Kayak** (☎ *298; Pedro Aguirre Cerda 545*). See Organized Tours in the Getting Around chapter for more agencies.

Places to Stay & Eat
Due to the town's isolated geography, most supplies have to be trucked in. Fresh vegetables can be in short supply sometimes, but locals do wonders with the many local fruits.

Fifteen kilometers from Puerto Ramíréz, **Cara del Indio** (*camping per person US$5*) is base camp for many kayakers. Run by Luis Toro and his family, the camp has six miles of riverfront, including the site of one of the proposed dams. Determined to keep the river from being dammed, Luis is active in getting locals involved in adventure tourism and offers a variety of activities. Sites along the river include hot showers and access to a wood-burning sauna. You can purchase homemade bread, cheese and beer from the family's house. December and March are more peaceful times to be here.

Camping Puerto Espolón (*per person US$3; open Jan-Feb only*), on eight hectares just before the entrance to town, has a sandy beach along a peaceful stretch of river and is the best camping option close to town.

Hospedaje Adolfo (☎ *721-256; O'Higgins 302; per person US$8*) has a few cozy upstairs rooms and serves a good breakfast in a quiet, pleasant family atmosphere.

Residencial Ely (☎ *721-205; Balmaceda 409; per person US$14*) is just slightly more upscale in a lovely white shingled house.

Hotel Continental (☎ *721-222; Balmaceda 595; per person US$5.50*) is a simple, ramshackle place with firm beds. Breakfast costs US$2.50.

Hostería Río Grande (☎ *721-320; O'Higgins 397; singles/doubles US$40/50*) caters mostly to sporty gringos on rafting packages. The quaint rooms are attractively decorated, each somewhat uniquely, with touches of wood, amber and blue. If it gets cold, management wheels in space heaters. The restaurant is known for pricey but well-prepared meals.

Encuentro (☎ 721-247; O'Higgins 633; mains US$5-9) is an adequate choice with large portions of so-so food.

SurAndes (Cerda 308; sandwiches US$2-3) is a mighty relaxed place serving oversized hamburgers and sandwiches made to order, plus fruit juices.

Lodge Frontera Patagónica (☎ 721-320; e fronterapatagonica@hotmail.com; 4-person cabins US$100), 5km south of town along Río Espolón, has three woodsy cabins with valley views and nearby swimming holes. Breakfast is included, and other meals, plus homemade liqueurs, are available. The owners arrange rafting, kayaking and fishing trips.

Getting There & Away
Futaleufú has no gas station, but the small grocery store on Sargento Aldea usually has some gas – sold by the wine jug. **Transportes Cordillera** (☎ 721-249; Prat 262) in front of the plaza, goes to the Argentine border (US$2.50) at 9am and 6pm Monday and Friday, but other companies make more frequent trips during high season.

Transportes Sebastián (☎ 721-288; Piloto Carmona 381), goes to Chaitén at 7:30am daily except Sunday, stopping at Villa Santa Lucía, Puerto Cárdenas and Termas El Amarillo. **Cuchichi** (Sargento Aldea) goes to Puerto Montt via Argentina at 8am on Tuesday (US$26, 13 hours).

PALENA
☎ 65 • pop 1700
Palena, 43km southeast of Puerto Ramírez, is only 8km west of the Argentine border, but the crossing is bureaucratically slow. Still, some visitors come here to enjoy otherwise inaccessible segments of the Río Futaleufú and February's **Rodeo de Palena**. For inexpensive accommodations, try **Residencial La Chilenita** (Pudeto 681; rooms per person US$7) or **Residencial Pasos** (Pudeto 661; per person US$12).

Buses Palena on the Plaza de Armas goes to Chaitén at 7:30am Monday, Wednesday and Friday.

LA JUNTA
Dusty and flat, La Junta is nothing much to look at, but this former estancia is growing in popularity, especially among rock-climbing enthusiasts and the fly-fishing set, who catch and release at Reserva Nacional Lago Rosselot and Lago Verde.

At the confluence of the Río Palena and the Río Figueroa, in an open valley, La Junta is just south of the boundary between Regions X and XI, making it an important stop for people hopping buses going north or south along the Carretera Austral. **Conaf** (☎ 314-128; Patricio Lynch & Manuel Montt) has some details on the nearby parks and reserves.

Residencial Valderas (☎ 314-105; Varas & Cinco de Abril; per person US$9) offers small rooms within a cute wooden house with loads of rose bushes. One of the double rooms has a woodburning stove in the bathroom. Breakfast is included.

Pension Hospedaje Tía Leti (☎ 314-106; Varas 569; per person US$10) has large attic rooms brimming with light, and a filling breakfast is included.

Espacio y Tiempo (☎ 314-141, fax 314-142; e espacio@patagoniachile.cl; singles/doubles/triples US$53/75/86) caters to anglers, but provides a nice alternative for anyone looking for an intimate, more comfortable spot to rest. It has classical music in the lounge, llamas grazing in the yard, and spacious rooms with central heating.

PUERTO PUYUHUAPI
☎ 67
At the northern end of the Seno Ventisquero, a scenic fjord that's part of the larger Canal Puyuhuapi, modest Puerto Puyuhuapi was settled by German immigrants in the 1940s. It's a gateway to Parque Nacional Queulat and to Termas de Puyuhuapi, one of Chile's most prestigious hot springs resorts.

Puerto Puyuhuapi's single biggest attraction is its **Fábrica de Alfombras**, which has produced handmade woolen carpets since 1945. Half-hour tours (adults/children US$2/1) take place weekdays at 10:30am, 11am and 11:30am and at 4pm, 4:30pm and 5pm; weekends and holidays at 11:30am.

Places to Stay & Eat
Many day visitors to Termas de Puyuhuapi spend the night in town, lending the place some quality lodging options.

Camping Puyuhuapi, alongside the gas station in town, is a free site (though it's customary to make a donation to the campsite's caretaker).

AISÉN

Hostería Marily (☎ 325-201; Uebel & Circunvalación; per person with shared/private bath US$10/12.50), the best bargain in town, is friendly and includes breakfast. It has firm beds and spacious common areas. During the high season rooms are shared.

Hostería Elizabeth (☎ 325-106; Circunvalación s/n; per person US$8.50) is another good choice. It's comfortable and has good meals. Rates include breakfast.

Aonikenk Cabañas (☎ 325-208; Hamburgo 16; 3-6 person cabins US$46-66) provide a fine escape in light, spacious cabins near the water. Ample breakfasts, served in a delightful café, cost US$3. The energetic owner is a good source of area information.

Hostería Alemana (☎ 325-118; Uebel 450; doubles US$41), cozy and meticulously maintained, has rooms with lake views, others with fireplaces. A wraparound wooden sun deck looks out onto flourishing flower and vegetable gardens. Reservations are a must.

Casa Ludwig (☎ 325-220; e l.ludwig@entelchile.net; Uebel s/n; singles to triples with shared bath US$16-41; triples to quintuples with private bath US$50-66) receives many accolades for its charm and coziness, all wrapped in a historic landmark. Small details, like hot water bottles, homemade bread and real coffee, make it a favorite for travelers. The owner, Luisa, keeps a few basic shared rooms available for backpackers (per person US$11). English and German are spoken.

Next door, **Lluvia Marina** (☎ 325-214; Otto Uebel s/n; meals US$10-15; onces US$6), intimate and well decorated with warm weavings and rustic pottery, is the best restaurant in town. There's a little something for any palate, from lentil soups to pastas and pizzas, plus an array of salads, homemade cakes and real coffee.

About 15km south of town, **Hospedaje Las Toninas** (Km 205; sites US$9, per person US$7) is a simple but attractive white Chilote-style shingled house, set among spectacular flower gardens. The beachfront campsites are protected and have firepits, while some of the upstairs rooms have beach views. Meals (about US$4), including garden fresh salads, steak and the occasional fresh crab salad, are available.

Getting There & Away

Buses that run between Coyhaique and Chaitén will drop passengers in Puerto Puyuhuapi. Buses Norte going southbound usually arrives between 3pm and 5pm. Transportes Emanuel leaves for La Junta, Puerto Cisnes and Coyhaique (on Sunday) from the store next to the police station.

TERMAS DE PUYUHUAPI

Chile's leading hot springs resort is the luxurious yet unpretentious **Termas de Puyuhuapi Hotel & Spa** (☎ 325-103, 02-225-6489, fax 274-8111; e info@patagoniaconnex.cl; Fidel Oteíza 1921, Oficina 1006, Santiago). Set in a lush forest on the western shore of the Seno Ventisquero, the buildings are tastefully designed with a medley of Chilote and Bavarian influences. Exclusive it is, however, and chances to enjoy the pools or spend a night are limited. On the days that their package-tour clients are transported to their next destination, nonpackage people can arrange to use the baths or spend a night (on Monday, Thursday or Friday).

Three outdoor baths, including a hot mud lagoon shaded by ferns, are right by the water, allowing for a fun pattern of steaming away then jumping in the refreshing inlet. The more elaborate indoor spa has a mélange of colorful cold-water pools, Jacuzzis and one large pool with different jets. Day use of the outdoor pools costs US$18 in high season (US$10 for children). Use of the indoor spa (hotel guests only) is US$15. Massages and seaweed treatments are also on offer and cost US$25 to US$30 for a 30-minute session.

Hotel rooms (doubles US$130-185) range from standards – smaller and with a forest view – to suites with heated floors and a sun deck. Rates include a continental buffet breakfast, and fixed-price lunches and dinners cost US$22. The cafeteria at the outdoor pools, open only in the daytime, is cheaper but has a more limited menu.

The spa attracts a mature crowd, but there's usually a handful of younger and middle-aged professionals. Most everyone dons plush white bathrobes to saunter around the grounds, with short trails to waterfalls and through the gardens of nalca, chilco, lavendar, canelo, tepa, coigue and notro.

Termas de Puyuhuapi is accessible only by water; the mainland dock is 11km south of Puerto Puyuhuapi at Bahía Dorita. Boat transfers cost US$8 each way. Launches leave the dock at 10am, 12:30pm, 3:30pm and 7pm, returning at 9:30am, noon, 2:30pm and

6:30pm, but there are often unscheduled crossings as well. For information on Patagonia Connection's package excursions, see Organized Tours in the Getting Around chapter.

PN QUEULAT

Straddling the Carretera Austral for 70km, midway between Chaitén and Coyhaique, 154,000-hectare Parque Nacional Queulat (admission US$3) is a wild domain of steep-sided fjords, rushing rivers, evergreen forests, creeping glaciers and high volcanic peaks, many over 2000m. Created in 1983, it has rapidly gained popularity, but is still an off-the-beaten-track destination, perhaps due in part to the almost constant rain (up to 4000mm per year) and the often impenetrable foliage. Despite its impressive size, there aren't that many hiking possibilities, and Conaf has struggled to maintain trailhead signs, most of which are either hidden by the aggressive growth or missing. The **Centro de Información Ambiental**, 22km south of Puerto Puyuhapi and 2.5km from the road, at the parking lot for the Ventisquero Colgante, is the main center to the park and where admission fees are collected. It has well-organized, informative displays of plants and glacial activity and rangers can help with hiking ideas.

Activities

Near the Centro de Información, there's a quick walk up to a lookout of the **Ventisquero Colgante**, the park's most popular attraction. Or take the hanging bridge across Río Ventisquero and follow a 3.2km trail along the crest of a moraine on the river's north bank to excellent views of the glacier and the occasional crash of ice onto the rocks below. Just north of the southern entrance to the park at Km 170, a damp trail climbs the valley of the **Río de las Cascadas** through a dense forest of delicate ferns, copihue vines, tree-size fuchsias, podocarpus and lenga. The heavy rainfall never directly hits the ground but seems to percolate through the multistoried canopy. After about half an hour, the trail emerges at an impressive granite bowl where half a dozen waterfalls drop from hanging glaciers.

Twenty kilometers south of the information center, on the left (there's nowhere to pull over), is **Sendero Padre García**, a 100m staircase that drops to an overlook of an impressive waterfall and its transparent pool.

Padre Garcia was a Jesuit priest who trekked through Queulat in search of the mythical Ciudad de Los Césares. Continuing on, the road begins to zigzag treacherously up the Portezuelo de Queulat between Km 175 and 178, from where the view of the Queulat Valley is outstanding.

Large streams such as the Río Cisnes and the glacial fingers of Lago Rosselot, Lago Verde and Lago Risopatrón offer excellent fishing.

Places to Stay

Camping Ventisquero (sites US$6; wood US$1.50), near the Ventisquero Colgante, has 10 attractive sites with covered barbecues and picnic tables, but the water that comes out of the showers in the spotless bathrooms is glacier cold. The sites themselves are a bit rocky for pitching tents easily.

Camping Angostura (Lago Risopatrón; sites US$6) is 15km north of Puerto Puyuhapi in a sopping rainforest, but the facilities are good (cold showers only).

Getting There & Away

Buses connecting Chaitén and Coyhaique will drop passengers at Puerto Puyuhapi or other points along the western boundary of the park. See the Chaitén and Coyhaique sections for details. Make seat reservations on the next bus you plan to take and be prepared to wait.

AROUND PN QUEULAT

At the southern approach to Parque Nacional Queulat, **Villa Amengual** is a pioneer village with a Chilote-style shingled chapel and basic services. It's at the foot of 2760m Cerro Alto Nevado. **Residencial El Encanto** (Francisca Castro 33-A) and **Hospedaje Michay** (Carmen Arias 14) are modest lodgings for around US$10 a night with breakfast.

Another 55km south, **Villa Mañihuales** was founded in 1962. It has a couple of hospedajes, including **Residencial Maniguales** (☎ 234-803; E Ibar 200; per person US$8), and some simple cafés.

Another 13km south, the Carretera Austral splits. The highway southwest toward Puerto Aisén and Puerto Chacabuco is completely paved, and access to Coyhaique is through a scenic route crossing the western-sloping Andes. The southern route may be paved by the time of publication.

PUERTO CISNES
☎ 67 • pop 5700

At the mouth of its namesake river and 35km west of the Carretera Austral, Puerto Cisnes' calm quaintness makes it an attractive detour. The road to the port, going past walls of blasted rock face, is in itself impressive. A small bridge and pedestrian walkway join the town's two sides – the first is a newer, cabin-centric area, and the second is the heart of town, with a small plaza and most of the services. At the plaza, the library, with a carved wooden faux-Greek faÁade, has a small **tourist office** with posted information. Close to 40% of the population works in the salmon industry, and a cottage industry of fish-skin crafts has grown. Fishermen arrange boat trips around the area (US$60-70 a day). West of Puerto Cisnes is **Parque Nacional Isla Magdalena** (not to be confused with the penguin colony near Punta Arenas). Rarely mentioned and with little infrastructure from Conaf, it could make an engaging trip for those who are looking for their own adventure. Talk to people in town about transport, which costs about US$100.

Places to Stay & Eat

Most places are in the main part of town.

Hospedaje Bellavista (☎ 346-408; Séptimo de Línea 112; per person US$9) is the best budget choice, with attractive 2nd-floor rooms that are warm and cozy, most with double beds, but the bathrooms are downstairs. Breakfast is included.

Hostal Michay (☎ 346-462; Gabriela Mistral 112; singles US$16), bedecked in Puyuhuapi rugs, has an impressive bone and shell collection, a stuffed ñandu, feather-stuffed couches, large beds with real mattresses and rooms with private bath.

Cabañas Brisas del Sur (☎ 346-587; Arturo Prat 51; 4-person cabin US$50), along the main road (easy beach access, not much privacy), has clean, ample and fully equipped cabins with comfortable beds, large bathrooms and TV, but bad reception. The owner, German Hipp Fuentes, is a good resource for fishing enthusiasts.

Donde La Oti (☎ 346-706; cnr Mistral & Cerda; lunches US$3) is the perfect hole in the wall to fill up on a large platter of fried salmon, potatoes and fresh salad.

El Guairao (☎ 346-473; Piloto Pardo 58; mains US$4.50), probably the best bet in town

and hard to miss, prepares wild river salmon and a local favorite, *puyes al pilpil* (tiny thin fish in garlic oil sauce).

K'cos (☎ 346-494; Arturo Prat 270; US$3-9) serves sandwiches and mains, which can be enjoyed on the patio overlooking the quiet bay.

Getting There & Away

Minibuses Hernández (☎ 346-929; Aguirre Cerda 048) leaves for Coyhaique (US$9) at 6am Monday to Saturday. Reserve in advance; they'll pick you up where you're staying. **Transporte Terraustral** (☎ 346-757) has similar service. If you're heading north, you can ask to be dropped at the junction with the Carretera Austral, but be prepared to wait. If your Spanish is up to it, you could try contacting northbound buses in Coyhaique to ask the driver to pick you up en route, but there is little guarantee they'll keep a seat open for you without payment. Your best bet may be hitchhiking.

COYHAIQUE
☎ 67 • pop 45,300

Coyhaique spreads over a barren valley lorded over by the impressive basalt massif of Cerro Macay. Rambles of houses, windmill energy farms and herds of semitrucks grunting along the paved highways comes as a shock to travelers emerging from the rainforests and fjords of the northern Carretera Austral. This is southern Aisén's center, the region's capital, an important link in the Bioceanic Corridor to Argentina, a highway development to increase transportation of industrial supplies to and from ports on the Pacific and Atlantic Oceans. It is also the supply center for the fly-fishing elite and anyone heading into southern isolation.

Back in 1929, just a small town was set up here, a service center for the properties of the Sociedad Industrial. As the town developed, the *carabineros* general Marchant González developed the city's plan, including a pentagonal Plaza de Armas based on the shape of the national police force's emblem. It's the city's most unusual feature and frustratingly confusing to visitors.

Orientation

At the confluence of the Río Simpson and the Río Coyhaique, Coyhaique is linked by a paved highway to Puerto Chacabuco to the west, and by partly paved roads to Puerto Ingeniero Ibáñez to the south and Chaitén to the north. It's also accessible from Argentine Patagonia to the east.

For travelers accustomed to the standard Latin American grid, Coyhaique's street plan can be disorienting. Its focus is the pentagonal Plaza de Armas, from which 10 streets radiate like spokes from a wheel, but within a block or two in every direction, this irregularity gives way to a more conventional pattern. One way to orient yourself is to walk once around the plaza, noting landmarks such as the cathedral, and then wander once around the outer pentangle bounded by Arturo Prat, General Parra, 21 de Mayo, Eusebio Lillo and Francisco Bilbao. This isn't foolproof, but it helps.

Av General Baquedano, which skirts the northeast side of town, eventually connects with the paved highway to Puerto Chacabuco and a gravel road east to the Argentine border at Paso Coyhaique. Av Ogana heads south to Balmaceda, Puerto Ibáñez and other southerly points on the Camino Austral.

Information
Tourist Offices Enthusiastic **Sernatur** (☎ 233-949; e sernatur_coyhaiq@entelchile .net; Bulnes 35; open 8:30am-9pm Mon-Fri, 11am-8pm Sat & Sun in summer; 9am-1pm & 3pm-7pm Mon-Fri rest of the year), half a block from the Plaza de Armas, is one of the best-organized, most helpful offices in the country. Check its board for updated lists of lodging and transportation. The staff also has lots of knowledge about developments further south.

Conaf (☎ 212-125; 12 de Octubre 382) has some information on the parks and reserves around the area.

Money Exchange cash and traveler's checks at **Turismo Prado** (☎/fax 231-271; 21 de Mayo 417) or **Cambios Emperador** (Bilbao 222). Along Condell, between the plaza and Av Baquedano, are a number of banks with ATMs.

Post & Communications The **post office** (Cochrane 202) is near the Plaza de Armas. There's also **Entel** (Arturo Prat 340), also with Internet access. **Telefónica (CTC)** (cnr Condell & 21 de Mayo) has Internet access, as does **Visual.com** (12 de Octubre 485-B), which has plenty of computers and a nonsmoking policy.

Travel Agencies Most agencies around town specialize in booking trips to Laguna San Rafael or organizing fishing holidays. But with more adventure seekers coming to town, loads more can help arrange off-the-norm adventures.

Patagonia Adventure Expeditions (☎ 219-894; w www.adventurepatagonia.com; Dussen 357), run by very knowledgeable US and English expats, organizes kayaking and rafting on many rivers, plus mountaineering expeditions around the region and in Puerto Bertrand. **Turismo Rural Río Baker** (☎ 522-646; San Valentín 438) also comes recommended for planning adventurous trips in the area. The more general travel agency **Cabot** (☎ 230-101; General Parra 177) is another good bet, as are **Los Andes Patagónicos** (☎ 232-920; Horn 48), within Café Ricer, and **Sur Nativo** (☎ 231-648; Baquedano 457). **Expediciones Lucas Bridges** (☎/fax 233-302, 09-892-5477; e lbridges@aisen.cl) is on the outskirts of town.

Language Schools The **Baquedano International Language School** (☎ 232-520, fax 231-511; e pguzmanm@entelchile.net; Baquedano 20) offers intensive Spanish-language instruction.

Laundry Try **Lavandería QL** (☎ 232-266; Bilbao 160) for prompt and efficient service, or **Lavamatic** (Simpson 417), which is near lots of hospedajes.

Medical Services Coyhaique's **Hospital Base** (☎ 231-286; Calle Hospital) is at the west end of JM Carrera.

Museo Regional de la Patagonia
Coyhaique's regional museum (Baquedano & Eusebio Lillo; admission US$0.75; open 9am-6pm daily in summer, limited hours rest of the year) is well worth a visit for its fine collection of labeled photographs on regional history, including some of the construction of the Carretera Austral. Also displayed are some pioneer artifacts, Marchant's uniform, Jesuit regalia and a minor collection of stuffed birds, fossils and minerals. Knowledgeable docents eagerly discuss the area's history.

Activities
The fishing season generally runs from November to May, but in a few popular areas it

AISÉN

COYHAIQUE

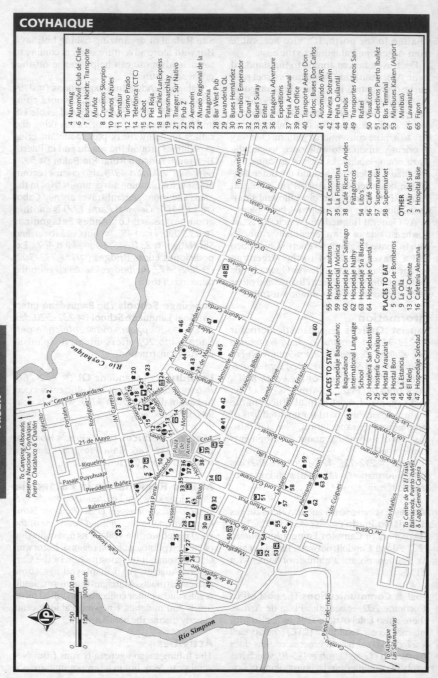

4 Navimag
6 Automóvil Club de Chile
7 Buses Norte; Transporte
8 Muñoz
10 Cruceros Skorpios
11 Manos Azules
12 Sernatur
14 Turismo Prado
15 Telefónica (CTC)
17 Cabot
18 Piel Roja
19 LanChile/LanExpress
21 Transmarchilay
22 Traeger; Sur Nativo
23 Pub Z
24 Aerohein
28 Museo Regional de la Patagonia
29 Bar West Pub
30 Buses Hernández
31 Lavandería QL
32 Cambios Emperador
33 Conaf
34 Buses Suray
36 Entel
37 Patagonia Adventure Expeditions
38 Feria Artesanal
39 Post Office
40 Transporte Aéreo Don Carlos; Buses Don Carlos
41 Automundo AVR
42 Naviera Sotramin
44 Peña Quilantal
48 Turibús
49 Transportes Aéreos San Rafael
50 Visual.com
51 Colectivos Puerto Ibáñez
52 Bus Terminal
53 Minibuses Kaiken (Airport Minibus)
61 Lavamatic
65 Figon

PLACES TO STAY
1 Hospedaje Baquedano; Baquedano International Language School
20 Hotelera San Sebastián
25 Hostería Coyhaique
26 Hostal Araucaria
43 Hostal Bon
45 La Estancia
46 El Reloj
47 Hospedaje Soledad
55 Hospedaje Lautaro
59 Residencial Mónica
60 Hospedaje Don Santiago
62 Hospedaje Nathy
63 Hospedaje Sra Blanca
64 Hospedaje Guarda

PLACES TO EAT
5 Casino de Bomberos
9 La Olla
13 Café Oriente
16 Cafetería Alemana
27 La Casona
35 La Florentina
38 Café Ricer; Los Andes Patagónicos
54 Lito's
56 Café Samoa
57 Supermarket
58 Supermarket

OTHER
2 Mar del Sur
3 Hospital Base

is restricted to a shorter period. Brown and rainbow trout are the most common species. Reservas Nacional Coyhaique and Río Simpson both have hiking options; see those sections later in this chapter.

From June to September, skiers can test the facilities at the **Centro de Ski El Fraile** (☎ 231-690; open 9am–5pm daily), only 29km south of Coyhaique. It has two lifts and five different runs, up to 2km in length and ranging in difficulty from beginner to expert. Rental equipment is available.

Places to Stay
Budget Besides camping options at nearby Reserva Nacional Coyhaique, **Camping Alborado** (☎ 238-868; per person US$3.50), only 1km from the city, has exceptionally clean and sheltered sites, lots of bathrooms and individual sinks, fresh water, firepits and electricity.

Albergue Las Salamandras (☎ 211-865; campsites US$5; per person US$10), in a woodsy area about 2km south of town on the road to the old airport, is an attractive lodge with ample common spaces, a TV loft full of lounge-around cushions, two kitchens, large bathrooms, laundry tubs and cozy dorm rooms with loads of blankets. The managers arrange off-the-beaten-track adventures as well as help organize more sedate excursions.

Hospedaje Soledad (☎ 254-764; 21 de Mayo 935; campsites US$3.50, rooms US$9) has two spots on either side of the street, one with independent lodging, kitchen use and garden camping.

Hospedaje Don Santiago (☎ 231-116; Errázuriz 1040; per person US$6) is a small, friendly family-run spot with bright rooms and kitchen use, and will probably grow to include rooms with private bath.

Hospedaje Nathy (☎ 231-047; Almirante Simpson 417; per person US$9) is pleasant and friendly with somewhat cramped rooms, and breakfast is included.

Hospedaje Sra Blanca (☎ 232-158; Simpson 459; per person US$11.50), with delightful owners, offers large rooms (no sharing), most of them in an independent annex. A couple of doubles with private bath are also available. Rates include an abundant breakfast.

Hospedaje Guarda (☎ 232-158; Simpson 471; per person US$12) has commodious rooms in a garden setting, but some of the mattresses are too soft.

Hospedaje Lautaro (☎ 238-116; Lautaro 269; per person US$9), open summer only, is in a spacious, convenient house with kitchen access for quick and easy meals. Late-night revelers note that it locks up around midnight.

Hospedaje Baquedano (☎ 232-520; Baquedano 20; camping US$5; per person US$10) has garden camping with spectacular views in the small backyard, plus an apartment with three beds, kitchen and bath to share.

Residencial Mónica (☎ 234-302; Eusebio Lillo 664; per person US$13) is a well-regarded small place with cozy rooms with private bath and breakfast, plus a decent restaurant on the 1st floor.

Mid-Range & Top End Hostal Bon (☎ 231-189; Serrano 91; singles US$24) is a bright and comfortable place that's managed with enthusiasm.

Hostal Araucaria (☎ 232-707; Vielmo 71; singles/doubles US$25/41), on a quiet street, has attractive rooms with private bath and lovely views from the breakfast nook.

La Estancia (☎ 250-193; Colón 166; 4-person cabins US$50), in a quiet neighborhood, has attractive log cabins bedecked in gingham and surrounded by daisy and rose bushes. It's a comfortable spot and a great deal for small groups.

El Reloj (☎ 231-108; Baquedano 828; singles/doubles/triples US$41/60/75) is Coyhaique's most attractive lodging option. It's in a renovated warehouse with touches of rusticity blending elegantly with a smart, clean design. Rooms are accessed from the comfortable lounge with a roaring fireplace, but buffered by an unobtrusive hallway that helps keep the rooms quiet. Upstairs rooms are slightly larger and brighter and have outstanding views. The kitchen provides sumptuous meals; breakfast is included and fixed-price lunches are US$6.

Hotelera San Sebastián (☎ 233-427; Baquedano 496; singles/doubles US$46/63) sports large rooms, each one with an exceptional view of the grassy valley below. Plush beds loaded down in duvets, plus central heating, keep the rooms cozy, and despite being on a main thoroughfare, the place is amazingly quiet.

Hostería Coyhaique (☎ 231-137; Magallanes 131; singles/doubles US$77/92), set among ample gardens, is highly regarded and favored by higher-end organized tour groups.

The rather cold slate lobby leads to wings of smallish rooms, some with garden views, others quite dark.

Places to Eat
Lito's (☎ 214-528; Lautaro 147; fixed-price meals US$4-6) might not look like much, but the service is excellent and the food consistently well prepared. A fixed-price meal, including a platter full of salad and a good portion of fish or meat, is quite a bargain.

Café Samoa (☎ 232-864; Prat 653) is a cozy little bar and restaurant with cheap meals and snacks.

Cafetería Alemana (☎ 231-731; Condell 119; US$3-5) serves up sandwiches, crepes and roasted chicken plates (the best deal) in an eatery that can get rather smoky.

Café Oriente (☎ 231-622; Condell 201; US$3-5), clad in tacky orange, is smaller and has excellent sandwiches.

Café Ricer (☎ 232-920; Horn 48; US$4-10), just off the Plaza de Armas, could possibly be the most touristy eatery south of Santiago. It's expensive, pretentious and can have apathetic service, but stays open longer, has a bilingual menu (including an assortment of breakfasts and vegetarian options), hosts slide shows, sells maps and local trinkets and plays the most awful throwback-to-the-'80s music around. Its upstairs restaurant has a more elaborate menu.

Casino de Bomberos (☎ 231-437; General Parra 365; fixed-price lunches US$5), within a basic windowless dining room, is packed at lunch with locals, and with reason: This is the best deal for a decent meal at a moderate price.

La Olla (☎ 234-700; Prat 176; lunches US$6-8) specializes in Spanish cuisine, including paella. While dinners are a bit pricey, the lunch specials are within reach of most budgets.

La Fiorentina (☎ 238-899; Prat 230; large pizza US$9) serves passable pizzas with lots of toppings, plus cold beers.

La Casona (☎ 238-894; Obispo Vielmo 77; fixed-price lunches US$7, meals US$10-12) provides patrons with an intimate formal dining option. While the chefs offer such usuals as salmon or congrio (conger eel) with a variety of sauces and pastel de jaivas (a creamy crab dish), they also offer more elaborately prepared meals, such as lamb stuffed with grilled vegetables with a reduced Merlot

sauce. An ample wine list and homemade desserts round out the meal.

Two large **supermarkets**, including Vyhmeister, are near each other on Lautaro, one at Prat, the other at Cochrane.

Entertainment
Coyhaique has a surprisingly active nightlife. **Piel Roja** (☎ 237-832; Moraleda 495) is a kaleidoscope of color and design. The downstairs circular bar and lounge, often swarming with the city's youth and with fly-fishing guides, is the mellow place to drink and chat, while upstairs, at least from 1:30am-5am, is a romping dance floor.

Pub Z (☎ 240-025; Moraleda 420) has live music in its converted red-brick galpón. It also hosts art exhibits and serves basic sandwiches and light fare.

Bar West Pub (☎ 210-007; Bilbao 110) brings the US West frontier here.

Peña Quilantál (☎ 234-394; Baquedano 791) features live folk music on weekend nights; shows may start considerably later than advertised.

Shopping
Several crafts outlets sell woolens, leather goods and wood carvings. The **Feria Artesanal** (Plaza de Armas) and **Manos Azules** (☎ 230-719; Riquelme 435) are worth a look.

Getting There & Away
Air LanChile (☎ 231-188; General Parra 402) has three daily flights (most leaving in the morning) to Puerto Montt (US$90) and Santiago (US$230) from the Balmaceda airport.

Transporte Aéreo Don Carlos (☎/fax 231-981; Cruz 63) flies small craft to Chile Chico (US$32) weekdays except Thursday, Caleta Tortel (US$30) Wednesday, and Cochrane (US$60) and Villa O'Higgins (US$93) Monday and Thursday.

For information on flights to Parque Nacional Laguna San Rafael, see that section later in this chapter.

Bus Bus transportation in and out of Coyhaique is just about as confusing as getting around the plaza. The dingy **bus station** (☎ 258-203; cnr Lautaro & Magallanes) is home to some bus companies, but most operate out of offices elsewhere in town, as indicated below. Bus service along the Carretera Austral is improving in frequency and quality, but it still has a long way to go. Most companies use small vans with tires that seem to blow in the most isolated spots (and when it's raining). The road is tough on vehicles, and most companies, in an effort to get the most money out of one run, cram in as many people and packs as they can and use just one driver – on the main Coyhaique-Chaitén route, drivers charge forth for 12 to 15 hours on the washboardy, blind-curve road, spend the night in Chaitén, and then barrel back the next day to pick up the next round of travelers. So, until that sad day when the road is completely paved and the large companies take over, companies and departures vary depending on demand. Most trips to Chaitén depart Coyhaique every other day (with one day's rest during the week), leave between 8am and 9am and charge about US$25. If you're planning to spend the night somewhere en route (besides La Junta), it is wise to reserve a spot on the next bus.

Companies going to Chaitén include **Buses Norte** (☎ 232-167; *General Parra 337*), **Transportes Muñóz** (☎ 251-266; *General Parra 337*) and **Buses California** (☎ 233-707; *bus terminal*).

Otherwise, take a bus to La Junta (US$12, seven to 10 hours), from where there are more buses to Chaitén: **Buses Pilchero** (☎ 239-218), **Buses Sao Paulo** (☎ 254-369) and **Los Ñadis** (☎ 258-203) all leave from the bus terminal.

To Puerto Cisnes, **Buses Hernández** (☎ 218-517; *12 de Octubre 337*) leaves daily except Sunday (US$9). There is also service to Puerto Cisnes from La Junta.

For Puerto Aisén and Puerto Chacabuco, **Buses Don Carlos** (☎ 231-981; *Cruz 63*) and **Buses Suray** (☎ 238-387; *Arturo Prat 265*) leave approximately every 1½ hours (US$2, one hour).

Colectivos and shuttle buses head to Puerto Ingeniero Ibáñez (US$5, 1½ hours) to connect with the Chile Chico ferry. These include **Colectivos Puerto Ibáñez** (*cnr Arturo Prat & Errázuriz*) and **Transportes Ali** (☎ 219-009, 250-346), which offers door-to-port shuttle service.

Villa Cerro Castillo (US$4 to US$5) is accessed by Buses Don Carlos, which continues south twice weekly to Puerto Murta (US$8), Puerto Río Tranquilo (US$9), Puerto Bertrand (US$12.50) and Cochrane (US$16). **Acuario 13** (☎ 232-067; *bus terminal*) and Los Ñadis also go to Cochrane four times weekly.

El Condor (☎ 210-452; *Freire 147*) goes to Puerto Río Tranquilo (US$10, five hours) at 4pm Thursday and Monday, from where connections can be made to Chile Chico.

For the long-haul trip north to Osorno and Puerto Montt (US$30, about 20 hours) via Argentina, **Turibús** (☎ 231-333; *Baquedano 1171*) leaves at 5pm Tuesday and Saturday.

For trips south to Punta Arenas (US$41) via Comodoro Rivadavia, Argentina, **Bus Sur** (☎ 211-460; *bus terminal*) goes at 4pm Tuesday, or take bus service to Comodoro from where other buses leave for Punta Arenas. Turibús leaves for Comodoro at 11am Monday and Friday (US$26, eight hours), and **Buses Giobbi** (☎ 232-067; *bus station*) leaves at 9:30am Tuesday and Saturday (US$28).

Boat Ferries to Chiloé, Chaitén and Puerto Montt leave from Puerto Chacabuco, two hours west of Coyhaique by bus, but ferry companies have their offices in Coyhaique. Schedules are subject to change. For transportation to Puerto Chacabuco, see Bus above.

Transmarchilay (☎ 231-971; *General Parra 86*) runs the ferry *El Colono* from Puerto Chacabuco to Puerto Montt (24 hours) once or twice a week, leaving in the evening. Reclining chairs cost US$33 to US$39, bunk beds US$75 to US$105 (based on double occupancy); meals are not included and must be reserved in advance. **Navimag** (☎ 223-306; *Presidente Ibáñez 347*) also sails from Puerto Chacabuco to Puerto Montt, on Sunday and Friday in summer, three or four times monthly the rest of the year. **Cruceros Skorpios** (☎ 213-755; *General Parra 21*) runs luxury trips to Parque Nacional Laguna San Rafael. For fares, see Getting There & Away for Puerto Montt in La Araucanía & the Lakes District chapter.

Ferries that cross Lago General Carrera to/from Puerto Ingeniero Ibáñez and Chile Chico have offices in town: **Naviera Sotramin** (☎ 233-515, 234-240; *Simón Bolívar 254*) runs the ferry *Pilchero* and **Mar del Sur** (☎ 231-255; *Baquedano 146-A*) runs the ferry *Chelenco*. If you're driving, make reservations early.

Getting Around

To/From the Airport Call-in shuttle services to the Balmaceda airport, 50km southeast of town, include **Minibuses Kaiken** (☎ 252-749; *12 de Octubre & Simpson*),

Transfer Coyhaique (☎ 210-495, 09-838-5070) and Transfer Aisén Tour (☎ 217-070, 09-489-4760). Most leave two hours before scheduled departure (US$4).

Car & Bicycle Because public transportation in this region is infrequent, sometimes inconvenient and focused on major destinations, many travelers rent cars. The local supply is limited, so advance reservations are advisable.

Shop around because prices vary considerably. Try Traeger (☎ 231-648, fax 231-264; Baquedano 457), Automundo AVR (☎ 231-621, fax 231-794; Bilbao 510), or Los Andes Patagónicos (☎ 232-920; Horn 48). The Automóvil Club de Chile (☎ 231-847; Carrera 333) is exceptionally friendly and helpful; staff meet clients at the airport and pick up the cars there as well.

Figon (☎ 234-616; Simpson 888) rents bicycles and does repairs.

RN COYHAIQUE
On the southern slopes of Cerro Cinchao, only 5km from town, spacious and forested Reserva Nacional Coyhaique (admission US$1) is a good day hike (about 1½ hours from Coyhaique), offering great views of the town and the enormous basalt columns of Cerro Macay in the distance.

Take Baquedano north, across the bridge, then go right at the gravel road, a steep climb best accessed by 4WD. Patagonia Adventure Expedition (see Coyhaique above) runs half-day inflatable kayaking trips (US$25) down Río Simpson with Class II and III rapids and full-day rafting trips (US$60) down Río Mañihuales (just north of the reserve).

Camping (US$6) is possible. From the park entrance, it's another 2.5km to Casa Bruja, with five campsites with firepits, hot water, showers and bathrooms, or 4km through coigue and lenga forests to Laguna Verde, where the campsites have more basic facilities. Hiking trails also lead to other small lakes – Laguna Los Sapos and Laguna Venus.

RN RÍO SIMPSON
Straddling the highway to Puerto Chacabuco, 41,000-hectare Reserva Nacional Río Simpson is an accessible, scenic area where streams from tributary canyons cascade over near-vertical cliffs to join the broad valley of the Río Simpson, 37km west of Coyhaique. Conaf's **Centro de Visitantes** consists of a

small natural history museum and botanical garden. A short walk leads to Cascada La Virgen, a shimmering waterfall on the north side of the highway.

Five kilometers east of the Centro de Visitantes, **Camping San Sebastián** (campsites night only/full day US$5/10) has protected sites and hot water. Near the confluence of the Río Simpson and the Río Correntoso, 24km west of Coyhaique, **Camping Río Correntoso** (☎ 232-005; sites per car/person US$11/4) has 50 spacious riverside sites within a bucolic setting. The showers are a tad rustic, but hot.

To get there, take any of the frequent buses between Coyhaique and Puerto Aisén; for details, see Bus under Coyhaique earlier in this chapter.

MONUMENTO NATURAL DOS LAGUNAS
On the road to Paso Coyhaique at the Argentine border, this 181-hectare wetland reserve (admission US$1.20) has abundant bird life, including black-necked swans, coots and grebes; the area is an ecological transition zone from southern beech forest to semiarid steppe. Around Laguna El Toro and Laguna Escondida, the two lakes that give the monument its name, Conaf maintains a self-guided nature trail, a campground (up to 6 people US$7.50) and a picnic area. While the park lacks regular public transport, Conaf (see Coyhaique earlier in this chapter) may be able to offer suggestions for getting there.

PUERTO CHACABUCO
☎ 67 • pop 22,000
Fumes from the fish meal processing plants permeate the air of Puerto Chacabuco, a hodgepodge town at the east end of a narrow fjord. Chacabuco is a frequent port of entry to Aisén, and it's reached by ferry from Puerto Montt or from the port of Quellón on Chiloé. It's also connected to Coyhaique, 82km away, by an excellent paved highway.

Catamaranes del Sur owns and runs the private nature reserve **Parque Aikén del Sur** (adults/children US$35/free), 5km from town. Visited mainly by its package-tour clients and guests at Hotel Loberías del Sur (see below), the park's exclusivity (it has a guarded gate) and entrance fees will deter most independent travelers, but those who do go might find it interesting. Five separate trails, most quite easy and ranging from three to five hours, wind through the native forests. Accessible only with a guide (that's really what you're paying for), the walks are geared toward educating visitors about the native trees and the area's ecosystem. Fortunately, the guides, most of whom speak English, do an impressive job.

Places to Stay & Eat
Hotel Moraleda (☎ 351-155; O'Higgins 82; rooms per person US$8), just outside the harbor compound, is convenient for late arrivals on the ferries, but it is mediocre and suffers from the smell of fish meal.

Hotel Loberías del Sur (☎ 351-115; JM Carrera 50; singles/doubles US$90/119) provides a level of luxury quite out of synch with its locale. Patronized mainly by folks on Catamaranes del Sur cruises, the hotel is five-star elegant, with fancy bathrooms with plush white towels and bright rooms with thick walls and windows to keep it quiet. The restaurant (mains US$8-12) is a worthwhile splurge. Service is outstanding, and the dishes, though perhaps a tad too complicated and salty, are tasty and very filling. Try a foil-baked salmon or congrio with centolla and mushroom sauce.

Getting There & Away
Buses from Coyhaique schedule departures to meet arriving and departing ferries, which go to/from Puerto Montt, Puerto Natales and Parque Nacional Laguna San Rafael. **Navimag** (☎ 351-111, fax 351-192) and **Transmarchilay** (☎/fax 351-144) have offices at the port. For bus and ferry details, see Coyhaique earlier in this chapter.

PN LAGUNA SAN RAFAEL
Established in 1959, the 1.7-million-hectare Parque Nacional Laguna San Rafael (admission US$5) is the region's most impressive and popular attraction despite the difficulty and expense of getting here. Dense with floating icebergs calved from the Campo Hielo San Valentín, part of the Campo de Hielo Norte, Laguna San Rafael is a memorable sight even beneath the somber clouds that so often hang like gloomy curtains over surrounding peaks, including 4058m Monte San Valentín, the southern Andes' highest peak. Most visitors arrive by sea, shifting to smaller craft and rubber rafts to approach the glacier's 60m face. Unfortunately, visitors arriving by sea spend only a few hours at the glacier and don't set foot on land. Those who fly get to hike to

---

What Is Alumysa?

While traveling around Coyhaique and Puerto Chacabuco, you'll probably hear reference to the 'Alumysa project,' which will alter the waterways and lifestyles of Puerto Aisén and Puerto Chacabuco. Alumysa is an aluminum smelter that Toronto-based Noranda, Inc, has proposed to build. The smelter would produce 440 tons of ingots per year for export. Alumina ore would be imported from Australia, Brazil and Jamaica for processing in southern Chile before export to Asia. Electricity for the plant would be generated from three hydroelectric power plants that Noranda also proposes to build on nearby rivers. Environmentalists are concerned that Chile could lose more rivers to dam projects, and they also point out that the plant will produce 600,000 to 800,000 tons of solid and toxic industrial waste each year. The increased possibility of contaminated water from the proposed plant and/or oil spills from barge traffic has prompted the salmon industry, which has cultivation centers in the nearby fjords, to join in the fight against the project.

the glacier, but with limited time as well. Well-equipped travelers in top physical condition and with the funds to organize transportation can stay to hike or climb around the area. A new road from Puerto Río Tranquilo to Bahía Exploradores on the Estuario San Francisco may improve access to the park in the near future, but this is still about 65km north of the glacier.

Visitors will see considerable wildlife, mostly birds, including flightless steamer ducks, black-browed and sooty albatross and Magellanic penguins. Otters, sea lions and elephant seals also frequent the icy waters, while pudú, pumas and foxes inhabit the surrounding forests and uplands.

The park is 225km southwest of Puerto Chacabuco via a series of longitudinal channels between the Chonos Archipelago and the Península de Taitao. Only the low-lying Istmo de Ofqui, linking Taitao and the mainland, impedes access to the Golfo de Penas. In 1940 the Chilean government began a canal to connect the two, abandoning the project after proceeding only 300m. Possibly as a result of global warming, the glacier has receded dramatically over the past several decades.

Camping Laguna Caiquenes near the Conaf office by the airstrip has five rustic sites (free with park entrance fee); there is water and a bathroom, fires are not allowed, and no food is available at the park.

Organized Tours

Charter flights from Coyhaique land at Laguna San Rafael's 775m gravel airstrip and usually spend only an hour at the glacier before returning. Contact **Patagonia Explorer Aviación** (☎ 09-817-2172; e stonepiloto@ hotmail.com), operated by recommended pilot Willy Stone; **Aerohein** (☎/fax 232-772; Baquedano 500, Coyhaique); and **Transportes Aéreos San Rafael** (☎ 232-048; 18 de Septiembre 469, Coyhaique). Small planes carry five passengers for about US$600 to US$700 roundtrip for the 1½-hour flight (or US$180 per person). For those planning to stay and camp, two roundtrip flights must be reserved and purchased.

The following sailings all leave from Puerto Chacabuco. For details on trips originating in Puerto Montt, see that section in La Araucanía & the Lakes District chapter.

Transmarchilay (☎ 231-971; w www .elcolono.com; General Parra 86, Coyhaique) runs the 230-passenger El Colono from Puerto Montt on Friday, picking up passengers at Puerto Chacabuco on Saturday. Roundtrip fares from Puerto Chacabuco to Laguna San Rafael range from US$202 for a reclining seat to US$404 per person for a bunk. A four-person suite costs US$604 per person. After spending most of Sunday at Laguna San Rafael, the ship sails back to Chacabuco at 6pm.

Navimag (☎ 233-306, fax 233-386; w www.navimag.com; Presidente Ibáñez 347, Coyhaique) sails the ferry M/N Evangelistas from Puerto Chacabuco (originating in Puerto Montt), every four or five days in summer but only three or four times monthly the rest of the year. Embarking at Puerto Chacabuco, rates per person are US$208 (reclining seat), US$321 (bunk beds) and US$480 (AA cabin) based on double occupancy. The trip takes two days, sailing to the glacier at night. Students (with ID) can get a 10% discount, senior travelers 15%.

Cruceros Skorpios (☎ 213-755; w www .skorpios.cl; General Parra 21, Coyhaique)

sails from Puerto Chacabuco once every seven days from September to March, with more limited trips until the end of May. The four- and five-day trips leave on either Monday or Friday, returning on the opposite day. It sails the fjords at night, unfortunately, but allows more time around the glacier. The trip also includes staying at its private hot springs resort, Quitralco. Four-day trips cost from US$520 to US$690. Five-day trips cost US$60 more. Rates include transfer from Balmaceda airport.

Catamaranes del Sur (☎ 351-112; w www .catamaranesdelsur.cl; JM Carrera 50, Puerto Chacabuco) runs a day trip from Puerto Chacabuco on the Iceberg Expedition, leaving at 8am, thereby ensuring you get to see the fjords to the glacier during the day, but with less time at the glacier face. Package trips including lodging at its hotel, Loberías del Sur, are also available. The 12½-hour trip costs US$286 per person, including meals.

Patagonia Connection (☎ 02-225-6489; w www.patagoniaconnex.cl; Fidel Ortiza 1921, Oficina 1006, Santiago) visits the glacier during one of its exclusive package tours including Termas de Puyuhuapi Hotel & Spa.

RN CERRO CASTILLO

Reaching nearly 2700m and flanked by three major glaciers on its southern slopes, the basalt spires of Reserva Nacional Cerro Castillo tower above southern beech forests in this sprawling 180,000-hectare reserve, 75km south of Coyhaique. Cerro Castillo has some fine but rarely visited treks and fishing spots. One excellent four-day trek leaves from Km 75, at the north end of the reserve, to Villa Cerro Castillo at the south end; it's described in Lonely Planet's Trekking in the Patagonian Andes.

Conaf operates a modest but sheltered and shady **campground** (per site US$5) at Laguna Chaguay, 67km south of Coyhaique. Backcountry camping is also possible, but check in with the ranger, since trekking is potentially hazardous.

Bus drivers will stop to let you out at the ranger station and campground.

VILLA CERRO CASTILLO

On a short lateral from the Carretera Austral about 10km west of the Puerto Ingeniero Ibáñez junction, Villa Cerro Castillo is a pioneer settlement with fantastic views of the Cerro Castillo peaks. For those looking for authentic rodeos, the town's Festival Costumbrista, usually held in February, definitely delivers. There is now a **tourist office** *(open 10am-8pm daily Jan-Feb).*

La Querencia *(O'Higgins 522; rooms US$8)* has rooms that are a bit dark, but are protected from the wind, and the shared bathroom is clean and large. Lunch in the quirky restaurant costs US$5.

Don Carlos buses shuttle daily to/from Coyhaique and twice weekly to Puerto Murta and Puerto Río Tranquilo (for details, see Coyhaique earlier in this chapter).

PUERTO INGENIERO IBÁÑEZ
☎ 67 • pop 2450

When Volcán Hudson erupted in 1991, Puerto Ingeniero Ibáñez, on the north shore of Lago General Carrera, got buried in ash. This forlorn little town has unearthed and repaired itself since that disaster, but anytime the wind picks up, the place gets clobbered with ashy dust storms that turn the sky dark and send townspeople scurrying inside. Ferries to Chile Chico, on the lake's south shore, leave from here; other than that, there's little of interest. **Residencial Ibáñez** *(☎ 423-227; Dickson 31; singles US$6.50),* opposite the ferry dock, has surprisingly nice, but unheated, singles with plenty of extra blankets. Breakfast costs US$3.50, and other meals are available.

For ground transportation from Coyhaique to Puerto Ibáñez, see Coyhaique earlier in this chapter. Ferry schedules seem to change year to year and season to season. **Naviera Sotramin** crosses to Chile Chico (2½ hours) in the ferry *El Pilchero* at 9am daily except Sunday; fares are US$3.50 per person, but students and children pay half-price. **Mar del Sur** runs *Chelenco,* a vehicle-only ferry (no passenger seating), on Tuesday, Wednesday, Friday and Saturday at 10:30am. Rates are passengers US$3, bicycles US$2.50, motorcycles US$6.50 and vehicles US$31-37. For contact information, see Coyhaique earlier in this chapter.

CHILE CHICO
☎ 67 • pop 4400

On the southern shore of Lago General Carrera, Chile Chico is a compact village only a few kilometers from the Argentine border at Los Antiguos. The winding gravel highway from the east straightens out suddenly into this windy town of paved roads, shaded with poplars and fruit trees. Founded in 1928 by immigrant fortune seekers, Chile Chico derived its early prosperity from copper, the blue-tinged ore still visible in the rocky hills. Today, locals earn their living from locally sold agriculture, livestock and from the gold mines to the west, run by US-based Coeur d'Alene Mines Corporation and opened in 1995. Most travelers zip through town, but there are a few worthwhile side trips.

The mountainous road known as Paso Las Llaves, west from Chile Chico to the junction with the Carretera Austral, is one of the region's highlights. It is a scary and stunning road trip of abrupt curves, blind corners, loose gravel, steep inclines high above the lake and no guardrails, giving the impression that its engineers were roller-coaster ride specialists. If driving, proceed very slowly; in some places the roadway is barely wide enough for a single vehicle.

Information
For area information, there's the **Oficina de Información Turística** *(☎ 411-123; cnr O'Higgins & Lautaro; open 8:30am-1pm & 2pm-5pm Mon-Fri)* and **Conaf** *(☎ 411-325; Blest Gana 121).*

Banco del Estado *(González 112; open 9am-2pm Mon-Fri)* changes US cash only and has reasonable rates, but it collects a commission on all traveler's checks.

Other services include the **post office** *(Manuel Rodríguez 121),* **Entel** *(O'Higgins)* and the call center **Fonosol,** near the fire station.

Antonio Rodríguez *(☎ 411-209; Pedro González 253)* rents horses (half/full day US$8/12) and arranges excursions to Laguna Jeinimeni, Cueva de las Manos (Argentina) and other nearby sites.

Casa de la Cultura
Chile Chico's museum and cultural center *(cnr O'Higgins & Lautaro)* features a ground-floor collection of works by regional artists and a second-floor assemblage of local artifacts, including minerals and fossils. Outside is the restored *El Andes,* which was built in Glasgow, Scotland, to navigate the Thames, but was brought here to carry passengers and freight around the lake.

Places to Stay

Camping Chile Chico (☎ 411-598; Pedro Burgos 6; per person US$4) is a tranquil but small campground protected from the wind by poplars. There are hot showers, and the kind owners sell firewood, share the bounty of local produce and organize an occasional *asado* or salmon bake.

Hospedaje No Me Olvides (per person: campsites US$2, rooms US$7.50), 200m from town on the highway to Argentina, is a popular, friendly budget choice with large clean rooms and camping in the apple and pear orchard. The owners allow kitchen use, but also cook up reasonable meals.

Hospedaje La Avenida (☎ 411-904; O'Higgins 420; per person US$6), upstairs from the Entel office and pushed by reps of the Argentine travel agency Chaltén Travel, is a small affair of foam beds stuffed close together. It's okay in a pinch and has kitchen access.

Hospedaje Brisas del Lago (☎ 411-204; Manuel Rodríguez 443; per person US$8) offers the best value rooms in town – they're clean, larger than other places and numerous, but service can be apathetic.

Hospedaje Eben Ezer (☎ 411-535; Rodriquez 302; per person US$5.50) has hot and stuffy upstairs rooms (you can't open the windows), but they are plenty large. Just don't expect too much from the people running it. Breakfast costs US$1.

Hotel Ventura (☎ 411-710; Carrera 290; per person US$13) has small creaky rooms with foam mattresses and lots of shared bathrooms. The dining area and bar are unfortunately monopolized by the TV.

Hostería de la Patagonia (☎ 411-337; camping US$4, singles/doubles with private bath US$20/35, with shared bath US$11/25), 200m from town on the highway to Argentina, was originally the home of an *estancia chacra* (small independent farm) owner, built by some of the area's first Belgian settlers. Rooms and common areas are attractively outfitted with many of the ranch's equine knickknacks, while outside there's a large lawn and flower gardens. Breakfast – ample and with an abundance of local jams – is included. The campsites overlook the gardens and have hot showers.

Places to Eat

Café Elizabeth y Loly (☎ 411-288; Pedro González 25; mains US$3-9, 3-course lunch US$10), opposite the plaza, is a good spot for snacks and ice cream, and supposedly Arabian cakes.

Aguas Azules (☎ 411-320; Manuel Rodríguez 252; lunches US$6.50), the town's better value, efficiently serves set-menu lunches in a small, unpretentious dining room.

Café Refer (☎ 411-225; O'Higgins 424; lunches US$5) is a good meeting spot, with large plates (chefs are keen on sauces), pizzas and a fun ambience. There's also a well-stocked bar, beer on draft and a selection of wines.

Getting There & Away

Air Transportes Aéreos Don Carlos (☎ 411-490; O'Higgins 264) flies weekdays except Thursday to Coyhaique (US$33). The airfield is just outside town, on the road to the Argentine border.

Bus A number of shuttle buses cross the border to Los Antiguos (US$3) just 9km east. **Acotrans** (☎ 411-582) leaves from in front of the Fonosol office on O'Higgins. Other shuttles leave from O'Higgins 420, which coordinate with Chaltén Travel's service along Argentina's Ruta 40.

From Los Antiguos, travelers can make connections in Argentina to Perito Moreno, Caleta Olivia, El Chaltén and southern Argentine Patagonia.

Transportes Ales (☎ 411-739; Rosa Amelia 800) goes to Cochrane (US$16, six hours) Wednesday and Saturday, stopping in Puerto Guadal (US$9) and Puerto Bertrand (US$13), returning along the same route on Thursday and Sunday.

Transportes Condor (☎ 419-500) goes Tuesday and Thursday to Puerto Río Tranquilo (US$11), stopping in Puerto Guadal (US$5). On Wednesday morning the shuttle continues from Río Tranquilo (you must spend the night) to Coyhaique (US$10). It offers a weekly transportation package (US$38) to Coyhaique, including lodging and breakfast in Puerto Río Tranquilo and a tour of Capilla de Marmól (see Puerto Río Tranquilo later in this chapter).

Boat Ferry schedules to Puerto Ingeniero Ibañéz (2½ hours) change from year to year and season to season. Check at the Entel office (see Information earlier in this section) for the latest posting.

Naviera Sotramin's auto-passenger ferry *Pilchero* leaves Chile Chico at 4:30pm Monday through Friday and at 2pm Sunday. Mar del Sur's ferry *Chelenco* leaves at 4pm Tuesday, Thursday and Friday and at 1pm Sunday. Rates are passengers US$3, bicycles US$2.50, motorcycles US$6.50 and vehicles US$31-37. For contact information, see Coyhaique earlier in this chapter; reservations for vehicles are highly suggested.

RN JEINEMENI

Within the transition zone to Patagonian steppe, little-visited Reserva Nacional Jeinemeni (*admission US$1*) covers 161,000 hectares, 52km southwest of Chile Chico. This is one of the area's least-appreciated beauty spots. Three private **camping areas** (*US$4*) are on the banks of the startlingly blue Lago Jeinemeni, about 400m from the Conaf office. A 5km hike leads to Laguna Esmeralda. Río Jeinemeni cuts across the road into the park, passable only by 4WD vehicles and only before midafternoon, when the water level gets too high. For those going as a day trip, leave early enough to cross on the way back before 4pm. En route to the reserve, about 25km south of Chile Chico, is an access road to an area with Tehuelche **cave paintings**. Getting to the cave requires a steep uphill climb (unmarked) and is best done with a guide.

A few locals with minivans arrange tours for groups, such as **Jaime Berrocal** (☎ 411-472, 411-461), who also arranges fishing trips. Multiday horse treks from Jeinemeni to Cochrane, via Paso Roballos and Paso La Leona, can be arranged with **Juan Luis Raty** (☎ 064-236-805 in Osorno).

PUERTO RÍO TRANQUILO

On the western shores of Lago General Carrera and one of the larger settlements between Coyhaique and Cochrane, Puerto Río Tranquilo is a decent place to rest, have a meal and load up on petrol (if they have any). Folks in town arrange boat trips to view the **Capilla de Marmól** (Marble Chapel), an intriguing geological formation – worth a visit if the water isn't rough. Just north of town is the new road being built northwest to Bahía Exploradores, which may improve access to Laguna San Rafael.

Residencial Carretera Austral (☎ 419-500; *1 Sur 233; per person US$11*), directly on the highway, also has a selection of inexpensive cabañas. **Residencial Los Pinos** (☎ 411-576; *2 Oriente 41; per person US$14*), painted in loud kelly green just west of the highway, has a restaurant with fixed-price meals for US$6. **Residencial Darka** (☎ 419-500; *Arrayanes 330; per person US$9*), a couple of blocks into the center of town, has a few decent rooms and a very kind owner.

Regular buses between Coyhaique and Cochrane will drop off and pick up passengers here. **Transportes Ales** goes to Chile Chico (US$16, six hours) Wednesday and Sunday mornings, returning on Tuesday, while **Transportes Condor** goes to Chile Chico at 6:30am Tuesday and Thursday, returning the same day around 9pm. For contact information, see Chile Chico earlier in this chapter.

CRUCE EL MAITÉN

Cruce el Maitén is nothing but a fork in the road. To the west, the Carretera Austral begins to wind its way to Puerto Bertrand, Cochrane and beyond. To the east is the beginning of the road alongside Lago General Carrera to Chile Chico. At and nearby this fork, a number of high-end fishing lodges have sprung up. Most offer a variety of activities, such as horse trekking, trips to Capilla de Marmól and, of course, fishing. Accommodations are usually in individual cabins overlooking the lake. Expect quality service, either a Jacuzzi or sauna and excellent food. Some of these include **Pasarela 2 Lodge** (☎ 411-425; *Km 265; cabañas for up to 5 people US$135*); **Bahía Catalina** (☎ 232-920; *Km 268; cabañas for up to 3 people US$63*); and **Hacienda Tres Lagos** (☎ 411-323; e hacienda@terra.cl; *Km 274; doubles US$150*), right at the junction.

PUERTO GUADAL

At the southwest end of Lago General Carrera on the highway to Chile Chico, 13km east of the junction with the Carretera Austral, Puerto Guadal's shingled houses are palpable evidence of Chilote immigration over the past two decades. This is a good place to rest before continuing on the highway: Most of the lodgings from here to Chile Chico are more exclusive and pricey. There's also a petrol station here.

Near the beachfront at the eastern edge of town there's **camping**, with rather exposed, rocky sites, but with some windbreaks. **Riconada** (☎ 431-224; *Las Camelias*

157; 5-person cabin US$55) is an alternative for small groups.

Hostería Huemules (☎ *411-202; Las Magnolias 382; per person US$9)* is a homey place with a good restaurant. If it looks closed, knock on the blue house next door.

Terra Luna (☎ *431-263;* e *t-luna@netline .cl; doubles US$80),* 1.5km along the highway to Chile Chico, provides small but attractive cabins and a forest Jacuzzi. All-inclusive adventure packages give guests a chance to trek, raft, ride and bike, accompanied by skillful guides (four- to nine-day packages, double occupancy, US$1380 to US$2700). This is a good spot for climbers and mountaineers.

Transportes Ales' shuttles to Chile Chico on Wednesday and Sunday mornings stop here. Enquire in Coyhaique about most recent service, as service changes frequently.

PUERTO BERTRAND
☎ 67

On the southeast shore of Lago Bertrand, 11km south of Cruce El Maitén, Puerto Bertrand is an unusual village of humble homes and high-end fishing lodges. With the quiet and spectacularly blue lake in the foreground and the enormous peaks of San Valentín and the Campo de Hielo Norte in the background, this is one of the most attractive spots along the stretch. It's also the base for mountaineering expeditions and rafting trips on Río Baker, Chile's most voluminous river.

About 40km south of Puerto Bertrand and 17km north of Cochrane, at the scenic confluence of the Río Baker and Río Nef, a decent gravel road climbs eastward up the valley of the Río Chacabuco to the Argentine border at Paso Roballos.

Organized Tours

Patagonia Adventure Expeditions (☎ *219-894;* w *www.adventurepatagonia.com; Dussen 357, Coyhaique)* offers rafting on the Río Baker (half-day trips, taking in Class III rapids, cost US$25), but its strength is five-day expeditions (per person US$590) into the region's wilderness. Focusing on 'cultural geography,' bilingual guides take groups (maximum six people) on journeys involving horse trekking through glacially carved valleys and old lenga forests, forging streams, climbing to Ventisquero Soler, ice climbing, and meeting up with gauchos for an asado. The price includes transfers to/

from Coyhaique. Ten-day trips are also arranged.

Places to Stay & Eat

Most places, except for the fishing lodges, take messages from the main public phone number (☎ 419-900).

Camping Municipal *(sites per person US$2-3),* on the riverside, is small but charming.

Hielos Norte Camping (☎ *72-491-779; per person US$3),* 3km south and just after Patagonia Baker Lodge, has sites in a shady coigue forest up from the riverbank, as well as a few protected picnic areas, a small dock and primitive but clean toilets.

Vista Hermosa *(campsites US$3; 4-person cabin US$66),* 4km south, has spacious grassy campsites near the riverbank with rustic toilets and firepits. Farther away, the two cabins are quite private and charmingly tacky. Look for the bright blue-and-green farmhouse.

Hospedaje Alicia Reyes *(Amador Esparza; camping US$3; singles/doubles US$5.50/9),* in the village, has tiny cramped rooms but an impressive bathroom. Breakfast costs US$3, but there is kitchen access for campers as well.

Hostería Puerto Bertrand *(per person US$13)* is rather run-down with rooms that lack views and ventilation. Breakfast is included; lunch or dinner costs US$8.

Fishing lodges around town have confusingly similar names.

Campo Baker (☎ *411-447, 236-373 in Coyhaique;* e *campobaker@entelchile.net; 4-person cabins US$240)* provides fully equipped cabins with wood stoves; most have spectacular views. The restaurant serves very filling meals (breakfast US$12, lunch or dinner US$24), or there's a quincho for asados. Multiday packages, with an emphasis on horse trekking or fishing, are arranged.

Lodge Río Baker (☎ *411-499;* w *www.rio baker.net; all-inclusive per person US$280),* 300 meters from the northern edge of town, takes full advantage of its great location right on the water, with floor-to-ceiling windows that drench the rooms and bedrooms in the river's intense blue color. Anglers can simply roll over in bed to see where the trout are jumping.

Patagonia Baker Lodge (☎ *411-903;* e *info lodge@pbl.cl; rooms from U$120),* about 3km south of town, provides upscale luxury in a friendly casual environment. The six rooms, all with two double beds and large bathrooms, have views of the river. The main lodge has an enormous sun deck with splendid views and a fly-tying loft. Fly-fishing programs start at US$250 per day.

COCHRANE
☎ 67 • pop 3000

Cochrane, 345km south of Coyhaique, lacks appeal, but it is a base from which many activities – namely fishing on Lago Cochrane, horse treks and hiking – can be organized.

It's also the last place on the Carretera Austral with a petrol station and the best place for information along this lonely stretch of road.

Head to **Red Río Baker** (☎ 522-646; **w** turismoriobaker.cl; San Valentín 438) for transportation details and the latest developments in Caleta Tortel and Villa O'Higgins. In summer, there's also a **tourist kiosk** (Plaza de Armas). Other services include **Conaf** (☎ 522-164; Río Nef 417), a **post office** (Esmeralda 199), a **call center** (cnr San Valentín & Las Golondrinas) and a **hospital** (☎ 522-131; O'Higgins 755).

Places to Stay & Eat
Hospedaje Cochrane (☎ 522-377; Dr Steffens 451; camping US$3) is a good choice for campers who need to stay in town. Sites are in the backyard orchard, firewood is available, and the one bathroom is shared with other lodgers.

Residencial Paola (☎ 522-215; Lago Brown 150; camping US$4, per person US$9) is a pastel-painted place with a precarious staircase and a lovely matron. Meals cost US$4.

Residencial Cero a Cero (☎ 522-158; Lago Brown 464; singles with shared/private bath US$9/15) is a good choice with comfortable beds and plenty of room.

Hotel Wellmann (☎ 522-171; Las Golondrinas 36; doubles/triples US$53/70) has bright rooms with real mattresses and heaters; breakfast is included.

Rogeri (☎ 522-264; Teniente Merino 502; lunches US$4) makes excellent fries and filling sandwiches and has decent beer.

La Costa Pub (Las Golondrinas 198; lunches US$6) specializes in 'El Patagón,' pan-fried pork or rabbit, boiled potatoes and a green salad. Basic sandwiches are also on offer.

Getting There & Away
Transporte Aéreo Don Carlos (☎ 522-150; Prat 281) flies from Coyhaique to Cochrane (US$62) and Villa O'Higgins (US$93).

Buses **Los Ñadis** (☎ 522-196; Los Helechos 490) goes to Coyhaique (US$12.50 to US$16, seven to 10 hours) at 8:30am Monday, Wednesday, Thursday and Saturday. **Buses Acuario 13** (☎ 522-143; Teniente Merino 481) goes at 8:15am Tuesday, Thursday and Saturday; in high season only, it also goes at 1pm Friday. **Transportes Ales** goes to Chile Chico (US$16, eight hours) Thursday and Sunday, stopping in Puerto Bertrand (US$3) and Puerto Guadal (US$6.50).

To get to El Vagabundo (US$9, three hours), from where there are launches to Caleta Gonzalo, Acuario 13 leaves at 9:30am Tuesday, Thursday and Sunday, and Los Ñadis leaves at 10am Sunday. For Villa O'Higgins (seven hours), Los Ñadis leaves at 8:30am Monday.

RN TAMANGO
The Reserva Nacional Tamango (also known as Reserva Nacional Lago Cochrane; admission US$3), covering a 7000-hectare transition zone to the Patagonian steppe, protects the largest population of the endangered huemul deer in the country, but sighting one is still a rare occasion. Trails (ranging from 1.5km to 7km) lead from the entrance to Laguna Elefantina, Laguna Tamanguito and 1722m Cerro Tamango. **Camping Las Correntadas** (Embarcadero, Playa Paleta; 6-person sites US$15, 4-person cabins US$40), provides large campsites (ask about individual rates) with potable water, wash basins and toilets. Cabins have bathrooms but not showers. The reserve is 6km northeast of Cochrane; there is no public transportation to the entrance. At the corner of Colonia and San Valentín, hikers can take Pasaje No 1 north and then east to access trails to the entrance. Red Río Baker distributes a trail map (see Cochrane above).

CALETA TORTEL
☎ 67 • pop 500

At the mouth of Río Baker and uniquely situated between two ice fields, Caleta Tortel is a picturesque fishing village of wooden houses linked together along the water's edge by wooden walkways and stairs. Launches down the Río Baker used to be the only way to access this gem, but a new road facilitates access. Hopefully, the village's status as a national monument will curb any unfavorable exploitation. Originally home to Alacalufes (Qawashqar), colonists didn't arrive until 1955.

The town's public **phone** (☎ 234-815) can take messages.

A few villagers organize all-day boat and hiking trips to Ventisqueros Montt (Campo de Hielo Sur) and Steffens (Campo de Hielo Norte). Trips for eight to 10 persons in high-speed boats cost US$130 to US$230. Interested parties should contact ☎ 211-876 or the public phone.

Sector Playa Ancha has free camping. **Hostal Costanera** *(Sra Luisa Escobar; ☎ 234-815; singles US$11)* is the largest lodging option. Other houses open to lodgers are **Sra Landeros**, **Sra Urrutia** and **Sra Quesada**, all of whom charge US$8 to US$9 with breakfast and about US$20 for full board.

Getting There & Away
Bus companies in Cochrane (see above) will have the latest details on transporta-

tion along the recently built road to Caleta Tortel. Los Ñandis drives to El Vagabundo, 20km north of Puerto Yungay, at 10am Sunday, and Acuario 13 goes at 9:30am Tuesday, Thursday and Sunday (US$9, three hours).

Municipal launch boats leave El Vagabundo. Check in Cochrane for their latest departure schedule. Private charters cost US$130, with a 12-person maximum.

SOUTH TO VILLA O'HIGGINS
South of El Vagabundo and the access road to Caleta Tortel, the Carretera Austral continues through wildly beautiful stretches. Unfortunately, the road is a mix of curves, washboards and potential slides, and it demands constant attention; only high-clearance vehicles should attempt this last stretch.

At **Puerto Yungay**, a government ferry hauls passengers and four cars to the east end of Fiordo Mitchell at Río Bravo, usually four times a day at 9am, noon, 3pm and 6pm (free, one hour). Space is limited so if you are driving, try to get there early and expect to wait.

Argentina, the Hard Way

Possibly the most alluring new development for intrepid travelers is the possibility to cross from Villa O'Higgins into Parque Nacional Los Glaciares and El Chaltén, Argentina. Consult tourist offices in Coyhaique, Cochrane and Villa O'Higgins before beginning your trip. Transportation along Lago del Desierto appears to be the most unpredictable. At time of research, travelers – backpackers and cyclists only – were able to cross in the following manner from December to March:

1. Chilean army boat (US$9, four hours) from Villa O'Higgins to Candelaria Mansilla on the south edge of Lago O'Higgins once a week, usually Saturday at 9am, leaving Mansilla at 3pm. Some lodging, guided treks and horse rental are available at Mansilla. Pass through Chilean customs and immigration here.

2. Trek or horseback to Laguna Redonda (two hours). Camping not allowed.

3. Trek or horseback to Laguna Larga (1½ hours). Camping not allowed.

4. Trek or horseback to north shore of Lago del Desierto (1½ hours). Camping allowed. Pass through Argentine customs and immigration here.

5. Ferry from north to south shores of Lago del Desierto (4½ hours). Camping allowed.

6. Shuttle bus to El Chaltén, 37km away (US$10, one hour).

Pack horses may be rented for the legs from Mansilla to Lago Desierto. Bring all necessary provisions (enough for at least four days), ID, Argentine visa and rain gear.

See PN Los Glaciares in the Magallanes & Tierra del Fuego chapter for a description of this area and accommodations. On the Argentine side, Rancho Grande Hostel, in El Chaltén, is the best source of information for the current details of this journey.

Another 100km of rugged road leads to the north end of a narrow arm of Lago O'Higgins (known as Lago San Martín on the Argentine side) and the isolated **Villa O'Higgins**, with its just over 450 inhabitants. First settled by English in 1914–16, the outpost attracted a few Chilean colonists, but wasn't officially founded until 1966. The road didn't reach here until 1999. Alluring in its isolation, O'Higgins provides spectacular country to explore on horseback or foot, and it has world-class fishing. Its popularity has also grown due to increasingly easy (but still arduous and complicated) transportation to El Chaltén and Parque Nacional Los Glaciares in Argentina (see the boxed text 'Argentina, the Hard Way'). The town's well-run **tourist office** (☎ 067-211-849; Plaza Cívica) can help with logistics and accommodations. The public **phone** (☎ 067-234-813) can also relay messages.

Locals organize **horse-ri...** US$12 per person. **Camping Do...** popular campground, or try **Isolde Ganga...** Río Mosco & Lago Cisne; US$3), with toilets and potable water. **Hospedajes** charge US$9 for a bed and breakfast, US$18 for full board. Many are on Pasaje Lago Salto. The more ample and tad more expensive **Hospedaje Patagonia** (☎ 234-813; Río Pascua) is worth a try, but also try **Hospedaje Apocalipsis 1:3**, **Hotel Branic** or **Hospedaje Mirta**.

Getting There & Away

Transporte Aéreo Don Carlos flies from Coyhaique (US$93, 1½ hours) Monday and Thursday, and from Cochrane (US$33, 45 minutes). **Los Ñandis** drives from Cochrane at 8:30am Monday (seven hours). If returning to Cochrane by bus, book your ticket in advance.

If driving, keep the headlights on, stop for huemuls and carry a spare tire.

Tierra del Fuego

...e's southernmost ...try's most historically ...ascinating. Región XII, ... art of Patagonia, takes in all of th... s territory beyond about 49° S, includ... e western half of the Isla Grande de Tierra del Fuego (whose eastern half is Argentine), the largely uninhabited islands of the Tierra del Fuego Archipelago, and the slice of Antarctica claimed by Chile. Travelers come the distance to trek in Torres del Paine, to gaze at the glaciers or simply to say they've been to the 'end of the world.' Whatever your reason for continuing this far south, keep in mind that the weather here can be extreme. Gusty winds and sudden rainstorms are regular occurrences in the summer, with temperatures varying seemingly at whim. And, once you're here, it only makes sense to extend your Patagonia travels into Argentina, where impressive parks, quirky towns and long, desolate roads provide a host of adventure.

See Books in the Facts for the Visitor chapter for a list of recommended histories of the region.

Traveling to Argentina

To visit just the Chilean destinations on this ragged scythe of land is like reading half a book. Fortunately, transportation between the countries is usually easy and plentiful, and crossing the border is effortless. This chapter includes the most-visited Argentine spots for Chilean travelers.

To the traveler's advantage, at least, the devaluation of the Argentine peso in 2001 has turned the country into one of South America's best bargains. As in Chile, traveling in Patagonia is more expensive than other areas, and because tourism is so linked, some services, mainly transportation, may reflect Chilean prices. Budget accommodations will cost between US$6 and US$10 and mid-range between US$20 and US$30. An average meal costs US$3 to US$6. You'll be able to find ATMs and exchange houses in most destinations.

Currently, visa requirements are the same as Chile's; you'll be given a tourist card upon entering as well. There is no Argentine consulate between Puerto Montt and Punta

Arenas, so if you will need a visa before you will be reaching either of these towns, get one at the Argentine consulate in Santiago. Also, don't cross the border where there are no officials to stamp you through. To do so is grounds for expulsion from the country. The most-used border crossings are at Cancha Carrera, between Torres del Paine and El

Highlights

- Trekking at Torres del Paine – one of the continent's best parks
- Kayaking in the iceberg lagoons of Glaciar Serrano
- Crouching down to the penguins at Isla Magdalena
- Soaking up the end-of-the-world feeling at Isla Navarino
- Spotting guanacos, ñandús and flamingos along the Patagonia roads

OTHER MAPS
Magallanes & Tierra del Fuego
pages 376-377
PN Torres del Paine, page 395

Puerto Natales
page 389

Punta Arenas
pages 378-379

Porvenir
page 403

MAGALLANES

Calafate, and Paso Integración Austral, between Punta Arenas and Río Gallegos.

Frequent buses link Puerto Natales with the Argentine towns El Calafate and El Chaltén, and Punta Arenas with Ushuaia; in fact, some travelers fly into Ushuaia as the starting point for southern tip explorations. Only the much-desired and hotly debated link across the Beagle Channel from Puerto Williams to Ushuaia has yet to be officially formed.

For expanded coverage of the places mentioned in this guide and for information on destinations farther into Argentina, see Lonely Planet's *Argentina, Uruguay & Paraguay* guide.

Magallanes

Battered by westerly winds and storms that drop huge amounts of rain and snow on the seaward slopes of the Andes, Magallanes is a rugged, mountainous area, geographically remote from the rest of the country. The only way to get here from the rest of Chile is by air or sea, or by road through Argentine Patagonia.

The Alacaluf (Qawashqar) and Yahgan (Yamaná) Indians, both canoe people who lived in the channels, subsisted on fishing, while the Tehuelche (Aonikenk) and Ona (Selk'nam) were hunters. Today, only a few individuals of pure descendent remain.

Magellan, who in 1520 became the first European to visit the region, left it his name, but early Spanish colonization attempts failed. Tiny Puerto Hambre (Port Famine), at the southern end of the Strait of Magellan, is a reminder of these efforts. Nearby, the restored wooden bulwarks of Fuerte Bulnes recall Chile's first colonization in 1843, when President Manuel Bulnes ordered the army south to the area, which at the time was sparsely populated by indigenous peoples.

Increased maritime traffic spurred by the California gold rush bolstered Punta Arenas, whose initial prosperity came from the ships that passed through the straits between Europe and California and Australia. With the opening of the Panama Canal and the reduction of traffic around Cape Horn (Cabo de Hornos), the port's international importance diminished. Later wealth was earned from the wool and mutton industries, which trans-

The Hole in the Sky

The continuing deterioration of the ozone layer over Antarctica has impacted southern South America more than any other permanently inhabited area on earth. The hole hovers over this region in the southern spring, and it affects both humans and livestock. Posters displaying the daily ozone danger level can be found throughout Punta Arenas. Most locals wear brimmed hats and sunglasses when outside, and travelers are wise to do so, too. Even when the sun doesn't feel strong, or there are clouds covering it, you'll most likely feel a slight stinging sensation as the sun slowly burns your face. Stay cautious and slather on the sunscreen.

formed both Argentine and Chilean Patagonia in the late 19th century.

Magallanes' modern economy depends on commerce, petroleum development and fisheries. Punta Arenas is the world's second-largest producer of methanol. It is a prosperous corner of the country, with some of its highest levels of employment and school attendance, and some of its best quality housing and public services.

PUNTA ARENAS
☎ 61 • pop 121,000
The most convenient base for transportation options around this area, Punta Arenas is an attractive mixture of elaborate mansions dating from the wool boom of the late 19th and early 20th centuries, good traveler's services and a variety of adventurers from all walks of life. Nothing sums it up more than the basement bar of the ornate Club de la Unión: Here, Antarctic explorers, geologists, Torres del Paine hikers and cruise-ship softies all gather together, faces red from the incessant winds and glaring sun, to share the thrill of being in such a spectacular corner of the world.

A busy place during the week, Punta Arenas shuts down on Sunday.

History
Founded in 1848, Punta Arenas was originally a military garrison and penal settlement that proved to be conveniently situated for

MAGALLANES

ships headed to California during the gold rush. Compared to the initial Chilean settlement at Fuerte Bulnes, 60km south, the town had a better, more protected harbor and superior access to wood and water. For many years, English maritime charts had called the site 'Sandy Point,' and this became its rough Spanish equivalent.

In Punta Arenas' early years, its economy depended on wild animal products (including sealskins, guanaco hides, feathers and guano, for fertilizer), mineral products (such as coal and gold) and timber, including firewood. None of these was a truly major industry, and the economy did not take off until the last quarter of the 19th century, after the territorial governor authorized the purchase of 300 purebred sheep from the Falkland Islands. This successful experiment encouraged others to invest in sheep, and by the turn of the century, nearly two million animals grazed in the territory.

The area's speculators (that is, the Menéndez-Brauns) could not have built their commercial and pastoral empires without the labor of immigrants, including English, Irish, Scots, Croats, French, Germans, Spaniards, Italians and others. Many locals trace their family origins to these diverse settlers. Today, evidence of this mass migration remains in the variety of street names throughout town and, most palpably, in the cemetery. Church services are also still held in English, while the many mansions created by the wealthy are now hotels, banks and museums. No longer the economic powerhouse it once was, Punta Arenas maintains a productive fishing and methanex extraction industry.

Orientation

Punta Arenas' regular grid street plan, with wide streets and sidewalks, makes it easy to walk around. The Plaza de Armas, or Plaza Muñoz Gamero, is the center of town. Street names change on either side of the plaza, but street addresses fronting the plaza bear the name Muñoz Gamero. Most landmarks and accommodations are within a few blocks of here. Mirador La Cruz, at Fagnano and Señoret, four blocks northwest of the plaza, provides a good view of the town and the strait. Av Costanera parallels the rocky coast, which is predominantly industrial. The avenue continues south of town toward Fuerte Bulnes. Both Av España and Av Bulnes are

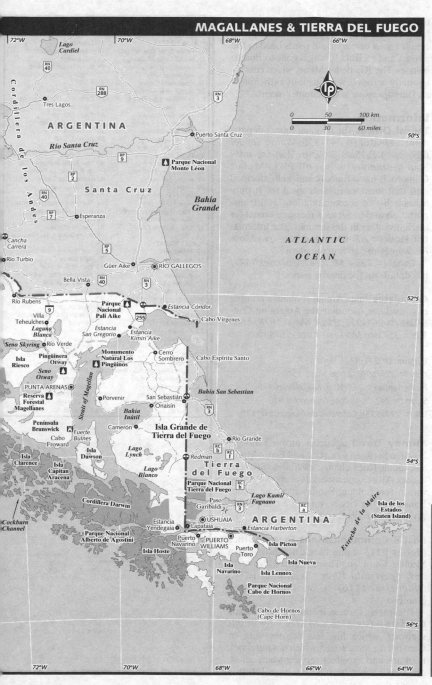

72°W · 70°W · 68°W · 66°W

Lago Cardiel

RN 40

RN 288

Tres Lagos

RN 3

0   50   100 km
0   30   60 miles

ARGENTINA

50°S

Río Santa Cruz

Puerto Santa Cruz

RP 9

Parque Nacional Monte Léon

RP 2

S a n t a   C r u z

Bahía Grande

RN 40

A T L A N T I C

RP 7

Esperanza

O C E A N

Cancha Carrera

Río Turbio

RP 5

Güer Aike

52°S

Bella Vista

RN 40

RN 3

RÍO GALLEGOS

Río Rubens

9

Parque Nacional Pali Aike

Estancia Cóndor

Villa Teheulches

255

Cabo Vírgenes

Laguna Blanca

Estancia San Gregorio

Estancia Kimiri Aike

Seno Skyring Río Verde

Isla Riesco

Pingüinera Otway

Monumento Natural Los Pingüinos

Cerro Sombrero

Cabo Espíritu Santo

Seno Otway

PUNTA ARENAS

Porvenir

San Sebastián

Bahía San Sebastián

Reserva Forestal Magellanes

Onaisin

RN 3

Isla Grande de Tierra del Fuego

Bahía Inútil

Península Brunswick

Camerón

Fuerte Bulnes

Cabo Froward

Isla Dawson

Río Grande

54°S

Isla Clarence

Isla Capitán Aracena

Lago Lynch

Lago Blanco

Redman

RC b   RC f

T i e r r a   d e l   F u e g o

Parque Nacional Tierra del Fuego

RC h

Lago Kami/ Fagnano

Cordillera Darwin

Paso Garibaldi

RN 3

RC a

Estrecho de la Maire

Isla de los Estados (Staten Island)

Cockburn Channel

Estancia Yendegaia

USHUAIA

Lapataia

Estancia Harberton

ARGENTINA

Parque Nacional Alberto de Agostini

Puerto Navarino

PUERTO WILLIAMS

Puerto Toro

Isla Picton

Isla Hoste

Isla Nueva

Isla Navarino

Isla Lennox

Parque Nacional Cabo de Hornos

Cabo de Hornos (Cape Horn)

56°S

72°W · 70°W · 68°W · 66°W · 64°W

main thoroughfares to the north of town, the latter accessing the large duty-free shopping center *(zona franca)*. Both roads head to the airport and to Ruta 9, which goes to Puerto Natales. The Río de las Minas, which cuts diagonally across town, is usually rather slow and unimpressive in the summer months.

Information

Tourist Offices The national tourist department, **Sernatur** *(☎ 241-330; Waldo Seguel 689; open 8:15am-6:45pm Mon-Fri, until 8pm in summer)* is just off Plaza Muñoz Gamero. It has a friendly and well-informed staff that includes English speakers. It publishes a list of accommodations and transportation and provides a message board for foreign visitors in the summer. The **information kiosk** *(☎ 200-610; open 8am-7pm Mon-Fri, 9am-8pm Sat)* is in the plaza.

Conaf *(☎ 223-841; José Menéndez 1147)* has details on the nearby parks.

Consulates Punta Arenas contains a number of consulates, including the **Argentine Consulate** *(☎ 261-912; 21 de Mayo 1878; open 10am-3:30pm Mon-Fri)*. Others include:

Belgium *(☎ 241-472), Roca 817*
Italy *(☎ 221-596), 21 de Mayo 1569*
Netherlands *(☎ 248-100), Magallanes 435*
Spain *(☎ 243-566), José Menéndez 910*
UK *(☎ 211-535), Cataratas de Niaguara 01325*

Money Travel agencies along Lautaro Navarro between Errázuriz and Pedro Montt and along Roca change cash and traveler's checks. All are open weekdays and Saturday, with a few holding Sunday morning hours. Banks dot the city, so finding a compatible ATM is no problem.

Post & Communications The **post office** *(Bories 911)* is one block north of Plaza Muñoz Gamero. There's **Entel** *(Navarro 957; open until 10pm)*. **Telefónica (CTC)** *(Nogueira 1116)* is on Plaza Muñoz Gamero.

For Internet access, try the lobby of **Hostal Calafate II** *(see Places to Stay later in this section)*, which has fast connections, or **GonFish** *(Croacia 1028)*, which has notebook hookups and excellent service. Many all-in-one backpacker hostels also have Internet

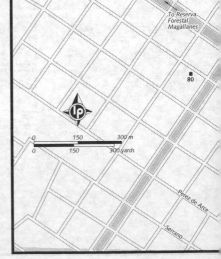

To Reserva Forestal Magallanes

80

0   150   300 m
0   150   300 yards

Perez de Arce

Serrano

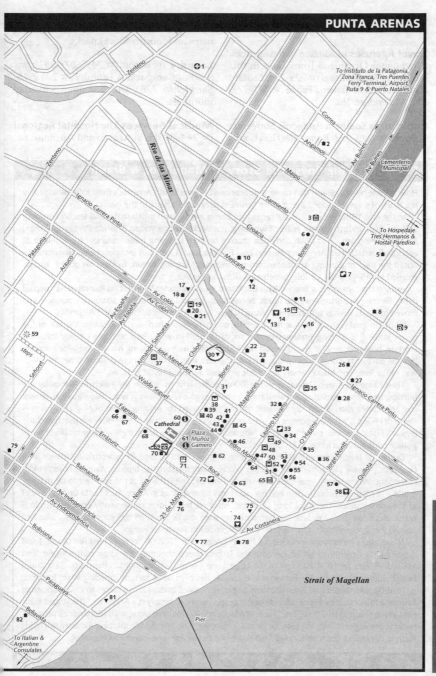

PUNTA ARENAS

access, as do many of the main telephone call centers in town.

Travel Agencies In addition to the agencies listed under Organized Tours, later in this section, try **Tecni-Austral** (☎ 223-205; *Lautaro Navarro 971*) and **Turismo Pehoé** (☎ 241-373; *José Menéndez 918*).

Bookstores Southern Patagonia Souvenirs & Books (☎ 225-973; *Bories 404*) has books

about the region, although most are in Spanish. It also has a decent assortment of maps and touristy knickknacks.

Laundry Try **Record** (☎ 243-607; *O'Higgins 969*) or **Backpackers Laundry** (☎ 241-516; *Sarmiento 726*), which is open Saturday mornings.

Medical Services The **Hospital Regional** (☎ 244-040) is at Arauco and Angamos.

Patagonia's Big Boys: The Story of Menéndez & Braun

How the Menéndez-Braun clan came together and became South America's most influential family is a story of swashbucklers, sheep, pure business savvy and affairs of the heart.

In the late 19th century, Punta Arenas had barely a thousand inhabitants, and sea lion hunting was the main industry. After years of working as a deck hand, a young illiterate Portuguese man, José Nogueira, arrived in town and soon started his own shipping business under the tutelage of an already established Argentine hunter, Luis Piedrabuena. Eager but inexperienced, Nogueira solicited the help of a young accountant from Lithuania, Mauricio Braun, to keep his books, and he married his 15-year-old Chilote sweetheart, Rosario Peralta.

Around the same time, a Buenos Aires bank sent José Menéndez to collect on Piedrabuena's unpaid debts. Sensing opportunity in the south, Menéndez instead bought out Piedrabuena's business and moved to Punta Arenas with his wife, María Behety, and his children, Josefina and Alejandro.

With the gold rush on, Nogueira's shipping company flourished, and he became the talk of the town, striking a dashing presence in the social scene. His wife, Rosario, didn't enjoy this new lifestyle, however, and Nogueira forced her to move to Uruguay, paying her a handsome monthly 'fee' as part of the deal. Meanwhile, José Menéndez was having a more difficult time; his office was ransacked, and María Behety was crippled after a violent revolt in town.

Then came the sheep. To begin with, 300 were brought over from the Falkland Islands by the territorial governor, providing the seed for a local economic revolution in wool. Separately, Nogueira and Menéndez each leased large swaths of land to be used for grazing. Most of Nogueira's was in Tierra del Fuego, while Menéndez focused on San Gregorio in Chile. Menéndez also purchased the region's first steamship, the *Amadeo*. As Nogueira's wealth and influence grew, he was able to renegotiate contracts and increase his land holdings.

During all this, Nogueira's abandoned wife, Rosario Peralta, died of tuberculosis. A year later Nogueira, possibly also suffering from tuberculosis, married again, this time to Mauricio Braun's older sister, Sara. When the 48-year-old Nogueira died in 1893, he left Sara as the sole heir to his massive estate and Mauricio (who by then had his own hefty landholdings in Argentina's Santa Cruz province) as the administrator. Then, not long after this, Mauricio fell in love, conveniently enough with José Menéndez's daughter, Josefina. The two socialites were married in 1895 by Señor Fagnano, who had started the Salesian mission to 'protect' the indigenous in Tierra del Fuego.

Menéndez's claims soon included 'La Primera Argentina' (60,000 hectares near Río Grande) and 'La Segunda Argentina,' which became the largest sheep-shearing operation in the world, and Mauricio Braun, by 1906, had one of the largest one-person landholdings in the south. Sara Braun herself managed a few of the *estancias* and created her own small fortune breeding foxes for pelts.

In 1908, Menéndez and Braun put any lingering rivalries aside, joining forces to create Sociedad Anónima Importador y Exportador de la Patagonia, or more simply 'La Anónima,' the largest business in the south at that time. Josefina and Mauricio's 10 children, along with Menéndez's progeny, became the region's reigning elite for decades to come. The Menéndez shipping industry still holds forth in Patagonia fjords with cargo ferries, known to the average traveler as Navimag.

Plaza Muñoz Gamero

Landscaped with exotic conifers and surrounded by many of the area's most opulent mansions, Plaza Muñoz Gamero is the heart of the city. In the plaza, note the monument commemorating the 400th anniversary of Magellan's voyage, donated by wool baron José Menéndez in 1920. (Rub the Ona's toe to ensure a return visit.) Facing the north side of the plaza is the **Club de la Unión** (☎ 241-489; admission US$2; open 11am-1pm & 4:30pm-8:30pm Tues-Sun), the former Sara Braun mansion, some rooms of which are open for public visits. Just east is the former Sociedad Menéndez Behety, now housing the Turismo Comapa offices. To the west is the cathedral.

Palacio Mauricio Braun

Housing a museum (☎ 244-216; Magallanes 949; admission US$1.50, plus to photograph inside US$2; open 10:30am-5pm in summer, to 2pm in winter), this opulent mansion, also known as Casa Braun-Menéndez, testifies to the wealth and power of pioneer sheep farmers in the late 19th century. One of Mauricio Braun's sons donated the house to the state, although it was against other family members' wishes. The rooms are divided; one part is a regional historical museum (booklets with English descriptions are available), and the other part displays the family's original French nouveau furnishings and details, from the intricate wooden inlay floors to the Chinese vases.

Museo Regional Salesiano

Especially influential in settling the region, the Salesian order collected outstanding ethnographic artifacts, but its museum (☎ 241-096; Av Bulnes 374; admission US$2.50; open 10am-12:30pm & 3pm-6pm Tues-Sun) takes a self-serving view of the Christian intervention, portraying missionaries as peacemakers between Indians and settlers. The rotting natural history specimens are nothing to speak of; the best materials are on the mountaineer priest Alberto de Agostini and the various indigenous groups. In the museum are also promotional exhibits of local industries – Enap, Methanex and the Fuerza Aérea de Chile.

Museo Naval y Marítimo

Punta Arenas' naval and maritime museum (☎ 205-479; Pedro Montt 981; admission

Kissing an Indian statue: said to bring luck

US$0.75; open 9:30am-12:30pm & 2pm-5pm Tues-Sat) has varied exhibits on model ships, naval history, the unprecedented visit of 27 US warships to Punta Arenas in 1908, and a very fine account of the Chilean mission that rescued British explorer Sir Ernest Shackleton's crew from Antarctica. The most imaginative display is a ship's replica, complete with bridge, maps, charts and radio room.

Cementerio Municipal

In death as in life, Punta Arenas' first families flaunted their wealth – wool baron José Menéndez's extravagant tomb is, according to travel writer Bruce Chatwin, a scale replica of Rome's Vittorio Emanuele monument. But the headstones among the topiary cypresses in the walled municipal cemetery (Av Bulnes 949; open daily) also tell the stories of Anglo, German, Scandinavian and Yugoslav immigrants who supported the wealthy families with their labor. There is also a monument to the Selk'nam (Ona).

The cemetery is about a 15-minute walk from Plaza Muñoz Gamero, but you can also take any taxi colectivo from the entrance of the Palacio Mauricio Braun on Magallanes.

Instituto de la Patagonia

Part of the Universidad de Magallanes, the Patagonian Institute's **Museo del Recuerdo** (☎ 207-056; Bulnes 01890; admission US$2; open 8:30am-11:30pm & 2:30pm-6:15pm Mon-Fri, 8:30am-1pm Sat) features a collection of antique farm and industrial machinery imported from Europe, a typical pioneer house and shearing shed (both reconstructed), and a wooden-wheeled trailer that served as shelter for shepherds. The library also has a display of historical maps and a series of historical and scientific publications. Any taxi colectivo to the zona franca (duty-free zone) will drop you across the street.

Reserva Forestal Magallanes

Only 8km from downtown, this 16,000-hectare reserve has a variety of hiking and mountain-biking trails through thick forests of lenga and coigue. A steady uphill hike goes to the top of Mt Fenton, also known as Cerro Mirador; views are spectacular – if you keep from being blown over by the wind. It is also possible to take the **chairlift** (weekday/weekend US$15/19) to the viewpoint. Other hikes, in the Valle del Río de las Minas section, meander around old coal mines. In winter the slopes provide a rare opportunity to ski while admiring the ocean. **Club Andino** (☎ 241-479) runs a quaint restaurant at the chairlift and rents ski equipment; cross-country rental costs US$6 for two hours, downhill rental US$16 per day. Turismo Viento Sur (see Organized Tours below) runs shuttles in the winter.

Organized Tours

Tours to the pingüinera at Seno Otway cost US$9, plus the US$4 entrance fee, and leave at 4pm daily December through March. Tours to Fuerte Bulnes and Puerto Hambre cost US$12, plus US$2 entrance fee, and leave at 10am daily, weather permitting. It is possible to do both tours in one day; however, renting a car and going at opposite times from the tours affords a chance to actually see the sites rather than the strings of tourist groups – this is especially beneficial at the penguin colony. Just about any lodging can help arrange tours with an agency, if the hotel doesn't run its own operation. Tours to Torres del Paine are abundant from Punta Arenas, but the distance makes for a very long day; it's best to head to Puerto Natales and organize transportation from there.

Travel agencies include **Turismo Pali Aike** (☎ 223-301; Lautaro Navarro 1129); **Turismo Aonikenk** (☎ 228-332; Magallanes 619), which is well regarded and has English-, German- and French-speaking guides; and **Turismo Viento Sur** (☎ 225-167; Fagnano 565). All of these agents can also arrange bus tours to Torres del Paine.

Tours to the penguin colonies on Isla Magdalena (Monumento Natural Los Pingüinos) cost US$30 per person (US$15 for children) on the Barcaza Melinka, leaving Tuesday,

Thursday and Saturday, December through February. Book tickets through **Turismo Comapa** (☎ 200-200; Magallanes 990), across from the plaza.

Turismo Yamana (☎ 221-130; Colón 568), organizes half- and full-day kayaking trips on the Magellan Strait.

Inhóspita Patagonia (☎ 224-510; Lautaro Navarro 1013) organizes two-day treks to Cape Froward for US$100, including equipment. It also features fly-fishing trips and trekking on Isla Navarino.

EcoTour Patagonia (☎ 221-339; Navarro 1091) is well liked for organizing a variety of excursions to fit individual traveling schedules.

Places to Stay

Budget A private school, **Colegio Pierre Fauré** (☎ 226-256; Bellavista 697; camping per person US$4, singles with/without breakfast US$7/6), six blocks south of Plaza Muñoz Gamero, operates as a hostel from December to February. Campers can pitch a tent in the side garden. All bathrooms are shared, but there's plenty of hot water.

Backpacker's Paradise (☎ 240-104; Ignacio Carrera Pinto 1022; dorm beds US$6) offers crowded rooms divided only by flimsy curtains. To its advantage are a well-stocked kitchen, Internet access and an oft-times party atmosphere. While the house dog is friendly, many have found it a bed hog.

Hospedaje Independencia (☎ 227-572; Independencia 374; camping US$3, dorm beds US$5), a casual place run by a young couple, has well-sized dorm rooms, kitchen use and camping in the small somewhat muddy front yard. Breakfast is an additional US$3.

Hospedaje Tres Hermanos (☎ 225-450; Angamos 1218; rooms per person US$7) offers quiet comfortable rooms in an old converted house; rates include breakfast. It's a friendly place and an excellent value.

Hospedaje Betty (☎ 249-777; Mejicana 576; rooms per person US$7) has a family atmosphere and allows use of the kitchen; breakfast is included.

Hospedaje Mireya (☎ 247-066; Boliviana 375; rooms per person US$9) has an independent annex with a full kitchen, but tiny bathrooms. Rates include breakfast. Rooms don't have heat, but it's still a great deal.

Hospedaje Manuel (☎ 245-441, fax 220-567; O'Higgins 646-648; singles/doubles

US$9/15) has all the necessary backpacker amenities, plus plenty of clutter. Dorm rooms upstairs are better quality.

Hostal O'Higgins (☎ 227-999; *O'Higgins 1205; rooms per person US$9, doubles with private bath US$26*) is well located in what used to be dormitories for the teams that would play at the adjacent gymnasium. It is spotlessly clean with large, gym-style bathrooms, kitchen privileges, hot showers and parking.

An HI affiliate, **Hostal Sonia Kuscevic** (☎ 248-543; *Pasaje Darwin 175; shared rooms HI members US$14, singles/doubles US$22/32*) offers cozy but cramped rooms with private bath and breakfast; the ambience is a bit formal, but Sonia treats her guests very well.

Hostal La Estancia (☎ 249-130; *O'Higgins 765; singles/doubles US$13/23*), run by a friendly young couple, has attractive upstairs rooms with shared bath, decent beds, but rock-hard pillows. A very filling breakfast is included and can be enjoyed while catching up on the news of the day on English-language TV.

Residencial Coirón (☎ 226-449; *Sanhueza 730; rooms US$13*) is right across from the Fernández bus terminal. Coirón's sunny singles upstairs are the best deal, but all rooms come with breakfast included.

Hostal del Rey (☎ 223-924; e *elrey@ enelmundo.com; Fagnano 589; dorm beds US$12, 2-person apartments US$21-26, 4-person $50*) has sweet dorms with down-comforter–covered beds, but the best bets are the downstairs apartments with full kitchens, hot water and TV.

Hostal Calafate II (☎/fax 241-281; e *hostal _calafate@entelchile.net; Magallanes 922; singles/doubles with shared bath US$23/32, with private bath US$37/45*), in the heart of downtown, feels more like a laid-back hotel than hostel, with long hallways, large rooms with TV, breakfast, free parking and friendly staff. The only drawback is the street noise. There's Internet service in the lobby.

Hostal Calafate (☎ 248-415; e *calafate@ entelchile.net; Lautaro Navarro 850; singles/ doubles US$25/38*) is in the owner's home, with serve-yourself breakfasts and comfortable common spaces. It's an inviting and intimate option.

Hostal Parediso (☎ 224-212; *Angamos 1073; singles/doubles with shared bath*

US$14/17, *with private bath US$22/28*), east of the cemetery, is another good choice with use of the kitchen and central heating.

Mid-Range Prices at more high-end establishments do not reflect the additional 18% IVA charge, which foreigners are not required to pay if paying with credit cards or in US cash. In the off-season, some places drop prices by as much as 40%.

Hostal de la Patagonia (☎/fax 249-970; e *ecopatagonia@entelchile.net; Croacia 970; singles/doubles US$31/50*) is a small, quiet and conscientiously run spot with perfectly adequate rooms with private bath. Breakfast is included.

Hostal Carpa Manzano (☎ 242-296; *Lautaro Navarro 336; singles/doubles US$42/54*) has pleasant rooms, most of which look onto a side path bedecked in flowers. All rooms come with a private bath, TV, breakfast, parking and kitchen privileges.

Hostal de la Avenida (☎/fax 247-532; *Colón 534; singles/doubles US$47/56*), near the Fernández bus terminal, is a simple mid-range option with pleasant, slightly dark rooms and breakfast. Unfortunately, it doesn't recognize the IVA discount.

Hostal del Estrecho (☎/fax 241-011; *José Menéndez 1048; singles/doubles with shared bath US$17/28, with private bath US$33/40*) has kindly owners and huge rooms, each full of bunk beds. Breakfast is included and served in the cozy dining area.

Hotel Plaza (☎ 241-300, fax 248-613; *Nogueira 1116; singles/doubles US$57/68*), in a converted mansion, brings to light the opulence of the city's history. Cozy rooms with high ceilings, some with great views of the plaza, and historic photos make this two-star hotel a worthwhile choice. Famous Everest climbers have rested their weary feet here many times.

Top End The **Hotel Tierra del Fuego** (☎/fax 226-200; *Av Colón 716; singles/ doubles US$98/109*) is rather drab in design and décor, but at least it has modern amenities, some nice views and an attractive, fairly active bar.

Hotel Isla Rey Jorge (☎/fax 222-681; e *rey jorge@ctcinternet.cl; 21 de Mayo 1243; singles/doubles US$116/143*), modern and chic, incorporates maritime details into its attractive rooms and common spaces. Its location close to the port makes it a popular choice for cruise passengers.

Hotel Cabo de Hornos (☎/fax 242-134; e rescabo@panamericanahoteles.cl; Plaza Muñoz Gamero 1025; singles US$126-140, doubles US$149-166), the king of the luxury hotels, offers solid rooms and sports nice views and attractive décor; the professional staff is quick to help. The bar is cozy but costly.

Hotel José Nogueira (☎ 248-840, fax 248-832; e nogueira@chileaustral.com; Bories 959; singles/doubles US$141/198), part of the Sara Braun Mansion, is equally regal. The highlight is accessible to even selective backpackers: dining or sipping a cocktail in the posh conservatory/restaurant beneath what may be the world's most southerly grape arbor.

Hotel Finis Terrae (☎ 228-200, fax 248-124; e finister@ctcreuna.cl; Av Colón 766; singles/doubles US$140/160) offers sunny standard rooms, which are a good deal, with attractive furnishings and courteous staff. The upstairs bar/lounge has spectacular views of town and the strait.

Places to Eat

The season for centolla (king crab) is from July to November, while erizos (sea urchins) are available from November to July. If heading to Torres del Paine, note that the variety of food supplies and trail snacks is better here than in Natales.

La Carioca (☎ 224-809; José Menéndez 600; pizzas US$3-7) is praised for pizzas, sandwiches and cold lager beer, plus a daily lunch special.

Rotisería La Mamá (☎ 225-829; Sanhueza 720; mains US$4-9), family-run, specializes in homemade pastas, including a hearty bowl of lasagna (the vegetarian option is bland). Read the praises and travelers' reports on the many napkins on the wall. This restaurant is right across from the Fernández bus terminal.

Lomit's (☎ 243-399; José Menéndez 722; sandwiches US$3-5), despite the slow and sometimes surly service, still attracts packs of locals and travelers alike, probably because it's open when other places are closed for the night. The made-to-order sandwiches are, however, generous and tasty.

El Mercado (☎ 247-415; Mejicana 617; mains US$5-10; open 24 hrs), a local institution, heaps on an assortment of seafood specials, from scallops stewed in garlicky

sauce to baked, creamed centolla to mussels a la parmesana. There is a 10% surcharge between 1am and 8am.

La Luna (☎ 228-555; O'Higgins 974; seafood pastas US$5), decked out in vibrant colors, with attentive service and a wide variety of dishes, is a favorite. Be sure to add a pin-flag to the world maps.

Santino Bar e Cucina (☎ 220-511; Colón 657; mains US$4-9), a hip spot, may be more popular as a bar, but it serves tasty pizzas and oversize savory crepes, plus plates of seafood with an assortment of sauces.

Sotito's Bar (☎ 243-565; O'Higgins 1138; dinners US$10-24) is one of the city's more long-lasting formal affairs and caters heavily to tourists. Salmon with mixed seafood sauce will put you back only US$9, but servings of fresh centolla are dearer.

Remezón (☎ 241-029; 21 de Mayo 1469; appetizers US$4-5, mains US$7-9) has a chef who impresses with delicately prepared and supremely delicious dishes, such as oysters and clams au gratin, fresh centolla with lemon, salmon smoked with black tea, or a salad of avocado with marinated beaver. Equally imaginative are the centolla canelones and baked sierra. To add to its appeal the service is unpretentious and welcoming and quick to pour a pisco sour to get you going.

Pachamama (Magallanes 698) is where you can purchase bulk trail-mix munchies, along with organic products.

Abugosh (Bories 647) and **Cofrima** (Navarro & Balmaceda) are large, well-stocked supermarkets.

Entertainment

Olijoe Pub (☎ 223-728; Errázuriz 970; open 6pm-2am), a faux-historic place, has an up-scale feel but relaxing ambience – it's a good place for a quiet drink and snack. Try the house special Glaciar, a potent mix of pisco, horchata, curuçao and milk.

La Taberna (☎ 241-317), in the dark, low-ceiling basement of the Sara Braun Mansion, is the place to huddle at a booth and swap tales of Antarctic and Andean adventures. The environment's tops but the mixed drinks could be better.

El Madero (Bories 655) gets packed with the pre-disco crowds saucing up on good strong drinks and bustling from table to table. Afterward, head downstairs to **Kamikaze** (ad-

One of Chiloé's historic churches

A Mapuche boy in rural Chile

Off to see the penguins: ferry passengers leave the boat behind on Isla Magdelena.

Braving a wild river at PN Queulat

Lush valley near Río Simpson, Aisén

High above the glaciers in southern Chile

Los Cuernos (the Horns) and Lago Pehoé in PN Torres del Paine

mission US$5), tripped out with tiki torches and South Pacific flares.

Disco Morena *(Menéndez 1173)*, a spacious place, keeps on thumping long after the rest of the city has turned in for the night.

For movies, head to **Teatro Cervantes** *(Plaza Muñoz Gamero)*, below the Centro Español, and **Sala Estrella** *(Mejicana 777)*, both of which are showing their age.

Shopping

The **Zona Franca** (Zofri, or duty-free zone), open daily except Sunday, is a chaotic maze of vendors in which finding anything can get annoying; however, it may prove fruitful if you're looking for camera equipment and film. Taxi colectivos shuttle back and forth from downtown throughout the day.

La Feria *(cnr Fagnano 607 & Chiloé)* sells inexpensive winter parkas.

Head to **Solovidrios** *(☎ 224-835; Mejicana 762)* if you need to replace a shattered windshield on a private car – not an unusual occurrence on Patagonia roads. Prices here are a fraction of what they are in Argentina.

Getting There & Away

Sernatur and the municipal tourist kiosk distribute a useful brochure with information on all forms of transportation, including those that go to or through Argentina and their schedules to and from Punta Arenas, Puerto Natales and Tierra del Fuego. Note that discount airfares are available from the major airlines between Punta Arenas and mainland Chile but usually involve some restrictions. *La Prensa Austral* newspaper lists transportation availability, contact details and schedules.

Air LanChile *(☎ 241-100, 241-232; Lautaro Navarro 999)* flies four times daily to Puerto Montt (US$213 one-way) and Santiago (US$300 one-way) and on Saturday to the Falkland Islands (US$460 to US$560 roundtrip).

Aerovías DAP *(☎ 223-340, fax 221-693; W www.aeroviasdap.cl; O'Higgins 891)* flies to Porvenir (US$22) and back twice daily except Sunday; it flies to Puerto Williams on Isla Navarino (US$70) Tuesday to Saturday. It also connects to Argentine destinations: to Ushuaia (US$100) on Monday and Wednesday; to El Calafate (US$50) twice daily on weekdays; and in summer to Río Grande (US$79) about once a week. Luggage is limited to 10kg per person. DAP also does three-hour excursion flights over Cabo de Hornos (Cape Horn; US$300) on Sunday, possibly also stopping in Puerto Williams en route.

Bus Punta Arenas has no central bus terminal, but at the time of writing, plans to make one near the port were underway. Each bus company has its own office from which its buses depart, although most of these are within a block or two of Av Colón. It makes sense to purchase tickets in advance by at least a couple of hours (if not by a day during summer). All at the same location and phone are **Buses Fernández**, **Turíbus**, **Queilen Bus** and **Buses Pingüino** *(☎ 221-812; Armando Sanhueza 745)*. Other companies are **Bus Transfer** *(☎ 246-242; Pedro Montt 966)*; **Central de Transportes de Pasajeros** *(☎ 245-811; cnr Magallanes & Colón)*; **Buses Pacheco** *(☎ 242-174; Av Colón 900)*; **Buses Ghisoni** *(☎ 222-078; Lautaro Navarro 975)*; and **Bus Sur** *(☎ 244-464; Menéndez 565)*.

To get to Puerto Natales (US$4, three hours), Bus Fernández, Bus Sur, Pacheco or Bus Transfer have three to eight departures daily; the first two companies have the most frequent departures. To Coyhaique (US$44, 20 hours), Bus Sur leaves at 10:30am Monday and Thursday. To Puerto Montt and Castro (US$44, 30 hours), Queilen Bus and Buses Pacheco leave twice weekly via Argentina.

Argentine destinations are well serviced. To Río Grande (US$19, eight hours), Buses Ghisoni and Pacheco have three to four weekly departures, each with some buses going via Porvenir.

To Ushuaia (US$36, 12 hours), Ghisoni buses continue direct, but travelers report Pacheco stops for too long in Río Grande – from Río Grande, shuttles to Ushuaia leave throughout the day and may cost slightly less (it depends on Chilean currency) than the through ticket. To Río Gallegos (US$12-18, four hours), El Pingüino has daily service, while Ghisoni and Pacheco leave three times weekly.

Boat From the Tres Puentes ferry terminal north of town (get taxi colectivos from Palacio Mauricio Braun), **Transbordadora Austral Broom** *(☎ 218-100; W www.tabsa.cl; Av Bulnes 05075)* sails to Porvenir, Tierra del Fuego (US$7, 2½ to 4 hours). Boats usually depart in the morning and return in the late afternoon. Travel times depend on weather conditions. Make reservations to ferry your vehicle (US$45) by calling or visiting the office .

A faster way to get to Tierra del Fuego (US$2, 20 minutes) is via the Punta Delgada–Bahía Azul crossing northeast of Punta Arenas. Transbordadora Austral Broom ferries leave every 1½ hours from 8:30am to 10:15pm. Call ahead for vehicle reservations (US$17).

Transbordadora Austral Broom is also the agent for the ferry *Patagonia,* which sails from Tres Puentes to Puerto Williams, on Isla Navarino, two or three times a month, Wednesday only, returning Friday, both at 7pm (US$120 to US$150 including meals, 38 hours).

From September through April, **Turismo Comapa** (☎ 200-200; *Magallanes 990),* runs weeklong luxury cruises on the 130-passenger *Mare Australis* from Punta Arenas through the Cordillera Darwin and the Beagle Channel to Puerto Williams and Ushuaia (Argentina) and back. Rates start at US$1152 per person double occupancy in low season (September, October and April) and reach US$2971 for a high-season single (mid-December through February). It is possible to do the leg between Punta Arenas and Ushuaia, or vice-versa, separately.

Navimag, which runs ferries from Puerto Natales to Puerto Montt is represented by Turismo Comapa. For schedules and fares, see Getting There & Away in Puerto Natales later in this chapter.

Getting Around

To/From the Airport The airport is 20km north of town. Bus Transfer has scheduled departures (US$3) throughout the day to coincide with departures and arrivals. **Turismo Sandy Point** (☎ 246-954; *Pedro Montt 840)* runs shuttles – US$2.50 from the office or US$3 for door-to-door service. DAP Airlines runs a shuttle service for its clients.

Bus & Colectivo Taxi colectivos, with numbered routes, are only slightly more expensive than buses (about US$0.50, a bit more late at night and on Sunday), but they are much more comfortable and much quicker. Catch northbound colectivos along Av Magallanes or Av España and southbound along Bories or Av España.

Car Punta Arenas has the most economical car rental rates in the area, and locally owned businesses tend to provide better service. Recommended **Adel Rent a Car** (☎ 235-471; *Pedro Montt 962)* provides attentive service, competitive rates and good travel tips for the area. Other choices include **Hertz** (☎ 248-742; *O'Higgins 987),* **Budget Rent a Car** (☎ 225-983, fax 241-696; *O'Higgins 964),* and **Lubag** (☎ 242-023, fax 214-136; *Magallanes 970).* There's the **Automóvil Club de Chile** (☎ 243-675; *O'Higgins 931).*

AROUND PUNTA ARENAS
Penguin Colonies

There are two substantial Magellanic penguin colonies near Punta Arenas: Easier to reach is **Seno Otway** (*Otway Sound; admission US$4),* with about 6000 breeding pairs, about an hour northwest of the city. Larger and more interesting, **Monumento Natural Los Pingüinos** has about 50,000 breeding pairs and is accessible only by boat to Isla Magdalena in the Strait of Magellan. Neither are as impressive as the larger penguin colonies in Argentina or the Falkland Islands. Tours to Seno Otway usually leave in the afternoon; however, coming in the morning would be better for photography because in the afternoon the birds are mostly backlit.

Since there is no scheduled public transportation to either site, it's necessary to rent a car or take a tour to visit them. For details, see Organized Tours in Punta Arenas earlier in this chapter. Admission to Isla Magdalena is included in the price of the ferry trip. There's a small snack bar at the Otway site.

Puerto Hambre & Fuerte Bulnes

Founded in 1584 by an overly confident Pedro Sarmiento de Gamboa, 'Ciudad del Rey don Felipe' was one of Spain's most inauspicious (and short-lived) South American outposts. Its inhabitants soon failed to conquer the ruthless elements and starved to death at what is now known as Puerto Hambre ('Port Famine').

In May 1843, Chilean president Manuel Bulnes sent the schooner *Ancud,* manned by Chilotes and captained by John Williams, a former English officer, to Magallanes to occupy this southern area, then only sparsely populated by indigenous peoples. Four months later, on September 21, when the *Ancud* arrived at Puerto Hambre, Williams declared the area Chilean territory and began to establish camp on a hilltop, dubbed Fuerte Bulnes. The exposed site, lack of potable water, rocky soil and inferior pasture soon made him abandon the site and move northward to a more sheltered area, called Punta Arenosa.

A good gravel road runs 60km south from Punta Arenas to the restored wooden fort, where a fence of sharpened stakes surrounds the blockhouse, barracks and chapel. There isn't any scheduled public transportation, but several travel agencies make half-day excursions to Fuerte Bulnes and Puerto Hambre; for details, see Organized Tours under Punta Arenas earlier in this chapter.

Cape Froward

The most southerly point on the continent, Cape Froward is 90km south of Punta Arenas and accessible by a two-day hike along wind-whipped cliffs. At the cape, a 365m hill leads to an enormous cross, originally erected by Señor Fagnano in 1913, but the latest one was erected in 1987 in anticipation of Pope John Paul II's visit. Camping is possible along the trail; ask at adventure travel agencies in Punta Arenas about guided hikes.

Río Verde

About 50km north of Punta Arenas, a graveled lateral leads northwest toward Seno Skyring (Skyring Sound), passing this former estancia before rejoining Ruta 9 at Villa Tehuelches. Visitors with a car should consider this interesting detour to one of the best-maintained assemblages of Magellanic architecture in the region.

Hostería Río Verde (☎ 311-122, fax 311-125; rooms with private bath US$30), 6km south of Río Verde proper, 90km from Punta Arenas, is more well known for its Sunday lunches (US$10), with large portions of lamb, pork or seafood. An enormous fireplace and views over Isla Riesco make it a welcoming place, and the rooms are plenty comfortable.

Isla Riesco

Just across the sound from Río Verde is Isla Riesco, whose western half is protected as the **Reserva Nacional Alacalufes**, an area that's close to impossible to access. Nearby, however, is a new private park **Monte León**, a 27,000-hectare estancia 140km from Punta Arenas. Preferring to protect the land than

sell it to logging interests, the owner of Monte León sold it to the conservation group **Fundación Yendegaia** (☎/fax 02-204-1914, fax 209-2527; e yendegaia@patagonia.com). Evergreen forests are found in the higher elevations, while near the ocean, trees are wind-battered into unnatural contortions. Condors soar overhead and the elusive huemul makes an occasional showing. The main house has **lodging** (per person US$16) and kitchen facilities, and a number of trails allow for multiday hikes in the area, but note that rain is a constant characteristic. Boats do make the trip to Isla Riesco across the sound, but they can be expensive. For information on the park, contact the conservation group.

Río Rubens

Roughly midway between Villa Tehuelches and Puerto Natales on Ruta 9, Río Rubens is a fine trout-fishing area and an ideal spot to break the journey from Punta Arenas, at least for travelers with their own transportation.

Hotel Río Rubens (☎ 09-640-1583; Km 183; rooms per person US$12), a cozy, comfy place, is the closest thing to an old country-style inn in the region, and at these rates, it's a bargain. The restaurant serves outstanding meals, including lamb and seafood. Rates include breakfast.

Estancia San Gregorio

Some 125km northeast of Punta Arenas, straddling Ruta 255 to Río Gallegos (Argentina), this once-enormous, 90,000-hectare estancia is now more a ghost town of faded yellow corrugated iron, but it is still maintained by a few people and the large shearing shed is still used. The skeletal remains of beached ships are a memory of the days when goods sailed to and from Punta Arenas.

Hotel El Tehuelche (☎ 198-3002; singles/doubles US$30/49) is at the junction to Punta Delgada. About 30km northeast of San Gregorio, this is the junction for the road to the ferry that crosses the Strait of Magellan from Punta Delgada to Chilean Tierra del Fuego. Until 1968, the hostería was the casco for **Estancia Kimiri Aike**, pioneered by the British immigrant family Woods, although they never lived here. High ceilings, fading floral wallpaper, warm yellow bathrooms with claw-foot tubs and antique furnishings plus gas fireplaces in some rooms make this a comfortable and entertaining

The Powers of a Calafate Berry

Local lore says if you eat the succulent blue berries from the Calafate bush, you are sure to return to Patagonia. So, keep your eyes peeled from December to March, when the fine bright yellow flowers of this low shrubby boxed-leaf barberry (Berberis buxifolia) turn into the sweet morsels of desired returns. Unfortunately, frequent-flier miles do not apply.

stopover. Downstairs, the restaurant serves sandwiches and meals either in the main room or, when it's sunny outside, in the large sunroom.

PN Pali Aike

Along the Argentine border, west of the Monte Aymond border crossing to Río Gallegos, this 5030-hectare park is an area of volcanic steppe where, in the 1930s, Junius Bird's excavations at **Pali Aike Cave** yielded the first Paleo-Indian artifacts associated with extinct New World fauna, like the *milodón* and the native horse *Onohippidium*.

The park has several hiking trails, including a 1700m path through the rugged lava beds of the **Escorial del Diablo** to the impressive **Crater Morada del Diablo**; wear sturdy shoes or your feet could be shredded. There's also a 9km trail from Cueva Pali Aike to **Laguna Ana**, where there's another shorter trail to a site on the main road, 5km from the park entrance.

Cueva Pali Aike itself measures 5m high and 7m wide at the entrance, while it is 17m deep. Bird's excavations in 1936–37 unearthed three cremated human skeletons plus milodón and native horse bones some 9000 years old.

Parque Nacional Pali Aike is 196km northeast of Punta Arenas via Ruta 9, Ruta 255 and a graveled secondary road from Cooperativa Villa O'Higgins, 11km north of Estancia Kimiri Aike. There's also an access road from the Chilean border post at Monte Aymond. There is no public transportation, but Punta Arenas travel agencies can arrange tours; see earlier in this chapter.

PUERTO NATALES

☎ 61 • pop 19,000

When the Navimag ferry comes in and unloads its cargo of sea-weary backpackers,

this port town comes alive. On the shores of Seno Última Esperanza (Last Hope Sound), 250km northwest of Punta Arenas via Ruta 9, Puerto Natales is the southern terminus of the ferry trip through the Chilean fjords, and it's the gateway to Parque Nacional Torres del Paine. Once dependent on wool, mutton and fishing, it now lives off the increasing number of outdoor adventure seekers who arrive each year, and it has loads of options for getting to the parks, to Argentina and out and about.

Orientation

A compact town along the Seno Última Esperanza, Puerto Natales is a very walkable town. Most services are found within a triangle delimited by Phillippi to the north, the Costanera Puerto Montt to the west and Bulnes to the south. The Plaza de Armas is a large open spot around which are found the municipal buildings, the church, some pubs and restaurants and a bank. Six blocks to the southeast of this plaza, along Baquedano, is another smaller plaza between Miraflores and Yungay, an area that is developing with more budget lodging. The Costanera provides a pleasant walk along the sounds, but is blocked off to the south by the main pier, where the Navimag ferry arrives.

Information

Tourist Offices The **municipal tourist office** (☎ 411-263; Bulnes 285), in the museum, has attentive staff and up-to-date listings on lodgings in and around town and in Torres del Paine. Not as helpful, **Sernatur** (☎ 412-125) is on the Costanera Pedro Montt at the junction with the Philippi diagonal. **Conaf** (☎ 411-438; O'Higgins 584) has an administrative office.

Money Stop Cambios (Baquedano 386) changes cash, as do many agents along Blanco Encalada. Most banks in town have ATMs. **Banco del Estado** (Plaza de Armas) changes US cash dollars.

Post & Communications Services include the post office (Eberhard 429) and the call centers **Telefónica (CTC)** (Blanco Encalada 298) and **Entel** (Baquedano 270). Internet connections are very slow throughout town; try **CyberCafe** (Blanco Encalada 226).

Travel Agencies Most travel agencies have similar services: tours to Torres del Paine, equipment rental and maps. **Path@gone** (☎ 413-291; e pathgone@chileaustral.com; Eberhard 595) is the central point for reserving refugios and campsites to the park, but long lines and lack of staff mean long waits. A handful of other agencies around town can also make reservations. **Fortaleza Expediciones** (☎ 410-595; Prat 234) has knowledgeable, English-speaking staff and rents camping equipment (per day, sleeping bags US$4, tents US$8). **Big Foot Adventure Patagonia** (☎ 414-611; Bories 206) arranges kayak trips, glacier hikes and individualized trekking expeditions with bilingual guides. Also well regarded, **Knudsen Tour** (☎ 411-819; Blanco Encalada 284) has trips to El Calafate, Torres del Paine and also alterna-

tive routes along Seno Último Esperanza. Readers have recommended **Turismo Yekchal** (☎ 413-591; Eberhard 564-A), which has details on tours to Puerto Edén and Glaciar Pio XI. In the winter months, Niko's Residencial (see Places to Stay later in this section) organizes one- to two-day trips to Torres del Paine.

Bookstores Southern Patagonia Souvenirs & Books (Bulnes 688) stocks a decent variety of books on the area (most are in Spanish).

Laundry Servilaundry (☎ 412-869; Bulnes 513) is the main washhouse in town, but many hostels offer service.

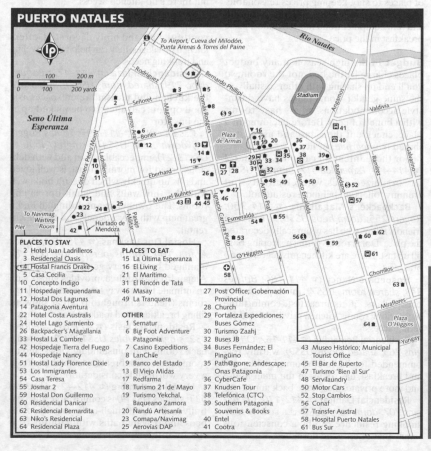

PUERTO NATALES

PLACES TO STAY
2 Hotel Juan Ladrilleros
3 Residencial Oasis
14 Hostal Francis Drake
5 Casa Cecilia
10 Concepto Indigo
11 Hospedaje Tequendama
12 Hostal Dos Lagunas
14 Patagonia Aventura
22 Hotel Costa Australis
24 Hotel Lago Sarmiento
26 Backpacker's Magallania
33 Hostal La Cumbre
42 Hospedaje Tierra del Fuego
44 Hospedaje Nancy
51 Hostal Lady Florence Dixie
53 Los Inmigrantes
54 Casa Teresa
55 Josmar 2
59 Hostal Don Guillermo
60 Residencial Danicar
62 Residencial Bernardita
63 Niko's Residencial
64 Residencial Plaza

PLACES TO EAT
15 La Última Esperanza
16 El Living
21 El Marítimo
31 El Rincón de Tata
46 Masay
49 La Tranquera

OTHER
1 Sernatur
6 Big Foot Adventure Patagonia
7 Casino Expeditions
8 LanChile
9 Banco del Estado
13 El Viejo Midas
17 Redfarma
18 Turismo 21 de Mayo
19 Turismo Yekchal, Baqueano Zamora
20 Ñandú Artesanía
23 Comapa/Navimag
25 Aerovías DAP

27 Post Office; Gobernación Provincial
28 Church
29 Fortaleza Expediciones; Buses Gómez
30 Turismo Zaahj
32 Buses JB
34 Buses Fernández; El Pingüino
35 Path@gone; Andescape; Onas Expeditions
36 CyberCafe
37 Knudsen Tour
38 Telefónica (CTC)
39 Southern Patagonia Souvenirs & Books
40 Entel
41 Cootra

43 Museo Histórico; Municipal Tourist Office
45 El Bar de Ruperto
47 Turismo 'Bien al Sur'
48 Servilaundry
50 Motor Cars
52 Stop Cambios
56 Conaf
57 Transfer Austral
58 Hospital Puerto Natales
61 Bus Sur

MAGALLANES

Medical Services Redfarma (Arturo Prat 158) is the best place to purchase motion sickness pills (Mareamin or Bonamina) before Navimag trips. The **hospital** (☎ 411-533) is at O'Higgins and Ignacio Carrera Pinto.

Museo Histórico

This museum (☎ 411-263; Bulnes 285; admission free; open 8:30am-12:30pm & 2:30pm-6pm Tues-Sun) has natural history items (mostly stuffed animals), archaeological artifacts, such as stone and whalebone arrowheads and spear points, plus a Yahgan canoe, Tehuelche bolas and historical photographs of Puerto Natales' development.

Places to Stay

For a small town, Puerto Natales is chock-full of places to stay, keeping prices reasonable. Many places can help arrange transportation and rent equipment, and most include a basic breakfast in the price.

Budget In the high season, many budget places charge by the bed, not the room, so you'll end up sharing with others, usually of the same gender. Some places have dorm-style accommodations, others have rooms with a bunch of beds. Before deciding on a place, check out the room and ask if it is shared (compartida) or not.

For those intent on camping, **Josmar 2** (☎ 414-417; Esmeralda 517; camping US$3) has organized sites with electricity but crummy toilets, all behind a restaurant.

Backpacker's Magallania (☎ 414-950; Rogers 255; dorm beds US$5) is run by a friendly fellow who has whimsically decorated the place. Dorm rooms (bring a sleeping bag) fill up fast. There are kitchen privileges, but no breakfast.

Hospedaje Nancy (☎ 411-186; Bulnes 343; shared rooms US$7), much praised by backpackers, offers breakfast, comfortable high-ceiling rooms, kitchen privileges and Internet access.

Residencial Bernardita (☎ 411-162; O'Higgins 765; shared rooms US$9), warmly recommended for its quiet rooms, kitchen use and breakfast, has rooms in the main house and more private ones in the back annex.

Residencial Danicar (☎ 412-170; O'Higgins 707; dorm beds US$6) is a strictly non-smoking residence run by a conscientious family that offers good dorm beds.

Hospedaje Tequendama (☎ 412-951; Ladrilleros 141; rooms per person US$7) is a converted house with small but pleasant rooms.

Los Inmigrantes (☎ 413-482; Ignacio Carrera Pinto 480; shared rooms US$7), part residencial and part equipment rental, is a good choice for serious hikers who want the inside scoop on the land. There are kitchen privileges, but no breakfast.

Hospedaje Tierra del Fuego (☎ 412-138; Av Bulnes 23; shared rooms US$7) is convenient to the ferry. Thin-walled but adequate, it offers breakfast and is a decent place to crash after a late-night ferry arrival.

Casa Teresa (☎ 410-472; Esmeralda 483; dorm beds US$7), with very kind owners, offers basic dorm beds and a good breakfast, but there's no kitchen access.

Patagonia Aventura (☎ 411-028; Tomás Rogers 179; shared rooms US$7), run by some youthful guys and hiply decorated, offers kitchen privileges; they can help with traveling and trekking needs.

Residencial Plaza (☎ 411-472; Baquedano 719; shared rooms US$8), with use of the kitchen and pleasant open spaces, is a good option; call ahead to be picked up at the bus stop.

Casa Cecilia (☎ 411-797; Tomás Rogers 64; dorm beds US$10, singles/doubles US$13/21), impeccably clean and with delicious bread for morning toast, is well loved and fills up quickly, which doesn't bode well with the thin walls and small dorms and rooms. The owners are multilingual and a great help with travel details and equipment rental.

Hostal Dos Lagunas (☎ 415-733; Barros Arana 104; rooms per person US$11), managed by the very gentle and attentive Alejandro and Andrea, provides guests with an intimate home away from home with large rooms (heaters brought in), great showers, filling breakfasts and loads of traveling tips.

Residencial Oasis (☎ 411-675; Señoret 332; singles/doubles US$13/22) has some back rooms with outstanding views, and all rooms come with breakfast, which makes it a very worthwhile consideration.

Hostal La Cumbre (☎ 412-422; Eberhard 533; singles US$14) is comfortable and centrally located, with high-ceiling rooms, plush beds and private baths with bathtubs. It is run by interesting, dynamic local women who make sure the place feels like the home it is to them.

Niko's Residencial (☎ 412-810, fax 413-543; e residencialnikos@hotmail.com; Ramírez 669; rooms with shared/private bath US$7/11) offers a separate kitchen for travelers and the added bonus of family-style dinner for US$5 more. Bring your own toilet paper and towel. Rates include breakfast.

Hostal Don Guillermo (☎ 414-506; O'Higgins 657; singles/doubles US$12/21) is a surprisingly pleasant spot with small boxy rooms with no windows, but with heat and incredibly clean shared bathrooms.

Concepto Indigo (☎ 413-609, fax 410-169; e indigo@entelchile.net; Ladrilleros 105; rooms US$15-35) has a range of rooms, some shared and others private, many with five-star views over the sound. It's a fab place to kick off your shoes and feel right at home, plus its great bar and restaurant are just downstairs. Climbers will enjoy the climbing wall along the wind-protected side of the building.

Mid-Range & Top End Prices at more high-end establishments do not reflect the additional 18% IVA charged, which foreigners are not required to pay if paying with credit cards or in US dollars cash. In the off-season, many places drop prices by as much as 40%.

Hostal Francis Drake (☎ 411-553; Phillipi 383; singles/doubles US$45/50), an attractive spot set apart from the main bustle, has pleasant rooms with plush beds; it's a good choice for couples.

Hotel Lago Sarmiento (☎/fax 411-542; Bulnes 90; singles/doubles US$50/70), a family-run place, is a worthwhile mid-range choice, with good bathrooms, lots of light and a great 3rd-floor living room. There's also a poolroom open in the evenings.

Hostal Lady Florence Dixie (☎ 411-158, fax 411-943; e florence@chileanpatagonia.com; Bulnes 659; singles/doubles US$60/75) has back rooms that are motel-style but clean and light, while rooms above the street are polished and a good value (but cost US$10 more). It's run by a smart, friendly woman.

Hotel Juan Ladrilleros (☎ 411-652, fax 412-109; e info@aventouraventuras.com; Pedro Montt 161; singles/doubles US$93/105), looking like a 1970s study in angles, has some great views, but the rooms smell slightly musty.

Hotel Costa Australis (☎ 412-000, fax 411-881; e costaus@ctcreuna.cl; Pedro Montt 262; singles/doubles with town view US$130/147, with harbor view US$164/181) has all of the amenities expected of luxury lodging, in addition to a pleasant street-level bar/restaurant with plush couches.

Places to Eat

El Rincón de Tata (☎ 413-845; Prat 236; sandwiches and meals US$3-10), dark and intimate, is a popular gathering spot with travelers for some of the better pizza in town, mixed drinks and Internet access. It's a shame that the musical selection tends too much to the '80s and the waiters have to wear such ridiculous outfits.

Masay (☎ 415-008; Bulnes 427; pizzas US$3.50-5) is well liked for fast service, oversize sandwiches and hamburgers and its abundantly topped pizzas.

El Living (Prat 156; sandwiches and salads US$2.50-5) focuses on vegetarian and gringo cravings, such as peanut-butter-and-jelly sandwiches, baked beans on toast and fresh crunchy salads, to name a few. It's also a fun spot to enjoy a coffee and muffin on a couch.

El Marítimo (☎ 414-995; Pedro Montt 214; seafood plates US$4-8), an informal eatery near the waterfront, caters heavily to tourists, but it does serve consistently good, cheap and heaping platters of fish and seafood.

Downstairs from the hotel, **Concepto Indigo** (☎ 410-678; Ladrilleros 105; meals US$3-7) is the spot to sink into a couch, order a healthy whole-wheat sandwich with fresh veggies, drip coffee and a brownie. Possibly the only thing to keep you from thinking you're in your favorite café back home is that incredible view out the window. During the high season, Indigo hosts slide shows.

La Tranquera (☎ 411-039; Bulnes 579; mains US$3-8), with friendly service and reasonable prices, is a worthwhile option for run-of-the-mill meat and fish plates or soups.

La Última Esperanza (☎ 411-391; Eberhard 354; dinners US$8-15) is good for a splash. It is a more formal affair, specializing in seafood and fish, that's worth the higher prices; main entrées come with side dishes and are exquisitely prepared. Or come for less-expensive, equally good soups and the powerful pisco sours.

Entertainment

El Viejo Midas (Tomás Rogers 169) is a lively ranch-style lounge across from the plaza with mixed drinks and some light meals.

El Bar de Ruperto (☎ 410-863; cnr Bulnes & Magallanes) has chess, dominoes and other board games and Internet access, all of which get mighty interesting after a few oversize drinks.

Shopping

Ñandú Artesanía (☎ 414-382; Eberhard 586) has shops all over town; all are good places for crafts, postcards and local maps.

Getting There & Away

Air Aerovías DAP (☎ 415-100; Bulnes 100) flies to El Calafate, Argentina (US$50, 30 minutes), at 9am and 6:30pm weekdays from the small airfield, a few kilometers north of town on the road to Torres del Paine. The local **LanChile office** (☎ 411-236; Tomás Rogers 78) can help with flights from Punta Arenas.

Bus Puerto Natales has no central bus terminal, though several companies stop at the junction of Valdivia and Baquedano. Carriers include **Buses Fernández** (☎ 411-111; Eberhard 555); **Bus Sur** (☎ 411-325; Baquedano 534); **Transfer Austral** (Baquedano 414); **Buses JB** (☎ 412-824; Arturo Prat 258); **Turismo Zaahj** (☎ 412-260; Arturo Prat 236); and **Buses Gómez** (☎ 410-595; Prat 234). Expect limited service in the off-season.

To Torres del Paine, most companies shuttle back and forth two to three times daily; Buses JB and Gómez are the best bets. Morning buses start picking people up at their respective lodgings around 7am. The afternoon bus leaves around 2:30pm. If you miss the morning bus, you'll have to pay again for the afternoon one. Note that if you're heading to Refugio Pehoé in the off-season, you need to take the morning bus (US$10 roundtrip, two hours) to meet the catamaran at Pudeto (see Getting Around under PN Torres del Paine later in this chapter).

To Punta Arenas (US$4, three hours), Buses Fernández is the best regarded, but also try Transfer Austral and Bus Sur. Book morning departures early the day before.

To Río Gallegos, Argentina (US$12, four hours), Bus Sur leaves Tuesday and Thursday; El Pingüino, at the Fernández terminal, goes at 11am Wednesday and Sunday.

To El Calafate, Argentina (US$21, 5½ hours), Zaahj and Bus Sur have the most service.

To Coyhaique (US$48, 22 hours), Bus Sur leaves Monday, heading first toward Punta Arenas but transferring to another bus before entering the city.

Boat A highlight of many people's travels in Patagonia is the four-day, three-night voyage through Chile's spectacular fjords aboard Navimag's car and passenger ferries *Puerto Edén* and the newer *Magallanes* to/from Puerto Montt.

To find out when the ferries are due to arrive in Puerto Natales, head to **Comapa/Navimag** (☎ 414-300; w www.navimag.com; Costanera Pedro Montt 262), a couple of days before and then on the estimated arrival date. The *M/N Magallanes* leaves Puerto Natales once a week, usually on Friday. Boats usually arrive in the morning and depart either later that day or on the following day, but dates and times vary according to weather conditions and tides. Passengers disembarking must stay on board a few hours for cargo to be transported first; those leaving may have to hang out in the tiny passenger lounge until boarding is allowed, or spend the night on board. Rate information is given in Puerto Montt in the La Araucanía & the Lakes District chapter.

Getting Around

Car rental is expensive; you'll get better rates in Punta Arenas. **Motor Cars** (☎ 413-593; Blanco Encalada 330) rents high-clearance vehicles for US$75-90 daily with 400km free. **Turismo 'Bien al Sur'** (☎ 415-064; Bulnes 433) charges around US$75; it also rents mountain bikes for US$16 per day, with discounts for multiday rentals.

CUEVA DEL MILODÓN

Just 24km northwest of Puerto Natales, Hermann Eberhard discovered the remains of an enormous prehistoric ground sloth in the 1890s. Nearly 4m high, the herbivorous milodón ate the succulent leaves of small trees and branches, but became extinct in the late Pleistocene. The 30m-high cave contains a tacky plastic life-size replica of the animal.

Conaf charges US$4 admission to the cave; camping (no fires) and picnicking nearby are possible. Torres del Paine buses will drop you at the entrance, which is 8km from the cave proper. Tours cost around US$5; see Puerto Natales above. Alternatively, you can take or share a taxi (about US$14 roundtrip with a one-hour wait).

PN BERNARDO O'HIGGINS

Daily in summer, weather permitting, **Turismo 21 de Mayo** (☎ *411-176, 411-978; Eberhard 560, Puerto Natales)* runs boat excursions (US$55) to the otherwise inaccessible Parque Nacional Bernardo O'Higgins *(admission US$3)*. The four-hour trip through Seno Última Esperanza passes by the meat freezer at Bories, several small estancias, numerous glaciers and waterfalls, a large cormorant rookery and a smaller sea lion rookery before reaching Glaciar Balmaceda. After admiring that glacier, the boat continues to the Puerto Toro jetty, from where a footpath leads to the base of Glaciar Serrano. The return trip goes the same way. Whether the trip justifies the cost is debatable; rather than expect tour excellence, consider this simply a way to access a very privileged spot. If weather is bad, the trips are aborted and a percentage of the cost refunded. Path@gone sells a similar tour for the same price on the galleon-style *Nueva Galicia*, which has more deck space and character, but takes a bit longer and exposes clients to a 'folklore' show on the way home.

An enjoyable way to access Torres del Paine is to take the boat to Glaciar Serrano and then hop on a Zodiac, which continues up Río Serrano, arriving at the southern border of the park at 4:30pm, where a bus waits to take passengers farther into the park. A brief portage is necessary because the Zodiac cannot climb or descend the Serrano rapids, but most passengers find this to be a relatively easy route, which includes a lunch stop alongside the river. The same trip can be done leaving Torres del Paine, but may require camping at Río Serrano to catch the Zodiac at 9am. The Zodiac trip, arranged at Turismo 21 de Mayo or **Onas Patagonia** *(☎/fax 412-707; e onas@chileaustral.com; Eberhard 599, Puerto Natales)*, costs an additional US$33. Trips are available until mid-March, when low water levels make the river too dangerous to run. Outfitters provide foul-weather gear and a sack lunch.

PN TORRES DEL PAINE

Considered one of the best parks and hiking circuits in the Americas, this 181,000-hectare park *(admission US$11)* is an unequaled destination, with a well-developed trail network and refugios and campgrounds at strategic spots allowing for single- and multiday treks. The spectacular peaks include the granite pillars of Torres del Paine (Towers of Paine), which soar almost vertically about 2800m above the Patagonian steppe, Paine Grande (3050m) and Los Cuernos (The Horns, 2200m to 2600m), beautifully carved with black sedimentary peaks. Around these, trails meander through ñire forests, alongside and over roaring rivers, past glaciers and up to jaw-dropping lookouts. Trails also access the vast openness of the steppe, heading to less-visited lakes and glaciers, all the while with the peaks in view. That is, anyway, when the weather is clear. Unpredictable at best, weather systems can sheath the peaks in veils of clouds that never break. Even then, the park has its allure, with azure and emerald green lakes, forests of ñire, wildflowers, herds of guanacos, flocks of ostrichlike rhea (known locally as *ñandú)*, Andean condors, flamingos and many other species.

From Backpack to Kayak

What better way to extend a trip at Torres del Paine than to slip into a kayak and let the arms do the hiking for a change. A three-day trip starts at the top of Río Serrano. The first night is spent along a secluded stretch of riverbank at the confluence of Río Tyndall and Río Serrano, followed by a day of paddling to reach Parque Nacional Bernardo O'Higgins. Camp the second night is set up in the absolute quiet of a coigue forest with Glaciar Serrano just meters away. The third day is spent kayaking among the beautifully shaped icebergs in Laguna Serrano, then paddling along the Fiordo Última Esperanza to Glaciar Balmaceda. **Big Foot Adventure Patagonia** *(☎ 414-611; Bories 206, Puerto Natales)* runs all-inclusive trips, with bilingual guides, for US$380 per person.

MAGALLANES

Flocks of ñandú make their home in the park.

Before its creation in 1959, the park was part of a large sheep estancia, and it's still recovering from nearly a century of overexploitation of its pastures, forests and wildlife. In 1978 it was declared a Unesco Biosphere Reserve.

Since the weather is changeable, with the strong westerlies that typify Patagonia – some say you get four seasons in a day – good foulweather gear is essential. A warm synthetic sleeping bag and wind-resistant tent are imperative for those undertaking the Paine circuit and recommended for those doing the 'W.'

Guided daytrips from Puerto Natales are possible, but they permit only a bus-window glimpse of what the park has to offer. Instead, plan to spend anywhere from three days to two weeks to enjoy the hiking.

Orientation & Information

Parque Nacional Torres del Paine is 112km north of Puerto Natales via a decent but sometimes bumpy gravel road that passes Villa Cerro Castillo, where there is a seasonal border crossing into Argentina at Cancha Carrera. The road continues 38km north, where there's a junction to the little-visited Laguna Verde sector of the park.

Three kilometers north of the Laguna Verde junction the highway forks west along the north shore of Lago Sarmiento de Gamboa to the Portería Sarmiento, the park's main entrance where entrance fees are collected. It's another 37km to the *administración* (park headquarters), where the **Conaf visitors center** *(open 9am-8pm daily in summer)* features a good exhibit on local ecology and videos that provide a good overview of the park. This visitors center, as well as Conaf *guarderías* throughout the park can provide park information, as can travel agents in Puerto Natales.

The park is open year-round, subject to the ability to get there. Conaf guarderías in the park stay open year-round, while the campgrounds and most refugios are open from mid-October to mid-March. Refugio Pehoé is open the longest, until the end of April. The passenger ferry (catamarán) runs once daily in October and April, twice daily in November and the last half of March, and three times daily in the high season, from December to mid-March.

If you're coming during the high season, plan your trip and make reservations for camping and/or refugio stays as far in advance as possible. Conaf and the concessions in charge of many of the lodgings may have to start regulating the flow of people into the most popular parts of the park in the near future.

Climbing Permits Conaf charges a climbing fee of US$100. Before being granted permission, climbers must present a current résumé, emergency contact numbers and authorization from their consulate.

Climbers must also get official permission from the Dirección de Fronteras y Límites (Difrol) in Santiago, which takes about an hour to get if in Santiago and up to five days if requested from Puerto Natales. Ask for plenty of time on the permission to avoid paying a separate fee each time you enter the park. Avoid delays by arranging the permissions with a consulate or a climbing outfitter, such as Big Foot Adventure Patagonia in Puerto Natales, before arrival in the country. For more information, contact the **Gobernación Provincial** (☎ 411-423, fax 411-954; Eberhard 417, 2nd floor), on the south side of the Plaza de Armas in Puerto Natales.

Books & Maps JLM maps, the most up-to-date of the park, are easily found in Puerto Natales.

For more information on trekking and camping, consult Clem Lindenmayer's Lonely Planet guide *Trekking in the Patagonian Andes*. Bradt Publications' *Backpacking in Chile & Argentina* and William Leitch's *South America's National Parks* both have useful chapters on Torres del Paine, but they're less thorough on practical information.

Dangers & Annoyances More than 74,000 tourists visited Torres del Paine in 2001, an almost 20% jump from the previous year, and the park's popularity continues to grow. In February, campgrounds look more like small towns and trails are foot to foot with hikers. Despite this increase in traffic, little is

being done to improve facilities or to limit entry. Whether in order to maintain minimal impact or because of a lack of initiative, Conaf restricts improving existing refugios, which would help circulate trekkers. Garbage has become an issue, but one that each trekker can solve: Pack it out.

Conaf intends to get more rangers on staff, but is short on cash to do so. Andescape, the current concessionaire for most of the campgrounds and refugios, is the subject of many criticisms about littered sites, broken bathrooms and neglected facilities. Both the concessionaires and Conaf could do a lot more to maintain the park, and hopefully they will have the time and money to do so in future years.

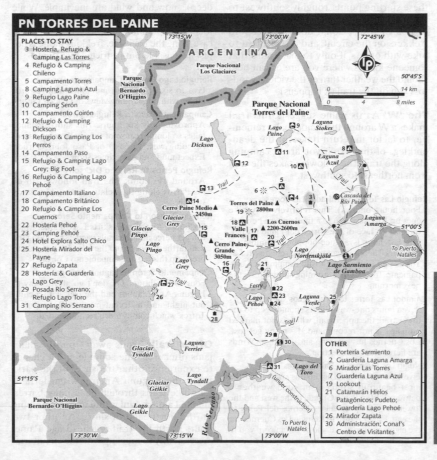

PN TORRES DEL PAINE

PLACES TO STAY
3 Hostería, Refugio & Camping Las Torres
4 Refugio & Camping Chileno
5 Campamento Torres
8 Camping Laguna Azul
9 Refugio Lago Paine
10 Camping Serón
11 Campamento Coirón
12 Refugio & Camping Dickson
13 Refugio & Camping Los Perros
14 Campamento Paso
15 Refugio & Camping Lago Grey; Big Foot
16 Refugio & Camping Lago Pehoé
17 Campamento Italiano
18 Campamento Británico
20 Refugio & Camping Los Cuernos
22 Hostería Pehoé
23 Camping Pehoé
24 Hotel Explora Salto Chico
25 Hostería Mirador del Payne
27 Refugio Zapata
28 Hostería & Guardería Lago Grey
29 Posada Río Serrano; Refugio Lago Toro
31 Camping Río Serrano

OTHER
1 Portería Sarmiento
2 Guardería Laguna Amarga
6 Mirador Las Torres
7 Guardería Laguna Azul
19 Lookout
21 Catamarán Hielos Patagónicos; Pudeto; Guardería Lago Pehoé
26 Mirador Zapata
30 Administración; Conaf's Centro de Visitantes

MAGALLANES

For those who expect some solitude within the park, consider going in the off-season (April is a great month to go) or focusing on the lesser-tramped trails.

Hiking

The most popular hiking routes are the 'W' and the circuit. Doing the circuit (basically the 'W' plus the backside of the park) takes from seven to nine days, while the 'W' takes three to five. When planning your trip, also add another day or two for transportation connections.

Most trekkers start both routes from Laguna Amarga and head west. However, it is also possible to hike from the Administración or take the catamaran from Pudeto to Pehoé and start from there (see Getting Around later in this section); hiking from these starting points, roughly southwest to northeast, along the 'W' presents more views of Los Cuernos. Conaf does restrict solo trekkers on the circuit, and it is prudent to hike with others, if only to make sure that someone knows where you are or can help should the weather turn or the vicious winds toss you off the trail (it happens).

The 'W' As its name suggests, this trail makes a W around the major peaks; remember to factor in return times for the dead-end legs of the hike if you aren't camping along the trail. The following takes the trail from northeast to southwest.

Refugio Las Torres to Mirador Las Torres
Four hours one-way. This relatively easy hike goes up Río Ascencio to a treeless tarn beneath the eastern face of the Torres del Paine proper. The last hour is a knee-popping scramble up boulders. There are camping and refugios at Las Torres and Chileno, with wild camping at Campamento Torres. For a stunning sunrise hike the next morning.

Mirador Las Torres to Refugio Los Cuernos
Seven hours one-way. Hikers should keep to the lower trail; the upper trail, which is not marked on maps, is not recommended – many get lost. Los Cuernos has camping and a refugio. Winds are fierce along this section.

Refugio Los Cuernos to Valle Frances
Five hours one-way. This hike is considered the most beautiful stretch – in good weather – between 3050m Paine Grande to the west and the lower but still spectacular Cuernos del Paine to the east. Either return to Refugio Los Cuernos for the night or camp at Italiano or Británico, if you're energetic enough to lug everything that far.

Valle Frances to Refugio Pehoé
Five hours one-way. This leg of the trek provides views of the Ventisquero Frances, a hanging bridge over a raging river. This moderately protected, fairly easy, well-marked trail runs near Lago Pehoé. Upon reaching the pampa, where the refugio is, be prepared for strong winds.

Refugio Pehoé to Refugio Lago Grey
Four hours one-way. This hike follows a relatively easy trail with a few bits of challenging downhill scampers. The glacier lookout is another half-hour farther. Camping and refugios can be found at both ends.

The Circuit Hiking the circuit takes in the 'W,' as described above, plus the backside between Refugio Lago Grey and Refugio Las Torres. You'll need foul-weather camping and trekking gear, as mud (sometimes knee-deep), snow and wind are inevitable. While the popularity of the 'W' means you'll meet lots of people along the way, that's not the case along the backside. Trekking alone is not just inadvisable but restricted by Conaf.

Refugio Lago Grey to Campamento Paso
Five to six hours. This moderate trail rewards hikers with outstanding views of Glaciar Grey.

Campamento Paso to Refugio Perros
Approximately six hours. This short distance takes so long because of the challenging ascent (if going west to east) of Paso John Garner. Expect mud and sometimes snow.

Refugio Perros to Refugio Dickson
Around 4½ hours. The trail follows Río de los Perros along this relatively easy but windy stretch.

Refugio Dickson to Campamento Serón
Six hours. As the trail skirts Lago Paine, winds can get fierce and the trails vague; stay along the trail farthest away from the lake. It's possible to break up this leg at Campamento Coirón.

Campamento Serón to Laguna Amarga
Four to five hours. Or, don't go all the way to Laguna Amarga, but end the trek with a chill-out night and a decent meal at Refugio Las Torres, which comes much recommended.

Other Trails Trails away from the main jams offer welcome solitude and a chance to experience other treasures of the park. From the Laguna Amarga Guardería, a four-hike leads through beautifully barren land to **Laguna Azul** where there is camping on the northeastern shore. Another two hours north the trail reaches Lago Paine. Accessibility to meet up with the circuit trail near the other side of the lake is made impossible by the river.

From Administración, the three-hour hike to Refugio Pehoé is an easy, mainly flat trail with fantastic views. For more solitude, a four-hour hike branches east after crossing Río Paine, zigzags up the skirt of the Sierra del Toro to access a string of lakes, ending with **Laguna Verde**. There is no camping along this route, but those inclined could splurge for a night at Hostería Mirador del Paine. This is a good hike for bird-watching.

From Guadería Lago Grey, a four-hour trail follows Río Pingo to Conaf's Refugio Zapata, from where hikes (about another 1½ to two hours) continue to a lookout with impressive views of **Glaciar Zapata** and to **Lago Pingo**. For true remoteness, plus a chance to view glaciers, this hike is well recommended.

For a shorter day hike, walk from Guadería Lago Pehoé, on the main park highway, to **Salto Grande**, a powerful waterfall between Lago Nordenskjöld and Lago Pehoé. Another easy hour's walk leads to **Mirador Nordenskjöld**, an overlook with superb views of the lake and *cordillera*.

Glacier Trekking & Kayaking

Big Foot Adventure Patagonia (☎ *414-611, 414-276; Bories 206, Puerto Natales*) is the only outfitter authorized to lead ice hikes on Glaciar Grey (US$75), which involve a quick Zodiac trip to the glacier, walking on the glacier with crampons and harnesses, and ice climbing before heading back. There's a tent shelter near the glacier in case of a change in weather, and snacks are provided. Treks leave daily in season at 9am and 3pm from the Big Foot refugio near Refugio Grey. For details on the kayaking trips down Río Serrano, see the boxed text 'From Backpack to Kayak' earlier in this section.

Horseback Riding

Due to property divisions within the park, horses cannot cross between the western sections (Lagos Grey and Pehoé, Río Serrano) and the eastern part managed by Hostería Las Torres (Refugio Los Cuernos is the approximate cut-off). **Baqueano Zamora** (☎ *412-911;* e *baqueano@terra.cl; Eberhard 566, Puerto Natales)* runs excursions to Lago Pingo, Laguna Amarga, Lago Paine and Lago Azul (all on the west side of the park). Half-day rides cost US$47, lunch included. **Fantástico**

Sur *(contact Hostería Las Torres; see Places to Stay & Eat below)* controls the eastern area and charges US$70 per day, snack included.

Places to Stay & Eat

Make reservations. Arriving at the park without them, especially in the high season, means you may be without any place to stay, either in the refugios or in the campgrounds. Unfortunately, the reservation system is slow and can be very nerve-racking. To make things easier, plan your trek as best you can *before* sitting down with an agent, and make sure that you receive a voucher for each reservation made; you'll need to give these to the staff at the refugios upon arrival. A number of travel agencies can call in reservations, or go directly to the main concessions – **Andescape** (☎ *412-592;* e *andescape@terra.cl)* in the Path@gone office in Puerto Natales and the **Hostería Las Torres/Fantástico Sur** (☎ *226-054; Magallanes 960, Punta Arenas)*. The latter manages Torres, Chileno and Los Cuernos refugios and campgrounds; the former manages Pehoé, Grey, Dickson and Los Perros. Once at a refugio, staff can radio your next destination to confirm the reservation. Also of importance is patience. The staffers at the campgrounds and refugios do their best to deal with the intense flow of trekkers, but they can't meet everyone's expectations.

Camping Campgrounds at **Las Torres, Chileno, Los Cuernos, Pehoé, Grey, Dickson** and **Los Perros** all charge between US$4 and US$5 for a campsite. Refugios rent equipment: a tent is US$9 per night, a sleeping bag US$4, a mat US$1 and a stove US$3. In high season it's prudent to bring your own equipment in case the refugios run out. They also have small stores with pastas, soup packets and butane gas. All other sites are administered by Conaf and are free and very basic (rain shelters and pit toilets). Rats and mice have become a problem at many campgrounds; hang food from trees to avoid packs and tents from being chewed through. Campsites at **Británico** are used mainly by climbers, but afford spectacular views and a welcome remoteness.

Refugios All of the refugios listed under the hiking descriptions have individual rooms with four to eight bunk beds, kitchen privileges (for lodgers only and during specific hours), bathrooms with showers and meals. At most, a bed costs US$17 to US$19, sleeping bag rental US$4, meals US$5 to US$11. Should the refugio be full, the staff will provide all necessary camping equipment. **Refugios Las Torres, Chileno** and **Los Cuernos** close at the end of March; **Lago Grey** closes in mid-April. **Refugio Pehoé** is the only one that stays open after that. Conaf-managed **Refugio Lago Toro** near Administración costs US$5 for lodging in one large dorm room (upstairs) with kitchen facilities and hot water (showers US$1 more).

All the other refugios mentioned in the text and shown on the map – **Refugios Dickson, Los Perros, Lago Paine** and **Zapata** – are managed by Conaf and are free. Don't expect leisure; these are basic shelters from the elements, not places of comfort.

Hotels & Hosterías
Posada Río Serrano (☎ 410-684, fax 412-349; doubles with shared/private bath US$66/90, quad with shared bath US$100), a remodeled estancia house near the Administración, has attractive rooms, some in cheery colors, with plenty of heat and thick blankets. Private baths have good water pressure, but you'll have to wait a while for the hot water. It's not maximum luxury, but it's the best value hostería in the park. Its restaurant serves surprisingly decent meals; lunches cost US$12. Reservations can be made through Baqueano Zamora (see Horseback Riding earlier in this section).

Hostería Mirador del Payne (Estancia Lazo; ☎/fax 228-712; e payne@mundosur.com; Fagnano 585, Punta Arenas; singles/doubles/ triples US$112/138/157), in the park's Laguna Verde sector, offers a Magallanes experience within a working estancia of red-roofed buildings, paddocks of horses and sheep, spectacular views, serenity a'plenty and fabulous service. Two separate houses have ample rooms with central heating and large showers with very hot water. Dinners (US$17) are served in the comfortable lounge area. Be sure to walk around the grounds to see the gardens, mud storage shed and the impressive wood-burning water heaters. The owners offer excursions around the area and can arrange transfers to other hosterías in the park and to/ from the Ruta 9 road junction.

Hostería Lago Grey (☎ 225-986; Sector Lago Grey; singles/doubles US$173/200), although at the outlet of iceberg-dotted Lago

Grey, has rooms that are cut off from the views by thick windbreaking trees, but the café enjoys a nice view. Zodiac boat tours are available on the lake, but not onto the glacier.

Hostería Pehoé (☎ 244-506; singles/ doubles US$145/160) is on a small island in the lake of the same name and linked to the mainland by a footbridge. It has panoramic views, but the rooms are small and simple. The restaurant and bar are open to the public, but service can be slow.

Hostería Las Torres (☎ 226-054; singles US$131-179, doubles US$149-197), constantly expanding, is 7km from Guardería Laguna Amarga. The wings of the hotel are all connected, separated by spacious living rooms, while the rooms are attractively decorated and warm. Buffet meals are elaborate, artistic affairs. Readers have commented that staff can be rather tired and rude.

Hotel Explora Salto Chico (☎ 02-206-6060, fax 228-4655 in Santiago; e reservexplora@ explora.com; singles/doubles for 2 days & 3 nights US$1347/2080, suites for 6 days & 7 nights US$5388/6738) is the most extravagant hotel around, at the outlet of Lago Pehoé. Rates include transfers from Punta Arenas, full board and all activities with knowledgeable bilingual guides. The modern building sits near the Salto Chico waterfall, unobtrusively blending in with the surroundings, while the interiors are gorgeously designed with fabrics that reflect the colors that stream in through the picture windows. Separate from the hotel is an indoor heated lap pool and outdoor Jacuzzi.

Getting There & Away
For details of transportation to the park, see Getting There & Away in Puerto Natales earlier in this chapter. A new road is being built from Puerto Natales to Administración, but it currently ends at Río Serrano, where the government has yet to finish a bridge. Hitching from Puerto Natales is possible, but competition is heavy.

Getting Around
Buses drop off and pick up passengers at Laguna Amarga, the Hielos Patagónicos catamaran launch at Pudeto and at park headquarters, coordinating with the catamaran schedule. Each transfer within the park costs US$3. The catamaran (US$14 per person with one backpack) leaves Pudeto for the Refugio

Pehoé at 9:30am, noon and 6pm December to mid-March, noon and 6pm in late March and November and at noon only in October and April. Another tourist boat runs between Hostería Lago Grey and Refugio Lago Grey, but does not have a regular schedule.

EL CALAFATE (ARGENTINA)
☎ 02902
From Puerto Natales, many buses make the trip to El Calafate, Argentina. This is a popular route for those hopping from Torres del Paine to Argentina's equally spectacular Parque Nacional Los Glaciares. El Calafate is a highly touristy town, which can be a shock if you've been trekking for ten days, but it does have the best traveler services before heading to Los Glaciares. And, of course, El Calafate's main claim to fame is the spectacular Moreno Glacier, 80km away.

The **municipal tourist office** *(Emcatur;* ☎ 491-090, 492-884; e *info@elcalafate.net;* w *www.calafate.com)* at the bus terminal keeps a list of hotels and prices; it also has maps, brochures and a message board, and there's usually an English-speaker on hand. The **national parks office** (☎ 491-755, 491-005; *Av Libertador 1302)* has brochures including a decent (though not adequate for trekking) map of Parque Nacional Los Glaciares. Along the main road, Av del Libertador General José de San Martín, travelers will find the post office, call centers and banks.

Places to Stay & Eat
Most places either have their own tours to the Perito Moreno glacier or can help line you up with one. Budget options range from US$4 to US$8 per person with shared bath. **Camping Municipal** *(☎ 491-829; José Pantín)* is a woodsy campground straddling the creek just north of the bridge into town. **Albergue del Glaciar** *(☎/fax 491-243;* e *info@glaciar.com; Calle Los Pioneros 251)* is a sociable HI affiliate, set away from the main part of town. **Calafate Hostel** (☎ 492-450, fax 492-451; w *www.hostelspatagonia.com; Gobernador Moyano 1226)* is an enormous and fun place. **Los Dos Pinos** (☎ 491-271, fax 491-632; e *losdospinos@cotecal.com.ar; 9 de Julio 358)* has camping, dorms (sleeping bag required) and regular rooms. **Cayupe Albergue** *(☎ 491-125; Manzana 355),* near Laguna Nimes, in an attractive, modern house with shared bunk-bed rooms.

Mid-range to top-end choices range from US$15 to US$25 per person. **Hotel La Loma** *(☎/fax 491-016;* e *lalomahotel@infovia .com.ar; Av Roca 849)* is in a quiet upper quarter of town, with ranch-style character. **Hostería Kalkén** (☎ 491-073, fax 491-036; e *hotelkalken@cotecal.com.ar; Valentín Feilberg 119)* has helpful staff and a quiet location. **Hotel Michelangelo** *(☎ 491-045, fax 491-058; Moyano 1020)* is an intimate hotel in the center.

In most restaurants, meals cost between US$3 and US$6, and the pasta plates and cuts of meat could easily feed two. **El Hornito** (☎ 491-443; *Buenos Aires 155)* has homemade pastas and large crispy pizzas. **La Tablita** (☎ 491-065; *Coronel Rosales 28)* serves parrilla and garlic-parsley french fries. Come to **El Rancho Pizza/Bar** (☎ 491-644; cnr *Gobernador Moyano & 9 de Julio)* for the pizza.

Getting There & Away
Chilean **Aerovías DAP** (☎ 491-143; *Av del Libertador 1329)* flies to Puerto Natales at 10am weekdays (US$50, 30 minutes). From the hilltop **bus terminal** *(Av Roca),* buses go to Puerto Natales (5½ hours) and El Chaltén (five hours) daily.

PERITO MORENO GLACIER (ARGENTINA)
To visit **Ventisquero Perito Moreno** (Moreno Glacier), one of earth's few advancing glaciers, is no less an auditory than a visual experience, as huge icebergs on the glacier's face calve and collapse into the **Canal de los Témpanos** (Iceberg Channel). From a series of catwalks and vantage points on the Península de Magallanes, visitors can see, hear and photograph the glacier safely as these enormous chunks crash into the water. Campgrounds near the glacier include **Camping Bahía Escondida** with woodsy sites and the not-as-well-maintained **Camping Correntoso**, 3km east of Bahía Escondida. The Moreno Glacier is about 80km from El Calafate via westbound partially paved RP 11. For a tour, ask at any hotel or hostel in El Calafate, or check for tour times at the bus station.

PN LOS GLACIARES (ARGENTINA)
☎ 02962
Indisputably one of the most majestic mountain areas of the Andes, the Fitzroy

MAGALLANES

range within Parque Nacional Los Glaciares, just on the Argentina side of the border, is a must destination for trekkers and mountaineers. It is less crowded than Torres del Paine to the south, but with an equal, if not greater, number of trails. Rustic, free campsites dot the trails; there are no refugios within the park. **Park rangers** (*guadaparques; ☎ 493-004*), at the entrance to El Chaltén, issue climbing permits and general information about the trails and surrounding area. There is no entrance fee, and like Torres, the park is ostensibly open year-round, but the main season is October through April.

El Chaltén

El Chaltén, a small village within the park and tattered from the winds whipping down the Río de las Vueltas floodplain, is base camp for trekkers heading well onto trails, most of which start from town. Park rangers, at the entrance to town just before the bridge over the Río Fitzroy, distribute a small map and town directory that is comprehensive but confusing in scale. Many of the rangers are bilingual; they provide trail updates and issue climbing permits from 8am to 8pm daily. But the several hostels in town are better sources for information about the town itself.

Money exchange, ATMs, Internet, cell phones and newspapers have yet to hit town, but there is phone service and a gas station. **Viento Oeste** (*☎ 493-021; San Martín & Brenner*), en route to Camping Madsen, rents some camping equipment, as may Rancho Grande Hostel, but call to reserve before arriving.

Hiking

The trail to **Laguna Torre** (three hours one-way) is mainly a level walk through beech forests and along the Río Fitzroy until a final steep climb up the lateral moraine to Mirador El Torre and breathtaking view of the majestic spire of 3128m Cerro Torre.

A bit more strenuous is the four-hour hike to **Laguna de los Tres**, named in honor of the three Frenchmen who first scaled Fitzroy. The trail leads to excellent backcountry **campsites** at Laguna Capri, continuing gently through windswept forests and past small lakes, meeting up with the **Madre y Hija** trail, which connects to the Laguna

Torre trail, described above. Carrying on through windworn ñire and along boggy terrain, Madre y Hija leads to **Río Blanco** and the woodsy **Campamento Poincenot**, passes the river and begins to zigzag up the tarn to the eerily still glacial lake and an extraordinary close view of 3405m Cerro Fitzroy.

At Campamento Poincenot, another trail heads northeast along Río Blanco to Valle Eléctrico and **Piedra del Fraile** (eight hours from town; five hours from the Río Blanco turnoff), where the privately owned **Refugio Los Troncos** has a campground with excellent services and the owners have information on many well-recommended trails within this private section.

Places to Stay & Eat

Plenty of places offer camping in El Chaltén. Try **Ruca Mahuida** (*☎ 493-018*), on Lionnel Terray; it has an oversize backyard that may get cramped.

Budget options range from US$4 to US$8 per person with shared bath. **Albergue Patagonia** (*☎ 493-019;* e *patagoni@hostels.org.ar; San Martín 493*) is a bit small but the owners are helpful. **Rancho Grande Hostel** (*☎/fax 493-005;* e *bigranch@hostels.org.ar; San Martín s/n*) is a spacious facility with dorm beds, a kitchen and restaurant. **La Base Hospedaje** (*☎ 493-031; cnr Lago del Desierto & Hensen*) has four private rooms, all in an independent bungalow with kitchen facilities.

For a meal, **Patagonicus** (*☎ 493-025; cnr Güemes & Madsen*) has pizza and salads. **Ruca Mahuida** (*☎ 493-018; Lionnel Terray*) serves hearty meals in a nonsmoking dining room.

Getting There & Away

El Chaltén is 220km from El Calafate via paved RP 11, rugged RN 40 and improved but still very rocky RP 23.

To get to El Calafate (five hours), **Los Glaciares** leaves daily from Av Güemes and Lago del Desierto; **Chalten Travel** leaves daily from the Rancho Grande Hostel; and **Cal Tur** leaves from the Fitz Roy Inn Monday, Wednesday, Friday and Sunday.

Adventurous travelers may be able to get to/from Parque Nacional Los Glaciares and El Chaltén through Chile from the north, but it's no cruise ship; see the boxed text 'Argentina, the Hard Way' in the Aisén & the Carretera Austral chapter.

Tierra del Fuego

Ever since the 16th-century voyages of Magellan and the 19th-century explorations of Fitzroy and Darwin on the *Beagle,* and even to the present, this 'uttermost part of the earth' has fascinated travelers. From the barren plains of the north, to virgin lenga forests draped in 'old man's beard,' to glaciers descending nearly to the ocean, the island never ceases to enthrall those who come to explore its mystery. The Yahgan Indians built the fires that inspired Europeans to give this region its name, now famous throughout the world.

The region comprises one large island, Isla Grande de Tierra del Fuego, and many smaller ones, few of them inhabited. The Strait of Magellan separates the archipelago from the South American mainland. This section covers the Chilean section of the island, including Isla Navarino, as well as the Argentine town Ushuaia.

If you are searching for the end of the world, Tierra del Fuego is it.

History

In 1520, when Magellan passed through the strait that now bears his name, neither he nor any other European explorer had any immediate interest in the land and its people. Seeking a passage to the Spice Islands of Asia, early navigators feared and detested the stiff westerlies, hazardous currents and violent seas that impeded their progress. Consequently, the Selk'nam, Haush, Yahgan and Alacaluf peoples who populated the area faced no immediate competition for their lands and resources.

These groups were mobile hunters and gatherers. The Selk'nam, also known as Ona, and the Haush subsisted primarily on hunting the guanaco and dressing in its skins, while the Yahgans and Alacalufes, known collectively as 'Canoe Indians,' lived on fish, shellfish and marine mammals. The Yahgans (also known as the Yamaná) consumed the 'Indian bread' fungus that feeds off the *ñire,* a species of southern beech. Despite frequently inclement weather, they wore little or no clothing, but constant fires (even in their bark canoes) kept them warm.

As Spain's control of its American empire dwindled, the area slowly opened to settlement by other Europeans, ensuring the rapid demise of the indigenous Fuegians, whom Europeans struggled to understand. Darwin, visiting the area in 1834, wrote that the difference between the Fuegians ('among the most abject and miserable creatures I ever saw') and Europeans was greater than that between wild and domestic animals. On an earlier voyage, though, Captain Robert Fitzroy of the *Beagle* had abducted a few Yahgans whom he returned after several years of missionary education in England.

From the 1850s, Europeans attempted to catechize the Fuegians, the earliest such instance ending with the death by starvation of British missionary Allen Gardiner. Gardiner's successors, including missionary GP Despard, working from a base at Keppel Island in the Falklands, were more successful despite the massacre of one party by Fuegians at Isla Navarino. Thomas Bridges, Despard's adopted son, learned to speak the Yahgan language and became one of the first settlers at Ushuaia, in what is now Argentine Tierra del Fuego. His son, Lucas Bridges, born at Ushuaia in 1874, left a fascinating memoir of his experiences among the Yahgans and Onas titled *The Uttermost Part of the Earth* (1950).

Since no other European power had had any interest in settling the region until Britain occupied the Falklands in the 1770s, Spain too paid little attention to Tierra del Fuego, but the successor governments of Chile and Argentina felt differently. The Chilean presence on the Strait of Magellan beginning in 1843, along with increasing British evangelism, spurred Argentina to formalize its authority at Ushuaia in 1884. In 1978 Chile and Argentina nearly went to war over claims to three small disputed islands in the Beagle Channel. International border issues in the area were not resolved until 1984.

Geography & Climate

Surrounded by the South Atlantic Ocean, the Strait of Magellan and the easternmost part of the Pacific Ocean, the archipelago of Tierra del Fuego has a land area of roughly 76,000 sq km, about the size of Ireland or South Carolina. The Chile-Argentine border runs directly south from Cabo Espíritu Santo, at the eastern entrance of the Strait of Magellan, to the Beagle Channel (Canal de Beagle), where it trends eastward to the channel's mouth at Isla Nueva.

TIERRA DEL FUEGO

The plains of northern Isla Grande are a landscape of almost unrelenting wind, enormous flocks of Corriedale sheep and oil derricks, while the mountainous southern part offers scenic glaciers, lakes, rivers and seacoast. The maritime climate is surprisingly mild, even in winter, but its changeability makes warm, dry clothing essential, especially on hikes and at higher elevations. The mountains of the Cordillera Darwin and the Sierra de Beauvoir, reaching up to 2500m in the west, intercept Antarctic storms, leaving the plains around Río Grande much drier than areas nearer the Beagle Channel.

The higher southern rainfall supports dense deciduous and evergreen forests, while the drier north consists of extensive native grasses and low-growing shrubs. Storms batter the bogs and truncated beeches of the remote southern and western zones of the archipelago. Guanaco, rhea and condor can still be seen in the north, but marine mammals and shorebirds are the most common wildlife along the Beagle Channel.

PORVENIR
☎ 61 • pop 5400

The largest settlement on Chilean Tierra del Fuego, Porvenir is most often visited in a daytrip from Punta Arenas, but this usually means spending only a couple of hours in town and more time than a belly might wish crossing the choppy strait. Spending a night in this quiet village of rusting, metal-clad Victorians and then proceeding to other destinations is a better way to gain a glimpse into Fuegian life.

When gold was discovered nearby in 1879, waves of immigrants, many from Croatia, endured the trip to come here. Whether or not anyone made a fortune is debatable. But when sheep estancias began to spring up, the immigrants found more reliable work. Chilotes (from the Chilean island of Chiloé) came down in droves for the fishing and estancia work and the chance of a better life. Today, most of the population is a Croat-Chilote combo.

The gravel road east, along Bahía Inútil to the Argentine border at San Sebastián, is in fine condition. Northbound motorists from San Sebastián should take the equally good route from Onaisín to Cerro Sombrero en route to the crossing of the Strait of Magellan at Punta Delgada-Puerto Espora, rather than the heavily traveled and rutted truck route directly north from San Sebastián.

Information
The **tourist office** (☎ 580-098; *Padre Mario Zavattaro 402; open 9am-5pm Mon-Fri, 11am-5pm Sat & Sun*) is upstairs from the museum. Information is also available at the artisanal shop on the Costanera between Phillipi and Schythe.

There's a **post office** *(Plaza de Armas)* and **Telefónica (CTC)** *(Philippi 277)*. Porvenir's **hospital** (☎ 580-034; *Carlos Wood)* is between Señoret and Guerrero.

Things to See & Do
The intriguing **Museo de Tierra del Fuego** (☎ 580-098; *Mario Zavattaro 402; admission US$1; open 9am-5pm Mon-Fri year-round, plus 11am-5pm Sat & Sun Jan & Feb)* on the Plaza de Armas, has some unexpected materials, including Selk'nam mummies and skulls, musical instruments used by the mission Indians on Isla Dawson, stuffed animals from the region, and an exhibit on early Chilean cinematography.

The tourist office can arrange tours of old gold-panning sites, horse-riding excursions and other ways to enjoy the area. **Explore Patagonia** (☎ 580-206; w *www.explorepatagonia .cl; Croacia 675)* organizes excursions, including a 'city tour' and a visit to Peale's dolphins around Bahía Chilote in a traditional Chilote-style fishing boat (US$65, including meals). It also runs longer camping and horseback-riding trips, including one to Río Condor (US$170 per day all-inclusive) and another, more intense six-day adventure in November that involves kayaking, *centolla* (king crab) fishing and riding to Glaciar Marinelli (US$190 per day all-inclusive).

Places to Stay & Eat
Residencial Colón (☎ 581-157; *Damián Riobó 198; singles US$7)* has basic rooms with shared bath and treacherous heating facilities, but it's still the best deal in town. Lunch costs US$4. Rates include breakfast.

Hotel España (☎ 580-160; *Croacia 698; singles/doubles US$9/11)* has a dark hallway leading to rooms with ample beds, large windows, private baths and cropped harbor views. Breakfast is US$2 extra.

Hotel Central (☎ 580-077; *cnr Phillipi & Croacia; singles/doubles with shared bath*

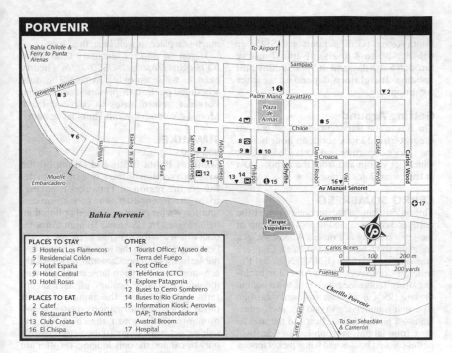

PORVENIR

Bahía Chilote &
Ferry to Punta
Arenas

To Airport

Sampaio

Teniente Merino

■ 3

1 ❶
Padre Mario Zavattaro

▼ 2

Plaza
de
Armas

4 ✉

Chiloé

■ 5

Williams

Jde la Rivera

Santos Mardones

Muñoz Camero

Silva

▼ 6

8 ❺
9 ■

■ 7

● 11

▢ 12

● 10

Philippi

Schythe

Damían Riobó

Croacia

Viel

Duble

Almeyda

Carlos Wood

Muelle
Embarcadero

13 14
▼ ▢ ❶ 15

16 ▼
Av Manuel Señoret

❹ 17

Bahía Porvenir

Parque
Yugoslavo

Guerrero

Carlos Bories

0   100   200 m
0   100   200 yards

Fuentes

Chorillo Porvenir

Santa María

To San Sebastián
& Camerón

PLACES TO STAY
3 Hostería Los Flamencos
5 Residencial Colón
7 Hotel España
9 Hotel Central
10 Hotel Rosas

PLACES TO EAT
2 Catef
6 Restaurant Puerto Montt
13 Club Croata
16 El Chispa

OTHER
1 Tourist Office; Museo de
   Tierra del Fuego
4 Post Office
8 Telefónica (CTC)
11 Explore Patagonia
12 Buses to Cerro Sombrero
14 Buses to Río Grande
15 Information Kiosk; Aerovías
   DAP; Transbordadora
   Austral Broom
17 Hospital

US$19/33, with private bath US$24/35) has
cozy and small rooms but not all have heat.
Prices don't include breakfast, but if you stay
longer than a day the owner may add it in.

Hotel Rosas (☎ 580-088; Philippi 296;
singles/doubles US$22/32) is a good choice
for clean rooms with heat and an owner who
knows heaps about the region. The restaurant serves up some great seafood dishes.
Lunch, with drinks, costs about US$9. Rates
include breakfast.

Hostería Los Flamencos (☎ 241-321; Teniente Merino; singles/doubles US$40/50),
overlooking the harbor, is the fanciest hotel
in town, but it's neglected by its owners. The
manager, however, is a charm and does what
he can to make your stay more inviting.

El Chispa (☎ 580-054; cnr Viel & Señoret;
breakfast US$1.50-3, lunches US$5-7), with
tattered green-hued paintings of European
garden parties, offers fresh seafood and large
breakfasts. Main meals include a side dish,
making this place a good deal for the money.

Club Croata (☎ 580-053; Manuel Señoret
542; mains US$4-10), a more formal expe-
rience, serves rich fish dishes. The owner can

fill you in on the Croatian history and influence in town.

Restaurant Puerto Montt (☎ 580-207;
Croacia 1169; mains US$3-6) is a more divey
place where the fishing crews come to feast
on huge portions.

Catef (☎ 580-625; Zavattaro 94; mains
US$7) offers creative dishes, all of which are
explained on the menu. Try the pichanga
caliente, a layer of tomato and avocado
topped with meat, fries and finally cheese.

Getting There & Away
Aerovías DAP (☎ 580-089; Manuel Señoret),
flies to and from Punta Arenas (US$25)
twice daily except Sunday.

To get to Río Grande, Argentina (US$17,
5½ hours), Tecni-Austral buses leave from
the corner of Philippi and Manuel Señoret
Wednesday, Friday and Sunday at 12:30pm.
Town buses transport workers from in front
of the DAP office to Camerón in Timaukel
(2½ hours) for free, but if the bus is full,
you're out of luck. To get to Cerro Sombrero,
buses leave from Santos Mardones, near
Manuel Señoret.

TIERRA DEL FUEGO

Transbordadora Broom (☎ 580-089) operates the auto-passenger ferry *Melinka* to Punta Arenas (US$7 per person, US$45 per vehicle, 2½ to 4 hours) at 2pm Tuesday through Saturday, and at 5pm Sunday and holidays. Travel times depend on weather conditions.

Getting Around

The bus to the ferry terminal departs from the waterfront kiosk about an hour before the ferry's departure and costs US$1. Taxis, which get you to and from the airport, cost at least four times as much.

CERRO SOMBRERO

This orderly but half-abandoned town at the north end of Tierra del Fuego, 43km south of the ferry crossing at Primera Angostura, is a company town belonging to Chile's Empresa Nacional de Petróleo (ENAP; National Petroleum Company). North American architects from Tennessee created the town plan in the late 1950s, giving it an awkward suburban style that is unnerving to find in these hinterlands – a pink A-frame church in the middle of a roundabout, surrounded by identical pastel-colored houses and white picket fences.

Rumor has it that ENAP may close business on this town, leaving the residents without much of a place to, well, hang their hats.

If you do stop for lunch, try **Club Social** (*O'Higgins s/n; meals US$5-7*) for a hearty cazuela while enjoying Muzac. The only scheduled public transportation comes from Porvenir; return buses to Porvenir leave Monday, Wednesday and Thursday at 8am.

TIMAUKEL
pop 420

South of Bahía Inútil and taking up the southern section of the Chilean Tierra del Fuego, the region of Timaukel is eagerly trying to reinvent itself as an ecotourism destination – a far more welcomed option than being logged by US-based Trillium Corporation, which was the plan just a few years back. Few roads lead into this region, with even less public transportation. **Camerón**, on the southern shore of the bay, is a large estancia owing its name to a New Zealand pioneer sheep-farming family. Here, the municipal **tourist office** may have information on latest developments. To the south, the cherished fly-fishing getaway Lago Blanco is accessible only by car and the only lodgings on offer are

---

Masks & Rituals in Tierra del Fuego

As Charles Darwin saw it, the Yamaná (or Yahgan) of the Beagle Channel – naked except for a loincloth and sealskin cape, paddling about in canoes with all their most important possessions, including bows, dogs and a constantly lit fire – were 'subhuman beings…without spiritual life.'

But theirs was a life rich in spiritual beliefs. They believed in a Supreme Being, Watauinewa, and their shamans talked to spirits who the Yamaná believed controlled the weather and the hunt. During the 'Kina' ceremony, in which boys were initiated to adulthood, the men dressed themselves as gods, painting their bodies with black carbon and the region's white and red clays and holding tall masks, and danced to represent the different spirits: Kina-Miami, the guardian; Tulema-Yaka, the tutor; Hani-Yaka, the energy giver.

North of the island's mountain range, another group held a similar ritual. The Selk'nam (or Ona to the Yamaná and, later, to the Europeans) believed in a Supreme Being, Temankel. They also believed that women once controlled the lands, keeping the men subordinate with clever sorcery. According to legend, the men learned of this ploy and decided the only way to gain control would be to kill all of the women except the youngest and to play the same game of fear. Thus the 'Hain' ceremony was created. Men painted their bodies using the same black carbon and red and white clays mixed with guanaco fat, and they created masks from the bark of trees. Boys went through the initiation process, learning about the different spirits as each body (zigzagged, striped or dotted) danced, leapt into the air and interpreted its symbolism, all the while instilling fear in the women and small children watching from afar. Spirits included Matan, the magic dancer and spirit of happiness; Kulan, the terrible vixen who descends from the sky, selects her man and then kidnaps him to make love to her; and Koshmenk, Kulan's jealous husband.

the nearby exclusive fishing lodges. A controversial new road may continue south of Lago Blanco to access Lago Fagnano, the new park administered by Fudación Yendegaia, and the Beagle Channel.

ESTANCIA YENDEGAIA

In the Cordillera Darwin, nestled between Argentina's Parque Nacional Tierra del Fuego and Chile's Parque Nacional Alberto de Agostini, Estancia Yendegaia consists of 40,000 hectares of native Fuegian forest, fingers of glaciers and serene bays – all of which is due to become a *Santuario de la Naturaleza*. A one-time estancia, this private park has in the works a series of hiking trails, including one to Glaciar Stoppani and others through Valle Lapataia to Paso de Las Lagunas, although the many river crossings make horse trekking a more viable option. For now only camping is possible.

Unfortunately, access is difficult and expensive. Transbordadora Austral Broom's ferry between Punta Arenas and Puerto Williams will drop passengers off if given advance notice; see Punta Arenas earlier in this chapter for contact information. From Puerto Williams, the trip takes seven hours. Infrequent naval boats from Punta Arenas to Puerto Williams will drop passengers at the southern approach.

For information on visiting the park, contact **Fundación Yendegaia** (☎/fax 02-204-1914, fax 209-2527; e yendegaia@patagonia.com).

ISLA NAVARINO

☎ 61 • pop 2200

Across the Beagle Channel from Argentine Tierra del Fuego, Isla Navarino has a truly end-of-the-world feel to it that makes it a unique destination. Trekkers seeking isolation and challenge are increasingly drawn to the **Dientes de Navarino** chain, through which there's a five-day circuit. Throughout the island, beavers introduced to Tierra del Fuego from Canada in the 1940s have wreaked havoc on the landscape.

Anglican missionaries in the mid-19th century tried over and over to maintain a presence here, but most often these efforts were ill-fated due to the wretched weather conditions. Fortune-seekers during the 1890s gold rush also helped establish a permanent European presence here.

The only town, **Puerto Williams**, is a ramshackle naval settlement of sterile gray military barracks and makeshift corrugated-iron houses. The center of town is little more than a concrete slab. It's an official port of entry for yachts en route to Cape Horn and Antarctica. Within minutes from town you can be deep in lenga and ñire forests dripping in old man's beard and on trails that lead past beaver dams and bunkers as they head deeper into forests and up into the mountains.

Information

The Centro Comercial near the main roundabout has call centers and the post office. Also inside the Centro Comercial, **Turismo SIM** (☎/fax 621-150; e sim@entelchile.net; w www.simltd.com) offers plentiful information about the island. Money exchange (US cash only) or Visa advances are possible at Banco de Chile; there is no ATM.

Things to See & Do

Near the entrance to the military quarters is the original bow of the *Yelcho*, which rescued Ernest Shackleton's Antarctic expedition from Elephant Island in 1916. The **Museo Martín Gusinde** (☎ 621-043; admission US$2; open 10am-1pm & 3pm-6pm Mon-Fri, 3pm-6pm Sat & Sun), honoring the German priest and ethnographer who worked among the Yahgans from 1918 to 1923, has mediocre exhibits on natural history and ethnography.

The most southerly ethno-botanical park in South America (and something of a work-in-progress), **Omora** contains trails showing regional foliage, which is described in Yamaná, Latin nomenclature and Spanish. Take the road to the right of the Virgin altar 4km toward Puerto Navarino. Entrance fees help the foundation further develop the park.

A lookout point, **Cerro Bandera**, can be reached via the beginning of the 'Dientes Circuit.' The trail ascends steeply through the mossy forest to a sparse alpine terrain with great vistas. For details on trekking in the Dientes de Navarino, refer to Lonely Planet's *Trekking in Patagonia* guide. Treks to some of the old **missionary houses** along the western corner of the island are being developed to promote environmentally sound tourism and protect the houses from further destruction. Consult Turismo SIM or Refugio Coirón for details.

TIERRA DEL FUEGO

local lodgings can arrange ...ounding areas. For yacht tours de Hornos and around the Beagle nel, as well as trekking, climbing and riding expeditions, talk to Turismo SIM.

Places to Stay & Eat

In the high season, some families offer rooms; check with Turismo SIM on the current status. Unless indicated, all of the below offer breakfast.

Refugio Coirón (☎ 621-150; e coiron@simltd.com; Ricardo Maragano 168; dorm beds US$13), catering to a backpacker clientele, has a welcoming atmosphere that makes it a top place to swap stories with other hikers. Rooms are shared, as is the one bathroom. Breakfast isn't offered, but there are kitchen privileges, and a large communal table helps promote group meals.

Residencial Onashaga (☎ 621-081; Upachun 290; dorm beds US$16) has plenty of rickety bunks, shared baths and a furnace made out of a ship's exhaust pipe. The owners are charming and offer tours to their estancia near Bahía Eugenia.

Residencial Pusaki (☎ 621-020, fax 621-116; Piloto Pardo 242; rooms US$12) is small, attractive and cozy. Owners Tano and Pati offer clean, warm rooms with shared bath and pleasant family surroundings.

Residencial Temuco (☎ 621-113; rooms with shared/private bath US$13/26) offers unheated rooms but the beds have electric blankets. Beware the stuffed beaver, Rambo, once the family pet. Guests are allowed to use the kitchen and laundry facilities.

Diente de Navarino (☎ 621-074; lunches US$5), an eatery/bar in the plaza, serves a huge 'fisherman's lunch' that will fill you up fast. During the evening the place fills with the fishing crowd enjoying schops.

Hostería Camblor (☎ 621-033; meals US$3-8), overlooking the town, is a good spot for lunch or dinner; it serves the best pan amasado in town. Thursday nights the place turns into a hopping discotheque.

There are a few supermarkets in town, **Simon & Simon** being the best of the lot, with fresher veggies and great pastries.

Entertainment

Club de Yates Micalvi, down at the harbor, serves drinks (US$1.50-8) and crab sandwiches (US$5), but the real reason to go here is to absorb one of the best atmospheres in Tierra del Fuego. Sailors and Antarctic explorers from around the world hold forth amid souvenirs of former adventurers, vying to outdo one another's stories, which grow louder and grander as the night progresses.

Pingüino Pub (Centro Commercial) is where you can throw down a couple of beers and handfuls of peanuts before heading to **Disco Extasis**, across from Residencial Temuco, on a Friday or Saturday night.

Getting There & Away

Aerovías DAP (☎ 621-051; Centro Comercial) flies to Punta Arenas Tuesday to Saturday (US$67). Seats are limited and advance reservations are essential. DAP flights to Antarctica make a brief stopover here.

The Transbordadora Austral Broom ferry leaves at 7pm Friday for the 38-hour trip to Punta Arenas (US$120 including meals, US$150 for a bunk); be forewarned that passenger berths are small and the reclining Pullman seats not as comfortable as one might wish on a trip this long.

Regular connections between Puerto Williams and Ushuaia, on Argentine Tierra del Fuego, may resume at some point. Private yachts making the trip sometimes take on extra passengers, usually for about US$50 each. For the most up-to-date information, ask at the Club de Yates or Turismo SIM.

USHUAIA (ARGENTINA)
☎ 02901

Built between the Beagle Channel and jagged glacial peaks rising from sea level to nearly 1500m, Ushuaia boasts an incredible location that few cities can match. In town, visit the **Museo Marítimo & Museo del Presidio** (☎ 437-481; cnr Yaganes & Gobernador Paz), with halls showing the penal life, a display on Antarctic exploration and an exhibit of scale models of famous ships.

A good hike from downtown leads to **Glaciar Martial**, from which one can enjoy the views of Ushuaia and the Beagle Channel; minivans leave from Maipú and 25 de Mayo every half-hour. **Parque Nacional Tierra del Fuego**, 12km west of Ushuaia via RN 3, is Argentina's first coastal national park and extends 63,000 hectares from the Beagle Channel in the south to beyond Lago Kami/Fagnano in the north with accessible day hikes and campgrounds.

The very helpful **municipal tourist office** (☎/fax 424-550, toll-free 0800-333-1476 on the island; San Martín 674; open 8am-9pm Mon-Fri, 9am-8pm Sat, Sun & holidays) has listings with current prices, activities and transportation options; after closing time it posts a list of available lodgings.

The **Club Andino Ushuaia** (☎ 422-335; e cau@tierradelfuego.org.ar; Fadul 50; open 3pm-10pm Mon-Fri) sells a comprehensive trekking, mountaineering and mountain-biking guidebook with rough maps and plenty of trail descriptions (in Spanish). The club occasionally organizes hikes and can link parties with hiking guides.

Places to Stay & Eat

Budget options (US$6 to US$10 per person with shared bath) are **Camping Municipal** (RN 3), 8km west of town en route to Parque Nacional Tierra del Fuego; **Hostal St Christopher** (☎ 430-062; e hostel_christopher@ yahoo.com; Deloqui 636); and **El Refugio del Mochilero** (☎ 436-129; e refmoch@ infovia.com.ar; 25 de Mayo 241).

For mid-range options (about US$20 per person), try **Alakaluf** (☎ 436-705; e alakalufes@arnet.com.ar; San Martín 146), family-owned and operated, with kitchen use; **Hotel Maitén** (☎ 422-733, fax 422-745; 12 de Octubre 140), south of downtown, quiet and well run; and **Hospedaje Malvinas** (☎ 422-626, fax 424-482; e hotelmalvinas@ arnet.com.ar; Deloquí 615) with pleasant carpeted rooms, some with great harbor views and a lovely owner keen on sailing.

Ushuaia has tons of restaurants. Try **El Turco** (☎ 424-711; San Martín 1440) for pizzas and quick-order meals; **Volver** (☎ 423-977; Maipú 37), for more upscale eating in a historic house, known for its centolla soup; **Café de la Esquina** (☎ 423-676; San Martín 621), with breakfasts, sandwiches and good people-watching; and **Kaupé** (☎/fax 422-704; Roca 470), a high-end spot with delectable creations and a fabulous view.

Getting There & Away

Aerovías DAP (25 de Mayo 64) flies Monday and Wednesday to Punta Arenas (US$100). Tecni-Austral buses for Río Grande (3½ hours), from where there is more service to Punta Arenas, and to Punta Arenas (10-12 hours) leave daily from the **Tolkar office** (☎ 431-408; Roca 157).

CABO DE HORNOS & ANTARCTIC PENINSULA

Destinations at this remote end of the earth beckon the intrepid traveler.

Cabo de Hornos (Cape Horn) is a synonym for adventure and the romance of the old days of sail – though for most of the poor sailors aboard ships attempting to double the Horn, there was no romance on a cold winter ocean with a gale blowing. It was 'discovered' in January 1616 by Dutchmen Jakob Le Maire and Willem Schouten, sailing in Unity. They named the cape for their ship Hoorn, which had accidentally burned at Puerto Deseado on the Argentine Patagonian coast.

Horn Island, of which the famous cape forms the southernmost headland, is just 8km long. The cape itself rises to 424m, with striking black cliffs on its upper parts.

The South Shetlands Islands at the northern end of the Antarctic Peninsula is one of the continent's most visited areas, thanks to its spectacular scenery, abundant wildlife and proximity to Tierra del Fuego, which lies 1000km to the north across the Drake Passage. The largest of the South Shetlands, King George Island, has eight national winter stations crowded onto it. Chile established **Presidente Eduardo Frei Montalva station** in 1969. Ten years later, Chile built Teniente Rodolfo Marsh Martin station less than 1km across the Fildes Peninsula from Frei station.

As part of Chile's policy of trying to incorporate its claimed Territorio Chileno Antártico into the rest of the country as much as possible, the government has encouraged families to live at Frei station, and the first of several children was born there in 1984. Today the station accommodates about 80 summer personnel.

Getting There & Away

Aerovías DAP (☎ 061-223-340, fax 221-693; w www.aeroviasdap.cl) has one- and two-day programs from Punta Arenas to Frei Base on King George Island, involving tours to Villa Las Estrellas, sea lion colonies and other investigation stations on the island. The one-day program costs US$2500, with departures from October through April. The two-day program costs US$3800, with departures throughout the year, mostly January through March. Note that the flight to Frei Base takes about three hours. Flights to Cabo de Hornos cost US$300 and leave

Monday and Wednesday from November to March.

Most Antarctica-bound ships depart from Ushuaia, Argentina. Some voyages take in the Falkland Islands and South Georgia, others go just to the Antarctic Peninsula, while others focus on retracing historic expeditions. The season runs from November to mid-February. The **Oficina**

Antarctica Infuetur (☎ *424-431, fax 430-694;* e *antartida@tierradelfuego.ml.org*), on Ushuaia's waterfront Muelle Comercial, serves as a clearinghouse for Antarctic tours; it's open 8am to 5pm weekdays; weekends only if there are boats. Tourist agencies All Patagonia, Antartur and Rumbo Sur, all in Ushuaia (ask for directions from the municipal tourist office),

---

When the Edge of the World Just Isn't Far Enough

Falkland Islands/Islas Malvinas
☎ **500 • pop 2826 humans, 700,000 sheep**

The sheep boom in Tierra del Fuego and Patagonia owes its origins to a cluster of islands 300 miles (500km) to the east in the South Atlantic Ocean. These islands – the 'Islas Malvinas' to the Argentines or the 'Falkland Islands' to the British – were explored but never fully captured either country's interest. Very little transpired on the islands until the mid-19th century wool boom in Europe, when the Falkland Islands Company (FIC) became the islands' largest landholder. The population, mostly stranded mariners and gauchos, grew rapidly with the arrival of English and Scottish immigrants. In an unusual exchange, the South American Missionary Society in 1853 began transporting Yahgan Indians from Tierra del Fuego to Keppel Island to catechize them.

Argentina has laid claim to the islands since 1833, but it wasn't until 1982 that Argentine president Leopoldo Galtieri, then drowning in accusations of corruption and economic chaos, decided that reclaiming the islands would unite his country behind him. However, British Prime Minister Margaret Thatcher (who was also suffering in the polls) didn't hesitate for a moment in striking back, thoroughly humiliating Argentina in what became known as the Falklands War. A severe blow to Argentina's national pride, the ill-fated war succeeded in severing all diplomatic ties between the two nations.

On July 14, 1999, a joint statement issued by the British, Falkland Islands and Argentine governments promised closer cooperation on areas of mutual economic interest. In August 2001, British Prime Minister Tony Blair visited Argentina in an effort to further improve ties between the countries.

Besides being an unusually polemic piece of property, what is there about the Falklands that might intrigue the intrepid traveler? Bays, inlets, estuaries and beaches create a tortuous, attractive coastline that is home to abundant wildlife. Striated and crested caracaras, cormorants, oystercatchers, snowy sheathbills, sheldgeese and a plethora of penguins – Magellanic, rockhopper, macaroni, gentoo and king – share top billing with elephant seals, sea lions, fur seals, some five species of dolphins and killer whales.

Stanley, the islands' capital, is an assemblage of brightly painted metal-clad houses and a good place to throw down a few pints and listen to island lore. 'Camp' – as the rest of the islands are called – is home to settlements that began as company towns (hamlets where coastal shipping could collect wool) and now provide lodging and a chance to experience pristine nature and wildlife.

Planning

The best time to visit is from October to March, when migratory birds and mammals return to beaches and headlands. Fun events around which to plan a trip are the sports meetings featuring horse racing, bull riding and sheepdog trials, which take place in Stanley between Christmas and New Year's and on East and West Falkland in late February. Summer never gets truly hot (maximum high is 24°C or 75°F), but high winds can chill the air.

Information

The **Jetty Visitors Centre** (☎ *22281, fax 22619;* e *jettycentre@horizon.co.fk*), at the public jetty on Ross Rd in Stanley, distributes excellent brochures on things to do in and around Stanley. The 'Visitor

handle last-minute bookings for many of the vessels. Tour companies charge anywhere from US$3000 to US$10,000, although some do allow walk-ons, which can cost as little as US$2000.

Antarctica XXI (**w** *www.antarcticaxxi .com)* offers a six-day tour to King George Island, leaving from Punta Arenas (see that section earlier in the chapter). Flights arrive at Teniente March station, from where the research vessel *Grigoriy Mikheev* proceeds to visit the peninsula and islands Livingston, Deception, Pleneau, Petermann, Cuverville and Half Moon. Passengers can disembark on some spots for hiking; specialists on board give presentations. Rates range from US$5300 to US$6900.

When the Edge of the World Just Isn't Far Enough

Accommodation Guide' lists lodgings and places that allow camping around the Islands. Another source of information is the **Falkland Islands Tourist Board** (☎ 22215, fax 22619; **e** *manager@ tourism.org.fk*; **w** *www.tourism.org.fk).* In the UK there's the **Falkland House** (☎ 020-7222-2542, fax 020-7222-2375; **e** *manager@figo.u-net.com; 14 Broadway, London SW1H 0BH).*

Visas & Documents
Visitors from Britain and Commonwealth countries, the European Union, North America, Mercosur countries and Chile do not need visas. If coming from another country, check with the British Consulate. All nationalities must carry valid passports. Everyone entering is required to have an onward ticket, proof of sufficient funds (credit cards are fine) and prearranged accommodations for the first few nights.

Money
Pound sterling and US dollars in cash or traveler's checks are readily accepted, but the exchange rate for US currency is low. There's no need to change money to FK£, which are not accepted off the islands. There is no ATM on the Falklands. In peak season, expect to spend US$70 to US$90 per day, not including airfare, within the islands, less if camping or staying in self-catering cottages.

Getting There & Away
From South America, LanChile flies to Mt Pleasant International Airport every Saturday from Santiago, Chile, via Puerto Montt, Punta Arenas and – one Saturday each month – Río Gallegos, Argentina. Santiago fares are US$410 one-way, US$680 roundtrip. Punta Arenas fares are US$320 one-way, US$490 roundtrip. From RAF Brize Norton, in Oxfordshire, England, there are regular flights to Mt Pleasant (16 hours, plus an hour layover on Ascension Island). The roundtrip fare is UK£2302, but reduced Apex fares cost UK£1414 with 30-day advance purchase. Travelers continuing on to Chile can purchase one-way tickets for half the fare. Contact the Travel Coordinator at Falkland House in London or, in Stanley, the **Falkland Islands Company** (☎ 27633), on Crozier Place.

Getting Around
From Stanley, **Figas** (☎ 27219) serves outlying destinations in nine-passenger aircraft. Travel within the Falklands costs approximately FK£1 (about US$1.60) per minute.

Byron Marine Ltd (☎ 22245, fax 22246) carries a few passengers on its freighter MV *Tamar* while delivering wool and other goods to outlying settlements. Berths are limited; day trips cost FK£20 (US$32), overnights cost FK£25 (US$40).

Several Stanley operators run day trips to East Falkland settlements, including Tony Smith's **Discovery Tours** (☎ 21027, fax 22304; **e** *discovery@horizon.co.fk);* Sharon Halford's **Ten Acre Tours** (☎ 21155, fax 21950; **e** *tenacres@horizon.co.fk);* and Dave Eynon's **South Atlantic Marine Services** (☎ 21145, fax 22674; **e** *sams@horizon.co.fk).* **Neil Rowlands** (☎ 21561; **e** *nrowlands@horizon.co.fk)* conducts fishing and wildlife tours. The **agricultural officer** (☎ 27355) or **Seaview Ltd** (☎ 22669, fax 22670) can arrange visits to Kidney Island, with its colonies of rockhopper penguins and sea lions.

Trekking and camping are feasible; however, there are no designated trails on the islands and getting lost is not unheard of. Permission must be sought, and details of movements given, before entering private land.

International operators arranging more in-depth Antarctic tours include:

Adventure Associates
(☎ 61-2-9389 7466; **w** www.adventure associates.com) 197 Oxford Street Mall, Bondi Junction, Sydney NSW 2022, Australia

Adventure Network International
(☎ 561-237-2359, 866-395-6664) 4800 N Federal Highway, Suite 307D, Boca Raton, FL 33431, USA
(☎ 44-1494-671-808; **w** www.adventure-network .com) Canon House, 27 London End, Beaconsfield HP9 2HN, England
(☎ 061-247-735) 935 Arauco, Punta Arenas, Chile

Mountain Travel-Sobek
(☎ 510-527-8100, 888-687-6235; **w** www.mt sobek.com) 6420 Fairmount Ave, El Cerrito, CA 94530, USA

Quark Expeditions
(☎ 203-656-0499 or 800-356-5699; **w** www .adventure-network.com), 980 Post Rd, Darien, CT 06820, USA
(☎ 44-1494-464-080) 19A Crendon St, High Wycombe HP13 6LJ, England

Those heading to Antarctica should pick up Lonely Planet's *Antarctica* guidebook, which has details on many possible voyages plus tons of background information on the great frozen continent.

Archipiélago Juan Fernández

Scottish maroon Alexander Selkirk left a peculiar legacy to the Juan Fernández Archipelago. Selkirk, who spent more than four years in utter isolation on the archipelago's main island, was the real-life model for Daniel Defoe's fictional character Robinson Crusoe. Though set in the Caribbean, Defoe's fictionalized account of Selkirk's experiences became the enduring classic for which Isla Robinson Crusoe is now named.

The history of Isla Robinson Crusoe, though, is much more than that of Alexander Selkirk's sojourn, and the island is much more than a hermit's hideaway. Singularly serene, it is also a matchless national park and a Unesco World Biosphere Reserve, with much to offer the motivated traveler. Despite the government's intentions, it and the other islands that comprise the Juan Fernández Archipelago – Isla Alejandro Selkirk and Isla Santa Clara – are not a major holiday destination and are not likely to become one because of the near impossibility and clear undesirability of significantly expanding their tourist infrastructure. Between December and March, about 40 to 50 foreigners per month visit the island; the rest of the year, visitation drops off dramatically.

If you are coming, then reading (or rereading) Defoe's classic *Robinson Crusoe*, now available in many editions, is an obvious must, but there are many accounts of voyages that stopped at least briefly in the islands. One of the most accessible is Captain Woodes Rogers' *A Cruising Voyage Round the World*, available in a Dover Publications facsimile edition (1970). The most thorough history in English is Ralph Lee Woodward's *Robinson Crusoe's Island* (1969).

History

Uninhabited when Spanish mariner Juan Fernández 'discovered' them in November 1574, the islands as a group still bear his name. The modest Fernández named them the 'Islas Santa Cecilia,' and two decades passed before Spain attempted even a temporary occupation. For more than two centuries, the islands were largely a refuge for pirates and sealers who sought the pelts of the endemic Juan Fernández fur seal *(Arctocephalus phillippi)*.

According to one account, North American sealers took nearly three million sealskins off the even more remote Isla Masafuera between 1788 and 1809. Single cargoes of 100,000 pelts were not unusual, bringing the species nearly to extinction by the early 19th century.

Juan Fernández Archipelago was most renowned for the adventures of Scotsman Alexander Selkirk, who spent more than four

Highlights

- Arriving at San Juan Bautista by Twin Otter and cliff-shadowed ferry to a pier full of people welcoming everyone home
- Cracking a fresh-caught lobster for lunch
- Hiking through the lush fern forests
- Watching the sunrise from Selkirk's lookout
- Snorkeling with the sea lions

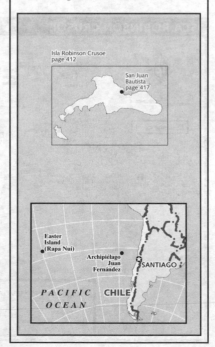

411

years marooned on what was then called Isla Masatierra. After a dispute with the captain of the privateer *Cinque Ports* in 1704, Selkirk was put ashore at his own request. This was tantamount to a death sentence for most castaways, who soon starved or shot themselves, but Selkirk survived, adapting to his new home and enduring his desperate isolation.

Ironically, the Spaniards, who vigorously opposed the presence of privateers in their domains, had made his survival possible. Unlike many small islands, Masatierra had abundant water, but the absence of food could have been a problem if the Spanish had not introduced goats. Disdaining fish, Selkirk tracked these feral animals, attacked them with his knife, devoured their meat and dressed himself in their skins. Sea lions, feral cats and rats – the latter two European introductions – were among his other companions.

Selkirk would often climb to a lookout above Cumberland Bay (Bahía Cumberland) in hope of spotting a vessel on the horizon, but not until 1708 did his savior, Commander Woodes Rogers of the British privateers *Duke* and *Duchess*, arrive with famed privateer William Dampier as his pilot. Rogers recalled first meeting with Selkirk when the ship's men returned from shore:

Immediately our Pinnace return'd from the shore, and brought abundance of Craw-fish, with a man Cloth'd in Goat-Skins, who look'd wilder than the first Owners of them.

After signing on with Rogers and returning to Scotland, Selkirk became a celebrity.

After Selkirk's departure, privateers (persona non grata on the South American mainland) frequented the islands for rest and relaxation, of a sort, and to hunt seals. In response, Spain reestablished a presence at Bahía Cumberland in 1750, founding the village of San Juan Bautista. Occupation was discontinued, though, until Chile established a permanent settlement in 1877.

Prior to this, after the turn of the 18th century, Masatierra played a notorious role in Chile's independence struggle, as Spanish authorities exiled 42 criollo patriots to the island after the disastrous Battle of Rancagua in 1814. The exiles, including prominent figures such as Juan Egaña and Manuel de Salas,

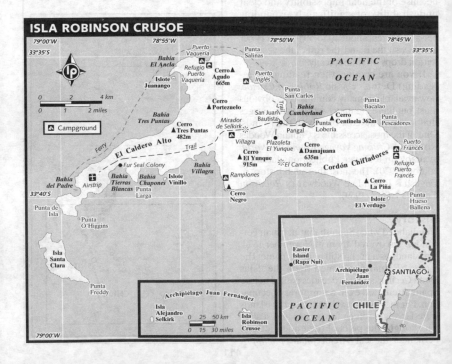

neither accepted nor forgot their relegation to damp caves above San Juan Bautista; for many years, the island remained a nearly escape-proof political prison for the newly independent country. Later, during WWI, it again played a memorable historic role, as the British naval vessels *Glasgow* and *Orama* confronted the German cruiser *Dresden* at Bahía Cumberland; the German crew scuttled their vessel before it could be sunk.

Since then, the islands have played a less conspicuous but perhaps more significant role in global history. In 1935, in order to protect the islands' unique flora and fauna, the Chilean government declared them a national park, and later it undertook a program to remove the feral goats (on whose predecessors Selkirk depended so much for his subsistence).

Isla Robinson Crusoe made the news again in 1998 when US communications engineer Bernard Keiser claimed to have detected a buried treasure near the site of Selkirk's house at Puerto Inglés. Keiser claims that the treasure was buried around 1713 by General Juan de Ubilla y Echeverría. The loot allegedly includes some 800 bags of gold, barrels full of gems and jewelry and a two-foot high trunk full of emeralds, gold and silver. For a few months every year, Keiser has permission to dig for the treasure. Despite the many years of work so far, he and his crew have yet to uncover anything except a few 'inspirational clues,' but they will continue to search until the government denies the right to dig.

Geography & Climate
Separated from Valparaíso by 670km of the open Pacific, the Juan Fernández Archipelago consists of Isla Robinson Crusoe (formerly Masatierra or 'closer to land'); tiny Isla Santa Clara (known to early privateers as Goat Island), just 3km off the main island's southern tip; and Isla Alejandro Selkirk (formerly Masafuera or 'farther out'), which is another 170km away from the continent.

The islands' land areas are very small, but their topography is extraordinarily rugged; geologically, the entire archipelago is a group of emergent peaks of the submarine mountain range known as the Juan Fernández Ridge, which trends east-west for more than 400km at the southern end of the Chile Basin. Isla Robinson Crusoe comprises only 93 sq km, with a maximum length of 22km and

a maximum width of 7.3km. However, it reaches an altitude of 915m on the peak of Cerro El Yunque (The Anvil), which hovers above the island's only settlement, the village of San Juan Bautista. Isla Alejandro Selkirk is even more mountainous, rising to 1650m on Cerro Los Inocentes, where snow has fallen. Isla Alejandro Selkirk is about two million years old, while Isla Robinson Crusoe is five million years old.

The archipelago is far enough from the continent for subtropical water masses to moderate the chilly subantarctic waters of the Humboldt Current, which flows northward along the Chilean coast. The climate is distinctly Mediterranean, with clearly defined warm, dry summers and cooler, wet winters. At San Juan Bautista the maximum mean monthly temperature is 21.8°C, while the minimum mean is 10.1°C. Mean annual precipitation is 1000mm, of which 70% falls between April and October; less than 10% falls in summer (December to February). Winds often exceed 25 knots.

Because of the islands' irregular topography, rainfall varies greatly over short distances. In particular, the Cordón Chifladores (of which Cerro El Yunque is the highest point) intercepts most of the rainfall, creating a pronounced rain shadow on the southeast portion of Isla Robinson Crusoe – a difference as great as that between the Amazon and the Atacama Desert. By contrast, the area north of the range is dense rainforest, with a high concentration of the endemic species for which the islands were designated a national park and biosphere reserve.

The seafloor drops abruptly to more than 4000m below sea level on all sides. This leaves relatively little continental shelf to support marine fauna and flora – according to one estimate, the total area exploited for fishing is only about 325 sq km. Those maritime resources that are present, particularly the Juan Fernández lobster (*Jasus frontalis*, really a crayfish), are in great demand on the mainland and provide a substantial income for some archipelago residents.

Flora
Like many oceanic islands, the Juan Fernández Archipelago is a storehouse of rare plants and, to a lesser degree, animals that evolved in isolation and adapted to very specific environmental niches. The indigenous biota have

suffered from the introduction of ecologically exotic species, particularly the goats that sustained Selkirk but devoured much of the original vegetation. More opportunistic plant species, resistant to grazing and to fires set by humans, colonized areas goats had degraded.

Still, a great deal of the native flora remains in sectors where even an invader as agile as the goat could neither penetrate nor completely dominate. In places, the terrain is so steep that one can only proceed by grasping branches of the nearly impenetrable foliage. Once, pursuing a feral goat, Selkirk plunged over a sheer cliff and survived only because the animal's body cushioned his fall.

The vegetation of the islands presents an extraordinary mixture of geographic affinities, from the Andes and subantarctic Magallanes to Hawaii and New Zealand. In its oceanic isolation, though, the plant life has evolved into something very distinct from its continental and insular origins. Of 87 genera of plants on the islands, 16 are endemic, found nowhere else on earth; of 140 native plant species, 101 are endemic. These plants survive in three major communities: the evergreen rainforest, the evergreen heath and the herbaceous steppe.

The evergreen rainforest is the richest of these environments, with a wide variety of tree species, such as the endemic *luma (Nothomyrcia fernandeziana)* and the *chonta (Juania australis)*, one of only two palm species native to Chile. Perhaps the most striking vegetation, however, is the dense understory of climbing vines and the towering endemic tree ferns *Dicksonia berteroana* and *Thyrsopteris elegans*. The forest was also a source of edible wild plants collected by the crews of visiting ships, as Rogers indicated:

The Cabbage Trees abound about three miles in the Woods, and the Cabbage very good; most of 'em are on the tops of the nearest and lowest mountains.

Evergreen heath replaces rainforest on the thinner soils of the highest peaks and exceptionally steep slopes. Characteristic species are the tree fern *Blechnum cyadifolium* and various tree species of the endemic genus *Robinsonia*. The steppe, which is largely confined to the arid eastern sector of Isla Robinson Crusoe and to Isla Santa Clara, consists of perennial bunch grasses such as *Stipa fernandeziana*.

Exotic mainland species have provided unfortunate competition for native flora. At lower elevations, the wild blackberry *(Rubus ulmifolius)* and the shrub *maqui (Aristotelia chilensis)* have proven to be aggressive colonizers, despite efforts to control them (incidentally, lobstermen use branches from the maqui for their traps). Visiting ships, seeking fresh provisions, not only collected edible wild species such as cabbage, but they even planted gardens that they, and others, later harvested.

Fauna

The only native mammal, the Juan Fernández fur seal, was nearly extinct a century ago, but has recovered to the point that nearly 9000 individuals now inhabit the seas and shores of Robinson Crusoe and Santa Clara. The southern elephant seal *Mirounga leonina*, hunted for its blubber, no longer survives here. Of 11 endemic bird species, the most eye-catching is the Juan Fernández hummingbird *(Sephanoides fernandensis)*. The male is conspicuous because of its bright red color; the female is a more subdued green with a white tail. Only about 250 hummingbirds survive, feeding off the striking Juan Fernández cabbage that grows in many parts of San Juan Bautista, but the birds do best in native forest.

Introduced rodents and feral cats have endangered nesting marine birds, such as Cook's petrel *(Pterodroma cookii defilippiana)*, by preying on their eggs or young. Another mammal that has proliferated since its introduction in the 1930s is the South American coatimundi *(coatí in Spanish)*.

Getting There & Away

Air From Santiago, flights to Juan Fernández leave almost daily in summer but less frequently the rest of the year. Flights may be postponed when bad weather makes landing impossible on Isla Robinson Crusoe's improved airstrip. Travel arrangements should be flexible enough to allow for an extra two or three days' stay on the island if necessary.

Lassa *(☎ 02-273-5209, 273-1458, fax 273-4309;* e *lassa@entelchile.net)* flies a 19-seat Twin Otter out of Aeródromo Tobalaba (Av Larraín 7941), in the eastern Santiago *comuna* of La Reina. The San Juan Bautista office is behind the gymnasium but most easily reached from the pier.

Transportes Aéreos Robinson Crusoe (☎ 02-534-4650, fax 531-3772; e tairc@cmet .net; Av Pajaritos 3030, Oficina 604, Santiago), in the southwestern comuna of Maipú, flies out of Santiago's Aeropuerto Los Cerrillos. There's also an **island representative** (☎ 751-099; La Pólvora 226). Round-trip fares to Isla Robinson Crusoe range from US$405 to US$495.

San Juan Bautista in Bahía Cumberland is about 1½ hours from the airstrip by a combination of 4WD (down a frighteningly

---

Who Was Friday?

Decades before Alexander Selkirk was left stranded on Isla Masatierra, later to be immortalized by Daniel Defoe as 'Robinson Crusoe,' a Miskito Indian from Nicaragua spent several years in solitary exile on the island, and did so with a style and resourcefulness Selkirk would have envied. That the Miskito's story was overshadowed by the Scotsman's should come as no surprise to anyone familiar with the long history of European explorers taking credit for achievements others accomplished first.

The young Miskito, Will, was accompanying the famous English privateer William Dampier to the Pacific when Spanish forces surprised Dampier's expedition at Cumberland Bay in 1681, and Will was inadvertently left ashore. For three years, he successfully evaded Spanish detection for, as Dampier wrote, 'The Moskitos are in general very civil and kind to the English…but they do not love the French, and the Spaniards they hate mortally.'

Will's life in the Caribbean prepared him well for his isolation in the Juan Fernández islands. Knowing the ingenuity and adaptability of the Miskito, Dampier was not surprised to find that Will had made the most of limited resources:

> He had with him his Gun and a Knife, with a small Horn of Powder and a few Shot; which being spent, he contrived a way by notching his Knife, to saw the Barrel of his Gun into small Pieces, wherewith he made Harpoons, Lances, Hooks and a long Knife, heating the pieces first in the Fire, which he struck with his Gunflint, and a piece of the Barrel of his Gun, which he hardened… All this may seem strange to those that are not acquainted with the Sagacity of the Indians; but it is no more than these Moskito Men are accustomed to in their own Country, where they make their own Fishing and Striking Instruments, without either Forge or Anvil.

In Central America, the Miskito lived by hunting, fishing, gardening and gathering in the forests and on the shores of the western Caribbean. On Masatierra, Will had no canoe or dory (a word adapted from Miskito into English) to ply the offshore waters, but he could fish the rivers and streams inshore. And as Selkirk later would, he could track and kill the island's feral goats; he used their skins to line his hut and his bed, a raised platform of sticks 2ft off the ground. In fact, wrote Dampier, Will was so comfortable that he could afford to be selective in his diet, eschewing seal entirely (which Will called a 'very ordinary meat').

The day before Dampier's ship returned to the island, Will spied it from shore and prepared three goats to greet the English sailors. Dampier's return also reunited Will with a countryman named Robin ('These were names given them by the English, for they had no Names among themselves'), who 'first leap'd ashore, and running to his Brother Moskito Man, threw himself flat on his face at his feet, who helping him up, and embracing him, fell flat with his face on the Ground at Robin's feet.'

This was extraordinary, but the Miskito were no strangers to remote places. It was no coincidence that Defoe placed Robinson Crusoe's fictional island in the Caribbean, where European interlopers had long depended on the Miskito for fishing, hunting and sailing skills by which 'one or two of them in a Ship, will maintain 100 Men…'

In reality, not just one but hundreds of Fridays helped thousands of Crusoes survive the unfamiliar and unwelcoming surroundings in the New World. While the fictional Crusoe may have overshadowed the genuine Selkirk, Friday's real-life Miskito predecessor was more than just a product of Daniel Defoe's imagination. Few knew the names of Will and his countrymen except the English privateers and others 'of whom they receive a great deal of Respect.'

—**Wayne Bernhardson**

steep dirt road; most people prefer to walk) to the jetty at Bahía del Padre and motor launch (the best part of the trip is sailing halfway around the island's awesome volcanic coastal escarpments). Both the flight and the rest of the voyage, however, can be rough, so travelers prone to motion sickness may want to consider preventative medication. The cost of the launch, normally about US$25 return, should be included in your air ticket, but check to be certain.

Sea Naval supply ships make the trip to the island about six times annually and are the cheapest option, carrying passengers for about US$32 per day, though their infrequency, the length of the trip (about two days) and the complete lack of comfort are obvious drawbacks. Try contacting the **Comando de Transporte** (☎ 032-506-354; *Primera Zona Naval, Plaza Sotomayor 592, Valparaíso).*

Naviera del Sur (☎ 032-594-304; *Blanco 1041, Oficina 18, Valparaíso)* sails to San Juan Bautista in the first fortnight of every month on the small freighter *Navarino* (US$110 oneway, 2½ days). Since the ship has only five bunks for passengers, reservations are essential. Bring a sleeping bag and extra snacks, although the food is passable.

Getting Around
Getting around Isla Robinson Crusoe presents no major problems but is not necessarily cheap, since it requires hiring a fishing boat or, perhaps more economically, accompanying the lobster catchers to their grounds. To arrange a launch, head to the Municipalidad offices across from the plaza and ask around. A launch to Puerto Inglés, for example, costs US$15 for up to eight passengers. With many areas of the island now restricted to guided hikes or tours, fee structures and departures may standardize.

SAN JUAN BAUTISTA
☎ 32 • pop 500

San Juan Bautista, Isla Robinson Crusoe's only settlement, is one of Chile's most tranquil places, with a relaxed island pace that is easy to slip into. A maze of muddy roads and concrete footpaths stretch along Bahía Cumberland and angle up and down through a disarray of small houses, lush gardens and horse paddocks, linking to trails leading up and out of town. El Palillo offers the best

place to swim or put on some snorkeling gear to see a variety of colorful fish.

The island economy depends on fishing, mostly for lobster that are afterward flown to Santiago. Most of the 120 fishermen work in open boats, leaving early in the morning to check on their 30 to 40 traps each. They return in the evening to sell their catch to individuals, hotels and the several mainland companies that purchase the lobsters for about US$20 each.

During the winter, the fishing boats search for *bacalao* (cod), which they salt and send to the mainland.

Many islanders rarely or never visit the 'continent.' Children attend school locally up until the age of 14, after which they can finish their secondary education elsewhere in Chile, usually in Santiago.

Orientation
Surrounded by forests of exotic conifers and eucalyptus (planted to stem erosion on the nearby hills), San Juan Bautista occupies a protected east-facing site on Bahía Cumberland. Launches from Bahía del Padre land at the jetty, a short walk from the main street, Larraín Alcalde, which intersects with the pleasant Costanera El Palillo a few hundred meters to the south. Other streets – La Pólvora, Subida El Castillo, El Yunque and Vicente González – climb steeply from the shore. There is a bridge across Estero Lord Anson, a stream that flows into the bay. This serves as San Juan Bautista's beach, but there is better swimming and diving off the rocks at El Palillo, at the southern end of the costanera.

Information
Conaf (*Larraín Alcalde),* runs a small kiosk near the plaza where it collects park admission and distributes some leaflets with decent maps. Its **Centro Información al Turista** (*open 8am-12:30pm & 2pm-6pm Mon-Fri, 9am-12:30pm & 2pm-6pm Sat & Sun)* is at the top of Vicente González; this large open hall has photo displays, a meeting room and more detailed information on the park and the history of the islands, all with decent English translations. Next door is **Conaf's administrative office** (☎ 751-004, 751-022). For information on visiting any part of the park outside the immediate environs of San Juan Bautista, it's advisable to contact Conaf in advance.

Ahu Akivi's seven moai face the setting sun.

The lake at Rano Raraku, birthplace of the moai

Rongo-Rongo tablet, one of few remnants of an ancient tradition

The 'birdman islands' off Rapa Nui

Anakena: Rapa Nui's largest beach

Moai towering above the harbor in Hanga Roa, Easter Island

Ask for a tour of its plant nursery, where over 40 endemic species are cultivated, the saplings then replanted in the park and given to locals to plant around the town.

There is no bank or other money-changing facilities on the island, so bring all the money you need from the mainland, preferably in small bills.

The **post office** is on the south side of the plaza, and magnetic phone cards are available there. The bar/restaurant **El Remo** on the other side of the plaza has a public phone.

The **Posta de Salud** (☎ 751-067; Vicente González), a government clinic, is just below the entrance to Conaf's grounds.

Casa de Cultura & Biblioteca Daniel Defoe

Half library, half museum, this converted house (open 10am-12:30pm & 4pm-8pm Mon-Fri, 11am-1pm & 5pm-8pm Sat) has a small exhibit of historic photos and artifacts.

Cemetery & Lighthouse

San Juan's cemetery, at the north end of Bahía Cumberland near the lighthouse, provides a unique perspective on the island's history, with its polyglot assortment of Spanish, French and German surnames – the latter survivors of the sinking of the Dresden.

Just beyond the cemetery, fur seals frolic offshore beneath a spot where, after missing the German cruiser Dresden, shells from British ships lodged in the volcanic cliffs. The Dresden, however, took enough disabling hits that its captain chose to scuttle it rather than let it fall into British hands.

Cuevas de los Patriotas

Reached by a short footpath from Larraín Alcalde and illuminated at night, these damp caverns sheltered Juan Egaña, Manuel de Salas and 40 other participants in Chile's independence movement for several years after their defeat in the Battle of Rancagua in 1814.

Fuerte Santa Bárbara

Built in 1749 to discourage incursions by pirates, these Spanish fortifications were reconstructed in 1974. To get there, follow the path from the Cuevas de los Patriotas, or

SAN JUAN BAUTISTA

PLACES TO STAY
6 Residencial Mirador Selkirk
11 Hostería Martínez Green
18 Hostería Aldea Daniel Defoe
19 Camping Los Cañones
20 Hostal Petit Breuilh
24 Cabaña Paulentz
26 Hostal Charpentier
27 Refugio Naútico

PLACES TO EAT
4 El Nocturno
13 El Remo
17 La Bahía

OTHER
1 Shell Holes & Dresden Plaque
2 Lighthouse
3 Casa de Cultura; Biblioteca Daniel DeFoe
5 Transportes Aéros Robinson Crusoe
7 Fuerte Santa Bárbara
8 Cuevas de los Patriotas
9 Municipalidad
10 Conaf
12 Post Office
14 Endémica Expediciones
15 Lassa
16 Power Station
21 Police
22 Conaf (Administrative Office)
23 Posta de Salud
25 Centro Información al Turista

else climb directly from the plaza via Subida El Castillo.

Organized Tours

Check with the Conaf kiosk on the plaza for a list of registered guides and tour schedules to visit areas around the island.

Endémica Expediciones (☎ 751-077; e endemica@ctcinternet.cl), on the east side of the plaza, provides city tours, scuba diving, hiking expeditions, kayaking and snorkeling trips. Single dives per person cost US$38 based on groups of six or more. Snorkeling with the sea lions costs US$42.

Special Events

June 29 is the Fiesta de San Pedro, in honor of the patron saint of fishermen. On November 22, the anniversary of the original Spanish discovery, islanders celebrate Día de la Isla. Two days later, there's a 13km footrace from Bahía Cumberland to Punta de Isla.

Places to Stay

Camping Los Cañones (☎ 751-050; Vicente González; US$2 per person), just above the costanera, has rocky sites that are barely flat and appear to be a favored grazing zone for horses. It is, however, central, woodsy and has bathrooms.

Camping Elector (☎ 751-066; US$5), en route to Plazoleta El Yunque, has three sites surrounded by flower bushes and quirky wooden structures in a more peaceful area. There are bathrooms, a BBQ and an inside kitchen.

Regular accommodations tend to be costly, but usually include full board. Visitors with special dietary requirements, such as vegetarians or those who cannot eat seafood, should inform their hotel prior to arrival in the islands. Rates below are per person based on double occupancy.

Refugio Náutico (☎ 751-077; e refugio nautico@123.cl; Carrera Pinto; with breakfast/half board US$20/30), also known as Club Náutico, in peaceful El Palillo, provides three light, attractive rooms all with great views and separate entrance. The common spaces are also modern, bright and comfortable. A selection of scientific books and music is available. The couple who own this lodge run Endémica Expediciones and are divers and registered guides.

Hostal Charpentier (☎ 751-070, fax 751-020; Costanera El Palillo s/n; cabin with breakfast US$41), with a large lawn, has a couple of cabins, one with an ocean view and three rooms.

Residencial Mirador Selkirk (☎ 751-028; Pasaje del Castillo; with breakfast/half board US$16/25) is a comfortable family home with three rooms and kitchen access, plus a deck with a spectacular view.

Hostal Petit Breuilh (☎ 751-107, 02-741-0186 in Santiago; Vicente González 84; with breakfast/half board US$20/31) has decent rooms overlooking a main terrace and fancy bathrooms. The dark living/dining room is cluttered with guns, cocktail sets, an enormous lobster and model ships.

Cabaña Paulentz (☎ 751-108; Costanera El Palillo s/n; with breakfast/half board US$18/33) is set among beautiful gardens with an independent entrance and kitchen, but more spartan rooms.

Hostería Martinez Green (☎ 751-039; Larraín Alcalde 116; with breakfast/half board US$20/41), opposite the plaza, has three levels of rooms in different annexes; the upstairs rooms have larger bathrooms and views of the town and bay. The lounge area has a selection of music to listen to while enjoying a meal.

Hostería Aldea Daniel Defoe (☎ 751-075; Costanera El Palillo s/n; cabins with breakfast/half board US$60/75) has seemingly ramshackle shoreline cabins that are surprisingly comfortable and full of character, although windows to the street don't allow for full privacy.

Hostería El Pangal (☎ 02-273-5209, fax 273-4309 in Santiago; singles with half/full board US$66/88), run by Lassa, caters mainly to package tours. Double rooms all have excellent views, especially at sunset, and have good beds, but it's inconvenient to town (either a 45-minute walk along some badly eroded area or by irregular launches) and suffers a lack in maintenance. It makes a better option for an afternoon saunter or a meal on the deck.

Places to Eat

If you want lobster (or in low season, a meal larger than a sandwich), it's best to let restaurants know several hours, if not a day, in advance. Vidriola is a particularly tasty fish that's worth trying.

El Remo (☎ 751-030; mains US$3-6), on the east side of the plaza, is a popular gathering spot that stays open till the wee hours and serves tasty sandwiches, lunches (fish with a salad usually) and, with advance warning, lobster for two (US$25). Ask to try the homemade *murtillado* – rum infused with murtillas, a blueberrylike red fruit.

El Nocturno (☎ 751-113; Alcalde Larraín s/n; lunches US$6), part of the Club Deportivo, has large portions of fresh fish and good french fries.

La Bahía (Larraín Alcalde s/n) is worth trying, despite its modest appearance.

Hostería Aldea Daniel Defoe (see Places to Stay above; mains US$8-11) whips up sandwiches, fish-and-chips, crab or langosta crepes and fixed-price meals. While the food is really no different from anywhere else, the restaurant/bar is the island's most colorful spot.

PN JUAN FERNÁNDEZ

Parque Nacional Juan Fernández (admission US$5 for 7 days) includes every square inch of the archipelago, a total of 9300 hectares, though the township of San Juan Bautista and the airstrip are de facto exclusions. In an effort to control access to the most fragile areas of the park, Conaf requires many of the hikes to be organized and led by local registered guides. A list of the guides with pricing information is posted at the kiosk near the plaza, where you are supposed to register before taking any self-guided hike. A day's hike for a group of six may cost around US$33. Still, a number of areas are accessible without guides. Another way to see the park is by boat. Local tour operators can arrange trips to see fur seal colonies at different points around the island. Camping is possible only in organized campsites, each with a one-night limit.

Self-Guided Hiking Trails

Mirador de Selkirk to Punta de Isla To see what Selkirk saw, hike to his *mirador* (lookout) above San Juan Bautista. The 3km walk, gaining 565m in elevation, takes about 1½ hours of steady walking but rewards the climber with views of both sides of the island. Start as early in the morning as possible and take at least a light cotton shirt, since the overlook, exposed to wind and weather, can be much cooler than at sea level. If it's been raining, the trail can be muddy and slippery.

On the saddle, there are two metal plaques commemorating Selkirk's exile on the island, one placed here by officials of the Royal Navy (1868) and the other by a Scottish relative (1983). The trail to the mirador begins at the south end of the plaza of San Juan Bautista, climbs the Subida El Castillo, and follows the north side of Estero El Castillo before zigzagging up Cerro Portezuelo to Selkirk's lookout – fill your canteen before continuing up the hillside through thickets of maqui and blackberry, which gradually give way to native ferns and trees. Conaf's inexpensive brochure (Spanish only) entitled *Sendero Interpretativo Mirador Alejandro Selkirk* is a detailed guide to the trail's environment.

Beyond Selkirk's overlook, the trail continues on the south side; it takes one hour to reach **Villagra** (4.8km), where there's a refugio (locked) and campsites. From here the wide trail skirts the southern cliffs to **Punta de Isla** (13km) and the airstrip, where there is also camping. En route is **Bahía Tierras Blancas**, the island's main breeding colony of Juan Fernández fur seals.

It is possible to walk to the airstrip to catch your flight or to walk from the flight to town, but make prior arrangements to be able to stash your pack on the boat and to confirm the actual date and time of the flight. If walking from town to the airstrip, start walking five hours before scheduled departure.

Plazoleta El Yunque Plazoleta El Yunque, half an hour's walk from town via a road that becomes a footpath, is a tranquil forest clearing with picnic areas. A German survivor of the *Dresden* once homesteaded here; the foundations of his house are still visible.

Starting at the plazoleta is a 1200m interpretive trail that loops through native forest, making this the easiest, if not the only, way to see this habitat without a guide.

Centinela Mount Centinela is the site of the first radio station on the island, established in 1909. The 3km hike is accessed from Pangal.

Salsipuedes At the top of Calle Pólvora, a trail zigzags through eucalyptus groves, then endemic ferns, then thickets of murtilla to reach the ridge Salsipuedes, which translates to 'Leave if you can.' With great views of Bahía Cumberland, the ridge also is home to a wind-energy research project.

JUAN FERNÁNDEZ

Guided Hiking Trails

Villagra to Cerro Negro From the Villagra refugio (camping only), guided hikes can carry on south to Plan del Yunque (base of Cerro El Yunque) and Cerro Negro (3.5km).

Puerto Inglés & Puerto Vaquería The 2.3km trail to Puerto Inglés starts at Salsipuedes and continues down a very precarious ridge to the beach area, where there is a reconstruction of the shelter in which Selkirk passed his years on the island. Puerto Inglés is the site of US researcher Bernard Keiser's search for millions of dollars worth of buried gold. Puerto Inglés has eight campsites with water and a bathroom.

A 4.3km continuation goes to Puerto Vaquería on the north side of the island, where there is a colony of about 100 seals. Conaf has two campsites and a refugio here with water and a bathroom.

Puerto Francés On the east shore of the island, Puerto Francés was a haven for French privateers, whose presence motivated Spain to erect a series of fortifications in 1779, the ruins of which have all but gone. A 6.4km trail continues from Mount Centinela to this spot, where there are five campsites, a refugio, water and a bathroom. From there guides can continue the trek 7.6km to **Rebaje La Piña** (a well-preserved area of native forest), **La Pascua** and **Cordón del Michay** on the southern side.

ISLA ALEJANDRO SELKIRK

When not out fishing for lobster, the 30-odd residents of this island can be found playing soccer, fixing boats, or perhaps going on a hunt for feral goats. Weathered and worn, their stories are intriguing and the island all the more enticingly isolated. During lobster season, a Conaf ranger stays on the island.

It's difficult and expensive but not impossible to get to Isla Alejandro Selkirk, which is rarely visited by foreigners. Contact the **Municipalidad** (☎ 751-001, or 751-046; **e** im_juan fernandez@entelchile.net) to arrange transportation, which usually costs about US$70 roundtrip with a local fishing boat. Take a sleeping bag and motion sickness remedies. If you do manage to get there, you may have to stay for months.

Easter Island (Rapa Nui)

Tiny Polynesian Rapa Nui (117 sq km) is one of the most isolated places on earth, but those who go the distance rarely regret it. Locals refer to their island as Te Pito o Te Henua, 'The Navel of the World' – and watching storms break over the endless ocean expanse, sun bursts and cloud shadows dance across volcanic angles, all as world-famous moai watch over, certainly does make one feel in the center of a magical place.

A Chilean territory since 1888, Rapa Nui is officially known by its Spanish name, Isla de Pascua (Easter Island). The nearest populated landmass, 1900km west, is even tinier Pitcairn Island of HMS *Bounty* fame, and the next nearest inhabited 'neighbors' are the Mangareva (Gambier) Islands, 2500km west, and the Marquesas, 3200km northwest. The South American coast is 3700km to the east.

In archaeology and the study of antiquity, Rapa Nui raises issues totally disproportionate to its size and population. The most obvious questions are where the original islanders came from, how they arrived at such an unlikely destination, what inspired them to build the imposing statues for which Rapa Nui is so famous, and how the islanders transported those statues from quarry to site.

History

How did such a tiny island become inhabited? While Thor Heyerdahl's *Kon Tiki* expedition theorized that the island was settled from South America, the most accepted answer is that the first islanders arrived from the Marquesas, as early as the 4th or 5th century; the Marquesas later also supplied the first settlers of Hawaii and New Zealand. It is thought that the islanders traveled by large double canoes capable of carrying the food and domestic animals that would have been required for colonization.

Intriguingly, Rapa Nui legends describe the arrival of two different peoples – the *Hanau Eepe* from the east and the *Hanau Momoko* from the west. These names, which Heyerdahl mistranslated as 'long ears' and 'short ears' because of the custom of earlobe elongation, would be more accurately rendered as 'corpulent people' and 'thin people.'

According to legend, the initial settlers were led by King Hotu Matua *(matua* is a Polynesian word for 'ancestor' and means

Highlights

- Imagining yourself as the birdman priest at Orongo Ceremonial Village, on the edge of a crater lake

- Deciphering *moai* construction from the carvings into the side of the Rano Raraku volcano

- Soaking in the serenity of a sunset behind the three restored moai at Ahu Tahai

- Appreciating the smooth blend of Polynesian and Chilean culture through language, food, music and dance in Hanga Roa and the Iglesia Hanga Roa

- Contemplating the navel of the world, Ahu Te Pito Kura, on the world's most isolated island

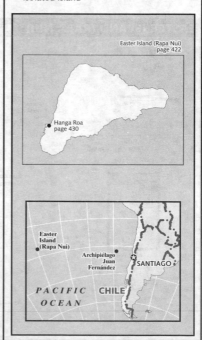

Easter Island (Rapa Nui)
page 422

Hanga Roa
page 430

EASTER ISLAND

'father' on Rapa Nui), who came from the east and landed at Anakena on the island's north coast. Some 57 generations of kings followed him. From this account, some experts estimate that Hotu Matua arrived around AD 450, though the earliest archaeological evidence of people dates from around 800. A second group of immigrants supposedly arrived later, from the west, led by Tuu-ko-ihu.

Clan Warfare & the Toppling of the Moai In local oral tradition, a gap exists between the arrival of Hotu Matua and the division of islanders into clans. The terms 'corpulent people' and 'thin people,' however, suggest a resource conflict in which the dominant Miru clan may have controlled the better soils and superior fishing grounds at the expense of the other. There appears to have been sustained clan warfare, resulting in damage or destruction of many of Rapa Nui's stone monuments.

Recent research suggests that, although islanders were few after Hotu Matua first landed at Anakena, their numbers grew over the centuries, first slowly and then rapidly.

Intensively cultivated gardens yielded an agricultural surplus sufficient to support a priestly class, the artisans and laborers who produced the moai and their *ahu,* and even a warrior class.

There were limits to this intensification, however, and sheer numbers eventually threatened the resource base. Irrigation, for instance, was difficult or impossible in an environment that lacked surface streams. Forest resources, probably used for timber to move the moai to their ahu, declined greatly, a situation exacerbated by the use of fire for military purposes. Marine food resources were too few and too dispersed to provide more than a supplement to agriculture.

Conflict over land and resources erupted in warfare by the late 17th century, only shortly before the European arrival; accounts by later European visitors provide snapshots of the results of what must have been a protracted struggle in which the population declined even before European slave raids in the mid-19th century. Population estimates for the early 19th century range from 4000 to 20,000.

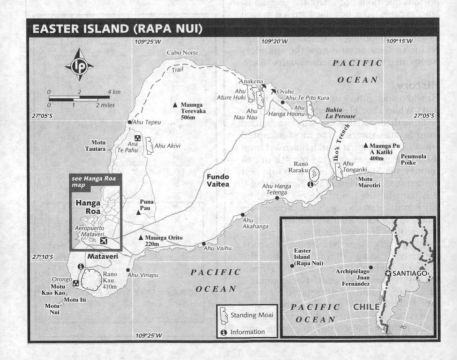

EASTER ISLAND (RAPA NUI)

Dissension between different families or clans led to bloody wars and cannibalism, and many moai were toppled from their ahu. According to one account, tribes or clans were highly territorial and proud of their moai. Enemy groups would topple the moai to insult and anger the statues' owners. Natural disasters – earthquakes and tsunamis – may have contributed to the damage. The only moai standing today have been restored during the last century.

Arrival of the Dutch Spanish vessels entered the Pacific from South America in the early 16th century, but on Easter Sunday, 1722, a Dutch expedition under Admiral Jacob Roggeveen became the first Europeans to set foot on Rapa Nui. Roggeveen recorded his observations in the ship's log, and another crew member, Carl Behrens, published an account of the voyage.

The Dutch found the islanders very friendly. The great moai, though, baffled them. According to Roggeveen:

What the form of worship of these people comprises we were not able to gather any full knowledge of, owing to the shortness of our stay among them; we noticed only that they kindle fire in front of certain remarkably tall stone figures they set up; and, thereafter squatting on their heels with heads bowed down, they bring the palms of their hands together and alternately raise and lower them.

Behrens recorded that the islanders:

relied in case of need on their gods or idols which stand erected all along the sea shore in great numbers, before which they fall down and invoke them. These idols were all hewn out of stone, and in the form of a man, with long ears, adorned on the head with a crown.

Behrens mentioned that some islanders wore wooden blocks or discs in their elongated earlobes – some of which were so long that, after removing the plugs, islanders hitched the lobe over the top of the ear to keep it from flapping. Behrens concluded that islanders with blocks or discs who also shaved their heads were probably priests. Those islanders who did not cut their hair wore it long, either hanging down the back or else plaited and coiled on the top of the head.

The Spanish Expedition Not until 1770 did Europeans again visit Rapa Nui, when a Spanish party from Peru under Don Felipe González de Haedo claimed the island for Spain and renamed it San Carlos. The Spaniards recorded that male islanders generally went unclothed, wearing only plumes on their heads, although a few wore a sort of colored poncho or cloak. Women wore hats made of rushes, a short cloak around the breasts and another wrap from the waist down.

Most islanders inhabited caves, but others lived in elliptical boat-shaped houses. The islanders' only weapons were sharp obsidian knives. The absence of goods and metal implements suggested no commerce with the outside world, but gardens with sugar cane, sweet potatoes, taro and yams provided a healthy subsistence.

Captain Cook In 1774, the celebrated Englishman Captain James Cook led the next European expedition to land on Rapa Nui. Cook, familiar with the Society Islands, Tonga and New Zealand, concluded that the inhabitants of Rapa Nui belonged to the same general lineage.

Cook conjectured that islanders no longer regarded the moai as idols and thought them monuments to former kings; the ahu appeared to be burial sites. His account is the first to mention that, though some moai still stood and carried their topknots, others had fallen and their ahu were damaged. Cook found the islanders poor and distressed, describing them as lean, timid and miserable.

It seems probable, then, that conflict had raged since the Spanish visit in 1770, reducing the population to misery and destroying some of the moai. It's possible that a number of moai had been toppled even before the Spanish and Dutch visits but that those sailors did not visit the same sites as Cook.

Only one other 18th-century European, the Frenchman La Perouse, visited Rapa Nui. After his two ships crossed from Chile in 1786, he found the population calm and prosperous, suggesting a quick recovery from any catastrophe. In 1804, a Russian visitor reported more than 20 moai still standing, including some at the southern coastal site of Vinapu. Existing accounts from ensuing years suggest another period of destruction, so that perhaps only a handful of moai stood a decade later.

EASTER ISLAND

European Colonization Whether or not the people of Rapa Nui experienced a period of self-inflicted havoc, their discovery by the outside world nearly resulted in their annihilation. By the late 18th century, European and North American entrepreneurs saw the Pacific as an unexploited 'resource frontier.' First came the whalers – many of them North American – who ranged the Pacific from Chile to Australia. Then came planters who set out to satisfy an increasing European demand for tropical commodities like rubber, sugar, copra and coffee. For labor, planters either enslaved indigenous peoples, made them wage laborers on their own lands, or imported foreign laborers where local labor proved insufficient, inefficient or difficult to control.

Then came slavers who either kidnapped Polynesians or – to give the trade a veneer of legitimacy – compelled or induced them to sign contracts to work in mines and plantations in lands as remote as Australia and Peru. Many islanders died from the rigors of hard labor, poor diet, disease and mistreatment. Christian missionaries, undermining and degrading local customs, also entered the region. Events on Rapa Nui in the 19th century closely followed this pattern.

In 1862, Peruvian slavers made a vicious and ruthless raid on Rapa Nui. The slavers abducted about a thousand islanders (including the king and nearly all the *maori* or 'learned men') and took them to work the guano deposits on Peru's Chincha Islands. After Bishop Jaussen of Tahiti protested to the French representative at Lima, Peruvian authorities ordered the return of the islanders to their homeland, but disease and hard labor had already killed about 90% of them. On the return voyage, smallpox killed most of the rest, and the handful who survived brought back an epidemic that decimated the remaining inhabitants of the island, leaving perhaps only a few hundred traumatized survivors. The knowledge and culture lost has never been fully regained.

Catholic missionaries converted the few remaining islanders in the mid-1860s.

Commercial exploitation of the island began in 1870, when the Frenchman Jean-Baptiste Dutroux-Bornier introduced the wool trade to Rapa Nui. Importing sheep, he intended to transform the entire island into a ranch and expel the islanders to the plantations of Tahiti. The missionaries, who planned to ship the islanders to mission lands in southern Chile or the Mangarevas, opposed his claims to ultimate sovereignty over the island and its people.

Dutroux-Bornier armed local followers and raided the missionary settlements, burning houses and destroying crops, leaving many people dead or injured and forcing the missionaries to evacuate. Most islanders reluctantly accepted transportation to Tahiti and the Mangarevas, leaving only about a hundred people on the island. Dutroux-Bornier ruled until the remaining islanders killed him in 1877.

Annexation by Chile Spain never pursued its interest in Rapa Nui and, in any event, lost all its South American territories early in the 19th century. Chile officially annexed the island in 1888 during a period of expansion that included the acquisition of territory from Peru and Bolivia after the War of the Pacific (1879–84).

With its vigorous navy, Chile was capable of expanding into the Pacific. It valued the island partly for its agricultural potential, real or imagined, but mostly for geopolitical purposes as a naval station, to prevent its use by a hostile power, for its location on a potentially important trading route between South America and East Asia, and for the prestige of having overseas possessions – any possessions – in an age of rampant imperialism.

By 1897, Rapa Nui fell under the control of a single wool company run by Enrique Merlet, a Valparaíso businessman who had bought or leased nearly all the land. His holdings were acquired by a shipping company, Williamson, Bafour & Company, which managed the island under lease from the Chilean government through its Compañía Explotadora de la Isla de Pascua (Cedip). The company became the island's de facto government, continuing the wool trade until the middle of the 20th century.

How islanders fared under this system is the subject of differing accounts, but there were several uprisings against the company. One result of foreign control was that islanders intermarried with immigrants of many countries. By the 1930s, perhaps three-quarters of the population were of mixed descent, including North American, British,

Chilean, Chinese, French, German, Italian, Tahitian and Tuamotuan stock.

In 1953, when Chile was seeking to consolidate its control over its far-flung, unwieldy territories, the government revoked Cedip's lease. The navy took charge of the island, continuing the imperial rule to which islanders had been subject for nearly a century.

Rapa Nui continued under military rule until the mid-1960s, followed by a brief period of civilian government, until the military coup of 1973 once again brought direct military control. In the 1960s, the islanders' grievances included unpaid labor, travel restrictions, confinement to the Hanga Roa area, suppression of the Rapanui language, ineligibility to vote (Chilean universal suffrage did not extend to Rapa Nui) and arbitrary naval administration. However, increased contact with the outside world soon developed after establishment of a regular commercial air link between Santiago and Tahiti in 1967, with Rapa Nui as a refueling stop.

For a variety of reasons, including islanders' dissatisfaction, increased immigration from the continent, international attention and tourist potential, and the assumption of power by former president Frei Montalva, the Chilean presence soon became more benevolent, with advances in medical care, education, potable water and electrification; Chile also paved many island roads. In August 1985, General Pinochet approved a plan allowing the USA to expand Aeropuerto Internacional Mataveri as an emergency landing site for the space shuttle, arousing opposition both locally and on the continent.

Land Reform The global impulse toward self-determination has reached this remote place, as some islanders argue for the return of native lands and speak hopefully of independence, or at least autonomy. Their aspirations are tempered by realism; when asked if he would like to expel the Chileans, one islander responded, 'We can't – but we'd like them to leave.'

Native Rapanui control almost no land outside Hanga Roa. A national park declared in 1935 comprises more than a third of the island, and nearly all the remainder belongs to Chile. Unesco has declared the park a world heritage site, though without consulting the local population.

In response, native groups have asked the Chilean government and the United Nations to return the park land to aboriginal hands, or at least to give them control of the resources to preserve the heritage sites. Mayor Pedro Edwards Poa says islanders will do the preserving themselves if given the money. In the words of the mayor, 'I cannot accept that a group of people claiming to be experts – I don't know who they are – take decisions behind our backs.'

In late 1996, the Frei administration agreed to return about 1500 hectares of land to islanders from the state development company, Corfo; local elected leaders were to determine the distribution of the land among the 200 applicants.

Two competing Consejos de Ancianos (Councils of Elders) represent native rights. The more traditional one, founded in 1888, represents the viewpoint of more people. The second, which formed in 1993, is more confrontational.

Tourism is keeping up, but not booming – approximately 20,000 visitors come to the island each year. Islanders have concerns that some tourist money goes off island (that is, profits from Hotel Hanga Roa are sent to its mainland owners), so although there are more tourists, there is less money for local families. Despite being 3700km from the mainland, Easter Island is considered part of the region of Valparaíso. The local government does not have the ability to levy taxes on tourist industries.

Geography & Geology

Rapa Nui, just south of the tropic of Capricorn, is a tiny volcanic island formed where lava from three separate cones of different ages coalesced in a single triangular landmass. Its total area is just 117 sq km, and its maximum length 24km. At its widest point, the island is only 12km.

All three of its major volcanoes are now extinct. Terevaka, the largest, rises 506m above sea level in the northern part of the island, and Pu A Katiki (about 400m) forms the eastern headland of the Poike peninsula; Rano Kau (about 410m) dominates the southwest corner. Rano Kau and Rano Raraku both contain freshwater lakes.

For the most part, Rapa Nui's volcanic slopes are gentle and grassy, except where wave erosion has produced nearly vertical cliffs. In contrast, rugged lava fields cover much of the island's interior. Despite this, several areas have soil that's adequate for cultivation.

Lava flow has left numerous caves, many in seaside cliffs. Some caves, consisting of larger and smaller chambers connected by tunnels through which a person can barely squeeze, extend for considerable distances into the lava. These were often used as permanent shelters, refuges in wartime and storage or burial sites.

Although some coral occurs in shallow waters, Rapa Nui does not have coral reefs. In the absence of reefs, the ocean has battered the huge cliffs, some of which rise 300m. Those cliffs composed of lava are usually lower but extremely rugged. There are a few shallow bays, but no natural sheltered harbor, and Anakena on the north coast has the only broad sandy beach.

Rapa Nui's rainfall supports a permanent cover of coarse grasses, but its volcanic soil is so porous that water quickly drains underground. Without permanent streams, water for both humans and livestock comes either from the volcanic lakes or from wells.

Climate

Winds and ocean currents strongly influence Rapa Nui's subtropical climate. The hottest months are January and February, and the coolest are July and August. The average maximum summer temperature is 28°C and the average minimum 15°C, but these figures understate what can be a fierce sun and formidable heat. The average winter maximum is 22°C and the minimum 14°C, but it can seem much cooler when Antarctic winds lash the island with rain. Light showers, however, are the most frequent form of precipitation. May is the wettest month, but tropical downpours can occur during any season.

Flora & Fauna

Vegetation was once more luxuriant on Rapa Nui – including forests with palms, conifers and other species now extinct – but islanders cut the forests long ago. Most of today's trees, like the eucalyptus, were planted only within the past century. Like other remote islands, Rapa Nui lacks entire families of plants and is particularly poor in native fauna; even seabirds are relatively few. Some plants are endemic, most notably the tree species

toromiro *(Sophora toromiro)* and several genera of ferns. Although the last native toromiro died in 1962, Conaf reintroduced 162 European-cultivated saplings into Rano Kau crater in 1995. About 30 of these have survived, but there is concern that the genetic pool is not large enough to conserve the species; competition from more than 60 other introduced trees and shrubs, coupled with a legacy of soil erosion from livestock, have made long-term viability unlikely.

Rapa Nui's original Polynesian immigrants brought rats and small domestic animals such as chickens, and the Norway (brown) rat escaped from European vessels; Europeans also brought horses and sheep in the 19th century.

Conaf's informational booklet *Vegetación de Rapa Nui: Historia y Uso Tradicional,* by Marcos Rauch, Patricia Ibáñez and José Miguel Ramírez, is a useful summary of the island's flora, including native and cultivated plants, medicinal properties and horticulture. The booklet also contains a selection of illustrations; it sells for US$5 at Conaf offices.

Society & Language

Most of the island's 3800 inhabitants live in Hanga Roa. About a third of the population is from the mainland or Europe. Large extended families bind all islanders together. Islanders have a great deal of respect for their elders. While not shown outwardly, some islanders disapprove of mainlanders on the island, and relationships and marriages joining the two are met with a small degree of criticism and a larger degree of teasing. Ask before taking photos.

Islanders speak Rapanui, an Eastern Polynesian dialect related to Cook Islands Maori, but also Spanish, the official language. Many people in the tourist business speak English. Essential expressions include *Iorana* – Hello; *Maururu* – Thank you; *Pehe koe* – How are you?; and *Riva riva* – Fine, good.

Planning

Maps Tourist maps, which are distributed freely at Sernatur and tour agencies, show the most important archaeological sites, but lack adequate road information. The 1:30,000-scale *Isla de Pascua-Rapa Nui: Mapa Arqueológico-Turístico* and the JLM *Isla de Pascua Trekking Map,* at 1:32,000, are available at local shops for about US$10 (cheaper if you can find them before arriving on the island).

What to Bring Long-sleeved shirts, sunglasses, a hat and powerful sunblock are essential. Also bring insect repellent to combat the pestering mosquitoes and *nonos* (fleas), and bring a flashlight to explore caves. Earplugs will help drown out the nightly chorus of dog howls that inevitably starts when you want to sleep.

Books & Film

Conaf's *Archaeological Field Guide, Rapa Nui National Park*, written by Claudio Cristino, Patricia Vargas and Roberto Izaurieta, contains useful material in a credible English translation. It's available at Conaf offices for US$3.

Thor Heyerdahl's *Kon-Tiki* and *Aku-Aku: The Secret of Easter Island* are both worthwhile books; the first is an account of his 1947 voyage to Rapa Nui in a balsa raft.

Englishwoman Katherine Routledge was head of the first archaeological expedition in 1914, which she describes in *The Mystery of Easter Island: The Story of an Expedition.*

Bavarian priest Sebastián Englert spent 35 years on Rapa Nui, until his death in 1970; his *Island at the Center of the World* retells the island's history through oral tradition.

For an account of the island from the mid-1800s almost to the present, see *The Modernization of Easter Island* by J Douglas Porteous. For a coffee-table-size photo book, try Michel Rougie's *Isla de Pascua*, with text in Spanish, French and English.

Georgia Lee has written several informative books on Rapa Nui, including *The Rock Art of Easter Island.*

The best source for current information on Rapa Nui research and travel is *Rapa Nui Journal*, published twice annually by the **Easter Island Foundation** (☎ 802-528-8558; **w** *www.islandheritage.org;* **e** *rapanuibooks@worldnet.att.net; PO Box 6774, Los Osos, CA, USA 93412-6774).* Rates are US$30 for one year. Besides the journal, the foundation also publishes books.

Rapa Nui has infinite potential for cinema, but Kevin Costner's badly reviewed, 1994 Hollywood megaproduction *Rapa Nui* was a colossal waste of money that marginalized

EASTER ISLAND

Rongo-Rongo Tablets

One Rapa Nui artifact that, until recently, resisted explanation was the Rongo-Rongo script. Eugene Eyraud, the first European to record its existence, noted that every house on the island contained wooden tablets covered in some form of writing or hieroglyphics. He could find no islander who could or would explain the meaning of these symbols. The complete name of the tablets was *ko hau motu mo rongorongo,* literally meaning 'lines of script for recitation.' According to oral tradition, Hotu Matua brought these tablets, along with learned men who knew the art of writing and reciting the inscriptions. Most of the tablets are irregular, flat wooden boards with rounded edges, each about 30cm to 50cm long and covered in tidy rows of tiny symbols including birds, animals, possibly plants and celestial objects and geometric forms. The hundreds of different signs are too numerous to suggest a form of alphabet. Only a few such tablets, carved of toromiro wood, survive.

Oral tradition describes three classes of tablets: One class recorded hymns in honor of the native deity Makemake or other divinities; another recorded crimes or other deeds of individuals; and the third commemorated those fallen in war or other conflicts. Tablets recording genealogies may also have existed. Bishop Jaussen attempted to translate the script in 1866, with assistance from an islander said to be able to read the symbols, but this and other attempts failed; informants appeared to be either reciting memorized texts or merely describing the figures, rather than actually reading them. The last truly literate islanders had by then died, either as a result of 1862's slave raid or the subsequent smallpox epidemic.

Researchers have proposed various theories, most of them fanciful, of the nature of the script. One researcher suggested that Rongo-Rongo was not readable text at all, but rather a series of cues for reciting memorized verse, and another claimed that the characters were ideographs like Chinese script. The accessible *Glyphbreaker* is linguistic expert Steven Fischer's account of his efforts to decipher the tablets.

local participants and damaged archaeological sites at Rano Raraku.

Getting There & Away

LanChile (☎ 100-920; Atamu Tekena; open 9am-1pm & 3pm-5:30pm Mon-Fri), near Av Pont, is the only airline serving Rapa Nui; it has two flights per week to/from Santiago and to/from Papeete (Tahiti), with more weekly flights during the high season. A standard economy roundtrip fare from Santiago can range from US$645 to US$1000. Flights are often overbooked, so it is essential to reconfirm your ticket two days before departure; LanChile claims that you don't need to reconfirm once you're on the island.

For travelers coming from Asia or Australia, a cheaper alternative is to stop here en route to (or from) South America, via Auckland, New Zealand. There you'll need to join a Qantas flight to Papeete and connect with LanChile's Papeete-Easter Island-Santiago service (see the Getting There & Away chapter).

The flight from Santiago takes 5½ tiring hours, but LanChile's service is excellent and attentive. The return flight is at least an hour faster because of the prevailing westerlies and the jet stream.

The airport departure tax is US$13 and is usually included with your airline ticket.

Those wishing to come by sea should note that the occasional cruise ship does stop here, but the few hours of shore time allowed is insufficient to gain any appreciation of island culture and history.

Getting Around

It's possible to walk around the island in a few days, but the summer heat, lack of shade and scattered water supply are good reasons not to do so. While distances appear small on the map, visiting numerous archaeological sites can be tiring and time-consuming. With good transportation, it's possible to see all the major archaeological sites, at least superficially, in about three days, but many people take longer.

Outside Hanga Roa, nearly the entire east coast road and the road to Anakena are paved. Side roads to the archeological sites are not paved, but most are in decent enough condition if you proceed with reasonable caution.

Within town, most visitors do a fair amount of walking around this very spread-

Site Distances

The following are approximate road distances to key archaeological sites from Hanga Roa:

site	distance from Hanga Roa
Ahu Tahai	1.5km
Orito	2km
Vinapu	5km
Orongo	6km
Vaihu	9.5km
Ahu Akivi	10km
Akahanga	12.5km
Puna Pau	15km
Rano Raraku	18km
Ahu Tongariki	20km
Ahu Te Pito Kura	26km
Ovahe	29km
Anakena	30km

out village, but taxis are also available. Aeropuerto Mataveri (Av Hotu Matua) is at the south end of Hanga Roa, about a 20-minute walk from downtown.

If you walk or ride a horse, mountain bike or motorcycle around the island, carry extra food and water, since neither is easily available outside Hanga Roa.

Car & Motorcycle Established hotels and agencies rent Suzuki 4WDs for US$55 to US$65 per eight-hour day, US$60 to US$90 for 24 hours; locals may charge less – ask at *residenciales* or at Sernatur. Hotels and agencies generally accept credit cards, but private individuals expect US cash. In Hanga Roa, **Comercial Insular** (☎ 100-480; Atamu Tekena) provides the best service for rentals. Also try **Tekena Inn Rent a Car** (☎ 100-366; Atamu Tekena & Tu'u Maheke) or look for signs in windows of businesses. Outside the high season, prices are negotiable. Insurance is not usually included and some cars are very far from perfect. Make sure the car has all the necessary fixings should a tire go flat (which is not uncommon).

Motorcycles are rented for about US$30 per eight hours, US$55 a day. Given the occasional tropical downpours, a jeep is more convenient and more economical for two or more people.

Gasoline, subsidized by the Chilean government, costs less than it does on the continent, so it's not a major expense for the island's relatively short distances.

Bicycle Mountain bikes, readily available in Hanga Roa for about US$11 to US$16 per eight hours, US$16 to US$22 per day, are more reliable than some horses. Be sure to take any bike for a test spin and make sure that the gears work and that the seat is at least bearable; many readers have complained about the poor conditions of rental bikes. Keep in mind that roads around the south part of the island are steep and winding. There's an air pump at the gas station near the airport.

Taxi Taxis cost a flat US$2 for most trips around town. Longer trips can be negotiated, with the cost depending mainly on the time. For example, a roundtrip to the beach at Anakena costs US$16 (per taxi); be sure to arrange for the taxi driver to pick you up at a predetermined time.

Horse Horses are good for visiting sites near Hanga Roa, like Ahu Tepeu, Ahu Vinapu, Ahu Akivi and Orongo, but for more distant places, like Rano Raraku and Anakena, motorized transportation is superior. Horses can be hired for about US$13 to US$38 per eight hours, but see the beast before renting it. Pastures are poor for the large number of animals, and you won't want to risk being impaled by protruding ribs as your mount collapses under you. Most horse gear is basic and potentially hazardous for inexperienced riders. Several residenciales, hotels and tour agencies can provide horses or arrange excursions. One recommended option is **Ernesto Pakarati Rapu** (☎ 100-595). Verify whether the price includes a guide. Wear long pants.

Organized Tours Plenty of operators do tours of the sites, typically charging US$35 for a full day and US$25 for a half day. You won't find much solitude on your tour; not only will you have your van mates for company, but many tours follow the same schedule, resulting in a pileup of vans at each site. Still, this is probably the easiest way to get to and learn about the archaeological sites.

Kia Koe Tour (☎ 100-852; *Atamu Tekena s/n*) is one of the best equipped, with the largest number of languages spoken and the widest variety of vehicles, from four-person Jeeps to full-size tour buses.

Haumaka Archeological Guide Services (☎/fax 100-274; e *haumaka@entelchile.net*), in the Aloha Nui Guest House (see Places to Stay later in this chapter), is run by guides Ramon Edmunds Pakomio & Josefina Nahoe Mulloy, who are fluent English speakers; Josefina is the granddaughter of archaeologist William Mulloy.

AO Tours (☎ 100-691; e *aotour2001@yahoo.com*) is operated by Patricio Ballerino Rojas, a mainland Chilean with nearly 30 years of living on the island. Patricio speaks passable English and takes only small groups (two to six people) on trips.

Steep drop-offs, abundant marine life and clear water make for good diving, available at **Orca Diving Center** (☎ 100-375; w *www.seemorca.co.cl; Caleta Hanga Roa*) and next door at **Mike Rapu Dive Center** (☎ 551-055; w *www.mikerapudiving.cl*). Dives, with all gear provided, cost about US$55 each. Bring proof of certification, although Mike Rapu offers beginning courses consisting of one guide per participant (US$80). Both shops also offer snorkeling excursions for $32 to $50 per person.

Before contracting a tour, clarify your expectations with the operator and determine what is included, the hour of departure and return, whether there is a meal, and the like.

HANGA ROA
☎ 32 • pop 3800

Nearly all Rapa Nui residents live in Hanga Roa. About 70% are predominantly Polynesian, considering themselves more Rapanui than Chilean, and most of the remainder are immigrants from the Chilean mainland. Nearly everyone depends directly or indirectly on the tourist trade, but there is some fishing, livestock (mostly cattle) ranching and kitchen gardens that grow fruit and vegetables within and beyond the village. Government agencies and small general stores are the only other source of employment.

For information on getting to and around Hanga Roa, see Getting There & Away and Getting Around earlier in this chapter.

Orientation

Hanga Roa, on the western shore of Rapa Nui, is a sprawling, decentralized tropical village with an irregular street plan. The main

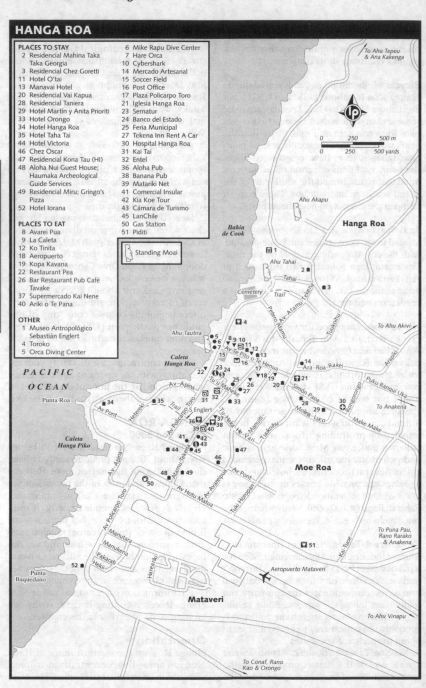

HANGA ROA

PLACES TO STAY
2 Residencial Mahina Taka Taka Georgia
3 Residencial Chez Goretti
11 Hotel O'tai
13 Manavai Hotel
20 Residencial Vai Kapua
28 Residencial Taniera
29 Hotel Martín y Anita Prioriti
33 Hotel Orongo
34 Hotel Hanga Roa
35 Hotel Taha Tai
44 Hotel Victoria
46 Chez Oscar
47 Residencial Kona Tau (HI)
48 Aloha Nui Guest House; Haumaka Archeological Guide Services
49 Residencial Miru; Gringo's Pizza
52 Hotel Iorana

PLACES TO EAT
8 Avarei Pua
9 La Caleta
12 Ko Tinita
18 Aeropuerto
22 Kopa Kavana
22 Restaurant Pea
26 Bar Restaurant Pub Café Tavake
37 Supermercado Kai Nene
40 Ariki o Te Pana

OTHER
1 Museo Antropológico Sebastián Englert
4 Toroko
5 Orca Diving Center
6 Mike Rapu Dive Center
7 Hare Orca
10 Cybershark
14 Mercado Artesanal
15 Soccer Field
16 Post Office
17 Plaza Policarpo Toro
21 Iglesia Hanga Roa
23 Sernatur
24 Banco del Estado
25 Feria Municipal
27 Tekena Inn Rent A Car
30 Hospital Hanga Roa
31 Kai Tai
32 Entel
36 Aloha Pub
38 Banana Pub
39 Matariki Net
41 Comercial Insular
42 Kia Koe Tour
43 Cámara de Turismo
45 LanChile
50 Gas Station
51 Piditi

Standing Moai

road is north-south Av Atamu Tekena, on which are a number of shops, the main supermarket, an artisans' market and several eateries. Old maps show this as Policarpo Toro, which now is just below it, along the waterfront (for some reason names of the two main streets keep switching). Caleta Hanga Roa is the town's small bay, where fishing boats come and go and body surfers catch a small swell or two.

Information

Sernatur (☎ 100-255; Tu'u Maheke; e sernatur_rapanui@entelchile.net; open 8:30am-1pm & 2:30pm-6pm Mon-Fri, also 9am-1pm Sat Jan-Feb) is at Policarpo Toro, near Caleta Hanga Roa. The useful **Cámara de Turismo** (☎ 550-055; e camararapanui@entelchile.net; Atamu Tekna s/n; open 9am-1pm & 3pm-6pm Mon-Fri), near Av Pont, is an organization of local businesses and has a useful orientation brochure. **Conaf** (☎ 100-236), on the road to Rano Kau, may give suggestions on hiking and camping.

Most businesses, especially residenciales and rental agencies, prefer US cash dollars. Travelers from Tahiti must bring US cash dollars. **Banco del Estado**, next to Sernatur, changes US dollars at reasonable rates but charges a US$10 commission on traveler's checks; there's also an ATM here. Exchange rates are better at the gas station on Av Hotu Matua. Some eateries and stores show prices in both dollars and pesos, but use a lower conversion rate, so using pesos saves money. Many residenciales, hotels and tour agencies take credit cards, but this is far from universal.

The **post office** (Av Te Pito o Te Henua) is half a block from Caleta Hanga Roa. **Entel,** easily located by its conspicuous white satellite dish, is on a cul-de-sac opposite Banco del Estado, but it has high rates. A public pay phone across the street from Entel can be used to make a collect or card call overseas.

Cybershark (☎ 100-600; Av Te Pito o Te Henua; open 1pm-8pm Mon-Sat), across from the soccer field, has Internet access, as do **Kai Tai** (Policarpo Toro) and **Matariki Net** (☎ 551-308; cnr Av Atamu Tekena & S Englert; open 9am-1pm Mon-Fri).

Standard ASA 100 to ASA 400 film is readily available, and some ASA 100 slide film can be found, though it's more expensive in many of the shops than on the mainland.

Supermercado Kai Nene has the cheapest prices (US$5 for 36 exposures).

No laundry is currently available on the island. Most residenciales and hotels can do your laundry, but beware of per-piece charges.

Hospital Hanga Roa (☎ 100-215) is one long block east of the church.

Things to See & Do

Iglesia Hanga Roa, the island's Catholic church, is well worth a visit for its spectacular wood carvings, which integrate Christian doctrine with Rapanui tradition. Mass is held at 7pm daily, and at 9am and 11am Sunday; visitors are welcome.

Overlooking the sea near Ahu Tahai, Hanga Roa's colorful **cemetery** is full of tombstones with Polynesian names, and it is also the site of ritual visits at Easter.

Locals make do with the tiny beach at **Playa Pea** (which is a good description of its size), on the south side of Caleta Hanga Roa. It even comes with a nearby rocky pool. **Caleta Hanga Roa** also provides an opportunity to catch a few waves. The shop **Hare Orca,** next to the Orca Diving Center, rents body boards (per half/full day US$16/27), surfboards (US$22/33), ocean kayaks (single kayak US$22/33, double US$33/55) and snorkeling gear (US$10 per day).

The interesting **Museo Antropológico Sebastián Englert** (adult/child US$2/1; open 9:30am-12:30pm & 2pm-5:30pm Tues-Fri, 9:30am-12:30pm Sat & Sun), north of town, uses text and photographs to explain the Rapanui people's history. It also displays moai kavakava (the strange 'statues of ribs'), replica Rongo-Rongo tablets, skulls from bodies originally entombed in ahu, basalt fishhooks and other implements, obsidian spearheads and other weapons, a moai head with reconstructed fragments of its eyes, sketches of elliptical houses, circular beehive-shaped huts and the ceremonial houses at Orongo.

Just outside the museum building stands the unusual reddish moai Mata Mea, about 2.5m high, found near the modern Hanga Roa cemetery and placed here by the Norwegians. With a triangular head and large sunken eyes, it appears crudely made, but may have been damaged or eroded. Within the museum are several oblong stone heads, known as 'potato heads,' with eye sockets and rudimentary features, including one with round ears. Thought to be the oldest carvings on the island, these may have preceded the Rano Raraku figures.

Signs are in Spanish, but translation booklets are available in English and a few other languages.

Hanga Roa contains several moai sites; for a description, see Parque Nacional Rapa Nui later in this chapter.

Special Events

Every February islanders observe the Tapati Rapa Nui, a fortnight-long celebration with music, dance and traditional cultural events, including moai carving, body painting and sliding down banana tree trunks. The event is organized by the Municipality of Easter Island.

Given the island's links to Christianity through the date of its European discovery, Easter has a special resonance, and the Sunday morning mass is a particular attraction. After mass, islanders and visitors gather for a *curanto* (seafood stew) near the church. Many saints days are celebrated throughout the year.

The June 21st Ceremonia Culto al Sol is a more indigenous event commemorating the winter solstice. Late November's Día de la Lengua Rapanui is a cultural festival celebrating the local language.

Places to Stay

Rapa Nui is not inexpensive, but visitors can control costs by staying at one of the many residenciales. Many offer other meals for about US$15 each, although it's easier to find cheaper food on the island, and it's not necessary to sign up for a package deal with your accommodations. Upon arrival at the airport, locals and residencial proprietors will attempt to woo you, sometimes with discounts. Make sure you are talking with a person from the residencial and not an agent.

Find out what the rates are in dollars and pesos; if you can, pay in the currency most favorable to you.

Reservations are only necessary in the peak times of August and January to February, when prices may be higher. It's considerably more expensive to book accommodations through agents on the mainland.

Budget Conaf operates a free, barebones **campsite** across the street from Anakena on the north coast of the island. Although a water tank provides drinking water (trucked in from Hanga Roa), it has been known to run out; concessionaires sometimes supply snacks and drinks at the beach, but it's best to bring your own food and water.

Residencial Miru (*☎ 100-365; Atamu Takena s/n; per person with shared/private bath US$10/15*) is basic and offers kitchen use; breakfast is US$5.

Residencial Kona Tau (*☎/fax 100-321; Avareipua s/n;* e *konatau@entelchile.net; members/nonmembers US$15/20*) is a pleasant HI affiliate, in a friendly family house, and serves large breakfasts. Members pay less but share the room, while nonmembers get their own rooms with private bath. Single rooms are hard to come by in the busy season. Rooms outside the main house are better.

Chez Oscar (*☎ 100-404; Av Pont; per person US$15*) is spotless and a great find, without breakfast (US$5 extra) but with kitchen use and private bath.

Residencial Taniera (*☎ 100-491, fax 100-105;* e *cguldman@entelchile.net; Simón Paoa s/n; singles/doubles/triples $35/60/80*) is quaint with basic rooms and includes large breakfasts with marmalades made from local fruits. The residencial is run by an artist who makes paper from local fibers and decorates it with drawings of island petroglyphs.

Residencial Vai Kapua (*☎ 100-377, fax 100-105;* e *vaikapua@entelchile.net; singles/ doubles US$25/40*), in a cul-de-sac off Av Te Pito o Te Henua, is a very good value. It's centrally located, friendly and quiet. It has plain but large and bright rooms (avoid the occasional musty room) and pretty gardens.

Residencial Mahina Taka Taka Georgia (*☎ 100-452, fax 100-105;* e *riroroko@entel chile.net; Atamu Tekena & Calle Tahai; per person US$30*) brims with the magic of the island. Knowledgeable and gregarious Lucia Riroroko Tuki encourages guests to mingle and may invite them to participate in family activities. Rooms are basic and a bit musty, but common areas are comfortable; Lucia says she offers *mas amor que lujo* ('more love than luxury'). The house is a 30-minute walk north of town.

Mid-Range An excellent value, **Residencial Chez Goretti** (*☎/fax 100-459;* e *chezmaria goretti@entelchile.net; Av Atamu Tekena s/n; per person with breakfast US$40*) is also a 30-minute walk north of town (or a short, US$2 taxi ride). Marvelous gardens spread out over the spacious grounds. Rooms are large and bright, and a superb gathering and dining area in the high-ceilinged lodge includes a bar. The staff can be a bit acerbic, though.

Hotel Orongo (☎/fax 100-294; Atamu Tekena s/n; singles/doubles US$45/75) is a friendly, intimate, five-room hotel, with pleasant gardens, large, bright rooms and an excellent restaurant. It's a good value.

Hotel Victoria (☎/fax 100-272; Av Pont s/n; singles/doubles US$55/75) is secluded and has panoramic views of the ocean from a hillock on the southeast edge of town, midway between the airport and the settlement. Rooms are disappointing for the price, however.

Hotel Martín y Anita Prioriti (☎ 100-593; w www.hostal.co.cl; Av Simón Paoa s/n; singles/doubles US$55/85) offers large rooms in a lush garden setting, some with AC. Martín and Anita operate a second nearby house for overflow business, where they put mostly solo travelers; this house is quieter but less lush.

Aloha Nui Guest House (☎/fax 100-274; e haumaka@entelchile.net; cnr Atamu Tekena & Hotu Matua; singles/doubles US$55/100) has decent, spacious rooms with private bath, set among attractive gardens. A large and varied breakfast, included in the rates, is served each day. English and German are spoken.

Manavai Hotel (☎ 100-670, fax 100-658; e manavai@entelchile.net; Av Te Pito o Te Henua s/n; singles/doubles US$74/106) is a central, family-run, friendly hotel with decent rooms, a swimming pool and a bar.

Hotel O'tai (☎ 100-250, fax 100-482; e otairapanui@entelchile.net; Av Te Pito o Te Henua s/n; singles/doubles US$70/95), the traditional favorite, is conveniently situated, pleasantly landscaped and often full. The hotel has a swimming pool. Superior rooms (US$130) are larger and include air-conditioning.

Top End Hotel Taha Tai (☎ 551-193, fax 551-192; e riroroco@entelchile.net; Av Apina s/n; singles/doubles/triples US$140/165/180) has a view of the ocean. Spacious and bright, it's popular with tour groups and often full. All rooms have air-conditioning; breakfast is included; and Internet access is available in

the bar. There's also a pool. The staff can be curt when harried.

Hotel Hanga Roa (☎/fax 100-299; e res hangaroa@panamericanahoteles.cl; Av Pont s/n; singles/doubles start at US$140/160), near Caleta Hanga Piko, is a walk from the middle of town. Standard rooms are large and bright, but older and bland; some have a sea view. Superior rooms (US$270) are in bungalows, all with an ocean view, ceiling fan, TV and minibar; some are near a noisy generator. The hotel also has a pool, bar, good restaurant and souvenir shops. Parts of the hotel are showing wear; there are better values in town. This hotel is owned by a mainland Chile corporation, so all profits go off the island.

Hotel Iorana (☎/fax 100-312; Policarpo Toro s/n; singles/doubles US$89/121) has rooms in a quiet area (except during the infrequent landings at the nearby airport) with outstanding coastal views, but it could use some maintenance, and restaurant service is questionable. There is a swimming pool.

Places to Eat

Besides great fruit juices and fish, the island's cuisine is rather bland and moderately expensive. Residenciales and hotels generally provide breakfast, and additional meals costs about US$15 each. However, Hanga Roa has several good, reasonably priced restaurants. Lobster is available but extremely expensive (US$25).

Supermercado Kai Nene (Atamu Tekena) has the best selection of basic goods.

In the mornings vendors sell fruits and veggies opposite the feria municipal.

Aeropuerto (Plaza Policarpo Toro) has the best fresh bread and cheeses, but get there early for the best selection.

Ariki o Te Pana (☎ 100-171; Atamu Tekena; lunches US$5-10), near the supermarket, has scrumptious empanadas (US$2 to US$3) that are a lunch in themselves, plus cold drinks and large lunches.

Bar Restaurant Pub Café Tavake (☎ 100-300; Atamu Tekena; set menú US$5, sandwiches US$3) is good for cheap meals, sandwiches and late-night snacks and drinks.

Gringo's Pizza (☎ 100-365; Residencial Miru, on Atamu Tekena s/n; small pizza US$6) serves up good pizzas, empanadas, vegetarian meals and great big juices.

La Caleta (☎ 100-607; Av Te Pito o Te Henua & Av Policarpo Toro; sandwiches

US$4, mains US$9) is a good bet for sandwiches and burgers, and it has a pleasant view of the harbor.

Avarei Pua (☎ 100-431; Av Policarpo Toro & Av Te Pito o Te Henua; mains US$9-10), around the corner, serves filling, well-priced meals, including excellent ceviche (US$6).

Ko Tinita (☎ 100-813; Av Te Pito o Te Henua; mains US$9) tends to be a bit touristy but makes up for the less-than-authentic ambience with good fish dishes, including options other than the ubiquitous tuna, such as toremo.

Kopa Kavana (☎ 100-447; cnr Av Te Pito o Te Henua & Av Avareipua; fish US$9-10)

Rapa Nui Antiquities

Although the giant moai are the most pervasive image of Rapa Nui, islanders created several other types of stonework, most notably the large ahu on which the moai were erected, burial cairns (large piles of rock where bodies were entombed) and the foundations of the unusual *hare paenga* (boat-shaped thatched houses). One of the most striking things about the island is the remarkable density of ruins, indicating a much larger population in the past.

Although many structures were partially demolished or rebuilt by the original inhabitants, and the moai fell during intertribal wars, Cedip's regime, lasting over a half century, was also responsible for major damage. Many ahu, burial cairns, house foundations and other structures were dismantled and used to build various structures, such as piers, stone walls and windmills. More recently, some stone houses were destroyed to construct the airport runway and east coast shore road.

Collectors have pillaged other sites. Only a few moai were removed, but museums and private collections in Chile and elsewhere now feature wooden Rongo-Rongo tablets, painted wall tablets from houses at Orongo, small wood and stone moai, weapons, clothing, skulls and other artifacts. Islanders themselves were responsible for removing building materials from sites like Orongo.

On the other hand, archaeologists have restored a number of sites over the last 30 years. These include Ahu Tahai, Ahu Akivi, the Orongo ceremonial village, Ahu Nau Nau and Ahu Tongariki. Others, such as Ahu Vinapu and Ahu Vaihu, lie in ruins but are nonetheless impressive.

Ahu

About 350 ahu form a line along the coast. They tend to be sited at sheltered coves and areas favorable for human habitation, but only a few were built inland.

Of several varieties of ahu, built at different times for different reasons, the most impressive are the *ahu moai* that support the massive statues. Each is a mass of loose stones held together by retaining walls and paved on the upper surface with more or less flat stones, with a vertical wall on the seaward side and at each end. The moai on these platforms range from 2m to almost 10m in height.

Usually a gently sloping ramp comprises the landward side of the platform. Next to the ramp is a large plaza. Sometimes there are small rectangular platforms, which may be altars, or large circles paved with stones, which are either burial sites (as at Ahu Tahai) or *paina* (as at Vaihu), places where feasts paid tribute to deceased ancestors. Reed boats were probably launched from *apapa* (stone ramps) leading into the sea alongside the ahu.

Researchers have learned little about the ceremonies connected with these ahu complexes. One theory is that the moai represented clan ancestors and that the ceremonies were part of an ancestor cult. Ahu were also burial sites, and some of the bodies were cremated. Whether these were bodies of deceased clan members or remains of sacrifices is unknown; oral tradition tells of sacrifice by fire.

Hare Paenga

Long and narrow, these houses resembled an upturned canoe, with a single narrow doorway at the middle of one side; the floor shape is outlined by rectangular blocks or curbstones with small hollows on their upper surfaces. To support the walls and roof, islanders inserted poles into these hollows, then arched them across the center of the structure and, where they crossed, lashed them to a ridgepole. These dwellings varied enormously in size; some could house more than 100 people, but others held but half a dozen. The foundations of hare paenga can be seen at the restored plaza at Ahu Tahai.

serves very good fish dishes, but service isn't always the friendliest.

Restaurant Pea (☎ 100-382; Av Policarpo Toro s/n; mains US$10), at Playa Pea, has fine tuna, steak and chicken dishes and friendly service. The ocean laps at the verandah here, and the restaurant has terrific views of the harbor and the small beach. Sandwiches

(US$4) are also available if you want the view at lower prices. For dessert, try the Polynesian Banana.

Entertainment
Aloha Pub (cnr Atamu Tekena & S Englert) has a pleasant atmosphere and is good for a drink and pub food. Shoot a game of pool at

---

Rapa Nui Antiquities

Moai
Although all moai are similar, few are identical. The standard moai at Rano Raraku has its base at about where the statue's hip would be. In general, the statues' arms hang stiffly, and the hands, with long slender fingers, extend across a protruding abdomen. The heads are elongated and rectangular, with heavy brows and prominent noses, small mouths with thin lips, prominent chins and elongated earlobes, which are often carved for inserted ear ornaments. Hands, breasts, navels and facial features are clear, and elaborately carved backs possibly represent tattoos. Moai mostly depicted males, but several specimens have carvings that clearly represent breasts and vulva.

Moai vary greatly in size; some are as short as 2m, and the longest is just under 21m. The usual length is from 5.5m to 7m.

Since the quarry at Rano Raraku contains moai at all stages of construction (the carvings were abandoned as work gradually ceased), it's easy to visualize the creation process. Most moai were carved face up, in a horizontal or slightly reclining position. Workers dug a channel large enough for the carvers around and under each moai, leaving the statue attached to the rock only along its back. Nearly all the carving occurred at this stage. The moai was then detached and somehow transported down the slope. At the base of the cliff at Rano Raraku, workers raised the moai into a standing position in trenches, where sculptors carved finer details on the back and decorated the waist with a belt surrounded by rings and symbols. Basalt *toki,* thousands of which once littered the quarry site, were the carving tools. In *Aku-Aku: The Secret of Easter Island,* Heyerdahl estimates that two teams working constantly in shifts would need perhaps 12 to 15 months to carve a medium-size moai.

When carving was finished, moai were moved to their coastal ahu (see the boxed text 'Moving the Moai,' later in this chapter). In total, islanders placed 300 moai on ahu or left them along the old roads in various parts of the island.

Topknots
Archaeologists believe that the reddish cylindrical topknots *(pukao)* on many moai reflect a male hairstyle once common on Rapa Nui. Quarried from the small crater at Puna Pau, the volcanic scoria from which pukao are made is relatively soft and easily worked.

Since only about 60 moai had topknots, and another 25 remain in or near the quarry, they appear to have been a late development. Carved like the moai, the topknots may have been simple embellishments, which were rolled to their final destination and then, despite weighing about as much as two elephants, somehow placed on top of the moai.

Moai Kavakava
Of all the carved figures that islanders produced, the most exotic are the moai kavakava, or the 'statues of ribs.' Each is a human figure carved in wood, with a large, thin and aquiline nose, protruding cheekbones that accentuate hollow cheeks, extended earlobes, and a goatee that curls back on the chin. Protruding ribs in a sunken abdomen imply starvation.

According to oral tradition, at Puna Pau, King Tuu-ko-ihu chanced upon two aku aku (sleeping ghosts) with beards, long hooked noses and pendulant earlobes reaching down to their necks. They were so thin that their ribs stood out. Tuu-ko-ihu returned home and carved their portrait in wood before he forgot their appearance, and since then islanders have always carved these statues.

Banana Pub *(Atamu Tekena)*, with cold beers and loud music.

Dancing through the night is a way of life here. **Toroko** *(Policarpo Toro)*, best on Thursday and Friday, jams with a mix of modern tunes and island pop. **Piditi** *(Av Hotu Matua)* is slightly less frenetic than Toroko and best on Saturday. The cover charge at both is about US$4, drinks are expensive, and nothing gets going until after 1am.

The elaborately costumed and talented group **Kari Kari** (☎ 100-595) performs island legends through song and dance 10pm on Wednesday and Saturday nights at the Hotel Hanga Roa (☎ 100-299), and 10pm Friday nights at the Hotel Iorana (☎ 100-312); check with your hotel or Sernatur for current schedules. Performances are followed by the obligatory 'let's watch the tourists dance this stuff' routine – which can be hilarious, until they pull *you* to the middle of the dance floor. Shows cost US$17. Buy tickets in advance during the busy season.

Shopping

Hanga Roa has numerous souvenir shops, mostly on Atamu Tekena (where they tend to be more expensive than elsewhere) and on Av Te Pito o Te Henua, leading up to the church. The best prices are at the open-air **Feria Municipal** *(cnr Atamu Tekena & Tu'u Maheke)*. The reconstructed **Mercado Artesanal** *(cnr Tuukoihu & Ara Roa Rakei)*, across from the church, has more choices. Both are open mornings and late afternoon Monday through Saturday.

For transit passengers or desperate last-minute shoppers, airport stalls have a selection of crafts and souvenirs, but prices are noticeably higher.

Look for small stone or carved wooden replicas of standard moai and moai kavakava, replicas of Rongo-Rongo tablets and cloth rubbings of them, and fragments of obsidian from Orito (sometimes made into earrings). It's possible to get custom-made carved stone moai of just about any reasonable size, though large ones take some time, and air freight may be prohibitively expensive. Ask at Sernatur for references.

Discourage reef destruction by not purchasing *any* coral products.

PN RAPA NUI

Since 1935, much of Easter Island's land and all the archaeological sites have been a na-tional park administered by Conaf, which charges admission *(non-Chileans US$11)* at Orongo, valid for the whole park for the length of one's stay. The park teems with caves, ahu, fallen moai, village structures and petroglyphs galore. Spending the extra cash on a guided tour or an islander who can explain what you are seeing is a very worthy investment. Respecting these sites is essential – avoid walking on the ahu (revered by locals as burial sites) or removing/relocating rocks of archaeological structures. Handle the land gently and the moai will smile upon you.

Although the government, in cooperation with foreign and Chilean archaeologists and local people, has done a remarkable job in restoring monuments and attracting visitors, it is worth mentioning that some islanders view the park as just another land grab on the part of colonialist invaders who differ little from Dutroux-Bornier or Williamson, Balfour & Company. Many islanders, however, work for Conaf and other government agencies.

Conaf *(☎ 100-236; open 8:30am-6pm Mon-Fri)* has a main office on the road to Rano Kau; there are ranger information stations at Orongo, Anakena and Rano Raraku. In case of emergency, rangers have two-way radios.

Northern Loop

West Coast Lined up along the island's west coast are four major ahu complexes. **Ahu Tautira** overlooks Caleta Hanga Roa, the fishing port in Hanga Roa at the foot of Av Te Pito o Te Henua. The torsos of two broken moai have been re-erected on the ahu.

A short walk north of Hanga Roa, **Ahu Tahai** is a site that contains three restored ahu, especially photogenic at sunset. North American archaeologist William Mulloy directed the restoration work in 1968. Ahu Tahai proper is the ahu in the middle, supporting a large, solitary moai with no topknot. On the north side of Ahu Tahai is Ahu Ko Te Riku, with a topknotted and eyeballed moai. Despite its size, it is relatively lightweight, only about a quarter the weight of the giant moai at Ahu Te Pito Kura on the north coast. On the other side is Ahu Vai Uri, which supports five moai of varying sizes. Along the hills are foundations of hare paenga and walls of 'chicken houses.'

Ahu Akapu, with its solitary moai, stands on the coast north of Ahu Tahai. North of

Around the Archaeological Sites

It's possible to take in all the major sites on three loops out of Hanga Roa – the Southwest Route, the Northern Loop and the Island Circuit. These three routes involve minimal backtracking.

Northern Loop

Take the route from Hanga Roa to the Puna Pau crater, source of the reddish volcanic scoria for the topknots of the moai. From here, continue inland to the seven moai of restored Ahu Akivi. From Ahu Akivi follow the track to Ahu Tepeu on the west coast, said to be the burial site of Tuu-ko-ihu. Then head south to Hanga Roa, stopping at Ahu Akapu, Ahu Tahai and Ahu Tautira, all of which have been restored and their moai re-erected. Because the trail-road is poorly marked between the coast and Ahu Akivi, it's easier to go from Hanga Roa to Ahu Akivi and then cut cross-country to Ahu Tepeu rather than the other way round.

Southwest Route

From Hanga Roa take the road south to the top of the Rano Kau crater and the Orongo ceremonial village. Backtrack to Hanga Roa; then follow the road, called Av Hotu Matua in town, along the northern edge of the airport to Orito, site of the old obsidian quarries. From here head southward to Ahu Vinapu, with its impressive, finely cut stonework.

Northeast Circuit

From Hanga Roa, follow the southern coast, stopping at Vaihu and Akahanga, with their massive ahu and giant toppled moai. Continue east from Akahanga and detour inland to Rano Raraku, source of the volcanic tuff for most of the island's moai. Leaving Rano Raraku, follow the road east to recently restored Ahu Tongariki, whose moai and masonry were hurled some distance inland by a massive tsunami after the earthquake of 1960.

From Tongariki, follow the road to the north coast to Ahu Te Pito Kura, which boasts the largest moai ever erected on an ahu. Continue west to the beach at Ovahe and then to Anakena, the island's main beach and the site of two more restored ahu. The paved road returns to Hanga Roa from here.

EASTER ISLAND

here, the road is rough but passable if you drive slowly.

Four kilometers north of Tahai is **Ahu Tepeu**. To the northeast rises Maunga Terevaka, the island's highest point, and to the south is a large grassy plain over a jagged lava flow. To the west, the Pacific Ocean breaks against rugged cliffs up to 50m high. The seaward side of the ahu is its most interesting feature, with a wall about 3m high near the center composed of large, vertically placed stone slabs. A number of moai once stood on the ahu, but all have fallen. Immediately east is an extensive village site with foundations of several large boat-shaped houses and the walls of several round houses, consisting of loosely piled stones.

Ana Te Pahu After visiting the moai along the coast, you can follow the faint, rough but passable track to Ana Te Pahu, a site of former cave dwellings whose entrance is via a garden planted with sweet potatoes, taro, bananas and other plants from the Polyne-

sian horticultural complex. The caves here are lava tubes, created when rock solidified around a flowing stream of molten lava.

Ahu Akivi This inland ahu, restored in 1960 by a group headed by Mulloy and Chilean archaeologist Gonzalo Figueroa, sports seven moai. Unlike most others, these look out to sea, but like all moai they overlook the site of a village. The site has proved to have astronomical significance: at the equinoxes, the seven statues look directly at the setting sun.

In raising the moai, Mulloy and Figueroa used methods similar to those used at Ahu Ature Huki (see Anakena later in this chapter) and steadily improved their speed and technique. Mulloy later wrote:

Clearly the prehistoric islanders with their hundreds of years of repetition of the same task must have known many more tricks than modern imitators were able to learn.

Mulloy believed that the large number of stones in front of Ahu Akahanga on the south coast were leftovers of stones used to raise the moai, and that one moai appeared to have fallen sideways in the process. He also pointed to the tremendous numbers of stones near many ahu, including Ahu Te Pito Kura, as evidence that the moai may have been erected using stones for support.

Mulloy calculated that 30 men working eight hours a day for a year could have carved the moai and topknot at Ahu Te Pito Kura, and 90 men could have transported it from the quarry over a previously prepared road in two months and raised it in about three months.

Puna Pau The small volcanic crater at Puna Pau has a relatively soft, easily worked reddish scoria from which the pukao were made. Some 60 of these were transported to sites round the island, and another 25 remain in or near the quarry.

Southwest Route

Orongo Ceremonial Village Nearly covered in a bog of floating totora reeds, the crater lake of Rano Kau appears to be a giant witch's cauldron. Perched 400m above, on the edge of the crater wall, the ceremonial village of Orongo occupies one of the island's most dramatic landscapes. Despite its ceremonial significance, it's a much later construction than the great moai and ahu. It is also demonstrably fragile, and visitors should keep to beaten paths and step carefully.

From the winding dirt road that climbs from Hanga Roa to Orongo, there are spectacular views of the entire island. Orongo, overlooking several small *motu* (offshore islands), was the focus of an islandwide bird cult linked to the gods Makemake and Haua in the 18th and 19th centuries.

Partly restored, the Orongo ceremonial village occupies a magnificent site overlooking the ocean. Built into the side of the slope, the houses have walls of horizontally overlapping stone slabs, with an earth-covered arched roof of similar materials, giving the appearance of being partly subterranean. Since walls are thick and have to support the roof's weight, the doorway is a low narrow tunnel, barely high enough to crawl through. At the edge of the crater is a cluster of boulders carved with numerous birdman petroglyphs with a long beak and a hand clutching an egg.

A short distance before the ceremonial village, a footpath descends into the crater, where the dense vegetation includes abandoned orange trees and grapevines, whose fruit local people collect in autumn. It is possible to hike around the crater, but it is slow

---

The Birdman Cult

Makemake, the birdman cult's supreme deity, is said to have created the earth, sun, moon, stars and people, rewarded the good and punished the evil, and expressed his anger in thunder. In times of trouble, he required the sacrifice of a child. Makemake is also credited with bringing the birds and presumably the bird cult to Rapa Nui, although Haua, another deity, aided him in this venture.

No complete record of the cult's ceremonies exists, and there are conflicting accounts with respect to schedules and duration. At a given time, worshipers would move up to Orongo, where they lived in stone houses, recited prayers, made offerings, held rites to appease the gods and participated in fertility dances.

The climax of the ceremonies was a competition to obtain the first egg of the sooty tern *(Sterna fuscata)*, which bred on the tiny islets of Motu Nui, Motu Iti and Motu Kao Kao, just off Cabo Te Manga. Each contestant or his *hopu* (stand-in) would descend the cliff face from Orongo and, with the aid of a small reed *pora* (raft), swim out to the islands. He who found the first egg became birdman for the ensuing year. If a hopu found the egg, he called out his master's name to a man in a cave in the cliffs below Orongo. The fortunate master's head, eyebrows and eyelashes were then shaved. His face was painted red and black, and he became birdman and was sequestered in a special house. The reasons for the birdman's celebrity are vague, but whoever found the first egg certainly won the favor of Makemake and great status in the community. The last ceremonies took place at Orongo in 1866 or 1867, a few years after the Peruvian slave raid that decimated the native community in 1862.

going – give yourself a full day and take plenty to drink, since the water in the crater lake is muddy and brackish.

Admission (US$11) to the Orongo ceremonial village is collected by rangers at the site. These fees are valid for the length of your stay.

Walking or cycling is possible, but it's a rather steep 9km trip from town.

Ahu Vinapu For Ahu Vinapu, follow the road from Mataveri Airport to the end of the runway. Then follow the road south between the airstrip and some large oil tanks to an opening in a stone wall. A sign points to nearby Ahu Vinapu, where there are two major ahu.

Both once supported moai that are now broken and lying facedown. Accounts by 18th- and early-19th-century visitors suggest that the moai were not overturned simultaneously but were all tipped over by the mid-19th century. Some had their foundations undermined, and others may have been pulled down with ropes.

One interesting find is a long brick-red stone, shaped rather like a four-sided column, standing in front of one of the ahu. Closer inspection reveals a headless moai with short legs, unlike the mostly legless moai elsewhere, resembling pre-Inka column statues in the Andes. Originally, this was a forked, two-headed moai between whose heads ran a wooden platform on which islanders placed corpses that, when desiccated, were finally interred.

Orito The early Rapanui made weapons from hard black obsidian quarried at Orito. The *mataa,* a common artifact, was a crudely shaped blade of obsidian used as a spearhead; embedded in the edges of flat wooden clubs, such blades made deadly weapons. Nonlethal artifacts included obsidian files and drill bits that would have been attached to a wooden shaft and used to drill bone, wood or stone.

From the slopes of Rano Kau, the quarry resembles an enormous gray rectangle on Orito's southern slope, but quarrying actually took place around its whole circumference. Orito is not the only obsidian quarry – there are others on Motu Iti off Cabo Te Manga, and another on the northeast edge of the Rano Kau crater.

Northeast Circuit

This loop takes in the three finest sites on the island and can be done in a long day with motorized transport. It's good to go counterclockwise, because Rano Raraku is a magnificent highlight in the late afternoon.

South Coast On the south coast, east of Ahu Vinapu, enormous ruined ahu and their fallen moai testify to the impact of warfare. Ahu Vaihu has eight large moai that have been toppled and now lie facedown, their topknots scattered nearby. Akahanga is a large ahu with large fallen moai, and across the bay is a second ahu with several more. On the hill slopes opposite are the remains of a village, including foundations of several boat-shaped houses and ruins of several round houses.

Also on the coast, the almost completely ruined Ahu Hanga Tetenga has two large moai, both toppled and broken into fragments. Just beyond Hanga Tetenga, a faint track off the main road branches inland toward the crater quarry of Rano Raraku, which is readily visible.

Rano Raraku Known as 'the nursery,' the volcano of Rano Raraku is the quarry for the hard tuff from which the moai were cut. Moai in all stages of progress cover its southern slopes and the crater, which contains a small lake. Most moai on the south slope are upright but buried up to their shoulders or necks in the earth, so that only their heads gaze across the grassy slopes. Park near the entrance gate (located in a stone wall). A trail leads up a slope from the gate to a 21m giant – the largest moai ever carved. Follow a trail to the right to several other large moai still attached to the rock, or turn left along the trail that leads over the rim and into the crater. At the top is a fabulous 360-degree view.

Within the crater are about 20 standing moai, a number of fallen ones and others only partly finished – about 80 in all. On the outer slope stand another 50. Note also the great holes at the crater rim that were used to maneuver the statues down the crater rim.

At the foot of the mountain and on the seaward plain lie another 30 moai, all fallen and, with few exceptions, facedown. In the quarries above are about 160 unfinished moai; this means that, when work stopped, some 320 moai had been completed but not yet erected on ahu, or were being worked on. The total

EASTER ISLAND

Moving the Moai

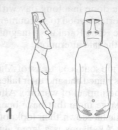

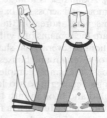

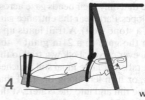

Just moving the moai (figure 1) to the site must have been an even greater problem than removing them from the rock and lowering them down the cliff. Legend says that priests moved the moai by the power of *mana*, an ability to make a moai walk a short distance every day until eventually it reached its destination. After suggestions that islanders could have moved the moai with a Y-shaped sledge made from a forked tree trunk, pulled with ropes made from tree bark, Thor Heyerdahl organized 180 islanders to pull a 4m moai across the field at Anakena and speculated that they could have moved a much larger one with wooden runners and more labor. Another explanation is that islanders inserted round stones under the moai, which were pushed, pulled and rolled to their destinations like a block on marbles, but this fails to explain how they were moved without harming the fine details carved at the quarry.

North American archaeologist William Mulloy proposed a different method of moving the moai that, though difficult, would have been physically possible with enough labor and is consistent with the shape and configuration of the moai. First, islanders would have fitted a wooden sledge to the moai (figure 2); the distribution of the statue's weight would have kept the relatively light and fragile head above ground when tipped over. The islanders would then have set up a bipod astride the statue's neck, at an angle to the vertical (figures 3 & 4) and tied a cable attached to the moai's neck to the bipod's apex and pulled it forward. The head of the moai would then rise slightly and the moai would be dragged forward. When the bipod passed vertical, the statue's own weight would carry it forward along its belly. By moving the legs of the bipod forward, the entire process could be repeated.

This repetitive series of upward and forward movements recalls the islanders' legend that the moai 'walked' to their ahu. It could also explain broken moai along the old transport routes; the rope or bipod may have slipped or broken when the moai was raised, and the statue fallen to the ground.

More recently, Charles Love and Joanne van Tilburg have experimented with moving statues on a sledgelike apparatus pushed along on rollers, and there is a broad consensus for this approach. Though it's unlikely the details will ever be known – feasibility doesn't prove the Mulloy and Love–van Tilburg methods were the actual means of moving the moai – both methods are theoretically possible.

Once at its ahu, the moai had to be raised onto an elevated platform. Restoration of seven moai in the 1960s by Mulloy and Gonzalo Figueroa (see Ahu Akivi earlier in this chapter) suggests that leverage and support with rocks may indeed have raised the moai.

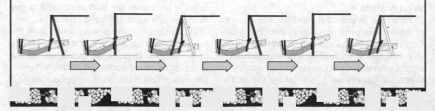

number of moai from the Rano Raraku quarries is nearly a thousand, but there may be evidence of even more in the mounds at the quarry.

A unique discovery at Rano Raraku is the kneeling Moai Tukuturi, which was almost totally buried when found. Slightly less than 4m high, it now sits on the southeastern slope of the mountain. Placing it upright required a Jeep, tackle, poles, ropes, chains and 20 workers. It has a fairly natural rounded head, a goatee, short ears, and a full body squatting on its heels, with forearms and hands resting on its thighs. It has a low brow with curved eyebrows, hollow and slightly oval eyes, and pupils marked by small, round cavities. Both the nose and lips are considerably damaged, but the cheeks are round and natural.

Ahu Tongariki Between 1992 and 1995, the Japanese company Tadano re-erected 15 moai at this site, the largest ahu ever built, east of Rano Raraku. A 1960 tsunami, produced by an earthquake between Rapa Nui and the South American mainland, had flattened the statues and scattered several topknots far inland. Only one topknot has been returned to its place atop a moai.

Several petroglyphs, near the bend of the road some distance from the moai, include figures of a turtle with a human face, a tuna fish, a birdman motif and Rongo-Rongo figures.

Península Poike The eastern end of the island is a high plateau called Península Poike, crowned by the extinct volcano Maunga Pu A Katiki. Its western boundary is a narrow depression called Ko Te Ava o Iko (Iko's Trench), which runs across the peninsula from north to south.

According to legend, this was a manmade trench that served a defensive function during clan warfare. Filled with branches and tree trunks, it was ready to be set on fire in event of an invasion from the west, but espionage allowed the invaders to penetrate the line and drive the defenders into their own firepit.

There is now consensus, though, that the legend was just that, a legend. While excavations revealed thick layers of ash and charcoal – evidence of a fire that produced very intense heat or else burned for some time – archaeologists have found no evidence of weapons, tools or bones that would have in-

dicated a battlefield site. Once covered with a giant palm forest, Poike could have been the site of a natural conflagration that left extensive charcoal remains.

Ahu Te Pito Kura On the north coast, overlooking a fishing cove at Bahía La Perouse (look for the sign by the road), is the largest moai ever moved from Rano Raraku and erected on an ahu. According to oral history, a certain widow erected the moai to represent her dead husband; it was perhaps the last moai to fall, although Heyerdahl's expedition has made that claim for the moai re-erected at Anakena. In height, proportion and general appearance it resembles the tall moai still buried up to their necks at Rano Raraku. If those standing at the quarry site are the last to have been made, the Te Pito Kura moai was probably the last erected on an ahu.

Nearly 10m long, the moai lies facedown on the inland slope of the platform. Its ears alone are more than 2m long. A topknot – oval rather than round as at Vinapu – lies nearby. The sheer density of remains at sites like nearby Hanga Hoonu is even more impressive.

The ahu's name comes from a particular stone called *te pito kura,* presumably meaning 'navel of light,' and legend claims that Hotu Matua himself brought this stone, symbolizing the navel of the world. The stone is magnetic and is about 40 meters to the left of the fallen moai.

Ovahe At Ovahe, between La Perouse and Anakena, is a small, attractive and less-frequented beach than Anakena, with interesting caves.

Anakena This sheltered, white-sand beach is Rapa Nui's largest; it's very popular for swimming and sunbathing. Anakena is a nice place to spend the afternoon or to overnight at Conaf's pleasant campground; bring food and water from Hanga Roa. A couple of concessionaires operate on the beach, but you won't want to depend on them for the basics. Conaf provides drinking water at its campground but has been known to run out.

Anakena Beach is the storied landing place of Hotu Matua. One of several caves is said to have been Hotu Matua's dwelling as he waited for completion of his boat-shaped house.

EASTER ISLAND

On the hillside above Playa Anakena stands **Ahu Ature Huki** and its lone moai, re-erected by Thor Heyerdahl and islanders. In *Aku-Aku: The Secret of Easter Island*, Heyerdahl described raising the moai onto its ahu with wooden poles:

The men got the tips of their poles in underneath it, and while three or four men hung and heaved at the farthest end of each pole, the mayor lay flat on his stomach and pushed small stones under the huge face…When evening came the giant's head had been lifted a good three feet from the ground, while the space beneath was packed tight with stones.

The process continued for nine days, the giant on an angle supported by stones and the logs being levered with ropes when the men could no longer reach them. After another nine days and the efforts of a dozen people, the moai finally stood upright and unsupported.

During the excavation and restoration of Anakena's Ahu Nau Nau in 1979, researchers learned that the moai were not 'blind' but actually had inlaid coral and rock eyes, some of which were reconstructed from fragments at the site. Of the seven moai at Ahu Nau Nau, four have topknots, while only the torsos remain of two others. Fragments of torsos and heads lie in front of the ahu.

Fundo Vaitea Midway between Anakena and Hanga Roa, Vaitea was the center of food and livestock production under Dutroux-Bornier and Williamson, Balfour & Company, who used the island as a gigantic sheep farm. The large building on the east side of the road is the former shearing shed. The property on the west side belongs to Corfo, which raises fruit and vegetables, but may be returned to the islanders.

Language

Every visitor to Chile should attempt to learn some Spanish, whose basic elements are easily acquired. If possible, take a short course before you go. Even if you can't do so, Chileans are gracious hosts and will encourage your Spanish, so there is no need to feel self-conscious about vocabulary or pronunciation. There are many common cognates, so if you're stuck, try Hispanicizing an English word – it is unlikely you'll make a truly embarrassing error. Do not, however, admit to being *embarazada* (which sounds like 'embarrassed') unless you are in fact pregnant!

Note that in American Spanish, the plural of the familiar *tu* is *ustedes* rather than *vosotros*, as in Spain. Chileans and other Latin Americans readily understand Castilian Spanish, but may find it either quaint or pretentious.

Chilean Spanish

Chile is not known for having eloquent Spanish. Even those fluent in Spanish as a second language will be stumped by the multitude of slang that Chileans use and the ofttimes confusing pronunciation. Chilean speakers relax terminal and even some internal consonants almost to the point of disappearance, so that it can be difficult to distinguish plural from singular. For example, *las islas* (the islands) may sound more like 'la ila' to an English speaker. Chileans speak rather more rapidly than other South Americans, and rather less clearly – the conventional *¿quieres?* (Do you want?) sounds more like 'querí' on the tongue of a Chilean.

Other Chilean peculiarities include pronunciation of the second person familiar of 'ar' verbs as 'ai' rather than 'as', so that, for instance, *¿Adónde vas?* (Where are you going?) will sound more like '*¿Adónde vai?*' More so in the south, speakers shorten the common interjection *pués* (meaning 'well', 'certainly') to 'pueh' or 'po' and add it as filler in sentences or at ends of words for emphasis, such as *sí po* or *No po*. Other vernacular includes *¿Cachai?/Te cacho*, meaning 'Do you get it (understand)?/I get it; *fome*, boring, drab; *luca*, a thousand pesos; and *pasarlo chancho*, have a great time. The most used slang term is *huevón*, which has been diluted from its literal meaning of 'big balls' to mean 'dude' or used as a verb, as in *No me hueves*, or shortened to *No me hue*, 'Don't fuck with me' or 'Don't put me on.' *Así con la hueva pu huevón* means, well, nothing really; ask a Chileno to explain it to you.

Vocabulary There are many differences in vocabulary between Castilian and American Spanish, and among Spanish-speaking countries in the Americas. There are also considerable regional differences within these countries not attributable to accent alone – Chilean speech, for instance, contains many words adopted from Mapuche, while the residents of Santiago sometimes use *coa*, a working-class slang. Check the glossary for some of these terms.

Chileans and other South Americans normally refer to the Spanish language as *castellano* rather than *español*.

Phrasebooks & Dictionaries

Lonely Planet's *Latin American Spanish Phrasebook*, by Anna Cody, is a worthwhile addition to your backpack. Another exceptionally useful resource is the *University of Chicago Spanish-English, English-Spanish Dictionary*, whose small size, light weight and thorough entries make it ideal for travel.

Visitors confident of their Spanish (and judgment) can tackle John Brennan's and Alvaro Taboada's *How to Survive in the Chilean Jungle* (1996), jointly published by Dolmen Ediciones and the Instituto Chileno Norteamericano, an enormously popular book that has gone through nine editions explaining Chilean slang to the naïve.

Pronunciation

Spanish pronunciation is, in general, consistently phonetic. Once you are aware of the basic rules, they should cause little difficulty. Speak slowly to avoid getting tongue-tied until you become confident of your ability.

Pronunciation of the letters f, k, l, n, p, q, s and t is virtually identical with English, and y is identical when used as a consonant; *ll* is a separate letter, pronounced as y and coming after l in the alphabet. *Ch* and *ñ* are also separate letters; in the alphabet they come after c and n respectively.

Vowels Spanish vowels are very consistent and have easy English equivalents:

a is like the *a* in 'father'
e is like the *e* in 'met'; at the end of a word, it's like the 'ey' in 'hey'
i is like 'ee' in 'feet'
o is like *o* in 'for'
u is like 'oo' in 'boot'; after consonants other than *q*, it is more like English *w*
y is a consonant except when it stands alone or appears at the end of a word, in which case its pronunciation is identical to the Spanish *i*

Consonants Spanish consonants generally resemble their English equivalents, but there are some major exceptions:

b resembles its English equivalent, but is indistinguishable from *v;* for clarification, refer to the former as 'b larga,' the latter as 'b corta' (the word for the letter itself is pronounced like the English 'bay')
c is like the *s* in 'see' before *e* and *i;* otherwise like an English *k*
d closely resembles 'th' in 'feather'
g before *e* and *i* is like a guttural English *h;* otherwise like *g* in 'go'
h is invariably silent; if your name begins with this letter, listen carefully when immigration officials summon you to pick up your passport
j most closely resembles an English *h,* but is slightly more guttural
ñ is like 'ni' in 'onion'
r is nearly identical to English except at the beginning of a word, when it is often rolled
rr is very strongly rolled
v resembles English, but see *b,* above
x is like *x* in 'taxi' except for very few words when it follows Spanish or Mexican usage as *j*
z is like *s* in 'sun'

Diphthongs These sounds are combinations of two vowels which form a single syllable. In Spanish, the formation of a diphthong depends on combinations of 'weak' vowels *(i* and *u)* or strong ones *(a, e* and *o).* Two weak vowels or a strong and a weak vowel make a diphthong, but two strong ones are separate syllables.

A good example of two weak vowels forming a diphthong is the word *diurno* (during the day). The final syllable of *obligatorio* (obligatory) is a combination of weak and strong vowels.

Stress Often indicated by visible accents, stress is very important, since it can change the meaning of words. In general, words ending in vowels or the letters *n* or *s* have stress on the next-to-last syllable, while those with other endings have stress on the last syllable. Thus, the words *cerveza* (beer) and *caballos* (horses) both have stress on their next-to-last syllables.

Visible accents, which can occur anywhere in a word, dictate stress over these general rules. Thus *sótano* (basement), *América* and *porción* (portion) all have the stress on the syllable with the accented vowel. When words are written all in capitals, the accent is often not shown, but it still affects the pronunciation nonetheless.

Basic Grammar

Nouns in Spanish are masculine or feminine. The definite article ('the' in English) agrees with the noun in gender and number; for example, the Spanish word for 'train' is masculine, so 'the train' is *el tren,* and the plural is *los trenes.* The word for 'house' is feminine, so 'the house' is *la casa,* and the plural is *las casas.* The indefinite articles (a, an, some) work in the same way: *un libro* (a book) is masculine singular, while *una carta* (a letter) is feminine singular. Most nouns ending in *o* are masculine and those ending in *a* are generally feminine. Normally, nouns ending in a vowel add *s* to form the plural – *unos libros* (some books), *las cartas* (the letters) – while those ending in a consonant add *es: los reyes* (the kings) is the plural of *el rey.* Gender also affects demonstrative pronouns: *este* is the masculine form of 'this,' while *esta* is the feminine form and *esto* the neuter; 'these,' 'that' and 'those' are formed by adding *s.*

Adjectives also agree with the noun in gender and number, and usually come after the noun. Possessive adjectives like *mi* (my), *tu* (your) and *su* (his/her/their) agree with the thing possessed, not with the possessor. For example 'his suitcase' is *su maleta,* while 'his suitcases' is *sus maletas.* A simple way to indicate possession is to use the preposition *de* (of). 'Juan's room,' for instance, would be *la habitación de Juan,* literally, 'the room of Juan.'

Personal pronouns are usually not used with verbs, except for clarification or emphasis. There are three main categories of verbs: those that end in 'ar' such as *hablar* (to speak), those that end in 'er' such as *comer* (to eat), and those that end in 'ir' such as *reir* (to laugh); there are many irregular verbs, such as *ir* (to go) and *venir* (to come).

To form a comparative, add *más* (more) or *menos* (less) before the adjective. For example, *alto* is 'high,' *más alto* 'higher' and *lo más alto* 'the highest.'

Greetings & Civilities
In their public behavior, Chileans are exceptionally polite and expect others to reciprocate. Never, for example, approach a stranger for information without extending a greeting like *buenos días* or *buenas tardes.* Most young people use the informal *tú* and its associated verb forms among themselves, but if in doubt, you should use the more formal *usted* and its forms.

hello	*hola*
good morning	*buenos días*
good afternoon	*buenas tardes*
good evening, night	*buenas noches*
good-bye	*adiós, chau*
please	*por favor*
thank you	*gracias*
you're welcome	*de nada*

Useful Words & Phrases
yes	*sí*
no	*no*
and	*y*
to/at	*a*
for	*por, para*
of/from	*de, desde*
in	*en*
with	*con*
without	*sin*
before	*antes*
after	*después*
soon	*pronto*
already	*ya*
now	*ahora*
right away	*en seguida, al tiro*
here	*aquí*
there	*allí*
Where?	*¿Dónde?*
Where is...?	*¿Dónde está...?*

Where are...?	*¿Dónde están...?*
When?	*¿Cuando?*
How?	*¿Cómo?*
I would like...	*Me gustaría...*
coffee	*café*
tea	*té*
beer	*cerveza*
How much?	*¿Cuanto?*
How many?	*¿Cuantos?*

I understand.   *Entiendo.*
I don't understand.   *No entiendo*
I don't speak much Spanish.
    No hablo mucho castellano.
Is there...? Are there...?
    ¿Hay...?

Getting Around
plane	*avión*
train	*tren*
bus	*ómnibus,* or just *bus*
small bus	*colectivo, micro, liebre*
ship	*barco, buque*
car	*auto*
taxi	*taxi*
truck	*camión*
pickup	*camioneta*
bicycle	*bicicleta*
motorcycle	*motocicleta*
hitchhike	*hacer dedo*
airport	*aeropuerto*
train station	*estación de ferrocarril*
bus terminal	*terminal de buses*
first/second class	*primera/segunda clase*
one-way/roundtrip	*ida/ida y vuelta*
left luggage	*guardería, equipaje*
tourist office	*oficina de turismo*

I would like a ticket to....
    Quiero un boleto/pasaje a....
What's the fare to...?
    ¿Cuanto cuesta el pasaje a...?
When does the next plane/train/bus
    leave for...?
    ¿Cuando sale el próximo avión/tren/
                ómnibus para...?
student/university discount
    descuento estudiantil/universitario
first/last/next
    primero/último/próximo

Accommodations
hotel	*hotel, pensión, residencial*
single room	*habitación single*

double room	habitación doble
per night	por noche
full board	pensión completa
shared bath	baño compartido
private bath	baño privado
too expensive	demasiado caro
cheaper	mas económico
May I see it?	¿Puedo verlo?
I don't like it.	No me gusta.
the bill	la cuenta

What does it cost?
  ¿Cuanto cuesta?
Can you give me a deal?
  ¿Me puede hacer precio?

Toilets

The most common word for 'toilet' is baño, but servicios sanitarios, or just servicios (services) is a frequent alternative. Men's toilets will usually bear a descriptive term such as hombres, caballeros or varones. Women's toilets will say señoras or damas.

Post & Communications

post office	correo
letter	carta
parcel	paquete
postcard	postal
airmail	correo aéreo
registered mail	certificado
stamps	estampillas
person to person	persona a persona
collect call	cobro revertido

Geographical Expressions

These are among the most common you will encounter in this book and in maps.

bay	bahía
bridge	puente
farm	fundo, hacienda
glacier	glaciar, ventisquero
highway	carretera, camino, ruta
hill	cerro
lake	lago
marsh, estuary	estero
mount	cerro
mountain range	cordillera
national park	parque nacional
pass	paso
ranch	estancia
river	río
sound	seno
waterfall	cascada, salto

Countries

The list below includes only countries whose spelling differs in English and Spanish.

Canada	Canadá
Denmark	Dinamarca
England	Inglaterra
France	Francia
Germany	Alemania
Great Britain	Gran Bretaña
Ireland	Irlanda
Italy	Italia
Japan	Japón
Netherlands	Holanda
New Zealand	Nueva Zelandia
Peru	Perú
Scotland	Escocia
Spain	España
Sweden	Suecia
Switzerland	Suiza
United States	Estados Unidos
Wales	Gales

I am from....
  Soy de....
Where are you from?
  ¿De dónde viene?
Where do you live?
  ¿Dónde vive?

Cardinal Numbers

1	uno
2	dos
3	tres
4	cuatro
5	cinco
6	seis
7	siete
8	ocho
9	nueve
10	diez
11	once
12	doce
13	trece
14	catorce
15	quince
16	dieciseis
17	diecisiete
18	dieciocho
19	diecinueve
20	veinte
21	veintiuno
22	veintidós
23	veintitrés
24	veinticuatro

25	*veinticinco*
30	*treinta*
31	*treinta y uno*
32	*treinta y dos*
33	*treinta y tres*
40	*cuarenta*
41	*cuarenta y uno*
42	*cuarenta y dos*
50	*cincuenta*
51	*cincuenta y uno*
52	*cincuenta y dos*
60	*sesenta*
70	*setenta*
80	*ochenta*
90	*noventa*
100	*cien*
101	*ciento uno*
102	*ciento dos*
110	*ciento diez*
120	*ciento veinte*
130	*ciento treinta*
200	*doscientos*
300	*trescientos*
400	*cuatrocientos*
500	*quinientos*
600	*seiscientos*
700	*setecientos*
800	*ochocientos*
900	*novecientos*
1000	*mil*
1100	*mil cien*
1200	*mil doscientos*
2000	*dos mil*
5000	*cinco mil*
10,000	*diez mil*
50,000	*cincuenta mil*
100,000	*cien mil*
1,000,000	*un millón*

Ordinal Numbers

1st	*primero/a*
2nd	*segundo/a*
3rd	*tercero/a*
4th	*cuarto/a*
5th	*quinto/a*
6th	*sexto/a*
7th	*séptimo/a*
8th	*octavo/a*
9th	*noveno/a*
10th	*décimo/a*
11th	*undécimo/a*
12th	*duodécimo/a*

Days of the Week

Monday	*lunes*
Tuesday	*martes*
Wednesday	*miércoles*
Thursday	*jueves*
Friday	*viernes*
Saturday	*sábado*
Sunday	*domingo*

Time

Eight o'clock is *las ocho,* while 8:30 is *las ocho y treinta* (literally, 'eight and thirty') or *las ocho y media* ('eight and a half'). However, 7:45 is *las ocho menos quince* (literally, 'eight minus fifteen') or *las ocho menos cuarto* ('eight minus one-quarter').

Times are modified by morning *(de la mañana)* or afternoon *(de la tarde)* instead of 'am' or 'pm.' It is also common to use the 24-hour clock.

What time is it?   *¿Qué hora es?*
It is….   *Es la una….*
                     or *Son las….*

Glossary

This list includes common geographical and biological terms as well as general terms from everyday speech. RN indicates that a term is a Rapa Nui (Easter Island) usage.

aerosilla – chairlift

afuerino – casual farm laborer

aguas – herbal teas; most commonly referred to as *aguitas*

ahu (RN) – large stone platforms on which *moai* (statues) were erected

alameda – avenue or boulevard lined with trees, particularly poplars

albergue juvenil – youth hostel

almuerzo – lunch

alpaca – *Lama pacos,* a wool-bearing domestic camelid of the central Andes, related to the llama but with finer and more valuable wool

altiplano – high plains of northern Chile, Bolivia, southern Peru and northwestern Argentina that are generally higher than 4000m

anexo – telephone extension

apapa (RN) – stone ramp used to launch boats

apunamiento – altitude sickness

Araucanians – major grouping of indigenous peoples, including the Mapuche, Picunche and Pehuenche Indians

arroyo – watercourse

ascensores – picturesque funiculars that connect the center of Valparaíso with its hillside neighborhoods

ayllu – indigenous community of the Norte Grande; ayllus are more kinship-based rather than geographical, although they usually possess community lands

Aymara – indigenous inhabitants of the Andean altiplano of Peru, Bolivia and northern Chile

bahía – bay

balneario – bathing resort or beach

barrio – neighborhood or borough

bencina – petrol or gasoline

bencina blanca – white gas used for camping stoves; usually available in hardware stores or chemical supply shops

bidón – spare fuel container

bodega – cellar or storage area for wine

bofedal – swampy alluvial pasture in the altiplano, used by Aymara to graze alpacas

boleadoras – weapon of round stones joined by a leather strap, used by Patagonian Indians for hunting guanaco and rhea; also called *bolas*

boleto inteligente – multitrip ticket for Santiago Metro; also known as *boleto valor*

cabildo – colonial town council

cacique – Indian chieftain

calefón – hot water heater; in most inexpensive accommodations, travelers must ask to have the calefón turned on before taking a shower

caleta – small cove

caliche – hardpan of the pampas of the Norte Grande; a dry, hard layer of clay beneath the soil surface from which mineral nitrates are extracted

callampas – shantytowns on the outskirts of Santiago, literally 'mushrooms,' since they seemed to spring up overnight around the capital. Some have now become well-established neighborhoods.

cama – bed; also a sleeper-class seat on a bus or train

camanchaca – dense convective fog on the hills of the coastal Atacama Desert; the camanchaca usually dissipates in late morning and returns with the sea breeze in late afternoon

camarote – sleeper class on a ship or ferry

caracoles – winding roads, usually in a mountainous area; literally 'snails' or 'spirals'

carretera – highway

casa de cambio – money exchange house that usually buys foreign cash and traveler's checks

casa de familia – modest family accommodations, usually in tourist centers

casco – 'big house' on a *fundo* or *estancia*

casino de bomberos – in many Chilean cities and towns, a fire-station restaurant, often run by a concessionaire, offering excellent meals at reasonable prices

cena – dinner

cerro – hill

certificado – registered, as in mail

chachacoma – *Senecio graveolens,* a native Andean plant; Aymara Indians brew a tea from the leaves that helps to relieve altitude sickness

charqui – dried llama or alpaca meat

chifa – Chinese restaurant; the term is most commonly used in the Norte Grande

Chilote – inhabitant of the archipelago of Chiloé; in certain contexts, the term has the connotation of 'bumpkin' despite the islands' rich cultural traditions

ciervo – deer

cine arte – arts cinema (in contrast to mass commercial cinema), generally found only in Santiago and at universities

ciudad – city

cobro revertido – reverse-charge (collect) phone call

cochayuyo – a variety of kelp

Codelco – Corporación del Cobre, the state-owned enterprise that oversees Chile's copper mining industry

colación – lunch

colectivo – shared taxi, also called *taxi colectivo*

comedor – inexpensive market restaurant; also, dining room of a hotel

comida corrida – a cheap set meal

comparsa – group of musicians or dancers

comuna – local governmental unit, largely administrative in the very centralized Chilean state

confitería – confectioner's shop

con gas – 'with gas'; carbonated, as in soft drinks

congregación – in colonial Latin America, the concentration of dispersed native populations in settlements, usually for political control or religious instruction; see also *reducción*

congrio – conger eel, a popular and delicious seafood

cordillera – chain of mountains, mountain range

costanera – coastal road; any road along a sea coast, riverside or lakeshore

criollo – in colonial times, a person of Spanish parentage born in the New World

curanto – Chilean seafood stew

desayuno – breakfast

desierto florido – in the Norte Chico, the flowering of dormant wildflower seeds in the desert during a rare year of heavy rainfall

DINA – Directoria de Inteligencia Nacional, or National Intelligence Directorate: umbrella organization created after the 1973 coup to oversee intelligence services of the police, army, navy and air force; it operated mainly as a secret police force to repress dissidents and maintained the detention centers where prisoners were routinely tortured

elaboración artesanal – small-scale production, often by a family

encomendero – individual Spaniard or Spanish institution (such as the Catholic Church) that exploited Indian labor under the *encomienda* system

encomienda – colonial labor system under which Indian communities had to provide workers for *encomenderos*, in exchange for which the encomendero was to provide religious and language instruction; in practice, the system benefited the encomendero far more than native peoples

esquí en marcha – cross-country skiing

estancia – extensive cattle- or sheep-grazing establishment with a dominant owner or manager and dependent resident labor force

estero – estuary

feria – artisans' market

Frontera – region of pioneer settlement, between the Río Biobío and the Río Toltén, dominated by Araucanian Indians until the late 19th century

fuerte – fort

fundo – Chilean term for hacienda, usually applied to a smaller irrigated unit in the country's central heartland

garúa – coastal desert fog; see also *camanchaca*

geoglyph – in the Norte Grande, pre-Columbian figures or abstract designs made by grouping dark stones over light-colored soil on hillside sites

golfo – gulf

golpe de estado – coup d'état, a sudden, illegal seizure of government

guanaco – member of the wild camelid (*Lama guanicoe*) family found in southern Chile; the term also applied to a type of police water cannon used in street protests

hacendado – owner of a hacienda, who usually resided in the city and left day-to-day management of his estate to underlings

hacienda – throughout Latin America, a large but often underproductive rural landholding, with a dependent resident labor force, under a dominant owner; in Chile, the term *fundo* is more common, though it generally applies to a smaller irrigated unit

hare paenga (RN) – elliptical (boat-shaped) house

hospedaje – budget accommodations, usually a large family home with one or two extra bedrooms for guests and a shared bathroom

hostería – inn or guesthouse that serves meals, usually outside the main cities

hotel parejero – urban short-stay accommodations, normally patronized by young couples in search of privacy

huaso – horseman, a rough Chilean equivalent of the Argentine gaucho

ichu – bunch grass found on the altiplano

IGM – Instituto Geográfico Militar; mapping organization whose products are available and useful to travelers

inquilino – tenant farmer on a *fundo*

intendencia – Spanish colonial administrative unit

invierno boliviano – 'Bolivian winter'; summer rainy season in the Chilean altiplano, so-called because of the direction from which the storms come

isla – island

islote – small island, islet

istmo – isthmus

IVA – *impuesto de valor agregado*, value-added tax (VAT) often added to restaurant or hotel bills

küchen – sweet, German-style pastries

kumara (RN) – Polynesian word for sweet potato

lago – lake

laguna – lagoon

latifundio – large landholding, such as a *fundo*, hacienda or *estancia*

lista de correos – poste restante or general delivery

llano – plain, flat ground

llareta – *Laretia compacta*, a dense compact shrub in the Chilean altiplano, with a deceptive, cushionlike appearance, used by Aymara herders for fuel

local – a numbered addition to a street address indicating that a business occupies one of several offices at that address; for example, Maturana 227, Local 5

lomas – in the Atacama Desert, coastal hills on which condensation from the *camanchaca* (convective fog) supports relatively dense vegetation

manavai (RN) – excavated garden enclosures

maori (RN) – learned men, reportedly able to read *Rongo-Rongo* tablets

Mapuche – indigenous inhabitants of the area south of the Río Biobío

marae (RN) – platforms found on Polynesian islands that resemble the *ahu* of Rapa Nui

marisquería – seafood restaurant, usually reasonably priced with excellent quality, in family-oriented beach resorts

mataa (RN) – obsidian spearhead

matua (RN) – ancestor, father; associated with Hotu Matua, leader of the first Polynesian immigrants

media pensión – half board, in a hotel

mestizo – a person of mixed Indian and Spanish descent

micro – small bus, often traveling along the back roads

minga – reciprocal Mapuche Indian labor system

minifundio – small landholding, such as a peasant farm

mirador – lookout point, usually on a hill but sometimes in a building

moai (RN) – large anthropomorphic statues, carved from volcanic tuff

moai kavakava (RN) – carved wooden 'statues of ribs'

momios – 'mummies'; upper-class Chileans resistant to social and political change

motu (RN) – small offshore islet

municipalidad – city hall

museo – museum

ñandú – large, flightless bird known in English as a rhea; similar to the ostrich

nevado – snowcapped mountain peak

Norte Chico – 'Little North'; the semi-arid region between the province of Chañaral and the Río Aconcagua

Norte Grande – 'Big North'; the very arid part of the country north of Chañaral

Nueva Canción Chilena – the 'New Chilean Song' movement, which arose in the 1960s and combined traditional folk themes with contemporary political activism

oferta – promotional fare, often seasonal, for plane or bus travel
oficina – in the Norte Grande, a 19th- and early-20th-century nitrate mining enterprise, in some cases almost a small city, with a large dependent labor force
onces – 'elevenses'; Chilean afternoon tea

palafitos – on the islands of Chiloé, rows of houses built on stilts over the water, where boats can anchor at their back doors on a rising tide
pampa – in the Norte Grande, a vast desert expanse where mineral nitrates were often mined
parada – bus stop
parque nacional – national park
parrilla – restaurant specializing in grilled meats
parrillada – grilled steak and other beef
pastel de choclo – maize casserole filled with vegetables, chicken and beef
peatonal – pedestrian mall, usually in the center of larger cities
peña – folk music and cultural club; many originated in Santiago in the 1960s as venues for the New Chilean Song movement
penquista – inhabitant of Concepción; derived from the city's original site at nearby Penco
pensión – family home offering short-term budget accommodations; may also take permanent lodgers
pensión completa – full board, in a hotel
picada – informal family restaurant
pingüinera – penguin colony
playa – beach
pora (RN) – small reed raft used for paddling to offshore islets *(motu)*
Porteño – a native or resident of the port city of Valparaíso
portezuelo – mountain pass
posta – clinic or first-aid station, often in smaller towns that lack proper hospitals
postre – dessert
precordillera – the foothills of the Andes mountains
propina – tip, at a restaurant or elsewhere
puente – bridge
puerto – port
pukao (RN) – the topknot on the head of a *moai;* once a common hairstyle for Rapa Nui males
pukará – a pre-Columbian hilltop fortress in the Andes

pulpería – company store on a *fundo, estancia* or nitrate *oficina*
puna – Andean highlands, usually above 3000m
punta – point

quebrada – ravine
quinoa – native Andean grain, a dietary staple in the pre-Columbian era, still grown by Aymara farmers in the precordillera of the Norte Grande

Rapa Nui – the Polynesian name for Easter Island
reducción – the concentration of Indians in towns modeled on the Spanish grid pattern, for purposes of political control or religious instruction; the term also refers to the settlement itself
refugio – a shelter, usually rustic, in a national park or other remote area
reserva nacional – national reserve, a category of land use
residencial – budget accommodations, sometimes seasonal; in general, residenciales occupy buildings designed expressly for short-stay lodging
rhea – large, flightless bird, called *ñandú* in Spanish, similar to the ostrich
río – river
rodeo – annual roundup of cattle on an *estancia* or hacienda
Rongo-Rongo (RN) – an indecipherable script on wooden tablets that some have thought to be an alphabet or other form of native writing
roto – 'ragged one'; a dependent laborer on a Chilean *fundo*
ruka – traditional thatched Mapuche house
ruta – route, highway

SAG – Servicio Agrícola Ganadero, the Agriculture and Livestock Service; its officials inspect baggage and vehicles for prohibited fruit and meat imports at Chilean border crossings
saladero – an establishment for salting meat and hides
salar – salt lake, salt marsh or salt pan, usually in the high Andes or Patagonia
salón cama – bus with reclining seats
salón de té – literally 'teahouse,' but more like an upscale *cafetería*
Santiaguino – native or resident of the city of Santiago

seno – sound, fjord

servicentro – large gasoline station with spacious parking lot, restaurants and toilet facilities, including inexpensive hot showers

sierra – mountain range

siesta – afternoon nap during the extended midday break of traditional Chilean business hours

sin gas – 'without gas'; noncarbonated mineral water

s/n – 'sin número'; indicates a street address without a number

soroche – altitude sickness

Southern Cone – in political geography, the area comprising Argentina, Chile, Uruguay and parts of Brazil and Paraguay; so called after the area's shape on the map

tábano – horsefly

tajamares – dikes built to control flooding of the Río Mapocho in late-colonial Santiago

tejuelas – in archipelagic Chile, especially Chiloé, shingles of varying design that typify the region's vernacular architecture

teleférico – gondola cable car

todo terreno – mountain bike

toki (RN) – basalt carving tool

toqui – Mapuche Indian chief

tortas – mine tailings, literally 'cakes'

totora (RN) – type of reed used for making rafts

turismo aventura – nontraditional forms of tourism, such as trekking and river rafting

Unidad Popular – 'Popular Unity'; a coalition of leftist political groups that supported Salvador Allende in the 1970 presidential election

vaina – common Chilean aperitif consisting of port, cognac, cocoa and egg white

Valle Central – Central Valley, the Chilean heartland that extends south from the Río Aconcagua to near the city of Concepción; this area contains most of Chile's population and its industrial and agricultural wealth

ventisquero – glacier

vicuña – *Vicugna vicugna,* wild relative of domestic llama and alpaca, found only at high altitudes in the Norte Grande

villa – village, small town

viscacha – *Lagidium vizcacha,* a wild Andean relative of the domestic chinchilla

volcán – volcano

Yahgans – indigenous inhabitants of the Tierra del Fuego Archipelago

zampoñas – pan pipes

zona franca – at Iquique and Punta Arenas, duty-free zone where imported goods are available at very low prices

Thanks

Many thanks to the travelers who used the last edition and wrote to us with helpful hints, useful advice and anecdotes. Your names follow:

Frederica Aalto, Maria Abel, Steven Abramovitch, Abinash Achrekar, Doug Adamson, Doug & Pat Adamson, Stephen O Addison Jr, Noel Aflague, Barbara S Ainslie, Laura Ainsworth, Erik Albrecht, Ximena Alfaro, Paul Alfers, Alvaro Alliende, Jeff Ames, Markus Amhof, Frederico Amorim, Duncan Anderson, Matt Anderson, Pat Anderson, Ruth Anderson, Lillemor Andersson, Corthout Andre, Jochen R Andritzky, Bill Angus, Cathie Archbould, Carolynn Archibald, Molly Arevalo, Robert Arevalo, Dominique Argenson, Diana Armstrong, Tone Arneberg, Vincent Arnold, Robert Aronoff, James Aronson, Fran Arp, Francine Arpin, Marc Arts, Paul Arundale, Hilmir Asgeirsson, Svein Otto Aure, Nicole Avallone, Megan Baccitich, Stan Bach, Christine Badre, Harris Baldascini, James R Ball, Carol Bank, Barbara Banks, Nancy Bannister, Paul Bardwell, Pamela Barefoot, CBH Barford, Steven Barger, Stephen Barnard, Stephen Barnes, Bernie Barnet, Valerie Barnich, Craig Barrack, Susan Barreau, Michael Barris, Michael C Barris, Alistair Basendale, Irmgard Bauer, Jane Beamish, JS Beard, Mirjam Beck, Irmengard Beckett, Michael Beckmann, John Beeken, Gina Behrens, Ben Beiske, Daniel Bekker, Carole Bell, Joanne Below, Kristel Beltman, Derek Benson, Kate M Berg, Petter Berg, Goran Berggren, Marloes Bergmans, Mauricio Bergstein, Karin Berli, Wayne Bernhardson, Loic Bertrand, Anne Bianchi, Simone Bianchi, Filippo Bianco, Jiri Biciste, Gillian Birkby, Vidar Birkeland, Ruth Bitterlin, Erwin Bittner, Caroline Black, Charles Blackham, Martin Blain, Bruce Blanch, An Blevi, Steve Blume, Robert Boardman, Andre Boessenkool, Gabriela Boiero, Jnrgen Boje, Inge Bollen, Robert Bond, Miguel Boo, Justin Boocock, Paul Boontje, Paul & Charlotte Boontje, Edgar Booth, Nila Boquin, Nick Borg, Christa & Hildegard Bornemann, Emmanuel Boutot, Carolyn Boyd, Gareth Brahams, Owen & Anna Brailsford, Virginia Brand, Kerstin Brandes, Sally & Nigel Branston, Elke Braun, Andrea Bravo Mendez, Harry Breemhaar, Annemarie Breeve, Katja Breitenbncher, N & S Brew, Elizabeth Briggs, Barbara Brons, Thomas Brostean, Berne Broudy, Fraukje Brouwer, Harro Brouwer, Jan Brown, Vanessa T Brown, Richard Brownsword, Robert Bruce, Ulrike Bruckmann, Maud Bruemmer, Marlis Bruse, Rod George Bryant, Sharon Buccino, Martin Bucheli, Alexander Bucka, Quentin & Nicky Buckingham, Sarah & GB Bucknell, Sergio Bueno, Bill Bullard, Jean Bullard, Tim Burford, Anne Burgess, Paige Burgess, Agi & Shanf Burra, Debbie Busler, Stuart Buxton, Neko Cabrera Vasquez, Miss Calderon, Laurence Campo, Edmur Caniato Arantes, Michael Cantzler, Paul Cardoen, Juan Carlos, Chris Carlson, Marianne Carpenter, Colin S Carr, TE John Carrington-Birch, Patrick Carroll, PJ Cary, D Case, Rufo Caufield, Mike Cavendish, Neil Chambers, Robert Chamerda, Jean Charles, Cindy Chin, Andrea Chittleborough, Alan Chong, Andreas Christen, Hansjuerg Christen, Becky Christiansen, Jeff Churchill, Tracy Cigarski, Helene Clappaz, Andy Clapperton, Lucy Claridge, Cameron Clark, Ali Clarke, Bjorn HB Clasen, Julia Clements, Grant & Heidi Clifford, Mike Clyne, Jack Cobb, Pat Coleman, Patricia Collins, Richard Collyer-Hamlin, Colleen Cook, Kit Cooper, Arnaud Corin, Sergio Cortez, Theresa Costigan, Bryce Coulter, Brian Council, Peter Coutts, Andrew Cowan, James Cowie, Bob Crabb, Paul Crovella, Brian Cruickshank, Claudia Crul, Dolores Cuadros, Meryl Cumber, Ryan Cummings, Fabio Cury, Ted & Sylvia Custovich, Leah Cutter, Andreas Dörr, Erin Daldry, Phillip A Dale, Craig Daly, F Damsteeg-Knapen, Elisabethe Dank, John Dank, Dan De Backer, Ingrid de Graaf, Martin de Ruiter, Daan de Vries, Frank de Vries, Emma Dean, Marine Delebecque, Uta Dempwolff, Matthew Dennigerq, Matthew Derham, Marian Dey, Jeffrey Dhont, Eileen Dietrich, Jorg Digmayer, Therese Dion-Renauld, Dave Diperna, Kamila Divisova, Raija Doertbudak, Eva Dolne, Dick Donaway, Luis Eduardo & Luciana Dosso, Dim Douwes, JP Drapkins, Katie Drew, Matt Dufort, George Dufour, Ross Duke, Jean-Marc Dumont, Kathy Dunham, James Dunlop, Julian Dunster, Alain & Margaret Duval, Denis Duysens, Jacqui Dyer, John Eastlund, Michael J Eatroff, Yasmin Ebrahim, Oliver Eck, David Edelstein, Alex Egger, Diane Eggerton, Ilona Ehrlich, Daniel Eisenberg, John Eklund, Johan Ekstrom, Elina Eldridge, Ryan Elliott, Don Ellis III, Donald C Erbe, John Eriksen, John & Lene Eriksen, Susan Erk, Jose Estay, Robin Ette, Ann Ez El Din, Alexandre Fage-Moreel, Peter Fahrney, Diego Falcone, Albert Fam, Pat Farrington, Carole Feldman, Marvin Feldman, Lucia Fell, Ninfa Fergadiotti, Jose Alberto Fernandez, Marjo Ferwerda, Christina Fetterhoff, Carsten Filthuth, Shiman Fink, Shiman & Maru Fink, Suki Finney, Alistair Firth, Molly E FitzGerald, Julia Fizer, Hubert Flahaux, Doug Fleming, Gabriel Flores, Pernille & Kennet Foh, John Foitzik, Josh Forde, Kent Foster, Gwyladys Fouche, Lisa Fowler, Jonathan Freeman, Lesley Freeness, Marjolein Friele, Carmen Frischenschalger, Dave & Lina Fuller, Jose Alberto Fernandez Gaete, Roman Gaiser, Paola Galasso, Tomasz & Anna Galka, Sanjay Gandhi, Jialiang Gao, Andres Garcia, Ignacio Garcia, Andres Garcia-Huidobro, Erica Gardner, Hillary J Gardner, Steve Garnsey, Dianne & Reg Gates, René Gautier, Ryan Gawn, Richard Geary-Cooke, Roy Gee, Katrin Geissler, Thomas Geke, Stephen George, Stephen & Tiffany George, Eva Geuder, Ian

Gilmore, Declan Gilmurray, Meghan Giulino, Lisa Glass, Katherine Glen, Roland Glockler, Petra Golja, Ricardo Gonzalez, Diane B Goodpasture, Andries Goossens, Leila Gorosito, Thorsten & Karina Gorski, John Gospodarek, Christophe Grandjean, Amanda Grant, Glenn Grant, Robert Grant, Peter Gravid Korning, Cathy Gray, Karen H Gray, Laura Grego, Vanessa Gregory, Jorrit Groen, Nienke Groen, Irena & Tony Grogan, Cesar Guerey, Alf Amund Gulsvik, Matthias Gutzeit, Rodrigo Guzman, Helen Hagan, Patrick Hagans, Marit Hagel, Hilda Haghighi, Caroline Hales, Pat Hall, Sarah Hall, Daniel Halse, Callem Hamilton, Duncan Hamilton, Duncan & Claire Hamilton, JT Hamilton, Vendela Hammarskjold, Robert Hammer, Doug Hanauer, Andrew Hanscom, Tim Hare, Nicky Harman, Lynda Harpley, S Harrel, Justin Harrison, Sherry Hart, Lynn Hartfield, Michael Hasan, Natasha Haslum, Jennifer & James Hatchell, Susan & Kent Hathaway, Sabine Hauptmann, Glenn Havelock, Francis Hawkings, Rhonda Hawkins, Patricie Ash & Godfrey Hawthorns, Jeremiah Hayes, Tom Hayes, Richard Haywood, Garry J Hazzard, Theresa Heasman, David Heatwole, John Hebert, Patricia de Heek, Patricia de & Rene Heek, Sue Heep, Henk & Eileen Heetveld, Susanne Heidmann, Onno Heijdens, Cyndi Heller, Ivar Hellesnes, Burkhard Helmedag, Imke & Andreas Hendrich, Siobhan Hennessy, Adolfo Henriquez, John Henzell, Neil & Christine Hepburn, Elmar Herhuth, Anders & Jonathan Hermansen, Mark Herrmann, Kathleen Hershner, Ben Herzog, Eitan Hess, Alan Hickey, Rodrigo Hidalgo, Kathryn Hiestand, David Higgs, Belinda Hill, Susanne Hillmer, Lorena Hirschberg, Muriel Hitchcock, Len Hobbs, Wilfred Hockfield, Gigi Hoeller, Eva Hoffman, Sabine Hoffmann, Brett Hogan, John Holborow, Vanessa Smith Holburn, Julie Hollar, Roos Hollenberg, R Dieter Hollstein, Mary Holozubiec, Andreas Holsten, William D Hood, Hester Hoogenboom, Elva Hoover, Jennifer Hoover, Christina Hoppe, Elizabeth Horton, Jean Houlder, Richard Howitt, Robert Hoysgaard, Hilde Hublou, Christine Hughes, Melissa Hunnibell, Patricia P Hunt, Sandy Hunter, Mike Hurd, Caleb Hurst-Hiller, Eva Huthoefer, Vickie Hutter, Eric P Hvolboll, Trebor Iksrazal, Holger Illi, Ricardo Imai, Christine Ingemorsen, Henry Ionescu, M Ismail, Niels Iversen, Remco Jaasma, Joe Jabaily, Michael Jacob, Nico Jacobs, David Jaffe, Christiane Jagailloux, Kazia Jankowski, Jack Janosik, Leonie Janssen, Mikki Jee, Nils Jenne, Colin Jerolmack, Ken Jewkes, David Jiron, Bob & Margaret Johnson, Carolyn Johnson, Lia Johnson, Christopher Jones, Erika Jones, Veronika Jonker, Jerry Jordan, Jacqueline Judah, Horst Jung, Marc Jurgens, Martin Kalista, Revital Kariv, C Karp, Frank Kaspereit, Roswitha Katscher, Michelle Katz, James C Kautz, George Kechagiouglou, Dion Keech, Shane Kehoe, Gloria & Jurgen Keil, Christopher D Keivit, Anne-Marie Kennedy, Pernillen og Kennet, Ton Kersbergen, Nancy Kershaw, Fred Ketting, Khalid Khan, Daniel Kiernan, Edwin Kirk, Konrad Klatt, Carlo Klauth, Kurt Kleiner, Lyn Kleiner,

Charles Kloch, Barbara Knapton, Karyn Knight, Holger Knoedler, Brigitte Knoetig, James Knox, Gabi Koch, Toni Konkoly, Herbert Konnerth, Martin Korff, Olaf Korr, Carl Koskey, Michael Kosnett, Kai Kottwitz, Thomas R Kraemer, Gen Kramer, Oliver Krause, Ulrich Kreuth, John Krieg, Tabea Krolzik, Carlo Krusich, Martina Kuhbandner, Eric Kuhn, Avril Kuhrt, Anne Kuiper, Agnieszka Kula, Bob Kull, Joe Kutza, Garrett Kwakkestein, Jan-Paul Kwasik, Kerstin Labatzke, Rene LaBerge, Marcelo Labre, Nicolas Laisney, C Lamb, Colin & Clare Lamb, Vicky Lamb, Peter Lambert, Xavier Lane-Mullins, Jessica Larsen, Allan Larsson, Monty Lasserre, Judith R Lave, Christine Law, Douglas Le Du, Andrea Lee, Sung Yun Lee, Toby Leeming, Barbara Leighton, Philip Leith, Macarena Leiva, Marcelo Leiva, John Lengacher, Albrecht Lenz, Manfred Lenzen, Sabrina Leombruni, Ronald Leong, Idan Levy, Jon Levy, Kathryn Lewis, Rebecca Lewis, Fernando Libedinsky, Gil Liberman, Ben Ligtvoet, Corina & Alfred Lindenmann, Konrad Lindner, Romeo Lipizzi, Kylie Little, RA Litton, Sarah Llewellyn, Francisco Lobos, James W Lockett, Magnus Lofqvist, Ida Longeri, Antoine & Agnes Lorgnier, Karl Loring, Anna Lovejoy, Richard J Lowe, Catherine Lowell, John Lucas, Philipp Luginbnhl, Diederik Lugtigheid, Doris Lundgreen, Eric Maar, Isabel MacDougall, Ian Mace, Ian Mackay, Elizabeth Maclaine-Cross, Bob Magnus, Antonia Maguire, Darcie Mahoney, Kate Mahoney, Joyce Majiski, Amy-Jocelyn Mandel, Francisco Mandiola, Mario Marchese, Hans Marcinkowski, Alessandro Marco Lindenmann, Claudia & Francois Maresquier, Sébastien Maret, Robert Marincin, Will Markle, Milena Marmora, Sonalle Maroo, Allegra Marshall, Herve Martin, L Martin, Trajan Martin, Andrea Martinez, Cristina Martinez de Murguia, Okumura Masato, Anna Maspero, Sharlene Matten, Gerhard Maucher, Chris Mazur, Laura McColm, Jason McCormack, Dave McCormick, Margaret McCormick, Edward McDonagh, Brian McDonald, Sara McFall, Philip McInerney, Anthony McInneny, Dave McJannet, Tony McKevitt, Dean McNally, Margaret McOnie, Amanda Mead, Peter Meaker, Mitja Medved, Arnout Meester, Olivia & Alain Meier, Sharon Meieran, Ulla Melchiorsen, Les Melrose, Daniel Mena, Jaime Mendez, Tan Meng Shern, Yael Meroz, Francois Mes, J Mickleson, Pete & Jay Mickleson, Christopher Milenkevich, DE Miller, Leila Miller, Marisa Miller, Doug Mitchell, Earle Moen, Jostein Moen, Olga & Earle Moen, John Moffat, Wilfred E Mole, Stefan Molenaar, Rodrigo Molina Henriquez, Mary Anne Moloney, Karin Momberg, Bruno Moncel, RS Moneta, Michael J Monsour, David Morawetz, Fernando Miguel Moreno Olmedo, Curtis Morgan, Michael Moritz, Paul Morris, Karim & Karen Moukaddem, Ken Moxham, Daniel Moylan, Patrick Moyroud, Daniela Mueller, Greg & Lisa Mueller, Terry Murphy, Martin Muscheid, Christopher Mutlow, Ishay Nadler, Kristin Nali, Alex Nash, Katrina Natale, John Naughton, Andreas Naujoks, Neal Neal, Nathan Nebbe, Rike Nehlsen, Marcia & Bruce Nesbitt, Pui Ng, DM Nicholls, Don Nicholls, Helen Nigg,

Gerardo Niklitschek, Mark Nilsson, Taly Noam, Irene Patricia Nohara, GB & Maria Norall, JC Noriyuki Kaitsuka, Justin Norman, Lennart Norstrand, Paul Nugent, Nyi Nyi Lwin, Evan Obercian, Patty A O'Connell, Donna O'Daniel, Paul Oldaker, Andres Olivares Pizarro, Leif & Monika Olsson, Justin Ooi, Jose Antonio Opazo, Mitzie V Ortiz, Dieter Ottlewski, Luz Ovalle, Carlos Ovalle Molina, Rick Owen, Nick Pace, Mercedes Pacin, Jenny Page, Amarnath Pai, Joan Paluzzi, Vijay Parbat, Aristea Parissi, Graham Parker, David Parson, Don Paskovich, Caron Patterson, Robert Patterson, John Payson, Luis F Paz, Nick Peacock, Rachel Peake, Richard Pearcy, Donna Peavoy, Cristina Pedrazzini, Elizabeth Pegg, Grace Peng, Carlos & Maria Peres de Costa, Carsten Perkuhn, Caterina Perrone, Earl Perry, Marlo Perry, Patrik Persson, James Grant Peterkin, Ginger & Jim Peterson, Huguette & Bill Petruk, Richard & Alison Pett, Lars E Pettersson, Severine Peudupin, Joshua Pevnick, Laura Pezzano, Anja Pferdmenges, Trish Phelan, Julie Pike, Kris M Piorowski, Adrienne Pitts, Mandy Planert, Thomas Pletzenauer, Cameron Plewes, Janice Plewes, Kevin Pluck, Mario Poblete, April Pojman, Tom Polk, Emma Pollard, Boris Popov, Felix Portmann, Robert Postle, Robbie Prater, Nicola Pratola, Jennifer Prattley, Chris Preager, Juergen Preimesberger, Lee J Price, Natalie Price, Bill Pringle, Allson & Bill Proctor, Julie Wood Prosperi, Rodrigo Proust, Donna Pyle, Trish Quilaran, Trish Quinhuan, Sabine Raab, Bruce Rae, Aldo Raicich, Sweet Rain, Torsten Ramforth, Timm Rampton, Chris & Peggy Raphael, Verena Raschke, Erin & Chris Ratay, Thomas Rau, Diederik Ravesloot, Diederille Ravesloot, Nick Read, Frances & Terence Reardon, Sofia Rehn, Malcolm Reid, Wim Reitsma, Tim Relyea, Charles Renn, Marco Antonio Reyes, Michael Rhodes, Mary Richards, Fabian Richter, Jens Riis, Caroline Rix, NRC Roberton, David Roberts, WN Roberts, Jacques Rocheteau, Ann Rodzai, Maureen Roe, Caroline Roels, Clive Rogers, Andrea Rogge, Tom J van Rooij, Rachael Rook, Eef Roon, Stefan Rooyackers, Assami Rosner, Jens Roth, Catherine Rourke, Karen Rowland, Andree Roy, Andrew Ruben, Debra Ruben, RF Rudderham, JD Ruehl, Bruce Rumoge, Robert Runyard, Philipp Rusch, Erica Russo, Patrick Ryan, Stig Rygaard, Daisy S, Marcelo Saavedra, Priti Sachdeva, Paul Sacki, Ofer Sadan, Robert Safrata, Enrique L Salgado, Mike Salusky, Stefan Samuelsson, Maria Sanchez de Campaña, Ron Sanchez, Tomás Sánchez, Marc Sanford, Christian Santschi, Ann Sargeant, Hedda Sasburg, Jacques Saskia, Todd Savitz, Emily Sayce, Peter Scheer, Andre Scherphof, Marnie Schilken, Hannelore Schimmer, Susan Schirber, Chris Schlager, Astrid Schloz, Olivier Schmeltzer, Gregg Schmidt, Susanne Schmidt, Caroline Andrews & Paul Schmutz, Michael Schneider, Nicole Schoenholzer, Natasja Scholz, Mark Schottlander, Anne Schreiber, Berit Schrickel, Toralf Schrinner, Sam Schulhofer-Wohl, Karin Schulte, Deborah Schwabowski, Torben Schwermann, Jens Schwyn, Laurent Schyns, Adam Sebire, Peter Seilern, Michael Sentovich, Fabian Seul, Jerome Sgard, Annik Shahani, Anjum Shariff, Paritosh Sharma, Peter & Florence Shaw, Yusuke Shimada, Michael Shohat, Ross Shotton, Karen S Shouse, Jane Shuttleworth, Christopher Siddon, Jay Sieleman, Bogdan Siewierski, Mark Sigman, Jacob Silberberg, Horst Simon, Anna Simonson, Charlie Simpson, Martin Sims, Diego Singer, Aruna Singh, Jenny Slepian, Stephan Sludts, Stuart Smeeton, Brian Smith, Duncan Smith, Sally Smith, Caroline Snare, Charlotte Snowden, Christoph Soekler, Vic Sofras, Tex Soh, Keith Sohl, Alejandro Sola, Luca Sorbello, HC Florian Sorensen, Judy Soukup, chris Spelius, Sandra Spies, Joshua Spillane, William Spurgeon, Dorothee Staeheli Egger, Richard Stanaway, Robert Stanich, Idahlia Stanley, Alex Starr, Wolf Staub, Roland Steffen, Gabriela & Franz Steiglechner, Andrew Stein, Corri Stein, Juerg Steiner, Sibylle Steiner, Edward Steinman, Hal Stephens, Britta Stina-Carlsson, Lea Stogdale, Mare Straetmans, Adrian Stuerm, Joseph R Sturgis, Wim Sturm, Janice Swab, Pieter Swart, Deborah Sweeney, Cate Swimburn, Francisca Tapia, Evert te Pas, Anamaria Tejos, Minden Ten Eyck, Joanne Tennyson, Paul Tetrault, Sabine Thielicke, Eric Thoman, Giles Thomas, Janie Thomas, Gordon Thompson, Jim Thomson, Chris Thorpe, Aranea Tigelaar, Frederik Tilmann, Timo Noko, Sara Tizard, Barbara Tomas, Donald Toney, Maria Torlaschi, Pablo Torlaschi, Irene Torres, Michele Tosi, Debbie Triff, Betty Tromp, Charlotte & Phill Trzcinski, Alois Tuna, Melissa Turley, Bill Turner, Jackie Turner, Susan Turner, Lena Tvede, Michael Uhl, MM Ulielander, BL Underwood, Heike Uphoff, Daniel Urbina, Cheyenne Valenzuela, Jeremy Valeriote, Marcelo Vallejos, Wineke van Aken, Llan van Berkel, Serge Van Cauwenbergh, Esther van den Akker, Maurits van den Boom, Koosje van der Horst, Michael van der Valk, Katy van Dis, Jann van Gaal, C van Hilten, Raoyl van Lennep, Silke & Ute van Os, Bart Van Overmeire, Tom J van Rooij, Jozef Varnagy, Paola Vega, Mariska Verplanke, Agustin Vezzani, RW Visser, Martijn Vlutters, Marcel Vos, Kfar Vradim, Kaspar Waelti, Jef Waibel, Robert Waite, Debbie Waldman, Michael Walensky, Elizabeth Walhin, Katharina Walldow, Stehpne Waller, Susanne Wallnöfer, Brooke Walters, Ricardo Wang, Darren Wapplington, Michael Ward, Rowena Ward, Joachim Warnecke, Sheldon Wasserman, Thomas Waters, JP Watney, Adrian Watson, Susan Webb, Joerg Weber, Thomas A Weber, Su Weekes, Barbara Wegman, Heidi Weiland, Shane Anna Weiss, Yishay Weiss, Claude Werner, Claude & Alexandre Werner, Wim van Westrenen, Richard White, Roxy Wicherts, Dean Wickens, Glen Widmer, Mieke Wieland, Anna Williams, Byron Williams, Gwyn Williams, Wayne & Pat Williams, Robert Williamson, Greer Wilson, Caroline Witzier, Paul Witzier, Peter Wonacott, Walter Wood, Andrew Woolley, Andy Worth, Neil Wray, Heather Wright, Sebastian Wright, Andrew Yale, Irit Yanay, Mong Yang Loh, Richard Yeomare, Rosemarie Yevich, Eric York, Bill Young, Robert Zenyik, Tymoteusz Zera, Oliver Zoellner, Vamosi Zoltan

Index

Bold indicates maps.

Bold indicates maps.

Boxed Text

Bold indicates maps.

MAP LEGEND

ROUTES

City   **Regional**

............Freeway
............Toll Freeway
...... Primary Road
......Secondary Road
......Tertiary Road
...... Dirt Road

.................Pedestrian Mall
.................Steps
.................Tunnel
.................Trail
.................Walking Tour
.................Path

TRANSPORTATION

............Train
............Metro

............Bus Route
............Ferry

BOUNDARIES

............International
............Región,
     Provincial

............County
............Disputed

ROUTE SHIELDS

ARGENTINA
RN 40   Ruta Nacional
RP 21   Ruta Provincial
RC 8   Ruta Complementaria

BOLIVIA
5   Red Fundamental
601   Red Complementaria

CHILE
5   Ruta Nacional

PERU
1   Carreteras Sistema Nacional
113   Carreteras Sistema Departmental

HYDROGRAPHY

............River; Creek
............Canal
............Lake
............Water
............Spring; Rapids
............Waterfalls
............Dry; Salt Lake
............Glacier

AREAS

............Beach
............Building
............Cemetery

............Forest
............Garden; Zoo
............Park

............Plaza
............Sports Field
............Swamp; Mangrove

POPULATION SYMBOLS

NATIONAL CAPITAL...... National Capital
REGIÓN CAPITAL......Región Capital

Large City............Large City
Medium City............Medium City

Small City............Small City
Town; Village............Town; Village

MAP SYMBOLS

............Place to Stay
▼ ....Place to Eat
● ....Point of Interest

............Airfield
............Airport
............Archeological Site; Ruin
............Bank
............Baseball Diamond
............Battlefield
............Bike Trail
............Border Crossing
............Buddhist Temple
............Bus Station; Terminal
............Cable Car; Chairlift
............Campground
............Castle
............Cathedral
............Cave

............Church
............Cinema
............Dive Site
............Embassy; Consulate
............Footbridge
............Gas Station
............Hospital
............Information
............Internet Access
............Lighthouse
............Lookout
............Mine
............Mission
............Monument
............Mountain

............Museum
............Observatory
............Park
............Parking Area
............Pass
............Picnic Area
............Police Station
............Pool
............Post Office
............Pub; Bar
............RV Park
............Shelter
............Shipwreck
............Shopping Mall
............Skiing - Cross Country

............Skiing - Downhill
............Stately Home
............Surfing
............Synagogue
............Tao Temple
............Taxi
............Telephone
............Theater
............Toilet - Public
............Tomb
............Trailhead
............Tram Stop
............Transportation
............Volcano
............Winery

Note: Not all symbols displayed above appear in this book.

LONELY PLANET OFFICES

Australia
Locked Bag 1, Footscray, Victoria 3011
☎ 03 8379 8000 fax 03 8379 8111
email talk2us@lonelyplanet.com.au

USA
150 Linden Street, Oakland, California 94607
☎ 510 893 8555, TOLL FREE 800 275 8555
fax 510 893 8572
email info@lonelyplanet.com

UK
10a Spring Place, London NW5 3BH
☎ 020 7428 4800 fax 020 7428 4828
email go@lonelyplanet.co.uk

France
1 rue du Dahomey, 75011 Paris
☎ 01 55 25 33 00 fax 01 55 25 33 01
email bip@lonelyplanet.fr
www.lonelyplanet.fr

World Wide Web: www.lonelyplanet.com or AOL keyword: lp
Lonely Planet Images: www.lonelyplanetimages.com